GUNI SERIES ON THE SOCIAL COMMITMENT OF UNIVERSITIES

Higher Education in the World 5

Knowledge, Engagement and Higher Education: Contributing to Social Change

GLOBAL UNIVERSITY
NETWORK FOR INNOVATION

palgrave
macmillan

First published 2014 by
PALGRAVE MACMILLAN

Palgrave Macmillan in the UK is an imprint of Macmillan Publishers Limited, registered in England, company number 785998, of Houndmills, Basingstoke, Hampshire RG21 6XS.

Palgrave Macmillan in the US is a division of St Martin's Press LLC, 175 Fifth Avenue, New York, NY 10010.

Palgrave Macmillan is the global academic imprint of the above companies and has companies and representatives throughout the world.

Palgrave® and Macmillan® are registered trademarks in the United States, the United Kingdom, Europe and other countries.

ISBN: 978–0–230–53556–5

This book is printed on paper suitable for recycling and made from fully managed and sustained forest sources. Logging, pulping and manufacturing processes are expected to conform to the environmental regulations of the country of origin.

A catalogue record for this book is available from the British Library.

A catalog record for this book is available from the Library of Congress.

Typeset by Aardvark Editorial Limited, Metfield, Suffolk

Printed and bound by CPI Group (UK) Ltd, Croydon, CR0 4YY

This publication has been produced with the financial support of the Agencia Española de Cooperación Internacional para el Desarrollo (AECID). Its content is the sole responsibility of GUNi and does not necessarily reflect AECID's opinions.

TEAM INVOLVED IN THE PREPARATION OF THIS PUBLICATION

PRINCIPAL EDITOR
GUNi

GUEST EDITORS
Budd L. Hall
Rajesh Tandon

EDITORIAL TEAM
Cristina Escrigas
Jesús Granados Sánchez
Budd L. Hall
Rajesh Tandon
Gemma Puig
Marta Forns

AUTHORS
Oga Steve Abah, Nigeria
Evangelos Afendras, Greece
Hatem Ali-Elaydi, Palestine
Luz Arabany Ramírez, Colombia
Alice Barnsdale, USA
Paul Benneworth, The Netherlands
Felix Bivens, USA
Janice Desire Busingye, Uganda
Matthieu Calame, France
Betty Cernol-McCann, The
Phillippines
Alfred Cheung-Ming Chan, China
Melba Claudio-González, Puerto Rico
Carlos Cortez Ruiz, Mexico
Michael Cuthill, Australia
Axel Didriksson, Mexico
Sophie Duncan, UK
Patricia Ellis, Barbados
Cristina Escrigas, Spain
Danielle Feinstein, USA-Jordan
Hiram E. Fitzgerald, USA
Juan Ramón de la Fuente, Mexico
Andrew Furco, USA
John Gaventa, USA
Katia Gonçalves Mori, Brazil
Jesús Granados Sánchez, Spain
Sylvie B. de Grosbois, Canada
Ayhan G. Hakan, Turkey
Budd L. Hall, Canada
Keith Hammond, UK
Robert M. Hollister, USA
Lorlene M. Hoyt, USA
Barbara Lethem Ibrahim, Egypt

Daniel Innerarity, Spain
Maria Ivanova, Bulgaria
Edward T. Jackson, USA
Mónica Jiménez de la Jara, Chile
Seçil Kaya, Turkey
Marek Kwiek, Poland
Sofia Lerche Vieira, Brazil
Alice Liu Cheng, China
Daniel Lumera, Italy
Carol Hok Ka Ma, Hong Kong, China
Mounir Mabsout, Lebanon
Paul Manners, UK
Simon Marginson, Australia
Yves Mauffette, Canada
Lorraine McIlrath, Ireland
Stela Meneghel, Brazil
Cynthia Mynnti, Lebanon
Claudia Neubauer, Germany
Joanna Ochocka, Canada
George Openjuru, Uganda
Michael Osborne, UK
Soheila Pashang, Morocco
B. Devi Prasad, India
Julia Preece, South Africa
Gemma Puig, Spain
Manuel Ramiro Muñoz, Colombia
Dzulkifli Razak, Malaysia
Uday Rosario, India
Brian Seilstad, USA
Jerome Slamat, South Africa
Anna Smolentseva, Russia
Paulo Speller, Brazil
Claudia Stengel, Bolivia
Rajesh Tandon, India
María Nieves Tapia, Argentina
Elif Toprak, Turkey
Crystal Tremblay, Canada
Oscar Valiente, Spain
François Vallaeys, France
Shirley Walters, South Africa
Paulo Wangoola, Uganda

MAPS
Clara Guixà Solé

BIBLIOGRAPHY
Melba Claudio-González and Jesús
Granados Sánchez

GUNi SECRETARIAT
Melba Claudio-González
Àngels Cortina
Cristina Escrigas
Marta Forns
Jesús Granados Sánchez
Gemma Puig

GUNi EXECUTIVE COMMITTEE

Founding Institutions

UNESCO

United Nations University (UNU)

Universitat Politècnica de
Catalunya BarcelonaTech (UPC)

GUNi President
Antoni Giró Roca (UPC rector)

GUNi Executive Director
Cristina Escrigas

Regional Offices
Peter Okebukola (Sub-Saharan Africa)
Juma Shabani (Sub-Saharan Africa)
Abdel Bagi AG Babiker (Arab States)
Yang Wei (Asia and the Pacific)
Playasakol Sakolsatayadon (Asia and
the Pacific)
Axel Didriksson (Latin America and
the Caribbean)
Denise Leite (Latin America and the
Caribbean)

ACKNOWLEDGEMENTS

The editors want to express our gratitude to all the authors that have contributed with their work and reflections to make this report a very special piece for the future of Community University Engagement. We also want to acknowledge all the networks that have provided us with the information about their outstanding activity in civic engagement. Also we want to express our recognition and gratitude to all those persons that with their work and support have contributed to make this project become real. We would especially like to thank: Agencia Española de Cooperación Internacional para el Desarrollo (AECID); Universia; Department of Education and Universities, Barcelona City Hall; Ministerio de Educación, Cultura y Deporte, Gobierno de España; and Ajuntament de Barcelona. To all of you thank you very much.

Editorial Team

CONTENTS

LIST OF FIGURES, TABLES AND MAPS

FIGURES

TABLES

MAPS

AAU	Association of African Universities	CACSL	Canadian Alliance for Community Service-Learning
ACIP	Advisory Council on Intellectual Property	CBPR	Community-based participatory research
ACU	Association of Commonwealth Universities	CBR	Community-based research
		CBRC	Community-Based Research Canada
AFL–CIO	American Federation of Labor and Congress of Industrial Organizations	CC	Campus Compact
AI/AN	American Indians/Alaska Natives	CCECS	Center for Civic Engagement and Community Service
AIDS	Acquired immune deficiency syndrome	CCM	Centre for Conflict Management
AIU	Albukhary International University	CCPH	Community-Campus Partnerships for Health
APUCEN	Asia-Pacific University-Community Engagement Network	CEBEM	Centro Boliviano de Estudios Multidisciplinarios (Bolivian Centre for MultidisciplinaryStudies)
ARWU	Academic Ranking of World Universities	CEDEFOP	European Centre for the Development of Vocational Training
ASEAN	Association of Southeast Asian Nations		
ASL	Academic Service-Learning	CERI	Centre for Educational Research and Innovation
AUB	American University of Beirut	CES	Community engagement scholarship
AUC	American University in Cairo	CHE	Council on Higher Education
AUCEA	Australian Universities Community Engagement Alliance	CHESP	Community–Higher Education Service Partnerships
AUI	Akhawayn University in Ifrane	CII	Cátedra Indígena Itinerante
AUS	American University of Sharjah	CKI	Community Knowledge Initiative
AUSJAL	Asociación de Universidades Confiadas a la Compañía de Jesús en América Latina	CLAYSS	Centro Latinoamericano de Aprendizaje y Servicio Solidario (Latin American Center for Service-Learning)
AUW	Ahfad University for Women	CLP	Community Learning Partnerships
BCS	Board of Community Services	COBES	Community Based Experience and Services
BRIDGE	Building Resources in Democracy, Governance and Elections	CONAES/MEC	National Commission for Higher Education Evaluation
		CSD	Commission on Sustainable Development
BTI	Business and Technology Incubators	CSL	Community service-learning
CAC	Community Action Center	CSO	Civil society organization

CSR	Corporate social responsibility		IARSLCE	International Association for Research on Service-learning and Community Engagement
CSU	Community Services Unit			
CTSA	Clinical and Translational Science Awards		ICT	Information and communication technologies
CUE	Community–university engagement		IESALC	International Institute for Higher Education in Latin America and the Caribbean
CU Expo	Community University Exposition			
CUNISAM	Centre for Mental Health			
CURA	Community-University Research Alliance		IISD	International Institute for Sustainable Development
DRC	Development Research Centre on Citizenship, Participation and Accountability		IIU	Indigenous Intercultural University
			IMU	International Medical University
			IRO	International research organization
EA	Elder Academy		IT	Information technology
EC	European Commission		ITMUA	Implementing the Third Mission of Universities in Africa
ECoC	European Capital of Culture			
EDUSOL	Programa Nacional Educación Solidaria		IUG	Islamic University of Gaza
EEU	Environmental Evaluation Unit		LC	Language Center
EHEA	European Higher Education Area		LK	Living Knowledge Network
EIB	European Investment Bank		LRU Law	Law of University Responsibilities and Freedoms
ESC	Engagement Scholarship Consortium			
ESR	Environmental and social responsibility		MCO	Management Consulting Office
			MDGs	Millennium Development Goals
EU	European Union		MERCOSUR	Mercado Comumdo Sul (Southern Common Market)
EUA	European Universities Association			
EWB	Engineers Without Borders		MHEI	Minority-serving higher education institution
FAU-UCV	Facultad de Arquitectura y Urbanismo, Universidad Central de Venezuela			
			MIT	Massachussets Institute of Technology
FHC	Facility Health Committee		MNISW	Polish Ministry of Science and Higher Education
FORFOREX	National Forum of Pro-Rectors of Public Universities in Brazil			
			MOOCs	Mass Open Online Courseware
GACER	Global Alliance on Community-Engaged Research		MSU	Montana State University
			MUPSF	Makerere University Private Sector Forum
GDP	Gross domestic product			
GER	Gross enrolment ratio		NCCPE	National Co-ordinating Centre for Public Engagement
GUNi	Global University Network for Innovation			
			NCED	National Center for Educator Development
HCBU	Historically black colleges and universities			
			NCSUE	National Collaborative for the Study of University Engagement
HCF	Humaniversity Competency Framework			
			NEPAD	New Partnership for African Development
HE	Higher Education			
HEFCE	Higher Education Funding Council for England		NGO	Non-governmental organization
			NPM	New Public Management
HEI	Higher education institution		NPO	Not-for-profit organization
HEQC	Higher Education Quality Committee		NRF	National Research Foundation
			NSF	National Science Foundation
HESA	Higher Education South Africa		NSS	National Service Scheme
HIV	Human immunodeficiency virus		NURI	New University for Regional Innovation
HSRC	Human Sciences Research Council			

OECD	Organisation for Economic Cooperation and Development	TVET	Technical Vocational Education and Training
OHEI	Other higher education institution	U3A	University of the Third Age
ORSALC	Observatory on Social Responsibility in Latin America and the Caribbean	UAB	Universitat Autònoma de Barcelona
		UAE	United Arab Emirates
		UBA	Universidad de Buenos Aires
OSL	Office for Service-Learning	UCP	Universidad Construye País
PAR	Participatory action research	UCP-SARnet	University-Community Partnership for Social Action Research
PATHS	Partnership for Transforming Health Systems		
		UCR	Universidad de Costa Rica
PE	Public engagement	UGC	University Grants Commission
PERARES	Public Engagement with Research and Research Engagement with Society	ULACAV	Regional Network of Housing Facilities
		ULEU	Unión Latinoamericana de Extensión Universitaria
PNA	Palestinian National Authority		
PRIA	Society for Participatory Research in Asia	UN	United Nations
		UNAM	Universidad Nacional Autónoma de México
PWC-CLAYSS	PricewaterhouseCoopers-CLAYSS		
QU	Qatar University	UNDP	United Nations Development Programme
RCUK	Royal College, UK		
R&D	Research and development	UNEP	United Nations Environment Program
REDIVU	Red Iberoamericana de Voluntariado y Compromiso Universitario	UNESCO	United Nations Educational, Scientific and Cultural Organisation
		UNICAL	University of Calabar
REF	Research Excellence Framework	UNICEF	United Nations International Children's Emergency Fund
RUN	Regional Universities Network		
SAHECEF	South African Higher Education Community Engagement Forum	UNILAB	University of International Integration of the Afro-Brazilian Lusophony
SAR	Systemic action research		
SARS	Severe acute respiratory syndrome	UNIMA	University of Malawi
SDG	Sustainable development goal	UniSol	Universidade Solidária
SEL	Social Entrepreneurship Lab	UNU	United Nations University
SLA	Sustainable livelihood approach	UPC	Universitat Politècnica de Catalunya BarcelonaTech
SLAN	Service Learning Asia Network		
SLRS	Service-Learning Research Scheme	UQAM	Université du Québec à Montréal
SODELA	Solidarity, Development, and Light Association	USM	Universiti Sains Malaysia (University of Science in Malaysia)
		USR	University social responsibility
SOPH	School of Public Health	UWC	University of the Western Cape
SSHRC	Social Science and Humanities Research Council	UWI	University of the West Indies
		VAE	*Validation d'acquis de l'expérience*
STEM	Science, technology, engineering and mathematics	VALUE	Volunteering and Lifelong Learning in Universities in Europe
TCU	Trabajo Comunal Universitario (University Community Work)		
		VNIL	Validation of informal and non-formal learning
TFD	Theatre for Development		
TFDC	Theatre for Development Centre	WB	World Bank
TOVAK	Türkiye Toplum Hizmetleri Vakfı	WCHE	World Conference on Higher Education
TRUCEN	The Research University Civic Engagement Network		
TV	Television		

AUTHORS OF CONTEXT, GLOBAL AND REGIONAL PERSPECTIVES

Oga Steve Abah is a Professor of Theatre for Development at Ahmadu Bello University, Zaria, Nigeria where he has taught since 1979. He is one of the leading theorists in Theatre for Development, an area in which he has researched since 1980. His current research has focused on the interaction of methodologies, especially between Theatre for Development, participatory learning and action and traditional social science research.

Evangelos Afendras is Professor in the School of Humanities and Social Sciences, Albukhary International University, Greece. He has taught in universities around the world since 1966, mostly in the Pacific and Asia. His teaching has ranged across many areas, from an early focus on language sciences and pedagogy to academic strategy, and recently entrepreneurship and innovation for poverty alleviation. His approaches are built on learner empowerment and enquiry-based learning.

Hatem Ali-Elaydi has a PhD in Electrical Engineering from New Mexico State University. He is currently an associate professor at the Islamic University of Gaza and Director of Administrative Quality Assurance. He has over 20 years of teaching and administrative experience. He is a member of IEEE, SIAM, Tau Alpha Pi and the Palestine Engineering Association.

Luz Arabany Ramírez is Associate Professor of the National University of Colombia, with a Master's degree in Environment and Development and a PhD in Sustainability, Technology and Humanism. She was Dean of the Faculty of Management at the National University of Colombia Campus Manizales from 2010 to 2012 and coordinated the Social Entrepreneurship for Eliminating Poverty in Caldas project 2012–2013. Her research interests are systems theory, complex thinking and knowledge cities.

Alice Barnsdale is a dual national of the UK and the USA and a BA graduate of English Literature and Creative Writing with a minor in Classical Arabic from the University of Cardiff, Wales. Alice moved to Morocco in 2006, where she worked as a freelance tour leader for educational and cultural activity groups visiting Morocco from abroad until March 2011. Since April 2011, Alice has been working as the Coordinator of Community Involvement at Al Akhawayn University, including acting as the In-country Morocco Coordinator for America's Unoffical Ambassadors and Field Coordinator for the ARANAS Service Learning Program of Al Akhawayn University.

Paul Benneworth is a senior researcher at the Center for Higher Education Policy Studies (CHEPS) at the University of Twente in the Netherlands and a visiting professor in university–community engagement at Central Queensland University, Australia. He is the editor of *Universities and Regional Development* (Routledge, 2012), *University-engagement with Socially Excluded Communities* (Springer, 2013) and the forthcoming volume *The Social Dynamics of Innovation Networks* (Routledge, 2014).

Felix Bivens is the founder and Director of Empyrean Research, a community-based research organization dedicated to enhancing the research and learning capacities of small voluntary organizations and to working with higher education institutions to build better community–university partnerships. Felix completed his PhD at the Institute of Development Studies in 2011. In addition to his current work with Empyrean Research, Felix serves as an adjunct professor at the Future Generations Graduate School (USA).

Janice Desire Busingye is a lecturer, adult educator and Head of Department of Adult and Community Education at the School of Distance and Lifelong Learning, Makerere University, Uganda. Her research interests lie in epistemology, community development and adult education. She is now involved in training and teaching adult educators in the department of Adult and Community Education and has been a coordinator of two projects on literacy and livelihoods.

Matthieu Calame is the Director of the Fondation Charles Léopold Mayer pour le Progrès de l'Homme, a Swiss foundation focusing on questions of governance, ethics and transition toward sustainable living modes. He is an agronomist and has planned and managed the conversion of the rural domain of 'La Bergerie de Villarceaux' France to biological farming agriculture. He is the author of numerous articles and has published three books on agriculture and science governance (www.eclm.fr/ ouvrages 320, 332, 348).

Alfred Cheung-Ming Chan has been both a practitioner in welfare services for older persons and an academic in social gerontology in China. Professor Chan has extensive skills and knowledge in health and social care services and policy-making. His academic interests are the interpretation of intergenerational relationships, ageing and long-term care policies in Asia-Pacific, the development of health and social care measurements, quality of life, the caring index, etc. He is also the expert consultant for the Division of Emerging Social Issues (Ageing) of the UN Economic and Social Commission of the Asia Pacific. He is currently the Director of the Asia-Pacific Institute of Ageing Studies and the Office of Service-Learning, which he founded in 2006 in the promotion of liberal arts education to university students through 'Serving-to-Learn; Learning-to-Serve'.

Melba G. Claudio-González holds a BBA from Puerto Rico University, a Master's in Arts and Cultural Policies, University of Barcelona (UB), Spain, and an Advanced Degree in Information and Documentation, UB. She obtained research proficiency presenting a work on *Management Models of Networking*. Currently she is working on a doctoral thesis on *Business Models of Publishing of Spanish Scientific Journals*.

Betty Cernol-McCann is currently Vice President for Programs of the United Board for Christian Higher Education in Asia, located in Hong Kong. In this capacity, she has promoted the development of service-learning programmes in various countries in Asia, including the Philippines. Prior to joining the United Board, she handled various tasks in Philippine higher education as a university administrator, professor, researcher as well as facilitator in training programmes of various community development projects.

Carlos Cortez Ruiz is a Doctor in Anthropology (UNAM), and a Professor in Postgraduate Studies on Rural Development at the Universidad Autónoma Metropolitana (UAM) in Mexico. He coordinates the Interdisciplinary Research Program on Human Development at the University, oriented to establish partnerships with social groups, through participative methodologies, to accomplish their human rights.

Michael Cuthill accepted, in 2012, a Chair in Regional Community Research at the University of Southern Queensland, Australia. His main task has been to build institutional research strength in this area. Over the past 15 years he has maintained a clear vision on the role of community-based research in supporting health and well-being outcomes for disadvantaged groups.

Axel Didriksson is Senior Researcher of the National and Autonomous University of Mexico (UNAM), at the Institute for University and Educational Research (IISUE). He is President of GUNI for Latin America and Director of the UNESCO Chair of University and Regional Integration. He was Minister of Education at the Mexico City Hall, Vice-president of the Latin American University Union (UDUAL), and the first general coordinator of the Latin American Public Macro-University Network.

Sophie Duncan is Deputy Director at the National Co-ordinating Centre for Public Engagement (NCCPE), UK and manages the overall work of the NCCPE including communications, partnerships and projects. A physicist by training, Sophie started her career at the Science Museum in London, where her work included exhibition development and public programmes. She became a programme manager with Science Year, before joining the BBC, where she managed the creation and delivery of national learning campaigns.

Patricia Ellis is a Caribbean educator, gender specialist and consultant in social development, human resource development and management, and in organizational development. Among her interests are continuing education and continuous learning, qualitative research, and facilitation and training. She is well known for her expertise and competence in using a participatory methodology in all aspects of her work and has written several articles on Adult Education in the Caribbean, as well as two books on Caribbean women, gender, and development.

Cristina Escrigas has been Executive Director at the Global University Network for Innovation (GUNi) since 2006. She holds Master's degrees in Organizational Development (GR Institute, Israel), Business Administration (Universitat Politècnica de Catalunya BarcelonaTech [UPC], Spain) and Teacher Training, Methodologies and Management of Education (UPC). She spent 12 years working in strategic management and institutional change at the UPC and five years as director of the Strategic Management of Universities seminar (UPC). As well as being Director of the UNESCO Chair in University Management (UPC), she has undertaken numerous advisory works and support for strategic planning process for Spanish and Latin American universities. She has participated in numerous research projects, conferences and seminars on higher education both nationally and internationally. Cristina is Master's-level teacher at UPC, the Universitat Pompeu Fabra (UPF) and the Universitat de Barcelona (UB) among others.

Danielle Feinstein is a Fulbright fellow based in Amman where she researches youth civic and political engagement in the Hashemite Kingdom of Jordan. She has a BA in Middle Eastern Studies from the Elliot School of International Affairs at The George Washington University in Washington, DC. Danielle has lived in Morocco, Egypt and Jordan in addition to other regional travels in the Arab World. She blogs about her experiences at afootinbothworlds.net.

Hiram E. Fitzgerald is Associate Provost for Outreach and Engagement and University Distinguished Professor at Michigan State University (USA). He received his PhD in Developmental Psychology from the University of Denver. His research focuses on the study of infant and family development in community contexts, the impact of fathers on early child development, the implementation of systemic community models of organizational process and change, the aetiology of alcoholism, and broad issues related to the scholarship of engagement. He is President of the Engagement Scholarship Consortium and serves on a number of national boards, including the steering committee of the Native Children's Research Exchange.

Juan Ramón de la Fuente earned his MD at Universidad Nacional Autónoma de México (UNAM) and trained in psychiatry at the Mayo Clinic in Rochester, Minnesota. He then joined the Faculty of UNAM where he was appointed Dean of the Medical School (1991–94) and Rector (1999–07). He served as Minister of Health of Mexico (1994–99) and as President of the Mexican Academy of Sciences. He has published extensively on health and educational issues and has

been awarded Honorary Degrees from the Universities of Montreal, Colombia, San Marcos (Peru), Córdoba (Argentina), Alcalá (Spain), Moscow, Santo Domingo, La Havana, San Carlos (Guatemala) and Arizona State. He is immediate Past President of the International Association of Universities.

Andrew Furco is the Associate Vice President for Public Engagement at the University of Minnesota (USA), where he also serves as an Associate Professor of higher education and Director of the International Center for Research of Community Engagement. Prior to this, he served as Director of UC Berkeley's Service-Learning Research and Development Center and a faculty member of Berkeley's Graduate School of Education.

John Gaventa is Director of the Coady International Institute and Vice President of International Development at St. Francis Xavier University (Canada). Before going to the Coady Institute in 2011, he was a Professor in the Participation, Power and Social Change team at the Institute of Development Studies, University of Sussex. He has also served as a leader of civil society organizations, including director of the Highlander Center in the USA, and chair of Oxfam Great Britain.

Katia Gonçalves Mori holds a bachelor's degree in Education from São Paulo University (USP), Brazil, and a Master's and Doctoral degree in Education: Curriculum from the Pontifícia Universidade Católica de São Paulo (PUC-SP). She is a consultant for the Organization of Ibero-American States (OEI, regional office in Brazil) and a member of the Latin American Centre for Service Learning (CLAYSS, Argentina).

Jesús Granados Sánchez holds a PhD in Education from the Universitat Autònoma de Barcelona (UAB), Spain, with a thesis on *Education for Sustainability and Teaching Geography*. Having graduated in geography from UAB, he also holds Master's degrees in Social Sciences Education and in Environmental Education and Communication. He was professor for nine academic courses at both Universidad de la Rioja and UAB. Since May 2011 he has been the Research and Content Coordinator at GUNi.

Sylvie B. de Grosbois is the Director of the Community Services Unit at Université du Québec à Montréal (UQAM) and Vice-President of Community-Based Research Canada. She holds a PhD in Epidemiology from McGill University. Having been involved with communities for several years as a researcher on issues related to occupational and environmental exposures, she developed this view of university–community engagement through her field work.

Ayhan G. Hakan is a Professor at the Faculty of Open Education, Anadolu University, Turkey. He previously worked at the Faculty of Educational Sciences, Ankara University and the Turkish Ministry of National Education. He has been involved in distance learning teacher training programmes for the last 30 years. He is the editor of many books in this field, the latest one entitled *'Community Service Training'* (*Topluma Hizmet Eğitimi*). He is now planning a lifelong learning programme for vocational training for teachers.

Budd L. Hall is Professor of Community Development and Founding Director of the Office of Community-Based Research, University of Victoria, Canada. He has a PhD in Comparative and International Education from the University of California, Los Angeles (UCLA). He holds the UNESCO Chair in Community-Based Research and Social Responsibility in Higher Education jointly with Dr. Rajesh Tandon. As well as being Secretary of the Global Alliance on Community-Engaged Research (GACER), he is a former Dean of Education and former Secretary-General of the International Council for Adult Education. He is also a poet.

Keith Hammond lectures in Open Studies at the University of Gaza, Palestine. He coordinates Lifelong Learning in Palestine, which is a European Tempus project. He has collaborated with Palestinian universities for many years and been involved in numerous Lifelong Learning projects.

Robert M. Hollister was Founding Dean of the Jonathan M. Tisch College of Citizenship and Public Service, Tufts University (USA) and is currently Executive Director of the Talloires Network. Previously at Tufts University, he was Dean of the Tufts Graduate School of Arts and Sciences, Director of the Lincoln Filene Center for Citizenship and Public Affairs, and Chair of the Department of Urban and Environmental Policy and Planning. He received his PhD from the Department of Urban Studies and Planning at Massachusetts Institute of Technology.

Lorlene M. Hoyt joined the Talloires Network as Director of Programs and Research in December 2011, and is responsible for directing programme activities and leading the design and implementation of new initiatives. From 2002 to 2011, she was Assistant Professor and then Associate Professor at the Massachusetts Institute of Technology (MIT) Department of Urban Studies and Planning (USA). While at MIT, Ms Hoyt founded and led the MIT@Lawrence Partnership, an award-winning collaboration between an impoverished community and several schools of the university.

Barbara Lethem Ibrahim is Founding Director of the John D. Gerhart Center for Philantropy and Civic Engagement, American University of Cairo (Egypt). She earned an MA degree from the American University of Beirut and a PhD in Sociology from Indiana University. She served for 14 years as regional director for West Asia and North Africa at the Population Council, where she published the first national youth survey on Egypt. From 1982 to 1990, she was Program Officer at the Ford Foundation regional office in Cairo, responsible for programmes in urban poverty, microenterprise lending and gender. She speaks internationally on the topics of higher education reform, engaged universities and philanthropy/social investing in the Arab world.

Daniel Innerarity is Professor of Political and Social Philosophy and Ikerbasque Researcher at the University of the Basque Country (UPV/EHU), Spain. His work mainly focuses on the cultural and political transformations of knowledge societies, on innovation in our systems of government, on democracy and on globalization. A visiting Professor at various European and American universities, he is currently Appointed Visiting Professor at the Robert Schuman Centre for Advanced Studies of the European University Institute of Florence. His latest books include *The Transformation of Politics* (3rd Miguel de Unamuno Essay Prize and 2003 National Prize for Literature in the Essay category), *The Invisible Society* (Espasa Essay Prize, 2004), *The New Public Realm* (Espasa, 2006), *The Future and its Enemies* (Paidós, 2009) and *The Democracy of Knowledge* (Paidós, 2011), all of which have been translated into into several languages.

Maria Ivanova is Assistant Professor of Global Governance and Co-director of the Center for Governance and Sustainability at the John W. McCormack Graduate School of Policy and Global Studies at the University of Massachusetts, Boston, USA. Her academic work analyses the history and performance of the international environmental architecture. Her policy work seeks to bring analytical rigour and innovative input to international negotiations on reforming the UN system for environmental governance.

Edward T. Jackson is a faculty member in the School of Public Policy and Administration and Senior Research Fellow, Carleton Centre for Community Innovation, at Carleton University, Canada. He is Co-editor of *Knowledge, Democracy and Action: Community-University Research Partnerships in International Perspectives* and Principal Investigator of the Community First: Impacts of Community Engagement Project, as well as advising the Canadian International Development Agency, the McConnell Foundation and the Rockefeller Foundation.

Mónica Jiménez de la Jara is currently Executive Director of the Forum Aequalis (www.aequalis.cl) and consultant on higher education issues. She was Minister of Education in the Government of President Michelle Bachelet in Chile and Rector of the Universidad Católica de Temuco. She is also a founder of the Project Universidad Construye País and part of the Talloires Network.

Seçil Kaya is an Assistant Professor at the Faculty of Open Education, Anadolu University, Turkey. Since 2005, she has coordinated the practical courses of the Faculty's PreSchool Teacher Training Program, including the community service course. She has been involved in many projects on teacher training and in open and distance education.

Marek Kwiek is Professor and Chairholder of the UNESCO Chair in Institutional Research and Higher Education Policy, Poznan University, Poland. His interests include university governance, the academic profession and academic entrepreneurialism. He is the author of *Knowledge Production in European Universities: States, Markets, and Academic Entrepreneurialism* (2013) and editor of the Higher Education Research and Policy book series (Peter Lang).

Sofia Lerche Vieira is Doctor in Education at the São Paulo Catholic University (PUC/SP), postdoctoral fellow at the Universidad Nacional de Educación a Distancia (UNED-Spain), Senior Professor at the Federal University of Ceará (UFC), Senior Professor at the State University of Ceará, Ceará State Secretary of Education (2003–2005), Researcher at the National Council for Scientific and Technological Development/CNPq, and Senior Visiting Professor at the University of International Integration of the Afro-Brazilian Lusophony/UNILAB.

Alice Liu Cheng is a visiting tutor in the Office of Service-Learning at Lingnan University. She received her Bachelor's degree in Psychology at the University of St Andrews at Scotland and then further studied an MPhil degree in Social and Developmental Psychology.

Daniel Lumera is an independent researcher, writer and lecturer who collaborates with various Universities in Master's and postgraduate courses in the field of communication and cultural processes. He has developed international projects focusing on innovative themes in the field of well-being and quality of life, examining in depth themes such as happiness, nature of conscience and meditation. He is responsible for Research and Development within the UNESCO Heritage International Club which aims for the enhancement of humanity's cultural heritage. He is the founder of 'My Life Design: A Conscious Design of our Own Life', an educational path that transmits an overall vision of reality, promoting a more conscious, peaceful and sustainable individual and collective development.

Carol Hok Ka Ma is currently an Adjunct Assistant Professor in the Department of Sociology and Social Policy and the Assistant Director in the Office of Service-Learning at Lingnan University, Hong Kong, China. She has been awarded a Women Together Award. In Asia, she is also the General Secretary for promoting service-learning initiatives by setting up the Joint Higher Education Network on Service-Learning in Hong Kong and the Service-Learning Asia Network (SLAN). Internationally, she is on the board of Directors of both the International Center for Service-Learning in Teachers Education and the International Association for Research on Service-Learning and Community Engagement.

Mounir Mabsout has been Professor of Civil Engineering at the American University of Beirut (AUB) since 1991, and Founding Director of the AUB Center for Civic Engagement and Community Service since 2008. Mounir earned his Bachelor's degree in Civil Engineering from AUB in 1981 and his PhD from the University of Texas at Austin in 1991. Through the Center, he is developing and coordinating the community-based learning initiative at AUB.

Paul Manners is Director of the National Co-ordinating Centre for Public Engagement (NCCPE), UK. Originally trained as a secondary school English teacher, he worked for 12 years at the Open University as a producer of TV, radio and multimedia before joining the BBC as an executive producer of a number of national public engagement campaigns. He advises a number of organizations on learning and engagement, including the National Trust and the Science Museum.

Simon Marginson is Professor of Higher Education at the Centre for the Study of Higher Education in Melbourne, Australia. He is one of two Editors-in-Chief of the world academic journal *Higher Education*.

Yves Mauffette has been Vice-President Research at the Université du Québec à Montréal (UQAM) since 2009. His main research interests are plant eco-physiology and higher education. He started as an associated professor in the biology department in 1986, where he founded the Problem-Based Learning programme in biology in 1996. He was Associate-Dean of studies and Dean in the Faculty of Science. In 2004, he received a 3M teaching fellowship from the Society for Teaching and Learning in Higher Education.

Lorraine McIlrath directs the Community Knowledge Initiative at the National University of Ireland, Galway, with responsibility for developing and supporting civic engagement activities across the university. She is a founding member of both Campus Engage and the Tawasol Project. Lorraine has published on the broad theme of civic engagement and higher education in books and journals and is Co-editor of the recently published *Higher Education and Civic Engagement – Comparative Perspectives* (Palgrave Macmillan, 2012).

Stela Meneghel is a Doctor in Education, Campinas State University/UNICAMP (2001), with teaching and research experience in educational policies, evaluation and higher education. She is a member of the National Commission for Higher Education Evaluation (CONAES/MEC; 2004–2006), and is involved in the Federal University of Latin American Integration/UNILA (2008–2010) and the University of International Integration of the Afro-Brazilian Lusophony/UNILAB (2010–2012). She is currently in charge of the General Coordination of Quality Control of Higher Education (CGCQES) from the Directory of Higher Education of the National Institute for Educational Studies and Research (INEP).

Cynthia Mynnti is Professor of Public Health Practice at the American University of Beirut (AUB), and directs the AUB Neighborhood Initiative. Cynthia earned her PhD in Social Anthropology from the London School of Economics in 1983, and has graduate degrees in public health (MPH, Johns Hopkins, 1986) and architecture (MArch, Yale, 2004). She has had a connection to Beirut since 1972 when she was a student at AUB.

Claudia Neubauer is Co-founder and Director of Fondation Sciences Citoyennes, a non-profit organization aiming at democratizing sciences and technologies so that they serve a common good and a socially and ecologically more just world. Claudia holds a PhD in Human Genetics and a Master's in Scientific Journalism. She has been working on issues such as scientific citizenship, national and European research systems, and the expertise and research capacities of civil society organisations.

Joanna Ochocka PhD is Director of the Centre for Community Based Research and Adjunct Professor at University of Waterloo, Canada. Joanna is one of the leaders in community based research and has directed a number of large-scale policy research studies including the Community-University Research Alliance on culture and mental health. She also led the organization of CUExpo2011. She is Vice Chair of Community Based Research Canada and board member of the Community Based Research Ethics Office and Global Alliance on Community-Engaged Research.

George Openjuru is an Associate Professor of Adult and Community Education and Dean of the School of Distance and Lifelong Learning, College of Education and External Studies, Makerere University, Uganda. He was formerly the Head of the Department of Community Education and Extra-Mural Studies, which was the community engagement department of Makerere University, founded in 1953. His research interests include formal and non-formal adult education, focusing on adult literacy education, lifelong learning in higher education institutions and university-community engagement.

Michael Osborne is a Professor of Adult and Lifelong Learning at the University of Glasgow, UK. He is experienced in adult and lifelong education, learning cities/regions, vocational education and training (VET) and Higher Education research, development and evaluation, particularly in the context of policy and pedagogy and engagement. Moreover, he is the Director of the Centre for Research and Development in Adult and Lifelong Learning within the Faculty of Education, and Co-director of the Pascal Observatory on Place Management, Social Capital and Lifelong Learning.

Soheila Pashang is a coordinator at the Social Service Worker – Immigrant and Refugee Program at Seneca College in Toronto, Canada. She is the editor of *Unsettled Settlers: Barriers to Integration* (2012), and is currently co-editing *Displacement, Migration and Trauma* book. Her poetry focuses on social justice issues.

B. Devi Prasad is currently Professor in the School of Social Work, Tata Institute of Social Sciences, Mumbai, Maharashtra, India having previously been Director of the Centre for Social Studies, Surat, Gujarat. During the last three decades, he has trained professional social workers, taught courses on development administration, participatory development and research methodology, and written on family studies, microcredit, etc. He is chairperson of Laya and People's Action for Research and Development (PARD), Visakhapatnam, Andhra Pradesh, India.

Julia Preece is Professor of Adult Education at the University of KwaZulu-Natal, South Africa. She was principal investigator, while working in Lesotho, for the Pan African research project, funded by the Association of African Universities. She is currently running a South African partnership (with the University of the Free State) funded by the South African National Research Foundation on the practice of adaptive leadership in linking community engagement with service-learning.

Gemma Puig is a PhD candidate in community engagement and higher education. She holds a degree in Pedagogy and an MA in Citizenship Education and Values from the University of Barcelona (UB), Spain. She was lecturer during three academic courses at UB and participates on the Intercultural Education Research Group. Since October 2012, she has worked at GUNi as a research assistant.

Manuel Ramiro Muñoz is Director of the Centro de Estudios Interculturales de la Pontificia Universidad Javeriana de Cali, Colombia. He is a philosopher with Master's in University Teaching (Pontificia Universidad Javeriana) and University Management Training (FES-ASCUN-MEN), and a Doctoral candidate in Education at the University of Barcelona (UB). Manuel is Higher Education Consultant of the International Institute for Higher Education in Latin America and the Caribbean (IESALC) and is responsible for IIESALC UNESCO's comparative study on higher education and indigenous peoples in Latin America and the Caribbean.

Dzulkifli Razak is Vice-Chancellor of Albukhary International University (Malaysia) and President of the International Association of Universities (IAU). He is former Vice-Chancellor of the Universiti Sains Malaysia (USM), a position he held from 2000 to 2011.

Dzul is a member of the Asia-Europe Meeting and the Education Hub Advisory Committee, and until 2012, the Executive Council of the Association of Commonwealth Universities and the Advisory Committee of World Universities Forum.

Uday Rosario has been involved with the Georgetown University School of Foreign Service campus in Qatar since 2005. He is presently the Community Engagement Administrator for the campus, where he coordinates and manages their local and international social justice programmes. Prior to Georgetown, he worked with a variety of civil society organizations focusing on young people and their inclusion in the political and social process. He is the founder of IndiaFirst, an organization dedicated to social development in urban Bangalore. Additionally, he was a member of the Youth Caucus at the United Nations and is involved in issues relating to human rights, international law and civic governance.

Brian Seilstad is a lecturer in the Language Center and School of Humanities and Social Science at Al Akhawayn University, Morocco. He holds an MA in Classical Languages from Bryn Mawr College, and was a Peace Corps Volunteer in Morocco from 2005 to 2007 and Deputy Director of Youth Service California from 2008 to 2010. His interests include the nexus of service-learning, civic engagement, language learning, and effective teaching in general.

Jerome Slamat is Senior Director of Community Interaction at Stellenbosch University in South Africa. His main source of wonder and interest is the institution called the 'university' and its different incarnations over the ages. He is interested in issues of complexity, sustainability, transdisciplinarity, solidarity and social justice. He believes that a different, more just world is possible.

Anna Smolentseva is a Senior Research Fellow in the Institute of Education at the Higher School of Economics, a National Research University in Moscow, Russia. She also specializes in higher education.

Paulo Speller has a PhD in Government (Political Science) from the University of Essex. He is Professor and former Rector of the Federal University of Mato Grosso – UFMT; an Advisor to the United Nations Educational, Scientific and Cultural Organization (UNESCO) on the Advisory Committee for the World Conference on Higher Education (WCHE) 2009 edition; a Member of the Economic and Social Development Board – CDES/Presidency of the Federative Republic of Brazil, civil society representative; and a former Member of the Higher Education Board of the National Council of Education; Pro tempore Rector of UNILAB (August 2010 until March 2013); and Secretary of Higher Education of the Ministry of Education in Brazil since April 2013.

Claudia Stengel is a pedagogue and project manager of the IIU-GIZ project, in which the German GIZ – Gesellschaft für International Zusammenarbeit GmbH, commissioned by the German Federal Ministry for Economic Cooperation and Development (BMZ), and has since 2005 accompanied and advised the Indigenous Peoples Fund and the Indigenous Intercultural University Network.

Rajesh Tandon is founder President of the Society for Participatory Research in Asia (PRIA). Under his leadership, PRIA has worked to promote citizen empowerment and democratic governance over the past 32 years. He is a pioneer in community-based participatory research and its applications in teaching and research in post-secondary educational institutions. He has a PhD in Organizational Behaviour from Case Western Reserve University, USA and has also received an Honorary Doctorate from the University of Victoria (Canada).

María Nieves Tapia is Founder and Director of the Centro Latinoamericano de Aprendizaje y Servicio Solidario (CLAYSS, Latin American Center for Service-learning). She directed the first service-learning programmes at the Ministry of Education in Argentina, and still acts as an advisor for Educación Solidaria, the National Service-learning Program. She has contributed to the promotion of service-learning throughout the region. The author of numerous books, articles and pieces of research, she has been honoured as National Service Fellow (1993) and with the 2001 Alec Dickson Servant Leader Award.

Elif Toprak is an Assistant Professor at the Faculty of Open Education, Anadolu University, Turkey. Since 2005, she has been involved in open and distance learning (ODL) projects such as the FORD Turkey e-Learning for Technical Staff, Teaching Turkish as a Second Language in Europe and EU Lifelong Learning Projects, for example ELBEP (Eliminating Language Barriers at European Prisons through Open and Distance Education Technology), in cooperation with EADTU (the European Association of Distance Teaching Universities).

Crystal Tremblay is a PhD candidate, Sessional Lecturer and Research Associate at the Department of Geography, University of Victoria, Canada. She has international community-based field experience working on projects related to the social economy, poverty reduction, governance, sustainable resource management, and participatory methodology.

Oscar Valiente joined the University of Glasgow in January 2013 from the University of Sussex. He has previously worked for the OECD in Paris, initially at the Centre for Educational Research and Innovation (CERI), and later at the Programme for Institutional Management in Higher Education (IMHE). Oscar is member of the Centre for Research and Development in Adult and Lifelong Learning and the Pascal Observatory on Place Management, Social Capital and Lifelong Learning.

François Vallaeys is a French philosopher who specializes in social responsibility and the ethics of sustainability. He has a PhD from the University of East Paris and was awarded the 2012 university thesis first prize by the General Council of Val-de-Marne. François taught at the Pontifical Catholic University of Peru for 15 years and was one of the founders of the university social responsibility movement in Latin America. He currently acts as an adviser to the Regional Observatory on Social Responsibility in Latin America and the Caribbean (ORSALC–UNESCO).

Shirley Walters is Founding Director and Professor of Adult and Continuing Education at the Division for Lifelong Learning, University of Western Cape, South Africa. She received her PhD in Adult Education from the University of Linkoping (Sweden). She is Chair of the network of government, civil society, higher education and labour, having for four years run the provincial Learning Cape Festival (2002–2005), and is Founding Chair of a grassroots women's non-governmental organization, the Women's Hope Education and Training Trust (WHEAT TRUST). In 2005, Shirley was inducted into the Adult and Continuing Education Hall of Fame, USA.

Paulo Wangoola is founder and Nabyama (President) of Mpambo Afrikan Multiversity, at the Source of the Nile, Uganda. His current area of academic interest and research is governance, mother-tongue and cognitive autonomy.

GU GLOBAL UNIVERSITY
Ni NETWORK FOR INNOVATION

GUNI IS

Guni is an international network created in 1999 by UNESCO, the United Nations University (UNU) and the Universitat Politècnica de Catalunya BarcelonaTech (UPC). It was founded after the 1998 World Conference on Higher Education to give continuity to and facilitate the implementation of its main decisions.

GUNi currently gathers 208 members from 78 countries among the UNESCO chairs in higher education, higher education institutions, research centres, networks related to higher education and other UNESCO Chairs and UNITWIN Networks established within the UNESCO/UNITWIN Programme that are involved in innovation and the social commitment of higher education.

GUNi has an office with regional representatives in Africa, the Arab States, Asia and the Pacific, Latin America and the Caribbean, Europe and North America. The Presidency and the Secretariat are located in UPC-BarcelonaTech.

GUNI'S MISSION

The mission is to strengthen the role of higher education in society, contributing to a renewal of the visions, missions and policies of the main issues of higher education across the world under a vision of public service, relevance and social responsibility.

At the beginning of this century, there is a strong need to establish new bases for a sustainable global society that, taking into account environmental limits, re-examines the dynamics of global economic, political, human, social and cultural models, as well as their local manifestations. We are currently experiencing a crisis of civilization, in which we must facilitate the transition towards a paradigm shift aimed at rebuilding society, with a collective desire and responsibility to attain a better world for future generations. There is a requirement to reconsider what the social contribution of higher education should be.

GUNi encourages higher education institutions to redefine their role, embrace this process of transformation and strengthen their critical stance within society.

GUNI'S GOALS

GUNi's goals are to:

- encourage higher education institutions to reorient their role for broadening social contribution, embrace this process of transformation and strengthen their critical stance within society;
- foster networking among higher education institutions and cooperation between them and society;
- help bridge the gap between developed and developing countries in the field of higher education, and foster north–south and south–south cooperation;
- promote the exchange of resources, innovative ideas and experiences in emerging higher education issues, while allowing for collective reflection and a co-production of knowledge regarding innovation, relevance and social responsibility.

GUNI'S MAIN ACTIVITIES

HIGHER EDUCATION IN THE WORLD REPORT

The Report is a collective work published as part of the GUNi series on the social commitment of universities. It is the result of a global and regional analysis of higher education in the world, with a specific subject chosen for each edition. The Report reflects on the key issues and challenges facing higher education and its institutions in the 21st century. It is currently published in English, Spanish, Chinese, Portuguese and Arabic.

INTERNATIONAL BARCELONA CONFERENCE ON HIGHER EDUCATION

The GUNi Conference is an international forum for debate on the challenges facing higher education. Each edition of the Conference deals with a hot topic that is chosen as a key working subject for a period. Held every two years in Barcelona and attended by renowned experts, university leaders, academics, policymakers and practitioners from all over the world, the Conference addresses innovative proposals and ideas, as well as the results of the latest research on each subject.

NETWORKING

GUNi reinforces and expands its network by encouraging the dynamic involvement of a wide range of actors in higher education in its activities. It fosters cooperation between them and promotes debate and the creation and exchange of knowledge on higher education worldwide through both onsite and online activities. The website and the monthly Newsletter are cornerstones of the accomplishment of this objective.

KNOWLEDGE COMMUNITY

GUNi.KC is created as a virtual meeting point with the objective of supporting the creation, transfer and application of knowledge. Through a variety of specific topics focused on the transformation of higher education and its role in responding to global challenges, GUNi.KC offers tools to stimulate the direct participation of the affiliates in order to facilitate the exchange of expertise, resources and good practices that will return as a knowledge gain to community members.

RESEARCH PROJECTS

GUNi undertakes research projects on higher education on its own initiative, alone or in collaboration with other institutions. So far, three Delphi surveys have been conducted — one for each of the first three Reports issued by GUNi — addressing research on Financing Higher Education, Accreditation and Social Commitment, and Higher Education for Human and Social Development.

In addition, GUNi undertakes research projects on higher education for public and private not-for-profit institutions.

www.guninetwork.org

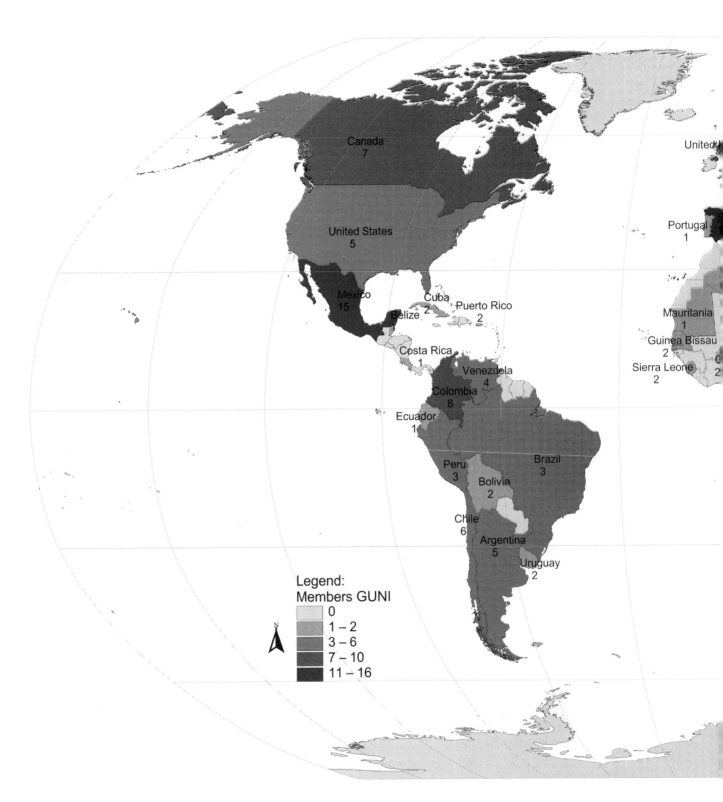

Legend:
Members GUNI

- 0
- 1 – 2
- 3 – 6
- 7 – 10
- 11 – 16

Canada 7

United States 5

Mexico 15

Cuba 2

Belize

Puerto Rico 2

Costa Rica 1

Venezuela 4

Colombia 8

Ecuador 1

Peru 3

Bolivia 2

Brazil 3

Chile 6

Argentina 5

Uruguay 2

United

Portugal 1

Mauritania 1

Guinea Bissau 2

Sierra Leone 2

Notes:
Members approved until December 2012
Classification method: natural breaks (Jenks optimization)
Vector layer source: ESRI Data; Projection: Robinson

MAP 1 **Number of GUNi Members per country**

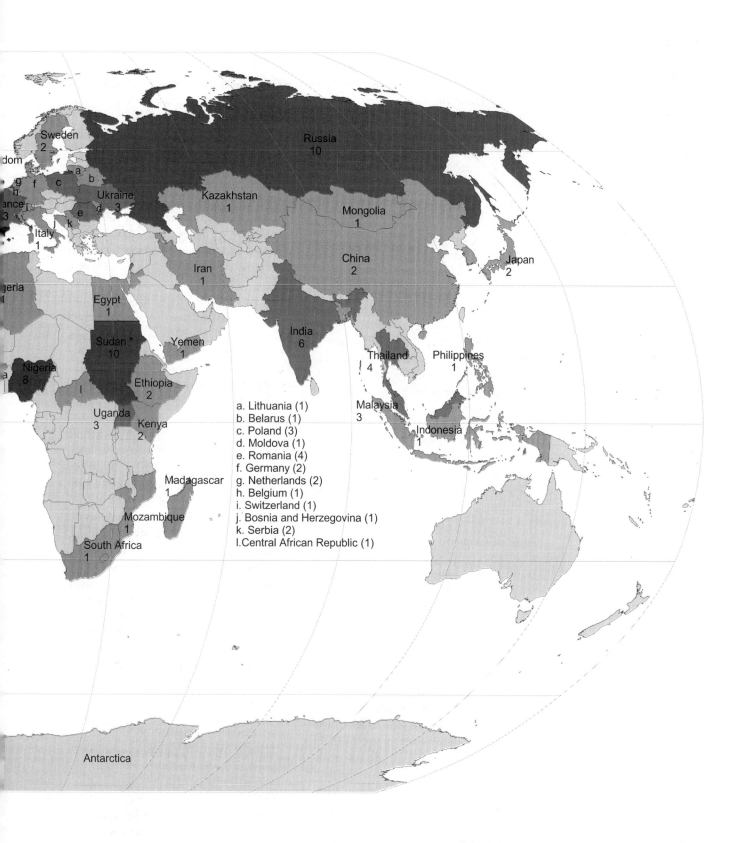

Sweden
2

dom

Russia
10

a

b

f
c
Ukraine
d 3
Kazakhstan
1

Mongolia
1

g
h
ance
3

e

Japan
2

j
k

Italy
1

China
2

eria

Egypt
1

Iran
1

India
6

Sudan
10

Yemen
1

Thailand
4

Philippines
1

Nigeria
8

l

Ethiopia
2

a. Lithuania (1)
b. Belarus (1)
c. Poland (3)
d. Moldova (1)
e. Romania (4)
f. Germany (2)
g. Netherlands (2)
h. Belgium (1)
i. Switzerland (1)
j. Bosnia and Herzegovina (1)
k. Serbia (2)
l. Central African Republic (1)

Malaysia
3

Uganda
3

Kenya
2

Indonesia
1

Madagascar
1

Mozambique
1

South Africa
1

Antarctica

MAP 1   xxiii

UNESCO'S INTRODUCTION

Paulina Gonzalez-Pose

In collaboration with its many partners, UNESCO is intensifying efforts to pursue this valuable mission to make quality education a reality for all, so that each and every one of us has the chance to realize our full potential and enjoy better health, improved living standards, and fuller social and political participation in society.

Dr Qian Tang
Assistant Director-General for Education

UNESCO's mission is building peace, eradicating poverty and promoting sustainable development and inter-cultural dialogue through education, the sciences, culture, communication and information. Today, UNESCO is committed to a holistic and humanistic vision of quality education worldwide, the realization of everyone's right to education, and the belief that education plays a fundamental role in human, social and economic development.

The extraordinary technological transformation that we have witnessed in the last dozen years has impacted our world in ways that were unsuspected a couple of decades ago. The advent of social networks such as Facebook, Twitter and Wikipedia have radically changed the way in which we communicate with each other and how we get information about the world surrounding us. The fast pace of globalization has increased economic interdependency and population mobility. In this context, the necessary internationalization of higher education has brought with it many challenges, but also wonderful opportunities to generate new knowledge and to use the ease of communication and mobility to engage better with each other, and to advocate for and affect the much-needed transformation of our institutions of higher learning into real agents of social progress.

In addition to the impressive scientific and technological advancements that they contribute, universities have an enormous responsibility to form the younger generations with a rooted sense of social responsibility towards their fellow citizens, towards peace and towards our planet. Much is said about the environment and the need to ensure sustainable development. We need to discuss and agree on ways to bring us closer to achieving those goals.

GUNi was created within the UNESCO UNITWIN Programme in 1999 to strengthen 'the role of higher education in society by contributing to the renewal of the visions, missions and policies of higher education across the world under a vision of public service, relevance and social responsibility'. The forward-thinking approach of the UNITWIN Programme seeks to impact socioeconomic development effectively, by building university networks and encouraging inter-university cooperation through the transfer of knowledge across borders.

The UNITWIN Networks have a double role as 'think-tanks' on the one hand and as 'bridge-builders' between the academic world, civil society, local communities, research and policy-making on the other. This new edition of the GUNi Report: *Knowledge, Engagement and Higher Education: Contributing to Social Change,* addresses the issue of community–university engagement. It is devoted to how to build these bridges between the several social actors and, in doing so, how to offer added value to society under a social responsibility point of view.

Following UNESCO's mandate, the second World Conference on Higher Education, held in 2009 in Paris, introduced in its Communiqué a special mention of the social responsibility of higher education. Some of its points were as follows:

Faced with the complexity of current and future global challenges, higher education has the social responsibility to advance our understanding of multifaceted issues, which involve social, economic, scientific and cultural dimensions and our ability to respond to them. It should lead society in generating global knowledge to address global challenges, inter alia food security, climate change, water management, inter-cultural dialogue, renewable energy and public health.

Higher education institutions, through their core functions (research, teaching and service to the community) ... should increase their interdisciplinary focus and promote critical thinking and active citizenship. This would contribute to sustainable development, peace, wellbeing and the realization of human rights, including gender equity.

Higher education must not only give solid skills for the present and future world but must also contribute to the education of ethical citizens committed to the construction of peace, the defense of human rights and the values of democracy.

This new edition of the *Higher Education in the World* Report explores how higher education institutions are committed to and engaged with their social realities. It analyses how engagement is a way to educate and generate knowledge to prepare new generations of citizens who are sensitive to their impacts in the world, and who have the sensibility to approach the global challenges of our time under new ways of thinking and acting. In this new approach of engagement, the key is how to address social change to overcome the side effects of our model of development and how to address new and imaginative ways of achieving progress in a sustainable and inclusive way. The Report brings up these issues and offers avenues for reflection and action to those interested in this emerging topic for higher education worldwide.

UNESCO is very proud to be a founding member and to be engaged in an active partnership with GUNi to look into issues of innovation, sustainability and social responsibility. We are also proud of the active work and networking done by the UNESCO Chair on Community-based Research and Social Responsibility in Higher Education, whose leaders are the guest editors for this 5th GUNi Report. Furthermore, I would like to mention the VI International Barcelona Conference in Higher Education that previously discussed the Report's issues, with more than 330 scholars, policymakers and civil society representatives from around the world. We applaud the choice of this year's topic, 'building transformative knowledge to drive social change', and we are impressed by the work already done in this regard.

I would also like to make reference to a notable initiative featured in this Conference: a set of short videos submitted by students around the world who felt motivated to respond to a call to express in a visual form their dreams of a better world. The short films were quite diverse, but they shared something in common: they were all made by young people who have the passion and the determination to do something to change the realities of this world for the better.

We at UNESCO give support to this new edition of the Report, which is bringing to the forefront regional analyses and global issues on how to transform higher education to exercise its social responsibility to citizens and societies, both locally and globally.

UNITED NATIONS UNIVERSITY'S INTRODUCTION

David Malone

In 1969, the UN Secretary-General U. Thant proposed the creation of a UN academic institution to be devoted to studying pressing global issues and promoting international understanding. Based upon that vision, the UN General Assembly approved the Charter of the United Nations University (UNU) on 6 December 1973. Ever since its inception, the UNU has conducted *research* through a worldwide nexus of now 15 institutes and programmes based in 13 countries, on topics related to the pressing global problems of human survival, development and welfare that are the concern of the UN, its peoples and its Member States. Our researchers are hired to work on specific policy areas of interest to the UN.

UNU also plays an important role as a *think-tank* for the UN system, and in this capacity it has been ranked among the top five global Government-Affiliated Think Tanks for the third year in succession, based on judgement criteria that include rigorous research, access to policy-makers and an ability to influence policy decisions. The UNU World Institute for Development Economics Research (UNU-WIDER), for example, has collaborated with or funded eight Nobel prize-winning economists.

The UNU occupies a specific and unique place in the worldwide landscape of higher education institutions. It operates under the joint sponsorship of the UN and UNESCO, but its Charter grants it 'autonomy within the framework of the UN' and guarantees it 'the academic freedom required for the achievement of its objectives'. Today, there is more than ever a need for such advanced research that is related directly to solving the pressing global issues currently faced by the world. This has been the driving force behind the creation of the UNESCO–UNU Chairs and Networks in 1994, which led to the creation of ten UNESCO–UNU Chairs, of which the Global University Network for Innovation (GUNi) is an inspiring example. Following the World Conference on Higher Education organized by UNESCO in 1998, GUNi was established in 1999 by three

parties: UNESCO, UNU and the Universitat Politècnica de Catalunya.

GUNi's mission is to help strengthen the role of higher education in society by reforming and innovating higher education policies according to a vision of public service, relevance and social responsibility. The UNU supports GUNi's objectives to: (1) help bridge the gap between developed and developing countries in higher education; (2) foster networking and cooperation among higher education institutions and society; and (3) promote the exchange of resources, innovative ideas and experiences to facilitate higher education's role in social transformation through institutional processes of change.

GUNi has developed into a very dynamic network with an international reputation. It has successfully fulfilled its mandate to share knowledge, stimulate networking and cooperation, identify good practices, track trends and establish research projects.

UNESCO and the UNU have made a long-term commitment to ensure that globalization benefits all. Education, and more precisely higher education, will play a major role in this respect because of its vocation to train young generations, who are the key drivers of social change. As the only university in the world that is not connected to a specific nation, UNU wants to explore fundamental questions about the future of higher education. That includes the questions 'for whose benefit are universities running?' and even 'what are universities for?'

One of the great challenges of today's higher education system is to enhance its role in stimulating and developing social change and social innovations. Everybody knows how technology and innovations have transformed the world. But every technological solution creates new problems, and we will always be faced with social problems. In today's globalized world, many of these problems have a global dimension. That is why we also need social innovations that lead to better local and global governance. Perhaps one of the most pressing social innovations needed is the rethinking of multilateral governance. The creation of the UN and the Bretton Woods institutions in the aftermath of Second World War was at that time a major social innovation. Today, almost 70 years later, the forces of globalization and regionalization, together with the shift towards multipolarity, call for a better functioning of that multilateral system.

The fifth GUNi *Higher Education in the World* Report is a major contribution to exploring the vital role that can be played by higher education in driving social change. I am sure we all agree on the importance of generating, transmitting and sharing knowledge to create a better world for future generations. Networking has emerged as a major means of action, and there is no doubt that GUNi has much to contribute towards shaping a better world.

UNIVERSITAT POLITÈCNICA DE CATALUNYA BARCELONATECH INTRODUCTION

Antoni Giró Roca

The Global University Network for Innovation (GUNi) is an international network created in 1999 by UNESCO, the United Nations University and the Universitat Politècnica de Catalunya BarcelonaTech, after the first UNESCO World Conference on Higher Education (WCHE). Ten years later, in 2009, GUNi played a significant role in the second WCHE, following its mandate for further reflection and action frameworks to facilitate the exchange of value between higher education and society. GUNi's mission is to strengthen the role of higher education in society, contributing to a renewal of the visions, missions and policies of higher education across the world under a vision of public service, relevance and social responsibility.

Higher Education in the World is a collective work published as part of the GUNi series on the social commitment of universities. It is the result of a global and regional analysis, with a specific subject chosen for each edition. The Report reflects on the key issues and challenges facing higher education and its institutions in the 21st century.

This new edition explores the critical dimensions in our understanding of the roles, and potential roles, of higher education institutions (HEIs) as active players in contributing to the creation of a more just and sustainable world. Within this context, the GUNi Report seeks to answer the call of the challenges of our time.

The world is facing a crisis of scale that is showing us a new paradigm for understanding life on Earth: interdependence. This has brought into our way of understanding reality the fact that life on Earth and its dynamics form a single Earth ecosystem that is highly sensitive to crossing impacts. This means that everything is interconnected and produces impacts on other issues at all levels. Because of this, we can clearly say that the post-industrial development model no longer works as it is neither extensible nor sustainable. In addition, the oversized dimension of the economic variable, supported on consumerism and material possessions, fails to meet the aspirations of human happiness and well-being.

We therefore need to readdress the way we handle economic, political, environmental and social issues to respond to new needs, overcoming the limitations that the system is experiencing at this moment. We should then review the priorities in the generation and use of knowledge in our societies. What we are really facing is the concept and the content of what progress is and how it can be achieved.

We are feeding an outdated system. In terms of social value, higher education's greatest challenge in the upcoming years is to materialize the contribution made by knowledge to build a sustainable future for humanity and for the planet. We must accommodate quickly and with priority the emerging idea of social innovation.

Building new social, economic and sustainable ways of thinking and acting requires the ability to imagine a different world. We need to stimulate the vision of the world we want and deserve, and also to be aware of its disconnection with the world that underpins teaching and research in HEIs today. Education has a big inter-generational responsibility in building the world we imagine.

We are key players in the model civilization. The responsibility of higher education systems consists in giving people the baggage of the past, preparing them to live in the present and to be critical, open-minded and creative to built a better world. Therefore, it is time for a general rethinking of the process, the purpose and the substance of education at all levels. It is time to go beyond educating professionals to educating citizens in ethical awareness and civic commitment.

Community–university engagement (CUE) is key in breaking the conformity of thought by renewing the world of ideas and transforming paradigms and beliefs that are supporting our current systems. CUE is central to the creation of a new citizenship. Because of that, it is not enough to just get engaged; it is necessary to analyse why, for what and how engagement takes place, to ensure a positive social process of transformation.

Therefore, one of the most important challenges involves a change of paradigm from a system that emphasizes the individualism and competitiveness to one that emphasizes the collaboration and the collective, building a new post-cosmopolitan citizenship. It is time for the whole society, at the local and global levels, to move from competitiveness, economic profitability and a short-term focus, to the collective, with human and social benefits and sustainable in the long term. It is time as well to link what we have previously disconnected.

In exploring CUE, the Report attempts to illustrate how this relevant issue is being developed within the different world regions. It shows peculiarities among countries and provides a current territorial and thematic map about how HEIs are engaging with society. It analyses how we are managing knowledge in society, the different ways in which it is created, how it is differently valuated, its ethical implications, the different understanding between what is knowledge and what is not, the ways of knowledge distribution and consumerism, and its social uses for addressing the current emerging issues and pressing problems.

The Report proposes integrating CUE into all institutional, teaching and research activities, as a way of thinking and acting. This is the new approach for a real social commitment of higher education, and it must be the social responsibility conception of our times. Finally, this publication aims to propose steps for advancing the contribution of CUE, offering a toolbox for higher education practitioners through examples of good practices, statements and political frameworks, structures at different levels and relevant experiences to move forward.

New engaged HEIs will require a metamorphosis with unavoidable transformations in their structures, culture, leadership and academic decision-making patterns, governance policy, management systems, research, teaching and learning, and engagement.

GUNi invites the global academic family to actively participate in the transformation of higher education, with the conviction that it is by taking action that we can introduce real changes in education and enlarge the transformative awareness of our societies. We encourage the analysis of how to build transformative knowledge to contribute to social change.

A POEM FOR THE GREAT TURNING*

Budd L. Hall

We have seen the images, the flames

We have seen the anger and the confusion in the faces of our friends.

But, we are told that perhaps ...

... perhaps is a special time

And sometimes we even feel that the turning has begun.

But we are unsure of the nature of the turning

And we are unsure of what it means for ourselves and even for our work.

And even more we ask how do we make the road together?

What are scholars and civil society leaders and public officials and funding agencies and artists and students for in this age?

What is the use of our power to read the world?

Do we have the skills to support the reenchantment of the Earth?

If you would be a person for the turning, make your work capable of answering the challenge of apocalyptic times, even if this means sounding apocalyptic.

You are Gandhi, you are Martin Luther King, you are Mandela, you are Wangari Mathaai, you are Audre Lorde, you are Neruda, you are Pasolini, you are Walter Rodney, you are every voice from every part of the Earth, you can conquer the conquerors with your words,

... and with your new knowledge.

If you would be a turner, write living works.

Be a scholar from outer space, sending articles to the journal of the new world rising, to a great new editor, an Indigenous woman, who cries out for contributions to this new reality and she does not tolerate academic bullshit.

If you would be a turner, experiment with all manner of words, all forms of representations of the new day dawning, of theatre and painting, of poetry, erotic broken grammars, ecstatic religions, heathen outpourings speaking in tongues, bombastic public speech, automatic scribblings, surrealist sensings, found sounds, rants and raves ... to create your own limbic, your own voice.

If you would be a turner, don't just sit there.

These are not the times of sedentary occupations; this is not a 'take your seat' time in history.

Stand up and let them have it.

Have a wide-angle vision, each look a world glance.

Express the vast clarity of the outside world, the sun that sees us all, the moon that strews its shadow upon us, quiet garden ponds, willows where the hidden thrush sings, dusk falling along the river banks, and the great spaces that open out upon the sea ... high tide and the heron's call ...

And the people,

the people,

the people ...

the people, yes the people all around the world ...

all around our wild and loving Earth,

the people speaking Babel tongues.

Give voice ...

give voice ...

give voice to all of them.

* Inspired by Lawrence Ferlingetti (2007) *Poetry as Insurgent Art*. San Francisco: City Lights.

EDITORS' INTRODUCTION: KNOWLEDGE, ENGAGEMENT AND HIGHER EDUCATION CONTRIBUTING TO SOCIAL CHANGE

Cristina Escrigas, Jesús Granados Sánchez, Budd Hall and Rajesh Tandon

INTRODUCTION

This Report looks at critical dimensions in our understanding of the roles, and potential roles, of higher education institutions (HEIs) as active players in contributing to social change and the creation of another possible world.

The first aim is to look at our changing understandings about who the agents of knowledge creation are and how the creation, distribution and use of knowledge are linked to our aspirations for a better world. The Report offers us elements of a vision for a renewed and socially responsible relationship between higher education, knowledge and society.

The second aim is to provide visibility for and critically examine one of the most significant trends in higher education over the past 10–15 years: the growth of the theory and practice of engagement as a key feature in the evolution of higher education. Recent years have seen the emergence of concepts such as 'engaged scholarship' (Boyer, 1990), the 'engaged university' (Watson et al., 2011), 'community-based research' (Strand et al., 2003a, 2003b), 'community–university research partnerships' (Hall, 2011), 'public engagement in higher education' (NCCPE, 2010) and more. At the very least, all are related to the new considerations about the creation and use of knowledge in society, broadening the idea of its social impact. The concept of engagement is intended to be redefined here, with new and deeper content that goes further than what is often called the 'third mission' of universities. It is about valuing knowledge (Innerarity, 2011).

This 5th GUNi Report is thus focused on 'Knowledge, Engagement and Higher Education: Contributing to Social Change'. In exploring this contemporary theme, the Report will attempt to go beyond the narrow and compartmentalized approach to engagement within higher education. In the present formulation, institutions of higher education are expected to serve three missions: teaching, research and service. The mission of 'service' is seen as being independent of teaching (or education) and research (or knowledge). In operational terms, primacy is attached to the teaching and research functions of HEIs; 'service' is undertaken afterwards. Many connotations of 'service' tend to assume that the knowledge and expertise available to HEIs will be transferred to communities and will thus help them to address their problems. No assumption is made that community engagement may, sometimes, actually contribute to improvements in HEIs, especially to their teaching and research functions.

In this Report, GUNi aims to approach the challenge of engagements by HEIs in the larger society in an integrated manner; it hopes to be able to explore ways in which engagement enhances teaching (learning and education) and research (knowledge production, mobilization and dissemination); it approaches engagement in ways that accept the multiple sites and epistemologies of knowledge, as well as the reciprocity and mutuality in learning and education through engagement. In this sense, this Report will call upon policy-makers and leaders of HEIs around the world to rethink the social responsibilities of higher education in being a part of society's exploration of moving towards a more just, equitable and sustainable planet over the next decades. The Report presents experiences and ideas that suggest directions for transformation of higher education and its diverse institutions so that it will exercise its social responsibility to citizens and societies both locally and globally.

THE CONTEXT: A TURNING POINT?

We are living in a significant historical moment, as Xercavins points out:

> I share the view held by analysts who claim that the quantitative and qualitative level of discontinuous changes in scale (which are in general related to exponential growth at the stage at which the curve is steepest) with regard to a multitude of

phenomena and phenomenologies (world population, world economy, environmental imbalances, social imbalances, knowledge and skills in science and technology, physical and virtual communication skills, etc.) is comparable, as a kind of macrostate, with the great revolutions in ways of living that have taken place on Earth, such as the agricultural and industrial revolutions from which new civilizational realities (in the most common and historicist meaning of the expression) have arisen. (Xercavins, 2008)

We write this Report in the recognition that there are many reasons indicating that our civilization paradigm is in crisis. Some of the characteristics of this crisis are the magnitude, acceleration, speed and interrelationship of the changes, and their quantitative and qualitative effects (Vitousek et al., 1997). Another is the interrelationships of the several crises that are currently taking place, including financial and economic ones.

The effect of the massive integration of the global scale that has taken place over the past two decades has made clear the interdependence of all areas of human activity. It has been shown that we integrate one lonely Earth ecosystem, which includes multiple ecosystems, and that the ways of organizing post-industrial political, social, economic and environmental issues do not work in this new order. We are living through a crisis of scale, a crisis that affects all systems and that requires a new understanding of reality, a new conscience and new ways of organizing the collective in all areas, overcoming the undesired affects of the old models.

The Organization of Economic Cooperation and Development (OECD, 2011) and United Nations International Children's Emergency Fund (UNICEF, 2011), as well as the 2012 Global Risks Report (World Economic Forum, 2012), are some of the mainstream organizations reporting on the nature and depth of this global crisis. Klaus Schwab, founder and Executive Chairman of the World Economic Forum, the gathering place of the global economic and political elite, has noted that:

As we begin the second decade of the 21st century, humanity is at a crossroads. We can either continue to work as lobbyists for our narrowly defined self-interests and keep doing the same old things that got us into the crisis in the first place. Or we can act together as true global leaders, with the long-term global public interest in mind and at heart. (Schwab, 2011)

The current crisis of civilization cannot be overcome by simply repairing the old engine. As Morin (2004) points out, it is time to rethink civilization and to think about and prepare a new way, the way of hope (Hessel and Morin, 2012). The new paradigm of civilization must consider the whole world as a global community (Raskin, 2010), with a common identity and a shared destiny. 'In a world where material acquisitions and consumptions are becoming the dominant ethos, there is an urgent need to bring spirituality to the core of human endeavour' (de Oliveira and Tandon, 1994).

The citizens' uprisings around the world (from the Arab Spring to the American summer and the European fall) have thrown up a wide range of citizen movements that are questioning the present social contract between the citizen and the state, at local, national and global levels. This challenge will require new world structures (on different scales, including the global) and a post-cosmopolitan citizenship (Dobson and Bell, 2006) equipped with a social consciousness (Goldberg, 2009), that will act and participate with their agency, and together with other people, social stakeholders and organizations, in the construction of a new world order.

The crises of civilization at this juncture of human history are manifested in three distinct, yet interrelated, trends. First, the scale of material prosperity achieved by many households and communities is unprecedented in human history; material well-being, quality of life, longevity of consumption and accumulation of wealth have now reached mind-boggling levels. Yet such prosperity coexists with unprecedented and widespread deprivations; shocking as it may seem, deprivation within seas of prosperity can be found around all societies today. If humanity has the means to generate such wealth and material well-being for some, how come those means are not applied for the well-being of all?

The second trend in the crisis of civilization is manifested in the large-scale disturbance to the larger ecosystem in which humanity has thrived over the centuries, and civilizations have been built and nurtured. The almost irreversible changes manifest in ecological systems and networks due to the exploitation of natural resources threaten the very foundations of current human civilization. The restoration of that delicate balance requires the use of inclusive intelligence from nature itself.

Third, there is a growing disconnect between the aspirations of individuals and the responses of the institutions of governance in societies. As aspirations for collective and shared well-being increase, deficits in the design and operation of institutions in governing human collectives have begun to show. Deficits in democracy, as the most respected and accepted form of governance for society, have become all too obvious even in those societies that have a longer tradition of democratic institutions.

In short, the challenge is not small. What is at issue today is the need for a new conception of human progress. We are on the verge of a change in the model of civilization, which cannot be built from the old paradigm of a system that has reached its limits (Escrigas, 2011). This changes the context of education, which has, in recent decades, been too focused on short-term instrumental performance within a socioeconomic system.

The way in which the world will evolve in the long term will depend on all of the responses that we will be able to articulate in the present and near future (Xercavins, 2008). In this respect, we consider knowledge to be a key element and HEIs to have a central role in its creation and in the promotion of its social use. It is important for HEIs to become, consciously and intentionally, analysts of the big changes that are happening and of possible initiatives in shaping, anticipating, intervening in and guiding these changes towards another possible world (Xercavins, 2008).

This cannot be accomplished with an educational model based on the old ways of thinking and values of an overcome order. As Einstein pointed out, problems cannot be solved from the same level of comprehension and conscience at which they were created. Thus, it is time to 'review and reconsider the interchange of value between university and society; that is to say, we need to rethink the social relevance of universities' (Escrigas, 2008).

KNOWLEDGE, SOCIETY AND GLOBAL CHALLENGES

Knowledge is defined in several ways: the facts, feelings or experiences of a person or group of people, a state of knowing or awareness, and/or the consciousness or familiarity gained by experience or learning. Knowledge is created through research, through the experience of the wise, through the act of surviving in the world, and is represented in text, poetry, music, political discourse, the social media, speeches, drama and storytelling. Knowledge is linked to practical skills, to our working lives and to universal and abstract thought. Knowledge is created every day by each one of us and is central to who we are as human beings. Knowledge tells us who we are and who we are not. Knowledge tells us how the world is and how to interact with it, how to live and prosper, what to do in life and how to do it in order to succeed and be happy,

and is even at the base of what we have collectively accepted by being successful.

At this moment in history, where the perception of truth and the comprehension of what things are is largely given to science, replacing the religious and traditional cosmovisions, the knowledge we value and the knowledge we manage (just a small part of the knowledge generated), lies at the basis of how we understand reality and how we live.

During the last years of the 20th century, we saw a dramatic increase in the importance given to the role of knowledge. The main way in which knowledge and society have been linked has been in a much more instrumental, productive and money-for-value relationship. Peter Drucker uses the concept of a knowledge economy to express how we have moved from an economy of goods to an economy of knowledge (Drucker, 1969), where ideas and knowledge have an economic value and have become a fundamental driver of society. Scholars working on what was called 'new growth theory' strengthened the ascendency of knowledge as a critical factor in economic growth. Romer noted that 'knowledge is the basic form of economic capital, and economic growth is driven by the accumulation of knowledge' (Romer, 1986, 1990). This relationship is also expressed by the World Development Report of 1999–2000, as follows:

> For countries in the vanguard of the world economy, the balance between knowledge and resources has shifted so far towards the former that knowledge has become perhaps the most important factor determining the standard of living – more than land, than tools, than labour. Today's most technologically advanced economies are truly knowledge-based. (World Bank, 1999)

National governments have, one after the other, taken up this language as they seek to build more skilled workforces, invest further in science and technological research and strengthen links between business and universities in the interest of global competitiveness. Higher education strategies around the world are often linked to the need to develop a workforce that would make a region or a nation more competitive within the global economy.

As Sörlin and Vessuri (2007) suggest, there is a 'democratic deficit' in the notion of a knowledge economy that they believe is overcome by the use of the concept of 'knowledge societies'. The UNESCO World Report *Towards Knowledge Societies* (2005) defines this concept as follows:

Knowledge societies are about capabilities to identify, produce, process, transform, disseminate and use information to build and apply knowledge for human development. They require empowering social vision that encompasses inclusion, solidarity and participation.

Waheed Khan notes that 'knowledge societies include a dimension of social, cultural, economical, political and institutional transformation' (Khan, 2005). There is growing attention to extending the discussions about the complex role of knowledge in our lives beyond the notions of knowledge economy and the knowledge society. Conceptual work linking knowledge, equity, democracy and engagement can be found in the thinking of de Sousa Santos (2006), Gaventa and Bivens (2011), Sörlin and Vessuri (2007), Hall (2011) and Tandon (2008). De Sousa Santos argues that, 'Social injustice is based on cognitive injustice' (2006, p. 19). Gaventa and Bivens note that, 'without cognitive justice, which focuses on whose knowledge counts, the larger struggles for social justice will not be realized' (2011, p. 1). A term that is increasing used to describe an active, engaged and values-based understanding of knowledge is 'knowledge democracy'. Knowledge democracy or cognitive justice (Van de Velden, 2004) is linked to the deeper transformations that our times appear to be calling for.

De Souza Santos provides arguably the richest conceptual approach to an inclusive understanding of knowledge. The global lines that he is referring to are those that separate the visible constituents of knowledge and power from those who are invisible. For de Souza Santos, the way forward lies in the concept of 'ecologies of knowledge'. An ecology of knowledge framework is centred on knowledge from the 'other side of the line', what others speak of as excluded knowledge.

Knowledge democracy is in part the idea that knowledge is to be measured through its capacity to intervene in reality and not just to represent it. An *intelligent society* must be ready to generate knowledge (ideas, instruments and procedures) corresponding with transnational knowledge societies and networks. The idea of an *intelligent society* recognizes that all human beings have the capacity to create knowledge in the context of creating a new way of living or a new society.

Now is the moment to widen the scope of knowledge in society and to move beyond creating socioeconomic well-being towards a true knowledge-based society,

through engagement with citizenry as a whole, at all scales of activity, to dealing with the problematic issues of the day and the global issues (GUNi, 2009). Knowledge must contribute to society's incorporation of sustainability shift paradigms. We need to connect different kinds and sources of knowledge and facilitate understanding between different cultures, forging links between knowledge and citizenship. This is necessary to breaking conformity of thought by proactively criticizing the world of ideas. The creation and dissemination of knowledge could contribute to transforming the paradigms and beliefs established in social, economic and political systems, and to moving forward to creative and innovative ways of thinking and imagining new realities.

Knowledge could also help in ethical awareness and facilitate the civic commitment of citizens and professionals. It is an important moment for looking more deeply at the ethical, social and environmental implications of the advance of knowledge, and to increase the resources invested in analysing the impact of science and technology in society. Knowledge is also linked with democracy, citizenship, inter-cultural relations, recognition of interdependence, new approaches to health and well-being, rights, mutual comprehension, peace-building and a deep understanding of life's dynamics.

Society needs to incorporate complexity and uncertainty in the way problems are analysed and assumed. We know there is a need to link multiple areas of knowledge that are complementary in the capacity to deal with complex problems and find solutions in the local and global context. Local needs require local proposals in global frameworks, and global challenges require global solutions that are locally acceptable. However, global solutions can come from local experience and vice versa. How we facilitate networking among a range of different social actors and levels of activity is also important. Coupling research, decision-making and development to inform political decisions that affect large segments of population is a key issue to tackle for the collective well-being (GUNi, 2008).

In the following section, we are extending the debate and making the case for HEIs and knowledge a playing central role in these new social needs. We suggest that our understanding of the creation and use of knowledge should move beyond the reproduction of society from generation to generation and beyond its link to the market and the economy, to an understanding of knowledge linked to values and active citizenship in a democratic knowledge society.

WHAT IS COMMUNITY–UNIVERSITY ENGAGEMENT?

Community–university engagement is a multifaceted, multidimensional umbrella term that may be applied to a vast range of activities, as well as to a certain view of the role the university has to play in society that underlies these activities. In this view, universities move from the agenda of simply increasing the general education of the population and the output of scientific research towards a model in which university education and research should work towards specific economic and social objectives, by means of co-creating and exchanging knowledge and by sharing resources, skills and processes with the public good in mind. It is of course important to recognize that there are some important critiques and limitations to the community–campus engagement literature.

First of all, the literature on community–university engagement is drawn nearly exclusively from the perspective of HEIs themselves. Whether the approach is how to position the university in a changing and complex world from a leadership perspective or how to support greater involvement of students and academic staff in knowledge contributions to community needs, the literature is heavily biased towards the university side of the engagement agenda.

Second, for a variety of historical and linguistic reasons, the literature is based in favour of North American and European scholars, and within that an Anglo-Saxon flavour. Rajesh Tandon, for example, has written about the 8th-century Taxila University (located in today's Pakistan), which had the motto 'Service to Humanity' (Tandon, 2008), but very little reference can be found in the dominant discourses of community–university engagement to the legacy of the Gandhian movement in India's universities, the history of popular education and participatory research, which has been strongest in Latin America, the impact of 'people's education' on post-secondary institutions in South Africa, or the community development work of the University of the West Indies in the 1960s and 70s. It is fair to say that the largest part of the world's knowledge about how HEIs relate to communities remains, to use de Sousa Santos's notion, 'on the other side of the line' or excluded. If we are to move beyond a narrow discourse of positioning universities in the global north to a broader movement re-examining the relationship of justice, democracy, knowledge, higher education and society, these limitations need to be addressed. We have attempted to address this gap in the literature through this Report by providing a full set of examples and practices from the global south and from communities of the global north.

Having noted the limitations of the community–campus engagement literature, it is valuable to get a sense of what the dominant discourse looks like as that is the language that is driving much of the action in this area. The term 'engagement' can be defined as collaboration between the university and a targeted community (regional, national or global) for the mutually beneficial exchange of knowledge and resources in a context of partnership and reciprocity. It started to gain currency within the world of higher education through the writings of Ernest Boyer, a former president of the Carnegie Academy for the Advancement of Teaching and Learning. Boyer (1996) proposed four interrelated – and, according to Boyer, necessary – forms of scholarship: discovery, integration, application and teaching. Together, these have become known in the literature as the 'scholarship of engagement'. During the 1990s, many universities used the term 'outreach' to signify their work that directly benefited external audiences. The activities conveyed by the term were defined as scholarly, reciprocal and mutually beneficial (Lunsford et al., 2006). However, many felt that the term 'outreach' implied a one-way delivery of expertise and knowledge, and suggested 'ownership' of the process by the university. Today, there is a clear tendency for the term 'engagement' either to replace or to be paired with the term 'outreach', as it is felt that it better conveys the idea of mutuality and the sharing of leadership. Some universities suggest a variation on the concept of engagement, calling for 'civic engagement', which Erhlich defines as:

> Working to make a difference in the civic life of our communities and developing the combination of knowledge, skills, values and motivation to make that difference. It means promoting the quality of life in a community, through both political and non-political processes. (Erhlich, 2000)

The practices and structures of engagement are rich and continually evolving. Some scholars speak of a community–university engagement movement (Talloires Network – see http://www.tufts.edu/talloiresnetwork), of service-learning (Campus Compact – see http://www.compact.org; McIlrath and Mac Labhrainn, 2007), of community-based research (Strand et al., 2003a, 2003b), of engaged scholarship (Boyer, 1996; Fitzgerald et al., 2012), of community–university research partnerships (Hall, 2011) and of knowledge mobilization and its variants, such as knowledge translation, impact or utilization (Levesque, 2010).

The strategies employed to reach these objectives are as various and creative as the objectives themselves. The most common engagement practices as seen from the university side of the partnership include: service-learning, in which students work in support of community groups; community-based research, participatory action research or engaged scholarship; knowledge mobilization or exchange; continuing education for community members; social advocacy (providing community groups with reliable information for interventions); community service-learning for students; business innovations or technological transfer activities; adaptive technology support for disabled individuals; and community-based programmes in support of specific communities such as indigenous peoples, unemployed youth, mothers returning to education.

National, regional and global networks have come into existence to support and promote various approaches to community–university engagement and knowledge democratization. Most of these networks are very new indeed, having been created within the past 10–12 years. They include such international networks as the Talloires Network, the Global Alliance on Community-Engaged Research (GACER – see http://communityresearchcanada.ca), the Living Knowledge Network, the Commonwealth Universities Extension and Engagement Network, the Latin American network CEBEM, the Society for Participatory Research in Asia (PRIA), the Ma'an Arab Universities Network, the Global University Network for Innovation, the Pascal International Observatory and more. On 23 September 2010, eight international networks supporting community–university engagement across the globe gathered to issue a call for increased north–south cooperation in community–university research and engagement. They called for 'all higher education institutions to make a strategic commitment to genuine community engagement, societal relevance or research and education and social responsibility as a core principle' (GACER, 2010).

Further evidence of these evolving global trends in community–university engagement can be seen in the Final Communiqué of the UNESCO World Conference on Higher Education of July 8 of 2009, which states that:

> higher education has the social responsibility to advance our understanding of multifaceted issues … and our ability to respond to them … It should lead society in generating global knowledge to address global challenges, inter alia food security, climate change, water management, intercultural dialogue, renewable energy and public health. (UNESCO, 2009)

Civil society, including community service organizations, global advocacy networks and social movement formations linked to issues such as climate change, anti-child labour, food security or homelessness, is increasingly involved both in the co-creation of knowledge through partnerships with HEIs and in the independent creation of knowledge. The academic monopoly on knowledge creation, if it ever existed, has ended. It can be argued, for example, that substantial amounts of knowledge on how to tackle issues of environmental change are found now in the large and sophisticated global civil society organizations such as the World Wildlife Fund or Greenpeace. Non-governmental research centres such as the Bonn Science Shop in Germany, the Centre for Community Based Research in Kitchener/Waterloo, Canada or PRIA in India, are but a few of the thousands of civil society groups carrying out research and influencing policy at the local, national and international level.

We are acknowledging the knowledge-creating processes, sometimes ancient, as in indigenous and Earth-based knowledge, where meaning and explanation are created and passed down completely outside the structure of a modern HEI. Another type of knowledge creation relates to the kind and form of knowledge carried out in civil society structures or social movements in the context of acting on critical issues in communities or on a larger scale. For example, women's groups around the world have over the years created new knowledge about gender, power, violence and justice. On the global scale, large global civil society networks and organizations have created much new knowledge in areas of human rights, climate change, citizenship and democratic engagement and the solidarity economy. A recognition of the capacities and processes of knowledge creation by social actors outside HEIs is key to understanding a transformative role for HEIs as we move towards engagement in a new way of organizing ourselves in this world.

But, in addition, and very importantly for the discussions in this Report, is the understanding of the very many forms of partnership research, what we speak of as the co-creation of knowledge between community or social movement sectors and HEIs. Let us be clear that there are few limits to the disciplines or knowledge domains where co-creation of knowledge happens. The Living Knowledge Network of science shops, for example, offers a multitude of examples of co-creation of knowledge in a broad area of science subjects (see http://bit.ly/xjf8kj). The Community-Campus Partnerships for Health network shares stories and techniques of the co-construction of knowledge in fields of health. In Canada, the partnership funding strategies of the Social Sciences and Humanities Research Council have seen a co-creation in areas of social economy, mental health, homelessness, food security, the revitalization of indigenous language and culture and much more.

The central principle in these kinds of community–university partnership is that the initial research question arises from the community or from the persons who are the intended beneficiaries of the research. Some issues regarding methodology of work for the co-creation of knowledge, and knowledge ownership, among others, must be clarified and negotiated from the beginning. The actual methodologies followed in community-based research are, however, as vast as both the scholarly and creative imagination. Keeping in mind that the methods should fit the purposes of the research, we can draw on the full range of quantitative and qualitative approaches and will provide further illustrations elsewhere in this Report. Before moving on, however, let us identify some of the main approaches to engagement by HEIs.

TENSIONS AND CHALLENGES

Collaborative, participatory, action or other forms of community-based partnerships bring their own set of challenges. The knowledge-making cultures of the academic world and the diverse community settings are different. Community wishes, aspirations, imaginations, visions and opportunities for research are often needed for a specific application being studied or planned at the moment. In such cases, there is need for clearness of language and unambiguous evidence or knowledge. While it is dangerous in the extreme to essentialize something as diverse as academic research, it is very often driven by intellectual curiosity linked to extended scientific discourse and is often expressed in a cautious and careful manner, admitting to considerable uncertainty. Community-based research can help to bring the capabilities and aspirations of communities and universities together through partnership practices that integrate community–university interests.

Similarly, community movements and local agencies are often looking for students to work in specific social change settings. They may be service organizations or they may be activist and social movement organizations. The university's role vis-à-vis students at this historical point is, however, to provide the best possible opportunities for them to learn and make a contribution to society. Service-learning, a term commonly used by educational institutions, does not imply social action.

A third set of challenges relates to the relative importance of relationships. There are obvious tensions when a research relationship engaged in and nurtured over a period of years disappears when the external funding runs out. Aboriginal community members have often stressed the importance of building long-term respectful relationships consistent with local protocols and cultural values. Relationships such as these must take precedence over short-term granting conventions or publication needs. These are challenges that need to be taken up within a context of developing a respectful capacity for community-based research at any university. This is particularly relevant for institutions such as the University of Victoria that are located as neighbours within the territory of First Nations who have an active interest in being partners in research and learning that involves their people, culture, language and land.

If we take the idea of relationship at its deepest, it means understanding the way in which the university is inserted into the community in a fundamentally different way. The boundaries between the university and the community need to disappear. The walls that separate scholarly knowledge from the others forms of knowledge in the world need to be broken down just as the Berlin Wall was destroyed in 1989. It means taking the notion of de-colonizing knowledge within the university seriously.

The challenges of relationships are related to another challenge of differing approaches to knowledge claims. Community groups, social movements, trade union locals, volunteer fish hatcheries and land- and sea-based Aboriginal communities have been creating knowledge since time began. They have evolved systematic approaches for the creation of knowledge that is needed to survive and prosper. The specific knowledge about homelessness, for example, is learned and re-learned everyday by the homeless themselves and by the agencies that work with them. Persons who are not formally trained or who were formally trained in universities and are now working in community settings as researchers or administrators are creating new knowledge in non-university settings. Universities sometimes see themselves as the creators or generators of new knowledge, with the challenge being to disseminate or mobilize the knowledge so that it can be of greater use to those outside the academic walls.

The elements of a global knowledge democracy,

new and transformed HEIs and deeper expressions of social responsibility and social justice already exist in isolated institutions or on a limited scale. For example, the strategic plan of the Universiti Sains Malaysia (University of Science in Malaysia) includes a pledge that the USM commits its academic staff, students and resources to the challenge of making a difference to the 'bottom billion' poorest people in the world.

This same university held an international conference in June 2011 on 'Decolonising the University'. The organizers of this conference agreed that we have for far too long lived under the Eurocentric assumption – drilled into our heads by educational systems inherited from colonial regimes – that our local knowledge, our ancient and contemporary scholars, our cultural practices, our indigenous intellectual traditions, our stories, our histories and our languages portray hopeless, defeated visions no longer fit to guide our universities – and therefore would be better given up entirely. The organizers of Decolonising the University issued a challenge that could serve as a global challenge for a dramatic breakthrough in the relationship between knowledge, engagement and higher education.

The recovery of indigenous intellectual traditions and resources is a priority task. Course structures, syllabuses, books, reading materials, research models and research areas must reflect the treasury of our thoughts, the riches of our indigenous traditions and the felt necessities of our societies. This must be matched with learning environments in which students do not experience learning as a burden, but as a force that liberates the soul and leads to the uplifting of society. Above all, universities must retrieve their original task of creating good citizens instead of only good workers.

CONCLUSION

In conclusion, we wish to emphasize three principal arguments. The first is the need to answer the call of the challenges of our time, while maintaining an eye towards the future. This means today actively supporting social change. The role of knowledge and HEIs in this is crucial. The second point is that we need to step back and look at our understanding of knowledge and its creation, distribution and use. It is necessary to break from the current conceptualization of our sense of higher education's role in the process of knowledge production. Facilitating socially engaged universities is paramount to the necessary creation of knowledge. We also see the collection and analysis of present community engagement practices as essential, both as a way

to share the efforts currently being executed by those in the higher education community, and as a platform for the evolution of these practices in responding to the challenges of the future.

REFERENCES

Boyer, E. (1990) *Scholarship Reconsidered: Priorities of the Professoriate*. The Carnegie Foundation for the Advancement of Teaching. San Francisco: Jossey-Bass.

Boyer, E.L. (1996) 'The scholarship of engagement', *Bulletin of the American Arts and Sciences*, 49(7), 18–33.

De Oliveira, M.D. and Tandon, R. (1994) 'An emerging global civil society'. In: De Oliveira, M.D. and Tandon, R., *Citizens: Strengthening Global Civil Society*. Washington DC: Civicus, pp. 1–17.

de Sousa Santos, B. (2006) *The Rise of the Global Left: The World Social Forum and Beyond*. London: Zed Books.

Dobson, A. and Bell, D. (eds) (2006) *Environmental Citizenship*. London: MIT Press/University of Edinburgh.

Drucker, P. (1969) *The Age of Discontinuity: Guidelines to our Changing Times*. New York: Harper & Row.

Erhlich, T. (2000) *Civic Responsibility and Higher Education*. New York: Oryz Press.

Escrigas, C. (2008) Acknowledgements. In: GUNi, *Higher Education in the World 3. Higher Education: New Challenges and Emerging Roles for Human and Social Development*. Basingstoke: Palgrave Macmillan, pp. xvi–xvii.

Escrigas, C. (2011) 'Sustainability and knowledge in contemporary society'. In: GUNi, *Higher Education in the World 4. Higher Education's Commitment to Sustainability: From Understanding to Action*. Basingstoke: Palgrave Macmillan, pp. xxv–xxvii.

Fitzgerald, H., Bruns, K., Sonka, S.T., Furco, A. and Swanson, L. (2012) 'The centrality of engagement in higher education'. *Journal of Higher Education Outreach and Engagement*, 16(3), 7–27.

Gaventa, J. and Bivens, F. (2011) 'Co-constructing Democratic Knowledge for Social Justice: Lessons From an International Research Collaborative'. Paper presented at the University of Tennessee, April 29, 2011.

Goldberg, M. (2009) 'Social conscience. The ability to reflect on deeply-held opinions about social justice and sustainability'. In: Stibbe, A. (ed.) *The Handbook of Sustainability Literacy. Skills for a Changing World*. Devon: Green Books, pp. 105–10.

GUNi (2008) *Higher Education in the World 3. Higher Education: New Challenges and Emerging Roles for Human and Social Development*. Basingstoke: Palgrave Macmillan.

GUNi (2009) *Higher Education at a Time of Transformation: New Dynamics for Social Responsibility*. Basingstoke: Palgrave Macmillan.

Hall, B. (2011) 'Towards a knowledge democracy movement: contemporary trends in community-university research partnerships'. *Rizoma Freireano*, 9 (Special Issue).

Hessel, S. and Morin, E. (2012) *El Camino de la Esperanza. Una llamada la la movilización cívica*. Barcelona: Editorial Destino-Paidós.

Innerarity, D. (2011) *La Democracia del Conocimiento. Por una Sociedad Inteligente*. Barcelona: Editorial Planeta.

Khan, A.W. (2005) 'Introduction. Which knowledge societies?' In: UNESCO, *Towards Knowledge Societies*. Paris: UNESCO, pp. 17–23.

Levesque, P. (2010) Knowledge Mobilization. Retrieved from http://www1.fpg.unc.edu/community/knowledge-mobilization.

Lunsford, C., Church, R. and Zimmerman, D. (2006) 'Assessing Michigan State University's efforts to embed engagement across the institution: findings and Challenges'. *Journal of Higher Education Outreach and Engagement*, 11(1), 89.

McIlrath, L. and Mac Labhrainn, I. (eds) (2007) *Higher Education and Civic Engagement: International Perspectives*. Aldershot: Ashgate.

Morin, E. (2004) 'En el corazón de la crisis planetaria'. In: Baudrillard, J. and Morin, E., *La violencia del mundo*. Barcelona: Paidós, pp. 53–94.

NCCPE (2010) *The Engaged University: Manifesto for Public Engagement*. Bristol: NCCPE.

OECD (2011) 'Divided We Stand: Why Inequality Keeps Rising'. Retrieved from http://www.oecd.org/els/social/inequality.

Raskin, P. (2010) 'Imagine all the people: advancing a global citizens movement'. In: *GTI Perspectives on Critical Issues*. Boston, MA: Tellus Institute. Retrieved September 2013 from http://gtinitiative.org/documents/IssuePerspectives/GTI-Perspectives-Imagine_All_the_PeopleSPANISH.pdf.

Romer, P.M. (1986) 'Increasing returns and long-run growth'. *Journal of Political Economy*, 94(5), 1002–37.

Romer, P.M. (1990) 'Endogenous technological change'. *Journal of Political Economy*, 98(5), 71–102.

Schwab, K. (2011) Davos WEF 2011 – Klaus Schwab: global economies face 'new reality'. Retrieved September 2013 from http://www.telegraph.co.uk/finance/financetopics/davos/8281279/Davos-WEF-2011-Klaus-Schwab-global-economies-face-new-reality.html.

Sörlin, S. and Vessuri, H. (eds) (2007) *Knowledge Society vs Knowledge Economy*. Paris: UNESCO.

Strand, K., Marullo, S., Cutforth, N., Stoecker, R. and Donohue, P. (2003a) 'Principles of best practice for community-based research'. *Michigan Journal of Community Service Learning*, 9(3), 5–15.

Strand, K.J., Cutforth, N., Stoecker, R., Marullo, S. and Donahue, P. (2003b) *Community-based Research and Higher Education: Principles and Practices*. San Francisco: Jossey-Bass.

Tandon, R. (2008) Civil Engagement in Higher Education and its Role in Human and Social Development. In: GUNi, *Higher Education in the World 3. Higher Education: New Challenges and Emerging Roles for Human and Social Development*. Basingstoke: Palgrave Macmillan, pp. 142–52.

UNESCO (2005) *UNESCO World Report: Towards Knowledge Societies*. Paris: UNESCO.

UNESCO (2009) *2009 World Conference on Higher Education: The New Dynamics of Higher Education and Research for Societal Change and Development*. Paris: UNESCO. Retrieved September 2013 from http://www.unesco.org/fileadmin/MULTIMEDIA/HQ/ED/ED/pdf/WCHE_2009/FINAL%20COMMUNIQUE%20WCHE%202009.pdf.

UNICEF (2011) *Global Inequality: Beyond the Bottom Billion. A Rapid Review of Income Distribution in 141 Countries*. New York: UNICEF. Retrieved September 2013 from http://www.unicef.org/socialpolicy/files/Global_Inequality_REVISED_-_5_July.pdf.

Van der Velden, M. (2004) 'From communities of practice to communities of resistance: civil society and cognitive justice'. *Development*, 47(1), 73–80.

Vitousek, P.M. Mooney, H.A., Lubchenco, J. and Melillo, J.M. (1997) 'Human domination of Earth's ecosystems'. *Science*, 227, 494–9.

Watson, D., Hollister, R., Stroud, S. and Babcock, E. (2011) *The Engaged University: International Perspectives on Civic Engagement*. London: Routledge.

World Bank (1999) *World Development Report 1999/2000: Entering the 21st Century. The Changing Development Landscape*. Oxford: World Bank/Oxford University Press.

World Economic Forum (2012) *Global Risks 2012* (7th edn). Geneva: World Economic Forum.

Xercavins, J. (2008) 'Higher education and its institutions and the civilizational paradigm crisis: reflections, analysis and proposals from the perspective of a forum of international civil society organizations'. In: GUNi, *Higher Education in the World 3. Higher Education: New Challenges and Emerging Roles for Human and Social Development*. Basingstoke: Palgrave Macmillan, pp. 35–9.

PART I
THE CONTEXT

Rajesh Tandon

We are living in an unprecedented era of human prosperity and well-being. Per capita incomes have been rising around the world; infant and maternal mortality rates have declined significantly in the so-called developing world; and life expectancy has visibly and significantly increased. Lifestyles have become more active, and the use of a wide variety of innovative technologies has reduced the drudgery of daily chores, especially for women. Levels of education have increased dramatically, showing an almost universal primary education coverage worldwide and increased enrolments at secondary and tertiary levels. The new information and communication technologies have made understanding the distant world a lot easier. Access to the rest of the world through new forms of communication has increased as nearly half the world's population is living in urban areas and more than 60% are using mobile telephones.

These are indeed impressive gains within our life time – these improvements in standards of living for all humanity are phenomena of the past half century, or less. The world today has wealth, technologies, knowledge, capacities and institutions that previous generations did not possess or even dream of; global air travel and even visits to space are now possible with ease.

Yet, in some quite visible and distinct ways, the world today is also facing enormous deficits and discontents. Nearly 1.2 billion people, about a fifth of all humanity, are living below a poverty line of $1.25 per capita per day. Nearly 40% of all children under five are malnourished, and half of all children live below the poverty line. Nearly half of all girls and women do not have functional literacy skills, and access to sanitation and safe drinking water has yet to be made possible for nearly 40% rural and urban households (World Bank, 2010). 'More than 2.5 billion people lack sanitation facilities, of which one billion continue to practice open defecation, a major health and environmental hazard' (UNDP, 2013a). There has been a considerable increase in inequality among the rich and the poor in all countries of the world. The top 5% of the world's households own and control nearly half the global wealth, while the bottom 40% own and control less than 5% of global wealth (UNDP, 2013a).

The recent reviews of progress on achievement of the Millennium Development Goals (MDGs) are not very encouraging in many parts of the world. The poor socioeconomic status of girls and women continues to be a cause of great concern; 'most maternal deaths are preventable, but progress in this area is falling short' (UNDP, 2013b, p. 5). Likewise, progress on the reduction of hunger has been rather slow and has been further exacerbated due to high food prices; nearly one billion people around the world do not get enough food to eat even today! These are aggregate percentages, so the incidence of deprivation is even more for socially excluded and marginalized households and communities; the achievement of MDGs for women-headed households in rural areas, tribals and indigenous communities, lower caste and minority groups, displaced and forced migrants families, and so on is even less satisfactory.

The recent global crises of food, fuel and finance have spread to the developed regions of the world. The recession in southern Europe has caused huge unemployment among the youth, and many households in countries such as Ireland, the UK, Italy, Greece and Spain are facing a reduction in standards of living for the first time since the Second World War. Nearly 300 million people are unemployed, with many more under-employed in low-paying, insecure and unprotected employment; youth unemployment is particularly severe in those societies where the majority of the population is under 25 years of age (World Bank, 2013).

Rapid economic growth and consumptive lifestyles worldwide have also resulted in enormous environmental problems. The degradation of land and forests has increased dramatically, and the pollution of bodies of water, air and soil has caused a wide variety of new diseases; indeed, the very survival of humanity on planet Earth is being threatened by huge climate changes. The UNDP (2011) has identified severe environmental trends that include land degradation (nearly 40%), desertification (one-third of world's population now living in such regions) and air and water pollution. Nearly 80 million cars and 215 million TV sets were sold in 2012, further reflecting consumptive lifestyles.

> In the last half century the use of natural resources (among them fossil fuels) has supported improvements in well-being, but when accompanied by resource degradation and climate change, such use is not sustainable. Neglecting the natural environment in the pursuit of growth, people have made themselves more vulnerable to natural disasters. (World Bank, 2010, p. 40)

There has been a significant increase in acceptance of democracy as a form of governance throughout the world since the Second World War. The fall of the Berlin Wall triggered the movement of many countries towards democracy, and recent changes in North Africa and the Arab region are also ushering in a new democratic era. Yet the citizens of these democracies find that their voices are not being heard by their own elected governments, and the recent wave of citizens' movements across the world is a manifestation of the disconnect between citizens and their leaders. The Occupy movement in Europe and north America focused world attention on growing economic inequalities; the student movements in Chile, Senegal and Quebec demonstrated the frustrations of the youth; and, outside party politics, citizens' movements in India, Bangladesh, Turkey, Indonesia, Brazil, Egypt and Russia are sending messages that the formal institutions of democracy are not working for most citizens of the world. These movements are calling for deeper engagement and participatory democratic practices where active citizens can contribute with their ideas, energies and creativity (Tandon, 2012). A recent study of civil society in 16 countries around the world concluded:

> Citizens' protests reflect the disconnect between their expectations and the performance of public authorities .... Rights, voice and dignity became part of everyday expectations of all citizens around the world, and in many cases those expectations have not been met. (Tandon, 2012, p. 7)

The world today is also much more unsafe. Human insecurity in daily life is creating isolation and gated communities, and many more regions of the world are in strife, with violence affecting the daily life of millions of citizens. It is not just about the 'big' conflicts in Syria, Libya, Afghanistan, Pakistan, Demcratic Republic of the Congo, Somalia and Mali; daily violent conflicts are erupting in India, China, the Philippines, Cambodia and Myanmar, as well as in Uganda, South Africa, Ivory Coast, Peru and Colombia. Military expenditures by governments worldwide rose to $1,400 billion in 2010 – the investment of that amount in health, education, water and sanitation would have solved these problems for all of humanity for a long time to come. As UNDP's Human Development Report (2013a) puts it, 'It will be neither desirable nor sustainable if increases in HDI [Human Development Index] value are accompanied by rising inequality in income, unsustainable patterns of consumption, high military spending and low social cohesion' (p. 23).

The most brutal effect of this violence is on girls and women, with increasing violence occuring against them around the world. Domestic violence, sexual harassment in the workplace, female foeticide, rape and custodial rape have created a situation where girls and women feel unsafe at home, in the community and in institutions. Such practices have enormous consequences not only for women, but also for the social and economic well-being of societies as a whole:

> sex-selective abortion and infanticide are artificially altering the demographic landscape, leading to a shortage of girls and women. This is not just a concern for gender justice and inequality; it also has major implications for democracy and could lead to social violence. (UNDP, 2013a, p. 32)

Finally, the relentless and almost universal pursuit of a model of development that focuses on economic growth at the exclusion of happiness, well-being and peace is causing enormous social isolation. The recent study of this phenomenon in North America has begun to show how a blind and sustained pursuit of narrow individual self-interests is making people disconnected from their families, communities and social networks (Packer, 2013). The consequent loss of intimacy and social support is affecting the happiness and well-being of many.

Clearly, these global trends affect different regions, communities and households differently. The cumulative impacts of these trends imply that humanity as a whole faces enormous global challenges. These challenges have arisen out of certain global forces, models and approaches being adopted around the world. Hence, the solutions to these global challenges have to be approached using a global lens. Although specific solutions to these challenges have to be contextually devised, it is critical that efforts at finding solutions are both local and global. New models of human development and well-being that place human happiness at the centre have to be consensually evolved. The United Nations has already agreed to promote the Gross Happiness Index as a counterfoil to the existing hegemony of economistic targets such as economic growth, stock market gains, gross domestic product and per capita income.

Societies' future directions have to be based on universally accepted values of equity, justice, inclusion, peace and sustainability. The pursuit of these values has to be integrated into the very design of productive economy, settlement-planning, community development and democratic governance. The building blocks of such a revolutionary transformation of our institutions, policies, economies, politics and social relations in families and communities have to be based on new ways of conceptualizing the interrelationships between the spiritual and material aspects of our beings. The invention of such models, approaches and formulations has to include at the forefront new ways of knowing, new ways of integrating cosmologies of knowledge and a diversity of perspectives.

What kinds of knowledge, knowledge epistemologies and knowledge ecologies are required to transform the world into such a place of peace, happiness, justice and equity for all citizens of the world? What roles, if any, can higher education institutions play in this regard? How can the transformative potential of knowledge be harnessed to address these global challenges globally?

REFERENCES

Packer, G. (2013) *The Unwinding: An Inner History of the New America*. London: Faber & Faber.

Tandon, R. (2012) *Civil Society @ Crossroads. Shifts, Challenges, Options?* New Delhi: PRIA (www.pria.org).

UNDP (2011) *Human Development Report 2011*. New York: Palgrave Macmillan.

UNDP (2013a) *Human Development Report 2013*. New Delhi: Academic Foundation.

UNDP (2013b) *MDG Report 2013*. New York: United Nations.

World Bank (2010) *World Development Report 2010*. Washington: World Bank.

World Bank (2013) *World Development Report 2013*. Washington: World Bank.

RIO+20: 'THE FUTURE WE WANT.' THE FIRST GLOBAL AGENDA OF THE XXI CENTURY

Cristina Escrigas

The conference, known as the Earth Summit on Sustainable Development (UN, 2012b), was an opportunity for governments, civil society and transnational structures to define the objectives and the common formal basis for establishing international agreements, with the aim of guiding human development and the global problems arising from it.

The document that arose from the conference, called *The Future We Want* (UN, 2012a), is, in expert in global governance Josep Xercavins' words, the first significant global political agenda of the 21st century. The document is the first message of a change of direction, moving towards a holistic and interconnected approach to the great problems of humanity. It presents an unfragmented global option of sustainable development, which includes the interconnection between social, environmental and economic issues, and reaffirms political commitment and the ways in which to implement it. The paper also proposes a participatory process to formulate the Sustainable Development Goals.

The Rio+20 summit was expected for many to be just another meeting with no real impact for change. For many, hope had already been lost and there were no expectations about positive results from the conference. For others, however, it was a new opportunity to do what was being delayed for several decades. As Ban Ki-Moon, UN Secretary General, said, a few days before the Rio+20 summit, to the *New York Times* (Ki-Moon, 2012):

> Clearly, the old economic model is breaking down. In too many places, growth has stalled. Jobs are lagging. Gaps are growing between rich and poor, and we see alarming scarcities of food, fuel and the natural resources on which civilization depends.

> Two decades later we are back to the future. The challenges facing humanity today are much the same as then, only larger. Slowly, we have come to realize that we have entered a new era. Some even call it a new geological epoch, where

human activity is fundamentally altering the Earth's dynamics.

> Global economic growth per capita has combined with a world population (passing 7 billion last year) to put unprecedented stress on fragile ecosystems. We recognize that we cannot continue to burn and consume our way to prosperity. Yet we have not embraced the obvious solution, the only possible solution, now as it was 20 years ago: sustainable development.

> Fortunately, we have a second chance to act. Rio offers a generational opportunity to hit the reset button: to set a new course toward a future that balances the economic, social and environmental dimensions of prosperity and human well-being.

> To secure our world for future generations we need … a transformative agenda for change to set in motion a conceptual revolution in how we think about creating dynamic yet sustainable growth for the 21st century and beyond.

This is perhaps the first time that the real situation has been as clearly expressed at that level. Ban Ki-Moon also stresses that Rio+20 should 'Inspire new thinking and action' and 'should be a people's summit that offers concrete hope for real improvements in daily lives'. He goes on to say that 'Now is not the moment for narrow squabbling. This is a moment for world leaders and their people to unite in common purpose around a shared vision of our common future, the future we want.'

On the other hand, Irina Bokova, UNESCO General Director, has talked about the pressing need for a global change in thinking and acting and the role of education in this area:

> Change must occur. We will reach our goal of green economies only if we build strong foundations, built on new ways of thinking and acting by people of all ages and by all parts of society. The signposts are clear: we need to change dramatically, beginning with

how we think about our relationship to each other, to future generations, and to the ecosystems that support us. [UN High-Level Panel on Global Sustainability, 2012] … This must start with education. Education that empowers women and men with new values and behaviors to find solutions to the challenges of today and tomorrow, education that develops new and relevant skills. Economic and technological solutions, political regulations or financial incentives are not enough. We need a fundamental change in the way we think and act. (Bokova, 2012)

Several other voices were raised about the urgent need for civilization to change its model in an obvious way. The president of Uruguay, José Mújica, was very clear regarding the current development model:

We are facing the need to fight for another culture … The crisis of the environment is not a cause, the cause is the model of civilization we have created and what we have to review is our way of living ... We have created a civilization that is daughter of the market and the competition … which has created market societies … Are we governing globalization or globalization governs us? … The great crisis of today is not ecological, it is political. (Mujica, 2012)

He also stresses a very peculiar matter in a political framework: the need to place values as happiness in the core of a new model of progress. 'We don't come to the planet to develop ourselves in general terms, we came into life trying to be happy … Development cannot fly in the face of happiness, it has to promote happiness, love and human relationships' (see http://www.youtube.com/watch?v=3cQgONgTupo).

This paper has been inspired by the tireless work of my colleague Josep Xercavins, whom I thank for his continued dedication to the pressing global issues, the state of the world and its governance. The object of this piece is to set the current context of the world and make a clear link with higher education activities.

Academia works worldwide training people who will show a way of understanding, of relating, of making decisions and of engaging with the world in which they live through their personal and professional activity. Collectively, we are more concerned to teach a specific professional content rather than the 'game rules'; the impacts we create; the deep understanding of reality and a responsible way of thinking and acting – held in conscience and ethics – in the exchange of value with society.

It is in the artificial separation of the activity and its impact – two sides of the same coin – that a gap opens up. This gap is about the ignorance that we have concerning our personal footprint on the world. This encourages victimhood and indignation against outside reality that lies at the same level as irresponsibility. The lack of attention to what is apparently not important is the gap by which we miss our capacity for transformative action in the world. As a result, we dilute our true responsibility – responsibility understood as the ability to respond and to create our reality – and therefore the ability to exercise our real freedom.

Everything that happens to us, as a human community, we have generated together, and together we can transform it. We create our reality with our attitudes, our behaviour and our daily contribution. We are living in an era in which the impact on the context of our personal and professional activity should concern us even more than the specific activities we undertake.

At GUNi, since we are aware of this, we dedicate a space in each report to the state of the world and its relationship to education and knowledge systems. Furthermore, in this report, we introduce the global agenda agreed by over 190 countries in June 2012 in Rio de Janeiro, Brazil, and adopted as a resolution by the UN General Assembly in its 123rd plenary meeting, on 27 July 2012.

We now have a global policy framework. As we all know, it is not binding, but it 'does its work' if we want to use it. Local governments, civil society organizations, individuals, public and private institutions, businesses and productive sectors in all areas of activity worldwide now have a place to contextualize their social responsible activity, if they choose to do so. Now is the time of consciousness, of will and implication, with no excuses.

What follows is a selection of several sections and articles from the resolution, along with some general comments, which allow us to understand its relevance, through both the nature of the content and the structure of the document. The full resolution is available at http://www.uncsd2012.org/thefuturewewant.html.

I. OUR COMMON VISION

1. We, the Heads of State and Government and high-level representatives, having met at Rio de Janeiro, Brazil, from 20 to 22 June 2012, with the full participation of civil society, renew our commitment to sustainable development and to ensuring the promotion of an economically, socially and environmentally sustainable future for our planet and for present and future generations.

3. We therefore acknowledge the need to further mainstream sustainable development at all levels, integrating economic, social and environmental aspects and recognizing their inter linkages, so as to achieve sustainable development in all its dimensions.

4. We recognize that poverty eradication, changing unsustainable and promoting sustainable patterns of consumption and production and protecting and managing the natural resource base of economic and social development are the overarching objectives of an essential requirement for sustainable development. We also reaffirm the need to achieve sustainable development by promoting sustained, inclusive and equitable economic growth, creating greater opportunities for all, reducing inequalities, raising basic standards of living, fostering equitable social development and inclusion, and promoting the integrated and sustainable management of natural resources and ecosystems that supports, inter alia, economic, social and human development while facilitating ecosystem conservation, regeneration and restoration and resilience in the face of new and emerging challenges.

II. RENEWING POLITICAL COMMITMENT

A. REAFFIRMING THE RIO PRINCIPLES AND PAST ACTION PLANS

18. We are determined to reinvigorate political will and to raise the level of commitment by the international community to move the sustainable development agenda forward, … We further reaffirm our respective commitments to other relevant internationally agreed goals in the economic, social and environmental fields since 1992. We therefore resolve to take concrete measures that accelerate implementation of sustainable development commitments.

B. ADVANCING INTEGRATION, IMPLEMENTATION AND COHERENCE: ASSESSING THE PROGRESS TO DATE AND THE REMAINING GAPS IN THE IMPLEMENTATION OF THE OUTCOMES OF THE MAJOR SUMMITS ON SUSTAINABLE DEVELOPMENT AND ADDRESSING NEW AND EMERGING CHALLENGES

20. We acknowledge that, since 1992, there have been areas of insufficient progress and setbacks in the integration of the three dimensions of sustainable development, aggravated by multiple financial, economic, food and energy crises, which have threatened the ability of all countries, in particular developing countries, to achieve sustainable development. In this regard, it is critical that we do not backtrack from our commitment to the outcome of the United Nations Conference on Environment and Development. We also recognize that one of the current major challenges for all countries, particularly for developing countries, is the impact from the multiple crises affecting the world today.

21. We are deeply concerned that one in five people on this planet, or over 1 billion people, still live in extreme poverty, and that one in seven – or 14 per cent – is undernourished, while public health challenges, including pandemics and epidemics, remain omnipresent threats …, we need to increase our efforts to achieve sustainable development and, in particular, the eradication of poverty, hunger and preventable diseases.

39. We recognize that planet Earth and its ecosystems are our home and that 'Mother Earth' is a common expression in a number of countries and regions, and we note that some countries recognize the rights of nature in the context of the promotion of sustainable development. We are convinced that in order to achieve a just balance among the economic, social and environmental needs of present and future generations, it is necessary to promote harmony with nature.

40. We call for holistic and integrated approaches to sustainable development that will guide humanity to live in harmony with nature and lead to efforts to restore the health and integrity of the Earth's ecosystem.

41. We acknowledge the natural and cultural diversity of the world, and recognize that all cultures and civilizations can contribute to sustainable development.

C. ENGAGING MAJOR GROUPS AND OTHER STAKEHOLDERS

It appeals to the necessary participation of all groups of society in achieving the sustainable development, including young people, children and indigenous people.

49. We stress the importance of the participation of indigenous peoples in the achievement of sustainable development. We also recognize the importance of the United Nations Declaration on the Rights of Indigenous Peoples in the context of global, regional, national and sub-national implementation of sustainable development strategies.

III. GREEN ECONOMY IN THE CONTEXT OF SUSTAINABLE DEVELOPMENT AND POVERTY ERADICATION

Another important contribution of Rio+20 was the questioning and the proposal for a new measure of the gross domestic product (GDP). Rio pointed out openly that this index has outlived its usefulness in a world in which natural resource scarcity, pollution and social exclusion are also becoming factors that determine whether a nation's wealth actually increases or decreases. This means revising and enlarging what we understand by development. The final document of the summit asked the Committee for Statistics of the UN to work with other United Nations agencies, including the UN Environment Program (UNEP) and other organizations, to identify new approaches to measure progress (UNEP, 2012).

38. We recognize the need for broader measures of progress to complement gross domestic product in order to better inform policy decisions, and in this regard we request the United Nations Statistical Commission, in consultation with relevant United Nations system entities and other relevant organizations, to launch a programme of work in this area, building on existing initiatives.

48. We recognize the important contribution of the scientific and technological community to sustainable development. We are committed to working with and fostering collaboration among the academic, scientific and technological community, in particular in developing countries, to close the technological gap between developing and developed countries and strengthen the science–policy interface, as well as to foster international research collaboration on sustainable development.

65. We recognize the power of communications technologies, including connection technologies and innovative applications, to promote knowledge exchange, technical cooperation and capacity-building for sustainable development. These technologies and applications can build capacity and enable the sharing of experiences and knowledge in the different areas of sustainable development in an open and transparent manner.

IV. INSTITUTIONAL FRAMEWORK FOR SUSTAINABLE DEVELOPMENT

A. STRENGTHENING THE THREE DIMENSIONS OF SUSTAINABLE DEVELOPMENT

75. ... The institutional framework for sustainable development should integrate the three dimensions of sustainable development in a balanced manner ... and [review] progress in implementing sustainable development. We also reaffirm that the framework should be inclusive, transparent and effective and that it should find common solutions related to global challenges to sustainable development.

76. We recognize that effective governance at the local, sub-national, national, regional and global levels representing the voices and interests of all is critical for advancing sustainable development. The strengthening and reform of the institutional framework should not be an end in itself, but a means to achieve sustainable development ....

B. STRENGTHENING INTER-GOVERNMENTAL ARRANGEMENTS FOR SUSTAINABLE DEVELOPMENT

Among other proposals, the Statement refers to the role of the General Assembly the Economic and Social Council and the High-level Political Forum.

HIGH-LEVEL POLITICAL FORUM

84. We decide to establish a universal, inter-governmental, high-level political forum, building on the strengths, experiences, resources and inclusive participation modalities of the Commission on Sustainable Development, and subsequently replacing the Commission. The high-level political forum shall follow up on the implementation of sustainable development and should avoid overlap with existing structures, bodies and entities in a cost-effective manner.

V. FRAMEWORK FOR ACTION AND FOLLOW-UP

A. THEMATIC AREAS AND CROSS-SECTORAL ISSUES

Poverty eradication	Food security, nutrition and sustainable agriculture	Water and sanitation
Energy	Oceans and seas	Health and population
Sustainable transport	Sustainable tourism	Oceans and seas
Promoting full and productive employment, decent work for all and social protection	Sustainable cities and human settlements	Disaster risk reduction
Climate change	Forests	Mountains
Biodiversity	Desertification, land degradation and drought	Chemicals and waste
Sustainable consumption and production	Mining	Education
	Gender equity and women's empowerment	

B. SUSTAINABLE DEVELOPMENT GOALS

247. We also underscore that sustainable development goals should be action-oriented, concise and easy to communicate, limited in number, aspirational, global in

nature and universally applicable to all countries, while taking into account different national realities, capacities and levels of development and respecting national policies and priorities. We also recognize that the goals should address and be focused on priority areas for the achievement of sustainable development, being guided by the present outcome document. Governments should drive implementation with the active involvement of all relevant stakeholders, as appropriate.

MEANS OF IMPLEMENTATION AND FINANCE

250. We recognize that progress towards the achievement of the goals needs to be assessed and accompanied by targets and indicators, while taking into account different national circumstances, capacities and levels of development.

251. We recognize that there is a need for global, integrated and scientifically based information on sustainable development. ... We further commit to mobilizing financial resources and capacity-building, particularly for developing countries, to achieve this endeavour.

EDUCATION

This is the first time that the Earth Summit statement has included a direct recognition of the role of education in the transformations needed for sustainable development.

229. We reaffirm our commitments to the right to education ... We further reaffirm that full access to quality education at all levels is an essential condition for achieving sustainable development, poverty eradication, gender equality and women's empowerment, as well as human development, for the attainment of the internationally agreed development goals, including the Millennium Development Goals, and for the full participation of both women and men, in particular young people. In this regard, we stress the need for ensuring equal access to education for persons with disabilities, indigenous peoples, local communities, ethnic minorities and people living in rural areas.

230. We recognize that the younger generations are the custodians of the future, and the need for better quality and access to education beyond the primary level. We therefore resolve to improve the capacity of our education systems to prepare people to pursue sustainable development, including through enhanced teacher training, the development of sustainability curricula, the development of training programmes that prepare students for careers in fields related to sustainability, and more effective use of information and communications technologies to enhance learning

outcomes. We call for enhanced cooperation among schools, communities and authorities in efforts to promote access to quality education at all levels.

232. We emphasize the importance of greater international cooperation to improve access to education, including by building and strengthening education infrastructure and increasing investment in education, particularly investment to improve the quality of education for all in developing countries. We encourage international educational exchanges and partnerships, including the creation of fellowships and scholarships to help to achieve global education goals.

234. We strongly encourage educational institutions to consider adopting good practices in sustainability management on their campuses and in their communities, with the active participation of, inter alia, students, teachers and local partners, and teaching sustainable development as an integrated component across disciplines.

There are two more points (231 and 233) that are devoted to education for sustainability in a very specific way.

FINAL REMARKS

Strengthening the links between science and policy and establishing a new mechanism for international cooperation and scientific collaboration in the field of sustainable development is the subject of the Future Earth initiative. Future Earth is a new 10-year international research initiative that will develop the knowledge to respond effectively to the risks and opportunities of global environmental change and to support transformation towards global sustainability in the coming decades. Future Earth will mobilize thousands of scientists while strengthening partnerships with policy-makers and other stakeholders to provide sustainability options and solutions in the wake of Rio+20 (Rockström, 2012).

The initiative aims to collectively produce knowledge that will meet the needs of sustainable development. To reach this goal, it will need to include scientific capabilities from all areas of knowledge in a multidisciplinary approach, including the natural sciences and social sciences as well as engineering, the arts and the humanities. This is a great opportunity for higher education institutions and scholars worldwide to engage with pressing global issues.

UNESCO, at the request of the UN, will lead the creation of a Scientific Advisory Board mandated with providing advice on the role of science and technology in the transition towards sustainability. This valuable interface between science and policy will also promote cooperation between the diverse UN agencies and the international scientific community.

It is now our job to know and disseminate this content and actively contribute to its effective implementation. The impact of this framework for higher education institutions in their role of creating knowledge and preparing professionals in all areas of activity is obvious. Also obvious is the huge delay that higher education institutions worldwide are showing in the incorporation of approaches, worldviews, ethics, values and specific knowledge to adapt the institutions' activity to the real needs of the world today. As with many other social sectors, we have settled into the known approaches. It is now time to recover the critical spirit and to show a stronger commitment to serve society.

REFERENCES

Bokova, I. (2012) 'Educating for a Sustainable Future.' Rio+20 side-event, Opening Address, Rio de Janeiro, Brazil, June 21, 2012.

Ki-Moon, B. (2012) 'The future we want.' *New York Times*, May 23.

Mujica, J. (2012) 'President of Uruguay presentation at Rio+20, 20 June 2012.' Retrieved August 22, 2013 from http://apuntesdeescritorio.wordpress.com/2012/06/26/discurso-de-jose-mujica-presidente-del-uruguay-en-la-cumbre-rio20/.

Rockström, J. (2012) *Future Earth: Research for Global Sustainability. A Framework Document* by the Future Earth Transition Team (Transition Team members are presented at: http://www.icsu.org/future-earth/transition-team). Final version – February 2012. Available online at http://www.icsu.org/future-earth.

United Nations Secretary-General's High-Level Panel on Global Sustainability (2012) 'Resilient People, Resilient Planet: A Future Worth Choosing.' Presented in Addis Ababa, January 30, 2012.

UN (2012a) 'The Future We Want.' United Nations General Assembly Resolution 66/288, 123rd plenary meeting, July 27, 2012. See also http://www.uncsd2012.org/thefuturewewant.html.

UN (2012b) United Nations Conference on Sustainable Development in Rio de Janeiro from 20 to 22 June 2012. See http://www.uncsd2012.org/.

UNEP (2012) 'Inclusive Green Economy Given Go Ahead by Heads of State at Rio+20.' Presented June 22, 2012 at United Nations Environment Programme (UNEP). Retrieved August 22, 2013 from http://www.unep.org/newscentre/default.aspx?DocumentID=2688&ArticleID=9195.

I.2.1 RIO+20: DYNAMICS, GOVERNANCE AND SUSTAINABLE DEVELOPMENT GOALS*
Maria Ivanova

* This paper is based on a longer analysis of Rio+20 by the author, 'The contested legacy of Rio+20,' which was published in the journal *Global Environmental Politics* in 2013.

In June 2012, nearly fifty thousand people gathered in Rio de Janeiro for the largest of four global environmental summits in four decades, the UN Conference on Sustainable Development (Rio+20). Long before the conference started, however, observers were predicting its failure. 'Designed with a wide range of objectives, the conference seems destined to fail,' noted Michel Rocard, former Prime Minister of France. 'Without consensus, no action can be taken, and consensus will be impossible' (Rocard, 2012). Indeed, as soon as Brazil's President Dilma Rousseff declared the conference closed, activists and analysts pronounced it a disappointment (Halle, 2012), a 'colossal failure of leadership and vision' (Center for American Progress,

2012) and evidence that 'governments have given up on the planet' (Monbiot, 2012). Many criticized the 50-page outcome document, entitled *The Future We Want*, as weak and lacking vision, a meaningless pot-pourri of issues. Greenpeace even dubbed it 'the longest suicide note in history' (*Time* Magazine, 2012).

Others, however, perceive the document as a successful outcome of a global gathering that many considered doomed to failure. They argue that it offers a global framework for sustainable development, and point out that the impact of Rio+20 goes beyond the official documents (Ong et al., 2012). The conference spurred hundreds of voluntary negotiated commitments by governments, businesses and non-governmental organizations to achieve specific sustainability goals. It generated pledges of over $513 billion to support the new initiatives.

Ultimately, the impacts of the Rio+20 conference have so far been subtle yet significant. The key to understanding them lies in discerning the detail in the broad political statements and numerous official and unofficial activities that constituted the conference. Three main areas stand out: a reform of international institutions, sustainable development goals (SDGs), and participation as principle and practice. The global decisions in these domains and the unprecedented local engagement provide critical junctures that are likely to shape global environmental and sustainability governance for the next two decades.

REFORM OF INTERNATIONAL INSTITUTIONS

Rio+20's most important legacy has been the reform of the international institutions for environment and sustainable development: it altered the institutional form of the United Nations Environment Programme (UNEP) and agreed to abolish the Commission on Sustainable Development. Reform of UNEP had been the subject of government deliberations for 15 years – starting with the 1997 Rio+5 Summit at UN Headquarters; it then continuing with the preparatory meetings for the 2002 World Summit on Sustainable Development and subsequently under various auspices in the UN General Assembly and UNEP's Governing Council (Ivanova, forthcoming).

Governments committed to 'strengthen and upgrade' UNEP by expanding its Governing Council from 58 countries to universal membership, by increasing its financial resources through greater contributions from the UN regular budget; and by expanding its role in capacity-building and implementation. The outcome document also explicitly affirmed UNEP's leadership role in environmental governance. These changes accord UNEP some of the key attributes of a specialized agency – universality, more stable and predictable finances, and formal authority – without the limitation of a lengthy treaty negotiation process.

As a result of Rio+20, UNEP became the only subsidiary organ of the UN with universal membership. This change is expected to grant UNEP greater legitimacy vis-à-vis member states and multilateral environmental agreements. Ultimately, however, UNEP has to earn the necessary influence to coordinate and oversee the work of the environmental conventions and produce a coherent response to environmental challenges.

Financially, UNEP also emerged in a stronger position. Affirming the need for 'secure, stable, adequate and predictable financial resources for UNEP' governments committed contributions from the UN regular budget in a manner that adequately reflected the organization's administrative and management costs. Contributions from the UN regular budget to UNEP's core operational needs would serve a role similar to that of assessed contributions in specialized agencies, a stable and predictable amount providing certainty for a core

budget. UNEP could then raise programme resources by entrepreneurial means. Indeed, support for UNEP at Rio+20 went beyond rhetoric and came from unexpected quarters. China's premier and Brazil's president announced contributions of $6 million each to UNEP's budget, putting them among the organization's top 20 donors (Ivanova, 2011). Finally, governments affirmed a greater role for UNEP in assisting nation states with capacity-building and in the implementation of environmental commitments, a role that would bring the organization closer to on-the-ground activities.

In a rare institutional reform move, governments decided to abolish the Commission on Sustainable Development (CSD) – the central institutional outcome of the 1992 Rio Earth Summit – and replace it with a High-level Political Forum within the UN General Assembly. Despite several attempts to revamp its programme of work and its format, the Commission failed to catalyse sufficient political commitment and action. Its futile negotiations (such as in 2007 on energy and climate change) illustrated the 'fundamental disagreements between states on the nature, scope and ambition of the sustainable development agenda and the role, relevance and value of the CSD itself' (IISD, 2007). Unable to address contemporary global challenges and add value to existing processes, the Commission had come to be seen as ineffective and even counterproductive. Moreover, opposition to the CSD came from many UN agencies, which saw its efforts as duplicative, particularly in the environmental field.

The core functions of the new universal, intergovernmental high-level forum would be to provide 'political leadership, guidance, and recommendations for sustainable development', to enhance and promote coordination in the UN system, to support evidence-based decision-making, and to provide a platform for collaboration for multiple stakeholders (UN General Assembly 2012, para 84). Unable to delineate the forum's format and organization during Rio+20, governments committed to an open and inclusive negotiation process under the General Assembly that would take place from January to May 2013, which Brazil and Italy were to lead. While Rio+20's outcome document sets out a comprehensive vision for a new UN institution, the potential for overlap, duplication and competition between the new forum, UNEP, other UN institutions and multilateral environmental agreements will remain significant unless there is a clear division of labour between the environment and sustainable development institutions; this also threatens to perpetuate the dynamic that led to the institutional reform in the first place.

SUSTAINABLE DEVELOPMENT GOALS

Many observers note that one of the most important achievements of Rio+20 was the agreement to set global SDGs. Inspired by the Millennium Development Goals (MDG), which are set to expire in 2015, SDGs will focus on priority areas for sustainable development and apply to both developed and developing countries. The MDGs have underscored the power of a global vision. They have mobilized political attention, fostered public awareness, harnessed resources and induced governments and others to collect and produce new data and information. The SDGs suggested by Colombia and Guatemala, and supported by multiple international scientific and political panels, have similarly gained political centre-stage. Envisioned as being comprehensive and universal, the SDGs will seek to frame the nexus between basic human needs, environmental sustainability, social equity and governance tools.

To develop the goals, governments established a new inter-governmental process, overseen by the UN General Assembly and open to all stakeholders. On 22 January 2013, the UN General Assembly adopted a decision (67/555) to establish the open working group on SDGs, which the Rio+20 outcome document envisioned as comprising 30 representatives from the five UN regional groups, nominated by member states. Selecting 30 countries, however, has proven more difficult than expected, as most member states demand to be engaged in the process, which they perceive will shape the new global goals. Once developed, the goals are likely to chart the course of sustainable development for the coming decades. They are also likely to influence official development assistance priorities, much like their predecessors, the MDGs, did. The final composition of the group has therefore grown from 30 to 70 countries.

PARTICIPATION AS PRINCIPLE AND PRACTICE

Rio+20 both called for and evidenced greatly increased global engagement in environmental governance. The outcome document reflected a new global norm for participation – from the 'full and effective participation of all countries in decision making processes' to enhancing the participation and 'effective engagement' of civil society in multiple aspects of governance (UN General Assembly 2012, para 76(e), 76(h)).

During the ten days of the conference, 4,000 side events took place in Rio, 500 of them at the official conference centre itself. Myriad local initiatives have sprung up from cities to campuses across the planet.

Governments, businesses, civil society groups and universities registered over 600 voluntary commitments in energy, transport, the green economy, disaster reduction, desertification, water, forests, agriculture and more, and mobilized over $513 billion to meet them. The People's Summit – organized as a counter-conference across the city – brought together 15,000 people looking for alternatives to the official government processes under the banner 'Come reinvent the world.'

Two hundred CEOs met in their own parallel event – the Business Action for Sustainable Development conference – to encourage business to improve environmental performance. Leaders of 37 banks, investment funds and insurance companies signed up to the Natural Capital Declaration, committing to 'help build an understanding of their impacts and dependencies on natural capital; embed natural capital into their products and services; report or disclose on the theme of natural capital; and account for natural capital in accounting frameworks' (Natural Capital Declaration, 2012). Thirty prominent insurance companies worth over $5 trillion launched the Principles for Sustainable Insurance, aiming to enhance the ability of the insurance sector to address environmental issues and provide insurance tools for risk management. Hundreds of judges, chief justices and prosecutor generals gathered at the World Congress on Justice in Rio to articulate the role of courts in environmental policy.

Thousands of students and faculty from across the world engaged in Rio+20 as thinkers and doers, articulating education and sustainability goals and initiatives in campuses and communities worldwide. The Brazilian government announced the creation of the Rio+ Centre, the World Centre for Sustainable Development, which will engage in the creation and dissemination of knowledge both locally and globally. Several UN organizations supported the launch of the Higher Education Sustainability Initiative, committing universities around the world to:

- teach sustainable development concepts as part of the core curriculum across all disciplines;
- encourage research on sustainable development;
- provide green campuses;
- support sustainability efforts in communities;
- engage with and share results through international frameworks.

RIO+20'S LEGACY

Despite its flaws, Rio+20 brought together political capital in ways that would not have been possible without the focus of the conference. As a result, governments completed the long-standing institutional reform process, offered options for rethinking financing, recommended the creation of SDGs and confirmed participation as a core principle and practice. In essence, Rio+20's lasting legacy is likely to be subtle yet significant through the institutions it has reformed, the values it has reaffirmed, the global goals it has launched and the local initiatives it has inspired. Indeed, it might just be the critical juncture catalysing the formation of a new group of leaders, the adaptive, perceptive leaders of tomorrow, attuned to local realities, globally.

REFERENCES

Center for American Progress (2012) 'Issues: How the Rio+20 Earth Summit Could Have Been Better'. Retrieved June 26 from http://www.americanprogress.org/issues/green/news/2012/06/26/11797/how-the-rio20-earth-summit-could-have-been-better/.

Halle, M. (2012) 'Perspectives on Rio+20: When the Best Options are Unavailable: What Space do we Really Have?' Retrieved from http://www.unep.org/environmentalgovernance/PerspectivesonRIO20/MarkHalle/tabid/55507/Default.aspx.

IISD (2007) 'Summary of the Fifteenth Session of the Commission on Sustainable Development: 30 April – 11 May.' *Earth Negotiations Bulletin,* **5**(254). Retrieved August 21, 2013 from http://www.iisd.ca/download/pdf/enb05254e.pdf.

Ivanova, M. (2011) 'Financing International Environmental Governance: Lessons from the United Nations Environment Programme.' Governance and Sustainability Issue Brief Series, Brief 1. Boston: Center for Governance and Sustainability, University of Massachusetts Boston. Available online from http://www.umb.edu/cgs/publications/issue_brief_series.

Ivanova, M. (2013) 'The Contested Legacy of Rio+20'. *Global Environmental Politics*, 13(4), 1–11.

Ivanova, M. (forthcoming) 'Reforming the Institutional Framework for Environment and Sustainable Development: Rio+20's Subtle but Significant Impact'. *International Journal of Technology Management & Sustainable Development.*

Monbiot, G. (2012) 'After Rio, we know governments have given up on the planet.' *The Guardian*, June 25.

Natural Capital Declaration (2012) '37 Finance CEOs Announce Commitment on Natural Capital at Rio+20.' Retrieved August 21, 2013 from http://www.naturalcapitaldeclaration.org/2012/06/37-finance-ceos-announce-commitment-on-natural-capital-at-rio20/.

Ong, S., Sampaio, R.S.R., Marcu, A., Maupin, A. and Sidiropoulos, E. (2012) 'Examining Rio+20's Outcome. Council on Foreign Relations. Expert Roundup.' Retrieved August 21, 2013 from http://www.cfr.org/energyenvironment/examining-rio20s-outcome/p28669.

Rocard, M. (2012) 'Don't Blame it on Rio.' Retrieved February 22, 2013 from http://www.project-syndicate.org/commentary/don-t-blame-it-on-rio.

Time Magazine (2012) Time Science. June 26.

UN General Assembly (2012) 'The Future We Want.' A/66/L.56. UN General Assembly. Retrieved October 2013 from http://www.uncsd2012.org/content/documents/727The%20Future%20We%20Want%2019%June%201230pm.pdf.

A BRIEF DESCRIPTION OF THE EXPERIENCE

Driven by our commitment to organize a plural and inclusive conference, the programme for 6th International Barcelona Conference on Higher Education included a special activity involving student participation. In the context of a debate on community–university engagement, we believed that this was the ideal opportunity to give young people a voice in the exercise of exploring new visions and future proposals for the construction of a transformative knowledge to drive real social change.

The role of students is essential, since they will be the main protagonists and change-makers of tomorrow. That is why GUNi took this challenge and, with the theme 'The World We Imagine', asked them to share through short videos their vision of a better world. The call asked for a no longer than three-minute creative short video inspired by the following: 'The world we imagine; What world would you like to live in?; What tools can make this imagined world work?' This call was answered by students from all continents. We also searched for more voices from civil society who have shared their ideas about the world they imagine through online digital platforms. In total, we collected more than 50 diverse and creative videos from around the world.

COLLECTIVE VIDEO COLLAGE

The videos were edited into a collage of clips representing the various themes inspired by the students and civil society. This collective video has demonstrated the urgency for inspiring and being open to a search for new ways of living and working together for the common good. It highlights that we, as individuals, have the capacity to create our own future, and that the path to our hopes and our dreams is through our own actions. It is clear that we need to generate individual commitments, because the sum of individual contributions shapes the collective commitment. Everyone has a role in this transformation,

in recognizing their own potential for being a change agent and in recognizing the capacity of collective action that builds a world based on cognitive justice, liberty and freedom.

The collective video was presented at the opening ceremony of the conference, creating an important space for the voices of students to participate in the collective discussions that continued over the following days. The opening session on 'The World We Imagine' also included a lively theatrical performance with music and powerful images bringing to light the need for an inclusive balance between all forms of life, between north and south, a world with equal rights for all, without exception.

Five main strands, inspired by the ideas that students and civil society shared through their videos, shaped the script of the performance:

1. Imagine a world without north and south, inclusive and in balance between all forms of life.
2. Imagine a world in which progress is not about having money.
3. Imagine that all are aware that life on Earth is a single ecosystem.
4. Imagine a world where cooperation replaces competition.
5. Imagine we can build the world that we imagine.

The audience had an opportunity to feel and experience living in a world where we are all one, as well as the possibility that we can build this future together. The theatre then evolved into an active participatory intervention with the audience in which participants worked in small groups and designed collaborative messages of what is needed for a global transformation, for a new world to be created.

THE VOICE OF THE STUDENTS

What world would you like to live in? What tools can make your imagined world work? Starting from those inspirational questions, young people around the world shared with us their desire for a better world. Some of

Melba Claudio-González and Crystal Tremblay

them also took the opportunity to express their worries about the world they had inherited. Despite blunt statements that denoted a deep discouragement among youth – such as 'Life is not what we were promised when we were kids' – they expressed their commitment to be involved in a process of social transformation. And for us, and for the GUNi conference participants, this result is really heartening.

By and large, the videos can be divided into three content types. The first group includes videos in which the students express broader concerns about one or more global issues. Having a more inclusive education system and being part of a strong civil society committed to environmental sustainability and a peaceful coexistence are the main topics covered in these videos. The second group collects together those videos that urge a change by underlining the desire to do something now, with young people expressing their commitment to partake in the transformation process and in social change. Finally, the third group includes videos that explain a concrete action and experience in an ongoing project of community engagement or denounce specific problems that are affecting directly their community.

Below we share some brief reviews of the videos that were presented during the conference. The videos can be viewed via our website: http://www.guninetwork.org/guni.conference/2013-guni-conference/video-gallery. It should be noted not only that GUNi recognizes and appreciates the work of all those who have been involved in this activity, but also that UNESCO, as an acknowledgement, has expressed its commitment to publish these videos on its website.

Colombia was the country with the greatest participation. We received some very interesting projects from the design and technological innovation centre SENA. Gonzalo Ulloa presented *Earth's Fate,* a video animation reflecting, from a futuristic aesthetic, the contradictions between the modern idea of progress and 'The consequences of searching for an ideal world'. Ulloa questions the benefits that technological breakthroughs offer for the sake of convenience in view of the impact on the deterioration of the environment and social isolation that sometimes results. The work entitled *Magic Dreams* recreates a utopian world where, only by reflecting on the wisdom of nature, can the wilderness become the real world in a beautiful and magical environment.

In the same vein of thinking about an ideal world, the students who presented the work *Transition* added a critique on those who care about themselves and do not care about ensuring the creation of a better world. *Zelcal* reflects a concern about the loss of natural resources through the eyes of a girl from the future,

who has only virtual reality to know the world of her ancestors when nature still existed. Pollution and the consequences of climate change are also the concern of the work entitled *My World*.

Several participants presented videos on the need for a change of attitude on the actions needed to conserve natural resources. Along these lines, other participants from Colombia presented their work called *On Time*, a video that appeals to the unconscious of those who, in their daily lives, do not care about environmental conservation.

What better time than graduation day to express how we imagine the future world? CQUniversity Australia is presented as one of the most engaged of Australia's universities in focusing on making higher education and research more accessible and relevant to all people. It has very high levels of participation among groups that are traditionally under-represented in higher education. Their video *The World We Imagine* captures how students graduating from CQUniversity feel about the world in which they live, and how their journey through higher education and beyond is creating a more positive future. While students acknowledge the major issues facing our modern world – poverty, injustice, discrimination, inequality and a lack of access to education – they also look to a future where they can contribute to making a change. They imagine a world in which people are equal, educated, positive, creative, progressive and at peace. Most importantly, they see themselves as being empowered to contribute towards a brighter future.

The security of peaceful coexistence is another outstanding issue that was tackled by the participants. Butrint Bozalija, from Alor Setar, Malaysia, states in *Dusk Till Dawn*: 'A safe place to live in is what we all look for … life is better than what we think if we all unite and take the right path'.

Sonam Dolma Lama from Albukhary International University in Malaysia presented *Humanity*. This video is a reflection on a world where people should to learn how to live together despite our differences: 'What is more beautiful than connecting a world with no barriers? United in ONE world, one dream … Unity in diversity and hope to humanity.'

Jose Consul Gonsalves, from the University of Melbourne, presented *Wire*, a video that offered a refreshing and optimistic touch, not only in terms of its colourful and cheerful aesthetic, but also because of its clear and forceful statements:

We as humans have crossed a significant threshold in human history when we adopted the Universal Declaration of Human Rights in December 1948. However, the broader concerns of human condition are still overpassed by our individualist narrow horizons. … Equal share is possible! One world, one planet.

The World Kavita Imagines is a touching but heartening story that encourages us to imagine a world where we help each other, a world where everyone gives back to the community what they have learnt.

Suzanne Gaulocher, from Wisconsin, USA, highlights the importance of hearing the voices of people who are not usually invited to the table to share their experiences:

We need to hear perspectives from all sorts of people in order to inform our work at all levels. … Bringing in a youth voice and communicating to a broad range of stakeholders can increase knowledge that supports health and place with a focus on equity.

Voice is a story by Linda Cavanaugh, from Nova Scotia, Canada. The world she imagines stresses the importance of learning to listen to each other and use an interdisciplinary format. Linda's voice urges us to challenge tacit assumptions and biases in order to learn to cross the invisible barriers created by our education.

Meanwhile, Faseeha Harthim, from Albukhary International University, in a work touchingly entitled *Let Me Be Who I Am*, says: 'The world we imagine did not exists'. This calls attention to the need for a change in rigid educational systems that do not allow for the passion or the ability to discover and develop what young people really want to be.

The students from Universidad Veracruzana, Mexico, pose the idea of *A World of Words*, a world in which progress rests primarily on the love of reading: 'Reading and studying is good to achieve great things … Someone that wants to learn wants to go far.'

We also received videos about ongoing project experiences. *The New Activists: Students in the Community* features the stories of three students who are using their creativity and knowledge to address challenges and act on opportunities in their communities. These students are already working on the world that they imagine. These engaged scholars are new activists because they have a new way of organizing to meet the challenges of our times. Underscoring the responsibility of higher education to address the issues that are critical to a sustainable future, their stories demonstrate the power of knowledge to transform our circumstances.

A service-learning experience was presented by participants from Canada. Thompson Rivers University's Service-Learning 1000 is a theory and practice course about service learning in which it is common for student volunteers to express that their worldview has changed through attention to others. In this video, each student is expressing a personal view about the world he or she imagines, and their second statement is an action call for how they might to achieve it. This is probably one of the videos that best captures the spirit of our invitation to the students and, by extension, the objective of the 6th GUNi Conference. That is, it goes beyond what we imagine, making concrete proposals and expressing a commitment to drive a social change.

A second service-learning project was presented from Chile: *Aprender Sirviendo* is a project based on solidarity as a teaching tool and uses the contents of the students' subjects to benefit the community.

Nanya Pérez Martínez and Carlomagno Gabriel from Universidad Veracruzana, Mexico, shared their desire to make the world a better place through music: 'We are learning to listen, to admire, respect, love and work. Through music we learn to work together, like in a band, to achieve our goals'.

From Canada, we received a video highlighting the voices of students and partners from Camosun College, who have worked with the Community Learning Partnerships (CLP) department to pursue educational and career opportunities. They shared with us their experience with this programme, which:

[gives] students the chance to pursue the 'world they imagine' and opens the door to many learning and employment opportunities. The programs offered by the CLP Department to Greater Victoria and Aboriginal communities have been described as 'transformative,' 'inclusive of culture' and 'life-changing.'

We also want to highlight the experience entitled *Global Call to Action Challenge* that was presented by Jody Williams, Nobel Peace Laureate. This video was prepared on behalf of Chautauqua Learn and Serve Charter School and the Peace Jam. It describes the efforts and accomplishments of the Chautauqua School's students as they strive to improve the community in which they live, as well as serve as models of civic engagement. Their hope is to inspire people who, like them, have disabilities to become the servers, not the served.

At first glance, the idea of imagining a different world probably seems to be an exercise that is a bit naive. However, in a context in which many social and economic matters across the world have been negatively impacted, it is heartening to see young people taking this opportunity to express their displeasure very seriously, stating that a change is urgent, but making proposals and reaffirming their desire to be the change-makers of *The World We Imagine*. Thanks to all!

TABLE I.3.1 The participants		
Country	Title	Name of participants
Australia	*Wire*	
		Jose Consul Gonsalves Junior, Nadia Faragaab
	The world we imagine: through the eyes of graduate students	
		Students from CQUniversity Australia – Rockhampton Graduation Ceremony (March, 2013)
Canada	*Community learning partnerships: Inspiring lives*	
		Jennifer Bennett, Camosun
	Voice	
		Linda Cavanaugh
	The world I believe	
		Wendy Krauza , Thompson Rivers University, Service-Learning 1000 (Winter 2013)
Chile	*Aprender sirviendo: Service-learning methodology*	
		Eugenia Cerna Hinojosa , Colegio Concepción
Colombia	*Magic dreams*	
		Johnny Muñoz Jiménez, Yulieth Acevedo Agudelo, Laura Franco Mejia, Marian Llano López, Mónica Ríos, Mónica Moreno
	Transition	
		Gustavo Arango Tabares, Erika Romero Correa, Alejandro Bueno Ossa, Héctor Zapata Ríos, Estafanía Rodriguez, Erika Álvarez, Leonardo Herrera, Giovanny Arango, Alejandra Hernández, Silvana Ortíz
	Zelcal	
		Andrea Montoya, Laura Uribe Valencia, Leidy Johanna Baena, Herly Sarry Morales, Oscar Aristizabal
	On time	
		Luis Carlos Monsalve, John Eduar Ramirez, Javier Vasquez, Leonardo Naranjo, Daniela García, Freddy Hinestroza
	My word	
		David F. Castaño López, Mario Quintero Gómez, David A. Tafur Rodríguez, Diana Salazar, Diego Díaz, Laura Sofía Tabares, Marcela Cardona, Mauricio Sánchez
	Earth fate	
		Gonzalo Ulloa

Country	Title	Name of participants
Malaysia	*Dusk till dawn*	
		Butrint Bozalija, Jasseh Fatou, Jammeh Zohene, Shpetim Sadriu, Ceesay Olimatou, Evangelos Afendras, Abdul Razaq, Muhammad Yahya, Hossen Ali Ahmad Hamud, Ardian Avdyli, Jammeh Zohene, Muhamed Simnica, Bilali Youssouf Said, Jasseh Fatou, Raja Sakib, Ceesay Olimatou, Malantugun Geraldine
	Humanity	
		Sonam Dolma Lama, Faseeha, Tsering, Afendrus, Pema, Kamoliddin, Tamba, Sukraj
	The world Kavita imagines	
		Mohamed Muizzu Abbas, Kavita Gurung, Dewi, Jeevan, Nasir, Zila, Tsosang, Muiz, Shamran
	Let me be who I am	
		Faseeha Harthim, Dolma Lama, Haseena Ahmed, Zeenath Zuhair, Yug Tara Moktan, Sylla Maimouna
Mexico	*Realeza musical - Universidad Veracruzana*	
		Nanya Pérez Martínez, Carlomagno Gabriel, Members of the Band
	A world of words	
		Arely León Sánchez, Pablo Romo Álvarez
United States	*Things aren't always what they seem*	
		Suzanne Gaulocher
	The new activists: Students in the community	
		Jamie Haft, Holly Zahn, Kevin Morrow, Ivan Akimov, Kaitlin Hardy, Danielle Preiss, Afua Boahene
	Peace Jam. Global call to action challenge, 2011 winners	
		Students & volunteers, Chautauqua Learn and Serve Charter School

FIGURE I.3.1 **Photo by: Shayna Hadley.**

I.4

PERSONAL TRANSFORMATION AND THE CONSCIOUSNESS REVOLUTION
Conscious life design in the holistic-biocentric evolutive model

Daniel Lumera

From an evolutive perspective, the profound transformation in collective and individual consciousness that is noted today could be considered to be a survival strategy that humans are adopting in order to enter a new evolutive paradigm. This revolution in consciousness could radically change our perceptions of self, others and reality.

It represents a spontaneous immunization strategy against a society that is irresponsible, materialistic and competitive, one that is based on individualism, anthropocentrism and the indiscriminate exploitation of nature and the planet's resources. The new consciousness is an antidote for humans who prefer personal gain to respect for all other forms of life and their suffering. Cooperation, a new sense of responsibility, personal, collective and planetary well-being, coherence, attention to quality of life and nutrition, meditation, the development of a humanitarian, ethical economy, new leadership based on consciousness and ethics, new spirituality and consciousness are just some of the concepts that, like antibodies, are gradually penetrating further into collective thought.

WHAT IS THE CONSCIOUSNESS REVOLUTION?

The revolutions we have seen to date have had two main characteristics: they have been *reactive* and *social*.

They were reactive because they were a reaction to a triggering cause: one or more external factors (for example, a dictatorship, a regime, the presence of abuses, a crisis, corruption, oppression, poverty, a power struggle, an ideal, an economic or other type of interest, the environment) triggered a reaction. Human beings have nearly always needed strong signals before reacting and being able to change, but these were always revolutions characterized by an impulsive phase and by the need to pass from a determined condition to a new status (as to adopt a reactive strategy means to react to an existing condition).

Today, we have the sufficient and necessary conditions for the first proactive revolution in the history of this evolution cycle: a re-evolution of consciousness. For the first time, there is a critical mass of people on our planet with a sufficient level of awareness to really manifest a new way of being human. In order for humanity to assist in an epochal change, different from all previous ones and based on truly new parameters, it is necessary to risk and to penetrate the roots of the nature of our perceptions and our consciousness, actively manifesting a new reality.

The proactive revolution is individual and interior. It concerns the consciousness of each individual, it does not stem from the need to change things and society, and it is not against anything or anyone but is the spontaneous expression of a deep interior consciousness. It does not stem from rage, discontent, a struggle for power, money, freedom or control, or even from a shift of balance. There is no need, desire or external trigger. It is like a blossoming flower. It does not open to the sunlight because it is indignant; it simply follows its nature of being a flower and reacts to the presence of the light. Its only scope is the consciousness of being, and everything else is simply the spontaneous consequence.

The consciousness revolution, therefore, is not the reaction to a specific condition and does not belong to the automatic dynamic of stimulus/reaction; it does not exist to host any fight for the conquest of something (either internal nor external). Freedom changes from being something to fight for and to conquer to our becoming natural condition of being.

The evolution strategy of this revolution is innovative because it does not consist of changing existing systems but is instead completely focused on the radical personal change of individuals: their identity, perceptions, emotions, life force, quality of thoughts, and so on. Each external stimulus, each problem, each change, becomes the simple means of interiorizing themselves, knowing themselves better and following their own spontaneous nature. This is the real power inside human nature: it is a power that is dominated not by a logic of conveniences, but by an expression of a deep existential happiness controlled only by mechanisms of wisdom and love, which spontaneously appear when the consciousness experience of our authentic nature occurs. External change will be a simple side effect of the enhanced level of internal awareness – not the aim of the developing process but a consequence of it. We are in a field of innovative experimentation because the original impulse of the consciousness revolution is not the need for change (which happens anyway as a simple consequence of internal work on awareness) but awareness itself and as an aim in itself.

FOCUS

The proactive revolution is based on *consciousness* and on absolute individual responsibility; it is completely focused on the individual as the author of reality. The strategy of change is based on individuals' work on themselves: internal change becomes the only real possibility to generate a change in the external world (people, relationships, society, and so on). For this reason, we can say that it is a real consciousness revolution: it consists of the full understanding that the external world is a simple reflection of the internal condition of each person and that it is useless to try to change the world by reacting to its stimulus, because the exterior changes more and more as individuals work on their own consciousness, on the roots of the perception of reality, so that they can express and experiment with their own nature.

External change will not be the main aim or the primary necessity. On the contrary, each stimulus, need or external problem will become a simple resource to develop more internal *awareness*, thanks to which correct actions, thoughts and words will be spontaneously expressed.

Fundamentally, the anthropocentric model based on the perception that humans are at the top of a universal evolutive ladder is no longer valid. The erroneous interpretation of this perspective has created considerable perceptual distortions, particularly the feeling that we are apart from or superior to nature, rather than an inseparable part of it and members of a complex, highly interconnected system.

The spontaneous evolutive strategy marks the path from a patriarchal, anthropocentric model to a holistic-biocentric model that focuses on respect for all forms

FIGURE I.4.1 The patriarchal, anthropocentric evolutive model

and expressions of life, and is based on an awareness of being closely connected to all forms of existence – one with every form of life.

The pyramid in Figure I.4.1 represents how the perception of evolution is expressed in the patriarchal, anthropocentric model, in which humans are at the top of a hierarchical ladder and all other forms of life are below them. This model lies behind the frenetic quest for success at any cost, the need to feel superior, the frustration of feeling inferior, the authoritarianism that replaces authority, the concept of evolution based on the law of the fittest, the use of violence to achieve goals and to dominate, and submission as a result of competition. In the past, education was strongly influenced by this approach.

However, before we can propose new, authentic education models, we must completely change ourselves and our convictions. How can we hope to clean up the world and society if we do not first start to clean up our inner selves? The construction of reality and society is rooted in the perception that we have of ourselves and of life, in the quality of our emotions and our thoughts, and in our capacity to be happy regardless of external events.

Figure I.4.2 represents the biocentric evolutive model and gives a new perspective on things and on ourselves. The peak-and-base shape is replaced by a circle in which humans are just one aspect of an extraordinary system that is interconnected in even the smallest details. The only approach that can provide an overall understanding of this system is a holistic one, as this can relate and connect all the multidimensional components. *Holos* is Greek for whole, all, and 'holistic' refers to a global, systemic way of considering

FIGURE I.4.2 The holistic-biocentric evolutive model

reality in which the focus is on the numerous interactions between the phenomena that occur at different levels of existence.

The fulcrum of the new holistic-biocentric paradigm is a deep awareness of the interconnection between all the planes of life (physical, biological-vital, emotional, psychic, relational, social, causal and spiritual) in an interdependent system (Lazlo, 1995). In this system, each individual part is not separate or isolated, but connected by an apparently invisible thread that is in fact evident and represented by consciousness. We know that the action of one individual, and even of one process, can influence thousands of events kilometres away. This awareness influences and completely changes our concept of individual and collective responsibility, and gives us the opportunity to be conscious guarantors who can maintain the balance needed for the natural world to persist, instead of being insensitive exploiters.

Phenomena such as the internet, Facebook, Twitter and all the social networks in general are the expression of a collective consciousness that is finally becoming aware of itself and is bringing to light all that consciously and unconsciously exists at the mental and emotional levels. This new dimension, in which there is an increased awareness of interconnectedness, is also reflected in an increasing need for interdisciplinarity and for an approach that can incorporate science and consciousness, spirituality and materiality, ethics and technology (Lazlo, 1996).

We can detect a spontaneous awakening of individual and collective consciousness that will lead to changes in our self-perception and our boundaries,

which will expand to include others, nature, the world and the universe. We will be able to experience 'the external' as a close reflection of our personal lives. We will truly understand that 'your well-being is my well-being, your happiness is my happiness, and your success is my success' and that 'my well-being is the collective well-being and vice versa.' However, this transformation requires new educational models, new ways of interpreting reality and new paths of knowledge that can freely express a higher level of consciousness, a new ethics and a new way of behaving.

In the holistic-biocentric paradigm and in a true peace culture and education, we need to uproot the feeling that we are separate from nature, things and others, as the origin of each conflict lies in this separation. We must completely free ourselves from the feeling of superiority or inferiority, from the perception that we are more or less developed than others, better or worse. The polarity between superior and inferior is replaced by the concept of 'complementarity', which enables us to structure our own identity through contact with diversity – an essential resource if we are to learn about ourselves. The holistic evolutive model requires an education based on unitary consciousness and on the experience of union: the feeling that we are one and at one with all forms of life and with life itself.

The emerging holistic-biocentric paradigm presupposes a higher level of inner consciousness and a radical alteration in our conception and perception of ourselves and of reality. Once the evolutive models have changed, we need a new human with a different cognitive and perceptual structure, free from the old parameters of measurement. We are completely reformulating the basic concepts that have defined what we call reality through the key word in this re-evolution: *consciousness*.

When we examine the two models (patriarchal, anthropocentric and holistic-biocentric) again in Figure I.4.3, we should bear in mind that they are basically simple perceptions of a cognitive system. The question that arises at this point is: which of the two evolutive models is the right one to ensure the survival of the human species and more harmonious development?

At first glance, the answer could be the second – the holistic-biocentric model. However, to answer the question correctly, we need a way of interpreting it that will help us find the real answer: deeper reflection will lead us to recognize that the real error is not in the model, but in the lack of consciousness of the observer. It is precisely on this consciousness that we need to work to reach a true understanding of things.

Here, we try to examine the two figures from a

FIGURE I.4.3 Perceiving the two models

transcendent perspective. We start with the observer's eyes, as it is through them that the perception of reality is first formed. On a second analysis, the two geometric figures that represent the two evolutive models (patriarchal, anthropocentric and holistic-biocentric) are really the same figure observed from two different perspectives: the cone, if seen from above, would appear to be a circle. Therefore, the observer's perspective changes the perception of the same reality and of reality itself. This leads us to reconsider the importance of the observer's individual responsibility, and of their level of maturity and self-realization in the entire evolutive process.

Consequently, the locus of control, interpretation and creation of reality is internal and depends on the consciousness of the observer and on their ability to see more than one point of view. The real question is not which model is right and which is wrong, but what is the observer's level of consciousness. Consciousness is the key to the new humanity.

FOCUS

Humans have always tended to focus on a specific perspective and to identify themselves with that perceived model, even to the extent that they will kill to defend it.

The solution to our many problems should be sought not in a new evolutive model, but in an individual and collective consciousness.

Therefore, there is a profound need for personal transformation through a new educational paradigm, based on consciousness as the path to learning to create reality itself and to drawing up a harmonious design for life – a life design. Education should be concerned with training 'internal' individuals, that is, conscious people who are strongly convinced that destiny is a choice and who can assume full responsibility for their existence. In these individuals, reality is controlled and created internally. In contrast, people with an external 'locus of control' tend to confer responsibility for their existence and for what they experience to external agents (their company, relatives, patients, luck, the government, politics, colleagues and the recession, among other factors), and thus lose the balance and awareness that is typical of individuals with an internal locus of control (Rotter, 1954).

The old educational model based on knowing how to *do* has been replaced by a model that is centred on knowing how to *be*. The essence of this model is not 'knowing how to do to be' (knowing how to make laws and regulations, knowing how to carry out actions and professions, and so on), but 'knowing how to be to do' – the true, deep consciousness that the right actions, ethics and models arise spontaneously, that they are the simple reflection of our level of self-realization. The new learning path is thus based on consciousness.

To this end, roles such as that of life designer are now needed. These are trainers who can facilitate and promote a pacific, eco-sustainable holistic culture and improve the quality of life, well-being, evolution and growth of individuals and society through consciousness. The concept of life design is based on the ability to consciously outline life (according to the real, deep needs of the individual that are considered to be an expression of consciousness), within a holistic-biocentric evolutive model.

The holistic-biocentric evolutive model needs new individuals who are fully aware of the fact that external reality is a simple projection of our internal level of consciousness, individuals who can totally revolutionize the concept of reality, fully internalize it and transform it by means of inner consciousness, so that it can then be projected outwards again as a reflection of a higher level of self-realization. Life designers will be able to consciously outline the path of existence and reality itself and, through this, will have a positive influence on the group.

There are three important indicators that mainly represent the characteristics of the individual and group transformation:

- Consciousness
- Happiness
- Responsibility.

If we follow these indicators, we will spontaneously develop an education that can create a generation of 'internal' individuals who are able to determine their well-being and happiness regardless of external events, individuals who have a deep feeling of self-efficacy and of being centred (Bandura, 1997). New humans are increasingly aware of being the cause of the reality that they experience, and therefore consider that they can have a profound influence on it.

A new educational paradigm based on consciousness should basically be developed around the following four parameters:

- A causal human, who can create all aspects of his or her reality: thoughts, emotions, perceptions, relationships, situations that are experienced and the level of happiness and well-being both internally and in the surrounding environment.
- A science of happiness: an education based on happiness, in which individuals gain and develop the ability to create their own happiness and to transmit it in their relationships and to society.
- A human who can assume full responsibility for his or her own existence, with a mind that clearly identifies the factors by which to create personal and collective reality, who can have a more incisive, deep interaction with this reality, which can in turn give rise to a higher order in line with the new needs.
- A culture based on consciousness, on knowing how to be, in which all individuals are educated to develop a conscious identity; that is, they consider themselves to be a conscience that uses the physical body, vital energy, emotions, mind and spiritual sphere to express, experience and manifest existence harmoniously.

THE SCIENCE OF HAPPINESS

An increasing number of people feel the need for profound personal transformation, to try out new ways of knowing and getting to know oneself, and to learn a new, completely different way of being human. Education has taught us that our aim is to try to be well and happy, and to seek this in success, family, love of and for our children, work, money, health and friendships, among other factors. However, this education model has to date not pushed us to experience a level of happiness and well-being that goes far beyond the commonly known standards and is independent of the numerous external factors described above.

It is possible to create a real science of happiness based on consciousness that can revolutionize the individual and collective way of being. We can learn to be happy, because we now have scientific, psychological, philosophical, spiritual and methodological knowledge that enables us to be the authors and protagonists of our own happiness (Ricard, 2009). We can train the body and nervous system to develop neural pathways of pleasure and to secrete the right hormones; we can train our vital energy itself to maintain an ideal level of vitality; we can train our mind, ideas, thoughts, convictions, impressions and emotional diet (the quality of our emotions) (Goleman, 1997) to be expressed according to superior parameters that enable us to maintain a very high level of happiness (Donovan et al., 1997).

We should clarify that we can live a new kind of experience that we have not been able to express on a mass scale before now, one that represents the heart of a new evolutive model: happiness as a natural condition of existence. This experience does not depend on any external factors, such as having or not having money, being successful or unsuccessful, having a satisfying relationship or being alone, and achieving or not achieving something. Instead, it is associated with a series of higher emotions that will be essential in the new emotional education and that are part of our heritage, connected to our right to exist.

Happiness in this existential nature is obtained through consciousness and persists regardless of external or internal changes. It has extraordinary secondary effects on the body, mind, emotions and spirituality: we are happy due to the simple fact that we are conscious of our existence and that we are life itself.

In this new way of being human, the concept of responsibility develops as the level of consciousness increases. In the new educational and pedagogical standard, each one of us is 100% responsible for everything that happens to us, for all that we feel and do, for the emotions that we create, for the quality of our thoughts, relationships and situations, for successes and failures, illnesses and healing, for having chosen our parents, and for the places in which we are born and die. The new humans are individuals who can self-determine and express this self-determination through their actions, and who represent the causal agent of reality itself, individuals who can take conscious decisions about the quality of their lives by acting as causal agents.

The individual is absolutely responsible for everything. This idea appears to be highly provocative, but it is at the same time a strong driver of evolution, with precise educational functions. First, it fosters the question 'Which part of me could affirm in perfect humility that I am completely responsible for everything?' Second, it leads to a search for a coherent, true response, which is the product not only of mental cogitation, but also of real awareness. This is a real puzzle for the mind that can be solved if the new humans can completely change how they consider themselves and feel that they are a consciousness that uses body, mind, emotions, vital energy, the past and the spiritual dimension to express themselves in existence and as existence. Clearly, we cannot approach the topic by following the existing models. Instead, we need to bring about internal change and enter into a new area of experimentation.

It is necessary to rethink completely many certainties that have represented the cornerstones of our think-ing until now. First of these is the idea that evolution is based on competition: the evolutive model based on belief in survival of the fittest created a system based on individualism and on the justification of violence as an evolutive force. The motor for evolution is, however, cooperation, through which more complex and inter-dependent systems develop, systems that are able to overcome difficulties that are insurmountable for the single individual. The foundation of the evolutive vision that originated in today's society is essentially an old-fashioned perceptual and cognitive system. It is a polar system, from which stems a divided (internally/externally) and dual perception of the world. New education will have to work on overcoming this gap in perception, which is, ultimately, the origin of all the distortions and problems that we know.

To synchronize with the standards of a holistic and biocentric evolutive paradigm, education must review its structure from its foundations and rethink the fundamental concepts on which it is based, working on three key concepts:

1. Everything is closely connected and interdependent. There will be a new idea of respect based on an awareness that apparent diversity is a complementary aspect of ourselves.
2. Everything is One. A unitary vision of reality and of self is developed, far removed from a polar and dual perception. To be one, to feel yourself whole, is to feel that everything is unified (and to develop responsibilities and respect in terms of this awareness). This awareness must not be a mentalization or the result of reasoning, but the result of an authentic and direct personal internal experience.
3. Evolution is based on cooperation and not on competition. By transmitting this concept, we can from the beginning eliminate the need for violence as an evolutive force, and purify the competitive, individualistic and ruthless aspects of society.

The vast majority of human beings have a polar perceptive and cognitive system, which is based on a fractured perception of everything surrounding them. Many individuals are unable to feel the unity that exists at the origin of creation and live in a subconscious state where they tend to satisfy only sensorial and instinctual desires. Reality is created on a basis of polar perceptions: inside/outside, right/wrong, life/death, and so on. To recuperate a unitary and holistic vision becomes a fundamental step in such a deep process of change.

The consciousness revolution will be expressed through holistic education, that is through being able to consider human beings as a complex system that is profoundly interconnected with the surrounding environment at seven levels: physical, vital, emotional, mental, causal, spiritual and of consciousness. Each of these levels should be developed in a balanced way and not, as has happened to date, favouring an essentially mental approach.

The holistic paradigm moves towards an education that is able to develop all these seven levels in a balanced way, as an interconnected and interdependent global system, really transmitting a different perception of self and of reality. Below is a brief example of some of the issues that could be developed for an understanding of each level in a holistic context:

- *The physical level*: a knowledge and health of the body as an integral part of nature and not as a separate entity; the interconnection between the physiological, vital, emotional and mental processes.
- *The vital level*: a knowledge of the vital energies and of their function in health; development of the capacity to regenerate your own vital energy; understanding the interconnection between this level and the others.
- *The emotional level*: understanding the nature and origin of emotions; the importance of the emotional dynamics of our health and psychophysical balance; how to control the quality of emotions and one's own emotional diet; development of the ability to create positive emotions to enhance personal and collective wellness.
- *The mental level*: the development of logical and rational processes; a knowledge of the nature of the mind and its dynamics; the origin of thoughts, ideas, beliefs, mental impressions and their harmonization; the development of a balanced mental diet; an understanding of the interconnection and interdependence between the mind, emotions, vitality, body and consciousness; an understanding of how thoughts and beliefs create and influence the internal, external, personal and collective reality.
- *The causal level*: understanding the internal causes structuring the perception of individual and collective reality; an awareness of the total responsibility and individual causality in the creation of reality.
- *The spiritual level*: meditation training and understanding its benefits (education should include all the basic meditation techniques for stress control and conflict management); an experience-based

study of higher states of consciousness. This level, like the others, should focus on the development of practical methods to develop a concrete, experience-based dimension that is related to the spiritual sphere and capable of being applied to the benefits of everyday life (personal life, relationships and work) (Goleman, 1996).

- *The level of consciousness*: developing a new identity of consciousness to be able to use the other six levels (physical, vital, emotional, mental, causal and spiritual) as a tool of personal expression without the need to identify oneself in them.

We can consider and imagine conscious and causal humans who can harmoniously create their reality in a way that is in line with deep needs; who can create their happiness and through this serve others and society; who are consciously interconnected with all surrounding forms of life; who are aware that they are one with life itself; who can understand the importance of collective well-being and perceive the needs of the collective consciousness as their own needs; who will ensure that an equilibrium is achieved with the natural environment and the planet's resources; and who are fully responsible for themselves and for their individual and universal role.

Conscious human beings must first change themselves before they can change the world.

REFERENCES

Bandura, A. (1997) *Autoefficacia: teoria e applicazioni*. Tr. it. Trento: Erikson.

Donovan, S., Murphy, M. and Taylor, E. (1997) *The Physical and Psychological Effects of Meditation: A Review of Contemporary Research*. Sausalito, CA: Institute of Noetic Sciences.

Goleman, D. (1996) *The Meditative Mind: The Varieties of Meditative Experience*. London: Thorsons.

Goleman, D. (1997) *Healing Emotions: Conversations with the Dalai Lama on Mindfulness, Emotions, and Health*. Boston: Shambhala.

Lazlo, E. (1995) *The Interconnected Universe: Conceptual Foundations of Unified Theory*. Singapore: World Scientific.

Lazlo, E. (1996) *The Systems View of the World: A Holistic Vision for Our Time. Advances in Systems Theory, Complexity, and the Human Sciences*. Cresskill, NJ: Hampton Press.

Ricard, M. (2009) *Il gusto di essere felici*. Milan: Sperling & Kupfer.

Rotter J.B. (1954) *Social Learning and Clinical Psychology*. New York: Prentice-Hall.

I.5

HIGHER EDUCATION IN THE WORLD: MAIN TRENDS AND FACTS

*Simon Marginson and
Anna Smolentseva*

Although higher education has a three thousand-year history in advanced learning and scholarship in India, China, Europe and the Muslim world, it became one of the core institutional components of human society only in the last century. The building of higher education and science has coincided with the building of the modern nation states that have been the chief conditions and facilitators of the growth in higher education and science. In much of the world, higher education systems took root only in the last 30 years. Yet higher education now seems ubiquitous and essential to all but the poorest communities.

Some countries, such as the USA and Canada, include two-year community college and shorter post-school learning programmes under the heading of 'higher education', but the most commonly accepted definition of 'higher education' embodies degree-level programmes of three full-time years or more. The larger group of post-school programmes is labelled 'tertiary'. In the nomenclature of the Organisation for Economic Cooperation and Development and UNESCO, degree-level higher education institutions (HEIs) are 'Tertiary Type A', and this will be the form of higher education discussed here, unless otherwise indicated as 'tertiary' (OECD, 2012; UNESCO Institute for Statistics, 2013; World Bank, 2013).

For the most part, HEIs are teaching and service-focused institutions. Only a small proportion of HEIs embodies substantial research activity and doctoral training programmes. However, research universities play especially important roles within national societies, within economies and in global relations, exercising much influence in higher education as a whole. One feature of the last 30 years has been the spread of research-based science both within countries and across the world (NSF, 2013). Here, the trend in research universities replicates the larger growth of higher education, although the role of these institutions remains distinctive and powerful. On the whole larger than they once were, research universities remain

intellectually (and often socially) elite. These are peak institutions in social selection and leadership preparation, in higher paid professional training and in access to codified knowledge, broadly connected within and between nations, with complex and variable patterns of social engagement.

Three common trends shape the evolution of higher and tertiary education. The first trend is the demographic growth of participation and the lifting of social literacy, including the spread of mass higher education across the world, the trend towards near-universal levels of participation among young people in many countries (UNESCO Institute for Statistics, 2013), the uneven but growing take-up of educated labour in the economy, and the spread and deepening of advanced training and scientific capabilities. In many countries, the advance in participation is also attended by a discernible increase in the differentiation and stratification of HEIs, processes encouraged by competition between HEIs and by government policy.

The second trend is the partial global convergence and integration of education and science on a global scale, so that they begin to constitute a single system, coupled with continued and in some respects more plural national and cultural differences in the practices of higher education (OECD Centre for Educational Research and Innovation, 2009).

The third trend is the growing social connectivity and omnipresence of HEIs, and the multiplication of their constituencies and agendas, within the framework of systems still largely regulated and partly funded by nation states (Marginson, 2011a, 2011b). With its capacity to form individual attributes on a large scale and to help in shaping communities, higher education is meant to address a growing range of social and economic developments and problems. Yet there are limits to its capacity to solve problems, especially unaided, and while higher education is growing and becoming more important, it is also being destabilized in some respects. Each of these three elements will now be reviewed in more detail.

TOWARDS UNIVERSAL PARTICIPATION

The advance of mass tertiary and higher education can be readily traced in statistical terms. In a growing number of countries, the gross enrolment ratio (GER) has passed 50% even in degree programmes, although it remains very low in sub-Saharan Africa and South Asia. Between the years 2000 and 2010, the overall GER in tertiary education rose from 67.8% to 91.5% in North America, from 44.7% to 58.3% in Europe and Central Asia, from 22.8% to 40.6% in Latin America and the Caribbean, from 21.4% to 30.6% in the Middle East and North Africa, and from 15.8% to 29.0% in East Asia and the Pacific, where the GER in China increased from 4% to 26% between 1990 and 2010. There has been an especially marked advance in the participation of females, now constituting more than 55% of the total tertiary enrolment in many countries, although comparatively few graduates from engineering, technologies and computing are female. Among high-participation systems are the Republic of Korea and Taiwan in East Asia; Canada, the USA and the rest of the English-speaking world; the Low Countries, Nordic countries, the Czech Republic, Slovenia, Poland, the Ukraine and Russia in Europe; and Chile and Argentina in South America (UNESCO Institute for Statistics, 2013).

The process of growth is nevertheless uneven and incomplete on the world scale. In the less modernized regions, the GER in tertiary education in 2010 was 23.2% in the Arab world, 15.3% in South Asia and only 6.8% in sub-Saharan Africa (UNESCO Institute for Statistics, 2013). The conditions for an expanding tertiary education system include a gross national income per person of about US $2,000 or more; a state capable of providing a stable regulatory environment and the necessary funding for salaries and an educational infrastructure and personnel, teachers and administrators; and a school system generating a flow of students qualified to enter the tertiary stage. In all three regions, there had been marked growth in students since 2000, but not in every country.

At the same time that there has been overall growth in participation in tertiary education, there has also been a notable advance in the number and strength of research-intensive universities in certain parts of the world. Even more than is the case with student participation, the overall pattern is near-universal growth, while at the same time the process is uneven. The research infrastructure is closely dependent on the level of national wealth. In Northeast Asia, China, Hong Kong SAR, Taiwan and Korea, together with Singapore in Southeast Asia, have joined the established science system in Japan, so that East Asia is becoming the third great region for research and development (R&D) after North America and Europe (Marginson, 2011c).

In China, the annual output of research papers has grown by 17% per annum and is already more than half the level of the world leader, the USA. Growth in the Republic of Korea has been almost as rapid as in China. The National University of Singapore has a total scientific output and a rate of high-citation papers not far below those of Oxford and Cambridge. Research paper output has also grown very rapidly in Brazil and Iran. In addition, there has been significant research growth in parts of Europe and Southeast Asia and in India. In 2009, 48 countries each produced more than 1,000 papers in the scientific literature, a proxy indicator for the presence of an indigenous research and research training capacity in at least some fields of knowledge, enabling the nation to share the worldwide exchange of science and innovative technologies. However, there are still many countries that are largely decoupled from the world science system. For example, scientists from Indonesia, with the fourth largest population in the world, produce fewer than 300 research papers per annum. This compares to more than 200,000 papers per annum in the USA, which has the third largest population (NSF, 2013).

When compared with non-graduates, tertiary graduates in almost every country – especially graduates from research universities – enjoy higher rates of labour market participation, lower unemployment rates, shorter average durations of unemployment and significant earnings advantages. Rates of return for first degrees typically vary between 7% and 15% depending on the country, the discipline and the student's gender (OECD, 2012). Graduate unemployment, especially in the first few months and for graduates from generic programmes in the humanities, the social sciences, business and science, is a source of public controversy in many countries, where it shades into the endemic discussion about whether graduates from education are or can be fully prepared for the rather different requirements of work. Nevertheless, for the most part, the labour market's deployment of graduates has advanced along with the increase in numbers. In addition, while many graduates end up working in fields that differ from those in which they were trained, and there has been a movement of graduate labour down the occupational scale, this very flexibility is a sign of the generic benefits conferred by degrees.

Social scientists variously attribute the returns on education to a function of the potential productivity of graduates ('human capital') or the role of educational credentials as a screening device for employers. Regardless of this, the net returns to higher education are sufficient to drive an increased private investment in higher education in many countries, in the form of tuition and income forgone while studying, in spite of the fact that state subsidies per student and grants for living costs have fallen away. Despite the fact that mass higher education is generally associated with a fall in the absolute level of graduate salaries relative to the workforce average – that is, graduates are less economically privileged than they were – the penalties attached to not having a degree have increased, maintaining the relativities. Overall, while the correlation between financial investment and demographic participation is not uniform – there being a closer relationship between public investment in R&D and scientific output (NSF, 2013) – total public and private investment has grown along with the reach of tertiary and higher education across the population and labour markets.

Countries with a gross national income per head of US $25,000 or more typically spend well over 1.0% of their gross domestic product (GDP) on tertiary education, as do some middle-income nations such as Russia, Chile, Argentina, Mexico, Malaysia and India (NSF, 2013). The OECD's country average was 1.6% in 2009, compared with 1.3% in 2005. The highest investors in tertiary education were the Republic of Korea and the USA, both at 2.6% of GDP in 2009, followed by Canada and Chile at 2.5%.

There is a variation in the public/private mix of funding by source, primarily depending on the extent to which tuition is covered by the state from general taxation revenue or financed directly by the families or students who are accessing that tertiary education. There is relatively high private investment in Korea, Japan, Chile, the USA, Canada and Australia. In most countries, the proportion of funding that is paid for from private sources is increasing. Between 2000 and 2009, the average OECD country saw the private share of funding increase from 22.9 to 30.0%, although it remains low in much of Europe, especially in the Nordic countries where domestic students pay no fees. Over that same period, the public funding of tertiary education institutions increased by 38% while private funding rose by 116% (OECD, 2012).

What drives the ever-advancing size and often-advancing cost of tertiary and higher education? Different trends in society, the economy, culture and government policy are coinciding, all pointing in the same direction. The vocational scope for graduates expands as agriculture becomes mechanized; the role of knowledge-intensive manufacturing advances in many countries; services come to demand a higher level of communications, information management, literacy and cultural competence; and cross-cultural skills become more useful as the weight of international trade within economic activity is increased. Governments believe that the quality of human capital is one key to productivity and global competitiveness, and that research generates potential benefits of innovation. However, the willingness of governments to invest in higher education and research at a given time is hostage to fiscal policy.

In North America and Europe, budgets have been hit by prolonged recession. Many American states have substantially reduced public appropriations for higher education, although federal research funding has increased, protecting the leading universities. In Europe between 2008 and 2012, there were decreases in public funding of more than 10% in 11 countries. This included the Netherlands, Ireland, Iceland, Latvia (a 57% reduction in government funding in 2008–2011), the Czech Republic, Hungary, Croatia, Greece, Italy, Spain and Portugal (EUA, 2013).

In the UK, the 2012 introduction of tuition fees of £9,000 per annum was associated with a sharp drop in the number of applications for places. Despite this example, however, the incremental shifts from public financing to tuition financing have not in the longer term been associated with reduced participation. This is because the most important single element driving the expansion of participation is the growing social demand for higher education, a political fact to which all governments must respond by directly funding increases in participation and/or supporting new infrastructure. One reason why student tuition is increasing is to enable governments to concentrate on growth.

Because higher education provides positional advantages, in that it is associated with above-average earnings and enhanced social gravitas, and in that the spread of participation increases the penalties attached to non-participation, an ever-growing number of families now aspire to higher education for their children. In that sense, the advancing frontier of participation directly feeds its own growth until age group participation reaches saturation levels, providing there are sufficient public and/or private resources to keep expanding the number of places available. Elite institutions prefer to restrain their own growth so as to enhance the selectivity and value of their degrees, but other institutions are often more volume dependent, and there is always the potential for new institutions.

Because the economic capacity to support participation has been growing in most countries, including developing countries, the trend to expansion of participation has been unabated, and this process will continue. The European Institute of Strategic Studies has estimated that, on present trends, the world middle class – those earning between US$10 and US$100 per day – will triple in size between 2009 and 2030, reaching 4.9 billion people – more than half the world population. In Asia alone, the middle class will grow from 0.5 to 3.2 billion, driven by the modernization of China and India as rural families migrate into mainstream urban capitalist economies (de Vasconcelos, 2012).

Most of the new middle-class families will want university education for their children as universities carry the most prestige, although some families will have to make do with other forms of tertiary education. It must be emphasized that tertiary participants do not all receive an education of equal value, although the institutional hierarchy is steeper in the vertical sense in some countries than others. The stratification is being enhanced by the governmental use of competition between HEIs as a tool of system management, designed to secure efficiencies and continuous improvement and to regulate the distribution of some resources, together with the fast-growing role of league table hierarchies at both national and global levels. In many countries, there is residual popular commitment to the idea of equality of opportunity. This requires more than the universalization of tertiary access: it requires public intervention in the competition between HEIs to ensure that all families have a good opportunity to access higher education that is well resourced and enjoys good social status. The associated issues have been and will continue to be a significant source of tension in the politics of higher education and/or the springboard for public programmes, whether these issues are urban/regional disparities in China, the position of Hispanic and African-American students in the USA or positive discrimination in favour of remote communities in Finland. However, the universal principle of equality of opportunity is impossible to fully implement in systems that are vertically stratified.

Tertiary and higher education systems are differentiated along both vertical and horizontal dimensions. In most countries, there is more than one formal sector of tertiary education, with technical-vocational institutes often focused primarily on local employment, or generalist community colleges, operating alongside academic universities. The quality of the second sectors varies greatly. Some, as in Germany and Taiwan, constitute a well-resourced and prestigious second university sector with an applied mission, while

others are at worst poorly funded educational ghettos that seem to have been designed primarily to lower the number of unemployed people.

However, it is likely that in future, given the potential costs of tertiary expansion, governments will want to channel much of it through other kinds of HEI for which they bear less responsibility. Growth in participation not only provides opportunities for HEIs to expand their tuition-related incomes and social reach; it also encourages the proliferation of new kinds of institution, such as private colleges with short programmes (including commercial delivery, which is growing in many places) and online delivery. In a minority of countries, including India, Brazil and the Philippines, there is a large mass private sector associated with weaknesses in quality and accreditation arrangements. More generally, marketing-biased educational cultures, inauthentic HEIs and the bogus qualification industry – because in some nations there is also an industry in bogus doctoral dissertations – are widespread problems. There has been much growth in officially sanctioned quality assurance arrangements, but these processes are unable to provide hard-edged data to fully protect and guide users, and in some countries they tend to become captured by HEI and government marketing departments.

GLOBAL CONVERGENCE AND THE NEW PUBLIC MANAGEMENT

The worldwide roll-out of the internet that began in 1990, together with the cheapening of air travel, triggered a new age of communicative and cultural globalization. This has been associated with a rapid growth of international trade, enhanced personal mobility, the ready spread of knowledge, ideas and technologies, the encouragement of policy borrowing, and a closer convergence of modes of government and social organization. Tertiary education, primarily the research-intensive universities, was always one of the most internationalized sectors of society. It has now become a primary conduit for the formation of cross-border relationships. In particular, knowledge, as published in academic journals in the English language, is increasingly taking the form of a single world system. This facilitates international collaboration – the number of scientific papers written by cross-national partners grew by more than 130% between 1995 and 2010 (NSF, 2013) – while at the same time tending to marginalize academic work in knowledges other than English, especially in the humanities and some social sciences, thus reducing valuable intellectual diversity.

This part-convergence and integration of higher education on a world scale has coincided with the adoption, to a greater or lesser degree, of New Public Management (NPM) principles in most national systems. NPM treats public services as if they were business corporations in a market, shaped by output targets, revenue-raising and competition with each other for customers and revenues. In a few systems, governments have attempted to introduce fully corporate HEIs, but professionalized executive leadership, selective market activity and entrepreneurial behaviours are now common. In many systems, policymakers place rhetorical emphasis on the role of higher education in producing private benefits for students and graduates, and declining emphasis on the role of higher education in producing public or social benefits, except in relation to three areas: internationalization, social inclusion and equity, and the engagement of HEIs with local communities, cities and regions.

While NPM has not been driven by globalization per se, global convergence has been the vehicle for the rapid take-up of NPM throughout the world (Rizvi and Lingard, 2010). In turn, NPM encourages the notion of the global higher education environment as a worldwide competition between individual HEIs and national systems for prestige and for people – leading researchers able to generate innovation benefits, and mobile students.

This vision of global higher education has been considerably facilitated by global rankings of research universities, led by the Academic Ranking of World Universities, which began at Shanghai Jiao Tong University in China in 2003 (ARWU, 2013). Global rankings encourage governments and leading HEIs to develop higher education along the lines favoured by rankings templates: research-oriented, comprehensive in the disciplines while especially strong in technologies and medical research, and publishing in English. This has encouraged investment in R&D and leading universities, but with negative side effects. Strategies oriented to global rankings often weaken primarily teaching-oriented institutions (no matter how strong they are), HEIs with primarily local or sub-national regional missions (even though these can be major contributors to social and economic development) and all smaller specialist HEIs. Governments that are focused on 'world-class universities' and the concentration of top researchers in favoured locations can neglect the all-round development of tertiary education systems and the broad-based reproduction of the academic profession. In developing countries, global rankings have also tended to encourage comparisons and policy goals inappropriate to emerging systems, such as expectations that nations with per capita incomes below the world average can achieve 'top 100 universities'.

A more positive outcome of globalization is regional-level cooperation in higher education and research. The formation of the European Higher Education Area and European Research Area, alongside Europe-wide labour markets in the professions, is associated with the streamlining of degree structures and programme contents to facilitate the mobility of persons and qualifications. There has been a major advance in research cooperation. The emergence of regional identity in higher education, albeit on a lesser scale, is apparent also in ASEAN in Southeast Asia and Mercusor in South America. The countries of Northeast Asia, despite continuing political tensions, collaborate in student mobility, elite university networking and research.

This trend to regionalization, together with the spread of science beyond North America and Europe, suggests an underlying theme within globalization: the coalescence of different cultural strands within the integrated global setting. For example, the rapid emergence of high-quality higher education and research in Northeast Asia and Singapore has been underpinned by a distinctive model of development, based in a comprehensive and formative state, strong Confucian educational traditions in the home that facilitate both high student achievement and household investment, and programmes of selective internationalization, especially in scientific research. Future years may see the strengthening of distinctive Spanish or Ibero-American approaches to system design and university organization, a revitalized Russian tradition in education and science, and perhaps distinctive South Asian models.

WILL THE POTENTIALS OF HIGHER EDUCATION BE REALIZED?

The continuing growth and multiplying connections of higher education are attended by a paradox: higher education is also becoming less coherent and its social roles more ambiguous and less stable. Expectations are multiplying faster than the capacity to meet them, more so given weakening state support in some countries, the interference in and corruption of HEIs and limits to academic freedom, perverse markets in bogus credentialing, and the partial fragmentation of the older public identity and purposes of higher education and of the consensus on its forms. Higher education has been both augmented and destabilized by changes in information and communications, and has been pulled in different directions by the semi-integration of HEIs into other social sectors.

Within the framework of the NPM, governments adopt an 'arms-length' relationship with HEIs so that the latter have greater economic responsibility, yet nation states often shape research more closely than before. In addition, HEIs in many countries have little opportunity to step outside business models, for example by grounding community relationships in participatory political structures. The NPM often seems to operate as a device enabling states to underinvest in tertiary and higher education while passing on to HEIs themselves the responsibility for a growing list of social and economic outcomes. There are tensions between the HEIs' management of programme contents and standards and the ideology of student-centred production in a consumer market; between social connectedness and the need to foster autonomous professionals of high calibre who contribute to world science; between the teaching and research functions of institutions; between institutional branding and corporate objectives, and disciplinary communities; between public and private goods; and between the heterogeneous logics of status-driven elite universities and massifying systems. The historical strength of HEIs as a social form has been their malleability, inclusiveness and adaptability in the face of changing social needs and policy agendas. There are, however, both material and structural limits to adaptability. Higher education cannot expand and transform to the level of society as a whole without losing the attributes that enable it to contribute while distinguishing it from other social forms.

There are worrying signs. There are, for example, tendencies towards the deprofessionalization of university teaching in many countries. Some governments are impatient with the lack of direct evidence for positive economic impacts of university research in economic innovation. Some surveys report that paid student work during the academic semester has become the norm and there is declining engagement in both educational programmes and extra-curricular activities. Mass Open Online Courseware (MOOCs) from leading American universities offers a user-friendly, internet-based mode of delivery, accessed free or at a low cost, that nevertheless constitutes a radical reduction in the global diversity of learning contents and empties out much of the teaching function. MOOCs could destabilize institutional delivery in many countries.

In short, higher education can contribute much to fostering social engagement and sustainability. At best, it could be a central instrument in tackling common human problems such as facilitating social adaptation to climate change, people mobility and issues of food and water; and it could be a primary instrument in building global society and even global polity. But these virtuous roles are not guaranteed.

REFERENCES

ARWU (2013) *2012 World University Rankings.* Shanghai: Shanghai Jiao Tong University, Graduate School of Education. Available online at http://www.shanghairanking.com/index.html.

de Vasconcelos, A. (ed.) (2012) *Global Trends 2030 – Citizens in an Interconnected and Polycentric World.* European Union Institute for Strategic Studies. Paris: EUISS. Retrieved August 22, 2013 from http://europa.eu/espas/pdf/espas_report_ii_01_en.pdf.

EUA (2013) 'Public Funding Observatory.' Retrieved August 22, 2013 from http://www.eua.be/eua-work-and-policy-area/governance-autonomy-and-funding/public-funding-observatory.aspx.

Marginson, S. (2011a) 'Imagining the global.' In: King, R., Marginson, S. and Naidoo, R. (eds) *Handbook of Higher Education and Globalization.* Cheltenham: Edward Elgar, pp. 10–39.

Marginson, S. (2011b) 'Strategising and ordering the global'. In: King, R., Marginson, S. and Naidoo, R. (eds) *Handbook of Higher Education and Globalization.* Cheltenham: Edward Elgar, pp. 394–414.

Marginson, S. (2011c) Higher education in East Asia and Singapore: rise of the Confucian model. *Higher Education,* 61(5), 587–611.

NSF (2013) 'Science and Technology Indicators 2012.' National Science Board. Retrieved August 22, 2013 from http://www.nsf.gov/statistics/seind12/.

OECD (2012) *Education at a Glance, 2012.* Paris: OECD.

OECD Centre for Educational Research and Innovation (2009) *Higher Education to 2030,* Volume 2: *Globalisation.* Paris: OECD.

Rizvi, F. and Lingard, R. (2010) *Globalizing Education Policy.* London: Routledge.

UNESCO Institute for Statistics (2013) 'Tertiary Indicators.' Retrieved August 22, 2013 from http://stats.uis.unesco.org/unesco/TableViewer/tableView.aspx?ReportId=167&IF_Language=eng.

World Bank (2013) 'Data and Statistics.' Retrieved August 22, 2013 from http://data.worldbank.org/indicator.

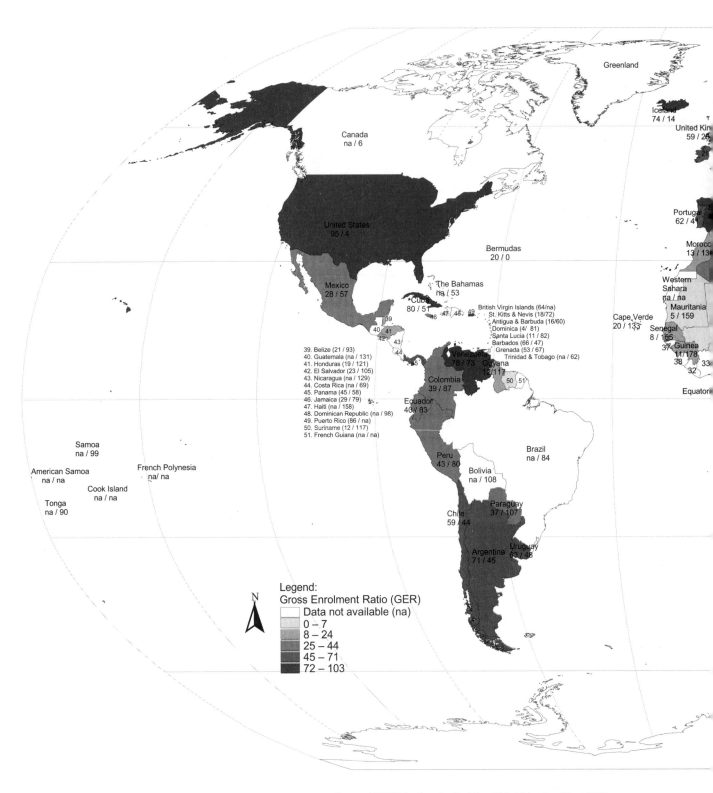

Legend:
Gross Enrolment Ratio (GER)
- Data not available (na)
- 0 – 7
- 8 – 24
- 25 – 44
- 45 – 71
- 72 – 103

39. Belize (21 / 93)
40. Guatemala (na / 131)
41. Honduras (19 / 121)
42. El Salvador (23 / 105)
43. Nicaragua (na / 129)
44. Costa Rica (na / 69)
45. Panama (45 / 58)
46. Jamaica (29 / 79)
47. Haiti (na / 158)
48. Dominican Republic (na / 98)
49. Puerto Rico (86 / na)
50. Suriname (12 / 117)
51. French Guiana (na / na)

British Virgin Islands (64/na)
St. Kitts & Nevis (18/72)
Antigua & Barbuda (16/60)
Dominica (4/ 81)
Santa Lucia (11 / 82)
Barbados (66 / 47)
Grenada (53 / 67)
Trinidad & Tobago (na / 62)

Notes:
This map shows a correlation: in general, countries with high GER have a better place in the ranking of HDI.

Sources: UNESCO Institute for Statistics, *Global Education Digest 2012.*
Comparing Education Statistics Across the World.
Available at: http://www.uis.unesco.org/Education/GED%20Documents%20C/
GED-2012-Complete-Web3.pdf

MAP 2 **Higher education enrolment ratio (GER) by country and position in the ranking of the human development index (HDI), 2011**

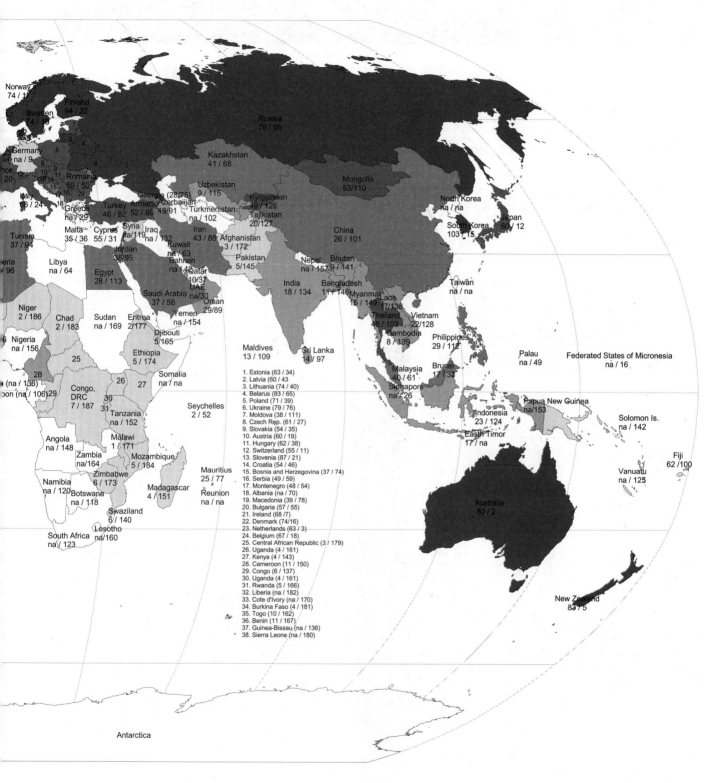

Norway
74 / 1?

Finland
94 / 22

Sweden
74 / 18

Germany
24 / na / 9
20...

France
20...

Romania
59 / 50

Italy
36 / 24

Greece
na / 29

Turkey
46 / 92

Georgia (28/75)

Armenia
52 / 86

Azerbaijan
19/91

Turkmenistan
na / 102

Tajikistan
20/127

Kyrgyzstan
49 / 126

Uzbekistan
9 / 115

Kazakhstan
41 / 68

Russia
76 / 66

Mongolia
53/110

North Korea
na / na

South Korea
103 / 15

Japan
60 / 12

China
26 / 101

Taiwan
na / na

Malta
35 / 36

Cyprus
55 / 31

Syria
na /119

Iraq
na / 132

Iran
43 / 88

Afghanistan
3 / 172

Kuwait
na / 63

Jordan
38/95

Bahrain
na / 48

Pakistan
5/145

Nepal
na / 157

Bhutan
9 / 141

Tunisia
37 / 94

Libya
na / 64

eria
96

Egypt
28 / 113

Qatar
10/37

UAE
na/30

Saudi Arabia
37 / 56

Oman
29/89

Yemen
na / 154

India
18 / 134

Bangladesh
11 /146

Myanmar
15 / 149

Laos
17 /138

Vietnam
22/128

Niger
2 / 186

Chad
2 /183

Sudan
na / 169

Eritrea
2/177

Djibouti
5/165

Nigeria
na / 156

28

Ethiopia
5 / 174

Somalia
na / na

Maldives
13 / 109

Sri Lanka
14 / 97

Thailand
48 / 62

Cambodia
8 / 139

Philippines
29 / 112

Palau
na / 49

Federated States of Micronesia
na / 16

(na / 136)
on (na / 106)29

Congo,
DRC
7 / 187

25

26

27

30
31

Tanzania
na / 152

Seychelles
2 / 52

Malaysia
40 / 61

Brunei
17 /33

Singapore
na / 26

Indonesia
23 / 124

Papua New Guinea
na/153

Solomon Is.
na / 142

Angola
na / 148

Zambia
na/164

Malawi
1 / 171

Mozambique
5 /184

Mauritius
25 / 77

East Timor
17 / na

Fiji
62 /100

Namibia
na / 120

Botswana
na / 118

Zimbabwe
6 / 173

Madagascar
4 /151

Reunion
na / na

Vanuatu
na / 125

1. Estonia (63 / 34)
2. Latvia (60 / 43)
3. Lithuania (74 / 40)
4. Belarus (83 / 65)
5. Poland (71 / 39)
6. Ukraine (79 / 76)
7. Moldova (38 / 111)
8. Czech Rep. (61 / 27)
9. Slovakia (54 / 35)
10. Austria (60 / 19)
11. Hungary (62 / 38)
12. Switzerland (55 / 11)
13. Slovenia (87 / 21)
14. Croatia (54 / 46)
15. Bosnia and Herzegovina (37 / 74)
16. Serbia (49 / 59)
17. Montenegro (48 / 54)
18. Albania (na / 70)
19. Macedonia (39 / 78)
20. Bulgaria (57 / 55)
21. Ireland (68 /7)
22. Denmark (74/16)
23. Netherlands (63 / 3)
24. Belgium (67 / 18)
25. Central African Republic (3 / 179)
26. Uganda (4 / 161)
27. Kenya (4 / 143)
28. Cameroon (11 / 150)
29. Congo (6 / 137)
30. Uganda (4 / 161)
31. Rwanda (5 / 166)
32. Liberia (na / 182)
33. Cote d'Ivory (na / 170)
34. Burkina Faso (4 / 181)
35. Togo (10 / 162)
36. Benin (11 / 167)
37. Guinea-Bissau (na / 136)
38. Sierra Leone (na / 180)

Swaziland
6 / 140

South Africa
na / 123

Lesotho
na/160

Australia
80 / 2

New Zealand
83 / 5

Antarctica

UNDP, *Human Development Report 2011*. Sustainability and Equity: A Better
Future for All.
Available at: http://hdr.undp.org/en/media/HDR_2011_EN_Tables.pdf
Vector layer source: ESRI Data; Projection: Robinson

MAP 2   33

Significative facts		Statements, declarations and global frameworks
Morrill Act creating Land Grant Institutions of Higher Education in the USA	1862	
Community Student Service became mandatory as a part of all degrees in Mexico	1910	
University Extension and Community Engagement Network was launched by ACU	1913	
	1918	The University of Cordoba Federation published the Manifiesto Liminar, the precedent for university reform for the whole of Latin America
For the first time, the term *service-learning* was used by William Ramsay, Robert Sigmon and Michael Hart at the Atlanta Service-Learning Conference	1966	
	1967	
Science shops were set up by chemistry students at Utrecht University	1972	
The regional network *Kuwait University's Deanship for Community Service and Continuing Education* was launched	1976	
	1978	
The National Student Volunteer Program (1971) became the National Center for Service-Learning	1979	
The Society for Participatory Research in Asia was launched	1982	
Campus Compact was founded by the presidents of Brown, Georgetown and Stanford Universities and the president of the Education Commission of the States	1985	
	1988	Magna Charta Universitatum (Europa)
The National Collaborative for the Study of University Engagement was established	1989	
The International Conference of University's Leaders was held in Talloires, France Boyer published *Scholarship Reconsidered* and coined the term 'engaged scholarship'	1990	Talloires Declaration on the role of universities in environmental management and sustainable development
	1991	
The First Cuban–Venezolano Cultural and University extension Directors Meeting was held in Cuba, and the Unión Latinoamericana de Extensión Universitaria (ULEU) was founded	1992	
	1995	
The UNESCO International Institute for Higher Education in Latin America and the Caribbean (IESALC) was launched	1996	
1st International Seminar on Education and Community Service was held in Argentina	1997	The Fourth of July Declaration on the Civic Responsibility of Higher Education was published The Wingspread Declaration Renewing the Civic Mission of the American University was published
The World Conference on Higher Education in the Twenty-first Century: Vision and Action was held in UNESCO Headquarters in Paris Community–Campus Partnerships for Health were established in Washington America Solidaria was established in Chile as a result of the Encuentro Continental de Jóvenes	1998	The World Declaration on Higher Education for the Twenty-First Century: vision and action, was stated by UNESCO The Community–University Research Alliance (Canada) was founded
The ASEAN University Network (AUN) was launched Imagining America was formally launched at a 1999 White House conference set up by the White House Millennium Council, the University of Michigan, and the Woodrow Wilson National Fellowship Foundation	1995	

Significative facts		Statements, declarations and global frameworks
The First Annual International Conference on Service-Learning Research was held in Berkeley and the International Association for Research on Service-Learning and Community Engagement (IARSLCE) was established in the USA The Center for Information and Research on Civic Learning and Engagement was established (USA) Project PERICLES was founded by philanthropist Eugene M. Lang in New York	2001	
PASCAL International was founded as one outcome of an OECD Conference in held in Melbourne on Learning Regions The Centro Latinoamericano de Aprendizaje y Servicio Solidario (CLAYSS) was founded in Buenos Aires	2002	
Strand coined the term *community-based research* The *Reunión de los responsables de proyección social de las universidades de AUSJAL* (author Gemma Puig) was held in Chile	2003	First Community–University Exposition: Community-University Research: Partnerships, Policy and Progress (Canada)
McConnell funded the establishment of the Canadian Alliance for Community Service-Learning	2004	
The Talloires Conference was convened by Tufts University as the first international gathering of the heads of universities devoted to strengthening the civic roles and social responsibilities of higher education	2005	Talloires Declaration on the Civic Roles and Social Responsibilities of Higher Education
	2006	Council of Europe Declaration on the Responsibility of Higher Education for a Democratic Culture – Citizenship, Human Rights and Sustainability
	2007	
The Global Alliance on Community Engaged Research (GACER) was established in Canada and India The Ma'an Arab University Alliance for Civic Engagement was launched at the Conference: Tadamunn: Towards Civic Engagement in Arab Education, Cairo, Egypt The Network Community-Based Research Canada (CBRC) was launched at the University of Victoria as a result of the Community University Expo Conference held in Victoria (Canada) The National Co-ordinating Centre for Public Engagement (NCCPE) was established in Bristol (UK) as part of the Beacons for Public Engagement Initiative	2008	Big Tent I – Declaration on Global Alliance on Community-Engaged Research
The South African Higher Education Community Engagement Forum was launched Campus Engage was founded in Ireland, and the Higher Education and Civic Engagement Partnerships: Create, Challenge, Change international conference was held in Dublin	2009	The UNESCO World Conference on Higher Education was held in Paris UNESCO launched the communiqué: 2009 World Conference on Higher Education: the New Dynamics of Higher Education and Research for Societal Change and Development
The Asia–Pacific University–Community Engagement Network (APUCEN) was launched at the Universiti Sains Malaysia The Research University Civic Engagement Network was launched in Boston	2010	Big Tent II – Communiqué on North–South Cooperation in Community–University Engagement The project Implementing the Third Mission of Universities in Africa, was initiated by the National University of Lesotho and funded by the AAU
The regional conference Community Engagement: The Changing Role of South African Universities in Development was held in East London, South Africa The International Conference on University–Community Engagement for Empowerment and Knowledge Creation was held in Chiang Mai, Thailand	2011	The Engaged University: *International Perspectives on Civic Engagement* is published by David Watson, Robert Hollister, Susan E. Stroud and Elizabeth Babcock
The Regional Conference on Higher Education-Industry-Community Engagement in Asia: Forging Meaningful Partnerships was held in Kuala Lumpur, Malaysia The Community-based Research and Social Responsibility in Higher Education UNESCO Chair is set up Rio+20 – the United Nations Conference on Sustainable Development – is held	2012	Big Tent III: Communiqué on Sustainability, Knowledge and Democracy The Future We Want: Outcome document adopted at Rio+20
	2013	Big Tent IV: The Grand Challenges and the Great Transformation International Barcelona Conference on Higher Education: Let's Build Transformative Knowledge to Drive Social Change, organized by GUNi

PART II
GLOBAL ISSUES ON KNOWLEDGE, ENGAGEMENT AND HIGHER EDUCATION

II.1.1 COMMUNITY–UNIVERSITY ENGAGEMENT – GLOBAL TERMS AND TERRAIN
Lorraine McIlrath

> Universities are both apart from and a part of society. They are apart in the sense that they provide a critically important space for grasping the world as it is and – importantly – for re-imagining the world as it ought to be. The academic freedom to pursue the truth and let the chips fall where they may isn't a luxury – in fact it is a vital necessity in any society that has the capability for self-renewal. But universities are also a part of our societies. What's the point unless the accumulated knowledge, insight and vision are put at the service of the community? With the privilege to pursue knowledge comes the civic responsibility to engage and put that knowledge to work in the service of humanity. (Higgins, 2012)

The current President of Ireland makes a compelling argument for community–university partnership that is pitched against a time of unprecedented global, economic, cultural, political, social crisis and change. His words highlight the need for universities to reject the taken for granted, to re-imagine a better future through an inherent duty to put scholarly knowledge towards the service of humanity.

The contemporary university faces many challenges, the greatest of which is both an ideological and a practical move from a narrow basis to one that is broad, meaningful and relevant to society and community. Hall (2009) highlights that 'community–university engagement is arguably the strongest theme cutting across all our university campuses', also noting the 'explosion' of recent writing on the theme. It is core that the sharing of knowledge across and through the boundaries of the community and the university plays a central role in the re-imagining and self-renewal of society. The purpose of this paper

is to briefly address community–university engagement from a definitional space in which the key terms and terrain will be briefly explored, and to touch on the emergence of institutional, national and regional policies that buttress engagement activities.

INTRODUCTION

The philosophy and practice of community–university engagement is historic and resonates with the foundations of many universities internationally, as many others elsewhere and within this volume note. But it is also evident that the attention of universities has swung like a pendulum over time from an economic to an engagement focus. However, community–university engagement has become increasingly overt and the terrain has expanded gradually since the 1970s, and more rapidly within the last ten years. Without doubt, the theory and practice of this work is as rich and diverse as the historical, political, social, civic and cultural roots that have given rise to regions, nations and continents, and the formation of universities and systems globally. One could say that community–university engagement is laced with *indigenous reference points* or *moments* emanating from local, regional, national and international priorities and contexts. No one institution, region or nation has travelled the same path towards this work, as other contributors within this volume explore and articulate. Consequently, the terrain and terms to describe and articulate community–university engagement are diverse and, at times, contested.

TERRAIN AND TERMS

Engagement as a concept implies activity, interaction, sharing, a dynamic that is in constant change and flux. It implies relationships between the university and the targeted communities, be this at local, regional, national, international or even virtual levels, for reciprocal benefits using knowledge-sharing and dimensions of co-creation that impact society and community, which are the central crux.

There is, however, no consensus on the 'engagement' terminology, and a plethora of terms abound in the terrain. In fact, there are great academic debates centring on the need and rationale for a common set of definitions, or otherwise. Wynne (2009) articulates the need for a common language for engagement thus: 'Without a uniform understanding, or engagement literacy, it is more difficult to develop a forum for discussing activities, or to devise a mechanism for reporting on initiatives and practices' so as to move it from the periphery to the centre (p. 180). Meanwhile, Salmat (2010) highlights definitional complexity within a highly complex and diverse higher educational landscape (drawing from the South African experience):

> Our definitional gaze (if indeed we should invest in a definitional project at all) will need to look cross-sectionally across the (virtually endless) breath of activities, as well as longitudinally back in time for how traditional and fashions arise, and are sustained or not. (p. 58)

'Definitional anarchy' (Sandman, 2008, p. 101) is central, and it would be both a utopian and a futile exercise within any paper to derive a cohesive or common understanding. What I will present is an exploration of the most popular or frequent broad terms that then lead to a set of engagement practices. These practices will be explored elsewhere within this volume.

In a recent review of the literature, Cuthill (2011) uncovered 48 keywords relating to community–university engagement, which encompass a broad range of concepts and in turn practices. What unifies these contemporary keywords, in general, is a movement away from service functions towards engagement, a renewed vision of democracy to one that is participative, and a commitment to the creation and sharing of knowledge. There are without doubt epistemological roots underpinning community–university engagement in moving from 'Mode 1' to 'Mode 2' ways of knowing and knowledge production; from a disciplinary base to one that is transdisciplinary; from hierarchical principles to one that is more participatory in nature; from linear to reflexive approaches (Gibbons et al., 1994). Hall suggests that perhaps the terrain of community–university is at an 'epistemological disjuncture' (Hall, 2010, p. 7) as there tends within the majority of the literature to be an evasion of the unpacking of terms and the provision of definitions due to contestation over ways of knowing. Those who define keywords and concepts are typically the large networking spaces – spaces that bring together cohorts of scholars and practitioners for networking and knowledge-sharing purposes.

In general, the definitions offered here tend to be all-encompassing and inclusive of all practices. For example, *community engagement*, the term adopted by the Carnegie Foundation (2013), is subsequently defined as:

> the collaboration between institutions of higher education and their larger communities (local, regional/state, national, global) for the mutually beneficial exchange of knowledge and resources in a context of partnership and reciprocity … to enrich scholarship, research, and creative activity; enhance curriculum, teaching and learning; prepare educated, engaged citizens; strengthen democratic values and civic responsibility; address critical societal issues; and contribute to the public good.

Again, the Association of Commonwealth Universities (2013), adopting the term *engagement*, define it as a 'core value' and as:

> strenuous, thoughtful argumentative interaction with the non-university world in at least four spheres; steering universities' aims, purposes and priorities; relating teaching and learning to the wider world; the back and forth dialogue between researchers and practitioners; and taking on wider responsibilities as neighbours and citizens.

Meanwhile, within the UK, the National Coordinating Council for Public Engagement (NCCPE, 2010) adopt *public engagement* as:

> the myriad of ways in which the activity and benefits of higher education and research can be shared with the public. Engagement is by definition a two-way process, involving interaction and listening, with the goal of generating mutual benefit.

Within the global north, many conceive of this word broadly under the umbrella of the *scholarship of engagement* or *engaged scholarship*, a term that was coined by Ernst Boyer. In 'Scholarship Rediscovered', Boyer's vision entailed 'connecting the rich resources of the university to our most pressing social, civic and ethical problem', and that campuses would be 'staging grounds for action' (Boyer, 1996, p. 20). Boyer's work has been influential, especially on the university landscape of the USA, where a *Boyerization* of higher education has been debated, commenced or taken root.

However, there are a wealth of additional philosophies and practices that have emanated from the global south but have very often not arrived on the northern literature radar. Ghandian philosophy has had a major bearing and influence on the creation and practice of university national service within India. In Mexico, the philosopher José Vasconcelos left an indelible mark on the education system through the adoption of a national service framework that buttressed his ideology on the connectivity between educational and social gains. In Argentina, the work of Frèire is an exception, as not only have his philosophies on 'other', dialogue and problem-posing influenced the engagement agenda in South America, but his work has also had an impact globally, although these roots are rarely articulated within the community–university engagement literature.

In other contexts, the term *civic engagement* abounds in the literature on community–university engagement but is infrequently qualified with definitions. This could be due to the contested nature of civic and citizenship, which is very much bound up within national belonging and issues of national civil and human rights; this has a grand bearing on those displaced, historically moving from the individual to the collective and back again. The emphasis placed within the realm of civic engagement is typically on the goal to create a citizenry that have the skills, knowledge, political literacy and competencies to be active agents of social change as a result of engagement activities; these agents include students, faculty and members of the wider community.

To extend the concepts of civic, Mcfarlane has written on the concept of 'academic citizens' and 'academic citizenship' (2007). Although these terms are not widely used within community–university engagement literature, they are extremely useful. Macfarlane (2007, p. 271) describes 'academic citizenship' as:

central to the success of the university as a collective entity rather than as a collection of individuals set on achieving personal goals ... academic citizenship is central to sustaining the infrastructure that supports academic life and the 'compact' between the university and society.

This conception draws from notions of public intellectualism, but as a collective force rather than an individual academic duty or activity.

The *engaged university* or *engaged institution* is an increasingly popular term within the literature (Holland and Gelmon, 1998; Hollander and Saltmarsh, 2000; Watson et al., 2011), and while it has a plethora of definitions, the Kellogg Commission typifies engaged university activities as cutting across all dimensions of institutional mission. In *Returning to Our Roots: The Engaged Institution* (1999), the Commission urges universities to reconfigure teaching, research, extension and service activities and become 'more sympathetically and productively involved with their communities, however community may be defined' (p. 9).

This could be at odds with another popular term within the literature – *third mission*. Mission debates ensue on the positionality of community–university engagement. Many describe community–university engagement as a *third mission* or a third pillar alongside the missions of research, and teaching and learning. Still others, fearful of conceptual and practical marginalization and peripherality, feel that the concept and practice of community–university engagement should transcend, align and influence the three domains of university life – namely, teaching and learning, research and service missions.

Perhaps another helpful lens to conceive of this work and enable the evolution of purposeful terms and definitions is through Wynne's (2010) conception of citizenship, contained in Table II.1.1.1. This resides in one lens or moves from and between 'civic', 'communitarian' and 'commonwealth' approaches that denote the underbelly or purpose and practice. In general, it

TABLE II.1.1.1 Conceptions of citizenship (adapted from Wynne, 2010)			
Purpose	Civic	Communitarian	Commonwealth
Citizen	Personally responsible; civic slug	Community; community as the locus of associational life	Justice-oriented; civic spark plug; civic responsibility
Education	Upholds the status quo; conformist; upholds cultural values	Maintains/rebuilds civic life	Renewal; system critique and reform
Educational approach	Traditional; citizenship content, legal aspect of citizenship	Progressive; service-learning; doing and action dimensions; civic engagement and common good	Advanced; critical dimension and pedagogies; system and root reform
Pedagogical approach	Didactic	Participatory	Critical pedagogies

can be said that the 'civic' domain is more conservative and concerned with the given status quo and with delivering of knowledge that is factual. Meanwhile, at the opposite end, in 'commonwealth', citizenship is underpinned by a sense of renewal through the values associated with social justice and a critical perspective, in which action and change are central. In the centre, 'communitarian', as denoted by its label, is community-oriented, seeks to effect change and rebuilds through participation and active doing.

POLICIES FOR COMMUNITY–UNIVERSITY ENGAGEMENT AT INSTITUTIONAL, NATIONAL AND REGIONAL LEVELS

Despite definitional anarchy, conceptual confusion, positionality and debates over epistemological disjuncture, many institutions, nations and regions have created and, at times, enacted a series of polices and rewards to support individuals, institutions and systems to enable the development of a range of practices related to community–university engagement. Some note the pivotal nature of policies in supporting engagement, as a commitment to engagement very often arises on a 'labour of love' basis and there is a danger of stagnation unless there is a policy-enabling environment (Lyons and McIlrath, 2011).

INSTITUTIONAL POLICIES
Macfarlane (2007) notes that the work of the 'academic citizen' is poorly rewarded and that while:

> many universities have redesigned their promotion
> and tenure policies in recent years to reward individual
> performance in research and teaching, few have
> addressed the more complex question of evaluating
> contributions for the collective good via academic
> citizenship. (p. 271)

There is evidence of some internal reward system alterations, but they tend to be both rare and few. One compelling example is the Albukhary International University in Malaysia, whose currently vice-chancellor articulates the institution as the *humaniversity*, which seeks to 'reclaim the ethos of education that upholds human beings as valued members of the community rooted in virtues that nourish humanity globally'. All academic staff must ascribe to the vision, mission and core values of the institution. These are in turn applied to work with the most economically disadvantaged, offering a free education while contributing

positively to community and society. In the words of the vice-chancellor, 'the policy and practice adopted by the institution becomes crucial … to enable transformative change … issues of governance, rewards and recognition … must be addressed by the policy and practice set for the institutions' (Razak, 2013, p. 61).

NATIONAL POLICIES
In many nations, the community–university partnerships movement has evolved at a grassroots level and very often within a policy vacuum; there is some recent evidence of explicit policy and other policy at nascent stages of development. In some contexts, engagement features as an aspect of other existing policies that relate to other 'sides' of higher education (such as policy aimed at the research agenda but pointing towards the importance of knowledge-sharing and exchange or acting through national frameworks for the recognition of education qualifications).

Within the context of Ireland, the 2011 government policy entitled the *National Strategy for Higher Education to 2030* seeks to rationalize and consolidate the higher education landscape in recessionary times and places a strong emphasis on engagement as one of three core and interconnected pillars of higher education (Department of Education and Skills, 2011). Pointers to manifestations of this work include engaged research, community/service-learning and outward-facing institutions to mention just a few. Meanwhile, the 1997 South African White Paper for the transformation of higher education frontloads the importance of community–university engagement:

> South Africa's transition from apartheid and minority
> rule to democracy requires that all existing practices,
> institutions and values are viewed anew and rethought
> in terms of their fitness for the new era. Higher
> education plays a central role in the social, cultural and
> economic development of modern societies. In South
> Africa today, the challenge is to redress past inequalities
> and to transform the higher education system to serve a
> new social order, to meet pressing national needs, and
> to respond to new realities and opportunities. It must
> lay the foundations for the development of a learning
> society which can stimulate, direct and mobilise the
> creative and intellectual energies of all the people
> towards meeting the challenge of reconstruction and
> development. (Department of Education, 1997, p. 3)

REGIONAL POLICIES
At a regional level, there is recent evidence of an evolving commitment to community–university part-

nerships. Of particular note is one that has emanated from Europe. The EU, through the Bologna Process and Declaration, which commenced in 1999 under the Modernisation of Higher Education in Europe, references through the preamble that a:

> Europe of Knowledge is now widely recognized as an irreplaceable factor for social and human growth and as an indispensable component to consolidate and enrich the European citizenship, capable of giving its citizens the necessary competences to face the challenges of the new millennium, together with an awareness of shared values and belonging to a common social and cultural space. The importance of education and educational cooperation in the development and strengthening of stable, peaceful and democratic societies is universally acknowledged as paramount, the more so in view of the situation in South East Europe.

While not a direct mandate, this does indirectly encourage the embedding of vision and practice related to community–university partnerships.

REWARDS

At a local level, some universities have sought to both showcase and affirm the work of community–university engagement through an annual competitive awards programme that has enabled further development of the work (see Southern Cross University in Australia's Excellence in Community Engagement Awards and Dublin City University's President's Award for Civic Engagement). At the global and national levels, a number of awards recognize the efforts of students, university staff and the community. Some of these include the MacJannet Award for Global Citizenship facilitated by the Talloires Network (2012), Campus Compact's annual student competitions entitled the Newman Civic Fellows Award, and the Thomas Ehrlich Civically Engaged Faculty Award aimed at academic staff or faculty.

FUTURE DEVELOPMENT AND CONCLUSION

To conclude, we recognize that there is global diversity in the terms associated with and the evolutionary terrain of community–university engagement; and although it is at times contested, is it clear that an enabling policy environment must meet grassroots practice for this work to survive. In addition, however we decide to term or describe the terrain, the underbelly or purpose

is central to community–university engagement. Is this work about the maintenance of the status quo? Or is it about renewal and rebuilding? Higgins (2012) calls us to image spaces 'for grasping the world as it is and – importantly – for re-imagining the world as it ought to be'. At the heart of the rebuild and renewal underbelly of engagement is the push towards tackling societal problems or 'knowledge-intensive challenges'. Bawa and Munck (2012, p. xi) stress:

> the effective interconnectedness of the societies, geographical spaces, economies, political systems and so on around a set of powerful global challenges such as climate change, the scourge of HIV/AIDS and other infectious diseases, the growing socioeconomic alienation of youth populations, and so on. These are all knowledge-intensive challenges.

Definitional richness is possible if we understand the possibilities for the underbelly of community–university engagement and strive with others towards attacking 'knowledge-intensive challenges', while creating policy-enabling environments to buttress, scaffold and value community–university engagement.

REFERENCES

Association of Commonwealth Universities (2013) 'Engagement'. Retrieved June 15, 2013 from https://www.acu.ac.uk/.

Bawa, A. and Munck, R. (2012) 'Foreword: Globalizing civic engagement'. In: McIlrath, L., Lyons, A. and Munck, R. (eds) *Higher Education and Civic Engagement – Comparative Perspectives*. New York: Palgrave Macmillan.

Boyer, E. (1996) 'The scholarship of engagement'. *Journal of Public Service and Outreach*, 1(1), 11–20.

Carnegie Foundation for the Advancement of Teaching (2013) 'Classification Description' Retrieved January 28, 2013 from http://classifications.carnegiefoundation.org/descriptions/community_engagement.php?key=1213.

Cuthill, M. (2011) 'Embedding engagement in an Australian "sandstone" university: from community service to university engagement'. *Metropolitan Universities*, 22(2), 21–44.

Department of Education (1997) *Education White Paper 3: A Programme for the Transformation of Higher Education*. Government Gazette No. 18207, August 15. Pretoria: Government Printers.

Department of Education and Skills (2011) *National Strategy for Higher Education to 2030*. Dublin: Government Publications Office.

Gibbons, M., Limoges, C., Nowotny, H., Schwartzman, S., Scott, P. and Trow, M. (1994) *The New Production of Knowledge: The Dynamics of Science and Research in Contemporary Societies*. London: Sage.

Hall, B. (2009) Higher education, community-engagement and the public good: the future of continuing education. *Canadian Journal of University Continuing Education,* 35(1), 11–23.

Hall, M. (2010) 'Community engagement in South African higher education'. *Kagiso*, 6, 1–52.

Higgins, M.D. (2012) Remarks by President Michael D. Higgins at the launch of the Irish Centre for Autism and Neurodevelopmental Research, Galway, February 24, 2012. Retrieved January 22, 2013 from http://www.president.ie/speeches/launch-of-the-irish-centre-for-autism-and-neurodevelopmental-research/.

Holland, B. and S. Gelmon (1998) 'The state of the engaged campus: what have we learned about building and sustaining university and community partnerships'. *AAHE Bulletin American Association for Higher Education*, 51(1), 3–6.

Hollander, E. and Saltmarsh, J. (2000) 'The engaged university'. *Academe*, 86(4), 29–32.

Kellogg Commission (1999) 'Returning to Our Roots: The Engaged Institution, Third Report of the Kellogg Commission on the Future of State and Land-Grant Universities'. Retrieved January 21, 2013 from http://www.aplu.org/NetCommunity/Document.Doc?id=183.

Lyons, A. and McIlrath, L. (2011) *Survey of Civic Engagement Activities in Higher Education in Ireland*. Galway: Campus Engage.

Macfarlane, B. (2007) 'Defining and rewarding academic citizenship: the implications for university promotions policies'. *Journal of Higher Education Policy and Management*, 29(3), 261–73.

NCCPE (2010) 'The Beacons Project'. Retrieved January 22, 2013 from http://www.publicengagement.ac.uk/about/beacons.

Razak, D.A. (2013) *Walking the Talk*. The Social Responsibility of Universities Conference Program, EICHE Conference 2013.

Salmat, S. (2010) 'Community engagement as scholarship: a response to Hall'. In: Hall, M., *Community Engagement in South African Higher Education*. South Africa: Council on Higher Education.

Sandman, L. (2008) 'Conceptualization of the Scholarship of Engagement in Higher Education: A strategic review, 1996–2006'. *Journal of Higher Education Outreach and Engagement, North America*, 12(1), 91–104.

Talloires Network (2012) 'The Talloires Declaration'. Retrieved January 27, 2013 from http://talloiresnetwork.tufts.edu/wp-content/uploads/TalloiresDeclaration2005.pdf.

Watson, D., Hollister, R., Stroud, S.E. and Babcock, E. (2011) *The Engaged University: International Perspectives on Civic Engagement*. New York: Routledge.

Wynne, R. (2009) *The Civic Role of Universities: General Concepts and Irish Practices*. Unpublished EdD thesis, University of Sheffield.

II.1.2 ENGAGEMENT AND PARTNERSHIP OF HIGHER EDUCATION INSTITUTIONS WITH SOCIETY: EXPERIENCES, LEARNING AND WORRIES
Carlos Cortez Ruiz

ENGAGEMENT AND PARTNERSHIP FOR HIGHER EDUCATION INSTITUTIONS TO ACCOMPLISH THEIR SOCIAL RESPONSIBILITY

The accelerated changes that characterize our society provide tremendous challenges for higher education institutions (HEIs), obligating them to address and redefine their traditional roles, to review their perspectives on social responsibility and to consider its implications. A fundamental issue is related to ways of establishing engagement and partnership, which have different meanings, purposes and implications for HEIs in different societies and are expressed through different political and ethical perspectives, behaviours, values, recognitions of responsibilities, uses of knowledge and ways of establishing relationships with different stakeholders.

The challenge for HEIs is to engage with society in an integral manner as a way of improving teaching and research, collaborating in social transformation. This engagement is expressed by HEIs around the world in ways that are based in diverse perspectives and epistemologies of knowledge, as well as in different ways of obtaining feedback for learning and education purposes. Partnership, one of the most important forms of developing community engagement that deals with people's issues, is a way of being and a way of working with others that implies mutual understanding, a common good, reciprocity, collaboration in decision-making and transparency regarding outcomes. In our unequal society, engagement and partnership mean assuming a shared responsibility with stakeholders through a democratic process.

In this paper, we present some reflections on the best way to construct partnerships. Most of the reflections were analysed in a dialogue with participants at the GUNi Conference in 2013, involving people from different HEIs around the world. It is not possible to identify each of the participants and the ideas they expressed in that open dialogue, but it is clear that this paper could not have been written without their participation and interest.

WAYS OF ENGAGEMENT AND PARTNERSHIP

There are different conceptions of engagement to accomplish social responsibility in HEIs, some of them placing emphasis on educative objectives. Among the most often mentioned are service-learning, community-based learning and community service learning. Service-learning is defined as an experience in which students or participants learn while they develop assistance and consultation activities through organized service. This meets the need of participants to gain a further understanding of their course content and discipline, while at the same time they gain a sense of civic responsibility.

Scholarship of engagement, public scholarship and community-engaged scholarship are defined as the collaboration between academics and individuals outside the academy for the exchange of knowledge and mutually beneficial resources, in a context of partnership and reciprocity. This explicitly includes democratic dimensions for encouraging the participants in ways that enhance engagement and deliberation about major social issues both inside and outside HEIs. Such collaboration is considered to be a mutually beneficial exchange of knowledge and resources in a context of partnership and reciprocity.

Partnership is an approach to research that puts an emphasis on the importance of collaboration for social justice through action and social change. It is an approach that tries to validate multiple sources of knowledge and promote the use of diverse research methods and the dissemination of the knowledge produced. Different terms have been used to describe these collaborative research processes between communities and HEIs: participatory action research (PAR), community-based research (CBR), community–university research partnerships and community–university engagement (CUE). Most of these processes have emerged in response to criticism that academics and HEIs are insufficiently responsive to the needs of communities.

CBR and community-based participatory research (CBPR) have their roots in a long tradition that has led to the consideration of very different experiences, from research that is controlled by the community to research developed within a community (Marullo and Edwards, 2000). The Loka Institute defines CBPR as an approach conducted for or with the participation of community members, not merely to advance understanding, but also to ensure that knowledge contributes to making a concrete and constructive difference in the world. This part-

nership is defined as innovation based and implies a significant effort in research and development (Hagedoorn et al., 2000).

In Latin America, there exists a tradition in higher education related to the community organizing for development and social change, with important contributions looking for solutions to some of the more complex problems, such as poverty, gender and ethnical inequalities, environmental damage and human rights violations. There are efforts to combine theoretical knowledge from different academic traditions and practical skills with developments in pedagogies and participative methodologies to improve students' capacities to collaborate with social actors in transforming their situation through innovative actions. The philosophy of praxis has been central in the development of popular education; the idea that 'without practice there is no knowledge' was the foundation on which was developed a pedagogy based in participatory methods that let people find their voice and speak to power (Freire). This provided an important advance in critical perspectives and a basis for an alternative discourse on the engagement of HEIs in social change.

Some authors (Sohng, 2013) describe the role of the participatory researcher in a similar way to how community organizers describe their work as a site of resistance and struggle. Participatory research developed a methodology for involving both disenfranchised people and researchers in the pursuit of answers to the questions arising in these people's daily struggle and survival. What participatory research is proposing is the generation of actions that can be carried out as an organized cognitive and transformative activity. This vision implies a new framework of politics for promoting research as collective action in the struggle over power and resources, and for the development of a change-oriented social theory (Sohng, 2013). The social change is about changing systems, and particularly about changing power structures. This kind of PAR means that the engagement will have different complications, including possible conflicts for academics and institutions.

The CUE approach is receiving more attention, considering that it offers significant benefits to society, young people and participating institutions. It is considered that the engagement of HEIs with different stakeholders is critical to the future success of higher education and will act as an important tool in addressing complex environmental, health and social problems.

THE CHALLENGES FOR HEIs IN DEVELOPING ENGAGEMENT MODELS AND PARTNERSHIP PRACTICES WITH SOCIETY

The engagement process is the result of an interaction between three elements: (1) a theoretical–conceptual framework, (2) a practical approach, and (3) a creative way to facilitate the expression of different experiences, approaches and knowledge.

Advancing critical reflection on the engagement process, based on this approach and considering these three elements, should consider how to engage and establish a relation with a collaborative perspective with social actors, particularly with those who are marginalized. This means that the priorities of and for the involved stakeholders will be defined. The best engagement approach is not just to support action on specific issues, but also to transform more broadly who produces knowledge, who influences the public knowledge and who controls the knowledge production process. This means that the engagement will redefine the research (the questions, knowledge production and interpretation and dissemination of results), the educative process (the learning, the consideration of different knowledge and the ways in which to evaluate the different related processes) and how to collaborate in achieving social priorities and in the actions required to advance transformative actions. These approaches are looking for different kinds of change: in how the research is produced with a perspective of collaboration; in how the academic participants assume their knowledge and capacities; and in how the social actors redefine their purposes and develop transformative actions to change their situation.

A central issue in the engagement is to define the actors with whom the relation must be established. It can be established that the work is with community-based organizations, but as there are many kinds of community-based organizations, there are also many ways to define the scope and the meaning of the engagement. CBR with good levels of participation by community members remains an ongoing challenge. Worldwide, communities are demanding to have greater decision-making power over studies that take place in their environment, while stakeholders and partnerships recognize the importance of collaborative approaches. In this sense, the interaction between academics, practitioners and community organizers opens up a broad space for reflection between the academic-theorist perspective and that of the activist-actor.

Most approaches do not assume that the knowledge and expertise of HEIs must be transferred to communities through service to help them address their problems. In the CBR approach, it is recognized that community engagement is fundamental not only to addressing communities' own problems, but also to contributing to improvements in HEIs. Only in some cases is the engagement considered to be a real interaction process between different kinds of knowledge (academic and popular) and as the confluence of different perspectives and interests.

Service programmes oriented to the community face different problems. Some programmes need to have an academic profile, which must work in teaching, research and service to society. One of the problems is that the timing and rhythms are very different for academics and for the community. Another issue is that, to address complex problems, different areas of knowledge and a transdisciplinary perspective are needed, while most of the developed activities derive from a particular discipline and are limited by institutional structures. In most cases, those interested in engagement, particularly those looking to work with the poorest people, face bureaucratic and economical problems.

Communication and information technologies are changing the means of learning and the exchange of knowledge, allowing HEIs to collaborate in research and posing new challenges and opportunities for the accomplishment of their social responsibility goals. We need to reflect on how these technologies can be used critically to facilitate engagement and collaboration for the creation of a more just and sustainable world. It is important that HEIs become analysts of the big transformations that are happening and the drivers of possible initiatives for another possible world.

The impact of engagement and partnership varies depending on the focus, scope and quality of a particular experience. According to François Vallaeys (Gaete, 2011), sociably responsible HEIs must be defined in terms of their impacts, identifying four possible types, each of which is related to specific forms of engagement: organizational, educational, cognitive and social impact.

There is no model for a relationship between HEIs with different partnerships. The central issues relate to how a partnership is established and how the problems, themes or worries are defined. It is clear that, as in any partnership, there are different interest groups and purposes, and it is very important whether these different interests and purposes are clear for all the participants.

The best way to strengthen relationships is by building trust, not just personal but institutional. Building trust needs time, needs to be amplified, is not a constant and can be easily lost by an a single attitude or action. A central issue on trust is how we can trust other people and how other people trust us. Sometimes we can acquire others' trust in us but institutionally not have the conditions to do the work they are waiting for. A possible solution here could be the construction of long-term activities.

HOW CAN WE ACHIEVE A HIGH LEVEL OF INVOLVEMENT OF ALL STAKEHOLDERS?

For some HEIs, the engagement is defined by their context, community engagement being built because students or academics have been working around equality. The issue in these cases is how to go from this instinctive way of working to a more institutional practice in which the relationship with others and the depth of research and engagement become deeper.

If we want a partnership that guarantees a desirable and successful relationship among the partners, one that enables real participation and shared leadership and power relations in the relationship between academics and the community, we need to consider whether both parties or only the HEI is exerting leadership. Another issue is related to how to relate the academic leadership to the local/popular leadership. This could be relatively easy with people who are academically and professionally qualified in the areas of interest, but sometimes the natural leadership comes from less educated people, those who are not qualified academically but can play an important role and provide important ideas because they hold other kinds of knowledge and experience.

Some experiences show how difficult it can be at times to be in agreement, even on the idea of the time that is available. A central issue in the partnership is respect for people's time, trying to ensure that the way in which projects are implemented will let them feel they are part of the project instead of this being something that is imposed on them. It is important for long-term relationships that involve using students as part of the process to recognize the differences between academic rhythm and community rhythm.

HOW CAN WE REACH A MUTUAL UNDERSTANDING AND A COMMON LANGUAGE?

A problem in multicultural societies – and indeed most societies have this characteristic – is how to find a common language between people with different cultures. This means not only translating verbally between languages, but also the interaction of knowledges, because there are different logics and ways of understanding reality. It is not only the language itself but the relation between the scientific-academic approach and the popular local knowledge that is important.

There are examples of members of HEIs establishing a dialogue with local communities and social actors who are looking for initiatives that respond to their priorities, needs and experiences. While there are cases where some academics have gained communities' confidence after years of work and have derived this from a collaboration between scientific and popular knowledges, there are other instances in which academics have appropriated popular knowledge on, for example, plants for their private purposes and even have patented this knowledge as being their own property.

The success of a partnership between HEIs and society in general is a complex process and depends on very different dimensions. One of these is policy itself, related to how governments set the direction for higher education. The second dimension that affects the process is funding – who gets access to resources? It seems that it is just a matter of HEIs, but what about the community partners? If the HEI's projects establish research goals and some standards that have to be accomplished in order to win financing, how does the HEI respond to the needs of the community and consider this problem in terms of standards to meet?

In the partnership, the role of each organization may be different. For instance, HEIs and community groups bring different perspectives. It is also important to think about the role of 'champions', who are different from leaders. Champions should exist in both the community and the university, but is important to have a sense of watching and approaching the champions.

A partnership has different characteristics in different social, economical and cultural contexts, and is also affected by different processes. In addition, it can have very different meanings depending on the kinds of actor with whom the partnership is established. If we want a partnership to guarantee a desirable and successful relationship among partners that enables real participation, mutuality and shared leadership and power relations, we must consider the key elements and values that must underpin a partnership.

Focusing on the long-term sustainability of partnership must start by creating engagements based on projects that flow from purposes. The fundamental key of long-term sustainability is to link action at the community level with policy. There needs to be attention not only to what is happening on the ground, but also to the policies encountered in the particular location.

HOW CAN WE MAINSTREAM COOPERATION AND PARTICIPATION?

Cooperation and participation form a process that requires the interaction of the three elements described above: (1) a theoretical–conceptual framework, which is mostly considered to be exclusive from the academic side of the partnership; (2) a practical approach, mostly deriving from local, communitarian or social partnerships, and (3) a creative way to express different experiences, approaches and knowledges.

If we are looking to develop and consolidate partnerships in a long-term perspective, we face different challenges. The basis is confidence, but this not sufficient. If the community is involved in a project, the results are different levels of relationship between the institutions and the community. Sometimes it is possible to establish a collaboration on basic issues between a group of students and the community, but sometimes the proximity is more a discourse than a kind of institutional practice.

To ensure a relationship that enables real participation, mutuality and shared leadership and power, the partnership must first adjust and grow as it evolves over time, adapting to changes of people, goals and even interests. There also needs to be some kind of result for both the local/community participants and the researcher, and some of the benefits may not be easy to articulate. For the researcher, there is very often a drive to get that research done, but the participant may not feel that impetus. So how can the participants and communities be engaged so that they pick up that sense of drive? Sometimes the engagement for the participants happens later in the process, and engagement may fluctuate as the process goes on. There is sometimes an effect of intimidation by the HEI. It is important not only to invite community members for the task or project, but also to make them feel that they are truly members of the community and make them feel that they are valuable if they come to the HEIs.

CONCLUSIONS AND FINAL COMMENTS

We need to debate the theory and practice of engagement, taking into account epistemological, methodological and pedagogical issues on how to develop engagement that is based in reflexivity and comprehensive knowledge, through collaboration with different actors working to generate change strategies for a sustainable human development.

A key feature is how to get that the population to be considered not as a target but as a stakeholder, taking a central role in the design, planning, execution and evaluation of the activities. The challenge lies in how to develop collaborative action, generating knowledge and using it for the different purposes of the participating academic and social actors. The impacts must consider the knowledge generated as well as the promoted changes in technical, social, economical, cultural or political relations.

It is necessary to conduct research on the approaches and practices of engagement that are developed in HEIs, considering the relationship between the educational content, the research problems addressed and more appropriate and ethical behaviour, to allow HEIs to advance in terms of accomplishing their social responsibility. For the students and academics of the HEIs, the challenge is to develop a methodological base that allows them to collaborate with social actors to spark their creative capacity, to develop their ability to advance in terms of sustainable human development, and to strengthen their capacity to express their ideas through action. In addition, participants should consider how to establish flexible forms of collaboration, investment in research and joint activities to promote HEIs in engaging with society, based on an ethical and humanistic perspective (Hall, 2011).

The engagement of an HEI with its environment involves establishing multiple relationships and different levels of co-responsibility, from the personal to the group or organizational and the institutional. This means the possibility of some kind of conflict between multiple interests and diverse epistemologies of knowledge. It is important to reflect on how to strengthen the interaction between the various sectors and actors of society, especially those who are most disadvantaged.

We can explore the conceptualization of engagement and partnership as the process of creating learning communities, based on the interaction between different stakeholders who bring different knowledge, skills and experiences for the generation of knowledge. The learning community is understood as a place of engagement to accomplish social responsibility in HEIs. It has several advantages for this purpose; it constitutes a reflection space in which participants can, if necessary, express and negotiate their interests, considering the objectives or impacts desired, differentiating between individual and collectives impacts, giving each party the opportunity to define the terms of their co-responsibility, and considering the possibility of working with wider social networks and establishing more permanent relations (Gaete, 2011).

HEIs have to connect different kinds and sources of knowledge and facilitate an understanding between different cultures, letting young people become aware of the social, cultural, economic and political relations that exist. The combination of a humanistic perspective and the use of new technologies with a participatory approach will provide the means and resources that will let young people play a part in generating alternatives to face the complex problems of our society.

REFERENCES

Gaete, R. (2011) 'La responsabilidad social universitaria como desafío para la gestión estratégica de la Educación Superior: el caso de España'. *Revista de Educación*, 355, 141.

Hagedoorn, J., Link, A.N. and Vonortas, N.S. (2000) 'Research partnership'. *Research Policy*, 29, 567–86.

Hall, B. (2011) 'Towards a knowledge democracy movement: contemporary trends in community–university research partnerships'. *Rizoma Freiriano*, 9, 2336–92. Available online from http://www.rizoma-freireano.org/.

Marullo, S. and Edwards, B. (2000) 'From charity to justice: the potential of university–community collaboration for social change'. *American Behavioral Scientist*, 43, 895–912.

Sohng, S. (2013) *Participatory Research and Community Organizing*. University of Washington, School of Social Work. Republished at www.cdra.org.za.

II.1.3 THE ARCHITECTURE OF ENGAGEMENT: FINANCING THE INSTITUTIONAL STRUCTURES THAT SUPPORT COMMUNITY–UNIVERSITY PARTNERSHIPS
Edward T. Jackson

INTRODUCTION

It's not about the ideas now. It's about the money.

After several decades of practice, experimentation and debate, more is known than ever before about the nature and scale of the structures that are necessary to plan, implement and launch effective community–university engagement. It is now widely understood that higher education institutions must do more than talk about engagement; rather, they must make significant investments in the infrastructure that nurtures partnerships and optimizes benefits for all stakeholders, especially those in the community. What is not as clear, however, is how the key actors involved can mobilize sufficient funds to execute those investments in the face of competing demands, often in a context of austerity and turbulence.

This paper reviews progress in putting in place structures for community engagement, examines the issues involved in the core challenge of financing these structures, and proposes strategies for addressing this challenge.

FROM INDIVIDUAL PARTNERSHIPS TO INSTITUTION-WIDE CHANGE

Across the globe, many universities have worked with community partners to set up individual partnership projects that, at their best, produce benefits for both sides of the relationship and are operated in a transparent and respectful manner. The substance of these initiatives can range from efforts to improve local livelihoods or governance, to strengthening biodiversity and sustainable resource management, as well as addressing many other issues. In Bolivia, for instance, the non-governmental organization Centro Boliviano de Estudios Multidisciplinarios (CEBEM) carried out cooperative research with three municipalities and local wood producers to generate a project to develop and test new value-added wood products in order to enhance household and community revenue (Hall et al., 2013).

Moreover, when these projects are successful and mutually beneficial, they are frequently converted into more permanent partnership mechanisms, such as research centres or service-learning or field-placement courses. A good example is that of the Mountain Development Research Centre in the mountains of Srinigar. The Centre is a joint initiative of Garhwal University and the Delhi-based civil-society organization Society for Participatory Research in Asia (PRIA). Among other activities, the Centre has used participatory research and training to support village groups in intervening in a resettlement dispute during the planning of a massive hydro-electric dam in the area (Hall et al., 2013).

Some universities, however, have mobilized the necessary leadership, will and resources to move decisively from individual partnership projects to an institution-wide commitment to engaged and partnered research, teaching and operations. A good case in point is that of Albukhary International University (AIU) in Malaysia. In this institution, *all* students (who are recruited from many cultures and countries) are required to participate in socially engaged and community-engaged activities throughout their time at AIU. Ultimately, this university aims to produce graduates who will 'not only be gainfully employed and become successful professionals' but 'will also have the passion to serve and contribute to their respective societies' (AIU, 2013). (For a detailed discussion on AIU's approach to engagement, see Razak and Afendras elsewhere in this volume.)

Still, such an institution-wide commitment to partnership and engagement remains exceptional in most countries. There are many obstacles to institution-wide change. Yet important gains have been made in all parts of the world, and more are being made every day.

PUTTING IN PLACE THE INSTITUTIONAL STRUCTURES THAT MATTER

While universities and their community partners have been experimenting with structures and processes of partnership for many years, it is particularly within the past ten years that higher education institutions have made visible and often impressive progress to establish the structures that effective community engagement demands.

Of course, it is not only universities that require institutional structures for effective community engagement. A range of supportive policies, programmes, infrastructure and funding is also needed inside and across *community-based non-profit* and other civil society organizations. A number of science shops in Europe and research brokers in North America are located outside the academy and are structured as stand-alone non-profit organizations. Some local Aboriginal governments in Canada operate their own research ethics boards to assess external proposals to study their communities. Such structures can only operate if they secure funds from public or private sources; where funding is not available, these structures rarely exist.

One of the most challenging, and slowest, areas to change within higher education institutions is that of *tenure and promotion* (Driscoll, 2008). To be sure, gains have been made here in the professions (for example, health, law, social work,

education and extension), but resistance to altering traditional criteria can be deeply rooted, even fierce, in certain disciplines, such as political science and economics. Pulling together best practices in this area, Community-Campus Partnerships for Health has produced excellent tools to create policies that reward community-engaged scholarship that is characterized by rigour, significant results, effective dissemination and ethical behaviour (Jordan, 2007). This institutional shift does not require money, but it does require a resilient coalition to press for change at all levels of the institution and across a range of disciplines.

Universities also establish structures, often *economic development* corporations or investment partnerships, to manage real estate projects on or adjacent to their lands. Housing, offices, classrooms, recreation facilities, commercial space – universities usually have strong capabilities in hard-asset investment, construction and property management. Sometimes, as in the case of the University of Pennsylvania's West Philadelphia Initiatives (Rodin, 2007), marginalized communities benefit through jobs and business opportunities, although the process is challenging. The US-based network Campus Compact and the UK-based Pascal International Observatory both document and promote regional 'learning economies' that lever university–civic partnerships for economic recovery and improved competitiveness. There is an opportunity for universities to deploy more of their capital for social purposes in the community while, at the same time, realizing a reasonable financial return and maintaining prudent stewardship of the institution's assets (Jackson, 2010).

SYSTEM-WIDE NATIONAL AND REGIONAL FUNDING PROGRAMMES

System-wide programmes that fund engagement also matter. In the broader policy environment in which higher education institutions operate, community engagement can be broadened and deepened through well-designed and well-executed grant programmes. One notable example is that of the Community-University Research Alliance Program of the Social Sciences and Humanities Research Council of Canada, which has directed more than $120 million since 1998 to a wide range of local, regional and national research partnerships on issues as diverse as Aboriginal languages, social enterprise and food security (Canadian Institutes for Health Research, Natural Sciences and Engineering

Research Council of Canada, and the Social Sciences and Humanities Research Council of Canada, 2010). However, this peer-reviewed, competitive programme suffered from the drawback that money had to be channelled first through universities and only then to community groups, a limitation that has since been partially addressed.

Another important case of a pro-engagement funding programme is that of the Seventh Framework Program of the European Commission, which supports the network of science shops across Europe, also catalysing the activities of individual science shops at the same time. Indeed, through its Fifth and Sixth Framework Programs, the Commission has funded science shop research, networking and conferences since 2000.

NATIONAL CERTIFICATION AS AN ANIMATOR OF CHANGE

The American experience suggests that a powerful animator for putting institutional structures for community engagement in place may be a national certification process. An elective component of the broader Carnegie Classification of Institutions of Higher Education, introduced 40 years ago to demonstrate and track the differentiation across American universities and colleges (McCormick and Zhao, 2005), the Community Engagement Classification is designed as a self-study process for institutions to reflect on and improve their partnership activities with communities. Since 2006, more than 300 institutions have successfully been classified as 'institutions of community engagement' (Carnegie Foundation for the Advancement of Teaching, 2012; Saltmarsh and Driscoll, 2013).

Among other things, applicants are required to report on institutional commitments to campus-wide infrastructure supporting engagement and through budgetary allocations, external funding, fundraising and the investment of financial resources. Studying the first cohort of applicants, Driscoll noted (2008, p. 40) that successful institutions demonstrated:

> a compelling alignment of mission, marketing, leadership, traditions, recognitions, budgetary support, infrastructure, faculty development, and strategic plans – the foundational indicators of community engagement.

In other words, they solved, to some extent at least, the funding problem. Nonetheless, there are still many hundreds (and perhaps several thousands) of other institutions in the USA that have not been able to meet the classification test. Their inability or unwillingness to allocate real, multi-year financial resources to engagement structures and processes remains a key factor holding them back.

NATIONAL CULTURE CHANGE INITIATIVES

Experience from the UK suggests that countries can also promote system-wide engagement through culture-change initiatives. There, the National Co-ordinating Centre for Public Engagement (NCCPE) – based at the universities of Bristol and West England, working with the BBC and funded by UK granting councils and the Wellcome Trust – promotes the EDGE Self-Assessment Tool for Public Engagement for higher education institutions; this aims to formalize and embed public engagement as 'a valued and recognized activity for staff at all levels, and for students' (NCCPE, 2013). Interest in the Centre's approach and tools is strong in other countries in the global north, such as the USA and Canada, and adaptations of this approach to European and southern countries could yield results as well.

TAKING AN ECOSYSTEM PERSPECTIVE

The foregoing suggests that the architecture of institutional structures that support community–university partnerships is multi-level, complex and dynamic. There are many moving parts. Indeed, it makes good sense, both strategically and tactically, to view all of these parts as an ecosystem of organic, interdependent components. If one component is weak or lacking capacity, the effectiveness of other components suffers. Conversely, if all parts of the ecosystem are robust and mutually reinforcing, the prospects of high-impact, successful partnerships are enhanced significantly.

Figure II.1.3.1 depicts this ecosystem of institutional structures that support community–university engagement. There are several levels of this system. First, there is the system-wide level of certification bodies and culture-change organizations, granting councils and programmes, and governments (both national and sub-national) that are responsible for higher education, as well as private, corporate and community foundations. At the institutional level, there are universities, colleges and other higher education institutions. And within those institutions, of course, are other levels: faculty, school and departmental or research unit.

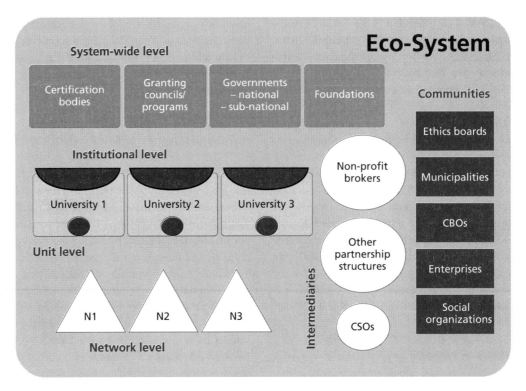

FIGURE II.1.3.1 Ecosystem of institutional structures in community–university engagement
Source: Jackson and Sánchez-Martí (2013).

The ecosystem also includes, of course, organizations at the community level, which can range from local ethics boards (in the case of Aboriginal communities in Canada), municipalities and civil society organizations, to private and social enterprises, and a diversity of social and cultural organizations, often taking the form of non-profit organizations or cooperatives. Furthermore, sitting between the higher education institutions and communities are intermediaries such as science shops, non-profit brokers and other partnership structures (consortia, round tables and so on) that facilitate engagement. Finally, the ecosystem includes networks that seek to advance the theory and (mainly) practice of partnership in the local, national and international spheres.

Taking such an ecosystem perspective has real advantages. In terms of the funding challenge, seeing the whole ecosystem enables practitioners and leaders in community–university partnerships to identify which components of the ecosystem are underfunded and to prioritize them for action. Moreover, this perspective clearly shows that the funding policies and decisions of the structures at the *system-wide* level are crucial to addressing funding needs in other parts of the ecosystem. That is, the most important sites of contestation are granting councils, government ministries responsible for higher education and foundations. If leaders and practitioners of engagement can influence the funding priorities of these bodies in a pro-engagement/partnership direction, and sustain those priorities and funding flows over an extended period of time, other components of the ecosystem will be more likely to be adequately funded – and the impacts of partnerships to be broadened, deepened and also sustained.

THE CONTRIBUTION OF INTERNATIONAL NETWORKS

In terms of the gritty, day-to-day work of institutional change, international networks may seem like a luxurious extra. However, in fact, the contributions of these structures can be very substantial in advancing the engagement agenda in general and the institutional structures it requires more specifically:

● Working for a renewal of the missions and policies of higher education institutions for public service, relevance and social responsibility, the *Global University Network for Innovation* (GUNi) produces an annual world report, organizes conferences, animates knowledge communities and commissions research projects. GUNi is supported by UNESCO, the United Nations University, the Polytechnic University of Catalonia, the Government of Spain, corporations and member fees.

- Promoting civic engagement and social responsibility in higher education, the *Tailloires Network* shares information among university leaders and builds institutional capacity through conferences, newsletters, tools and experts. Tailloires is supported by member fees, foundations and corporations, as well as Tufts University, where its secretariat is based.

- The *Living Knowledge Network* (LK) uses conferences, magazines, tools and research to promote best practices and knowledge-sharing among an international network of science shops. With its members primarily based in Europe, and its coordinating office in Bonn, LK is funded mainly by the European Commission's Seventh Framework Program.

- The *Global Alliance on Community Engaged Research* (GACER) is an emerging network of engaged faculty members and academics from the science shop and participatory research traditions working to promote the effective use of community-engaged research in higher education, public policy and civil society. It is supported by the University of Victoria, PRIA and other member organizations.

- For *its part, the Pascal International Observatory*, a non-profit organization with members and affiliates in 50 countries, is a knowledge network that undertakes grant- and contract-based policy, research and evaluation projects on social capital, lifelong learning and the renewal of place, including social, economic and cultural development.

- Finally, *Community-Campus Partnerships for Health* (CCPH), a mainly US-based network, has built a large repository of tools and policies on structuring partnerships, conducting participatory research and reforming tenure and promotion policies for engagement. CCPH is funded by foundations, health funding agencies and its members.

While each of these organizations has developed its own funding model, finding the money to coordinate and administer active international networks – that is, financing their core functions – is a constant challenge for their proponents. The fact is that these networks can rarely, if ever, become self-sustaining; their activities almost always must be subsidized. One way of strengthening the case for multi-year core support is to carry out evaluations of the outcomes and impacts of these networks. Value for money and social return on investment studies could provide compelling evidence for core support. A second approach would be for networks to convene current and potential donors and partners to discuss their network's strategy, plans and expected results over the next five to ten years – and to offer funders an opportunity to shape, and of course invest in, the next phase of work. As in all fundraising strategies, diversification of sources of support is as essential as expanding the absolute quantum of funding.

WHY ARE INSTITUTIONAL STRUCTURES FOR ENGAGEMENT DIFFICULT TO FUND?

There is a cluster of issues that combine to obstruct, defer and delay the allocation of appropriate and adequate funds to community-engagement structures within higher education institutions and the systems of which they are a part. First and foremost is *austerity*. Owing to structural economic change and shrinking tax bases, publicly funded higher education budgets in most countries of the global north today are stagnant or are, in fact, experiencing real cuts in absolute terms. Moreover, rich-country universities and the systems in which they operate continue to cope with increasing enrolment levels, a trend that is several decades old (see, for example, Clark et al., 2009).

In addition, universities in very poor countries in the global south have, typically, been badly underfunded since their inception. Such conditions result in budgets that focus on basic operating expenses and little else. Of course, the situation of the new economic powers – China, India, Brazil, Korea and others – is very different. In those countries, public funding of higher education and research is massive and has grown markedly in recent decades. Notwithstanding recent economic challenges faced by the new powers, these trends in higher education funding are likely to continue, although perhaps at a slower pace.

The second issue is internal *competition*. Scarcity of funds, the culture and traditions of disciplinary 'tribalism' within the academy, and broad-based participation by faculty, staff and students in university governance, are among the factors that torque intense competition for funds within universities. Added to this is the simple fact that executives and faculty in some disciplines are actually energetic *opponents* of community engagement, rejecting it as unscholarly and irrelevant to the pursuit of knowledge. Finally, there is the path dependence and bureaucratic inertia of large *funding bodies* such as ministries of higher education and granting councils that are also remarkably resistant to changing their policies and procedures to become more supportive of community–university partnerships.

STRATEGIES THAT CAN WORK

These are formidable obstacles. What, then, should pro-engagement executives and faculty members and their allies in the community do to remove or reduce these barriers? How can they mobilize the funds that pivotal engagement structures require? Several strategies have shown potential:

- *Continuously improving through certification and culture-change processes.* The Carnegie Community Engagement Classification process in the USA has demonstrated that individual universities seeking certification as 'an institution of community engagement' use self-study and external standards to drive financial commitments to under-gird important institutional structures for effective engagement. The NCCPE's self-assessment tool in the UK also promotes institutional culture change in this direction.
- *Authentically aligning engagement with mission.* It is also possible for individual universities to authentically align engagement with their mission. When engagement is understood by decision-makers to be part of the core business of the university (that is, aligned with student recruitment and revenue generation), the business case for funding its structures becomes very clear and attracts broader support.
- *Building a resilient coalition for change.* In order to drive and achieve an authentic alignment of community engagement with mission, engagement proponents can mobilize a university-wide taskforce or working group that encodes a coalition of pro-engagement faculty members, administrators, staff and students, as well as community allies, to work over a period of years to prepare a report and push for reform horizontally and vertically across the institution.
- *Shaping the policies and programmes of system-wide public-funding agencies.* While this strategy make take many years, it has been shown in several jurisdictions that when pro-engagement advocates are able to influence the design and implementation of system-wide funding programmes, good things happen – for many years, and for many institutions.
- *Building alliances with progressive private foundations and endowments.* Pro-engagement advocates in the academy and community alike should seek out and build productive working relationships with leaders and officers in philanthropic institutions that are interested in animating change for engagement.
- *Converting the credibility of international innovation into local institution-level and system-wide change.* University boards of trustees, funding agencies and even government cabinets often react more positively to innovative ideas that are brought from outside than to home-grown ones. Engagement structures bolstered by international experience and profile have more success attracting budget support.

These and other strategies for funding community engagement structures are worthy of testing and elaboration by leaders and practitioners in the engagement field. Furthermore, young, emerging leaders should be introduced to these strategies early in their careers, through training, mentoring and action.

CONCLUSION

Much is known around the world today about what structures are required inside and outside universities in order to broaden, deepen, render more effective and sustain community engagement. What is needed now is for university leaders, faculty members, students and their community allies to organize to not only institute such structures, but also mobilize the funds necessary to operate them. Budgetary allocations and targeted fundraising inside universities, and well-designed, pro-engagement funding programmes across the higher education system, are essential elements in addressing the financing challenge. Indeed, taking an ecosystem approach to promoting change in funding arrangements has important strategic and tactical advantages. And international networks can also contribute credibility, tools and connectivity to reinforce these actions for change. Looking ahead, if community engagement proponents can focus at least some of their efforts on solving this money problem, their prospects of success will be much brighter.

REFERENCES

AIU (2013) 'About Albukhary University'. Retrieved July 18, 2013 from http://www.aiu.edu.my/about-aiu/.

Canadian Institutes for Health Research, Natural Sciences and Engineering Research Council of Canada, and the Social Sciences and Humanities Research Council of Canada (2010) *Tri-Council Policy Statement on the Ethical Research Involving Humans.* Ottawa: Tri-Council, Chapter 9.

Carnegie Foundation for the Advancement of Teaching (2012) *2015 Documentation Reporting Form: First Time*

Classification Documentation Framework. Stanford, CT: Carnegie Foundation for the Advancement of Teaching.

Clark, I.D., Moran, G., Skolnik, M.L. and Trick, D. (2009) *Academic Transformation: The Forces Reshaping Higher Education in Ontario.* Montreal: McGill-Queen's University Press.

Driscoll, A. (2008) *Carnegie's Community-Engagement Classification: Inventions and Insights.* Stanford, CT: Carnegie Foundation for the Advancement of Teaching, pp. 39–40.

Hall, B., Jackson, E., Tandon, R., Lall, N. and Fontan, J.-M. (eds) (2013) *Knowledge, Democracy and Action: Community University Research Partnerships in International Perspectives.* Manchester: Manchester University Press.

Jackson, E.T. (2010) 'University capital, community engagement and continuing education: blending professional development and social change'. *Canadian Journal of University Continuing Education,* 36(2), 1–13.

Jackson, E.T. and Sánchez-Martí, A. (2013) 'Eco-system of Institutional Structures in Community–University Engagement'. Diagram presented to the Institutional Structures Workshop, Sixth International Barcelona Conference on Higher Education, Global University Network on Innovation, Barcelona, Spain.

Jordan, C. (ed.) (2007) *Community Engaged Scholarship Review, Promotion and Tenure Package.* Peer Reviewed Work Group, Community Engaged Scholarship for Health Collaborative. Seattle, WA: Community-Campus Partnerships for Health.

McCormick, A.C. and Zhao, C.M. (2005) *Rethinking and Reframing the Carnegie Classification.* Stanford, CT: Carnegie Foundation for the Advancement of Teaching.

NCCPE (2013) *The EDGE Self-Assessment Tool for Public Engagement.* Bristol: University of Bristol and University of West England.

Rodin, J. (2007) *The University and Urban Revival.* Philadelphia, PA: University of Pennsylvania Press.

Saltmarsh, J. and Driscoll, A. (2013) 'Carnegie Invites Institutions to Apply for 2015 Community Engagement Classification or Reclassification – Applications Due April 15, 2014'. Letter distributed via Campus-Community Partnerships for Health, January 15.

II.2.1 REDESIGN PROGRESS NOW! THE USE OF KNOWLEDGE FOR A RECONCEPTUAL- IZED HUMAN PROGRESS

Claudia Neubauer and Matthieu Calame

INTRODUCTION

Human activity has exercised an unprecedented impact on the integrity of the biosphere. In the era of anthropocene, the human species as a bio-geological force systematically transforms nature, causing climate change, soil erosion, loss of biodiversity, scarcity of natural resources, and water, soil and air pollution. After decades of furious techno-economic development, two main observations can be made: poverty and social injustice have barely declined or may even be rising again, and our planet is approaching its limits. Therefore, a radical change, a 'quantum leap', is necessary in our conception of progress. Many factors are now gathered to allow such a leap – that is, the ecological transition – provided that courageous decisions are taken to drive a multi-scale change within a short period of time.

WHY THERE IS A NEED TO RECONCEPTUALIZE HUMAN PROGRESS

During the 17th and 18th centuries, the Age of Enlightenment, rose an idea of progress that was quite simple and easy to understand. Through the action of rationality, humankind would be able to master Nature, to improve well-being and production, to overcome disease and hunger, and also to defeat religious superstitions, lack of knowledge and prejudices of all kinds (racial, social, gender, cultural ...), which were considered to be the roots of exploitation and misery. Because

the origin of the problems was seemingly so clear, the solution seemed obvious. By improving education, knowledge and intellectual skilfulness, by giving the power to philosophers, engineers and scientists, modern society would guarantee a better life for the majority of its citizens. From the *New Atlantis* of Francis Bacon (1626), where 'generosity and enlightenment, dignity and splendour, piety and public spirit' are ruling, to the *Esquisse d'un tableau historique des progrès de l'esprit humain* ('Outline for a historical picture of the progress of the human mind') of Condorcet (1794), a large range of books have expressed this faith in reason. From a European perspective and despite numerous contradicting facts (for example, colonialism and growing tensions between European powers), the 19th century established the triumph and unchallenged domination of the idea of progress as it was born in Western Europe.

The 20th century, however, shattered this and witnessed the crisis and failure of the ideology of progress due to two major collapses: the two World Wars and the planetary boundaries. The conflicts over the period 1914–1945, which precipitated Europe into an unforeseen and inconceivable apocalypse, swept away the myth of a regular and irreversible step forward for Human Progress, and made it clear that most intelligent, cultivated and 'reasonable' people could become cruel killers. The illusion of a natural link between technical progress and moral progress was broken.

And yet, during the second half of the 20th century in large parts of the world, an unprecedented technical development and economic growth continued to unfold by exploiting and polluting seemingly unlimited natural resources, be these oil, water or land. If the first warnings rose in the 1960s (for example, in *Silent Spring* from Rachel Carson in 1962, and in *Limits to Growth* from the Club of Rome in 1973), and if the environmental debate has been established at the highest international level, notably through the Kyoto protocol, no country has up to now seriously taken into account what have been identified in the past few years as the *planetary boundaries*:

Anthropogenic pressures on the Earth System have reached a scale where abrupt global environmental change can no longer be excluded ... Transgressing one or more planetary boundaries may be deleterious or even catastrophic due to the risk of crossing thresholds that will trigger non-linear, abrupt environmental change within continental- to planetary-scale systems. (Rockström et al., 2009)

However, *progress* remains nowadays a prominent narrative in the world. It continues to disseminate all over the globe through the dogmatic vectors that are economic growth, competition, new technologies and communication.

For a long time, technoscientific developments such as nuclear power plants, pesticides, genetically modified organisms, aeroplanes and space shuttles, big and fast cars, household appliances for all and everything, as well as fashion clothes and faraway holidays, were presented as the ultimate marks of modernity and progress. The modern 'hero' does not know limits; the world is his. We are told: this is in human nature – always reach beyond limits. And science does just the same. The modern mind neither knows nor accepts boundaries. But if the mind of man cannot be constrained, his acts should be (and indeed are, for example by laws), and anyway physical planetary boundaries will be, since they are not a frontier that can be pushed back. Numerous countries will have to undertake major changes in their current or upcoming modes of living to reduce the impact on nature.

We have to consider seriously the notions of sufficiency and prosperity without growth, and to redefine the role of technical development. We have to move from conquest to stewardship: maintaining before obtaining. This is the profound psychological background for the ecological transition – which has to be followed by accordant action. Therefore, the promise of a universal prosperity based on unlimited production and consumption for all appears henceforth not only like an illusion, but also like a dangerous and unreasonable objective.

WHAT HAS TO BE CHANGED IN OUR CONCEPTION OF PROGRESS

Several questions arise: Which progress do we consider real and indisputable? What should be discarded? How do we assess and measure what is progress and what

is not? Our model of society needs close scrutiny since 'Patterns of power in society may thus be seen not only as outcomes, but also as determinants of our understandings of progress' (Stirling, 2009).

We value the freedom of consciousness and thriving of happiness, the sense of personal responsibility and compassion, the idea of improving living conditions by social, moral or technical innovations. We acknowledge that equal dignity between all human beings and equality of rights are important objectives. We know that no *natural* order of society exists and that we have choices.

But several assumptions should be strongly deconstructed: the idea that competition and greed are the sources of human progress, that there is a linear relation between consumption and happiness, that increasing power by technology will solve all problems, that an unregulated market is the final path to prosperity, that unlimited property rights lead to an optimized use of rare resources, and that a struggle for and accumulation of power is the law of nature.

However, if it is (relatively) easy to underline what is wrong and why, it is much more challenging to figure out what kind of society we can imagine and create.

ON THE NATURE OF PROGRESS

Four fields of improvement can neither be confused nor reduced: truth, efficiency, good and beauty. It is *true* that we are able to kill. But this does not mean that it is *right*. Neither is it *beautiful*. Metallurgists of the early Bronze Age were *efficient* enough to create *wonderful* masterpieces without having a concrete idea of *exactly* what happened. Scientific *truth* and technical *usefulness* can say nothing about the *value* of a flower. And so on. *Truth* is the issue of science, *efficiency* the issue of craft, *good* the issue of moral and justice, and *beauty* the issue of art. Our modern societies are characterized by a shared confusion of what relates to truth, efficiency, beauty and good, and their respective importance for societal life. Not only do modern societies pretend to be science-based, but they also merge science and craft, science and good (where 'technical progress' is inextricably positively connoted).

Real and balanced progress can only occur if we restore both the clear distinction and the constructive dialogue between Beauty, Good, Technology and Truth. We need a better and different comprehension of nature and society, more social and environmental justice, smart production and beauty in our common life. But, as Plato pointed out in his text *Protagoras*, if a society can fulfil its technical and artistic needs through specialized people, the sense of justice must be common to all people. We need doctors, farmers, engineers … but we need them first of all as citizens. Thus (higher) education should not only train engineers but citizen engineers, not only researchers but citizen researchers, not only lawyers but citizen lawyers, and so on. Knowledge can be used for any kind of (political, economic, legal) target, be it bad or good. But who can say what is bad or good, what we need to know or not, what is just or unjust? Kant gave three moral imperatives: 'Act in such a way that you could will that the maxim of your act become a Universal Law', 'Act in such a way that you treat Humanity, whether in your own person or in the person of another as an end in itself and never merely as a means', and 'Act so that through your maxims you could be a legislator of universal laws'. The German philosopher Hans Jonas added a fourth one: 'Act so that the effects of your action are compatible with the permanence of genuine human life'. Those four principles frame the essence of the ecological humanism we need now.

A MULTI-SCALE TRANSFORMATION

Every existing societal system builds its own coherence between the individual and the collective level, the local and the international level. A quantum leap – the ecological transition and a shift in the *cosmovision* – requires simultaneous changes at every scale in a limited time period.

At the individual level reappears the question of the meaning of human life. We have to (re)learn to appreciate what is useful rather than what is big, to enjoy what is fruitful rather than what is powerful, what is close rather than far, what is supporting rather than dominating us, what is given and vital rather than rare and expensive. We should abandon the race to power. We should teach our children how extraordinary ordinary life is. We have to teach them self-esteem, self-respect, and esteem and respect for others. If the mind capacities of children, such as are needed for mathematics or natural sciences, are today highly valued in the (Western) school system, abilities that call for artistic and craft skills or social and collective behaviour suffer from lesser consideration. Solidarity, creativity, critical thinking and collective acting should gain ground as central elements of education. In other words we need a 'Wiederverzauberung der Welt' ('re-enchantment of the world') as a response to the 'Entzauberung der Welt' ('disenchantment of the world') through science (Weber, 1917). There is no reason why the knowledge of reality through science should lead to a disenchant-ment of the world. Modern sciences such as ecology or evolution of life tell us pleasant narratives.

WE NEED TO CHANGE OUR FIGURE OF THE MODERN HERO FROM THE WARRIOR TO THE GARDENER

What exactly is a society? What kind of society do we wish to build? Just a few short reflections to underline the purpose. In the last century, the domination of nations states and limited liability companies led to both the loss of consciousness in individuals and the loss of their capacity to cooperate in societies. In both cases, obedience to a leader or struggle for power seemed to be the only viable behaviour. If the model might be efficient for the purpose of mobilizing a lot of people very quickly for a single objective, it however shows its limits in the management of a complex reality and may (or surely does) even prove to be counterproductive.

Nineteenth-century federalists such as Proudhon pointed out the weaknesses of centralized systems and dreamt of a 'federation of free communes of the world', thus meeting the thoughts of Aristotle, Locke, Condorcet and Tocqueville. They claimed that the commune was the basis of all the civilized world, not least because the local economy is closely connected with social and environmental issues, and because they encourage direct participation of citizens (active and responsible citizenship). A third reason could be added: the commune (or community) is the ideal place for innovative answers to overcome commonly identified problems. Reinforced communities are thus a pathway for progress.

A decentralized organization would also bring change in the production and use of knowledge. It would make technoscientific innovation subject to democratic scrutiny, open new paths through a cooperation between academia, citizens, not-for-profit civil society organizations and local companies, lead to a sharing and co-production of knowledge and thus a sharing of power, and strengthen the local dimension and relevance of research, while valuing different forms of knowledge, be this local, professional, empirical, women's, traditional or indigenous.

Regarding the economic sphere, at least three policies have to be deeply overhauled: the status of *limited liability* of companies, property rights and the currency system.

How can we achieve a society with a high level of responsibility if we admit that one of our major activities – the economy – is managed through organizations with 'limited' responsibility? This in fact often leads to no responsibility at all. With an 'unlimited' responsibility (both economic and legal) of companies, stakeholders would rather focus on how money and profits are made than on their return on investment.

Over the centuries, *property rights* have been mostly limited. A large part of human activity was managed according to the 'right of use'. Later, property rights were enforced to secure the improvement that people could bring to their properties. However, what was meant to protect individual property became an unlimited property right dogma resulting too often in monopoly and misuse. 'Because property rights define relationships between people in respect of things, and almost all things are subject to some form of property, the regulation of property has a fundamental role to play in the management of the world's resources' (Barnes, 2013). If state and private property are nowadays the dominant property forms, their use and importance would have to be reconsidered in relation to common property and open access, and to effects on the capability of property to sustain social, ecological and economic resilience. We need to redevelop the notion of the 'Commons' (common pool resource management) (Ostrom, 1990) and a broad range of property rights according to the nature of the resources, the community concerned and the local situation.

Last but not least, *currency*. How to manage a diverse world with a single unit: the dollar? How long will the Earth accept the dollar as a counterpart of its deregulation? Some economists (for example, Kirk Barrett, David Fleming, Mayer Hillman and Tina Fawcett, Suryapratim Roy and Edwin Woerdman) suggest the creation of a carbon-unit. Beside a labour-currency (what the dollar is), would we not need a water currency, an energy-currency, maybe a bio-currency to measure what our ecological footprint is (as suggested by William Rees and Mathis Wackernagel)? In addition, local currencies already (re)appear in numerous places all over the world to enforce local economies.

Instead of gross domestic products and stock exchange prices, we need human well-being in reinforced democracies and in unison with nature (and respective indicators to measure this) (UNDP, 2002; Sen et al., 2009).

At the global level, we have learned from history that institutions tend to become corrupted, and a mighty corrupted universal state would be a dreadful thing. However, we do need a worldwide harmonized system that would be mainly responsible to go as far as possible in the definition of common objectives, with the means to reach them being left to the discretion of lower levels. Unity of the questions, diversity of the responses. To make this power transparent, limited, binding and the most democratic would require power-ful means of control, systematic collegial and transparent decision-taking and a huge level of accountability of those who decide. Between unbearable dependency and impossible independence stands interdependency. For man, by nature, is a Zoon Politikon.

CONCLUSION: FROM NATURAL ORDER TO NATURAL LIMITS

The Enlightenment refused an order that was presented as 'natural', according to the law of God. Natural the right of the king to abuse his people, natural the right of a man over his wife and children, natural the right of Man over animals, natural the superiority of the winner over the loser, the right of the master over the slave. The Enlightenment claimed that only the right of people was natural and not their submission. Nevertheless, the great ideologies of the following centuries – liberalism, fascism and communism – pretended that they were ruling society according to scientific 'natural' laws. It would be very dangerous to consider ecology as a new set of 'laws'. We have to manage the City of Men not according to the laws of nature but according to its limits. The Earth is not a fierce master but just an exhausted and weak tree carrying all of us and giving us shelter. But as Charlie Chaplin said it at the end of his movie *The Great Dictator* (1940):

> In this world there is room for everyone. And the good Earth is rich and can provide for everyone. The way of life can be free and beautiful, but we have lost the way. Greed has poisoned men's souls, has barricaded the world with hate, has goose-stepped us into misery and bloodshed. We have developed speed, but we have shut ourselves in. Machinery that gives abundance has left us in want. Our knowledge has made us cynical. Our cleverness, hard and unkind. We think too much and feel too little. More than machinery we need humanity. More than cleverness we need kindness and gentleness. Without these qualities, life will be violent and all will be lost …

We should remember that we are all human in the deepest sense of the word. Ultimately, the choice in front of us is between life and death. We should choose life!

REFERENCES

Barnes, R.A. (2013) 'The capacity of property rights to accommodate social-ecological resilience'. *Ecology and*

Society, 18(1), 6. Available online from http://dx.doi.org/10.5751/ES-05292-180106.

Ostrom, E. (1990) *Governing the Commons: The Evolution of Institutions for Collective Action.* New York: Cambridge University Press.

Rockström J., Steffen, W., Noone, K. et al. (2009) 'Planetary boundaries: exploring the safe operating space for humanity'. *Ecology and Society*, 14(2), 32.

Sen, A., Stiglitz, J.E. and Fitoussi, J.-P. (2009) *Report by the Commission on the Measurement of Economic Performance and Social Progress.* Paris: OFCE – Centre de recherche en économie de Sciences Po.

Stirling, A. (2009) *Direction, Distribution and Diversity! Pluralising Progress in Innovation, Sustainability and Development.* STEPS Working Paper No. 32. Brighton: STEPS Centre.

UNDP (2002) *Human Development Report 2002. Deepening Democracy in a Fragmented World.* New York: Oxford University Press.

Weber, M. (1917) *Wissenschaft als Beruf.* Oral presentation on November 7, 1917. Cited in Weber, M. (1984) *Wissenschaft als Beruf*, 7. Berlin: Duncker & Humblot.

II.2.2 THE CHALLENGES OF KNOWLEDGE IN A KNOWLEDGE DEMOCRACY

Jesús Granados Sánchez and Cristina Escrigas

At this point in history, we need to review the idea of what reality is and the mechanisms by which we produce knowledge. It is not possible to build a new world order if it does not change our perception of what reality is and what is true. It is time for a revision and an enlargement of the conception of knowledge.

UNDERSTANDING REALITY IN A KNOWLEDGE DEMOCRACY

Thanks to the contributions of socio-constructivism, we can affirm that internal aspects of an individual's cognition and collectivity issues are involved in the development of knowledge, which means that subjects construct their own knowledge from their perceptions and through the subsequent restructuration that makes in terms of society. Therefore, we nowadays believe that knowledge relates partly to genetic potential, and that it is also a social product and a personal reconstruction (Benejam, 2005).

According to Simmons (1993), we can say that humans occupy, in addition to an ecological world, a social and a psychological world. The ecological world refers to the place we are, the physical reality that is governed by the laws of nature, which is unique and objectified. The social world constitutes the organization of people and the knowledge that groups have developed to explain the ecological reality that surrounds them. Every civilization has a collective mentality that has shaped its own cultural rationality

(Leff, 2004). The ways of thinking about and interpretations that different cultures have of the position of the human species on Earth have had enormous importance because, somehow, they have legitimized humans' development, which means the relationship between humans and between humans and their environment. The social sphere also has to do with governmental politics and actions which create structures that can enable, or not, the conditions for the development of a collective intelligence (Innerarity, 2011).

Although science and cultural backgrounds provide a framework of common social knowledge, endless personal versions derive from this framework. Each individual's cultural learning is unique due to that person's particular experience in the community, which is established by factors such as education, geographical context, social relationships, occupation, and so on. This experience is also established by personal cognitive factors (which form the so-called psychological world) such as memory, imagination, experience, values, evaluation, understanding, thought processing, command of the language (very important during the learning process), sensations and personal emotions, which are conveyed by the ecological and the social world. Ultimately, we can say that every person creates for themselves a subjective image of the world according to their life in society and their experiences and personal history. This is what Fien (1992) called *personal geography* and Simmons (1993) *lifeworld*. The great diversity of personal records is very valuable since it brings to humanity different ways of reading our surroundings, and getting to know the 'world' of the others both helps and enriches us in restructuring our own ideas and visions.

The ecological, social and psychological worlds are spheres that act simultaneously in each individual, enabling the creation of a personal reality through the processes of perception and cognition that enable action (Figure II.2.2.1). But, as Chambers (1997) pointed out, not all realities count, and some individuals impose their realities on others (those they deem 'lower' than them). The result is the implementation of hierarchies of knowledge or regimes of truth that are sustained through discourses, institutions and practices, and that determine which knowledge is true, assuming that some individuals and groups know better than others, and therefore that decisions over action must fall on them. This is the case with science. For Bunge (1998) 'Science is the source of knowledge that provides the different societies the basis of their knowledge.' Along the course of history, Western society has valued and trusted both science and technology, and these have been converted into a myth. We have to admit that scientific knowledge has helped in the conceptual reconstruction of the world, and it keeps getting wider and deeper all the time. But one of the most prominent contributions to the epistemology of the last century has also been the consideration that science is showing the limits of reason and the impossibility of reaching a true knowledge.

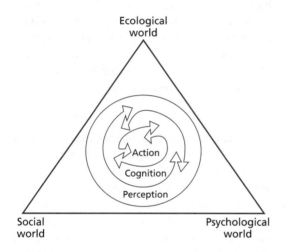

FIGURE II.2.2.1 **Key spheres in knowledge creation**
Source: After Granados (2010).

Science is defined as the group of answers that the scientific community gives to the problems of the moment. It seems clear that if these scientific answers to theory are provided by certain people, these people cannot be separated from their context. This means that their answers are affected by the acknowledgement of the problems of the moment, by the social urgencies and the necessities that make certain issues the centre of attention, by how they understand and see reality according to the knowledge available to them, and by the interests of the power groups and structures that rule the world in every period. If we accept that scientific knowledge is a social product elaborated by people through time, this implies that knowledge is a

historical product and therefore that it remains subject to interpretation and change (Benejam, 2005).

Given the fact that science is an instrument to understand the world, and seeing that the world is changing at a fast pace, it is somehow perceived that science and the scientific method (which were conceptualized and created and emerged in a world that is not the world of today) can no longer give answers to many demands, especially to the large changes and challenges that occur on a planetary scale (Clark et al., 2005). Therefore, this perception creates a need for a new relationship between science and society that corresponds to the new demands.

THE CHALLENGES FOR KNOWLEDGE

Figure II.2.2.2 expresses the need to enlarge the conception of knowledge through six main domains: a recognition of the plurality of sources and cosmovisions of knowledge, and the need for a dialogue among them; a knowledge that is comprehensive; the use of knowledge to take action; the creation of holistic and complex knowledge to understand the whole; the democratization of knowledge and power through the co-creation of knowledge; and the assumption of a dynamic and creative knowledge.

FIGURE II.2.2.2 **Key issues for enlarging the conception of knowledge**
Source: Granados (2013).

PLURALITY AND DIALOGUE: THE ECOLOGY OF KNOWLEDGE

We must move on from considering that the only criteria of truth and validity of knowledge are found in science, in the sense that other knowledge is considered non-existent or irrelevant and assuming that any knowledge is incomplete. Therefore, the ecology of knowledge recognizes the plurality of knowledges and establishes the necessary epistemological dialogue between the different constellations or sources of knowledge, which must be complementary.

The debate on the relationships between science and other knowledges (de Sousa Santos et al., 2007) is a critical aspect for scientific knowledge and the hegemony of Western thought. Dominant Western scientific knowledge currently obscures or underprivileges other forms of knowing and the voices of other knowers. For Boaventura de Souza Santos (2007, pp. 3–4):

> this monopoly is at the core of the modern epistemological disputes between scientific and nonscientific forms of truth. Since the universal validity of a scientific truth is admittedly always very relative, given the fact that it can only be ascertained in relation to certain kinds of objects under certain circumstances and established by certain methods, how does it relate to other possible truths which may even claim a higher status but which cannot be established according to scientific methods, such as reason as philosophical truth or faith as religious truth … On the other side of the line, there is no real knowledge; there are beliefs, opinions, intuitive or subjective understandings, which, at the most, may become objects or raw materials for scientific inquiry.

The ecology of knowledge is an epistemological and political option of a new kind of solidarity among social actors or groups. According to Simmons (1993), it is necessary to consider 'other plants in the garden', since with them and with their cultivation the universal benefit can be greater. It is more than a recognition of the invisible; it is about valuing all our indigenous ancestral heritage and placing it in an equal position with other sources of knowledge. We also have to recover the value of tacit knowledge, of everyday knowledge, of the knowledge of rural and indigenous cultures as other legitimate and complementary forms of knowledge (Novo, 2006). What matters is the epistemological dialogue and complementarity among constellations of knowledge:

Being infinite, the plurality of knowledge existing in the world is unreachable as such, since each way of knowing accounts for it only partially, and from its own specific perspective alone. On the other hand, however, since each way of knowing exists only in the infinite plurality of knowledge, none of them is able to understand itself without referring to the others. Knowledge exists only as a plurality of ways of knowing, just as ignorance exists only as a plurality of forms of ignorance. The possibilities and limits of understanding and action of each way of knowing can only be grasped to the extent that each way of knowing offers a comparison with other ways of knowing. Such comparison is always a reduced version of the epistemological diversity of the world, the latter being infinite. What I call ecology of knowledge lies in this comparison … The limits and possibilities of each way of knowing reside, thus, ultimately, in the existence of other ways of knowing. They can only be explored and valorized in comparison with other ways of knowing. The less a given way of knowing knows the limits of its knowing about other ways of knowing, the less aware is it of its own limits and possibilities. This comparison is not easy, but herein lies the learned ignorance we need in our time. (de Sousa Santos, 2009, p. 116)

Each exercise of ecology of knowledge implies a selection of ways of knowing and a field of interaction in which the exercise takes place. An unlimited number of ecologies of knowledge is possible, as unlimited as the epistemological diversity of the world. For de Sousa Santos (2009), the ecology of knowledge faces two problems: how to compare ways of knowing given the epistemological difference; and given that plurality of knowledge is infinite, how to create the set of ways of knowing that partake of the ecology of knowledge. To deal with the former, de Sousa Santos (2009) proposes translation; to deal with the latter, artisanship of practices.

COMPREHENSIVE KNOWLEDGE

Traditionally, rational knowledge has been considered to be of a higher order. Novo (2006) states that the value of feelings, emotions and affection has been expelled from the rational discourse. We think that knowledge must be considered as an equilibrium and a mixture of different human ways of knowing and capturing reality that includes intuitive, experiential and emotional knowledge and reason.

Knowledge also should seek a balance between personal aspects, such as values, affective and cognitive learning, rationality and intuition, the object and the subject, the material and the spiritual, and collective aspects, such as economics and ecology, present and future, local and global, individual and community (Sterling, 2001).

USE OF KNOWLEDGE TO TAKE ACTION

The creation of knowledge needs not only to describe, but also to prioritize its capacity of transformation, taking into account the context of phenomena and acquiring a problem-solving perspective and the creation of alternative futures. Thus, knowledge has to integrate a scalar variable in all forms (local, national, regional, global, and so on) and in all its interrelationships, and it must also incorporate the time variable in its different forms (circular time, cyclical time, and so on) and considerations.

In terms of social change, we find that action and intervention are as important as cognition and rationality in the knowledge-creation process. Therefore, knowledge is to be guided by ethical criteria, especially regarding their technological applications and the repercussions arising from their impact. It is about including ethics attached to precaution (Novo, 2006).

HOLISTIC AND COMPLEX KNOWLEDGE

Knowledge must integrate its humanistic and technological orientations, and must have multiple perspectives and be built upon cross-disciplinary bases and complexity. Complexity implies the limits of knowledge and an assumption of ignorance, uncertainty and insecurity. The aim of knowledge is to understand the whole.

DEMOCRATIZATION AND POWER: SOCIAL CO-CREATION OF KNOWLEDGE

Knowledge is seen as being in the hands of a monopoly of expert knowledge producers, who exercise power over others through their expertise (Hall, 2002; Tandon, 2002). Power relationships affect both those who participate and those whose knowledge counts (Gaventa, 2006), as well as how knowledge is socialized and used.

The current polycentric production of knowledge must consider the universities, the new centres of expertise, as well as all the agents that can and want to be involved in hybrid, horizontal and cooperative spaces of reflection and action, with the purpose of co-creating the needed knowledge in each situation. This reflective modernization is also a promotion of equity in the spread, use and creation of knowledge. This view of knowledge moves from knowledge that is privately produced and for private consumption, to a commitment to the socialization of knowledge for the common public good. The current emphasis in knowledge production and consumption is based on the assumption that knowledge is a commodity; in contrast, the knowledge commons view informs the significance of social control over the production and utilization of knowledge. In such a shift, commitment to knowledge as a contribution to the common public good may transform meanings and practices in public spheres.

DYNAMIC AND CREATIVE KNOWLEDGE

Today, information and communication technologies, the so-called social web, enable us to access and share information and knowledge, and to interact and collaborate with others easily and instantly through communities with the same interests, while at the same time contributing to enhanced sociability. This scenario presents a total revolution for knowledge: the chaotic interaction allows different ideas and types of knowledge to be brought into contact, which results in multiple combinations or mutations that favour creativity and innovation. The processes of knowledge creation, knowledge management and validity are short in time, and their evolution is unpredictable.

BEING KNOWLEDGIASTIC

The leitmotiv of the 6th International Barcelona Conference on Higher Education organized by GUNi was 'Be Knowledgiastic' (Figure II.2.2.3).[1] We suggested this new term to designate an attitude of being: 'Being knowledgiastic is to show enthusiasm about and actively encourage the co-creation of transformative knowledge'. 'Being knowledgiastic' implies actively incorporating six changes into the way we handle, use, build and understand knowledge. There must be:

- a movement from a mono-culture of scientific knowledge to an ecology of knowledge;
- a passage from rational knowledge to comprehensive knowledge;
- a move from descriptive knowledge to knowledge for intervention;
- a change from partial knowledge to holistic and complex knowledge;
- abandonment of the isolated creation of knowledge in order to start building a social co-creation of knowledge;
- a change from conceiving a static use of knowledge to a dynamic and creative knowledge.

FIGURE II.2.2.3 'Be Knowledgiastic'

Universities are already beginning to make some of these shifts. A practice of knowledge democracy linked to an intelligent society would be supported by dramatic increases in the varieties of community–university engagement that are arising now in thousands of creative and imaginative ways in universities in literally every part of the world. This would build on a vision for a new architecture of knowledge and an activist sense of social responsibility in higher education.

NOTE

1   The term 'knowledgiastic' was first presented during the plenary session 'Building the World We Imagine' at the 6th International Barcelona Conference on Higher Education, where the chair of the session engaged the audience with an unexpected activity: about 30 boxes were passed to the attendees for expressing their wishes and commitments for the world they imagined, by drawing and writing in the boxes. As a result of the activity, a wall was created and became the leitmotiv of the conference: 'Be Knowledgiastic'.

REFERENCES

Benejam, P. (2005) *Una reflexió sobre educació i algunes experiències*. In: Benejam, P., Castellanos, J., Fontana, J., Jou, D. Torrents, R. and Tuson, J., *Mirades al Segle XXI*. Barcelona: Eumo Editorial, pp. 81–126.

Bunge, M. (1998) *La ciencia: su método y su filosofía*. Buenos Aires: Editorial Sudamericana.

Chambers, R. (1997) W*hose Reality Counts? Putting the First Last*. London: Intermediate Technology.

Clark, W.C., Crutzen, P. J. and Schellnhuber, H.J. (2005) *Science for Global Sustainability: Toward a New Paradigm*. CID Working Paper No. 120, Center for International Development. Cambridge, MA: Harvard University.

de Sousa Santos, B. (2007) 'Beyond abyssal thinking: from global lines to ecologies of knowledges'. *Review*, XXX(1), 45–89.

de Sousa Santos, B. (2009) 'A non-occidentalist West? Learned ignorance and ecology of knowledge'. *Theory, Culture and Society*, 26(7–8), 103–25.

de Sousa Santos, B., Nunes, J.A. and Meneses, M.P. (2007) 'Opening up the canon of knowledge and recognition of difference'. In: de Sousa Santos, B. S. (ed.) *Another Knowledge is Possible*. London: Verso, pp. xix–lxii.

Fien, J. (1992) *Geografia, sociedad i vida quotidiana*. Documents d'Anàlisi Geogràfica 21. Barcelona: Universitat Autònoma de Barcelona, Departament de Geografia, pp. 73–90.

Gaventa, J. and Cornwall, A. (2006) 'Challenging the boundaries of the possible: participation, knowledge and power'. *IDS Bulletin*, 37(6), 122–8.

Granados, J. (2010) *L'Educació per la Sostenibilitat a l'Ensenyament de la Geografia. Un estudi de cas*. PhD thesis, Universitat Autònoma de Barcelona. Retrieved September 2013 from https://www.educacion.gob.es/teseo/imprimirFicheroTesis.do?fichero=18803.

Granados, J. (2013) 'Enlarging the Conception of Knowledge'. Presented to the 6th International Barcelona Conference on Higher Education, May 14, 2013. Retrieved September 2013 from http://prezi.com/_

kmstilqyiuk/enlarging-the-conception-of-knowledge-be-knowledgiastic/.

Hall, B. (2002) 'Breaking the monopoly of action knowledge: research methods, participation and development'. In: Tandon, R. (ed.) *Participatory Research: Revising the Roots*. New Delhi: Mosaic Books, pp. 9–21.

Innerarity, D. (2011) *La Democracia del Conocimiento. Por una sociedad inteligente*. Madrid: Paidós.

Leff, E. (2004), *Racionalidad Ambiental. La reapropiación social de la naturaleza*. Mexico: Siglo XXI editores.

Novo, M. (2006) *El desarrollo sostenible. Su dimensión ambiental y educativa*. Madrid: Pearson Educación.

Simmons, I. (1993) *Interpreting Nature. Cultural Constructions of the Environment*. London: Routledge.

Sterling, S. (2001) *Sustainable Education: Revisioning Learning and Change*. Schumacher Briefings 6. London: Green Books Publishers.

Tandon, R. (2002) 'A critique of monopolistic research'. In: Tandon, R. (ed.) *Participatory Research: Revising the Roots*. New Delhi: Mosaic Books, pp. 3–8.

II.2.3 ENLARGING THE CONCEPTION OF KNOWLEDGE: THE DIALOGUE BETWEEN ANCIENT KNOWLEDGE AND SCIENCES

Manuel Ramiro Muñoz and Paul Wangoola

The following text is the dialogue that Paul Wangoola and Ramiro Muñoz had at the 6th International Barcelona Conference on Higher Education, Let's Build Transformative Knowledge to Drive Social Change (Barcelona, May 2013). The two speakers contributed to enlarging the conception of knowledge from the dialogue between ancient indigenous knowledge and scientific knowledge. Both of them are part of these two worlds. Paul Wangoola, who comes from Uganda, from the African ancestral tradition, is the founder and president of the Mpampo African Multiversity. He plays diverse advising roles related to heritage, history and reconciliation in Uganda. Manuel Ramiro Muñoz comes from Colombia and is the Director of the Intercultural Studies Center at the Pontificia Universidad Javeriana of Cali, Colombia.

WHICH ARE THE PRINCIPAL CHARACTERISTICS OF ANCIENT HOLISTIC KNOWLEDGE?

Paul: One main characteristic of African ancient and indigenous knowledge is that knowledge has a common source. That common source was there before God, before time and before matter. It is sometimes called the creative force or the vital force – a force that is responsible for the creation of all beings and all living things. And living things and every creation share the characteristics of this vital force, which is coherent and multiple in its being, but also coherent and a complementary unity of opposites. That is a very

enduring characteristic of ancient knowledge: having a common source, complementarity, unity and both internal and external coherence.

Now, everything that was created is also internally and externally interconnected, coherent and at peace. This knowledge and great awareness are distributed in creations and living things – in the rocks, in the plant world, in the animal world and in human beings. So if you want knowledge, you need to be surrounded by all these things, because that is where knowledge is, and you learn from them. In our case, to ensure that we do not lose any knowledge, we deeply believe that everything that is living is our brother. The rock is our senior brother and sister; the plant world is also our senior brother and sister, and the animals are our senior brothers and sisters. To demonstrate that, each one of us has a totem to emphasize our unity with the rest of beings and nature.

Manuel: The characteristics of ancient African indigenous knowledge, described by Paul, are not very different from those of ancient indigenous knowledge in Central and South America. I would add that the criteria of truth and validity are totally different from those we have in the scientific world. I would like to express this through an aphorism from the Nasa people which says that 'The word without the action is empty; the action without the word is blind; the word and the action outside the spirit of the community is death.' To avoid being empty, any word has to be supported by action, in a relation that, in our jargon, would be that between theory and practice. To avoid turning into activism, the action needs the word. And here is a high value given to knowledge built through the word, either oral or written.

But the ultimate criterion of truth and validity for the word and the action, as the aphorism ends saying, is in the community praxis. What makes a word, an action or both valid and relevant is the extent to which it builds community. And, as Paul said, the community does not only belong to human beings. All peoples, for example the Inkal Awás, who live in the south of Colombia, or the Nasas, located nearer the middle of the country, do not refer only to the human being when they name themselves. Nasa, for instance, is the rock, the river. In other words, that same concept is for all, as Paul said, communing with things, nature and so on, and surely at the same hierarchical level. Not the way we consider the human being as the fundamental part of the pyramid – theirs is really a community vision. So there, in the community, is where the criterion of truth and validity lies.

The method, using our jargon, is of course not linear. I would not say it is circular either, because the circle is closed, and any closed circle inclines towards dogmatism. So it is more spirally shaped, moving outwards and upwards in constant growth. Sometimes the same topics are repeated, the same things are discussed, but at a deeper level or with greater understanding.

As Paul says, the knowledge of these peoples is normally about life, to be used in real life, to defend life. I think life is the fundamental value, even above justice itself, above liberty and other values. If a hierarchy of values could be created, life would be the top value that connects and integrates everything.

I would finally like to emphasize the linear, circular and spiral matter. I think there is an interesting point here, because the spiral needs time and rest, what is circular probably works faster, and what is linear works using a different and much faster time.

WHAT IS KNOWLEDGE? WHO DETERMINES WHAT KNOWLEDGE IS? WHY SHOULD WE ENLARGE THE CONCEPTION OF KNOWLEDGE THAT WE HAVE IN THE DEVELOPED WESTERN WORLD?

Paul: When we speak about ancient knowledge, it is not that this knowledge has expired and been tucked away in some museum. For us, this is living knowledge. And it is living knowledge at the source of the Nile, the cradle of humanity, where I have been since the beginning of time. So when I talk about these matters, I speak with that kind of historical perspective.

Knowledge is the understanding of the interconnectedness of all beings – the understanding that the purpose of life is abundant life. And the way to abundant life is to live in great harmony with all living things. Knowledge is also the understanding that the being of one depends on the being of everything else (what has been summed up as the *Ubuntu* philosophy). I am an extension of you, and you are an extension of me. My well-being is consummated in your well-being.

So my doing good to you, my neighbour, is not an act of charity but an act of self-interest because you are my own interest. So knowledge is anything that enables you to understand the interconnectedness of life, and to live in such a way that your living does not diminish any other being.

You have to realize that you need tools to know, to keep knowing and to keep renewing your knowledge. For that reason, God or the creative force directly gave each one of us the assets, the divine assets, to enable us to keep knowing. And that is land. We know that everybody else was given land because we were given, as black African people, only the continent of Africa. Although God only created black people, at the time he created us, he gave us only Africa. The rest of the world was set aside for the rest of you. Additionally, we got the divine assets of language and culture directly from God. And God said that each one of us would be able to excel in knowledge through our respective languages and culture.

Manuel: To define what knowledge is, I would like to start from the academic world and try to get to this dialogue that we have held for a long time with wise people from different indigenous communities. As Manfred Max Neef, Alternative Nobel Prize-winner, says, we are definitely in a world where we know more than we understand. And I think the knowledge that ancient peoples possess is a kind of knowledge that allows understanding.

Let's make the difference between knowing and understanding. Knowing involves at least three movements. The first one is to move away from that object to be known; that is the key. Scientists establish a distant relationship of subject and object, but then penetrate reality through their analytical capacity. That capacity allows them to build differential awareness about that whole they are going to know, any matter. When doing that exercise, they fragment reality in order to penetrate it and thus know it. Finally, there is a third step: to name that process. Theories tell how one has been able to do, and then describe. It is likely to be a more descriptive knowledge, and that is very valuable, even in this dialogue with ancient peoples – knowledge as a valuable factor. Why? Because knowledge allows the multiple activities and actions that humanity needs today; it is not about fighting with scientific knowledge and with rational knowledge. Instead, we need to know and penetrate reality, if possible, in a more specialized way each time. That allows us numerous benefits, inventions and so on, which make our lives better.

But maybe we do not understand all what we know,

because understanding involves a different logic, one that even works the other way around. Instead of a distant subject–object relationship, ancient peoples establish a merging relationship with what they are going to know – there is no distance in between. You experience what you want to understand. And instead of doing an analytical exercise, a differential awareness of things, what you do is a synthetic exercise – you understand the whole. That is why it is holistic. And what follows is not the description of the process, the name of the process, the theory. What comes afterwards is the action or silence, not the word, not the theory, the article, the book or the paper.

These are in my opinion two edges, two ways of approaching reality, the scientific knowledge and the ancient knowledge, among others – both valid and very important. What probably occurs is a mirror relationship between the scientific world and ancient knowledge. What is lacking in one is what is plentiful in the other, and vice versa. We probably know more than we understand, hence the topic of science without conscience, science without sense. But in communities, it is necessary not only to understand, but to know too, because – among other reasons – knowledge is power. We coexist in relationships of power. Otherwise we would be naive to believe that harmony itself is possible, ignoring the fact that we live in a society and a world where there are asymmetrical relationships, and those asymmetrical relationships are of power.

In addition, knowledge is part of the most important powers today, in the 21st century. Today, knowledge is the factor that produces the highest value added in the world economy, as we all know. And that knowledge is necessary. Perhaps that knowledge, that science, needs conscience. But it is not bad for that conscience, that particular way ancient peoples have of understanding the world, if we can build with them and at the same time they can take ownership of the Western scientific tradition of knowledge. In that sense, I would even vindicate scientific knowledge – of course, that science with conscience, that science that not only knows but also understands, and therefore gets engaged.

I would end by referring to what one of the wise Indians from my country says about the worst invisibility and denial they have suffered. We do not see them – they are invisible to society, to scholars, to politicians. But we also deny them. He says that there is legal and political invisibility and denial. (The ancient peoples from my country, from South and Central America, have just been recognized in constitutions in the last 20 years.) There is also an economic and social invisibility and denial, as well as a cultural and educational one.

But all these denials are based on an epistemological denial. He says the following: centuries ago, in the first globalization, it was the European scholars who said, with theological, legal and philosophical reasons, that black people did not have souls. Therefore there were not human beings, therefore they had no rights, and therefore they were objects. And that was the justification for slavery. Millions of human beings were taken from their native Africa as objects and enslaved in our continent. But the basis for it came from knowledge, from the philosophers, theologians and jurists of that time, who said, 'They have no souls.' Now, about indigenous peoples they said, 'They have incipient souls.' That is, small souls. That invisibility and that epistemological denial are the origin of all asymmetries and problems. And this wise man says that it is the same today. Now academia says, 'They do not have kinds of knowledge, but beliefs; they do not have a religion, but superstitions; they do not have a culture, but folklore; they do not have languages, but dialects.' So it is the same. They did not have souls before; now they do not possess knowledge. And since they do not possess knowledge, they are 'under age'. They need to be guided; they need to be directed. That same invisibility and epistemological denial are still present today.

Paul: I would like to add that the appearance that we understand more than we know comes a result of having been occupied, our assets having been taken away and our centres of learning and higher learning closed. Just imagine if the Chinese were to come and take over Europe, and they closed all your universities, all your churches and everything for 200 years. You would be in a situation similar to where we are. And, just as you said, you cannot correct the situation within the framework in which it was caused. I think the Western university today has the responsibility to go and look out for the African indigenous mother tongue scholar spaces, to link up with them and give them space. If you want cooperation, co-dialogue, dialogue means two. The two must be viable and comparable. So we truly require a resource basis and resource support to be able to engage with you and have multiple centres of knowledge creation.

WHAT COULD BE THE RECOMMENDATIONS FOR MOVING FORWARD AND CREATING A REAL PRODUCTIVE DIALOGUE BETWEEN THESE TWO KINDS OF KNOWLEDGE?

Paul: It is interesting to come here in 2013 and find a

debate saying that we are on the wrong track or that we have missed something in respect of knowledge; that we are in deficit and need some transformation to be able to catch up in terms of knowledge creation. This same debate broke out at the source of the Nile about 50 years ago when, according to professors there, the Western paradigm and the Western sustainable domination of the world actually collapsed in 1966. Since then, we have been walking on a knowledge base to carry us into the new epoch. So in 2016 we shall be celebrating 50 years of the new epoch, which we call *Mulembe Mutinzi.*

In Uganda, we are first of all lucky to have a tradition of indigenous scholarship with generations of mother-tongue scholars. They have been at the source of the Nile for thousands of years and have been the keepers of knowledge. Besides, these are people who have lived conquered, by Arabs and Europeans, but have remained steadfast. Right now, we are reorganizing them around the Mpambo African Multiversity to generate a knowledge-based philosophy of life in consonance with the new epoch.

We have many weaknesses and many strengths. We can learn a lot with and from you. So I think this is the space for engaging in some dialogue to see how such space can be supported, to identify a variety of such spaces, to see how they can come together, to exchange learning with one another and strengthen each other. In the long run, we should be better off if these centres of knowledge are engaged in the deep questions of finding a solution to today's knowledge crisis. I think the greatest knowledge crisis we face is that the resources of the world are in institutions that are part of the problem and cannot be part of the solution. We need to find a way of identifying margins in these institutions and seeing how they can link up with other spaces. We need to see how the transformative forces and energies in the Western university can also reorganize themselves to move things forwards. But as it is, the university was formulated as an instrument to suffice the needs of the global system, and it has turned out to be a global system of mass oppression. So we also need to look into that, and to see how you can really extricate yourselves here and globally link up with transformative forces.

Manuel: I understand these as two different edges, as two different types of logic, so I make recommendations for each one. First, I think that, in the university world, we can become more prepared to engage in dialogue with other cultures and with other kinds of knowledge if we make at least two steps.

The first one is to be true universities. Let's remember the concept of university. It is that of *universitas, unus verto* in Latin, which means one, let's say, within diversity. Diversity is the real reason for the university; not only monocultural knowledge, but knowledge, the possibility of being a meeting place, of having a knowledge dialogue.

The second step is to become true scientists. When humanities, physics, chemistry and social sciences repeat or keep hold of positivist epistemologies of the 19th century that cannot make others see reality today, it is not possible to enter into that dialogue and that knowledge.

Now, as in the view of ancient peoples, it is necessary to make room for dialogue, avoiding ethnocentrism. The possibility of having dialogue with others, of being enriched with others, is very positive. So is the recovery of their knowledge, their traditions, which could recognize the word of the communities to a higher degree.

Paul: When my sister was here, she started by saying that we are all Africans. And the truth is that we are all Africans because we come from the source of the Nile. I can assure you that people there know that everybody in the world comes from there. They have stone monuments in recognition of the other colors of the peoples of the world. They also say that we are facing the crisis today because, since you left the source of the Nile, you have forgotten the good manners you were taught, the rules, regulations, everything you learned – with good reason because it has been a long time and it is a long distance from there. So it is now time for all of us to go back to where we started, so that we get new instructions and a new message. Then we will be able to go back where we came from.

II.3.1 KNOWLEDGE DEMOCRACY, COGNITIVE JUSTICE AND THE ROLE OF UNIVERSITIES*

John Gaventa and Felix Bivens

* This paper is drawn in part from a longer paper, 'Co-constructing democratic knowledge for social justice: lessons from an international research collaboration', presented at the conference on Social Justice and the University, University of Tennessee, April 28–30, 2011 and forthcoming in a volume on the same theme.

Much has been written in recent years on the process of deepening democracy – that is, on building democratic societies that go beyond an institutional form to include more inclusive, expansive and deliberative forms of participation and power on the part of all citizens. Similarly, much has been written on the knowledge society and its potential to support development and participation. In 1997, in a speech at a World Bank Conference on global knowledge, Kofi Annan said, 'if information and knowledge are central to democracy, they are the conditions for development. It is that simple' (Annan, 1997). A 2005 UNESCO report further observed, 'Knowledge societies are about capabilities to identify, produce, process, transform, disseminate and use information to build and apply knowledge for human development. They require an empowering social vision that encompasses inclusion, solidarity and participation' (UNESCO, 2005, p. 27).

For many theorists and policy-makers, knowledge is considered to be a critical, driving force for the democratization process. The projects of deepening democracy and of harnessing the potential of a knowledge society are assumed to go together.

And yet such a linear relationship between democracy and knowledge cannot be assumed. The promises of both the democratic and the knowledge society are mediated by power relationships that affect both who participates and whose knowledge

counts. Those who write about democracy often see knowledge as a way to inform and educate the citizenry, who remain passive consumers of knowledge, not active participants in its very production. And those who write about knowledge often assume that knowledge will serve the needs of the people, but do not necessarily consider whether or how the people participate democratically in its creation.

This brief paper puts forth another view – any vision of democracy that includes the meaningful participation of people in decisions that affect their lives must also consider their participation in the production of knowledge itself. Without a consideration of how, why and for whom it is produced, knowledge is not necessarily a force for democracy. From this, it follows that universities as knowledge institutions may or may not be part of the democratization and development process. Much depends on how they see their research and knowledge mission. As a colleague and I wrote some years ago, 'Researching for democracy also implies democratizing research, a shift that poses a fundamental challenge to many university-based researchers' (Ansley and Gaventa, 1997, p. 46).

THE IDEA OF COGNITIVE JUSTICE

While mainstream debates on the 'knowledge society' and the 'democratic society' have often assumed that one leads to the other, the relationships between knowledge, power and participation have long been critically interrogated by another set of scholars, especially from the global south. Paulo Freire's seminal work *The Pedagogy of the Oppressed*, published nearly 50 years ago, launched an important debate on how the objects of knowledge and research by others became subjects in their own knowledge creation (Freire, 1971). Throughout the 1970s and 80s, thinkers such as Orlando Fals Borda (1984), Rajesh Tandon, Budd Hall and Robert Chambers also began to challenge dominant views about knowledge, and to argue for the importance of people's own knowledge in both the research and the development process. Each of these scholars has also challenged us to become more critical about our roles as academics and about the power of knowledge itself. Who creates knowledge? And for whom is it created? Whose knowledge counts?

In 1982, Anisur Rahman, a Bangladesh economist and researcher, called our attention to this relationship between knowledge inequalities and other forms of injustice:

> The dominant view of social transformation has been preoccupied with the need to change existing oppressive structures of relations in material production. But … by now in most polarized countries, the gap between those who have social power over the process of knowledge generation – and those who have not – has reached dimensions no less formidable than the gap in access to means of physical production … For improving the possibilities of liberation, therefore, these two gaps should be attacked, wherever feasible, simultaneously. (quoted in Gaventa, 1993)

Other southern intellectuals have begun to articulate this as the struggle for 'cognitive justice', that is, as overcoming the domination of certain forms and types of knowledge over others. As Boaventura de Santos Sousa writes, 'Social injustice is based on cognitive injustice' (2006, p. 19).

Visvanathan, an Indian scientist and activist, further articulates five principles of cognitive justice (quoted in Van der Velden, 2004):

- All forms of knowledge are valid and should coexist in a dialogic relationship to each other.
- Cognitive justice implies strengthening the 'voice' of the defeated and marginalized.
- Traditional knowledge and technologies should not be 'museumized.'
- Every citizen is a scientist. Each layperson is an expert.
- Science should help the common man and woman.
- All competing sciences should be brought together into a positive heuristic for dialogue.

Such an approach also assumes, as does democracy, certain values of tolerance and respect for diverse forms of knowledge and ways of knowing. As de Sousa Santos (2006) has argued, modernity must remember and recognize that an 'ecology of knowledges' exists and is necessary for understanding the world in its full complexity; such an ecology is necessary to augment the 'monoculture of scientific knowledge,' which has often been understood as universal, thus invalidating alternative forms of knowing. He writes:

> The ecology of knowledge aims to create a new sort of relationship between scientific knowledge and other kinds of knowledge. It consists in granting 'equality of opportunities' to the different kinds of knowledge … maximizing their respective contributions to building 'another possible world,' that is to say a more democratic and just society. (2006, p. 21)

THE ROLE OF UNIVERSITIES

If we can accept the argument for cognitive justice as being central to social justice, and of the democratization of knowledge as central to a democratic society, we must also ask 'What is the role of the universities as centres of knowledge production?' How can universities create knowledge that contributes to human development and more robust democracy, in ways that are inclusive and participatory?

From the ancient Indus valley to 19th-century America, universities have often been strong supporters of social justice, using knowledge as a force for social change. South Asian scholar Rajesh Tandon has written about the 8th century BC university Taxila (located in what is now Pakistan), which had as its motto 'service to humanity' (Tandon, 2008). Likewise, America's rapid transition from an agricultural to a modern economy was largely under-girded by the massification of higher education, enabled for instance by land grant universities. In the UK in the early 20th century, institutions such as the London School of Economics were founded on the proposition that universities could aggressively support the development of knowledge and government policies that could combat urban poverty. Even in recent popular uprisings across the Middle East, we see young, university-educated people leading the way, using their knowledge and ideas to bring justice and change to their homelands.

However, in many parts of the world, this capacity of universities to support change and to question power in the name of justice is increasingly being challenged because of changes in the political economy upon which the universities depend. For decades, governments have been reducing public spending on higher education, and this trend seems to be accelerating in this new age of fiscal austerity. As universities lose state funding, they are expected to become more market-oriented, branding and selling their knowledge or contracting with private sector companies to support them in research and innovation for their products. Moreover, the emergence in recent decades of the 'knowledge economy' has raised the commercial value of certain forms of knowledge – but not all – and as a result some forms of knowledge, and some disciplines, are becoming marginalized because they are not income-earners for their institutions. In this for-profit environment, there is often a loss of the space for teaching critical thinking, for building citizenship and for harnessing the ecology of knowledges to address development and democracy issues.

On the other hand, although the context in which universities operate is challenging, if one looks deeper it is also possible to locate spaces and opportunities for democratic engagement in social change that exist alongside, and actually because of, these same structural challenges. Despite the current state of higher education, Hall and Dragne argue that 'universities remain the single largest underutilized source for community development and social change available' (Hall and Dragne, 2008, p. 271). Likewise, de Sousa Santos (2008) maintains that universities remain a 'counter-hegemonic force', particularly if they can play a role beyond the market. Although marketization has driven universities into greater collaboration with the private sector, this concept of the '3rd stream' – of working with actors outside the university – need not be exclusively limited to businesses. Around the world, university leaders have pushed to broaden this concept to include partnerships with non-profit and civil society organizations. Global networks have begun to form that actively promote universities as agents of democratic change.

In this context, arguments about cognitive justice and the need to challenge knowledge inequalities have now become much more accepted than they were 20 years ago. Programmes of participatory research, community–university partnerships and community-based knowledge movements exist around the world. Yet many of these are at the local level. The challenges of knowledge inequality become even greater when we look globally. As we face increasingly complex global problems, knowledge from one location or one point of view is no longer sufficient to deal with problems that manifest themselves in thousands of ways across diverse global contexts. Knowledge must be multi-sited and pluralistic in its underlying assumptions and worldviews.

A CASE IN POINT: THE CITIZENSHIP DRC

One example of this new form of large-scale participa-tory knowledge production can be found in the decade-long work of the Development Research Centre on Citizenship, Participation and Accountability (DRC), a network involving academics, activists and practition-ers from universities and think-tanks in seven core countries,[1] with dozens of others also involved from an additional 15 countries in the global south. The DRC took shape in 2001, emerging out of questions of how respond to the growing failures of democracy to meet the challenges of inequality and social justice in countries of the north and south alike. It was also concerned about the lack of democratic structures and accountability at the international level, particularly regarding processes of globalization.

Perhaps more importantly, its researchers sought to question the very concepts of democracy and citizen-ship. Were the traditional views of democracy and citizenship sufficient to deal with the challenges of participation and representation in a globalized world? Was part of this perceived deficit a result of other forms and practices of citizenship, which existed outside the Western model, simply not being recognized? (For more on this theme, see Gaventa, 2006.)

In order to better understand and respond to these challenges, the DRC aimed to produce new insights on various conceptions and practices of citizenship and democracy in divergent national and political contexts from around the world. Over a ten-year period, the Citizenship DRC compiled over a hundred case stud-ies that have revealed a vast ecology of democratic practices and ways through which citizens mobilize to claim their rights. (For further information see www. drc-citizenship.org and Citizenship DRC, 2011).

From the beginning, the Citizenship DRC had a broad mission of producing research and using that research to bring about change. Its partners were diverse, cutting across many disciplines. Some came from within universities; others were practitioners within non-governmental organizations. Some already had long histories of using committed research approaches, such as participatory action research, in the pursuit of social justice. Others came from more conventional research backgrounds.

But it was also clear from the beginning that, to pursue its mission of producing research and capacities for using knowledge to address issues of democratic justice – inclusive citizenship, rights, accountability and participation – the network would also have to deal with issues of how such knowledge was produced, and whose voices and agendas were to be important within the network. The programme was to be up to ten years long, with substantial sums of money involved. Funded by the Department of International Development, this programme is an example of a much larger field of development research, much of it funded from the north, but with the stated goals of promoting development processes for overcoming poverty in the global south. Yet, historically, such research had been carried out with little active engagement of those from the global south: research questions, methods and issues were set from the north; southern researchers were often treated as subcontractors to gather data, but with little voice in how it was analysed or used. In such a system of research, often linked to an extractive set of relationships that are deeply colonial in their nature and roots, there is little scope for 'cognitive justice'.

The Citizenship DRC set out to be different. It sought to develop a way of working in which all partners could help to construct the research agenda and work with one another – as well as with the communities they were researching – to gather, analyse and use knowledge to engage with the issues of rights and democracy that it sought to explore.

In its first few years, the Citizenship DRC sought to shift the received top-down, northern-driven way of producing knowledge to a more collaborative and participatory way of working. In particular, in the early years, it focused internally on the process of building shared values and purposes, developing relationships and trust, and creating a more decentralized and participatory architecture, which could distribute formal and informal power across the network (Brown and Gaventa, 2008, 2010).

Over the course of working together for ten years, the members of the Citizenship DRC produced a great deal of research on citizenship, democracy and citizen action. However, along the way, we also learned a great deal about how research could be conducted differently, which gave us insights into how to create inclusive knowledge networks, across universities and activists, based on principles of cognitive justice and linked in turn to larger issues of social and democratic justice. These lessons have focused on (1) the value of a collaborative, co-construction of knowledge; (2) the importance of iterative ways of knowing that link different forms of knowledge over time, and which ground the universal in the contextual; (3) the multiple ways of linking knowledge to action, at all levels; and (4) the value of linking research on democracy and citizenship to the pedagogies of democracy and citizenship in the classroom.

In this way, the theme of the work became its methodology as well. We found that our work was deeply enriched by the participatory inclusion of voices and methods from all of our partners. Producing democratic knowledge required a democratic process, not only the inclusion of all voices in decision-making, but also an inclusion of their different epistemic perspectives, which were grounded in specific contexts and experiences. By operating within a framework of knowledge democracy within the DRC itself, we found that not only were our research outputs transformed, but our relationships to each other were likewise deepened and improved, with residual effects that stretched into our home institutions, affecting the attitudes, pedagogies and positionalities of many of the collaborators.

The themes reflected in the DRC's work have important implications for universities as they seek to contribute to social justice in the wider world. As universities become more marketized and market-driven, it is increasingly common to think of knowledge purely as a product or commodity. The DRC's work makes a strong counterclaim to this by demonstrating that knowledge is also a process, and that the process of how knowledge is constructed is fundamental to the counterhegemonic value of that knowledge. Knowledge production that is driven by motivations of efficiency or market value is unlikely to be transformative or contribute to social justice. Space and time have to be left for iteration, relationships and imagination. As our exploration of cognitive justice has emphasized, knowledge itself has been and should remain a fundamental tool in constructing a more just world. However, universities must go beyond their old ways of constructing knowledge as they strive to address the complex, global problems of our age. These challenges require knowledge that is adaptable and epistemologically pluralistic, knowledge that draws on the experiences and diversity of the world in all its fullness.

Looking more broadly at the global context of the higher education sector, several specific implications for universities can be drawn from the lessons of the Citizenship DRC case:

- *Universities must engage.* Universities can be a monoculture of knowledge. Despite differences in disciplines and training, academics share a similar worldview. In order to challenge that homogeny, university researchers must step outside the university and look for partners to learn with rather than subjects to learn about.
- *Global challenges demand diverse local insights.* Global questions are too vast and complex to be solved from any one perspective or location. Knowledge must be multi-sited, fluid and capable of surfacing the dialectic between global patterns

and local realities. While not all universities will be as international in their membership as the DRC, decades of internationalization have made the vast majority of universities sites of significant diversity. As such, most universities have global networks latent in their faculty and student bodies that can be activated and utilized more intentionally.

- *Communities are reservoirs of knowledge.* Rather than a core–periphery binary in which universities are the owners and producers of knowledge and communities are empty vessels to be filled, cognitive justice emphasizes the *a priori* existence of knowledge in non-academic groups and communities. However, these alternative forms knowledge have been so long suppressed and marginalized that they may be difficult to bring to the surface. University researchers have methods for and experience in elucidating such hidden knowledge. Rather than extracting that knowledge as 'data', universities can help communities to recognize, own and mobilize their own untapped knowledge reserves as a means of catalysing social change from within communities.

The case of the Citizenship DRC suggests those concerned about the social responsibilities of universities need to think about not only how they contribute to social justice, but also how they shape cognitive justice and knowledge democracy. Without cognitive justice – which focuses on whose knowledge counts – the larger struggles for social responsibility will not be realized. And struggles for cognitive justice also include the need to learn and link globally with others in collaborative and participatory ways.

NOTE

1   Core partners included ADRA (Angola), BRAC University (Bangladesh), CEBRAP (Brazil), PRIA (India), the Universidad Nacional Autónoma and Universidad Autónoma Metropolitana (Mexico), Ahmadu Bello University (Nigeria), University of the Western Cape (South Africa) and Institute of Development Studies (UK).

REFERENCES

Annan, K.. (1997) 'Address to Global Knowledge '97' World Bank Conference', Toronto, Canada.

Ansley, F. and Gaventa, J. (1997) 'Researching for democracy and democratizing research'. *Change: The Magazine of Higher Learning*, 29(1).

Brown, L.D. and Gaventa, J. (2008) *Constructing Transnational Action Research Networks: Observations and Reflections from the Case of the Citizenship DRC.* IDS Working Paper. Brighton: IDS.

Brown, L.D. and Gaventa, J. (2010) 'Constructing transnational action research networks: observations and reflections from the case of the Citizenship DRC'. *Journal of Action Research*, 8(1), 5–28.

Citizenship DRC (2011) 'Blurring the Boundaries: Citizen Action Across States and Societies'. Retrieved April 14, 2011 from http://www.drc-citizenship.org/system/assets/1052734700/original/1052734700-cdrc.2011-blurring.pdf.

de Sousa Santos, B. (2006) *The Rise of the Global Left: The World Social Forum and Beyond.* London: Zed Books.

de Sousa Santos, B. (2008) 'Democratic reform and emancipation in higher education: a focus on institutional policies'. In: GUNi, *Higher Education in the World 3.* Basingstoke: Palgrave Macmillan.

Fals Borda, O. (1984) 'The challenge of action research'. In: *Development: Seeds of Change 2.* Rome: Society for International Development.

Freire, P. (1971) *Pedagogy of the Oppressed.* New York: Continuum.

Gaventa, J. (1993) 'The powerful, the powerless and the experts: knowledge struggles in a information age'. In: Park, P., Hall, B. and Jackson, T. (eds), *Participatory Research in North America.* Amherst, MA: Bergin & Hadley.

Gaventa, J. (2006) *Triumph, Deficit or Contestation? Deepening the Deepening Democracy Debate.* IDS Working Paper 243. Brighton: IDS.

Hall, B. and Dragne, C. (2008) 'The role of higher education for human and social development in the USA and Canada'. In: GUNi, *Higher Education in the World 3.* Basingstoke: Palgrave Macmillan.

Tandon, R. (2008) 'Civil engagement in higher education and its role in human and social development'. In: GUNi, *Higher Education in the World 3.* Basingstoke: Palgrave Macmillan.

UNESCO (2005) *Towards Knowledge Societies.* Paris: UNESCO.

Van der Velden, M. (2004) 'From communities of practice to communities of resistance: civil society and cognitive justice'. *Development*, 47(1), 73–80.

II.3.2 COMMUNITY AND CIVIL SOCIETY AS SOURCES OF KNOWLEDGE
Rajesh Tandon and PRIA Team

Gitga indigenous community has been living on the west coast of Canada for several thousand years. They have been leading a healthy life based on sea food, and marine plants. Their communities built canoes and navigated the rivers and oceans throughout the year. They have survived all these centuries with their competencies in navigating their natural habitats and in harvesting, processing and storing their foods. (Turner et al., 2008)

Women vendors in Mumbai (India) have organized their homes on the informal settlements. Keeping their living and working requirements in view, they have designed and built these small homes accordingly. The local authorities do not provide any services to them as their informal settlement is not recognized by the municipality. The young boys and girls of the settlement conducted a detailed survey of their settlement and prepared a map which they have given to the municipality now. (www.sparcindia.org)

Local men's group in South Africa began to share their experiences of visiting local AIDS clinics. In the process, they learnt about the possibility that treatment was possible, and that HIV need not necessarily result in AIDS and death. Based on this understanding, a nationwide campaign was mounted in South Africa for effective treatment and care of affected population, and desirable preventive steps. It was led by the affected women and men themselves. (Robins, 2010)

The above stories are manifestations of different forms of knowledge embedded in the lives of communities. Gitga communities would not have been able to survive all these centuries if their community knowledge had not been *authentic* and *valid*. Women vendors would not have been recognized by local authorities if their knowledge of their housing requirements had not been serving their livelihoods. The South African government and international pharmaceutical companies would not have changed their policies and practices of the treatment and pricing of drugs if the *experiential knowledge* of the affected populations had not been synthesized into an actionable agenda.

Therefore, the community as a source of knowledge

is no longer imaginary. During the past couple of decades, there has been growing evidence suggesting that community and civil society are significant sites of knowledge. It is not only that new knowledge is being produced in such community settings, but that local civil society actors are actively engaged in systematizing, storing, disseminating and using such knowledge for the larger public good. Summarizing the discourse, Tandon (2002, p. vii) concludes:

Therefore, the first significant contribution of participatory research has been to challenge the *mythical and artificial divide between mental labour and manual labour*, intellectual pursuits. It has questioned the belief that capacity for intellectual work resides in only a few. It argued that popular knowledge, ability to produce and use knowledge, is a universal human phenomenon.

COMMUNITY KNOWLEDGE SYSTEMS

The knowledge system comprises elements related to its *creation*, *storage* and *dissemination*.

In the creation of knowledge, the first step is to *frame the research question* – what new knowledge needs to be generated? The framing of research question is rooted in the political economy of knowledge. Who is interested in finding answers to these research questions? Who considers these questions important and why are they important? Sometimes, practical considerations influence the choice of research questions. For example, who is willing to fund this research? What is the time frame for funding such research? What kinds of outputs do the funders want? What kinds of uses would the funders would like to put this research to?

When community is a source of knowledge, in some real ways, this step of framing research questions is embedded in the everyday life of the community itself. The practical realities of everyday life need to be navigated to ensure the survival and well-being of the community itself. As a result, the urge for knowledge creation emerges from the challenges of living life holistically. Research questions emerge from the everyday challenges of life in its myriad complexity.

In a community in America, research was driven by the existential problems facing it:

Families of the leukemia victims were the first to discern a geographical pattern in the proliferation of disease. Anne Anderson, whose son Jimmy had leukemia, began gathering information about other sick children based on chance meetings with victims' families and word of mouth. She theorized that the proliferation had something to do with the town water supply and asked the State officials to test the water. She was rebuffed. The affected families responded by initiating their own epidemiological research. Eventually they were able to establish the existence of a cluster of leukemia cases and then relate it to industrial carcinogens leaked into the water supply. (Sclove et al., 1997, p. 79)

The second most critical step in knowledge creation is the choice of *methodology*. What methods and tools of data collection and analysis could be deployed to find answers to the chosen research questions? This choice is generally made on the basis of *epistemological considerations*. If it is believed that knowledge is produced through cognitive processes, the methodology tends to exclude several other options. If the epistemology suggests that *feelings and actions are equally legitimate means of knowing* (in addition to cognition), observations, arts, music, dance, theatre, photography, emotions, stories, journeys, audiovisual items, and so on all become relevant elements of the research methodology. Knowledge from communities tends to use an *inclusive* research methodology as the community's epistemological repertoire is more inclusive and broad based. It combines all three modes of knowing – cognition, emotion and action.

The case of poor rural women discovering themselves in research has been depicted by Khot:

These women were dalits (scheduled castes) themselves and came from economically weaker sections, with little formal education. Once they believed in their ability to acquire more knowledge about their own situation, they were able to do so. It proved that only they know about their problem, its causes and possible solution. The whole process of using theatre for projecting, studying and analysing problems was initiated by dalits themselves, which was integrated by dalit women in their own interest. (Khot, 2002, p. 319)

The primary purpose of the *storage* of knowledge is to enable easy *access* to it when the need arises. In general, new knowledge generated through research is stored in written form as books and papers. Digital space is another method of storing the written form, although it has also made audiovisual storage a lot simpler in terms of access. Modern search engines have nowadays made access to information quite easy and inexpensive.

Much community knowledge is stored in a variety of forms. By its very nature, the community's knowledge is in its *mother tongue*, the language of life of the community. The community's oral traditions mean that the knowledge is stored in the souls of its people, especially those who are elderly. If access to such knowledge is to be gained, the elders of the community should be listened to . Community archives and records frequently take the form of *local artefacts* – community halls, religious places, spiritual locations, forests, rocks and other public spaces. The indigenous communities of western Canada store their knowledge in the 'big house':

In the past, and in some cases up to the present, learning about cultural traditions has been an ongoing process of observing, listening, practicing, and participating in all aspects of daily life through the seasons and the years, in the home and 'big house' (feast and ceremonial hall) and out on the land and waters. (Turner et al., 2008, p. 51)

The *dissemination* of knowledge is critical for its recognition and appraisal. When new knowledge is disseminated in the public domain, others can assess its relevance, authenticity and applicability. The primary audience for disseminating knowledge is determined by the funders of research in general. In addition to funders, dissemination to the research fraternity and professional peers takes place through journals, books and conferences. Dissemination to policy-makers is enabled through policy briefs or dialogues.

In the case of knowledge from the community, all the above forms of dissemination are also used. In addition, the dissemination of new knowledge is primarily within the community for its own immediate usage. Practical actions follow from such dissemination within the community. The community of practice actually refers to the peers of a community sharing their knowledge across communities. Describing the South African community process:

in *Living Learning*, they discuss one important space for this within *Abahlali* – the 'night camps'. These monthly meetings start in the evening and will typically run throughout the night. Anyone can participate in these, anyone can speak, anyone can question. (Harley, 2012, p. 10)

Sometimes the community employs other audiovisual and cultural tools for knowledge dissemination.

These tools are designed and deployed by the community itself. Many civil society actors also get engaged with communities in disseminating the knowledge they have. They support the process of translation, recording, storage and dissemination to other stakeholders and fraternities whom the communities themselves cannot reach so readily.

TYPOLOGY

The descriptions and illustrations presented above make it clear that community and civil society as sources of knowledge are universal, historical and contemporary. As sites of knowledge, they have been at times ignored, at times undermined and mostly labelled as being 'unscientific'. However, the various social movements of the recent past – women's, indigenous, peace, labour, ecological – have demonstrated the validity and authenticity of knowledge residing in, and generated from, communities and civil society. This realization makes it now possible to create synthesis and coherence with knowledge from the community and civil society.

Much of this knowledge from the community and civil society can be classified under three different headings. A brief description of these three types is provided below.

INTERGENERATIONAL ACCUMULATION

This type of knowledge from the community is directly related to the daily rituals and practices of the community over several generations. By virtue of living life, knowledge is created, stored and utilized; it is then passed on to the next generation largely through oral traditions. In the process, it is refined and reassessed for its utility in everyday life.

The most significant illustrations of the domains of such knowledge are ecological and health. Many of the practices related to water harvesting, forest regeneration, horticulture, land fertility, fisheries, animal husbandry, and so on have been found to be of immense value to contemporary society: 'They argue that traditional knowledge is a complex system of learning and understanding that is essential to community adaptation and resilience' (Lutz and Neis, 2008, p. 9)

Similarly, various types of knowledge about human health that evolved through practices relating to the prevention and cure of illnesses have now become a significant form of knowledge through intergenerational accumulation. Holistic health, acupressure, yoga, and so on are today examples of universally accepted health knowledge. Herbal medicine, naturopathy and the selection of healthy foods for different seasons and life stages are various examples of the intergenerational accumulation of knowledge in the domain of health.

ENDOGENOUS CONCEPTUALIZATION

Which concepts are relevant from the perspective of community and civil society? While describing subaltern studies, some scholars have suggested that the same phenomenon appears to be different when viewed from below, from the grassroots level of the community. Mother-tongue scholars view concepts entirely differently; in fact, the conceptualization of phenomena in the mother tongue appears rather different. Take the case of knowledge itself. Knowledge is viewed in a functional, empowering sense through the community's lens. Knowledge enables individuals and collectives to improve their life. In this sense, knowledge has practical use; it has a collective praxis; its access is universal for public use – open source, so to speak. Knowledge liberates; as the Sanskrit saying goes, '*Sa Vidya Ya vimuktaye*'. A group of African parents provided an alternative perspective from below to challenge the push for immunization programmes:

> Thus parental mobilization around MMR did not just dispute scientific claims that there was no link between MMR and autism, but exposed the biases in the science producing claims of MMR safety, arguing that this was linked to political interests in mass-vaccination and commercial interests in selling vaccines. (Leach and Scoones, 2007, p. 17)

Therefore, endogenous conceptualization is a valuable contribution of knowledge from the community and civil society.

GAINING VISIBILITY

A third type of knowledge from the community gives visibility to hitherto invisible phenomena. Several phenomena in society do not gain visibility until the experiences of the community are not listened to and the knowledge derived from those experiences is not articulated. Informal settlements in cities, domestic violence against women and the pollution of groundwater from agriculture are just a few examples of phenomena that came to light only when the community's knowledge was articulated. Describing one situation:

> In the case described above, aspects and nuances of sexual harassment in a field setting were uncovered

through such a collaboration. Women field workers in the role of researchers began to articulate dynamics of harassment that their male, urban counterparts could not perceive. (Tandon and Farrell, 2008, p. 289)

Gaining visibility for such phenomena at an early stage of their development makes it easier to understand them, deal with them and improve the lives of people and communities before the problems become intractable. Such visibility can then be utilized to undertake a more systematic investigation of these phenomena for improved understanding.

CHALLENGES

It is clear that knowledge from the community and civil society can be very valuable in enabling higher education institutions (HEIs) to contribute to social transformation. The transformative potential of knowledge can only be fully realized in pursuit of the 'world we want' if knowledge from the community and civil society is acknowledged, accessed, incorporated and synergized with knowledge from other sites and sources. Recognizing the value of community and civil society as sources of knowledge is the key first step to be taken by HEIs and other knowledge centres.

There are some other challenges that have to be addressed if an organic, ongoing and seamless synergy of this knowledge is to be achieved with knowledge from other sites such as HEIs. Three particular challenges need to be addressed in this regard.

WEAK SYSTEMATIZATION
By its very nature, knowledge from the community remains fragmented, sporadic and raw. The community does not have the capacity, motivation or resources to undertake such systematization, which may make this knowledge more accessible and usable by other knowledge producers. Some form of *intermediation* becomes essential for this systematization. Sometimes, a local civil society organization facilitates and undertakes this systematization; sometimes a local HEI supports this process with its students and faculty. But whatever the process of intermediation is, systematization needs to be undertaken if such knowledge from the community is to be made more visible and accessible.

FORMAL DISSEMINATION
Most formal channels of the dissemination of knowledge from the community are not easily accessible;

such knowledge does not find its place in journals or conferences. The language of dissemination becomes another constraint, and resources and capacities for translation into globally dominant languages (like English) are not easily available. Even when dominant-language documents are available, they do not get referenced as they are not part of the global accession code system (ISSNs). Digital spaces are making this somewhat more accessible, but there is still a huge challenge in this regard.

With the world becoming increasingly digital, these numbers are becoming critical for organizing the distribution and marketing of books and serial publications. If the majority believe that knowledge that is available in 'libraries' (both physical and increasingly online) is the only valid knowledge, written (or even audio and video) documents will not be accessioned into the library, and hence will not become available to or validated for a wider audience.

GENERALIZABILITY
By its very nature, knowledge from the community is locally embedded and contextual. Its local relevance is manifest, and its authenticity is defined by its local rootedness. Hence, questions are posed about the wider relevance of such knowledge. Knowledge from the community does not pass the standard tests of generalizability. In order to assess its wider relevance, further innovation in parameters of generalizability needs to be achieved. Greater effort in the synthesis of knowledge from community in multiple sites needs also to be made. 'Higher Education Institutions (HEIs) can acknowledge the multiplicity of knowledge traditions and create spaces and opportunities for practitioners (from government, community and civil society) to engage with scholars in HEIs in the *co-production of knowledge*' (Tandon, 2008, p. 150).

CONCLUSION

In conclusion, it is important that the community as a site of knowledge gains recognition and respect in the pursuit of social responsibility in higher education. The contributions of civil society to producing new knowledge and synthesizing community knowledge for wider access need to be acknowledged and supported. Resources and capacities to allow greater access to and dissemination of such knowledge from the community and civil society need to be made available so that their use in finding solutions to everyday challenges of humanity can be harnessed.

REFERENCES

Harley, A. (2010) '"We are poor, not stupid": learning from autonomous grassroots social movements in South Africa'. In: Hall, B.L., Clover, D.E., Crowther, J. and Scandrett, E. (eds) (2012) *Learning and Education for a Better World: The Role of Social Movements*. Rotterdam: Sense.

Khot, S. (2002) 'Popular theatre'. In: Tandon, R. (ed.), *Participatory Research: Revisiting the Roots*. New Delhi: Mosaic Books.

Leach, M. and Scoones I. (2007) *Mobilising Citizens: Social Movements and the Politics of Knowledge*. IDS Working Paper No. 276. Brighton: IDS.

Lutz, J.S. and Neis, B. (eds) (2008) *Making and Moving Knowledge: Interdisciplinary and Community-based Research in a World on the Edge*. Kingston: McGill-Queen's University Press.

Robins, S. (2010) 'Mobilising and mediating global medicine and health citizenship: the politics of AIDS knowledge production in rural South Africa'. In: Gaventa, J. and Tandon, R. (eds), *Globalising Citizens*. London: Zed Books, p. 56.

Sclove, R., Murphy, D. and Scammell, M. (eds) (1997) *Doing Community Based Research: A Reader*. Amherst, MA: Loka Institute.

SPARC (Society for the Promotion of Area Resource Centers). Retrieved November 25, 2013 from http://www.sparcindia.org.

Tandon, R. (ed.) (2002) *Participatory Research: Revisiting the Roots*. New Delhi: Mosaic Books.

Tandon, R. (2008) 'Civil engagement in higher education and its role in human and social development'. In: GUNi, *Higher Education in the World 3*. Basingstoke: Palgrave Macmillan, p. 150.

Tandon, R. and Farrell, M. (2008) 'Collaborative participatory research in gender mainstreaming in social change organisations'. In: Shani, A.B., Mohram, S.A., Pasmore, W.A., Stymne, B. and Adler, N. (eds), *Handbook of Collaborative Management Research*. Thousand Oaks, CA: Sage, p. 289.

Turner, N.J., Marshall, A., Thomson, J.C. (Edosdi), Hood, R.J., Hill, C. and Hill, E.A. (2008) '"Ebb and flow": transmitting environmental knowledge in a contemporary Aboriginal community'. In: Lutz, J.S. and Neis, B. (eds), *Making and Moving Knowledge: Interdisciplinary and Community-based Research in a World on the Edge*. Kingston: McGill-Queen's University Press, p. 51.

II.3.3 SHIFTING TO INTELLIGENT SOCIETIES
Daniel Innerarity

In a world in which common goods are severely limited for those who lack recourse to institutional decision-making bodies, a world in which radical changes of scale have taken place and in which we are confronted by problems of governance, political disaffection and insufficient consensus, the demand on us is to examine our tools for shaping the political will, paying special attention to the ways in which we socially construct collective intelligence. How societies succeed or fail in harnessing distributed intelligence will determine our collective destiny.

Decision-making is typically organized on the assumption that governments possess the best knowledge of any situation. However, in reality, knowledge is highly dispersed throughout society, and governments have no alternative but to avail themselves of this dispersed knowledge. This is particularly true at a time when the collective generation of knowledge has grown exponentially with new technologies. At the same time, it is also clear that collective rationality cannot be constructed simply by aggregating individual utilities: the market cannot operate without an institutional framework that includes other kinds of logic, and the sound organization of society requires ways to allow for the political articulation of interests. The question of how to shape intelligent democracies through networked intelligence or 'smart governance' is a crucial issue. One formulation is the notion of 'wiki government' (Noveck, 2009). Whatever the case may be, however, the institutions of government need to be redesigned in an age of networks. Effective governance in the 21st century requires organized collaboration. Hierarchies need to be transformed into collaborative knowledge ecosystems. Radical change is needed in the culture of government, moving away from centralized expertise towards a collective grappling with social problems.

The appeal to the intelligent self-organization of society – for example, in the neoliberal model of self-regulating markets – and the disdain for public opinion voiced by an elite cadre of experts reflect a highly simplified view of the way in which societies generate collective knowledge. Such simplifications typically fail to take into account that it is the same society that gives rise to collective knowledge and yet, when badly organized, is liable to slide down a slippery slope into errors that ramify as they spread through society. This ambiguity or indeterminacy is especially typical of global knowledge societies, and it leads neither to the wisdom of crowds nor to the madness of mobs, but rather to opportunities that can transform common action into collective intelligence.

COLLECTIVE INTELLIGENCE

Whatever name we use to characterize our contemporary societies – post-industrial society, information society or knowledge society – all of these concepts point to a profound change that has taken place in recent decades in the developed nations of the world. These concepts refer to the powerful growth of information and knowledge resources in relation to material and energy resources. Knowledge generation and transfer are now of great significance. They play a fundamental role in social, economic and territorial development. We could sum up the nature of the period in which we live in this way: the great challenge of humanity no longer lies in the mastery of nature but in our joint progress in information and organization. The chief enemy facing us is not so much poverty or fear as ignorance. Our major challenges concern knowledge in the broadest sense, and the most critical strategies focus on policies that address knowledge, science, technology, innovation, research and training. The real wealth of nations lies in what people know. What does this mean for politics? And what challenges does it pose for governance?

The future of democracy depends on its ability to rise to the challenges of a knowledge society. The knowledge society requires the political system to raise the level of its knowledge and decisions so that governance also becomes knowledge work. This implies a radical shift in our routines, because the prevailing approach to decision-making remains prescriptive and it needs to be complemented by a cognitive style. Social organization must increasingly place an emphasis on knowledge tools and abilities, such as analytical reasoning, critical thinking, imagination, a view of diversity as a resource, independent judgement, collective deliberation and the ability to cope with uncertainty and complexity.

Charles Lindblom (1965) spoke of the 'intelligence of democracy' to refer to a centuries-old triumph that has crystallized in structures, procedures and rules. Democracy has gradually taken shape as a system of representation, procedures for decision-making and the provision of public goods. The intelligence of democracy has replaced hierarchy and authoritarianism with an inclusive structure to take decisions on collective issues; it has pushed aside procedures of divine or hereditary authority in favour of representative voting systems and regular changes of government, and it has transformed eternal rules into systems of rules that are open to review and alteration.

If a knowledge society calls for a special cognitive effort, the reason for this is because there is an element of ungovernability in an active society with distributed intelligence. Professionals and specialists operate under their own standards, with professional ethics that cannot be imposed or controlled from outside. None-

theless, there is still room for politics in the management of negative externalities, the demand for accountability, the ability to anticipate the need for change before it becomes desperately obvious, the provision of framework conditions for the development of each and every one of the autonomous systems present in a society, and so forth. At any rate, politics needs to abandon its prescriptive obsession with 'telling people what they have to do', while at the same time not shirking its responsibility to create the opportunities required by an emerging knowledge society. A complex knowledge society needs to be able to carve out a set of spaces for distributed and decentralized collective intelligence, and the job of politics is to coordinate and moderate the interaction between these autonomous units.

Collective intelligence is the only possible way to counter the risks inherent in complex systems, such as in the case of financial risks. Individual people and actors appear to be blind to the properties of a linked, interdependent system. In modern societies, social actors and systems must be able to function as complex, interacting wholes, not as a mere aggregation of elements.

However, it would be wise to have an adequate understanding of what we mean when we propose a concept such as collective intelligence (Salomon, 2003; Rheingold, 2004; Sunstein, 2006; William, 2007; Willke, 2007). First, it is necessary to distinguish individual knowledge from collective knowledge, because a specific aspect of organizations or societies is that they generate specific knowledge that is additional to the knowledge of their members and even greater than the sum of those members' knowledge. There is a difference between learning in societies and societies that learn, just as there is a difference between actors who cooperate and institutions that learn. While individual expertise is a private matter, the framework for achieving collective intelligence is a genuinely public task.

It is often said that knowledge in an organization is simply the result of adding together the knowledge of its members. Of course, the competence of organizations depends on the knowledge of their members. However, just as a jumbled assortment of geniuses and Nobel laureates does not make for an intelligent organization, neither does a rise in the number of university graduates automatically produce an intelligent society. It makes little sense to pay too much attention to individual qualities, rely too heavily on people's virtues or be content with our indignation at the defects of individuals or institutions when what we should be doing is paying attention to how these factors are interconnected.

In the case of matters involving group dynamics, there is always a question of whether the whole is greater than the sum of the parts, of whether there is a supra-individual aspect – that is, the system, the organized whole, an emergent phenomenon – 'that cannot be reduced to the intentions of the participating individuals' (Heintz, 2004, p. 3). The term *emergence* is used precisely when there are general properties that cannot be reduced to the characteristics of their elements. A knowledge society is not a society with many experts, but a society in which the systems are expert. It is not enough for individuals to learn and innovate; there is little value in citizens acquiring new competences while the rules, routines and procedures – in other words, public, organizational intelligence – stand in the way of harnessing these new competences. Change happens only when collective structures, processes and rules change as well. The knowledge of a society amounts to more than the mere accumulation of existing knowledge, just as an organization is intelligent by virtue of the synergies produced by its systems of rules, institutions and procedures, and not by the mere summation of the intelligence of its members. Knowledge generation arises out of communicative acts or, to put it another way, knowledge is a relational good.

POLITICAL MIRACLES

It was Hannah Arendt who said that, in politics, we have a right to expect miracles. Not because we are superstitious, but because human beings are, when acting freely and in concert with one another, 'able to perform what is infinitely improbable' (1993, p. 35). I have always interpreted these words of the Jewish philosopher as a definition of democracy and, more specifically, of the collective intelligence that makes democratic life possible. Today's landscape, however, is bleak, and public opinion is rife with discourses that run counter to Arendt's view: routine, predictability, disaffection and more. Any of us who still believe in politics as a transformative force in society may be viewed as deluded or credulous, just as we may once have believed things in the past that we can no longer support today.

But why must we give up this hope? The entire organizational complexity of democracy is a triumph of humanity in the pursuit of something like collective wisdom. Let me put it more provocatively: a handful of fools have produced something wise. But we can also posit a more refined formulation: a group of average people, who did not start out in agreement ideologically and who had diverse interests, have been able to generate – and not despite their diversity but because of it – a society that is more intelligent than each person taken individually. This is what we could call the miracle of politics – a politics that is more intelligent than the people who are engaged in it.

The enemies of democracy have always been sceptical of this miracle. Their preference is to point to the stupidity and madness of the mob. The problem is that they have spread belief in another miracle that is even more difficult to swallow: that right is on the side of the few, the elites, the experts, those who have somehow been declared the best. If, however, in spite of everything, democracy exists, it is because we do not know how to determine who the best are and because, above all, even if we could identify them, nothing guarantees that their decisions, too, would be the best.

For a number of years, neoliberal ideology has circulated a self-serving notion that is even harder to believe: that human beings are intelligent as consumers and stupid as voters. This thinking rests on Schumpeter's observation that the individual will is on a firmer footing in the case of an individual's consumer decisions (given that the individual has direct experience of his choices), while the experience and will of the electorate are imprecise (Schumpeter, 1942, p. 256). Neoliberal economists have applied this principle of the wisdom of crowds to the marketplace, but the principle of the madness of the mob to politics (Surowiecki, 2004). The conclusion that follows is disturbing: 'If people are rational as consumers and irrational as voters, it is a good idea to rely more on markets and less on politics (Caplan, 2007, p. 114).

Although the idea of perfect information in the markets has long been disproved, some persist in the belief – which now takes on the character of an outright superstition – that an actor in the market possesses perfect information. By contrast, they claim that the voter lacks the necessary information, and therefore political decisions must be reduced to a minimum and transferred to the marketplace. This contrast between the supposed knowledge of the consumer and the ignorance of the voter lacks any empirical evidence. How can people have fewer erroneous beliefs when they pursue individual ends than when they work towards collective ends? After a careful examination of both assumptions, it is clear that neither is true: there is structural ignorance both in the marketplace and in politics, and this ignorance must be borne in mind and compensated for with frameworks of governance that prevent incorrigible mistakes or enhance our collective ability to exercise foresight, take balanced decisions, work out corrective procedures, and so forth. In politics, there is representation and participation, and in the markets there are prices and rules. This is precisely to avoid or correct some of the mistakes that tend to arise from the adoption of a unilateral viewpoint, such as acting without heed to the long term, putting too much reliance on immediate decisions or eliminating checks and balances.

Not only is democracy the least bad of all systems, as Churchill put it, but it is also the least stupid. The traditional rationales for democracy have stressed arguments of values, making appeals to equality, justice or freedom. They have not resorted to instrumental arguments. While all of this is true, however, a defence of democracy can also draw on instrumental criteria, that is, that democracy is epistemically superior to other systems and makes for better decisions (Coleman, 1989; Elster and Landemore, 2010, pp. 9ff). As Josiah Ober maintains, the primacy of Athens over its rivals lay in the character of its institutions, particularly the deliberative body of the council of 500 (Ober, 2009). This superiority was specifically due to the council's harnessing of the collective intelligence.

Our democracies need leadership and our complex societies require governance that must be able to articulate these various levels of government, with their social subsystems and differing forms of logic, all in the midst of vigorous civil societies with dispersed knowledge, if we are to have the best possible combination emerge. To illustrate the interrelationship of these elements, consider the metaphor proposed by the anthropologist Edwin Hutchins (1995): the calculation involved in steering a naval vessel is not carried out in the head of any one person but in the coordination of many different people with navigational instruments, charts, communications networks and organizational functions. Not even in this area, where giving orders carries greater weight than giving reasons, is the exercise of authoritarian leadership enough. There is more power in shared power, and also more intelligence of the sort needed for the self-organization of democratic societies.

'Democratic reason' is the epistemic superiority of the rule of the many over the rule of the few. The reasons against aristocracy, oligarchy or a regime of experts are also cognitive in nature. Even if it were possible to identify the most intelligent people and guarantee their virtue, many individuals with average intelligence and varied ways of thinking have greater epistemic competence than a few individuals, however great their intelligence may be.

This is not to say that the many are infallible. The social production of knowledge also has its dark side, and there is no shortage of examples of collective stupidity. Indeed, we should not overvalue the possibilities of aggregation. There are subjects about which the average citizen is not only ignorant, but also makes systematic mistakes. Often, however, this also applies to the experts whose judgement nevertheless does need to be included in decision-making processes, albeit balanced against other democratic criteria. The 'intelligence of democracy' can be seen precisely in rightly articulating knowledge, decision-making and legitimacy.

Collective wisdom is not produced automatically, as though it were a guaranteed outcome whenever a number of individuals come together to take decisions. There is a need for the framework of rules and procedures that we designate loosely as democratic governance. It is also fundamental to fulfil what we may call 'the condition of diversity'. If we can be more intelligent collectively than each of us on our own account or than the select few, it is because we can, in our immense diversity, bring to bear a wide range of viewpoints, interpretations, predictive models, social media, professions, ideologies, interests and life experiences.

The theorem of Scott Page (2006) on the primacy of diversity over expertise says the following: a cognitively diverse group of people is more valuable than a group of highly intelligent people who think alike. Cognitive diversity (the ability to see reality from different points of view) is fundamental for the emergence of collective intelligence. As with any emergent phenomenon, nothing wholly ensures that diversity translates into intelligence, but we can be certain that environments with little diversity (whether as a result of explicit exclusion or sectarianism, or because of a shortfall in representation or participation) do not give rise to the collective intelligence that lies at the heart of the best public decisions.

A 'moral' approach to human relationships typically emphasizes intimacy and trust, as though social capital involved a store of emotion. This over-emphasis tends to make us lose sight of the epistemic advantages of distance and diversity, which have their own logic. In social systems, weak bonds are more effective for cognitive purposes than strong bonds. The more intimate a relationship is, the less information it provides. Friendship is a strong bond, but generally our acquaintances give us more information than our friends do. The reason for this is easy to grasp: people with whom I have weak bonds move in circles to which I have no access. Conversely, intimacy provides a maximum of emotion, but a minimum of information.

This potentiality of pluralism offers a stark contrast

to the fanaticism and blindness of overly homogeneous groups. Rational thought requires cognitive dissonance at the personal level and for societies as a whole. When we look for reality to prove us right, when we seek out somebody too much like ourselves to confirm that we are correct (an almost unconscious mechanism that is quite common among human beings), we sharply narrow our epistemic field, which is usually the prelude to poor decision-making. For collective reason to work, therefore, we need conditions in the political culture that we could call 'liberal' in a broad sense, that is, the free circulation of ideas, respect and open confrontation, and a willingness to engage in argument. In short, the need is for a culture that safeguards cognitive differences and does not see them as a drawback or a mere stepping stone on a path towards unanimity.

THE SOCIAL CONSTRUCTION OF INEPTITUDE

We cannot account for the nature of the knowledge society without also coming to grips with why it can produce enormous collective failures that may outstrip even the failures committed by societies where knowledge has not held such a central place. A number of explanations for this singular paradox have been proposed (Tuchman, 1984; Tainter, 1988; Garzón Valdés, 2004; Diamond, 2006) in the context of questions such as: Why do societies collapse? What reasons can explain how, given that a society may be more intelligent than its members, we may also be more inept, more incompetent, than we are when considered individually?

To account for our peculiar vulnerability to collective errors and poor decisions, the explanation lies not in any lack of adequate tools, but rather in how misled we can become by the sophistication of our capabilities. Let us take, for instance, economic swings between euphoria and disappointment. These swings would not have reached the critical dimensions of today if it were not for the financial power of our economic systems; the spread of rumours increases with the density of our communications and gives rise to phenomena on the internet such as 'trolling' and 'flaming'. What has been called 'the tragedy of the commons' (Hardin, 1968) astutely encapsulates this fatal mix of interdependence, contagion and organizational inability that can lead to an aggregation of decisions with catastrophic effects.

One explanation for 'wiki errors' is the fact that we are handling second-hand information and must put our reliance in others. This is true of any society, but even more so of a complex society. Our world itself is second hand, mediated, and it could not be otherwise: we would know very little if our knowledge consisted solely of what we personally know. We make use of a great number of epistemological prostheses. We enhance our brain power on the basis of trust and delegation. Second-hand experiences affect human life with at least as much force as first-hand experiences, if not more. Nearly everything we know of the world we know by means of specific mediations. We have no choice but to rely on others and the information they give us. Some who consider themselves well informed actually have first-hand experience of very few things. This state of affairs has resulted in the greatest triumphs of humanity, but has also produced our gravest mistakes (Sunstein, 2006). Too much or too little trust can be shown, rumours can spread wildly without sources of objectivity to halt them, and panic can become even more contagious in a world based on assessments that are hard to refute.

There are sound reasons to think in many cases that, when an opinion is widely shared, we should probably take it as true. However, the opposite experience is also fascinating: from the most harmless types of commonplaces to the infamy of lynch law, our collective mistakes can reverberate. Many live in information bubbles, which have dynamics that can sometimes lead to echoes that spread, link into a chain reaction and grow even stronger, resulting in enormous collective failures. And let us not think that such a spread of errors is limited only to those who know least about the matter in question. There are also errors typical of the aggregation of experts' knowledge and decisions, the failings of specialists, which are usually even more maddening insofar as we feel entitled to expect these individuals to have special foresight.

THE DRAWBACKS OF 'BEING TOO RIGHT'
A root cause of many collective errors is something that we could call the drawback of 'being too right'. This refers to the fact that some errors stem from the fragmentation that prevents us from stepping outside the circle of people who think like us. In this way, we lose the advantages of heterogeneity. The possibilities afforded by the information explosion are one example of this paradoxical state of affairs.

Some have welcomed the potential of 'Daily Me', a personally customized information product (Negroponte, 1995, p. 153). The 'customization' of information highlights how informational options and the ability to make personal choices increase with advances in technology. Customization can, however, also lead to impoverishment because it reinforces individuals' prejudices and deprives them of exposure to opposing viewpoints and undetected problems. In this way, new communication technologies can also lead to misunderstandings and rifts when citizens join groups in which the members think alike and jealously guard against cognitive dissonance. Sunstein studied this phenomenon and found that the members of a deliberative group frequently gravitate towards extreme positions (2002). It is not uncommon for one cause of fanaticism and radicalism to be found in ideologically closed groups linked by technology. When people who think alike exchange information and opinions and are not exposed to differing viewpoints, it is easy for them to become radicalized. The internet has encouraged the gathering of like-minded individuals, the formation of stovepipes, including sectarian ones, and the creation of spaces where monolithic views prevail. If the new technologies can broaden the horizon of information, they can also enable us not to see what we do not wish to see, allowing us to build an echo chamber that prevents us from examining our own biases.

Recently, commentators on the role of the internet in politics have coined the terms 'cocoons' and 'echo chambers' to denote people's propensity to form networks of the like-minded (Huckfeldt and Sprague 1995; Rogers and Kincaid 1981). This propensity increases in networks in which the defining rationale is 'like': you 'click' on the people that you 'like', that is, the people who are like you. Differences are filtered out. The same logic appears even in commercial contexts: if I buy a book from Amazon, I receive a message saying, 'If you bought book X, you may also like book Z'. Indeed, democracy would be better served if (as Benjamin Barber recently observed) we were instead told, 'If you liked book X, you should get to know the alternative viewpoints found in book Z'.

The world of the internet can have the effect of reducing our cognitive dissonance. The customization of internet search engines has transformed our experience of the world to the point at which we are thrown back into a Ptolemaic universe in which the sun and everything else revolves around us. Such customization hails the end not only of serendipity – the kind of search that blends method and chance and can bring us to unexpected discoveries – but also of bridging capital. As Eli Pariser puts it, 'In the early days of the World Wide Web, the online terrain felt like an unmapped continent, and its users considered themselves discoverers and explorers' (Pariser, 2011, pp. 1415–20), while 'Google is great at helping us find what we know we want, but not at finding what we don't know we want' (pp. 1226–32).

THE INVISIBILITY OF THE COMMONS

Another source of collective ineptitude lies in what we could call 'the invisibility of the commons'. For interactions to result in virtuous circles, it should be possible for actors to receive some return on the impact of their personal action on the group. Making visible any membership in a group aimed in the same direction increases the utility of decisions taken by the group's representatives and improves implementation by the group's members. However, this mutual sense of belonging is barely noticed when individual actions are uncoupled from the context and the group. Many collective mistakes stem from an initial difficulty in taking a comprehensive view of the consequences of an action.

How can this relationship be made visible? Let us look at an example in the area of taxes. A study in Minnesota, USA, examined four possibilities for combating false tax returns. One group of taxpayers received a letter explaining how the money raised would be used. A second group was reminded of the punishment for anyone filing a false return. A third group received a document with information on how to get help to fill in their tax forms. And a fourth group was informed that 90% of taxpayers fulfilled their filing obligations. The campaign showed that only the fourth option was effective at reducing fraud. Looking at personal action from a collective perspective had the effect of making the action of fraud socially illicit; it marginalized fraud (Thaler and Sunstein, 2008). In a city in California, the electricity bills for a group of neighbours were appended together so that each neighbour could place himself in relation to the group. Those whose consumption was greater than the average sharply reduced their consumption. The first step to restraining individual behaviours that have a negative impact on the commons is to show this impact. Making the connection visible may not be a guarantee of responsible behaviour, but its invisibility is definitely a source of irresponsibility.

There are many proposals to reverse the current invisibility of personal taxes and bring them more in line with the logic of the gift, whose operation was studied in primitive tribes by Marcel Mauss. The increase in the computer processing of taxes and financial flows permits a level of traceability that was unthinkable in the past. If we customize the solidarity represented by taxation and indicate as precisely as possible what percentage of our tax bill goes to which public buildings or to which social actions, it may serve to increase the personal utility of this collective action. The ability to see the impact of solidarity with as much detail as possible encourages its acceptance and fosters responsibility for public actions and infrastructure. Other measures such as leaving a margin for personal action could increase the personal meaning of taxes, raising everyone's responsibility and individual satisfaction. Success would lie in making others less unknown to us and in ensuring that the flows of collective life are not wholly mediated by a cold black collection box set up by the State.

THE FAILURES OF AGGREGATION

Many poor decisions at the root of collective failures can be attributed to a poor aggregation of decisions, which were simply the addition of individual preferences in the short term. Let us consider, for instance, the self-destructive character of the impulse for protectionism (which was the actual cause of the economic crash of 1929) or the problem of financial bubbles in 2008 (the difficulty of halting a process in which everyone is better off right now and the disaster lies in the long run). Markets, for example, are systems to aggregate knowledge and preferences, and everyone knows at this stage how beneficial this procedure usually is for the coordination of our actions. However, we are also aware of its limitations, its catastrophic ramifications and now, above all, the fiasco that usually results from thinking that we are so intelligent that any regulatory intervention is superfluous. When financial euphoria predominates, any hypothetical crisis seems far off and therefore fails to trigger reactions that prudence would otherwise counsel.

Thinking and acting in real time hampers our ability to take coherent decisions. When the time horizon is narrow, we run the risk of yielding to the 'tyranny of small decisions', as Kahn has put it. By simply going from decision to decision, we can eventually arrive at a situation that we did not want at the outset. Anybody who has ever examined how a traffic jam develops, for example, will recognize the problem. Each consumer, through private consumption, can contribute to destroying the environment, while each voter can contribute to destroying the public space – a result that voters do not want and that can, in addition, make it impossible for them to satisfy their needs. If they could have anticipated the outcome and reversed or at least moderated their immediate private interest, they would have acted differently.

There is no collective intelligence if societies fail to govern their future rationally. The future is constructed, and its construction requires forward thinking and a certain degree of coherence. When decisions are taken with a short-term view, without taking negative exter-

nalities and long-term implications into account, when decision-making cycles are too short, the rationality of agents must necessarily be short-sighted. When the time horizon is narrow and only the most immediate interest is borne in mind, it is very hard to prevent matters from taking a catastrophic turn.

Today, society possesses many sources of inertia that not only work against the maximization of the common good in the long run, but also work systematically to divert us from this objective. Overhauling the concept of responsibility could contribute to removing fatalism from the process of modernization, so that it is perceived not as a realm of uncontrollable powers, but as a civilizing process undertaken by human beings, in which we are confronted by processes that lie beyond our control but that can be partly regulated. In an era of second-hand consequences, we are not condemned merely to choosing between total responsibility and total irresponsibility. Rather, the task before us is to determine for ourselves, drawing on procedures of democratic legitimacy, how we wish politically to construct our responsibility.

REFERENCES

Arendt, H. (1993) *Was ist Politik? Aus dem Nachlass.* Munich: Piper.

Caplan, B. (2007) *The Myth of the Rational Voter: Why Democracies Choose Bad Policies.* Fairfax, VA: Mason University Press.

Coleman, J. (1989) 'Rationality and the justification of democracy'. In: Brennan, G. and Lomasky, L.E. (eds), *Politics and Process.* Cambridge: Cambridge University Press, pp. 194–220.

Diamond, J. (2006) *Colapso.* Barcelona: Debate.

Elster, J. and Landemore, H. (eds) (2010) *La segesse collective'.* In *Raison Publique* 12. Paris: Presses de l'université Paris-Sorbonne.

Garzón Valdés, E. (2004) *Calamidades.* Barcelona: Gedisa.

Hardin, G. (1968) 'The tragedy of the commons'. *Science,* 162, 1243–8.

Heintz, B. (2004) *'Emergenz und Reduktion. Neue Perspektiven auf das Mikro-Makro-Problem'.* In: *Kölner Zeitschrift für Soziologie und Sozialpsychologie,* 56, 1–31.

Huckfeldt, R. and Sprague, J. (1995) *Citizens, Politics, and Social Communication.* New York: Cambridge University Press.

Hutchins, E. (1995) *Cognition in the Wild.* Cambridge, MA: MIT Press.

Lindblom, C. (1965) *The Intelligence of Democracy: Decision Making Through Mutual Adjustment.* New York: Free Press.

Negroponte, N. (1995) *Being Digital.* New York: Knopf.

Noveck, B.S. (2009) *Wiki Government: How Technology Can Make Government Better, Democracy Stronger, and Citizens More Powerful.* Washington, DC: Brookings.

Ober, J. (2009) *Democracy and Knowledge: Innovation and*

Learning in Classical Athens. Princeton, NJ: Princeton University Press.

Page, S. (2006) *The Difference: How the Power of Diversity Creates Better Groups, Firms, Schools and Societies*. Princeton, NJ: Princeton University Press.

Pariser, E. (2011) *The Filter Bubble: What the Internet is Hiding from You*. New York: Penguin, Kindle Edition.

Rheingold, H. (2004) *Multitudes Inteligentes*. Barcelona: Gedisa.

Rogers, E. and Kincaid, L. (1981) *Communication Networks: Toward a New Paradigm for Research*. New York: Free Press.

Salomon, G. (2003) *Distributed Cognitions*. New York: Cambridge University Press.

Schumpeter, J. (1942) *Capitalism, Socialism and Democracy*. New York: Harper.

Sunstein, C.R. (2002) *Republic.com*. Princeton, NJ: Princeton University Press.

Sunstein, C.R. (2006) *Infotopia – How Many Minds Produce Knowledge*. Oxford: Oxford University Press.

Surowiecki, J. (2004) *The Wisdom of Crowds*. New York: Doubleday.

Tainter, J. (1988) *The Collapse of Complex Societies*. Cambridge: Cambridge University Press.

Thaler, R. and Sunstein, C. (2008) *Nudge: Improving Decisions About Health, Wealth, and Happiness*. New Haven, CT: Yale University Press.

Tuchman, B. (1984) *The March of Folly*. New York: Knopf.

William, A.D. (2007) *Wikinomics*. Barcelona: Paidós.

Willke, H. (2007) *Smart Governance: Governing the Global Knowledge Society*. Frankfurt: Suhrkamp.

Legend:
CO₂ Emissions
CO_2 Emissions

28. Belize (1.2 / 21)
29. Guatemala (1.1 / na)
30. Honduras (1.1 / 19)
31. El Salvador (1.0 / 23)
32. Nicaragua (1.8 / na)
33. Costa Rica (1.8 / na)
34. Panamá (2.3 / 45)
35. Jamaica (3.2 / 29)
36. Haiti (0.2 / na)
37. Dominican Republic (2.1 / na)
38. Puerto Rico (na / 86)
39. Guyana (2.1 / 12)
40. Suriname (4.8 / na)
41. French Guiana (na / na)

British Virgin Islands (na / 64)
St. Kitts & Nevis (na / 18)
Antigua & Barbuda (5.3 / 16)
Dominica (1.9 / 4)
Santa Lucia (na / 11)
Barbados (5.8 / 66)
Grenada (2.4 / 53)
Trinidad & Tobago (35.8 / na)

N

Data not available (na)
0 – 3.9
4 – 7.9
8 – 11.9
12 – 14.9
15 – 44

Notes:
This map shows the relation between the CO_2 emission per country and the higher education enrolment ratio (GER). Classification method: natural breaks (Jenks optimization)

Sources: UNESCO Institute for Statistics, *Global Education Digest 2012.* Comparing Education Statistics Across the World.
Available at: http://www.uis.unesco.org/Education/GED%20Documents%20C/ GED-2012-Complete-Web3.pdf

MAP 3 CO₂ Emissions and higher education enrolment ratio (GER) by country, 2011

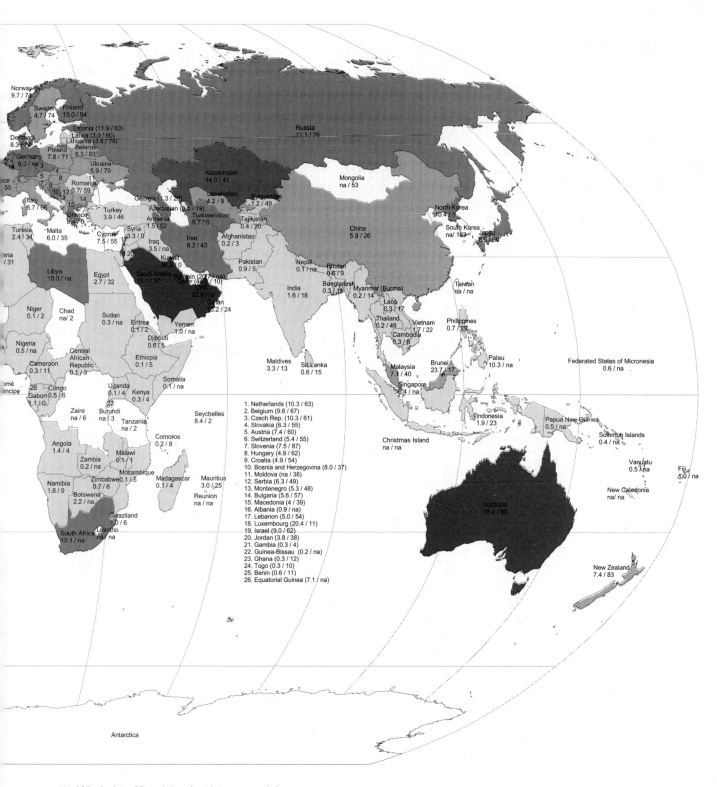

Norway
9.7 / 74

Sweden Finland
4.7 / 74 10.0 / 94

Denmark
8.3 /
Germany   Belarus
9.0 / na   6.3 / 83
Poland
7.8 / 71
Estonia (11.9 / 63)
Latvia (3.0 / 60)
Lithuania (3.8 / 74)

Ukraine
5.9 / 79

Russia
11.1 / 76

Romania
3.7 / 59

Italy
6.7 / 66

Greece
8.4 /

Georgia (1.3 / 28)
Azerbaijan (3.8 / 19)
Armenia
1.5 / 32

Turkey
3.9 / 46

Kazakhstan
14.0 / 41

Mongolia
na / 53

North Korea
10.4 / 0

Tunisia
2.4 / 34

Malta
6.0 / 35

Cyprus
7.5 / 55

Syria
3.3 / 0

Turkmenistan
9.7 / 0

Uzbekistan
4.2 / 9

Kyrgyzstan
1.2 / 49

Tajikistan
0.4 / 20

China
5.8 / 26

South Korea
na / 103

Japan
8.5 / 80

Libya
10.0 / na

Egypt
2.7 / 32

Iraq
3.5 / na

Iran
8.2 / 43

Afghanistan
0.2 / 3

Pakistan
0.9 / 5

Nepal
0.1 / na

Bhutan
0.6 / 9

Taiwan
na / na

Niger
0.1 / 2

Chad
na / 2

Sudan
0.3 / na

Saudi Arabia
16.1 / 37

Kuwait
30.3 / 0

Bahrain (20.1 / na)
Qatar (44.0 / 10)
UAE
22.6 / na
Oman
15.2 / 24

India
1.6 / 18

Bangladesh
0.3 / 11

Myanmar (Burma)
0.2 / 14

Nigeria
0.5 / na

Eritrea
0.1 / 2

Djibouti
0.6 / 5

Yemen
1.0 / na

Laos
0.3 / 17

Philippines
0.7 / 29

Palau
10.3 / na

Federated States of Micronesia
0.6 / na

Cameroon
0.3 / 11

Central
African
Republic
0.1 / 3

Ethiopia
0.1 / 5

Somalia
0.1 / na

Thailand
0.2 / 48

Vietnam
1.7 / 22

Cambodia
0.3 / 8

Congo
0.5 / 6

Gabon
1.1 / 0

Uganda
0.1 / 4

Kenya
0.3 / 4

Seychelles
8.4 / 2

Malaysia
7.1 / 40

Brunei
23.7 / 17

Zaire
na / 6

Buruhdi
na / 3

Tanzania
na / 2

Comoros
0.2 / 8

Maldives
3.3 / 13

Sri Lanka
0.6 / 15

Singapore
6.4 / na

Angola
1.4 / 4

Malawi
0.1 / 1

Mozambique
0.1 / 4

Madagascar
0.1 / 4

Mauritius
3.0 / 25

Christmas Island
na / na

Indonesia
1.9 / 23

Papua New Guinea
0.5 / na

Solomon Islands
0.4 / na

Zambia
0.2 / na

Zimbabwe
0.7 / 6

Reunion
na / 4

1. Netherlands (10.3 / 63)
2. Belgium (9.6 / 67)
3. Czech Rep. (10.3 / 61)
4. Slovakia (6.3 / 55)
5. Austria (7.4 / 60)
6. Switzerland (5.4 / 55)
7. Slovenia (7.5 / 87)
8. Hungary (4.9 / 62)
9. Croatia (4.9 / 54)
10. Bosnia and Herzegovina (8.0 / 37)
11. Moldova (na / 38)
12. Serbia (6.3 / 49)
13. Montenegro (5.3 / 48)
14. Bulgaria (5.6 / 57)
15. Macedonia (4 / 39)
16. Albania (0.9 / na)
17. Lebanon (5.0 / 54)
18. Luxembourg (20.4 / 11)
19. Israel (9.0 / 62)
20. Jordan (3.8 / 38)
21. Gambia (0.3 / 4)
22. Guinea-Bissau (0.2 / na)
23. Ghana (0.3 / 12)
24. Togo (0.3 / 10)
25. Benin (0.6 / 11)
26. Equatorial Guinea (7.1 / na)

Vanuatu
0.5 / na

Fiji
1.0 / na

Namibia
1.6 / 9

Botswana
2.2 / na

Swaziland
1.0 / 6

South Africa
10.1 / na

Lesotho
na / na

Australia
18.4 / 80

New Caledonia
na / na

New Zealand
7.4 / 83

Antarctica

World Bank, data. CO_2 emissions (metric tons per capita)
Available at: http://data.worldbank.org/indicator
Vector layer source: ESRI Data; Projection: Robinson

MAP 3   87

UNIVERSITY SOCIAL RESPONSIBILITY: A MATURE AND RESPONSIBLE DEFINITION

François Vallaeys

SOCIAL RESPONSIBILITY THEORY: VIRTUE, JUSTICE AND SUSTAINABILITY FOR 3D ETHICS

Social responsibility, a new core responsibility that complements moral and legal responsibilities, is a collective, not a personal, responsibility that fosters political creativity (Vallaeys, 2011). Whereas moral and legal responsibilities govern our acts, social responsibility governs our impacts; that is, the latter governs not what has immediate and local consequences, but what has to do with distant systemic and global emergencies. Once we understand that social responsibility is responsibility for impacts and that impacts are not the same as acts, we can explore the theoretical and practical richness of the social responsibility of organizations, in particular of universities.

The problems that require responsibility to be socialized refer to systemic issues arising from the social routines of a multitude of cohabiting people, with impacts that are often invisible unless supported by scientific research (for example, as seen with climate change). Since these routines, tied to a particular way of life, produce chronic, unwanted and socially damaging side effects, citizen co-responsibility becomes necessary for people, first, to recognize that their way of life generates endemic, unsustainable problems, and second, to institute the social changes necessary to solve these problems. The shift from unquestioningly experiencing social problems at the individual level to active co-responsibility regarding consensual solutions for common problems is what the philosopher Dewey (1984 [1927]) referred to as the constitution of a 'Public', that is, the emergence of a political collective capable of taking its destiny into its own hands, innovating and acquiring a proper, fair and sustainable political constitution, with adequate mechanisms for regulating collective action. Social responsibility is the quintessential political responsibility because it is relational – it is not the individual responsibility of elected representatives, but of all citizens united.

It is nowadays obvious that our collective problems are linked to the risk of our planet becoming ecologically uninhabitable due to industrial productivism and a lack of control over a modern social society – especially its economic, financial, scientific and technical systems – that is developing autonomously at a frantic pace. It is no longer possible to feel sure that these systems continue to be piloted in a socially responsible way by legitimate powers. The world's ecological problems are the outcome of a global political control problem. In early modernity, we had to figure out how to control the political domain and how to collectively resolve the problem of scarcity; therefore, we invented democracy and industrial technoscience. Today, our biggest problem is to take back democratic control over the powers unleashed by technoscience and handed over to the lucrative interests and 'blind intelligence' (Morin, 2004) of scientists, who, inadvertently, confirm Gabor's law: 'Everything that can be done will be done, whatever the consequences.' Reining in one's own power lest it becomes uncontrolled is the duty of the responsible individual. The political risk of before was that of an excess of political power; the political risk of today is that of a lack of political power, reflected in the impossibility of governing social powers unleashed by industrial modernity. Our era is the era of responsibility and reflexivity, of dominion over the domain (Serres, 1990), of the 'responsibility principle' (Jonas, 1979). Yet it is a strange and difficult responsibility to take on board: it is not the individual responsibility of a person or an organization, but a collective, mutualized, shared responsibility. It is, in short, a 'social', meta-subjective responsibility.

Distinguishing between the three core responsibilities – moral, legal and social – is therefore a fitting philosophical task that avoids confusion when analysing corporate social responsibility (CSR) and university social responsibility (USR); above all, it avoids mistaking these for the kinds of philanthropic act that result in greenwashing. The complex ethics that we need to take on board is now simultaneously viewed in three distinct windows (Table II.4.1); in other words, our ethics are three-dimensional (3D) ethics (Morin, 2004; Vallaeys, 2011):

In this complex ethics, it is important to highlight three issues:

- No dimension can operate in isolation from other dimensions without ethical pathology developing as an outcome, whether this is moral fanaticism, legal dogmatism or ecological totalitarianism.

- Sustainability should not be reduced to ecology (the protection of nature) but should be understood in more complex terms as nourishing continued freedom and intergenerational justice, respect for the autonomy and dignity of upcoming generations, and respect for the ethical efforts of previous generations.

- Governance begins when government is no longer possible, that is, when stakeholders jointly regulate their collective actions and when no one stakeholder gives orders to (governs) any other stakeholder. A situation of government implies a hierarchical chain of obeyed orders and guaranteed sanctions in the event of disobedience (Luhmann, 1975). A situation of governance implies the need for mutual regulation regarding a common good (planetary habitability, global financial balance, international tax arrangements, overcoming social dumping, and so on) in the absence of a government coercing all stakeholders by law. Governance produces co-responsibility agreements according to rules whose implementation is mutually overseen by peers. Most of our current negative impacts call for us to build regulations via governance, since they involve transnational and meta-governmental coordination of multiple stakeholders for whom market self-regulation and national laws are insufficient (Ostrom, 1990). Liberal ideologues reject governance, because they believe that the market is perfectly capable of regulating collective action. Socialist ideologues also reject governance since it can never efficiently oblige social agents and so needs laws. Neither liberals nor socialists understand what is meant by social responsibility: the liberals view it as a form of corporate philanthropy (the moral responsibility of the good and virtuous manager or director), and the socialists reject it in favour of legal responsibility (obligations imposed by the State). In reality, socially responsible regulation requires, at the very least, both legislation and the market. Hybrid regulation involves peer associations and social innovations, over and above laissez-faire liberalism and legal coercion. Thinking in terms of real social responsibility removes us from the ongoing battle between liberals and socialists and also presents us with the challenge of establishing genuine co-responsibility for present and future generations of humans by simultaneously using all the possibilities for regulating collective action (Table II.4.2).

TABLE II.4.1
3D ethics (Vallaeys)

3D ethics	1st dimension: personal ethics	2nd dimension: social ethics	3rd dimension: anthropological ethics
Type of obligation	Virtue	Justice	Sustainability
Subject	The individual (personal obligations)	Community (interpersonal obligations)	Humanity (transgenerational obligations)
Object	Acts	Laws	The world
Obligation framework	Personal conscience	The rule of law	International governance
Type of responsibility	Moral responsibility	Legal responsibility	Social responsibility
Generator of responsibility	One's own ills and the pain of others	Illegal acts and injustice	Negative impacts and systemic unsustainability
Regulation mode	Morality	Law	Politics

TABLE II.4.2
Four kinds of regulation of collective action: hybrid regulation (Vallaeys)

Ethics	Non-programmed self-regulation: personal undertaking	I oblige myself	My law
Market	Non-programmed hetero-regulation: systemic feedback	Necessity obliges us	No law
Law	Programmed hetero-regulation: legal coercion	The law obliges us	Hard law
Partnership	Programmed self-regulation: mutual obligation	We oblige ourselves	Soft law

ORGANIZATIONAL SOCIAL RESPONSIBILITY STANDARDS: IS IT ENOUGH TO AVOID NEGATIVE IMPACTS?

Our philosophical reconstruction of a definition of social responsibility in terms of co-responsibility (for negative social and environmental impacts arising systemically from our collective lifestyle) is not an ad hoc invention but corresponds to an international consensus stated clearly in the ISO 26000 social responsibility standard (2010): an organization's social responsibility is its responsibility for impacts in its local and global social environment. Nonetheless, since impacts are not acts, nobody can assume this responsibility alone without linking up with other stakeholders. This inherently collective dimension of social responsibility is still not very well understood.

An ethical sensitivity for the traceability of links between individual acts and global impacts is, however, developing. The prioritization of environmental unsustainability and economic globalization injustices in the international public agenda is making us increasingly aware of the footprints left by our daily acts of purchase, transport, consumption, production, and so on. We are learning to develop ethical concerns for issues that are not necessarily directly visible to us. Is the way I shop sustaining an unfair system of exploiting workers without rights? Does my transport increase carbon emissions into the atmosphere? Does my work promote collusion between the sciences and the private interests of multinationals? By asking questions, we increasingly demand more socially responsible management from the companies, organizations and institutions with which we are associated.

A number of standards for good business practices have been developed in recent decades (ISO 14000, EMAS, SD 21000, AA 1000, SA 8000, SGE 21, GLOBAL GAP, GRI, Dow Jones Sustainability Index, ISO 26000, and so on). These standards define the best management practices for organizations to follow, according to their own core business and irrespective of the laws of their state. These standards are voluntary (since they are not laws), but the combined pressure of customers, investors, governments, professionals, managers, and so on makes them universal. They are often defined by experts, sometimes in multi-stakeholder round-table discussions and even in lengthy negotiations between public and private national and international social stakeholders, as was the case for ISO 26000 (Capron et al., 2011). These standards endeavour to acquire legitimacy in terms of ethical relevance (the definition of universally good actions) and technical effectiveness (evaluable and successful quality management). They also endeavour to supplement, as 'soft law', the inevitable inadequacies of the 'hard law' of states, which are limited to legislating at the national level even though problems now occur globally. It nonetheless remains clear that soft law should complement or anticipate, not replace, hard law.

Universities are now entering this dynamic of regulated good practice and are beginning to formulate, as well as their own socially responsible initiatives, management tools intended to serve as a model and paradigm: STARS in the USA, LIFE in the UK, AISHE in Holland, PLAN VERT in France and Sustainability and Social Responsibility Reporting in Spain, not to mention the United Nations Academic Impact initiative (2010) and the Principles for Responsible Management Education applying to business schools. Latin America, since the early years of the new century, has also invested efforts in promoting USR, culminating in the publication of guidelines entitled *Responsabilidad Social Universitaria: Manual de Primeros Pasos* (Vallaeys et al., 2009).

Does this mean that all is well and that we can trust this voluntary movement of organizations abiding by increasingly socially responsible standards for a more just and sustainable world? In fact, if one examines these rules and the organizations that claim to practise them a little more deeply, it becomes apparent that they merely define 'best practices' for each organization to implement in isolation in 'their' management process with 'their' employees and 'their' stakeholders. Since this, no doubt, promotes more virtuous behaviour within organizations (good environmental practices, gender equity in leadership positions, better treatment of employees, participation in acts of solidarity with vulnerable populations, and so on), we can certainly speak of greater *moral responsibility* on the part of organizations concerned about CSR. Nonetheless, much remains before this moral responsibility is converted into the kind of *social responsibility* that will bring about changes in the entire social field – not just within organizations, but both between them and over and above them.

Current social responsibility standards do not encourage, over and above best practices, any movement towards inter- and transorganizational co-responsibility partnerships that would break with the current unjust and unsustainable system and result in social innovations capable of overcoming the chronic negative impacts of the 'global risk society' (Beck, 1986). For example, they encourage reductions in the carbon footprints of individual organizations but do not foster the implementation of new economic systems, such as the 'circular economy' or the 'economy of functionality', which require inter- and transorganizational management. The question remains: How can we expect to reduce our overall carbon footprint if we persist with an economic system that is fuelled by a focus on ever-growing sales and planned obsolescence?

The philosophical error of social responsibility standards is to confuse acts with their systemic impacts. Such confusion condemns to failure any attempt to address the root causes of systemic adverse impacts, because sustainability cannot be ensured merely by asking a few stakeholders to behave. On the contrary, good deeds can hide bad impacts (greenwashing) and bad impacts – like systemic impacts – need a reorganization of the system (political co-responsibility) and not just good initiatives within an unchanged system (ineffective philanthropy). Considering just the problem of USR: What use is it to adopt initiatives regarding a sustainable campus if the economic faculty continues to teach neoclassical economics that ignores environmental costs? What good is it implementing solidarity projects with indigenous populations if we continue to reject non-Western medicine in medical schools? What is the point of talking about socially responsible management at the university if we fail to address the underlying epistemic prejudices that have led modernity to its current state of unsustainable social and environmental development?

We can easily criticize CSR for being little more than discourse that barely changes the realities of the human exploitation of other humans and the chronic destruction of the habitability of our planet (AFL-CIO, 2013). But so too can we accuse USR of making superficial changes that barely reduce the 'blind intelligence' of academics and scientists, so expert in their tiny disciplinary niche that they fail to see the negative impacts they are generating in the transdisciplinary social fabric (Morin, 2004). As long as university USR evades transdisciplinarity, it will fail to suppress the main negative impact of university education. Yet fostering transdisciplinarity requires a reorganization of the entire education, research and knowledge management structure.

WHAT FORM SHOULD USR TAKE?

It is evident that we need a more rational and more coherent theory of USR than currently exists. We will remain close to the core definition of responsibility for

impacts, bearing in mind, moreover, that, since impacts are social, they cannot be managed alone. From there, we can suggest that *social responsibility should consist of a dynamic partnership for transforming a system that is reproducing the wrong impacts in which the university is participating.* The unifying thread in a definition of USR therefore reflects types of university impacts and the associated risks. The specificity of USR in relation to the social responsibility of other organizations (particularly corporations) depends on the specificity of university impacts, which in turn depend on what universities do, with whom they do this, who they affect and how they participate in the goal of all social responsibility, which is the local and global, social and environmental sustainability of society as a whole.

What is the university really doing? What and who are affected? What is its role in the current world crisis of human planetary unsustainability? Is it aggravating the crisis or does it, in fact, open up windows of opportunity? How does it reproduce or reduce social inequalities transmitted via each tranche of newly admitted students? How can the university be an agent of social change, weave new networks and help external social stakeholders to build new knowledge and new processes for equitable and sustainable development? If the university is functioning as a cloister, how can it project its learning beyond its walls? If the university is promoting knowledge and education that is entirely divorced from its social context, how can it become anchored in its territory? What attitudes does it promote in its academic and non-academic staff, what values does it foster, what processes does it encourage? Universities have to answer all these questions if they want to take social responsibility beyond the sententious and pompous speeches and meaningless social commitment statements that barely affect institutional routine. To help members of the academic community to respond to the questions listed above, it is necessary to identify the impacts and risks associated with the daily routines of the university and to consider how to promote reflection and initiatives in favour of positive impacts from the university community (managers, administrators, researchers, lecturers and students).

Following a dual organizational–academic axis, we can distinguish between four types of impact that are of relevance to the university (Figure II.4.1):

- internal organizational impacts affecting the university's community and the environment (organizational impacts);
- academic impacts related to educating people (educational impacts);

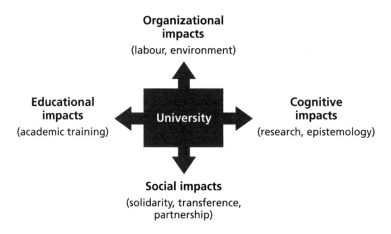

Organizational
impacts
(labour, environment)

Educational
impacts
(academic training)

University

Cognitive
impacts
(research, epistemology)

Social impacts
(solidarity, transference,
partnership)

FIGURE II.4.1 Four kinds of university impact

- academic impacts related to building knowledge (cognitive impacts);
- external organizational impacts affecting society in general (social impacts).

ORGANIZATIONAL IMPACTS

Like any other employer, the university has an impact on the lives of its community, including its administrative staff, academics and students. The way in which it organizes its routine tasks also has environmental impacts, in the form of waste, deforestation, energy costs, transport costs, and so on. Organizational impacts affect both people and the environment, and the responsible university is concerned with its social and environmental footprint. What are the values that we live by from day to day on the campus? How can we live in the university in a responsible way, caring for nature and for the dignity and well-being of the university community?

EDUCATIONAL IMPACTS

The university provides education to young people and professionals and has a bearing on their ethics and values and their way of interpreting the world and behaving in it. It also has an impact on codes of ethics and, consciously or otherwise, guides the definition of the professional ethics and social roles of individual disciplines. Responsible universities ask what kind of professionals and citizens they are shaping and also reflect on the proper organization of education that ensures socially responsible students. What kind of professionals and people are we educating? How should we structure our educational system to build citizens who care for sustainable human development? Will our graduates be able and willing to redirect the currently unstable and unjust course of global development or will they simply want to find a job?

COGNITIVE IMPACTS

Universities guide the production of knowledge and have a bearing on the definition of what we socially call truth, science, rationality, legitimacy, utility, education, and so on. They incentivize (or not) the fragmentation and separation of knowledge by delimiting the scope of each specialism or course. They consolidate the relationship between technoscience and society, enabling (or not) social control and the appropriation of knowledge. They influence the definition and selection of problems to be placed on the scientific agenda. Responsible universities ask about the kind of knowledge they produce, its social relevance and its beneficiaries. What kind of knowledge are we producing, why and for whom? What kind of science do we foster – a democratic science or a science in the hands of the elite? What knowledge should we produce, and how can we disseminate it to meet the cognitive deficits that hinder sustainable development?

SOCIAL IMPACTS

The university is a social referent that may (or may not) foster progress, build social capital, prepare students for outside realities, provide access to knowledge, and so on. A university may close in on itself and act as an 'academic cloister' in imparting knowledge unrelated to its immediate context. It may want to just imitate what is done internationally and be unconcerned for its immediate surroundings. Alternatively, it may be anchored and deeply bound to its surroundings and wish to help solve its specific problems. The responsible university asks how it can contribute to societal development and to resolving its fundamental problems: What role can it play in the development of society, with whom and why? How can the university, given its function and specific expertise, participate in social progress and promote education and knowledge for territorial social responsibility? With whom should universities associate to achieve territorial social responsibility?

Impacts, in general, imply risk: the risk of failing to comply with a mission, of being incongruent in declarations (for instance, regarding commitment to society and to excellence) and in actions, of failing to perceive the systematic reproduction and proliferation of social and environmental pathologies. Visualizing negative impacts is essential for an organization to be able to assume its social responsibility. Like any responsible person, a responsible organization is attentive to what it does, prevents potential adverse events, remains vigilant and takes precautions to avoid regret.

The statement that the university in itself and of itself is socially responsible given its educational and scientific goals is entirely misleading. Even well-meaning intentions to do good can produce negative impacts. Just as a law may be unjust, so too can education fail to educate and science fail to solve human problems. No organization is immune to the negative impacts that it generates in its social and environmental surroundings. If our universities educate the professionals and leaders of our currently socially and environmentally unsustainable world, then, given how they teach and generate knowledge, they are certainly co-responsible for the social pathologies they induce. Guilty, maybe not, but co-responsible, yes!

The negative impacts (Figure II.4.2) that threaten the relevance and congruence of the university function are, in fact, powerful prods to waken, warn and motivate us to do something creative, different and innovative to change daily life on campuses, in classrooms, in research laboratories and in our social interactions with external agents. They should serve as a compass, so that we do not become complacent, even when we can be proud to comply with good practices (which, happily, do exist in universities).

But the battle against negative impacts has to be managed rationally. Enabling the university to be vigilant with regard to incongruences and the risk of producing negative impacts are four basic processes that avoid, in turn, the four pitfalls of the irresponsible organization: corruption, autism, blindness and egocentrism. These processes are as follows:

● *Good university governance (or good government).* Defining and complying in a consistent manner with the organizational mission, implementing a code of ethics and creating an independent committee responsible for promoting and monitoring compliance, complying with the highest international labour, social and environmental standards as well as with national laws, ensuring a good workplace climate, combating discrimination and gender inequality, defending human rights, reporting results in a transparent and reliable way – these are just some recommendations promoted in USR management instruments, which aim essentially to combat *corruption* in the organization.

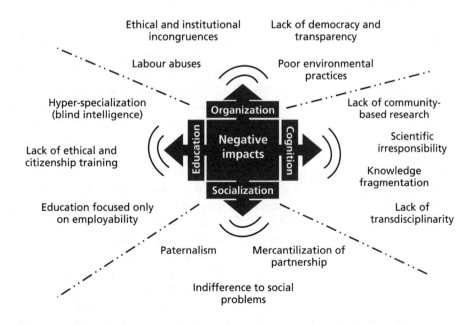

FIGURE II.4.2 **Possible negative impacts of universities**

- *Dialogue and accountability for stakeholders.* The stakeholder model views the university as an open space where interests and risks intersect for many individuals belonging (or not) and related (or not) to the university community, and affected (or not) by its performance and in turn having (or not) the power to affect performance. The university must properly respond to its stakeholders, establish a transparent and democratic relationship with them and reliably and honestly report the outcomes of joint decisions. It must listen to internal stakeholders (students, fixed-term and permanent lecturers, researchers and administrative staff) and external stakeholders (alumni, local communities, suppliers, the State, employers, non-governmental organizations [NGOs] and other universities). This process of socially responsible regulation through dialogue reduces the risk of *autism* in the organization.
- *Self-diagnosis of environmental and social impacts.* The social responsibility management philosophy invites universities to take stock of the possible consequences of their strategies and actions on persons, society and the environment. In promoting sustainable development, the university must become aware of its internal and external impacts on society and the environment, and must either resolve the problems diagnosed or mitigate them to a legally and socially acceptable level. Without adequate and ongoing self-diagnosis by the members of the university community itself, very little can be done to change established habits and foster improvements. Indeed, without measurement, improvement is difficult. Social responsibility thus becomes a management policy that forces the university to examine itself and to responsibly assume the risks of negative impacts. Self-diagnosis, because it is democratic and transparent, is also crucial as a way to practise good governance and to listen to, enter into a dialogue with and render accounts to community stakeholders. In this way, the risk of *blindness* in the organization is reduced.
- *Local social and environmental alliances for sustainable development.* Compliance with the university's mission and values, impact management and stakeholder participation combined lead from a reactive to a proactive logic in two areas: first, an involvement in solving social problems in the university environment; and, second, social anchorage and the creation of networks and alliances aimed at jointly tackling social problems. This partnership strategy for social responsibility – not only in the university as such, but also in the territory in which it operates – will be sustainable if external participation by the university yields returns in the form of better education, better campus management, better scientific innovation and the creation of more relevant knowledge. The constitution of alliances for local development does not mean one-off philanthropic gestures. USR, in overriding the arrogance of the deep-rooted belief that the university is the only source of knowledge, helps universities to build networks with other stakeholders (local authorities, NGOs, businesses, local communities, central government, international organizations, national and international universities, and so on) so as to achieve more ambitious social transformation goals. USR thus helps fight against the risk of *egocentrism* in the organization.

This last process tends to be overlooked, although it is, in fact, essential for a single, simple reason: no one can effectively control 'their' impacts on their own, whether eliminating them or mitigating them. As we have seen, as social agents we become 'entangled' in impacts that draw us into social networks shared with many other local, national and global stakeholders. It would be unrealistic to think that organizations operating in isolation could solve their unsustainable carbon footprint problem or the problem of the reproduction of poverty among those most marginalized by the current economic system. If social responsibility is responsibility for impacts on society and the environment (and this is the only precise definition of social responsibility that we have), any volition to deal with these impacts requires partnership with other stakeholders to try to redirect systemic processes that exceed the possibilities of an organization acting alone. Thus, organizational social responsibility, when properly understood, leads to a duty of partnership and of alliance-building for just and sustainable development. In other words, it leads to *territorial social responsibility* between partners located – depending on the extent of alliances and the problems to be resolved – in a specific local, regional, national, international or even global arena. It is pointless to consider social responsibility as an issue for an organization to deal with in isolation, as if it were the simple moral responsibility of performing good deeds and refusing to perform unlawful and unjust deeds. Responsibility is either social, that is, shared by all, or individual; and when it is individual, it is simply moral or legal responsibility.

The four types of impact defined above enable us to define four socially responsible management areas for the university (Figure II.4.3).

FIGURE II.4.3 Four areas of social responsibility in universities

USR FOR A UNIVERSITY ANCHORED IN ITS TERRITORY AND PROMOTING PUBLIC AND DEMOCRATIC KNOWLEDGE AGAINST THE MERCANTILIZATION OF EDUCATION AND SCIENCE

In these times of financial liquefaction of the entire economy, everything is a good that can potentially be traded, and knowledge is no exception to this trend. Two ground-breaking innovations in higher education are currently presented as innocuous, although they may portend gloomy horizons for a university system that may eventually be controlled by transnational corporations: massive open online courses, and the triple helix (Etzkowitz and Leydesdorff, 1997) that brings the public and private sectors and universities together in a economic innovation model that promotes 'corporate science'.

Online courses – as offered by Stanford and Harvard Universities, MIT, and so on (the Coursera, Udacity and edX websites) – are currently free and claim to transcend the walls of the faculty to ensure access to the best knowledge by all; however, they also unintentionally represent a knowledge model that is uprooted and unanchored and also, just like any purchasable commodity, capable of being produced and disseminated, irrespective of any associated history, location, language or social context. The teaching–learning process is thus optimized as a flow of uniform information made available to the greatest possible number of equally uniform students. The hidden curriculum behind this model is the denial of the personal and unique nature of the teaching–learning process as a *trans*formative and not just an *in*formative process. Valued knowledge is that which can be unanchored from territorial and intersubjective conditions of production and comprehension. On the horizon too is the disappearance of university diversity worldwide, and also the domination of English (already depleted as 'globish') and the rise of the monopolization of higher education by multinationals.

The triple-helix model, meanwhile, has the hidden – or maybe not so hidden – agenda of the privatization of knowledge through public and private demand for 'profitable' science. Markets undoubtedly have a role to play in promoting social welfare improvements and innovations. But the profitable exploitation of certain goods or services always requires that free public access be expressly prohibited to ensure sale and not free use. So once science becomes a commodity, it is no longer a common good or a transparent democratic activity open to the criticisms of peers (Apel, 1973; Habermas, 1981). The privatized commercial use of science, a direct contradiction of a production process that requires free examination and universal criticism, is only possible if we abandon the desire for true knowledge legitimized by an open community of scientists existing in an 'open society' (Popper, 1945) and if we instead practise a science that seeks to make or do, not a science that seeks knowledge. Naturally, scientists who seek knowledge, and especially the whistleblowers who warn about the dangers of scientific innovations, are systematically marginalized by the triple helix.

Against this commodification of education and science, USR is constructed as the model of a university anchored in its territory, open to dialogue, concerned about its local and global social and environmental impacts and active in promoting democratically produced science as a public and non-commodified good. USR encourages ongoing self-reflection by the academic community regarding epistemic horizons and the repercussions of its task. A 'green' university cares for its people and environment, aspires to worldwide academic diversity, rejects monopolies and the standardization of knowledge production, and encourages sustainable and equitable learning and research in communities of knowledge. There is no indication that its contribution to the universal cognitive and spiritual progress of humanity might be less than that of the model that holds science and knowledge to be commercial goods. It is time for universities to choose which model of society they aspire to. Here lies their moral responsibility regarding social responsibility.

REFERENCES

AFL–CIO (2013) 'Responsibility Outsourced: Social Audits, Workplace Certification and Twenty Years of Failure to Protect Worker Rights'. Retrieved July 4, 2013 from http://www.aflcio.org/content/download/77061/1902391/CSReport+FINAL.pdf.

Apel, K.O. (1973) *Transformation der Philosophie*. Frankfurt: Suhrkamp Verlag.

Beck, U. (1986) *Risikogesellschaft*. Frankfurt: Suhrkamp Verlag.

Capron, M., Quairel-Lanoizelée, F. and Turcotte, M.F. (2011) *ISO 26000: une norme 'hors-norme'? Vers une conception mondiale de la responsabilité sociétale*. Paris: Economica.

Dewey, J. (1984 [1927]) *The Public and its Problems*. Carbondale, IL: Southern Illinois University Press.

Etzkowitz, H. and Leydesdorff, L. (ed.) (1997) *Universities in the Global Economy: A Triple Helix of University–Industry–Government Relations*. London: Cassell Academic.

Habermas, J. (1981) *Theorie des Kommunikativen Handels*. Frankfurt: Suhrkamp Verlag.

Jonas, H. (1979) *Das Prinzip Verantwortung*. Frankfurt: Insel Verlag.

Luhmann, N. (1975) *Macht*. Stuttgart: Lucius & Lucius Verlagsgesellschaft.

Morin, E. (2004) *La Méthode 6: l'éthique*. Paris: Seuil.

Ostrom, E. (1990) *Governing the Commons. The Evolution of Institutions for Collective Action*. New York: Cambridge University Press.

Popper, K. (1945) *The Open Society and its Enemies*. London: Routledge.

Serres, M. (1990) *Le contrat naturel*. Paris: Editions François Bourin.

Vallaeys, F. (2011) *Les Fondements Éthiques de la Responsabilité Sociale*. PhD thesis, Université Paris Est. Retrieved July 4, 2013 from http://blog.pucp.edu.pe/item/149507/these-de-doctorat-les-fondements-ethiques-de-la-responsabilite-sociale.

Vallaeys, F., de la Cruz, C. and Sasia, P. (2009) *Responsabilidad Social Universitaria, Manual de Primeros Pasos*. México: McGraw-Hill Interamericana Editores and Banco Interamericano de Desarrollo. Retrieved July 4, 2013 from http://idbdocs.iadb.org/wsdocs/getdocument.aspx?docnum=35125786.

II.5

ENGAGEMENT BEYOND THE THIRD MISSION: THE EXPERIENCE OF ALBUKHARY INTERNATIONAL UNIVERSITY

Dzulkifli Razak and Evangelos Afendras

THE MALAYSIAN CASE: INTRODUCTION

In 2008, the Ministry of Higher Education of Malaysia decided to establish the Division of Industry and Community Liaison at all public universities in the country. This was in addition to the existing Divisions of Academic and International Affairs, and Research and Innovation. Like the other two, the new division is also headed by a deputy vice-chancellor.

This marked the beginning of a new phase for tertiary education in the country, at least at the level of the public sector. Community services that had at one time been introduced as part of the university's mission were now being expounded conceptually into what is known as 'community engagement', of which the industry is a subset. While the traditional missions of any Malaysian university are generally understood to lie within the realm of teaching, research and services, the latter area is being expanded to include full-scale 'collaborative' activities with their own research and teaching dimensions.

In doing this, the 'third (civic) mission' of Malaysian universities is seeking to establish a mutually beneficial relationship with the community and display a stronger commitment to the welfare of the surrounding society. Indeed, several Malaysian universities are located in relatively underserved areas so that they can develop a closer rapport and more meaningful relations with the community at large. This includes creating the relevant industry to serve the needs of the community by using the universities' expertise and facilities. The idea that a university is an ivory tower detached from the everyday needs and life of the surrounding community is now waning following the move taken by the Ministry of Higher Education.

Also waning is the 'tokenism' that was previously related to community activities but was biased only towards benefiting the universities, especially in the areas of research and publication. In the case of teaching, the university assumed a 'university knows best' stance and proceeded to 'teach' the community in a unidirectional way. Similarly, services were being rendered without an in-depth understanding of the corresponding needs of the community. All this was seemingly being done at a superficial level in the pursuit of academic excellence and intellectual 'truth' at the expense of the community. By moving beyond the third mission under the Office of the Deputy Vice-Chancellor, Division of Industry and Community Liaison, universities are now more conscious of the participatory roles of the various stakeholders in nurturing education in the country's development partners. Partnering, promoting and protecting the public in a more direct way is now increasingly being regarded as the social responsibility of universities – 'university social responsibility'. More so in modern societies where knowledge is seen as key to progress, not just economically, universities are called upon to play this 'new and expanded' role beyond the third mission.

Generally, this role revolves around the major themes of (1) education, (2) economic enhancement, (3) healthcare, (4) environment ethics, and (5) heritage and culture. Where possible, these themes are dealt with in an integrated or transdisciplinary way so that a greater impact or outcome can be realized for all partners. One way to do this is by adopting a sustainable livelihood approach (SLA), as discussed below. The overall aim is to build awareness, partnerships and capacities by directly engaging the community within a systematic and methodic framework. That said, the heart of this mission is the same as for any part of the academy: to discover, develop, disseminate and transfer knowledge for the benefit of society.

THE SLA

Working beyond the third, particularly civic, mission of universities can be realized through the SLA that is currently being adopted by the Albukhary International University (AIU) in Malaysia, especially in the context of alleviating poverty. The two key components of the SLA are:

- a *framework* that helps in understanding the complexities of poverty;
- a set of *principles* to guide action to address and overcome poverty (International Fund for Agricultural Development, undated).

The SLA seeks to provide a way of thinking about the livelihoods of poor people that will stimulate debate and reflection on the many factors that affect livelihoods, the way they interact and their relative importance within a particular setting. This should help in identifying more effective ways to support livelihoods and reduce poverty.

In addition, the SLA has seven guiding principles that are very much in line with the third mission to engage the community. People, rather than the resources they use or their governments, are the main concern. The guiding principles are therefore as follows:

- *Be people-centred.* The SLA begins by analysing people's livelihoods and how they change over time. The people themselves actively participate throughout the project cycle.
- *Be holistic.* The SLA acknowledges that people adopt many strategies to secure their livelihoods and that many actors are involved, for example the private sector, ministries, community-based organizations and international organizations.
- *Be dynamic.* The SLA seeks to understand the dynamic nature of livelihoods and what influences them.
- *Build on strengths.* The SLA builds on people's perceived strengths and opportunities rather than focusing on their problems and needs. It supports existing livelihood strategies.
- *Promote micro–macro links.* The SLA examines the influence of policies and institutions on livelihood options and highlights the need for policies to be informed by insights from the local level and by the priorities of those who are poor.
- *Encourage broad partnerships.* The SLA counts on broad partnerships drawing on both the public and private sectors.
- *Aim for sustainability.* Sustainability is important if poverty reduction is to be lasting.

The guidelines generally do not prescribe solutions or dictate methods. Instead, they are flexible and adaptable to diverse local conditions, which makes the approach appropriate for projects that go beyond the third dimension.

In the case of AIU, participation in the SLA is compulsory for all students as part of the core curriculum. It is organized into a number of projects, each extending over 10 trimesters (that is, over a three-year period), in which the students work in groups of 10–15 to implement the projects with the community. They are equipped with theoretical as well as practical dimensions so that they can draw on the interplay of the various main factors to effect change in the community. Students are able to identify the constraints and opportunities present in the community, as well as engage and empower the community to arrive at the most desirable 'solutions'.

In one case study, where the community is made up of indigenous Kensiu people, some of the SLA outcomes have been as follows:

- *Entrepreneurial aspects.* Identify skilled handicraft makers from the Kensiu community and streamline production by focusing on specific bamboo products; source the appropriate machines to enhance the production of indigenous handicrafts; connect the community to ready suppliers for the commercialization of the handicrafts.
- *Empowerment aspects.* Plant honey bamboo around the community as the first step in being self-sufficient in the supply of bamboo and in moving towards a 'Bamboo Village'; empower more community members to learn new types of bamboo handicrafts; regarding health, conduct awareness campaigns on the dangers of tobacco, alcohol and glue-sniffing.
- *Sustainability aspects.* Involve the Department of Orang Asli Development and local community leaders; create 'Bamboo Village' eco-tourist projects; set up an awareness programme for better hygiene and sanitary practices; increase access to and awareness of the importance of education – including the compilation of a 'Kensiu dictionary.'
- *Triple Bottom Line.* Planet – the community is now able to live in a more ecologically sustainable environment; People – healthier lifestyles will be adopted and a better quality of life achieved; Prosperity (Profit) – the community will become more entrepreneurial and empowered by learning new skills and getting access to the marketplace for additional income.

The overall reach over a 2-month period has involved about 20 families in the community. This is expected to expand over time as the project develops even further.

COMPETENCY FRAMEWORK AND MEASUREMENTS

In order to help implement the SLA in a systematic

and methodical way, AIU is developing a specialized competency framework called the AIU Humaniversity Competency Framework (HCF). This is aimed at developing a set of core competencies that will enable students to better engage with the community in achieving the right outcomes. It is also intended to foster a consistent documentation and reporting format, as well as a reliable monitoring and assessment system. This is an effort to make the third mission more acceptable based on a more defined framework and measurement to support it.

The AIU HCF is designed to ground the university's vision and mission, as well as the core values based on the concept of 'the humaniversity' – which is the AIU tagline. The HCF serves as the foundation for student development efforts underpinned by a comprehensive, well-balanced, structured and standardized approach. It addresses both the academic and the behavioural development components. The latter is assessed separately throughout the students' years at AIU to complement the academic aspect, but it does not supersede it (Figure II.5.1).

As a working definition, the 'competency model' is intended to provide 'a structured guide enabling the identification, evaluation and development of targeted behaviours in individuals'. It encompasses 'a set of observable, measurable and improvable behaviours comprising of knowledge, skills, abilities and other characteristics, including values (KSAV)' (see https://www.opm.gov/policy-data-oversight/human-capital-management/reference-materials/#url=Glossary).

The university believes that the competency model, as designed for AIU, can enhance further the third mission based on desired behavioural qualities and values, to take the mission beyond what it is today. The five domains in the AIU HCF are: beingness, togetherness, leadership and management skills, effective communication, and critical thinking. They collectively mirror the set of six core values of AIU that would facilitate their long-term engagement with society and industry. The five domains in the HCF are subdivided into a number of core competencies (Table II.5.1).

For example, under 'beingness' would be included aspects of personal development, emotional intelligence, and perseverance and resilience, whereas 'togetherness' would cover social awareness (local and global), interpersonal skills, teamworking, fair play, valuing diversity, compassion, being recreationally active and sustainability orientation. In all, there are 26 competencies that are further broken down to 'observable' criteria that allow them to be 'measured' on a five-level scale of proficiency (for example, the quality of being competent ranging from very unsatisfactory to outstanding). The purpose of this is to enable monitoring and assessment to be conducted as objectively as possible based on a set of 'scoring guidelines.' This then allows for the necessary 'interventions' to be carried out on a regular basis where indicated.

All these mechanisms are purposefully designed to ascertain not only whether students are well prepared to engage with the community but, equally importantly, can have a sustainable impact on the livelihood of the

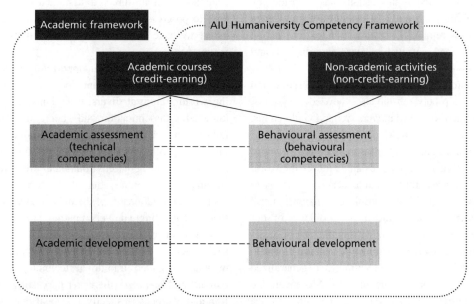

FIGURE II.5.1 **Behavioural competency assessment**
Source: © 2012 Albukhary International University & Deloitte Consulting Malaysia Sdn. Bhd.

TABLE II.5.1					
The domains and competencies of AIU's HCF					
AiU's Humaniversity Competency Framework					
	Domains				
	Beingness	Togetherness	Leadership and management skills	Effective communication	Critical thinking
Competencies	Personal development	Social awareness (local & global)	Demonstrating initiative and being proactive	Practical communication	Analytical and reasoning skills
	Perseverance and resilience	Interpersonal skills	Achievement orientation	Presentation skills	Conceptual creativity
	Emotional intelligence	Team working	Decision making	Facilitation skills	Problem solving
		Fair play	Planning and organising	Negotiation skills	Effective questioning
		Valuing diversity	Building effective teams		
		Compassion	Resourcefulness		
		Recreationally active	Time management		
		Sustainability orientation			
© 2012 Albukhary International University & Deloitte Consulting Malaysia Sdn. Bhd.					

community as a whole. This will be the foundation to go beyond the third mission. In so doing, it will create opportunities for research and innovation, and for various windows for learning and co-creating 'new' knowledge, while (re)discovering the old from within the community. In this respect, the aspect of knowledge diversity – with a special emphasis on local/traditional knowledge – is an important dimension of taking the third mission beyond what it is today.

In October 2012, AIU hosted an international conference on integrating knowledge diversity within the higher education system to understand this dimension further. The conference was organized on the assumption that, just as biodiversity has been the key to sustainability in nature, the diversity of knowledge systems must remain a significant ingredient in the maintenance and survival of our own distinct and unique cultures.

The conference addressed leadership issues and the relationship between modern knowledge systems, as represented by the university, and indigenous, traditional and local knowledge systems that are part and parcel of the survival toolkit transcending the third mission involving communities and cultures the world over. It recognized that higher education today is in the throes of a crisis of multiple dimensions: moral disengagement vis-à-vis the major problems of our age; uselessness of course contents in the face of societies' challenges; increasing student cynicism related to the ideals of a university education; and generalized reluctance to provide public funding. Moreover, the university systems in Asia, Africa and South America are confronting a 'relevance deficit' associated with the uncritical appropriation of an imported hegemonic 'modern' knowledge system based on a region-specific and culture-bound epistemology (first in Europe and now the USA) with non-transferable cognitive validity.

All these are factors that call for the third mission to be widened as an attempt to reconcile the role of modern-day universities and the community at large. Otherwise, the university, as a system dedicated to knowledge, will be forced to continue with the processes of colonization and homogenization instead of encouraging the resumption of the processes that have been so displaced or halted. Many of these processes have generated violence, corrupting all societies, as all are forced to assume a single universal path to progress. This is the biggest problem. This is where we have to go beyond the third mission as it is understood today.

This provides a singular opportunity to reconsider the sphere of traditional and local knowledges from the world's cultural diversity as a major agenda for knowledge dissemination and generation. This could not only unlock the wisdom of ages from the community in our collective quest for viable solutions to our shared concerns about environmental preservation and sustainable economies, but also, more importantly, lead to an abandonment of the delusionary assumption that there is a single universal path to progress.

During the conference, several speakers highlighted such practical wisdom and science that infused much of what is called traditional technology, including *qanauts* and *khettaras* (the water-harvesting systems of Iran and Morocco, respectively), local pharmaceutical and pharmacological knowledge (in Asia and Africa), and architectural and home-building techniques as represented by the Malay house in Malaysia.

In furthering the cause of the third mission, some of the proposed affirmation expressed at the conference could be of relevance to carving a new meaning in the forging of closer community–university engagement. This includes:

- the integration of local knowledge as practised by indigenous communities within the framework of academic knowledge taught in modern universities;
- the indigenization of the academic curriculum after having decided that it was no longer relevant to use knowledge created in other social and cultural contexts;
- the participation of university students within communities designated as knowledge sites as an integral complement of their academic work;
- the location of universities that have decided to place themselves within communities and orient their research and teaching programmes in the direction of communities and their needs.

The conference further affirmed that universities are an integral part of society and that it is incumbent upon them to become an effective instrument for achieving sustainable societies beyond the third mission. The latter challenge can only be achieved if universities commit themselves to a thorough reappraisal of the indigenous cultural inheritances of our societies and what they have to offer in terms of sustainable solutions as they engage the community in more equitable and substantial ways.

PREAMBLE TO OUR INTERNAL DIALOGUE

We address here what we consider to be central issues in fulfilling the third mission of universities, by examining prerequisites for developing a strategy and setting it opposite our current practice. This is a perspective that derives from our own special situation but, *mutatis mutandis,* may apply to others in similar situations as well.

We turn first to the identification of our reference community and the engagement processes and objectives. Next, we focus on our external environment, including the reference community, the array of stakeholders with their respective needs and requirements as well as their relative power over higher education institutions (HEIs), the organizational needs of HEIs, including organizational learning, and other matters. Models of organizational management are key to strategic planning and are discussed in the context

of conflicting paradigms and trends in practice. The external environment can be seen as the global forces prevalent in our time that have left us with a deep crisis of human values, in a financial abyss with an exacerbation of differences among the haves and the have nots, with a natural environment that is under direct threat and with an uncertain future for all.

We then reflect on the learning issues and approaches, complex precisely because of constraints resulting from our institutional position of limited autonomy in pursuing our vision. If we are to live up to our role as both an international university and one with a strong sense of the space beyond the third mission, we are faced with a Herculean task.

OUR REFERENCE COMMUNITY

An important and specific challenge posed for our university, a truly international one since 80% of our students are not local, lies in defining our reference community. Is it limited to our immediate geographical environs or should it more appropriately refer to our 'catchment area', something that encompasses our students' (and employees') communities? We need even to change the prevalent terminology and not speak of 'foreign' students, as this already casts them outside 'our' community. Addressing the issue of our reference community takes us through expanding circles of engagement:

- the immediate one, our physical neighbourhood, within walking distance, meaningful because it is the space within which our students, and many of our staff, move and relate, frequenting shops, interacting with neighbours and performing their religious worship; it is also the focus of some of our community projects such as tuition for school children, the orphanage adjacent to our campus, support for the disabled, and so forth;
- the city/state where we are located and, *de facto,* the geographically proximal area where crucial projects are running (SLAs and microfinance);
- our host country, Malaysia, where we move and interact in various capacities (administrative, financial, educational and political);
- Southeast Asia/ASEAN, from which we draw large numbers of our students and with which we share much from the environmental, cultural and historical points of view;
- our students' places of origin (50 nations at present and many sub-national regions);
- the global locus of sustainability and action.

Obviously, our approach should be one whereby we start with the inner circle and expand outward as both staff and students develop their requisite abilities. This will also afford us the time and effort needed to plan for our geographically more distant engagement.

Now, if we are to change in substance and not merely in nomenclature, what ideological or organizational changes should we develop and implement? How do we tap into and integrate this tremendous wealth of perspectives, values and cognitive systems into our learning and teaching (and assessing and managing and planning and …)? What is the framework of pedagogic approaches within which we can achieve all this? In carrying on with prevalent imported educational practices while gazing at traditional sources of wisdom, do we risk retaining tools from the 'other' universe, the one we are trying to leave behind, while attempting to fulfil our lofty objectives?

GOVERNANCE AND ORGANIZATIONAL MATTERS

In reflecting upon the transitional university by using our own university as a case study, we are forced to consider the contradictory forces and tendencies, the dialectics of operating a vision within a real world, a world of constraints, external controls and powers, a world where we have to overcome contextual obstacles and where we need to project our vision and persuade decision-makers to adopt it. Our academic autonomy seems at best relative, indeed fragile, and at worst an illusion. Our instructional and other content is subject to strict administrative controls by the relevant ministry within its dominant perceptions of academia. It is also dependent, through our necessary operational finances, on external consent and is subject to continuous negotiation with the offices that control our *waqaf,* the charitable foundation behind our existence. The officers in charge are business people with perceptions and procedures that are not academic.

A vital part of our strategy is the development of the university itself as a learning organization, with learning approaches that encompass not only classroom pedagogy, or learning from practice while in the field, but, significantly, learning by the entire institution across all levels, tasks and functions – action research as well as action teaching and indeed action management. Engaged, indeed, the university must be, and if we are to embrace the community, the university community itself and the immediate stakeholders must be the first circle of engagement. Learning, then, starts 'backstage' in every organizational unit (Eikeland, 2012).

Within this context, what kinds of changes in internal organization can we envisage? Where do we start in identifying what is necessary and the process for attaining it? Universities, AIU included, are organizations, and general organizational management principles and findings ought to be considered in running it. To some of us, a process-relational rather than systems operational approach seems necessary (Watson, 2006).

Now, reflecting on this first circle of achieving empowerment and sustainable environmental and economic practice, where are we? We are still pondering our first steps towards sustainability within the process of also taking our first steps as a university. But these are essential steps to take before we go out to the 'community' lest we be perceived as hypocrites who preach and do not practise.

In their contribution to GUNi 4, Filho and Manolas (2012) surveyed a number of universities and the manner in which they were implementing sustainability programmes internally. Many alternative approaches are given as examples – University of British Columbia, for instance, has a 'Campus Sustainability Office'. So for us too, such options are on the table, but is it all a matter of creating yet another administrative unit or of deeper changes in mentality and 'action management'? How would such an effort be integrated and coordinated with the existing ones?

We are exploring pedagogical approaches and models of internal governance (as, at present, participation in governance on the part of either the students or the staff is mostly lacking), present patterns of decision-making and control, power and how to interface with various stakeholders in decision-making and finances.

ENGAGEMENT

We can now take stock of our trajectory and the distance remaining ahead. We have reached out to the nearby community with solid projects, but these are still *our* projects, conceived and initiated by us. However, we yearn for input, for a joint generation of knowledge, and not merely passive participation. Yes, we serve the community; yes, our students forge their academic and ideological arsenal out there – but is something still missing?

It should be mentioned at this point that another essential element of our institutional identity, and engagement, is student recruitment – one of the most important processes in defining our connection with the 'other' communities. Students' socioeconomic statuses, as well as their academic quality, are the key selection criteria. Future engagement and employment or placement after graduation are also very important, otherwise we really may 'lose' students to the pull of market opportunities, or worse to unemployment. In any case, students' concern with 'jobs' or gainful employment when they graduate is something we have to support within our engagement strategy.

CURRICULA – 'FIRST MISSION' PEDAGOGIC PRACTICE

As we enter our third year of operation and see cohorts advance from language to foundation courses and the first subjects in a range of areas currently becoming available, matters of pedagogy come to the fore. Are we lugging with us, on our own and our learners' shoulders, vestiges of consumer industry trends in higher education, which many of us had hoped to jettison? How can we graduate students into this empowered space under the constraints of an industrial model of education, of the managerialist corporation where rules for behaviour reflect Taylorian assembly line practices and the knock-on constraints on thinking and relating? Are we trapped, some willingly, in the competing model of higher education that is emerging especially in North America, which is very much subject to the strict requirements of the industry, this in turn dictating the 'profile of the graduate' stripped of humanistic content, and with the power to enforce through reference to the 'job market' and other processes? Is questioning the dominance of this model to be interpreted as engaging in academic arrogance through knowledge? Or do we otherwise run the risk of replacing the tyranny of academic ivory towers with that of the Taylorian factory? Humanism and measurement – a cross-eyed vision?

The driving force for our students to learn, to be and to behave should be a passion for learning, being and doing good, not compulsion brought about by the obsessive measurement of every iota of their behavior, or by fear or even apprehension brought on by punishment. Pedagogy impacts on learners' values and skill sets. Is it, then, reasonable that we are at present being 'trained' how to teach by consultants who know demonstrably little about teaching? Does the much touted competency framework merely produce the illusion that something has been assessed?

Yet, we push forward with our development of approaches enhancing the reflective learning processes. Foundation subjects, ethics, current affairs, fieldwork on SLAs or projects on persons with disabilities have generated lively courses and are certainly preparing the soil for planting the seeds of thinking and feeling about sustainability and our interconnected humanity. Practice-based learning, which is what Eikeland is calling for, is eminently taking place.

LANGUAGES, COMMUNITY LANGUAGES, MEDIA OF INSTRUCTION AND WORKING LANGUAGES

English is presently AIU's 'medium of instruction', but Bahasa Melayu is used in the field through the intermediary of our local students and staff, and we will soon be introducing courses in it. Other languages are *de facto* part of our running projects, the outstanding example being Kensiu, an indigenous 'orang asli' language. A draft of Kensiu–Malay–English has been compiled, and additional working material will be elaborated to ensure language sustainability as well.

And more languages, world languages as tools and community languages for sustainability, will slowly be added over the next trimesters and will be oriented to community use. There is naturally a certain contradiction in running community programmes with a colonial language as the main medium of programme management and communication, and we have been addressing this issue in our planning; however, we are far from reaching an acceptable solution. The complexity of our situation, as mentioned above, lies in the delimitation of our boundaries, the definition of our community of reference. Herein also lies the great challenge: developing a dedicated programme that will cover a rich array of very different languages from 50 nations and more regions, utilizing our students as primary resources.

FUNDING: CONTEXTUAL FACTORS AND POWER RELATIONS

As mentioned above, our situation is precisely such that we cannot ignore the decisive powers of both our benefactor foundation or the control mechanisms or the Ministry of Higher Education's Quality Assessment office through the control they exercise over our structure, our content and our pedagogic approaches. Our choices have to be approved and authorized by them. Moreover, our context, the surrounding community, has its own culture, its own practices and its own image of who we are and what we do. Religion forms a very important part of this culture, and it is therefore incumbent on us to negotiate our beliefs and identity. The political landscape and dynamics in Malaysia at this point are in turmoil with imminent elections, and this too is defining the profile of our engagement.

CONCLUSION

Undertaking a journey beyond the third mission in a new, international university funded by philanthropy is like embarking on an Odyssey. Every day brings uncharted matters, challenging vistas. We have cleared some of the obstacles, we have learned much, yet much, most of it unknown, remains ahead. Part of the excitement! Part of the enchantment!

REFERENCES

Eikeland, O. (2012) 'Symbiotic Learning Systems: Reorganizing and Integrating Learning Efforts and Responsibilities Between Higher Educational Institutions (HEIs) and Work Places'. Retrieved September 6, 2013 from http://link.springer.com/search?query=Symbiotic+Learning+Systems%3A+Reorganizing+and+Integrating+Learning+Efforts+and+Responsibilities+Between+Higher+Educational+Institutions+%28HEIs%29+and+Work+Places.

Filho, W.L. and Manolas. E. (2012) 'Making sustainable development in higher education a reality: lessons learned from leading institutions'. In: GUNi, *Higher Education in the World 4. Higher Education's Commitment to Sustainability: from Understanding to Action.* Basingstoke: Palgrave Macmillan.

Watson, T. (2006) *Organising and Managing Work. Organisational, Managerial and Strategic Behaviour in Theory and Practice.* Harlow: Pearson-Longman.

II.6

REBUILDING UNIVERSITY SOCIAL ENGAGEMENT

Juan Ramón de la Fuente and Axel Didriksson

INTRODUCTION

Social engagement has become part of the ethos and the raison d'être of universities, as well as an ethical duty that creates a natural link between educational institutions and all sectors facing the emerging challenges of the 21st century and seeking to resolve serious issues regarding our basic needs.

Higher education must take the lead in society and promote the overall acquisition of knowledge to address global challenges, food security in all regions, climate change, water resource management, inter-cultural dialogue, renewable energy and population health. As such, continuous reflection regarding social commitment is the sign of the higher education systems of the future, where this commitment is understood as the service that education provides in terms of a public good. In this sense, the aim of public universities is not to serve private capital, but rather to become a catalyst for individual and social development and a source of critical and independent thinking.

The social commitment of the university encompasses many fields related to reproducing and perfecting the social model: equality, science, professional efficiency, culture and identity, ideological pluralism, social ethics, the conservation of historical memory and the universality of knowledge, and the formation of a critical mass. From this perspective, university social engagement is the connection between educational institutions and societies with the values, traditions and culture that give us our identities, and should remain the force that defines public universities as the critical conscience of our people.

REBUILDING A SENSE OF UNIVERSITY SOCIAL ENGAGEMENT

Economic globalization has brought about new patterns of production, consumption and commercialization that (1) disrupt all areas of daily life, (2) provide a new view of the nation state and geopolitical borders, (3) favour an unprecedented circulation of capital, goods

and people, and (4) incorporate the acquisition of knowledge, information and symbolic communication as the most important productive forces of the economy. Moreover, the science and technology revolution has had a profound cultural and economic impact.

Universities have a responsibility and a fundamental commitment to the goals and interests of a society that is moving towards a new profile. The educational and cultural functions of universities as well as their organic and historical identity make them a space in which to ponder the complexity of our times and reflect upon ourselves as fundamental pieces of the puzzle. On this point, it cannot be overlooked that universities:

> have a singular position in society, as they have extremely high density of management, creation and knowledge dissemination capacities. At a time of global challenges, universities are well placed to work on issues of human and social development on the global and local level. The role of higher education will determine the place of knowledge in providing solutions to these challenges. (Escrigas, 2009, p. 7)

The 21st century is an opportunity for universities to participate in building a new social design that favours the emergence of critical globalization processes resisting the hegemonic perspectives that tend to commercialize knowledge. It is imperative at this moment to assume that education is a public good, and as such must be distributed for the benefit of each and every sector of society.

The autonomous nature of institutions of higher education is a pillar of university social engagement in defining their policies and priorities. However, this involves designing alternatives aimed at ensuring social inclusion and coordination with national development, learning and innovation, and recognizing our multicultural nature. Hence it cannot be assumed that this is such an obvious proposition whose framework is universal and accepted by all; that would make it an article of faith. Rather, university social responsibility has a specific content depending on the concrete context in which a university exists, and on the framework of complex and historically and socially determined problems.

THE DEBATE SURROUNDING THE PUBLIC NATURE OF KNOWLEDGE

Knowledge has become the engine of new development, which opens up the possibility to extend the basis of support for the right to higher education, its universalization and the spread of knowledge and high-level learning in a socially extended way. In light of this, the central issue for universities is oriented towards the breakdown and redefinition of institutional borders between universities and society, as has occurred before. The central argument is not a stern defence of the type of university carrying out this transformation towards the socialization of knowledge and learning, but rather the social utility and the positive impact it generates for the welfare of citizens and communities.

In a knowledge democracy, the creation of wealth from assets related to science and technology or business innovation seeks assurance of high levels of quality and collective well-being for its people, as well as more profound and true democracy. In other words, it is about how a society freely decides how it is organized with the use of knowledge acquired.

With this, it can be said that each phase in building a society comes with different features and characteristics, with new tools and technologies, processes and products that give meaning to their cultural, social and political lives, and this is reflected in a certain stage of collective life that takes advantage of education, learning and knowledge, either very broadly or in favour of minority interests. Today, this is beginning to be decisive in countries' national and regional structures. The nature of these transition periods is crucial in defining the path to follow regarding the type of society to which we aspire.

From the perspective of the knowledge democracy, autonomous universities have a new direction to take. The previously developed theoretical construct shows that the overall organic structure of universities that decide to make serious, and even radical, changes begins to undergo transformation, to positively frame itself on the constitution as a knowledge production mode (Gibbons et al., 1997, 2001).

All this reinforces the idea that, going back to our main subject, the idea that public good and social responsibility should guarantee the existence and future of the university has seriously been thrown into doubt in a society dominated by the variables of a knowledge economy.

This is because, in the current conformation, products and inter-company, inter-institutional conglomerates are dominant, interwoven with a profit-seeking knowledge economy, in a polarized society, mired in recurring crises, with authoritarian and anti-democratic governments that constantly provoke social conflicts or wars.

However, a knowledge economy is mainly dependent upon scientific and technological production and social innovation. In these economies, science is not entirely dependent upon universities, but it does have a specific and unique role, mainly because of its ability to generate organized knowledge acquisition in certain disciplines or areas of academic or educational work, without which science could not exist in the modern sense. Without the contribution of universities to generating this knowledge acquisition, there could not be a knowledge economy (Didriksson, 2007; UNESCO, 2009).

It is therefore important to stress that current knowledge economies do not work (as was thought in the past) based on a direct and one-dimensional relationship between universities and companies with government support. The context of knowledge application has become somewhat more complex, especially because of the pervasive condition of the sustainability of knowledge as a public good and social benefit that can reach broader bases for development while still benefiting from marketing and commercialization, or even exclusive use by individuals.

> It therefore seems relevant to recall that saying a good (for example knowledge) is a public good, on the basis of the properties of non-excludability and non-rivalry, does not mean that this good must necessarily be produced by the state, that markets for it do not exist, or that its private production is impossible; it simply means that, considering the properties of the good, it is not possible to rely exclusively on a system of competitive markets to guarantee production efficiently. (Foray, 2006, p. 119)

Therefore, the production of this general social good, knowledge, and also the learning that enables the accumulation and innovation of knowledge in time and space, are crucial and essential. It is almost a paradox, as is almost everything we experience. The guarantee and manifestation of the autonomy of universities is thus essential for the accumulation of knowledge that is transformed into technologies, products and goods that are cumulative and standardized, and that generate most of the profits for the private sector, to such an extent as we have never before seen. And this is the basis of current knowledge economies.

THE DEBATE SURROUNDING THE DEFENCE OF THE UNIVERSITY AS A PUBLIC GOOD TO BUILD A DEMOCRATIC SOCIETY OF KNOWLEDGE

The university as a public good and a fundamental human right contributes to achieving higher levels of development and welfare in a democratic society of knowledge, understood as the organization of the State, society and its institutions, based on using knowledge, learning and education, all for the purpose of general welfare, equal development, justice and sustainability, and with the guarantee of the full democratic participation of its citizens.

The overall impact is multiple and of comprehensive benefit to society as a whole because public goods are not subject to competition or exclusion, but rather are a highly valuable social right. Even as an economic good, knowledge is 'unconditional,'[1] and markets do not have the ability to offer it as such, or in the required quantity or quality. Moreover, as a public good, higher education is not limited to purely achieving economic or labour goals, but can set its sights on cultural and democratic objectives, citizens, the expansion of knowledge and explanations of the dynamics of society and nature, to help provide solutions to fundamental problems of common interest. The risks of maintaining a wider reproduction of higher education as a commodity, excessively driven by all parties involved, implies an enormous danger for the essence of this level of study and for society as a whole.

The responsibility for ensuring this public good falls directly to public and State authorities, and to actors that must guarantee it, particularly teachers, researchers and students, on the basis of initiatives and guidance to defend the educational and academic public good. Boaventura de Sousa Santos (2005), among others, framed the following initiatives:

Confront the new with the new: for the democratization of university public good, in other words, the specific contribution of the university in defining and providing collective solutions for social, national and global problems.

– Strive to define the crisis: from conventional university knowledge to multi-university, multidisciplinary, contextualized and interactive knowledge, which is produced, distributed and consumed using new information and communication technologies. On the one hand, this has changed the relationship between knowledge and information and, on the other, it has changed the relationship between education and citizenship.

– Seek to define the university: a university only exists when there is undergraduate and postgraduate study, research and extension. Without these programmes, there may be higher education but it would not constitute a university.

– Regain legitimacy: the university must overcome the triple crises of hegemony (it no longer has a monopoly on research), legitimacy (it is perceived as an institution that blocks access for the most disadvantaged) and institution (because of the difficulties in preserving its autonomy under the pressure of market demands and because of the tendency to see universities as businesses), which have existed since the 1990s. This involves implementing reforms in line with a feasible national project that considers education as a public good and prepares its graduates to build sustainable development and equity. (de Sousa Santos, 2009, p. 45)

As involved as universities are, they face a dissonance and duality regarding their duties and the perspectives used to define their changes, structures and most intimate processes. These institutions would promote and encourage academics, students, administrative staff and top administrators to stick to the principles of autonomy, academic freedom and the open, free and social generation of knowledge, enabling private appropriation and entrepreneurial and economic innovation. This is even more true when the public domain of knowledge is an irreversible trend that must face enormous constraints and interests arising from the risks of altering the modes and rhythms of cooperation and the free exchange of knowledge from the perspective of a social good that is profoundly disrupted when the relationship becomes one-dimensional by serving contracts with companies and laboratories.

Because of this, the need has arisen to reinforce new strategies of cooperation, networking and substantive changes that, by promoting and ensuring quality service with equality and autonomy, enhance the building of social capacities to produce and transfer science and technology-based knowledge, as well as significant, large-scale learning (De la Fuente, 2010).

The development of production capacity and knowledge or learning transfer, and its local and national promotion, should be *the aim of new inter-institutional agreements to make a government reform possible*. Such a reform should ensure and promote these objectives over time, with local people serving as the main actors in charge of the design and formulation of proposals, programmes and projects of change and transformation. This government reform, on behalf of the university as a public good, should explicitly seek a new stage of social valuation of knowledge and learning to cope with society's new demands and requirements for universities and the education system as a whole.

This scenario of new educational and university reform enables a number of situations: integration into different networks, community participation in internal and public democratization and the generalization of environments for lifelong learning. It would be a change to the prevailing pedagogical and organizational model, which understands that education is based on contributing something different, building new objects of knowledge, reflecting on others and on the whole, driving self-learning plans and recognizing diversity, based on broadly participative and autonomous social management. This implies a *paradigm shift* of what educational changes mean in contemporary times, towards a focus on the design of an open organization, with a number of people involved in different ways. This system would be flexible, self-regulated and have a strong social, local and institutional orientation.

This role of new collective responsibility (State policy), from which it may be possible to advance to a sustainable society of knowledge, also assumes that knowledge is multiplied by research, as well as new learning systems, defined by the context in which knowledge and its public utility are applied. Therefore, the production and transfer of knowledge refers to a connected process, from existing knowledge towards knowledge that is produced and recreated. As such, this knowledge includes a set of elements and components of expertise and savoir-faire, techniques and varied capabilities, mechanisms, programmes, institutions, agencies and players in the process. An institution organized to produce and transfer knowledge to society should therefore be complex, dynamic and differentiated.

We understand this not as the prospective action of an isolated policy, but rather as a set of diverse yet consistent and joint short-, medium- and long-term efforts, arising from the public system, society and educational and academic communities. These will advance changes enabling a new educational management relationship in building new knowledge areas, equally expanding social security coverage and contributing to the education of new citizens, where universal higher education is a right for all, understood as a continual process of academic and life careers. This should be permanent and linked to other levels of education, in order to make a real contribution to human development in all of its dimensions. This will largely depend on changes initiated by institutions of higher learning, especially public universities, to join the efforts of a very active and emerging society based on the new conformation of its actors and leaders.

This change will be a race against time, because it will always be a challenge for society and government as long as equal opportunities and rising welfare levels among the population increasingly depend on greater equal access to knowledge. Over the coming years, governing will be synonymous with education, and living in society will be understood as an everyday experience of multiple, diverse and permanent forms of learning. Thus, the very concept of education will be different then, based on the paradigm of learning, which will have gone back to, surpassed and transformed the old paradigm of rigid and limited teaching, based on memorization and repetition.

Education will be understood as a set of social and institutional practices that offer all kinds of opportunities and incentives for learning, production and the transfer of knowledge and technology. The organized system of learning for all will be an open, flexible and lifelong system in which differences in gender, economic status, race or age will not affect access to or graduation from the system. There will be multiple ways in which this lifelong education will unfold (formal, informal, open, distance, network, and so on), although formal schooling will remain the core element of formal education, especially because it will be geared towards learning multiple skills, abilities and competencies to develop *social culture and intelligence.*

The creation of this new, permanent and lifelong system will be the product of a new education policy. This will be understood as a set of principles, goals and objectives for the public and private sectors, State government, society, social groups and individuals. This new education policy will bring together a strong political will, built from a wide social consensus giving this policy a popular mandate in the short, medium and long term.

Achieving these objectives will be a task for all sectors of political and civil society. Transforming learning paradigms and establishing and developing a permanent educational system cannot occur without the participation and harmonious cooperation of institutions, or the support and supervision of the community and State government. Education becomes a right, but also a duty of all and for all.

In this way, universities, which are extremely important for economic, cultural and social development, are creating enormous expectations regarding the production and transfer of knowledge among academic conglomerates, especially among university networks and associations with strong international partnerships. Universities are both provoking and providing incentives for substantive changes, taking positions with regard to the cyclical economic and social crises and demanding the redefinition of policies and plans, as well as more resources to carry out their key roles in a high-quality, relevant manner. The vital function of universities is to serve as the social institutions that best contribute to the social development of a knowledge society related to the welfare of the majority of its population.

What is happening, in terms of the general trends and variables impacting the future that have been presented in this paper, is a dialectic of scenarios that have significantly altered what was known as a university until around 20 years ago. These changes have occurred related to their functions, areas of focus and ability to exercise autonomous governance, and will build programmes of study and find a place in society.

In reality, the process has become slightly more complex, because instead of clear steps advancing towards a knowledge society, education, learning and consecrated human thought are polarizing societies, opening up huge gaps in their levels of development. This process is seriously improving living conditions for those who have information, providing them with substantial added value compared with those who do not. This is a danger for our planet and its species, altering the genetic patterns of entire societies, significantly changing food consumption and increasing the chances of extinction, bringing about a society with a constant risk of partial destruction.

If an ideal society is a knowledge democracy, those that exist are so few and far between that they appear to be mere ideals given the welfare of their populations. It would almost be a mockery to mention the signs of this ideal society, as it is so far from the future prospects for the next two or three decades of the new century. As such, what is indeed being imposed is a new way of using and managing human intelligence, knowledge and information that can produce, organize and provide for the social transfer of logical gains and extreme competition. This is an economy that values the human workforce in new proportions and fosters links between entire institutions and knowledge production centres to achieve new profit rates and higher levels of financial speculation to alter the basis of economic relations and mediations – the value-in-use of labour in exchange for the changing value of learning – in the constitution of a new mode of production: knowledge-supported production.

Universities and higher educational complexes are indispensable. They produce a sort of new educational, socio-institutional and organizational education of social value and meaningful learning. They may follow an erratic path of evolution, but they are dominant and increasingly authoritarian.

In the context of successive changes, this paper has discussed the concept of university autonomy, not in an abstract or idealized way, but rather seeking the integration of autonomy in new conformations that over-determine it.

In any case, it is a certain conclusion that autonomy as a concept has undergone change. This is not a concept that has been fully altered, but it is frequently modified and used with different expressions in the current age as a principle that continues to stay afloat.

However, this paper suggests that, faced with the debate both caused by and surrounding autonomy, academic freedom and the relevance and social responsibility of universities, it is time to take a firm stance. This work believes that public universities have built refreshing, multiple and differentiated thought, rich in content and at the same time orthodox, historical and deeply rooted in these public institutions. This paper sought to express this idea and provide more current references to follow up on this debate. This is our opinion, and this is how it is presented, arguing the possibility of a fundamental change in universities that seek and demand their own spaces, which have been long lasting and ever present.

CONCLUSION

Self-assessment and evaluation processes are closely related to the management of social engagement and university responsibility, and should be guided by six criteria. The first is relevance, whose core is analysing the social value of knowledge produced and the mechanisms promoted to spread and transfer knowledge for the benefit of society. The second is quality, which evaluates a university's ability to critically and comprehensively educate a student.

The responsible exercise of social and political criticism is the third criterion. This is highly important because it establishes that universities must be assessed in terms of the contributions they make to the production of useful knowledge for the development of citizenship and civic awareness that is necessary for the exercise of democratic life, the strengthening of civil society and the increase in society's capacity to hold dialogue about public policy. It also implies strengthening proactive governance and building spaces for participation through education and culture.

The fourth criterion assesses the contribution of universities to economic development, because knowledge is a key factor for economic growth and social development. Public universities should therefore be evaluated by their participation in the production and transfer of new knowledge, but from the perspective of their social value. Here, it is essential to evaluate their ability to offer solutions to the problems of the growth, welfare and development of the majority of the population, especially the poorest segments.

The fifth criterion concerns the university's availability to expand the frontiers of knowledge. This provision assesses academic freedom, plurality, the linkage of various disciplines and the proliferation of methods and languages derived from different theoretical and methodological perspectives, among other aspects.

The last of the criteria that guide the processes of assessment and self-assessment of social engagement is the commitment of universities to disseminating culture. Public universities must participate in the development of culture and contribute to making all aesthetic and artistic demonstrations available to the public.

Planning the course of change for universities that make social engagement the backbone of their substantive and procedural functions requires a strategic approach that favours the development of new governmental, management and organizational models that incorporate both the university and non-university sectors.

The route to a university model characterized by a high degree of social responsibility requires, as a starting point, that the university transform itself by designing structures that bring together all of its sectors around a common project. This transformation also includes a strong commitment to the social distribution of knowledge and the implementation of programmes with non-university sectors, ensuring the critical appropriation of information and knowledge. In other words, it requires that new synergies be created between economics, society, education and culture.

However, to ensure their character as a public good that plays a vital part in the current transition phase, universities must maintain and reinforce their role as politically, ethically and scientifically autonomous independent institutions, although this does not make them exempt from accountability.

University social responsibility involves universities knowing how to govern themselves and provide extensive and high-quality training for competent and cultured citizens with solid ethics when performing their scientific and professional tasks and social responsibilities. They must be able to assert their right to be free, to experience democracy with a full knowledge of their rights and duties, and to express egalitarian values and dialogue with the diversity of cultures.

In the 21st century, universities must be more critical and comprehensive of public or market policies that do not coherently match the depth of changes. For universities to start to redefine themselves, they must initiate a virtuous cycle that drives the education of a new citizenship and critically incorporates diverse ways to understand, engage and commit to the world. From this perspective, universities must provide new ways for our region to become a society of learning, ensuring the highest levels of general human welfare and reaching the ideal of sustainable human development.

NOTE

1 'What is a public good? Economists … define public goods as those that are non-excludable and non-rivalrous, that is, such goods cannot be provided exclusively to some: others cannot be excluded from consuming them; second, non-rivalrous means their consumption by some does not diminish other people's consumption of the same goods. Public goods generate a large quantum of externalities, simply known as social or public benefits. Public goods are available to all equally; marginal utility is equal, and the marginal cost of producing public goods is zero. They are also collective consumption goods. Economists consider all public goods that strictly satisfy all the above conditions as pure public goods; alternatively, other public goods that do not necessarily fully satisfy all the conditions are seen as semi or quasi-public goods. Further, if the benefits of public goods are limited geographically, they are called local public goods … and the public goods whose benefits are available to the whole world are called global or international public goods … By contrast, private goods are altogether different; they do not satisfy any of these conditions' (Jandhyala B.G. Tilak. 'Higher education: a public good or a commodity for trade?'. In: UNESCO, *World Conference on Higher Education, 2009*. Paris, 2009, p. 17).

REFERENCES

De la Fuente, J.R. (2010) 'Research and innovation in Latin America'. In: Weber, L.E. and Duderstadt (eds), *University Research for Innovation*. London: Economica, pp. 199–208.

de Sousa Santos, B. (2005) *La universidad en el siglo XXI. Para una reforma democrática y emancipadora de la universidad*. Argentina: Miño y Dávila editores.

de Sousa Santos, B. (2009) 'Role of the university in the construction of an alternative globalization'. In: GUNi, *Higher Education in Changing Times, New Dynamics for Social Responsibility*. Barcelona: GUNi, p. 164.

Didriksson, A. (2007) *Universidad y sociedades del conocimiento*. Mexico: UNESCO-México.

Escrigas, C. (2009) *'Nuevas dinámicas para la responsabilidad social'*. In: GUNi, *La educación superior en tiempos de cambio*. Spain: Ediciones Mundi-prensa, pp. 3–16.

Foray, D. (2006) *The Economics of Knowledge*. Cambridge: MIT Press.

Gibbons, M., Limoges, C., Nowotny, H., Schwartzman, S., Scott, P. and Trow, M. et al. (1997) *La nueva producción del conocimiento, la dinámica de la ciencia y la investigación en las sociedades contemporáneas*. Barcelona: Ed. Pomares.

Gibbons, M., Nowotny, H. and Scott, P. (2001) *Rethinking Science, Knowledge and the Public in an Age of Uncertainty*. Cambridge: Polity Press.

UNESCO (2009) *World Conference on Higher Education*. Draft Communiqué. Paris.

PART III
RESEARCH ON KNOWLEDGE, ENGAGEMENT AND HIGHER EDUCATION

Currently, the main activities of the Global University Network for Innovation (GUNi) are focused on the growth of the theory and practice of community–university engagement (CUE) as one of the most significant trends in higher education over recent years. Within this framework, GUNi held the 6th International Barcelona Conference on Higher Education, entitled 'Let's Build Transformative Knowledge To Drive Social Change' (http://www.guninetwork.org/guni.conference/2013-guni-conference). The Conference provided a space for discussing how higher education institutions (HEIs) are advancing in engaging with the community and broader society all around the world.

The aim of this paper is to discuss the trends and progress of CUE initiatives by presenting the main findings of the study that analysed all the initiatives featured at the Conference in both oral communications and poster presentations. The paper is structured in four parts. An initial look at the theoretical framework that guided the Conference's call is followed by the study methodology. The third part of the paper is focused on the data analysis and shows the main findings from the study. The last part summarizes the main conclusions on the main trends of the initiatives and discusses how to make progress on CUE.

CUE: A THEORETICAL FRAMEWORK

According to the Carnegie Foundation for the Advancement of Teaching, CUE can be defined as 'the collaboration between institutions of higher education and their larger communities ... for the mutually beneficial exchange of knowledge and resources in a context of partnership and reciprocity' (Driscoll, 2008, p. 39). The centrality of engagement will be critical to the success of higher education in the future (Fitzgerald et al., 2012).

The concept of community is linked to aspects such as territory and geographical location, identity, the circumstances of a common problem, interest in and affiliation to

a group, occupation and professional practice, faith, kin, and so on. The concept of engagement can be related to activities of research, teaching and service and even to commercialized activities. As a result of this range of possibilities, the practices and structures of engagement in the CUE movement are rich and continually evolving, as the Talloires Network highlights on its website. The main ways or practices of engagement are: service-learning (McIlrath and Mac Labhrainn, 2007); engaged scholarship (Boyer, 1996; Fitzgerald et al., 2012); academic enterprise; community-based research (Strand et al., 2003), in which we include science shops and community–university research partnerships (Hart et al., 2007; Hall, 2011); and knowledge mobilization and its variants, such as knowledge translation and knowledge utilization or impact, among others.

Engagement is the key element for enabling the integration of teaching with research, knowledge creation and community development and involvement to form one unique thing. Bivens (2011) adds to this integration a call for the institutionalization of engagement as a core value in all the structures, processes and relationships throughout the HEI system.

From a knowledge democracy perspective, partnership is the main aspect to consider in the shaping of a truly engaged university, as it is central in developing community engagement initiatives. A partnership is a way of being and a way of working with others that implies mutual understanding, common good, reciprocity, collaboration in decision-making, shared leadership and transparency regarding outcomes. CUE partnerships have as their primary purpose enhancing the role of knowledge in the strengthening of democratic principles and practices in society, in order to address systemic and complex common challenges.

For us, partnerships can be described through two main dimensions: the operational processes and the components (Figure III.1). The operational processes are the stages of partners' relationships, which can

III

COMMUNITY–UNIVERSITY ENGAGEMENT INITIATIVES: TRENDS AND PROGRESS

Jesús Granados Sánchez and Gemma Puig

be conceptualized temporally. Bringle and Hacther (2002) talk about four important points:

- initiating a partnership;
- developing the partnership after having agreed common objectives;
- sustaining and maintaining the partnership;
- knowing when to end the partnership.

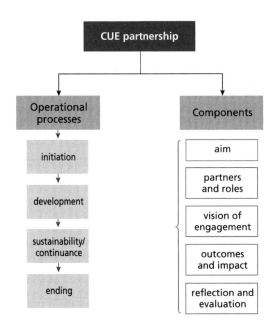

FIGURE III.1 The main dimensions of CUE partnerships

The components for a successful partnership are as follows:

- *The aim of the partnership.* What is the aim of the partnership? What kinds of partnership do we need? How is the process of constitution developed? What composition does the partnership have?
- *The partners and their roles.* Partnership involves mutual understanding and trust, a definition of leadership (or shared leadership) and participation in decision-making or how the power relations are established. Also important is the self-consciousness of the partners' participation in and contribution to the partnership. All the members of the partnership have their own knowledge, expertise and agency and contribute to shaping the collective agenda. This allows the contributions of all partners to be defined, recognized and valued.
- *The vision of engagement.* This implies defining the culture, vision and mission regarding community engagement, in order to define the type and meaning of community and the level of partnership or involvement. The Clinical and Translational Science Awards

(CTSA) (2011) highlight the level of community involvement linked to impact, trust and communication flow, resulting in a community engagement continuum that starts from outreach and moves to consultation, involvement and collaboration to reach a shared leadership. For Hartley and Huddleston (2010), there are five levels of partnership: exchange, dialogue, networking, collaboration, and partnerships that address social problems and build democracy.

- *The outcomes and impact.* There must be reciprocity and mutual benefit. The impact on each partner and on society (the collective impact) must be clear, as must the product or service that has been developed. The self-transformation and collective transformation also have to be measured in order to acknowledge the social change. The outputs and impacts of the CUE partnerships are diverse. Granados (2011) reports they are related to: creating and implementing solutions; acting as mediators for developing actions and solutions to problems by third parties; taking action to alleviate problems; making contributions in the form of knowledge, reports, material goods, art, and so on; reporting and informing on problems, with the aim of raising social awareness; and providing capacity training and learning.
- *Reflection and evaluation.* There must be an evaluation of the difficulties, weaknesses, strengths and opportunities, a revision of agreements and a contemplation of people's replacement. After that, planning for continuance can be established. Funding sources must be assured, and it is worth expanding the partnership by joining networks and through other mechanisms.

METHODOLOGY: THE CONFERENCE'S CALL AND THE STUDY

The aim of this exploratory study was to analyse the main features of the CUE initiatives that were presented at the 6th International Barcelona Conference on Higher Education.

The Conference's call was created as an online questionnaire. In line with the theoretical reflection based on the relevant literature, the questionnaire was organized into the following conceptual sections:

- The first section consisted of basic data from the initiative (contact details, title, theme, and so on).
- The aim of the second section was to detail the creation of the initiative and the partnership, and what the initiative was about. In this section, we expected to gather information related to the follow-

ing questions: Where did the idea come from? Who are the members of the partnership? What is the aim of this initiative? What is the vision of engagement and community that the partnership has? We also wanted to determine the level of partnership (from the leadership, power relations, commitment and participation of all members of the partnership) and the specific role of each member of the partnership, especially concerning their contribution to the project, and the mechanisms and structures developed to support the initiative.

● The third section was centered on the type of CUE. By looking at the description of the initiative, it aimed to see how research, teaching, learning and engagement were linked.

● The fourth section concerned the main outcomes and the impact of the project on each partner.

● The final section tackled the sustainability or continuance of the initiative and included the self-assessment and any recommendations for overcoming difficulties. This part was also expected to contain data on how the completed initiatives ended.

The questionnaire included both scaled response-type questions and questions requiring evidence of a more qualitative nature (see Annex 1 at the end of the paper).

The scope of the study was based on a database of initiatives and good practices on CUE found in different HEIs. In preparing the document, we had access to the following sources:

● Good practices awards (the McJannet Prize, Ernest A. Lynton Award, Vermont Campus Compact awards and Campus Engage network awards).

● University Networks (CLAYSS, Australian Universities Community Engagement Alliance, Campus Compact, Canadian Alliance for Community Service-Learning, ResearchImpact, Project Pericles, Opción Latinoamérica, Campus Engage Network and Coalition of Urban and Metropolitan Universities).

● Projects supporting service-learning (for example, tawasol.org).

● Conferences and congresses (Living Knowledge Conference, ApS(U)3, and so on).

● The webpages of various universities and HEIs.

● Based on the information GUNi has about institutions that usually offer good practices and a noteworthy engagement between the institutions and their communities, the research has been focused on those institutions that have historically shown social responsibility.

GUNi gathered together 2,088 projects and programmes (Table III.1). This database was used for the

call of the Conference and was sent to the contact persons on several occasions. As a result of the call, a total of 167 initiatives were accepted for presentation at the conference, either as oral communications or as posters. These initiatives formed the random sampling pool for this exploratory study.

| TABLE III.1 | |
| Initiatives in the database, by region | |
Region	Number of initiatives
Africa	410
Arab States	50
Asia and the Pacific	200
Europe	250
Latin America and the Caribbean	850
North America	328

MAIN FINDINGS

The main aspects that were analysed from the data provided for each initiative were the location of the initiative, the diversity of types or modes of engagement, the origin of the initiative, the thematic area, the aim of the initiative and the features of the partnerships that were created.

LOCATION OF THE INITIATIVES

The CUE initiatives that were presented at the Conference came from all over the world. The majority were from Europe (30.7%) and the USA/Canada (23.8%), followed by Asia and the Pacific (15.7%), Africa (14.5%) and Latin America and the Caribbean (12.1%). The region that was least represented was the Arab States, with only 3.8% of the initiatives (Figure III.2).

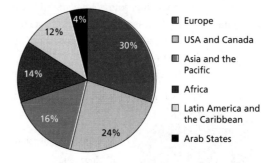

FIGURE III.2 Regional origin of the initiatives

At a country level, 37 different countries were represented (Table III.2). The countries that submitted the highest number of initiatives were Spain, the USA, Canada, South Africa and the UK.

TABLE III.2			
Number of initiatives per country			
Country	Number of initiatives	Country	Number of initiatives
Argentina	7	Lebanon	2
Australia	4	Malawi	1
Bahrain	1	Malaysia	2
Belgium	2	Mexico	1
Bolivia	1	New Zealand	2
Botswana	1	Nigeria	2
Brazil	4	Palestine	1
Canada	19	Peru	1
Chile	4	Russian Federation	2
Colombia	7	Portugal	1
France	2	Saudi Arabia	1
Greece	1	South Africa	13
Hong Kong – China	1	Spain	25
India	8	Sweden	1
Indonesia	1	Tunisia	1
Ireland	8	Uganda	1
Japan	1	UK	10
Kenya	2	USA	25
Korea, Republic of	1		
	TOTAL	37	167

TYPES OR MODES OF CUE

The authors and/or representatives of the initiatives were asked to classify them according to one or more of the following types or modes of CUE: service-learning, community-based research (specifying whether it was a science shop), engaged scholarship, knowledge mobilization or academic enterprise.

Figure III.3 shows the proportion of each type of CUE in relation to the total number of the initiatives that were presented at the Conference. The majority of these were of service-learning (41%), accounting for almost half of the total. The three next most common types – engaged scholarship, knowledge mobilization and community-based research (including science shops) – made up similar proportions, and academic enterprise was the least represented.

If we compare the classification that each initiative

makes of the CUE typology in relation to the appearance of the chosen type (as a concept) in the description of all requested parts of the questionnaire, some interesting results emerge: almost all service-learning initiatives repeatedly use the concept in their text. This makes us think that they are aware of what they are doing. When it comes to knowledge mobilization and community-based research, something similar happens: the respective concepts are used in the text in most cases, despite the fact that we have noticed a usage of other equivalent concepts such as knowledge transfer, community–university partnerships, and so on. In the case of engaged scholarship, the concept is mentioned in half the cases. Finally, academic enterprise contains a wide variety of initiatives in which the concept is never mentioned.

It should be mentioned that, after reading the initiatives, we were able to check how a large a proportion of them combined more than one type of CUE, although in the actual description of the activity not all of them were acknowledged, only the main one being reported. We can relate this aspect to the lack of knowledge that initiatives have of CUE types other than the ones they are used to working with. Another factor related to this point is the integration of engagement with teaching, research and its institutionalization. Despite the fact that integration is incipient and appears in very few cases, in those cases where it does appear, there is a lack of explicit recognition of such integration, which opens up the question of whether there is a lack of awareness on this matter.

THE ORIGIN OF THE INITIATIVE

It is relevant to know where the initiative came from, because this provides information on the level of the engagement in terms of people, institutional implications, scale and geographical scope, and impact. The responses on the origin of the initiative could be grouped into the following categories (Figure III.4):

- personal motivation (the project emanated from the personal motivation of a specific individual);
- research group project (as a new project or as a continuance of a previous one);

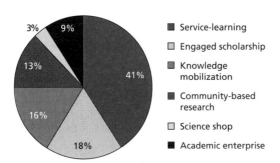

FIGURE III.3 Types of CUE initiatives

Service-learning
Engaged scholarship
Knowledge mobilization
Community-based research
Science shop
Academic enterprise

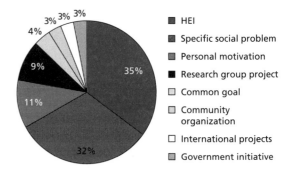

FIGURE III.4 Origin of the initiative

HEI
Specific social problem
Personal motivation
Research group project
Common goal
Community organization
International projects
Government initiative

- HEI (a department or faculty decided to undertake a project together with the community);
- a specific social problem or requirement (the focus was on one of the most relevant social needs);
- the common goal of social actors and the university (a specific group work agreement emerged between the university and social actors);
- government initiative (the government took interest in CUE and promoted it);
- community organization (an organization in the community created and developed a project);
- international project (the initiative was born as an international project among several universities).

We found that 35% of the initiatives explained the origin of their experience as a university initiative (either as part of the range of studies offered within the university, as an institutional university project, as a departmental initiative or as part of the syllabus of a particular subject). A similar percentage – 32% – of the answers indicated that the generation of the initiative arose from the urgency of a relevant social problem, the university not appearing as a central focus. It is very significant that the third most common choice was that of personal initiative, which, at 11%, showed the importance of projects that are motivated and propelled by professors and students individually. In many cases, these projects are the forerunners of bringing CUE into many HEIs.

The initiatives that were started by research groups (9%) were mostly linked to research, either to the development of the research methodology (as happens with community-based research) or to research on the initiative itself (as happens in some cases with service-learning).

Of the remaining initiatives, 4% specified that the project had emerged as an objective of the HEI and social actors, 3% of the projects had been promoted by social groups, and another 3% were international projects among universities (which was seen only with European projects). Finally, 3% of the initiatives came from governments.

THEMES OF THE INITIATIVES

The initiatives were classified according to a wide range of proposed themes, grouped into five main thematic areas: access and equity for disadvantaged groups, democratization of knowledge, contribution for solving pressing problems, citizenship, and others (Figure III.5).

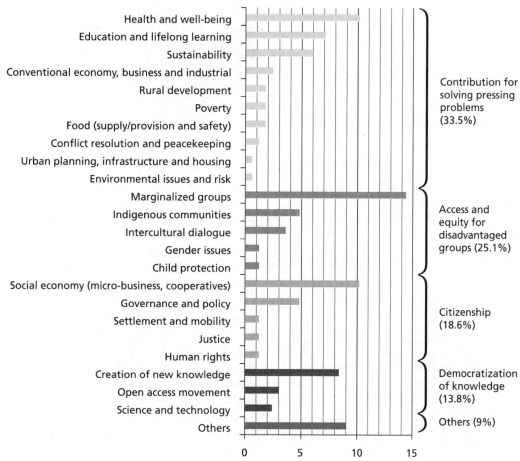

FIGURE III.5 Diversity of themes and their proportion

The main treated themes were marginalized groups, health and well-being, social economy, the creation of new knowledge, education and lifelong learning and sustainability. These six themes covered 57% of the initiatives.

AIM OF THE INITIATIVES

According to the descriptions of the objectives of each initiative, we were able to extract as a first conclusion the fact that the majority of initiatives (94%) had as an objective the development of a type of CUE. It is important to point out that some other initiatives focused on the institutionalization and research of the CUE phenomenon itself (Figure III.6).

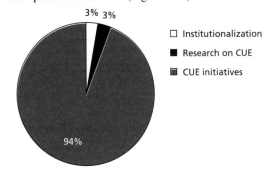

3% 3%

☐ Institutionalization
■ Research on CUE
■ CUE initiatives

94%

FIGURE III.6 Purposes of the initiatives

Table III.3 shows a classification of the aims of 94% of the CUE initiatives. These aims are a combination of elements such as the participation of the members of the partnership, the outcomes and their impact, and especially whether the initiative was centred on solving complex and pressing social prob-

TABLE III.3 Typology of aims of the initiatives	
Aim of the initiative	Description
Co-creation of knowledge	To co-create knowledge and technology to solve specific problems or to address social needs
Designing a solution	To design solutions to specific problems, to be implemented by the corresponding bodies
Developing a corrective action	To design a corrective action that would help to relieve the symptoms of a problem even though further attention to the root of the problem would be needed in the future
Capacity-building	To offer capacity-building to students and other stakeholders, enabling them to acquire knowledge, new perspectives and skills and apply them to real social problems through engaged fieldwork and research
Reporting on problems	To report and inform on problems, with the aim of raising social awareness
Transferring knowledge	To transfer knowledge and technology to society
Contribution in terms of art and culture	To create knowledge, art or culture that contributes to the community in another way (aesthetics, and so on)

lems or on making a more testimonial or symbolic contribution. The aims of the initiatives ranged from the co-creation of knowledge, the design of a solution, the development of a corrective action, to offer capacity-building, to report on problems, to transfer knowledge and to contribute to the community in terms of art or cultural goods.

Almost half of the initiatives (47%) aimed to offer capacity-building to students, enabling them to acquire knowledge, new perspectives and skills and to apply them to real social problems through engaged fieldwork and research (Figure III.7). Next, some way off but still with a relevant proportion of the initiatives (13%), were the aims of both the transfer of knowledge and technology to society and the reporting and information on problems, with the aim of raising social awareness. The aims of designing solutions, developing corrective actions and co-creating knowledge each accounted for 8–9% of the initiatives. The category that was least significant was contributing in terms of art and culture (Figure III.7).

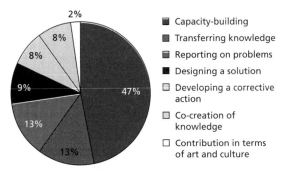

2%
8%
8%
9%
47%
13%
13%

■ Capacity-building
■ Transferring knowledge
▦ Reporting on problems
■ Designing a solution
☐ Developing a corrective action
▨ Co-creation of knowledge
☐ Contribution in terms of art and culture

FIGURE III.7 Proportion of initiatives per aim

Tables III.4–III.6 provide more information on the type of CUE and the aims of the initiatives. As it can be seen from Table III.6, there are some relationships between the aim of the initiatives and the type of CUE. The service-learning initiatives mainly pursued as their principal aim the creation of capacity-building. Through this description, they focused on the students' learning more than on service. The other service-learning initiatives were suggested to report on problems or develop a corrective action. Knowledge mobilization initiatives aimed to transfer knowledge, to create capacity-building and to report on problems. Community-based research focused on reporting on problems and the co-creation of knowledge, which was the principal type of CUE to achieve co-creation of knowledge. Engaged scholarship aimed to transfer knowledge and design a solution. Finally, academic enterprise initiatives had as their goals capacity-building and the co-creation of knowledge.

TABLE III.4

Proportion of initiatives for each aim in terms of the type of CUE*

		Type of CUE					
		CBR	SS	ES	AE	KM	SL
Aim of the initiative	To transfer knowledge	5.6%	5.6%	33.3%	11.1%	33.3%	11.1%
	To design a solution	16.7%	0%	33.3%	8.3%	25.0%	16.7%
	To develop a corrective action	27.3%	0%	18.2%	9.1%	0%	45.5%
	To report on problems	27.8%	0%	11.1%	5.6%	27.8%	27.8%
	Contribution in terms of art and culture	50.0%	0%	0%	0%	0%	50.0%
	Capacity-building	3.1%	6.2%	4.6%	4.6%	9.2%	72.3%
	The co-creation of knowledge	36.4%	0%	9.1%	27.3%	9.1%	18.2%

Note: CBR, community-based research; SS, science shop; ES, engaged scholarship; AE, academic enterprise; KM, knowledge mobilization; SL, service-learning.

**Note:* each row/aim adds up to 100%.

TABLE III.5

Proportion of initiatives for each type of CUE in terms of the aim of the initiatives*

		The aim of the initiative						
		To transfer knowledge	To design a solution	To develop a corrective action	To report on problems	Contribution in terms of art and culture	Capacity-building	The co-creation of knowledge
Type of CUE	CBR	6.1%	11.2%	16.6%	27%	6.1%	11.2%	21.8%
	SS	20.0%	0%	0%	0%	0%	80.0%	0%
	ES	29.3%	20.8%	12.4%	12.4%	0%	16.7%	8.4%
	AE	18.1%	9.7%	9.7%	9.7%	0%	26.4%	26.4%
	KM	27.8%	14.8%	0%	23.5%	0%	27.8%	6.1%
	SL	3.6%	3.6%	8.1%	8.1%	2.2%	70.8%	3.6%

Note: CBR, community-based research; SS, science shop; ES, engaged scholarship; AE, academic enterprise; KM, knowledge mobilization; SL, service-learning.

**Note:* each row/type of CUE adds up to 100%.

TABLE III.6

Relationship between the type of CUE and the aim of the initiatives

		Type of CUE						
		SL	KM	CBR	SS	ES	AE	Total
The aim of the initiative	To transfer knowledge	1.4%	4.3%	0.7%	0.7%	4.3%	1.4%	13%
	To design a solution	1.5%	2.3%	1.5%	0%	3%	0.7%	9%
	To develop a corrective action	3.6%	0%	2.2%	0%	1.5%	0.7%	8%
	To report on problems	3.6%	3.6%	3.6%	0%	1.4%	0.7%	13%
	Contribution in terms of art and culture	1%	0%	1%	0%	0%	0%	2%
	Capacity-building	34%	4.3%	1.5%	2.9%	2.2%	2.2%	47%
	The co-creation of knowledge	1.5%	0.7%	2.9%	0%	0.7%	2.2%	8%
	Total	46.6%	15.2%	13.4%	3.6%	13.1%	8%	100%

Note: CBR, community-based research; SS, science shop; ES, engaged scholarship; AE, academic enterprise; KM, knowledge mobilization; SL, service-learning.

PARTNERSHIP

According to Hartley and Huddleston (2010), CUE partnerships are built on democratic principles and exist not only to pursue specific goals, but also to foster democratic practices and values. CUE partnerships see communities and their social actors as having assets and as being critically important partners, because they bring their own knowledge, expertise and agency. Therefore, all partners shape the collective agenda and their contributions need to be defined, recognized and valued. Not all the respondents linked up CUE initiatives with the need to form a partnership between HEIs and other social actors from the community. Of those participants who understood the need for the partnership, some did not provide clear information about who the partners were and what their roles were. Six levels of partnerships, in terms of involvement, trust, communication, outcomes and impact, have been detected from those who were aware of the importance of the partnership and described it; we have conceptualized these in descending order as funding source, outreach, exchange–consult, collaboration, involvement and partnership (Table III.7).

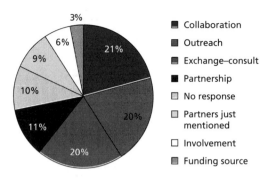

FIGURE III.8 Proportion of initiatives for each type of CUE in term of the aim of the initiatives

TABLE III.7 Level of partnership through involvement, trust, communication, outcomes and impact	
Level of partnership	Type of activity
Funding source	Partners are considered as just a funding source
Outreach	Communication flows mainly in one direction to provide other groups in the community with information. The main outcomes are communication and outreach channels
Exchange–consult	Communication flows to other groups in the community and back again, generating feedback. The main outcomes are the build-up of networks and information-sharing
Collaboration	Communication flow is bidirectional, forming working groups in the community with different levels of participation and commitment. The main outcome is trust-building
Involvement	The flow of communication is multidirectional and participatory. The main outcomes are increased cooperation and greater visibility of each partner
Partnership	There is a strong bidirectional and multidirectional relationship, with shared leadership, participation and commitment. Entities have formed strong partnership structures. Final decisions are made at partnership level. The main outcomes are strong multidirectional trust and a broader community impact of decisions

Collaboration, outreach and exchange–consult are the main levels of partnership, each accounting for approximately 20% of the initiatives (Figure III.8). The categories that were least common where those that recognized the partnership as a funding source and of a degree of involvement. It is worth mentioning that 11% of respondents identified their level of partnership as the highest one ('partnership'), while the answers about the origin of the initiatives showed just 4% of them as having been initiated jointly by social actors and HEIs. The main ideas that respondents expressed regarding partnerships are those of developing trust, the importance of having a common language, the maintenance of regular communication, dialogue, negotiation and collective reflection, the understanding of different timings and to formalize and systematize the process.

CONCLUSION

In recent years, the CUE movement has seen a great expansion worldwide. Many scholars and people from civil society are working to provide a strong theoretical framework for the field and a systematization of its processes. The vast majority of CUE initiatives or projects are being generated by the universities themselves, or by individual scholars, and are not a response to issues raised by civil society or social movement sectors. This study highlights mainly university-based work but does not provide many insights into CUE initiatives initiated by civil society groups themselves. And initiatives instigated together by HEIs and social actors for a common goal are rare. This raises a serious concern from a knowledge democracy framework point of view as to the transformative power of much of this work and the quality of partnerships.

The initiatives that have been analysed show either very reflexive works or some other intuitive projects. In those cases where reflection is higher, partnerships are seen as a process and an opportunity to learn how to work for common purposes and how this helps in self-transformation and collective change. In contrast, when projects are made from intuition, the collective impact is not guaranteed as, in many cases, the impact is limited to just one group.

Also, a disconnection between the existing typologies of CUE has been noted: for instance, some of those working in a manner of engagement, such as service-learning, ignore what is being done in initiatives of engaged scholarship and others. This also explains the fact that there are few examples of activities that integrate teaching, research and engagement. Efforts must be made to bring together the complementarity of the diverse ways of engagement. Figure III.9 shows different scenarios that result from combining the levels

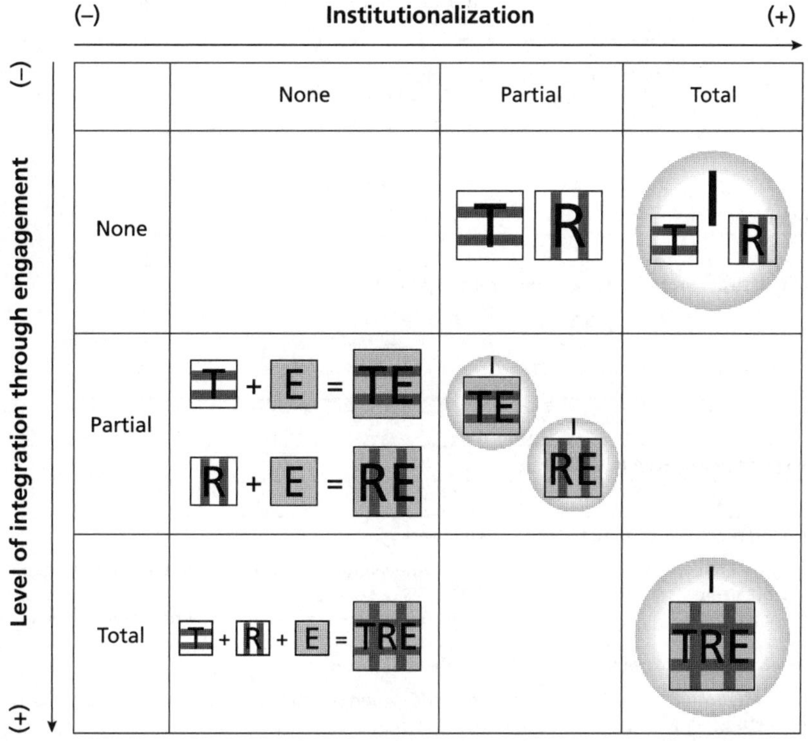

FIGURE III.9 Levels of integration and institutionalization
Note T, teaching; R, research; I, institutionalization; E, engagement.

of integration of the three main activities of universities (teaching, research and engagement) and how this integration is institutionalized.

ACKNOWLEDGEMENTS

We want to thank all participants of the CUE initiatives that were presented at the 6th International Barcelona Conference on Higher Education that provided the data from their initiatives and made possible this research study.

Also we want to thank Melba Claudio and Marta Forns for their help.

REFERENCES

Bivens, F.M. (2011) *Higher Education as Social Change: Seeking a Systemic Institutional Pedagogy of Social Change*. PhD thesis, Institute of Development Studies, University of Sussex, Brighton. Available online from http://sro.sussex.ac.uk/6942/.

Boyer, E.L. (1996) 'The scholarship of engagement'. *Bulletin of the American Arts and Sciences*, 49(7), 18–33.

Bringle, R.G. and Hatcher, J.A. (2002) Campus-community partnerships: the terms of engagement. *Journal of Social Issues*, 58(3), 503–16.

CTSA (2011) *Principles of Community Engagement* (2nd edn). Durham, NC: NIH Publications, Duke University. Retrieved from http://www.atsdr.cdc.gov/communityengagement/pdf/PCE_Report_508_FINAL.pdf.

Driscoll, A. (2008) 'Carnegie's community-engagement classification: intentions and insights'. *Change*, Jan/Feb, 39–41.

Fitzgerald, H.E., Burns, K., Sonka, S., Furco, A., and Swanson, L. (2012) 'Centrality of engagement in higher education'. *Journal of Higher Education Outreach and Engagement*, 16(3), 7–33.

Granados, J. (2011) *La evaluación de iniciativas de aprendizaje participativo para una acción responsable y de servicio*. In: Miralles, P., Molina S. and Santisteban, A. (eds) *La Evaluación en el Proceso de Enseñanza y Aprendizaje de las Ciencias Sociales*. Múrcia: APUDCS, pp. 343–52.

Hall, B. (2011) 'Towards a knowledge democracy movement: contemporary trends in community university research partnerships'. In: *Rizoma Freireano*, 9 (Special Issue).

Hart, A., Maddisson, E. and Wolff, D. (2007) *Community-University Partnerships in Practice*. Leicester: National Institute for Adult and Continuing Education.

Hartley, M. and Huddleston, T. (2010) *School-Community-University Partnerships for a Sustainable Democracy: Education for Democratic Citizenship in Europe and the United States*. EDC/HRE Pack, Tool 5. Strasbourg: Council of Europe.

McIlrath, L. and Mac Labhrainn, I. (Eds.). (2007). *Higher Education and Civic Engagement: International Perspectives*. Aldershot: Ashgate.

Strand, K., Marullo, S., Cutforth, N., Stoecker, R. and Donohue, P. (2003) 'Principles of best practice for community-based research'. *Journal of Community Service Learning*, 9(3), 5–15.

1. Contact details:

Author 1:	Author 2:
Name:	Name:
E-mail:	E-mail:
Website:	Institution/organization:
Institution/organization:	Country:

Institution

Status: [ ] Public [ ] Private profit [ ] Private non-profit [ ] Mixed

Country:

Position:

Postal address:

2. Title:

3. Summary of the good practice (up to 150 words):

4. Keywords:

5. Categorize the good practice according to the following tracks:

[ ] 1. Community-based research
[ ] 2. Engaged scholarship
[ ] 3. Academic enterprise

[ ] 4. Knowledge mobilization and research utilization
[ ] 5. Science shops
[ ] 6. Service-learning, community-based learning and community service

6. Categorize the good practice according to the following thematic areas:

[ ] 1. Access and equity for disadvantageous groups
   – Indigenous communities
   – Marginalized groups
   – Gender issues
   – Intercultural dialogue
   – Child protection
   – Others

[ ] 2. Democratization of knowledge
   – Creation of new knowledge
   – Open access movement
   – ICT uses
   – Others

[ ] 3. Contribution for solving pressing problems
   – Poverty
   – Environmental issues and risk
   – Food security and local food production
   – Sustainability
   – Rural development
   – Housing affordability
   – Renewable energy
   – Food supply/provision and security
   – Health and well-being
   – Conflict management and peacekeeping
   – Community economic development
   – Others

[ ] 4. Citizenship
   – Human rights
   – Safe communities (security and protection)
   – Justice
   – Settlements and mobility
   – Governance and policy
   – Others

[ ] 5. Others

7. Duration:

Starting date: _____

[ ] Active [ ] Completed   Date: _____

8. Background (context in which the initiative was developed) (300 words):

9. Objectives (maximum 100 words):

10. Type of partnership (leadership, role and commitment of partners, etc.) (maximum 200 words):

11. Description of the initiative (maximum 500 words):

12. Outcomes of the initiative (maximum 100 words):

13. Main impacts on each partner (maximum 150 words):

14. Innovative aspects (Please select the innovative aspects)

[ ] 1. A transformative and relevant impact on solving problems, improving existing systems and satisfying community needs
[ ] 2. New pedagogical approaches to teaching, learning and training
[ ] 3. How research, learning and engagement were integrated and linked
[ ] 4. The way the initiative was assessed

[ ] 5. The process of partnership creation and engagement, and the way of working and the empowerment of social actors
[ ] 6. The transformative impact on the institution (institutional management)
[ ] 7. The way of communicating between partners and with the community during the process and on the results
[ ] 8. The knowledge produced, the service or the product developed as a result of the project

Explain the innovations (maximum 100 words):

15. Recommendations (maximum 100 words):

16. Sustainability of the project (maximum 100 words):

A Campus-Community-School Transformational Partnership, Robert Bringle, Starla Officer, James Grim, Appalachian State University, United States.

A framework for learning, a framework for application: Increasing the capacity of students to engage in successful community development, Mary Emery, South Dakota State University, United States.

A+S Universidad Católica de Chile Chantal Jouannet, José Tomás Montalva Carmona, Chile.

Aboriginal women's trajectories and perspectives on homelessness: a collaborative research project, Julie Cunningham, Université de Montréal, Canada.

Academic and social participation in sustainability and University Social Responsibility (SyRSU): Case Study, Azul Alférez, Silvia Albareda, Mónica Fernández, Jordi Puig, Salvador Vidal, Universitat Internacional de Catalunya, Spain.

Academy of Community Engagement Scholarship (ACES), Patricia Sobrero, North Carolina State University, United States.

Acquiring and evaluating transversal competencies through solidarity activities: The practical case of the UdG, M. Rosa Terradellas, Sílvia Lloveras, Martí Casadesus, Universitat de Girona, Spain.

Active Pharmacy, Mike Ellis-Martin, Beth Thomas-Hancock, University of Brighton, United Kingdom.

African higher education and the creation of employment through community engagement, Idowu, Biao, University of Botswana, Botswana.

An emergent model of Research Ko knowledge Mobilization to Policy Impact, Fay Flecher, Christie Schultz, University of Alberta, Canada.

An-Najah National University: Serving the Community, Katie Flanagan, An-Najah National University, Palestine.

Artistas en los barrios: Estrategias de inserción laboral y aprendizaje de oficios para jóvenes en riesgo, María Mónica Caballero, Universidad Nacional de la Plata, Argentina.

Arts-based adult education, research and knowledge mobilisation with homeless/street-involved women in Victoria, Darlene Clover, University of Victoria, Canada.

Balancing indigenous and western research paradigms in a community-based participatory research project, Melissa Daniels, Lola Baydala, Natasha Rabbit, Barb Mclean, University of Alberta, Canada.

Best practice of Ural Federal University on generation and development of student entrepreneurship, Alexey Klyuev, The Ural Federal University named after the first President of Russia B. N. Yeltsin (UrFU), Russian Federation.

Beyond the third mission - the PASCAL PUMR Initiative, James Powell, PASCAL University of Glasgow, United Kingdom.

Bright smiles for Manungara, Federico Alejandro Álvarez Echeverri, Colombia.

Bringing Medical Research Skills/Laboratory research to the Community, Lynn O'Connor, National University of Ireland Galway, Ireland.

Building a new understanding of ESD through community university engagement in Catalonia, Jesús Granados Sànchez, Josep Bonil, Genina Calafell, Mercè Junyent, Rosa Maria Tarin, Universitat Autònoma de Barcelona, Spain.

Building Educational Institutional Capacity to Address Skills Shortages, Dianne Paez, University of Southern Queensland, Australia.

Building Engagement and Aspirations through Mentoring in Schools (BEAMS) project: Assisting students from low socio-economic backgrounds to aspire to further education and achieve their potential, Marie Kavanagh, Natasha Levak,

& Anita Williamson, Springfield, University of Southern Queensland, Toowoomba, Queensland, Australia.

Building identity. Knowledge sharing in the process of building the habitat. Experience with the Community originating in Berisso mocovíes, Natali Rodriguez, Argentina

Building research capacity for sustainable development, Zinaida Fadeeva, United Nations University Institute of Advanced Studies, Japan.

Camins Open Course Ware: Open Teaching Strategy + Open Quality Material, M. Rosa Estela, Mercè Oller, Universitat Politécnica de Catalunya, Spain.

Catalyst! Citizens Transforming Society: tools for change, Jon Whittle Pi, Debbie Stubbs, Lancaster University, United Kingdom.

Chance 2 Advance programme, Genevieve James, Unisa, South Africa.

Changing the Culture: Involving the Entire University in Community University Engagement, Leslie Brown, University of Victoria, Canada.

Citizen Science, Joy McManigal, Erin Cannan, Bard College Center for Civic Engagement (CCE), United States.

Collaborative Campaign of Community, Civil Society and Academia to End Female Foeticide and Sex Selective Abortion, Martha, Farrell, Society for Participatory Research in Asia (PRIA), India.

Community Based Experience and Services: An Innovative Medical Education of the University of Ilorin, Nigeria, Temidayo Oladiji, Abdul Ganiyu Ambali, Olugbenga Mokuolu, University of Ilorin, Nigeria.

Community Based Research and Innovative Practice; Mental Health and Cultural Diversity, Joanna Ochocka, Centre for Community Based Research, Canada.

Community based research and post secondary vocational training in indigenous and afrocolombian communities in Colombia, Sandra Frieri, Maria Clara Van Der Hammem, Tropenbos International Colombia, Colombia.

Community Connections: Knowing what we do, Gary Tennant, Douglas College, Canada.

Community Covenantal Ethics: The Use of Structured Ethical Reflection to Guide Community-Based Research, Mary Brydon-Miller, University of Cincinnati, United States.

Community Engagement with Service Learning: a community development approach, Julia Preece, Desiree Manicom, University of KwaZulu Natal, South Africa.

Community Learning Partnerships: Inspiring Lives, Jennifer Bennett, Camosun College.

CommunITy: Putting IT in the community, Pat Byrne, National University of Ireland, Galway, Ireland.

Community–University Engagement for Economic Empowerment: The Nigerian Experience, Chineze Uche, Onyewuchi Akaranta, Joseph Ajienka, Bene Abbey, University of Port Harcourt, Nigeria.

Community-university engagement in social economy, the Quebec's experience, Sylvie Boucher De Grosbois, Vincent Van Schendel, Université du Québec à Montréal, Canada.

Community-university engagement initiatives TALENTS. Academic Leveling Project for public High School Students, Ángela Maria Franco, Universidad del Valle, Colombia.

Consequences of the use of street pesticides for pest control on children's health, Judith Favish, South Africa.

Constraints and Alternatives for Community Engagement Scholarship of University Faculty, Patricia M. Sobrero, North Carolina State University, K.S.U. 'Jay' Jayaratne, North Carolina State University, United States.

Cooperative University of Colombia Student Retention Program Enlace, Yency Paolo Avila Gutierrez, Universidad Cooperativa de Colombia, Colombia.

Creating 'Comediantes' in the Classroom, for the Community, Ellen Frye, William Paterson University of New Jersey, United States.

CROMA programme: from the primary and secondary schools to the university, learning together, Elsa Espinosa, Universitat Autònoma de Barcelona, Spain.

Crossing boundaries: Teaching socially responsive psychology through service-learning, Luzelle, Naude, University of the Free State, South Africa.

Culture as a manner of relation: the co-creation of a new city, Richard Alonso Uribe Hincapié, Universidad Pontificia Bolivariana /Metro de Medellín, Colombia.

Dare to dream: Creating an international centre for community engagement and scholarship, Heather McRae, Katy Campbell, University of Alberta, Canada.

EcoSPORTech: Young entrepreneurship linking sport, nature and new technologies, Salvador Simó, Xavier Ginesta, Albert Juncà, Jordi San Eugenio, Universitat de Vic, Spain.

Educating for innovation: within and beyond the arts, Tara, Daniel, Perth Insitute of Contemporary Arts (PICA), Australia.

Educational change for social justice: A service-learning experience in teacher education, Pilar Aramburu-Zabala, The Autonomous University of Madrid, Spain.

Enabling and Measuring Student Learning through Volunteering, Lorraine Tansey, National University of Ireland, Ireland.

Engaged Partnership Transforms Academic Practice: Authentic Engagement with a Metis Settlement in Alberta, Canada, Alicia Hibbert, Fiona Robertson, Susan Ladouceur, Fay Fletcher, University of Alberta, Canada.

Engaging for sustainable rural water supply in Cambodia, Zulkifli Yusop, Nur Naha Abu Mansor, Masputeriah Hamzah, Azlan Abdul Rahman, UTM team, Malaysia.

Engaging our clients'; building capacity through participatory research within services for the homeless, Josephine Boland, National University of Ireland Galway, Ireland; Seamus Morrisey, Galway City Partnership, Ireland; Ena Norris, Lisa Silke, COPE Galway, Ireland.

Engaging Students in Jail-Based Service-Learning Projects, Megha Ramaswamy, University of Kansas School of Medicine, United States.

Engaging the community: Activate and The BA Community Development at the university of Glasgow, Helen Martin, Margaret Layden, United Kingdom.

Engaging with communities - an empowerment approach to university-community engagement, Pierre Viljoen, CQUniversity, Australia.

Engaging with the Private Sector at Makerere University: A case of the Private-Public Partnerships, Janice Desire Busingye, Makerere University, Uganda.

Establishing the criteria for 'good practice': Evaluating a model of a university-community knowledge partnership, Janice Mcmillan, Suki Goodman, Tanja Winkler, University of Cape Town, South Africa.

External participation in university governance: the stakeholders in the Universidad Nacional de Río Negro (Argentina), Juan Carlos del Bello, Graciela Giménez, Universidad Nacional de Río Negro, Argentina.

Family Substance Use and Head Start Teachers' Perceptions of Children's Behavior, Hiram E. Fitzgerald, KyungSook Lee, Jessica V. Barnes, Patricia Farrell, Hope Gerde, Michigan State University; Ann Belleau, Inter.Tribal Council of Michigan, United States.

Forming the future University Students as socially respon-
sible beings, just from school: Learning by Serving, Eugenia Verónica Cerna, Concepción Private School, Chile.

Free Aid: Business Students for Not-for-profits, Irena Descubes, ESC Rennes School of Business, France.

From Practicum to Service Learning Project: a pilot experience in University of Barcelona, Esther Luna, Spain.

Good Practice: The Service Learning. An Experience in the Degree in Social Work, Carmina Puig Cruells, Universitat Rovira i Virgili, Spain.

Guide to implement disability issues in the University Social Responsibility management, Daniel Guasch, Universitat Politècnica de Catalunya, Spain; Pilar Dotras, Universitat Ramon Llull, Blanquerna, Spain; Maria Hortensia Alvarez, Yolanda Guasch, Universitat Politècnica de Catalunya, Spain; Raquel Vallez, Universitat Politècnica de Catalunya Spain.

Health and society, community participation for action, César García Balaguera, Alba Yise Rojas Caballero, Universidad Cooperativa de Colombia, Colombia.

Higher Education Service Learning Engagement for Students with Disabilities: An Inspiring and Replicable International Partnership, Mary Pat Zebroski, Chautauqua Learn and Serve Charter School, United States.

How the University of Chicago forms reciprocal relationships with the community through the arts and humanities, Joanie Friedman, Erika Dudley, University of Chicago's Civic Knowledge Project, United States.

IKD Gazte: self-managed learning to develop the sense of initiative within the curriculum in Higher Education, Julieta Barrenechea, Idoia Fernández, UPV/EHU and Euskampus Fundazioa, Spain.

Implementation of the policy of social development: a strategy of engagement of the university, Ines, Amaro da Silva, Pontifícia Universidade Católica do Rio Grande do Sul, Brazil.

Innovation in Science Shop practices: A case study from Queen's University Belfast, Emma Mckenna, Queen's University Belfast, United Kingdom.

Innovative Practice to Enhance Health Professionals' Training Capacity in Developing Countries: Experience of Saudi Arabia, Hisham, Aljadhey, King Saud University, Saudi Arabia.

Inquiry-based e-learning in community health, Christina, Severinsen, Massey University, New Zealand.

Integrating a Youth-based Stigma and Discrimination Reduction Curriculum in Higher Education, Lancelot D'Cruz, S.J., Sebastian Vadakken Antoney.

Integrating Coaching Psychology into Education, Ruth FitzGerald, Bahrain Polytechnic, Bahrain.

Integrating community-based learning into the student experience, Kate Miller, Maggie Leggett, United Kingdom.

Integrating service to the community in undergraduate studies at San Jorge University: Service-Learning as best practice, Arantzazu Martinez-Odria, A. Gil-Albarova, N. Nashaat, San Jorge University Spain.

Intergenerational Service-Learning: Elder Academy at Lingnan, Carol Ma Hok Ka, China.

International Advocacy NGO Workshop: A Practice Research Engagement, L. David, Brown, Hauser Center for Nonprofit Organizations, Harvard University, United States.

International Cooperation between European and Latin America Higher Education Institutions, José Beltrán, Universitat de València; António Teodoro, Manuela Guilherme, Universidad Lusófona de Humanidades e Tecnología, Portugal; Alejandra Montané, Universitat de Barcelona, Spain.

Learning by serving, Eugenia Veronica, Cerna Hinojosa, Colegio Concepción, Chile.

LOW3 – A living Lab approach for a holistic learning and open innovation platform for sustainability at UPC – Barcelona Tech, Torsten Masseck, Universitat Politècnica de Catalunya, Spain.

Macheo Achievement Programme, Roselyne Mwangi, Strathmore University, Strathmore University, Kenya.

Making engaged learning integral to the student experience in a research intensive university, Kate Miller, Maggie Legget, Centre for Public Engagement, University of Bristol, United Kingdom.

Managing stakeholder relations: Using co-operative governance for effective higher education strategy, Jeanette Botha, University of South Africa, South Africa.

Mentoring for Change: An East African Case Study, Tashmin Khamis, Aga Khan University, Kenya.

Miquel Marti i Pol garden, Salvador Simo, Maria Kapanadze, Ivan Cano, Universitat de Vic, Spain.

Mobilizing universities to adress the global crisis of youth unemployment, Amy Newcomb, Talloires Network, United States.

Modernizing a Curricular Artifact. Can Graduate Students Write Theses That Don't End Up Moldering on Library Shelves?, Lorlene Hoyt, The Talloires Network, Tuft University, United States.

Mukondeni Ceramic Water Filter Business, Vhonani, Netshandama, University of Venda, South Africa.

Niehoff Urban Studio: Thematic Strategies and Didactic Methods, Mehri Mohebbi, University of Cincinnati, United States.

Nordic Nuances Meeting Global Challenges: Learning for Sustainable Development in the Spica Network, Kerstin Sonesson, Malmö University Sweden, Ane Fleischer, University of Greenland, Roar Krakenes, Telemark University College Norway, Britta Lohman, University of Greenland; Mikkjal Mikkelsen, University of the Faroe Islands, Kristin Norddahl, University of Iceland, Birgitte Stougaard, University College Lillebaelt Denmark.

One minute against Malaria, Aranzazu Martínez-Odria, A. Gil-Albanova, N. Nashaat, MITLHE Research Group, Spain

Open odyssey, Ismael Sene, France.

Piloting Integrated Youth Based Stigma and Discrimination Curriculum in Higher Education, Lancelot D'Cruz S.J., St. Xavier's College, Ahmedabad, India.

Practical education in sustainability, Miren Onandia, Jasone Unzueta, University of the Basque Country, Spain.

Practice-Based Learning and Improvement for Medical Students: Engaging an Emergency Department in Knowledge Transfer and Exchange, Andrew Park, United States.

Practices Leading to an Academy of Community Engagement Scholarship: Timeline, Patricia M. Sobrero, North Carolina State University, Katy Campbell, University of Alberta, United States.

Professional Development Diagnostic Tool for Business and Community Engagement, Simon Whittemore, Bob Bell, Anne Craig, Linda Baines, Marc Dobson, Carl Vincent, Anthony Gladdidh, United Kingdom.

Programa de Apoyo al Desarrollo Local: PADEL (Lambayeque – Perú), Juan Carlos Pérez Bautista, Juan Carlos, Universidad Señor de Sipán, Peru.

Project Aahaar, reclaiming life the culinary way, Abhay Kumar, India.

Project Life On Wheels, let them own what they owe, Abhay Kumar, India.

Promoting Sustainable Livelihoods: Revealing/addressing a silent public health scourge in South Africa through community engagement, Andrea Rother Judith Favish. University of Cape Town, South Africa.

Putting academic knowledge into public policy proposals, Ignacio, Irrazaval, Catholic University of Chile, Chile.

Relief to Recovery to Rebuilding: University & Community Engagement in a Post-Disaster City, Billy O'Steen, University of Canterbury, New Zealand.

Reviving Community Engagement: Teaching Cardiopulmonary

Resuscitation to Primary School Children – A Special Study Module in Community Based Service Learning, Aoife Jackson, Lorraine McIlrath, Gerard Flaherty, Mauren Kelly, National University of Ireland, Galway, Ireland.

Rural Women's Action Research Programme, Dee Smythe, Aninka Claassens, South Africa.

Science Shop at University of Groningen, Henk A.J. Mulder, Groningen University, The Netherlands.

SCS-CEL: Community based Learning Method for Transforming University Principals (Tri Dharma PerguruanTinggi) – Education, Research and Community Services, Irfan Diwidya Prijambada, Puji Astuti, Irkham Widiyono, RCE Yogyakarta, Institute for Research and Community Services, Universitas Gadjah Mada, Indonesia.

Sense of Initiative Learning Module from Students to Students, Maddi Suárez, IKD Gazte, Spain.

Servers, Not the Served, Mary Pat Zebroski, Cyntia McCauley, Chautauqua Learn and Serve Charter School, United States.

Service learning as a successful methodological strategy in training social responsible professionals, Gracia Navarro, Gladys Jiménez, Margarita Baeza, Manuel Ardiles, Chile.

Service Learning in Ethics, Values and Social Education, Mariona Graell, Spain.

Service learning in universities. Description of an experience in the Faculty of Pedagogy at the University of Barcelona, Anna Escofet, Mariona Graell, Josep Puig, Montse Freixa, Xus Martín, Laura Rubio, Maribel de la Cerda, Mireia Páez, University of Barcelona, Spain.

Service Learning: Fiber Glass Technology for Small Boats Development in Rural Areas, Saman Kader, NurHaha Abu Mansor, Beni Widarmar, UTM team, Malaysia.

Service-Learning as a Bridge from Local to Global Communities, Sook-Young Ryu, Sulggy Park, Seoul Women's University, Republic of Korea.

Setting internationally shared research agendas by CSOs and research institutes through a science shop case, Jozefien De Marrée, Audrey Van Scharen, Nicola Buckley, Rachel Teubner, Halliki Voolma, Vrije Universiteit Brussel, Belgium.

SFU Public Square, Philip Steenkamp, Andrew Petter, Shauna Sylvester, Simon Fraser University, Canada.

SFU's Community Engagement in Vancouver's Downtown Eastside, Philip Steenkamp, Simon Fraser University; Canada.

Shared Learning in Our Community; The Creation of New Knowledge in Higher Education, Cyndi Rickards, Drexel University, United States.

Shere Rom: A learning service programme for minority empowerment, José Luis Lalueza, Marta Padrós, Autonomous University of Barcelona, Spain.

Siem Smun'eem: The Indigenous Child Welfare Research Network, Leslie Brown, Qwu l'sih'yah'maht (Robina Thomas), University of Victoria, Canada.

Social enetrepreneurship LAB, Luz Arabany Ramirez, Steffany Fisher, Julian Ramirez Nieto, Universidad Nacional de Colombia, Colombia.

Social Mission of Higher Education in training of professional personality, Natalya, Shkurko, Moscow institute of public administration and law, Russian Federation.

Socially Engaged Art as Transformative Education: The Dublin 1913 Tapestry Project, Gary Granville,National College of Arts and Design, Ireland.

South Line Program - A model of planning university associations and intercultural, Graciela Giménez, Argentina.

Strategic Initiatives to Impact the Institutionalization of Community Engagement at a Public, Research University, Andrew Furco, University of Minnesota, United States.

Strategies for Engagement in Regional Development, Edward

Jackson, Katherine Graham, Todd Barr, Andre Spitz, Carleton Centre for Community Innovation, Canada.

Student Community Engagement in a Changing Economic Context, Dr Juliet Millican, University of Brighton, United Kingdom.

Student supporting permanence program, Yenci Paola Avila, Universidad Cooperativa de Colombia, Colombia.

Student-staff-community partnerships using fiber glass technology for small boats, Nur Naha, Abu Mansor, Universiti Teknologi Malaysia, Malaysia.

Support for Implementation of Experiential Learning in Faculties, Mary Ho, Gallant Ho Experiential Learning Centre, The University of Hong Kong, Hong Kong.

Taking the Pulse of the New Saskatchewan: A Case of Community Engaged Scholarship, Harley Dickinson, University of Saskatchewan, Canada.

Taking the University to Grassroots Communities in Vhembe District of South Africa: Processes and Experiences, Joseph Francis, Institute for Rural Development, University of Venda, South Africa.

TANDEM PROJECT Josep Holgado García, Universitat Rovira i Virgili, Spain.

Teaching–Learning the Practice of Empowerment: Reflections on ANANDI as a 'field placement' for students, Jahnvvi Andaharia, Anandi, India.

Technipedia - From idea to business, Najda Gmelch, Catalan Association of Public Universities, Spain.

The Classroom Assessment Scoring System (CLASS) in American Indian/Alaska Native Head Start Programs: Implementation, Evaluation and Cultural Relevance, Jessica Barnes, Ann Belleau, Inter-Tribal Council of Michigan; Michelle Sarche, Centers for American Indian and Alaska Native Health. University of Colorado Anschutz Medical Campus; Hope Gerde, Patricia Farrell, Hiram Fitzgerald, Michigan State University, United States.

The Environmental Law Clinic at Universitat Rovira i Virgili, Maria Marquès, Aitana de la Varga Pastor, Universitat Rovira i Virgili, Spain.

The IDEA Portal – Innovative Approaches to Doctoral Education in Africa, Nadja, Gmelch, Catalan Association of Public Universities, Spain.

The Inclusive Neighborhood: Ras Beirut, Lebanon Mounir Mabsout, Cynthia Myntti, American University of Beirut, Lebanon.

The Indigenous Intercultural University Network - a place for dialogue on knowledge, Roberto Alulima, Homayra Condarco, Claudia Stengel, UII-GIZ, Bolivia.

The Interuniversity Framework Programme for Equity and Social Cohesion Policies in Higher Education, María Manuela Guilherme, António Teodoro, José Beltrán, Alejandra Montané, Universidade Lusófona de Humanidades e Tecnologias, Portugal.

The MacJannet Prize: Recognising Sustained Community-University Partnership Around the Globe (2009-2013), Maureen Keegan, The Talloires Network, Tufts University, United States.

The Olifants River Harder Fishery Co-management Project, Judith Favish, University Of Cape Town, South Africa.

The Practice of Transmedia Storytelling Edutainment in E-Learning Environments, Stavroula Kalogeras, The Business College of Athens, Greece.

The Project of Learning-Service in the University of Zaragoza: taking care of professional futures integral formation, Pilar Arranz, Marta Liesa, Diana Aristizábal, Belén Dieste, Tatiana Gayán, Rebeca Soler, Sandra Vázquez, Alberto Abán, Universidad de Zaragoza, Spain.

The role of the university in the transformation of a territory of poverty, Paulo Speller, Sofia Lerche Vieira, University of International Integration of the Afro-Brazilian Lusophony, Brazil.

The social clinic and supervision as the construction of a reflexive position socially committed to service learning in the university. An experience in the degree in Social Work, Carmina Puig Cruells, University Robvira i Virgili, Spain.

The Tawasol Project – A Case Study of EU and Arab World Universities through Civic Engagement and Service Learning, Lorraine McIlrath, Michele Lamb, Rhanda Mahasneh, Mounir Mabsout, Hashemite University in Zarqa, Al Al-Bayt University, Jordan, University of Balamand, Lebanon, American University of Beirut, Lebanon, Nui Galway, Ireland, University of Gothenburg, Sweden, Hashemite University, Jordan, Plovdiv University, Bulgaria, Roehampton University, United Kingdom, Zarqa Private University, Jordan.

The UGA Tunisia Educational Partnership: A Holistic Global engagement Paradigm, Takoi Hamrita, University of Georgia, Tunisia.

The UK Community Partner Summit, Sophie Duncan, Deputy Director, Sharon Court, Kim Aumann, National Co-Ordinating Centre For Public Engagement, United Kingdom.

Thematic Strategies and Didactic Methods, Frank Russell, Mehri Mohebbi, M. Arch, University of Cincinnati Niehoff Urban Studio, United States.

Towards a University Social Commitment: Building Together, Estefanía Buzzinini, Juan Cruz Hermida, Universidad Católica Argentina, Argentina.

Towards networks research governance model? Isabel Pinho, University of Aveiro, Portugal; Denise Leite, Universidade Federal do Rio Grande do Sul, Brasil.

Towards Participatory Planning & Education: Citywide Enumerations in Uganda, Mara, Forbes, The New School, United States.

Transformational Relationships and Social Change: Learning to Speak Good Community Corey Dolgon, United States.

Transformative Reynolds University of Victoria, Kathy Sanford, University of Victoria, Canada.

UNESCO Chair in 'Equity and Non-Discrimination, Martha de la Mora Gómez, University of Guadalajara, Mexico.

Universities and their environments: Engagement, partnerships, and conditions of mutual relationships, Margo Fryer, Hans G. Schuetze, University of British Columbia, Canada.

University relations company strategy to promote sustainable development on business environment care in Bogota. Nubia Edith Céspedes Prieto, María Silvana Ballestas Alemán, Juan Bautista Carda Catello.

University-Community Engagement: Nyanya Group Village Headman Project, Dorothy Nampota, University of Malawi, Malawi.

Violence Against Women, Judith Favish, University of Cape Town, South Africaaki Andharia, Anandi, India.

Visualizing Community and Justice, Nicholas Longo, Eric Sung, Providence College, United States.

Women from indigenous communities researching food shortages: Towards methodological advancement of community research, Neeta Hardikar, Jan 'Are you ready? The Community Readiness Model as a tool for Engagement and Partnerships', Christine, FitzGerald, National University of Ireland, Galway, Ireland.

Youth Academy. A University Experience for 10 Year Olds, Geraldine Marley, Lorraine Mcllrath, Community Knowledge Initiative, NUI Galway; Caroline Heary, School of Psychology, NUI Galway; Mary Dempsey, College of Engineering and Informatics, NUI Galway, Ireland.

Youth economic participation initiative (YEPY). Mobilizing Universities to Address the Global Crisis of Youth Unemployment, Jennifer Catalano, Rantini Oluwasegun, Amy Newcomb, Edwin Nelson, Tufts University, United States.

PART IV
REGIONAL DEVELOPMENTS

Evidence from engaged universities around the world demonstrates that there is a global movement of universities dedicated to civic engagement and social responsibility. This movement contributes to societal change by enlarging existing notions of knowledge generation and impact. Experience and perspectives from the global south are essential to growing and strengthening this movement, and national and regional networks constitute a key dimension of the movement's infrastructure and momentum. Our regional overview synthesizes information from the regional papers and from the research and experience of the Talloires Network to describe this global movement; it also provides a collective vision and agenda for civic engagement in higher education.

INTRODUCTION

Developing alternative methods of knowledge production, mobilization and dissemination is an increasingly urgent task in a rapidly changing world. Dominant conceptualizations of higher education's role in the process of knowledge production are insufficient and, in some instances, antiquated. Although knowledge production through research is a valued function within many institutions of higher education, it can be substantially and strategically enhanced in combination with teaching and service functions. The integration of research, teaching and service through civic engagement expands both the sites and the epistemologies of knowledge, focusing attention on the production of knowledge that is relevant and crucial to solving pressing societal problems. Engaged universities are moving beyond the ivory tower, blending research, teaching and service functions with guidance and support from local community partners. Collecting, analysing and sharing university civic engagement practices from different regions of the world can foster dialogue and learning as national, regional and global networks of engaged universities craft an agenda for change.

The regional portraits of university civic engagement prepared for this volume describe a growing global movement with a high level of common vision and strategy, led by dynamic national and regional coalitions, and illustrate the distinctive experience and perspectives of the global south. In all parts of the world, these national and regional coalitions are growing in size and strength. Impressive examples include the Latin American Center for Service-Learning, the Ma'an Arab University Alliance for Civic Engagement, the South African Higher Education Community Engagement Forum, AsiaEngage, Engagement Australia, Campus Engage in Ireland, and Campus Compact in the USA. These coalitions are further evidence that there is a global movement underway. In addition, they are influential vehicles for promoting and growing the movement – through an exchange of experience and mutual support, and through collective voice and action.

This global movement is therefore characterized by both a diversity and a universality – of goals, approach and programmatic direction. While there is significant variation across and within regions, the larger story is one of a common vision, strategy and cause. These commonalities are striking, especially as their geopolitical contexts vary dramatically. The regional papers present powerful examples of individual and collective leadership for change by university professors, administrators, staff, students and their community partners.

AN EXPANDING GLOBAL MOVEMENT

Combining observations from the regional papers with our own observations from research and practice with engaged universities, we believe there is strong evidence that there is a global movement of civic engagement in higher education (Bjarson and Coldtream, 2003). The presence of a global movement is supported by the growth in the number of engaged universities, the increased

Lorlene M. Hoyt and Robert M. Hollister

collaborative action among these institutions, the rise of university conferences dedicated to the topic, the growing body of scholarship and publication in the field, and increased support for university civic engagement within communities and from funders.

The first observation to support the existence of a global movement is the steady growth in the number and type of universities that are expressing a commitment to civic engagement. Gradually, universities around the world are refining their missions, joining national and regional networks of engaged universities and signing declarations that affirm their dedication to social responsibility. For example, the membership of the Talloires Network has increased dramatically. The Network is the primary global alliance committed to strengthening the civic roles and social responsibilities of higher education. It mobilizes its members to improve community conditions and, in the process, to educate students to be leaders for change. At the network's founding conference in Talloires, France, in 2005, 29 university heads from 23 countries created and signed the Talloires Declaration on the Civic Roles and Social Responsibility of Higher Education. Today, the Talloires Network has a total of 301 members in 71 different countries around the world. With 48 in Africa, 34 in the Asia-Pacific region, 56 in Europe and Central Asia, 42 in Latin America and the Caribbean, 16 in the Middle East and North Africa, 63 in North America, and 42 in South Asia, substantial geographical diversity is a defining feature of the coalition (Talloires Network, 2013).

Additionally, the numerous regional examples in this paper illuminate the scale and steady growth in the number of university administrators, faculty, staff and students as well as community partners that participate in civic engagement activities. Such activities move higher education beyond the ivory tower and include curricular and co-curricular efforts to increase problem-solving skills through interdisciplinary collaboration, as well as to broaden the kind of knowledge that is valued inside and outside the academy. University civic engagement activities include community-based research as well as research applied to policy development and public decision-making. It may also include extensive collaboration between university faculty, staff and students and external constituencies with regard to educational goals and the conduct of research. The most powerful civic engagement programmes aim to achieve mutual benefit between institutions of higher education and the communities in which they are located.

Many diverse sectors are involved in university civic engagement programmes, including the private sector, community-based organizations, governments and philanthropists. Although there is tremendous variation in the way in which universities engage with local communities, common issues emerge from these diverse contexts, such as economic development, alleviation of poverty, physical and mental health, early childhood education and recovery from disaster.

By definition, movements are concerted group action focused on specific issues. Engaged universities not only sustain collective action within their own communities, but also engage with one another. Much like movements targeting issues regarding labour, women's rights and the environment, the university civic engagement movement aims to influence public opinion, government policies and cultural norms by questioning and working to reorient the relationship between higher education and society at large. This movement contributes to societal change by enlarging existing notions of knowledge; it calls into question whose knowledge is valued, where knowledge is managed and how knowledge can serve society.

In-person regional, national and global conferences that critiqued the dominant methods of knowledge creation and dissemination were first held several decades ago in South America and Africa and continue to expand and proliferate throughout the world. Leaders in the Asia-Pacific region are now organizing networks, major events and conferences to share ideas and advance new pedagogies and epistemologies. There are also prominent annual conferences on university engagement in North America, Europe and Australia. Modern movements often utilize the internet to mobilize ideas and people globally, and the civic engagement movement in higher education is no exception. Webinars and other virtual meetings are on the rise and are accelerating the rate of exchange among participants of the movement.

In addition to the regional, national and global networks that have formed and united for the purpose of 'leading, developing and promoting university-community engagement' (part of Engagement Australia's tagline), there are other higher education agencies and organizations for whom social responsibility and civic engagement have become more prominent (Brown and Gaventa, 2009), even in monarchies such as the Kingdom of Saudi Arabia and Malaysia. In 2013, Saudi Arabia's Ministry of Higher Education held its third International Exhibition and Conference on Higher Education in Riyadh. The themes for the first two gatherings were 'research' and 'teaching', in 2011 and 2012, respectively. Suggesting, possibly, that engagement should also be a core mission for institutions of higher education in Saudia Arabia and beyond, the theme of the conference was 'social responsibility.' At a recent conference, presenters from different regions of the world discussed models of civic engagement and 'the importance of engaging broad-based participation in higher education and civic society' (Ministry of Higher Education in Saudi Arabia, 2012).

Additionally, the civic engagement movement in higher education has generated significant public scholarship including books, book chapters, articles, films, reports, blog posts, websites and social media outlets. For example, there are about 20 peer-reviewed journals dedicated to university civic engagement, which regularly publish public scholarship including articles that are co-authored with community partners. These contributions to knowledge and community-building demonstrate how communities and institutions of higher education are being transformed through civic engagement. In addition, the people and organizations in this realm of activity all around the world regularly reference each other's work and describe themselves as part of a global movement.

The growth and diversity of institutional changes taking place within institutions of higher education suggest that this movement is gaining momentum. From resource allocation to faculty recruitment and evaluation, from ethics reviews to student graduation requirements, universities around the world continue to integrate aspects of civic engagement into their missions, operations and cultures (for example, faculty assessment policies at the University of Notre Dame in the Philippines, the National University of Malaysia and Portland State University; mandatory service-learning courses at the Hong Kong Polytechnic University; and the Community Based Research Ethics Review Board in Kitchener, Canada).

Movements, especially those that have achieved some level of sustained success, often incorporate and leverage resources from intersecting groups into their own activities. The civic engagement movement in higher education in recent years has witnessed a rise and spread of related movements with common strategies, visions and values. For example, social entrepreneurship and corporate social responsibility are gaining traction in many regions. These ideas and practices are often aligned with university civic engagement. In Hungary's South Transdanubia region, community activists, including the Mayor of Karasz, work collaboratively with the higher education sector to 'restore traditions and to generate income.' This community–university partnership creatively blends elements of corporate social responsibility and civic engagement. In Europe, there are innovative forms of civic engagement such as the Science Slam and Living Laboratories and Social Innovation emerging from universities, yet the focus is largely on business engagement as policy-makers struggle to make public engagement with society a cornerstone of university missions.

This global movement also encourages and reflects increased public and private support for civic engagement in higher education. National governments, private foundations and development agencies are investing in university civic engagement (Bloom et al., 2006). For example, in the USA, the National Institutes of Health Director's Council of Public Representatives created a community engagement framework, including a peer-review process for evaluating research that engages communities. Their aim is to increase accountability and equality between researchers and the communities with whom they partner.

Furthermore, engaged university partnerships with corporate and other foundations are on the move. In July 2012, the Talloires Network launched a new $5.9 million global Youth Economic Participation Initiative funded by the MasterCard Foundation. This programme aims to address the global crisis in youth unemployment by supporting the efforts of engaged universities in developing countries to create and test innovative models that enable university students and recent alumni to become successful employees and entrepreneurs in their communities. In Russia, the national government has consolidated many existing universities and called on them to elevate their contributions to regional social and economic development. To help the higher education sector navigate this transition, the New Eurasia Foundation, a Russian non-profit organization located in Moscow, is sponsoring a multi-year series of conferences and training to encourage and guide Russian universities to develop new and expanded civic engagement programmes. And several major donor programmes, including Tempus (European Union) and the United States Agency for International Development, are providing funding for higher education partnerships for development and civic engagement.

THE POWER OF REGIONAL NETWORKS

International and regional networks that focus specifically on university civic engagement are playing a major role in supporting universities in all parts of the world. These coalitions have grown in number, size of membership and capability in recent years, displaying impressive leadership, energy and momentum. Such coalitions are effective vehicles for the exchange of experience as well as capacity-building and collective voice in policy advocacy. International networks collaborate with regional networks and include the Global Alliance for Community-Engaged Research, the International Consortium for Higher Education, Civic Responsibility, and Democracy, the Global University Network for Innovation, the Association of Commonwealth Universities and the Talloires Network.

Regional networks such as the Ma'an Arab University Alliance for Civic Engagement and the South African Higher Education Community Engagement Forum are at different stages of development, and appear to be experiencing a similar development trajectory. They typically begin with convening informally, move to greater organizational formality and structure, focus initially on an exchange of experience and later on joint programmes, and successfully transition from founding leaders to subsequent leaders with increasing support both regionally and locally.

The Ma'an Arab University Alliance for Civic Engagement emerged in 2008, among broad acknowledgement that higher education in the Arab region was in crisis. The Gerhart Center for Philanthropy and Civic Engagement at the American University in Cairo then invited senior staff, faculty and students from Arab universities to a conference in Cairo to explore potential interest in civic engagement in higher education institutions. They discovered a high level of interest from people at universities across the region. Rather than wait for major public policy changes, participants expressed a belief that civic engagement might be a way to substantially reform higher education from within (Watson et al., 2011). Civic engagement leaders believe institutions of higher education in the Arab world need engaged forms of research and teaching as well as practical relationships with communities in this time of rapid change. The nascent Ma'an Alliance is an effective vehicle for exchanging experience and knowledge with other regional networks towards this aim (Ibrahim, 2014).

Additionally, such networks are often motivated in part by efforts towards higher education policy reform. From Mexico to Malaysia to South Africa to Australia and beyond, national governments in different parts of the world are undertaking higher education policy reform. In Malaysia, the Ministry of Higher Education launched the Strategic Enhancement Plan for University–Industry and Community Collaboration to support the New Economic Model, adopted in 2010. The latter

has as its principal goal 'to enhance the quality of life for the "rakyat" (people of the nation).' The success of this strategy will depend to a large extent on the ability of universities to create a knowledge economy and conduct innovative research and development (Watson et al., 2011). In many instances, including these two, higher education policy reform fuels the creation of regional networks as well as profound institutional change within universities.

In South Africa, the 1997 White Paper on Higher Education mandated that universities be more responsive to society's needs and called for a new relationship between higher education institutions and communities. This policy is situated within the government policy of development and reconstruction in the post-apartheid era (Hall, 2010). To jumpstart civic engagement in South African universities after the adoption of the White Paper, the Ford Foundation invested in the development of the Community–Higher Education Service Partnerships (CHESP) project, which created an initial network of seven universities and eventually became a broader forum with government and other institutions of higher education. When the CHESP ended, staff at many South African universities decided that there was a need for a forum for institutional managers for community engagement. In 2008, faculty and staff at the University of the Free State began a conversation with colleagues at other universities about the need for a network to sustain their work, which led to the launch of the South African Higher Education Community Engagement Forum (SAHECEF) in 2009. All 23 public universities are currently members.

Today, community engagement is institutionalized in many South African universities (Watson et al., 2011). Even Stellenbosch University, an Afrikaner university and the intellectual birthplace of apartheid, has made a significant turnaround by institutionalizing community engagement with its own governance structure, budget lines, academic work and student activities (Talloires Network, 2010). SAHECEF represents a substantial departure from the past, when African universities aimed to promote colonial ideology, weaken tribal authority and prevent students' exposure to progressive ideas. Numerous historical shifts explain the emergence of the engaged university in South Africa. In the early 1940s, for example, several institutions of higher education were established and implemented policies designed to transform the people from 'colonial subjects' to 'future equal partners.' In recent years, a Pan African Action Research study funded by the African Union Commission explored how the Millennium Development Goals, especially poverty reduction, were being addressed through community–university engagement (Preece et al., 2012).

Engagement Australia, which aims to lead and facilitate the development of best practice community–university engagement in Australia, became an independent legal entity in 2005 with start-up funding from the University of Western Sydney. Known then as the Australian Universities Community Engagement Alliance, Engagement Australia's roots took hold in the 1990s and early 2000s after the Australian government decreed that all colleges of advanced education would be merged with existing institutions or become new universities; many new universities were located in rural and disadvantaged communities and adopted a mission as 'universities without walls.' In 2002 and 2003, the University of Western Sydney organized a forum on community engagement, which has evolved into Engagement Australia (Watson et al., 2011).

As we have noted, national and regional networks of engaged universities often emerge in response to changes in the higher education policy environment. According to Lorraine McIlrath at the Centre for Excellence in Learning and Teaching at the National University of Ireland Galway, the Universities Act, 1997 for Ireland provided a foundation of the expansion of civic engagement in higher education. In 2006 and in response to concerns raised by Robert Putman's seminal book, *Bowling Alone* (Putnam, 2001), the *Taoiseach* (Prime Minister of Ireland) convened a taskforce on 'active citizenship' that developed a set of recommendations about the civic life of Ireland. The taskforce produced two crucial recommendations for higher education: that students' civic activities should be recognized, and that a network of universities should be formed to encourage greater levels of civic engagement. The government then made funding available specifically for the purposes of forming and supporting a network, which was named Campus Engage (Watson et al., 2011).

In most European societies, universities are an early stage with regard to civic engagement. Because, in part, all national systems of higher education have faced pressure from the European Union to prioritize teaching and research through the Bologna and European Research Area processes, civic engagement is often part of an institution's 'third mission,' although there are some noteworthy exceptions. In the Netherlands and Sweden, for example, universities are required by law to interact with and make their knowledge available for society, but their mandates lack a corresponding funding stream. France, however, is a good example of a country where there is strong legislation

and a significant system of financial rewards; French universities are legally required 'to engage with various communities, including working adults, the unemployed, socially excluded young people and the disabled with associated funding at national and regional level' (Benneworth and Osborne, 2014).

In contrast, civic engagement is increasingly becoming central to the missions of higher educational institutions in North America. A wide array of institutional structures and national organizations and initiatives are actively broadening the definition and practice of civic engagement. Over time, the idea of civic engagement has evolved from an emphasis on service to a focus on partnership and to a means for co-creating knowledge to solve pressing problems.

As engaged universities become an integral part of the communities in which they are located, national and regional networks and their community partners are producing new knowledge that is contextual and relational, and in turn making headway on pressing local problems. For example, Auburn University's Living Democracy Project in Alabama aims to enhance the civic agency of students through immersion experiences that foster community relationships and interactions. During the summer of 2012, students lived in Hobson City, Alabama, for 10 weeks and executed a project planned with local citizens. They documented their summer on blogs and Facebook.

A decade earlier, the Universidad Veracruzana created University Social Service Brigades, a novel approach to the compulsory social service that Mexican students must complete before graduation. In 2001, the first 'university house' was built to provide a permanent infrastructure for student community work in the impoverished and indigenous communities in the state of Veracruz. Universidad Veracruzana now has eight such houses in operation. Similarly, in 1994, Brigadas Comunitarias at Tecnológico de Monterrey (ITESM Campus Querétaro) began building bridges between government, civil society and philanthropic organizations. Brigadas supports interdisciplinary teams of 6–8 students who live and work with the local community for 2–4 weeks while on summer or winter break. Together, they have improved the textile industry and started new enterprises, including a company that transforms wine and beer bottles into eyeglasses.

In Africa, Strathmore University's community outreach programme connects students with people living in the nearby Kibera slum in Nairobi, Kenya. Spearheaded by students in 2004, the programme has grown substantially and now includes 250 students, 10 faculty and more than 500 community members.

Strathmore has a 200-hour compulsory volunteer unit taken by all degree students during their 3-month holiday in the first academic year. Through 'work camps,' students and staff live and work with the community for periods of 7–21 days.

EXPERIENCE AND PERSPECTIVES OF THE GLOBAL SOUTH EXPERIENCE

The authors of these regional papers and others observe that the literature about higher education engagement is distorted and dominated by the lens of the global north (Watson et al., 2011; McIlrath et al., 2012; Tapia, 2014). The regional accounts in this volume and other writing make a significant contribution to remedying the predominance in the literature of perspectives from the global north (Bawa, 2007; Connell, 2007). The global south provides the following distinctive experiences and perspectives.

In comparison with the community work of northern universities, those in the south are driven more by the pressing needs of local communities and their countries (Bawa, 2007). While southern universities have clear goals with respect to educating their students to be leaders for change, they show a different balance between goals of community development and of student development. It is more common in the north to find a primary emphasis on student development. This contrast reflects a fundamental difference in driving forces – greater societal demand in the south, a greater institutional push in the north. A related contrast is apparent in the kinds of issue that are the focus of civic engagement in the south and the north – in the south, there is a greater concentration on work to combat poverty and to improve public health (Talloires Network, 2013).

The university approach to political activity also differs between north and south. University civic engagement efforts of northern universities are shaped by the relative political stability in which they operate, and a common goal of university civic engagement is to encourage students to be more politically active. By comparison, in many southern settings, university students are already intensely politically active, compelled to act by unacceptable and sometimes life-threatening realities. Furthermore, there are repeated examples in the global south of universities whose teaching, research and service work is steered and constrained by authoritarian regimes. In some instances, universities may be shut down because they are viewed as sources of political opposition to the ruling party; university professors and students may also risk the danger of disappearance, physical harm or death if they speak out against the regime. In a period we characterize as 'moving beyond the ivory tower', it is important to remember and to celebrate examples of when firm walls between the university and elements in its surrounding communities had positive and courageous meanings. The South African universities that were centres of resistance and political change in the apartheid era are an inspiring example.

In the global south, there are more instances where government policies substantially influence university civic engagement. These include several countries that require university students to complete a specified amount of volunteer service in order to graduate or that offer a civilian alternative to compulsory military services Examples, not all in the south, include Angola, Algeria, Austria, Denmark, Finland, Greece, Mexico, Paraguay and Switzerland. Another set of countries has organized national commissions to advance civic participation and/or formally require universities to contribute to national priorities. Witness the Irish National Task Force on Active Citizenship and the South African government policies noted above that have called on institutions of higher education to advance reconstruction and transformation in the post-apartheid era.

Also important are specific innovative models that hold promise and may represent opportunities for learning, adoption and adaptation elsewhere. Here are just a few examples:

- In 2007, the national government of Malaysia directed the country's four research universities to create new offices of Industry and Community Partnerships, each headed by a deputy vice-chancellor. This organizational approach holds promise for facilitating greater coordination and mutual support between industry partnerships and community partnerships, realms that in many institutions of higher education are quite separate and that fail to connect effectively with each other (Watson et al., 2011).
- For more than ten years, the Pontifical Catholic University of Chile has operated PuentesUC (BridgesUC), a partnership with 14 municipalities in the Santiago metropolitan area. Each year, the municipalities specify unmet community needs and PuentesUC organizes teams of professors and students to address these issues. The university teams help to fill gaps in heathcare, environmental support and community development. Innovative features of this model are its large scale, its formal mechanism for expressing community priorities and

negotiating the university response, the financial commitment by both the community and the university partners, and the high level of accountability of the university actors to their municipal colleagues.

- In a movement that has been long on rhetoric but short on hard evidence, Tecnológico de Monterrey has exerted pioneering leadership in measuring student learning outcomes. Based in Monterrey and operating across Mexico through 36 campuses, the university has for several years surveyed current students and recent graduates to assess their learning of values and skills with respect to ethics and citizenship. Tecnológico de Monterrey's research tools and growing body of experience in using its survey results are a rich resource for the rest of higher education.

Harry Boyte and others have advocated that community–university collaboration move from partnership activities to a next stage in which universities are an integral part of the communities in which they are situated (Boyte, 2004). An inspiring area of innovation in the global south has been the creation of new universities whose primary mission is to advance social and economic development in their local settings. For these institutions, civic engagement sits at the very core of their purpose; it is a purpose that pervades the entire institution and all of its functions. More than a 'third mission,' it is the overarching mission. For example, when Universidad Señor de Sipán in Peru was created in 1997, a primary motivation was to accelerate development of the impoverished Northwest region of the country.

Similarly, in 1992, the government of Ghana established the University for Development Studies to 'blend the academic world with that of the community in order to provide constructive interaction between the two for the total development of Northern Ghana, in particular, and the country as a whole' (University for Development Studies, 2011). The mission of Ashesi University College, created in Ghana in 2002, 'is to educate a new generation of ethical, entrepreneurial leaders in Africa, to cultivate within our students the critical thinking skills, the concern for others and the courage it will take to transform a continent' (Ashesi University, undated). At Ashesi, service-learning opportunities abound. Students and their professors participate in a series of substantial long-term projects that focus on people in and around the community where it is located. The College sees itself as, and acts as, a full part of the community.

Since its beginning in 1990, EARTH University in Costa Rica has focused on 'preparing young people from Latin America, the Caribbean and other regions, including Africa and Asia, to contribute to the sustainable development of their countries and construct a prosperous and just society' (Tiemens, 2012). While many universities work to expand service-learning courses, at EARTH University service-learning is a defining strand in its institutional DNA. Multi-year sustainable development projects are an essential dimension of the university's programme – including rural community development projects in Northern Costa Rica and a carbon-neutrality initiative to reforest much of the university's 8,500-acre campus. A notable feature of both EARTH University and Ashesi University College is that they are supported by special purpose foundations located in the USA. The focus of each of these philanthropies is to build and support an institution that is deeply embedded in its local context, in contrast to investing in external efforts to assist local development activities.

Southern university civic engagement programmes demonstrate forcefully what such institutions can do with fewer resources. Just as the whole higher education sector in the north is better funded than are counterpart institutions in the south, the same is true of university civic engagement programmes. Such lessons are especially important and relevant in a period of austerity. The north can benefit from studying civic engagement approaches from the south and applying them to their own contexts.

Within several of the points discussed above, there are examples of a similar approach and experience of northern as well as southern universities. These instances are a reminder that higher education is a highly segmented sector. The civic engagement practices of different types of southern universities may have more in common with northern institutions of the same category than with those of another category in the same region. A disproportionately large number of the most prestigious universities in the world are located in the global north, so there may be a tendency to equate the practices of that elite group with those of the full spectrum of northern institutions. Just as many of the most innovative and substantial civic engagement programmes in the south can be found in less elite universities, so the same is true in the north.

FUTURE DIRECTIONS – A WORLD OF UNIVERSITIES MOVING BEYOND THE IVORY TOWER

There is an ambitious collective vision that arises from the regional accounts, but achieving this future will not happen automatically. There will inevitably be many challenges and numerous setbacks in the years ahead. Nonetheless, this is an eminently practical vision because it is already beginning to take shape (Goddard, 2009; Watson, 2010). The impressive examples and directions of higher education civic engagement emerging around the world represent seeds that, if nourished, can yield substantial change. This is our vision of what the movement could look like in another decade.

Many universities have moved beyond the ivory tower, and many others are moving in that direction. In addition, an increasing number of new institutions entirely avoided the ivory tower syndrome because they were created with a strong commitment to civic engagement. The fully engaged university has become the preferred model, even the gold standard. This movement has been led by institutions below those in the top tier of prestige. But now many of the most elite universities have started to embrace the forms and levels of engagement that have been innovated by those with less lofty reputations.

Both the absolute number and the proportion of institutions of higher education that are engaged with their communities have grown substantially. A defining feature of the new generation of engaged universities is a network of community partners – non-governmental organizations, government agencies and private businesses – that work closely with them in both planning and implementing community-collaborative teaching and research. These are long-term, sustained working relationships. Both universities and their community partners assess these collaborative efforts in terms of their impacts on teaching and research and also the impacts on community conditions. At the same time, a growing number of universities do not describe their community presence in the vocabulary of 'community–university partnerships', but rather in terms of being integral parts of the communities in which they are located.

There exists a much larger body of fresh knowledge that has been co-created by universities and their community partners. This knowledge has been generated through their complementary insights, skills and access – about issues such as the effectiveness of alternative approaches to local economic development, the dynamics of cultural change, the health impacts of environmental pollutants, and electoral participation and alternative governance structures.

Internal organizational changes have accompanied these advancements and have, of course, played a large role in achieving them. Many universities have created new high-level positions responsible for coordinating and supporting university civic engagement. In addition, a growing number of institutions have adjusted their faculty assessment and advancement policies to give greater weight to the quality and the impacts of professors' community-engaged teaching and research.

National and regional networks of universities that focus specifically on civic engagement have grown in number, the size of their membership and the robustness of their programmes. Constituting a key dimension of infrastructure, these coalitions are primary vehicles for the exchange of experience, capacity-building and collective voice in policy advocacy.

University civic engagement has emerged as an important aspect of the rapidly expanding online educational offerings. Areas of vigorous innovation include courses and training modules for community partners, and also for combined community and university constituencies. An exciting area of collaboration among universities is the development of online and hybrid courses that analyse the causes of societal problems that are the focus of university engagement activities. Universities have shared the costs of curriculum development in this realm, and have pooled their expertise, community expertise and other resources to create curricular units that are used by many institutions. This trend complements service-learning that is embedded in individual courses.

The impressive impacts of the UNESCO Chair for Community Based Research and Social Responsibility in Higher Education have stimulated the development of several regional analogues, professorships that are platforms for inter-university leadership.[1] People realized that the UNESCO Chair was the global equivalent of a university professorship, the kind of institution-wide position employed in many places to recognize distinguished scholars and to enable them to teach throughout the university. A number of regional bodies have created such professorships that both transcend and knit together individual universities. At the same time, several universities have established professorships in the social responsibility dimensions of varied disciplines.

University civic engagement has come to encompass basic institutional operations as well as their teaching and research. It is increasingly the case that universities meet a higher standard of institutional citizenship. They pay their employees a living wage and require that their contractors do likewise. They practise environmentally sustainable policies in the design of buildings and in energy consumption. These operational practices reinforce community-engaged teaching and research.

Reinforcing these developments is a major expansion of international exchange programmes for both professors and staff, and also for students, that have a core component of civic engagement. These exchange programmes both build the capabilities of the individual participants and also accelerate the exchange of experience. Students from universities in Argentina and Mexico, and from Indonesia and Vietnam, spend periods of time that combine study and community service at each other's institutions. They return to their home universities cross-pollinating the knowledge and inspiration they have acquired at their sister institutions. Professors and community partners who focus on community-engaged research have similar opportunities for exchange – south to south, as well as south to north, and vice versa. These exchanges emphasize mutual learning, based in an attitude of humility and respect for cultural differences and differences in ways of knowing in the host environment. Their cross-national experiences accelerate the sharing of alternative models and strengthen their own skills in knowledge creation.

The most prominent global ranking systems in higher education now fully recognize and reward university civic engagement. They first added civic engagement as a new criterion. A subsequent stage was then to integrate civic engagement in the working definitions and assessment of educational programmes and research. There is increased evidence that engaged teaching and research is an effective pathway to higher quality teaching and research.

As a result of these changes, public and private support for higher education has continued to grow. The increased visibility of positive community impacts and the production of graduates who are leaders for social change have created a powerful rationale for greater investment. Government, non-profit and business leaders have witnessed the positive impacts of university work in their own communities, and are more inclined to provide greater financial support. Portions of that increased investment are tied directly to sustaining and continuing the growth of collaborative community programmes. Private foundations and development aid agencies have embraced investment in university civic engagement as a promising strategy for addressing their grant-making priorities. Such funders are less sceptical about supporting universities; they are more confident about the strategy of leveraging university resources to combat poverty, improve public health and restore the environment.

There are, of course, powerful forces that obstruct progress towards these future elements of vision and will continue to do so. These counterpressures include:

- The trend of reduced public spending for institutions of higher education is likely to continue as governments around the world are slow to recover from the 2008 economic downturn. Reduced investment and competing claims for resources weakens countries' research capacities and knowledge base, puts additional financial pressure on families and students, and limits campus contributions to local economies through the procurement of goods and services. These conditions may result in cuts to civic engagement and other programmes, as well as a decline in student volunteerism.

- Technical rationality reigns supreme in the global higher education system and its culture. A concept of scientific knowledge is highly valued and rarely called into question, and institutions of higher education are slow to change. This narrow perspective on knowledge limits our capacity to understand reality and generate innovative solutions to perennial problems. The dominant culture of higher education values individualism and competition above equity and collective prosperity.

- Higher education is experiencing a period of 'massification' or rapid expansion of systems. The overwhelming emphasis in some countries – China being a prominent example – is on very quickly creating new universities and growing total student enrolment. In such a system, it is difficult to do anything more than construct new facilities, recruit new professors and implement traditional curricula.

- Many institutions of higher education are located in societies with ongoing political division and opposition. In these contexts, powerful forces actively oppose the priorities expressed by other groups, such as economic participation and self-sufficiency for women and ethnic minorities. The political implications of community-engaged teaching and research and its prospects in unstable or undemocratic contexts varies and presents a host of risks where university engagement with the community could be seen as a threat to the government.

RECOMMENDATIONS

The experience of engaged universities around the world suggests there are a set of strategies that can help to achieve elements of the vision and overcome the obstacles mentioned above (Watson, 2008):

- Align civic engagement with other core priorities of the university. When civic engagement programmes are seen by either their advocates or others mostly as an end in themselves, they will inevitably be treated as competing with other institutional needs. An alternative strategy is to develop civic engagement activities that accelerate institutional progress towards priorities such as student and faculty recruitment, fundraising and educational and research productivity – to reframe civic engagement as a route to high-quality teaching and research.

- Connect institutional goals and strategies with respect to social inclusion and student/faculty recruitment, retention and success, with institutional aspirations and approaches relating to civic engagement. There is increasing evidence that effective civic engagement programmes contribute positively to advancing social inclusion and to strengthening the recruitment, retention and success of groups that are under-represented in higher education, in both staff and student roles.
- Develop and expand new sources of funding for engaged universities. Encourage public and private funders to understand that university civic engagement programmes are a promising investment opportunity, one with a high potential for accelerating achievement of the priorities of private foundations and development assistance agencies.
- Participate in, and contribute to, the higher education engagement movement. Mobilize the power of collective action. Benefit from others' experience and contribute to their efforts to transform their own institutions.
- Document and publicize broadly the emerging impacts of effective university civic engagement programmes. During the current period when the civic work of higher education is growing rapidly, a sizeable gap exists between the extent and results of these activities and the awareness and therefore support for these programmes on the part of opinion-leaders and decision-makers.

CONCLUSION

In closing, our vision is that a decisive majority of universities worldwide should collaborate actively with the communities where they are located. We see a future where institutions of higher education become more effective engines of social and economic development, systematically partnering with non-governmental organizations, government agencies and private businesses to achieve positive community impacts and academic excellence. Such partnerships will move society from a monoculture of scientific knowledge to an ecology of knowledge capable of serving society with innovative solutions to common issues such as physical and mental health, alleviation of poverty and recovery from disasters. In our vision of the future, the ivory tower is a relic of a bygone era and the gold standard in higher education is the engaged university.

NOTE

1 Based at the University of Victoria in Canada and the Society for Participatory Research in Asia, the newly established UNESCO Chair supports partnerships that enhance north–south and south–south policy development and knowledge transfer.

ACKNOWLEDGEMENTS

We thank the regional paper contributors for their thoughtful observations. They include: George Openjuru and Shirley Walter (sub-Saharan Africa), Jerome Slamat (sub-Saharan Africa), Carol Ma and Lean Chan Heng (Asia Pacific), Maria Nieves Tapia (Latin America/Caribbean), Barbara Ibrahim (Arab states), Michael Osborne and Paul Benneworth (Europe) and Hiram Fitzgerald and Sarena Seifer (USA/ Canada). Together, their papers have provided valuable, contemporary insights into the civic engagement movement in higher education – what it has accomplished and how, and where it can head in the future. Additionally, we gratefully acknowledge the feedback, guidance and editorial support we have received from Talloires Network secretariat staff (Jennifer Catalano, Elisabeth Holden, Maureen Keegan, Amy Newcomb Rowe and John Pollock), as well as GUNi staff and affiliates (Cristina Escrigas, Jesús Granados, Budd Hall and Rajesh Tandon).

REFERENCES

Ashesi University (undated) 'Ashesi's Mission and Vision'. Retrieved September 7, 2013 from http://www.ashesi. edu.gh/about/mission-and-vision.html.

Bawa, A.C. (2007) 'Rethinking the place of community-based engagement at universities'. In: McIlrath, L. and I. Mac Labhrainn (eds), *Higher Education and Civic Engagement: International Perspectives*. Hampshire and Burlington: Ashgate, pp. 55–63.

Benneworth, P. and Osborne, M. (2014) 'Knowledge, engagement and higher education in Europe'. In: GUNi (2014) *Knowledge, Engagement and Higher Education: Contributing to Social Change*. Basingstoke: Palgrave Macmillan.

Bjarnson, S. and Coldstream, P. (eds) (2003) *The Idea of*

Engagement: Universities in Society. London: Association of Commonwealth Universities.

Bloom, D., Canning, D. and Chan, K. (2006) *Higher Education and Economic Development in Africa*. Human Development Sector. Washington, DC: World Bank. Available online from www.arp.harvard.edu/AfricaHigher Education/Reports/BloomAndCanning.pdf.

Boyte, H. (2004) *Everyday Politics: Reconnecting Citizens and Public Life*. Philadelphia, PA: University of Pennsylvania Press.

Brown, D. and Gaventa, J. (2009) *Constructing Transnational Action Research Networks: Observations and Reflections from the Case of the Citizenship DRC*. Working Paper No. 32. Brighton: Institute of Development Studies.

Connell, R. (2007) *South Theory: The Global Dynamics of Knowledge in Social Science*. Cambridge: Polity Press.

Goddard, J. (2009) *Reinventing the Civic University*. London: National Endowment for Science Technology and the Arts.

Hall, M. (2010) 'Community engagement in South African higher education'. *Kagiso*, 6, 1–52.

Ibrahim, B. (2014) 'Knowledge, engagement and higher education in the Arab States'. In: GUNi (2014) *Knowledge, Engagement and Higher Education: Contributing to Social Change*. Basingstoke: Palgrave Macmillan.

McIlrath, L., Lyons, A. and Munck, R. (2012) *Higher Education and Civic Engagement: Comparative Perspectives*. New York: Palgrave Macmillan.

Ministry of Higher Education in Saudi Arabia (2012) International Exhibition and Conference on Higher Education, Riyadh, April 17–18.

Preece, J., Idowu, B., Nampota, D. and Raditloaneng, W.N. (2012) 'Community engagement within African contexts: a comparative analysis'. In: Preece, J., Ntseane, P.G.,

Modise, O.M. and Osborne, M. (eds), *Community Engagement in African Universities: Perpective, Prospects and Challenges*. London: NIACE.

Putnam, R.R. (2001) *Bowling Alone*. New York: Simon & Schuster.

Talloires Network (2010) The Talloires Network: Higher Education Responding to Social Needs, Bellagio Center, Italy, March 23–27.

Talloires Network (2013) 'Talloires Network Members'. Retrieved September 7, 2013 from http://talloiresnetwork. tufts.edu/what-is-the-talloires-network/talloires-network-members/.

Tapia, M.N. (2014) 'Knowledge, engagement and higher education in Latin America and the Caribbean'. In: GUNi (2014) *Knowledge, Engagement and Higher Education: Contributing to Social Change*. Basingstoke: Palgrave Macmillan.

Tiemens, T. (2012) 'The MasterCard Foundation and EARTH University Partner to Create $19.5 Million Scholarship Program. MasterCard Foundation Press Release: 26 April'. Retrieved September 7, 2013 from http://www. mastercardfdn.org/newsroom/press/2620-2.

University for Development Studies (2011) 'Facts and History'. Retrieved September 7, 2013 from http://www. uds.edu.gh/history.php

Watson, D. (2008) 'The university in the modern world: ten lessons of civic and community engagement'. *Education, Citizenship and Social Justice*, 3(1), 46–57.

Watson, D. (2010) 'Universities' engagement within society'. In: Peterson, P., Aker, E. and McGaw, B. (eds), *International Encyclopedia of Education*, 4. Oxford: Elsevier.

Watson, D., Hollister, R., Stroud, S. and Babcock, E. (2011) *The Engaged University: International Perspectives on Civic Engagement*. New York: Routledge.

IV.1.1

Global networks on community–university engagement

Association of Commonwealth Universities (ACU) University Extension and Community Engagement Network

SECRETARIAT: London (UK).
INSTITUTION: The Association of Commonwealth Universities.
WEBSITE: https://www.acu.ac.uk/ (accessed 28 June 2013).
MEMBERS: n/a.

The Network provides a forum for the exchange of good practice in community engagement and outreach. The Network looks to enable a sharing of experiences in building and sustaining links between universities, policy-makers, enterprise and public stakeholders.

Campus Compact

SECRETARIAT: Boston, MA (USA).
INSTITUTION: n/a.
WEBSITE: http://www.compact.org/ (accessed 6 March 2013).
MEMBERS: Almost 1,200 college and university presidents from the US and from 6 other different countries.

Campus Compact advances the public purposes of colleges and universities by deepening their ability to improve community life and to educate students for civic and social responsibility. Campus Compact envisions colleges and universities as vital agents and architects of a diverse democracy, committed to educating students for responsible citizenship in ways that both deepen their education and improve the quality of community life. They challenge all of higher education to make civic and community engagement an institutional priority (text taken from http://www.compact.org/about/history-mission-vision/ [accessed 6 March 2013]).

Global alliance on Community-Engaged Research (GACER)

SECRETARIAT: Victoria (Canada) and New Delhi (India).
INSTITUTION: University of Victoria (Canada).
WEBSITE: http://www.gacer.org/ (accessed 28 June 2013).
MEMBERS: n/a.

The main objective of the Alliance is to facilitate the sharing of knowledge and information across continents and countries to enable interaction and collaboration to further the application and impact of community-based research for a sustainable just future for the people of the world. Organizations involved in community-based research from around the world are invited to participate in an open and democratic Alliance that adds value to existing networking and collaborative endeavours (text taken from http://www.gacer.org/about-gacer/ [accessed 28 June 2013]).

Global University Network for Innovation (GUNi)

SECRETARIAT: Barcelona (Spain).
INSTITUTION: Universitat Politècnica de Catalunya (UPC), UNESCO and United Nations University (UNU).
WEBSITE: http://www.guninetwork.org/ (accessed 25 July 2013)
MEMBERS: 208 (as of 15 March 2013).

GUNi's mission is to strengthen the role of higher education in society, contributing to the renewal of the visions, missions and policies of higher education across the world under a vision of public service, relevance and social responsibility. Furthermore, GUNi's main objectives are to encourage higher education institutions to reorient their role for broadening their social value, embrace this process of transformation and strengthen their crucial stance within society; promote the exchange of resources, innovative ideas and experiences to facilitate higher education's role for social transformation; foster networking among higher education institutions and cooperation between them and society; help bridge the gap between developed and developing countries in the field of higher education and foster cooperation north–south and south–south; and allow collective and cooperative reflection, and the exchange and production of knowledge regarding what social responsibility and relevance should mean in the emerging planetary era (text taken from http://www.guninetwork.org/about-guni/mission_objectives [accessed 25 July 2013]).

International Association for Research on Service-learning and Community Engagement (IARSLCE)

SECRETARIAT: New Orleans, LA (USA).
INSTITUTION: Tulane University Center for Public Service.
WEBSITE: http://www.researchslce.org/ (accessed 6 March 2013).
MEMBERS: n/a.

IARSLCE's mission is to promote the development and dissemination of research on service-learning and community engagement internationally and across all levels of the education system. Their objectives are to advance the fields of service-learning and community engagement research across the educational spectrum (primary, secondary, post-secondary and further education) (text taken from http://www.researchslce.org/about/ [accessed 6 March 2013]).

Living Knowledge – the International Science Shop Network

SECRETARIAT: Bonn (Germany).
INSTITUTION: n/a.
WEBSITE: http://www.livingknowledge.org/livingknowledge/ (accessed 6 March 2013).
MEMBERS: n/a.

The international Living Knowledge Network (LK) is set up for people interested in building partnerships for public access to research. Members use the network platform and its tools for documentation and to exchange information, ideas, experiences and expertise on community-based research and science and society relations in general. LK focuses on strategic issues and is active within political settings. The Network's activities range from strategic networking to the training of individual skills, and from information to mentoring of old and new practitioners in public engagement with research.

Pascal International Observatory

SECRETARIAT: Glasgow (Scotland).
INSTITUTION: University of Glasgow.
WEBSITE: http://pascalobservatory.org (accessed 6 March 2013).
MEMBERS: 39 (as of 6 March 2013).
REGIONAL OFFICES: Northern Illinois University (USA), University of South Africa (South Africa), Royal Melbourne Institute of Technology (Australia), University of Glasgow (Europe).

PASCAL International Observatory aims to connect the communities of policy-makers, practitioners and researchers through an innovative approach to the sharing and exchange of cutting-edge best practice research, ideas and policies. PASCAL is focused on creating new knowledge, sharing and exchanging current knowledge and best practice wisdom, consolidating, interpreting and applying state-of-the-art knowledge in policy and practice development, and creating and facilitating opportunities for knowledge-sharing and mutual learning (text taken from http://pascalobservatory.org/about/what-we-do [accessed 6 March 2013]).

Talloires Network

SECRETARIAT: Medford, MA (USA).
INSTITUTION: Tufts University.
WEBSITE: http://talloiresnetwork.tufts.edu/ (accessed 6 March 2013).
MEMBERS: 300 (as of 1 June 2013).
REGIONAL PARTNERSHIPS: AsiaEngage, Campus Compact, Campus Engage, Latin American Center for Service-Learning

(CLAYSS), Engagement Australia, Ma'an Arab University Alliance for Civic Engagement, Russian Community Universities Network, South African Higher Education Community Engagement Forum (SAHECEF).

The Talloires Network is an international coalition of universities committed to strengthening the civic roles and social responsibilities of higher education. The Network works to advance university civic engagement as a strategy to address societal challenges and improve research, teaching and learning. The goals of the Network are to: foster connections between individuals and communities of practice to facilitate the exchange of ideas and strengthen the global movement of engaged universities; generate, share and use knowledge about university civic engagement; increase awareness and support for university civic engagement among communities, governments, funders and other stakeholders; and facilitate collective action among university leaders, faculty, staff, students, and community partners to reform policy and practice in higher education (text taken from http://talloiresnetwork.tufts.edu/what-is-the-talloires-network/ [accessed 6 March 2013]).

University-Community Partnership for Social Action Research (UCP-SARnet)

SECRETARIAT: Tempe, AZ (USA).
INSTITUTION: Arizona State University
WEBSITE: http://ucpsarnet.org/ (accessed 4 October 2013).
MEMBERS: About 1,600 individual members (students, university faculty members, community activists and governmental officials) and 42 organizational members (as of 6 October 2013).

UCP-SARnet is a global network of students, universities, community organizations and local governments engaged in finding solutions to the most pressing global issues as articulated in the United Nations Millennium Development Goals (MDGs). Its vision is to contribute to the MDGs by building, inspiring, promoting and facilitating cross-sector collaborations, and multi-cultural dialogues (text taken from http://ucpsarnet.iglooprojects.org/aboutus/ourmission [accessed 4 October 2013]).

IV.2
KNOWLEDGE, ENGAGEMENT AND HIGHER EDUCATION IN AFRICA*

Shirley Walters and George Openjuru

* This chapter is devoted to Sub-Saharan Africa following the UNESCO regional classification.

Africa's wide diversity of culture, language, socioeconomic conditions, climate, politics and history is reflected in the diversity found in its multiple community–university engagement (CUE) approaches. African scholarship has an ancient and diverse multi-ethnic base that has been impacted by the historical forces of slavery and colonialism. Recent shifts from regarding communities as 'beneficiaries' to a view of 'equal collaborative partnership' between communities and universities are beginning to gain momentum and to yield mutually beneficial outcomes. A constructivist framework describing 'scholarly', 'benevolent', 'democratic' and 'professional' discourses is used to describe and illustrate CUE approaches in Africa. Examples are given of national policies and legislative CUE frameworks, and challenges to implementation are discussed. These require 'boundary-spanners' who understand cross-cultural dynamics and have the ability to co-create hybrid cultural spaces where people can collaborate to develop shared visions. The scholarship of CUE brings into focus questions of belonging and identity, which in Africa can manifest as a bricolage of traditional and modern elements of culture. CUE in Africa suggests directions for the transformation of higher education as a social responsibility to citizens and societies both locally and globally. CUE is, however, under-theorized, and more research is required to understand, learn and teach how to mediate the complex relationships that CUE requires.

INTRODUCTION

Africa is a vast continent with a great diversity in terms of culture, religion, socioeconomic conditions, language, climate, politics and history. In this paper, we have contextualized CUE in Africa within a history of oppressive power relations that continues to influence debates and scholarship across much of the continent. We have traced the discourses influencing CUE and discussed competing understandings, national policies and practices, and implementation structures, and highlighted contemporary trends and concerns, as reflected in available CUE literature within selected African universities.

HISTORICAL BACKDROP

Given the vast size of continental Africa, perhaps one of the most distinctive features of African scholarship is its diverse roots, coming from indigenous African, Islamic and European-Christian origins, each with unique ways of understanding the world and engagement with community. One of the world's oldest centres of scholarship, dating from 3300 BC onwards, existed in Egypt, where the Alexandria Museum and Library (3rd century BC) became the largest centre of learning in the ancient world. By the 10th century, the al-Karaouine mosque in Morocco and the Al-Azhar mosque in Egypt had been founded. These are considered to be the oldest continuously run universities in the world. During the 15th century, Sankore was part of an active centre of scholarship, with thousands of students and numerous private libraries situated in Timbuktu (Mali). Today, these institutions of Islamic scholarship in Africa remain deeply influential. However, Cleaveland (2008) points out that:

> scholars did not acquire their skills in universities … they acquired their knowledge through informal institutions that may have been in many ways distinctively West African, but were also clearly multi-ethnic and multiracial.

The indigenous education system was fully integrated with and served the communities' ways of life (Marah, 2006), and continues in many ways across much of Africa. Mbiti (1990) explains the Ubuntu principle, in which personhood and identity are considered to be totally embedded in the collective existence – 'the individual can only say: "I am because we are, and since we are, therefore I am."'

The development and furtherance of a scholarship rooted in African values, with its unique cosmovision describing a holistic and anthropocentric ontology, was truncated by major, disruptive historical forces in the form of slavery and colonial domination, which reached their apex during the 19th century. Although slave trading in Africa has been documented from 3000 BC onwards, by the 19th century up to 50 million people had been forcibly removed from their homes and traded to external sources across the Atlantic and Indian oceans. Colonialism brought with it the legacy of European-style universities where structure and mandate were rooted in the residential model. Together with Judaeo-Christian beliefs of control over nature, individuality and autonomy (Nobles, 1991), Cartesian duality and Newtonian linear causality were major influences on the development of modernist thinking. It was a worldview from which to observe the physical world as separate from the human mind and its capacity for formulating thoughts. Science was believed to be objective, universal and rational, and as being able to bring order, security and social understanding through intellectual pursuit. The belief that Europe was the most enlightened and civilized part of the world was used to justify the subordination of other parts of the world through colonization.

In sub-Saharan Africa, early elementary education, originally introduced by slave traders, was taken over by missionaries and gradually augmented by the activities of the ruling colonial governments (Sicherman, 2005). One of the earliest universities in Africa was Fourah Bay College, founded in 1826 in Sierra Leone (Preece et al., 2012). From the 1920s, several other universities, notably Makerere in Uganda (1922) and Fort Hare in South Africa (1916), were established following the commissioning of the British Advisory Committee on Education in the colonies. In the British tradition of community outreach, an extra-mural unit was established at Makerere in 1953 and at the University of Cape Town in the 1940s. However, universities were established mainly to promote colonial ideology, to weaken the authority of local chiefs, to reduce students' exposure to liberal ideas from universities in other parts of the world and to train local staff to assist in colonial administration (Akin Aina, 1994; Sicherman, 2005).

Towards the early 1940s, several institutions were created that promoted and implemented policies to develop the British colonies as 'future equal partners' rather than as colonial subjects. Alongside the Colonial Development and Welfare Fund, the Colonial Research Fund included the appointment of the Asquith and Elliot

Commissions in the British East African and West African regions to guide policy for the development of higher education in the colonies. Their recommendations have had a lasting influence on the development of higher education (Basu, 2012). In 1945, the Asquith Commission emphasized the importance of universities in preparing educated leaders for self government and promoted the need of 'a strong, fully staffed Department of Extra-Mural Studies [that would] have a vital contribution to make to the development of the community as a whole' (Saunders, 1961).

By the late 1950s and 1960s, several African countries had gained independence. Their presidents made strong pleas for the recognition of African scholarship and an orientation towards community needs in line with indigenous African beliefs and values. In 1961, Nkrumah inaugurated the University of Ghana with a speech drawing on the history of education in Africa (Cleaveland, 2008). The message was echoed in 1963 by Nyerere, who made a plea to African universities to shake off their elitist colonial mentality and contribute to society:

> let us be quite clear; the University ... has a very definite role to play in development in this area, and to do this effectively it must be in, and of, the community ... The University of East Africa ... must direct its energies particularly towards the needs of East Africa ... it's in this manner that the university will contribute to our development ... In this fight the university must take an active part, outside as well as inside the walls. (Nyerere,1963, cited in Mwaikokesya, 2012)

This shift in orientation was reinforced in 1962 during the UNESCO conference at Tananarive on the development of higher education for social and economic transformation and by the founding of the Association of African Universities (AAU) in 1967 to promote the Africanization of African universities through ownership of the curriculum and management, and by serving national and regional development needs through CUE (Preece et al., 2012).

Despite the rise of postmodernism in other parts of the world, the European colonial influence left a lasting impression on African universities (Ajayi et al., 1996) through the positivist orientation of knowledge production that had been incorporated into African universities during the 1950s. This resulted in universities aiming to produce subject/discipline-specific, professional specialists, while subjects such as sociology and psychology were imbued with quantitative methods in order to be 'more scientific'. This orientation was hostile to certain African knowledge systems and traditions and was characterized by:

> Separation and alienation from the rural majority, particularly in the Anglophone countries, reflecting the ivory tower nature of the colonial institutions ..., research that was not related to the needs of the majority and limited access to higher education since the universities were geared towards serving the elite. (Ng'ethe et al., 2003)

At the same time, while the nationalist movements were overtly anti-colonial, the universities 'emulated the goals of their colonial masters in producing an elite population for the bureaucracy and private sector' (Zeleza, 2004).

By the 1970s, African governments were struggling to meet the challenges of matching pre-liberation ideals to post-independence realities in the face of harsh economic conditions, unfulfilled expectations from their constituents and growing inequality between the ruling elites and the masses. While there were inspiring efforts to promote popular participation by President Nyerere in Tanzania in his campaign to imbed 'education for self-reliance', Tanzania was by the early 1980s in the midst of a severe economic crisis, and President Nyerere admitted that the policy had failed to be fully realized.

The neoliberal model of development, promoted by global financial institutions such the World Bank (WB) and the International Monetary fund, had a severely crippling effect on African universities and education in general, not least with respect to community engagement and lifelong learning. Tensions mounted as some nationalist governments grew increasingly intolerant of the criticism that often emanated from staff and students at the universities. Governments responded by restricting their autonomy through exercising increased control over university appointments and funding. In the 1980s, the WB tended to disinvest from universities in favour of primary and vocational education, which led to a rapid decline in capacity across African universities, and impacted the development of Africa-centric knowledge systems, research strategies and the capacity to address local problems with local solutions (Brock-Utne, 2003; Teferra and Greijn, 2010) and community outreach. Externally imposed fiscal policies encouraged:

> an increase in user fees at the universities ... and the reduction of funding support for books, food and tuition fees – making universities ... become places

of learning only for the children of the well-to-do. (Modise and Mosweunyane, 2012)

While the WB has since reversed its policy towards universities, it remains directed within a narrow neoliberal orientation driven by competitive market forces. An important measure of quality in universities is the publishing of research papers in leading, peer-reviewed journals. As quantitative research studies are deemed to be more scientific and therefore more trustworthy and legitimate (Grant et al., 1987), they have a greater impact on policy and public opinion. This underlying bias towards positivist-oriented quantitative research, together with the 'free-market' approach, severely hampered the development of African scholarship uncoupled from Western perspectives. As Nobles (1976) argued:

> As long as Black researchers ask the same questions and theorise the same theory as their White counterparts, Black researchers will continue to be part and parcel of a system which perpetuates the misunderstanding of Black reality, and consequently contributes to our degradation.

It is also important to note that, in the mid-1970s to early 1980s, a group of adult education researchers such as Kemal Mustapha, Linzi Manicom, Yousuf Kassam, Marja-Liisa Swabtz, Marjorier Mbilinyi and others introduced an alternative community-based research methodology called 'participatory research' that was partially theorized. This process culminated into the formation of the Participatory Research Network based in Tanzania and an African Regional Workshop on Participatory Research held in Mzumbe, Tanzania in 1979 (Kassam and Mustafa, 1982). This participatory research approach introduced very well the idea of involving local communities in research projects that concerned them, and its principles are in consonance with CUE philosophy.

More recently, the Implementing the Third Mission of Universities in Africa initiative, a Pan African Action Research study funded by the African Union (2010–2011), explored how the Millenium Development Goals, specifically with respect to poverty reduction, were being addressed through CUE (Preece et al., 2012). The shift:

> was brought about by the realisation that just as knowledge, technology and skills reside in universities, so public and private sectors also command knowledge bases from which the university can

learn and leverage its entrepreneurial and innovative capabilities. (Openjuru and Ikoja-Odongo, 2012)

In summary, the tension inherent in producing African scholarship located within indigenous African philosophies and those which are driven externally persists and remains a central conundrum with which African scholars continue to grapple. The impacts of the socioeconomic and political contexts at different periods in the history of the different countries and regions of Africa have shaped different and often competing approaches to CUE.

DIVERSITY OF TERMS AND CONCEPTS OF CUE

In Africa, CUE varies widely in its terminology, application and outcomes, and stage of development. O'Brien (2012) developed a constructivist framework (Charmaz, 2006) employing four CUE discourses, namely 'scholarship', 'benevolence', 'democracy' and 'professionalism', which describe a series of power relations and development processes inherent in CUE. Its simplicity allows it to be broadly applied as a descriptive tool for CUE approaches in Africa. These are briefly summarized below, followed by illustrative examples.

The 'scholarly' discourse is oriented towards research and theoretical development at the individual as well as at the institutional level. Academics and students remain dominant with respect to the roles of participating communities, with knowledge diffusing from the central core of a discipline, but also emanating from communities. Student reflection about the learning process is key, while engagement between the university and other partners involves the patronage of highly regarded academics to increase legitimacy. 'Scholarly' CUE recognizes the interdisciplinarity of knowledge, but is presented within the confines prescribed by the dominant discourse 'separated from the engagement and service' (Grossman, 2009) where it is incorporated into academic programmes and published in journals rather than as community projects, services or physical structures. Thus, students' learning through reflection is regarded as the key focus of the CUE, compared with practical off-campus work and the provision of services.

The 'benevolent' discourse intends to foster a sense of social responsibility or 'good citizenship' within the student to benefit others. Engagement typically consists of consultations, needs surveys, planning, service provision and evaluation by outsiders who have come to help the beneficiaries (O'Brien, 2012). Typically, the lead role-player is a government department or not-for-profit organization (NPO), assisted by the university; together, they provide the community with a physical product, facility or service. The development of students' skills in planning, performance of services and reporting to the universities' funders is emphasized. Communities are judged on whether they can achieve their goals independently from the service providers. Power relations are highly skewed but not transparent, as service providers determine the service to be provided to beneficiaries in need, thus 'both students and communities perceive the provision of services to be a means of empowerment ... [yet] services are delivered in environments of scarcity' (O'Brien, 2012).

The 'democratic' discourse is explicitly concerned with power relations, social justice and diversity, with the focus on '[affirming] commonality and unity, while ... [validating] diversity and individuality among human beings' (Goduka, 1999):

> The discourse defines engagement as dialogue, with the emphasis on understanding the other's life space rather than necessarily converting that space to mirror one's own. Engagement is characterised by mutuality and the flattening of the hierarchies prominent in the previous two discourses. (O'Brien, 2012)

Rather than being defined by what is lacking in their lives, participating communities are defined by their roles or place of residence. Stakeholders recognize each other as equal partners in knowledge creation and development for interdependence and cohesion between them. The co-creation of multilayered knowledge is emphasized, as are personal skills such as sensitivity to power inequalities, mutual accountability and the use of participatory methods. Power-brokering is the direct focus of the curriculum as the different parties work together towards eliciting social change.

The 'professional' discourse perceives engagement as a transaction that serves to 'facilitate the development of ... future leaders who are not only knowledgeable and competent, but also socially conscious and ethical professionals' (O'Brien, 2010). Engagement between communities, service providers and representatives from universities interacts formally through the use of logical frameworks, contracts, timetables and budgets. Professionalism is displayed as a preoccupation with human and organizational development; marketplace language dominates, with the service provider holding the dominant role. 'Community members are regarded as clients, learners, patients or users of the professional service rendered by students under the supervision of the service provider', while 'Higher education staff highlight their roles as administrators, monitors, accreditors and managers in the service learning process' (O'Brien, 2012).

The application of knowledge, with both specialized practical skills and experiential knowledge, is prioritized in the university curricula. Power is held by those with the resources to undertake service-learning and by external professional bodies who give accreditation for professional practice. Community members, although they may benefit materially, are merely a means to an end, and hence agreements for service-learning 'can often fail or be sabotaged due to insufficient attention being given to skewed power relations' (O'Brien, 2012). O'Brien (2012) recommends that, despite inherent flexibility in the application and implementation of CUE, curricula need to be coherent in terms of the goals and (un)articulated philosophies behind the modules, as well as to avoid unnecessary confusion for students, staff and communities regarding practical realities.

Below, we use this framework as a lens to briefly examine power relations as well as application, implementation and challenges according to the prevalent discourse. Four examples of CUE from different African countries are provided in contexts that have emerged from authoritarianism, war or other forms of oppression and trauma. The relations of power are complex with regards to race, gender, ethnicity and class and have a direct bearing on the dominant CUE discourse employed.

Example 1 is the National University of Rwanda, which, despite the loss of staff, students and resources during the 1994 genocide, reopened the following year. Its mission statement now includes community service, termed 'outreach'. The Centre for Conflict Management (CCM) and the Centre for Mental Health (CUNISAM) were specifically created in response to the genocide. The CCM generates local knowledge about the deep causes of conflict, and aims to develop policies and potential strategies for the development of durable peace. The CUNISAM clinic, run by the Department of Clinical Psychology, provides free outpatient treatment in a country where many still struggle with the aftermath of genocide-related trauma disorders. CUE programmes for 'genocide ideology prevention' include 'Community Dialogue for Peace' and 'Rwandan Reconciliation and Democratic Citizenship', while the 'Civic and Peace Education' module is compulsory for all first-year students. In addition, a free legal advice clinic for local people is run by staff and students at the Faculty of Law to provide ongoing legal support for persons affected by the events of 1994, as well as for other matters. The CUE programme encompasses aspects of all four discourses, but due to its goal to address specific and immediate national needs and the transitional state of the nation, the CUE programme is more aligned with the 'scholarly', 'benevolent' and 'professional' discourses (National University of Rwanda, 2013).

Example 2 comes from the University of the Western Cape (UWC) in South Africa, respected for its long-standing and varied approaches to CUE with its roots as a 'struggle university' during the period of opposition to the apartheid government. Its School of Public Health (SOPH) has built a reputation over 20 years of being a leader in African public health education. It has provided access for more than 700 health professionals, some to Master's level, from more than 20 African countries (Alexander et al., 2009). Its aims include the provision of community-based field training that fosters community partnership, and to empower communities to participate in debates around ethical issues (University of the Western Cape, 1992). The SOPH collaborates widely with international and local parties. Its CUE discourse employs aspects of both 'democratic' (in its interaction with communities) and 'professional' (in its delivery) discourses. However, the SOPH is facing challenges in delivery, capacity and funding, as well as organizational challenges associated with the delivery of a distance learning programme in a university originally structured around contact and residential training (Commonwealth of Learning, 1994).

Example 3 concerns a recent CUE initiative in Mozambique that involved a quadruplicate agreement between women from the local farming communities, an international NPO, an international research organization (IRO) and the Eduardo Mondlane University. The project aimed to empower poor women by linking the research capacity of the IRO with the field operations of the NPO, whose staff had been trained by the university. Although a forum was established at the start of the project to bring all parties to the same table, local government structures were isolated almost from the outset. After two years, it was found that the project had been taken over by the more powerful men and a few wealthier women, while most of the poor women had 'disappeared'. When the project was assessed by external consultants, the IRO research manager observed that 'Participant communities have experienced research fatigue due to prolonged exposure from visits by different researchers' (van Oosterhout and

Chitsike, 2012). Yet, after a participatory field exercise with the consultants, a farmer from one of the participant communities commented:

> We would like to continue having these exercises. We learned (through this participatory work) that we can improve by exchanging experiences. The project should give us a hand, and we are stronger together. In this way we can improve our lives. (van Oosterhout and Chitsike, 2012)

This example, originally employing the 'scholarly' discourse, illustrates the benefits of more equal power-brokering between scientists and communities through the 'democratic' discourse. Yet implementation structures are often problematic in that research contracts state specific outputs at specified dates that need to be adhered to in order to attract funding, while programmatic engagement between communities, university bodies and other partners advances and regresses during its evolution.

In example 4, Favish and McMillan (2009) describe the processes that were put in place in 2006 when the Senate of the University of Cape Town approved a definition of social responsiveness that included 'an intentional public purpose or benefit'. They demonstrate how a range of 'socially responsive' practices feed back into the university's mainstream teaching and research, thus dispelling the myth that socially responsive CUE is a discrete activity, marginal to the core functions and activities of the institution. Rather, it involves feedback loops that embed CUE within teaching and research itself. Similar participatory approaches are embedded at the Centre for Applied Social Sciences and the Agriculture Faculty of the University of Zimbabwe. These examples deal with the epistemology of participation (Umpleby et al., 2004) and the depiction of the resultant changes in social systems (Auerswald, 1990), thereby demonstrating an integrated approach to CUE that stretches O'Brien's four discourses to the second- and third-order levels.

O'Brien's framework is different but complementary to Budd Hall's (personal communication, 1 January 2013) four principles of expression of CUE, which cover a student engagement focus, a community-based research focus, an academic staff policy focus and a 'knowledge mobilization' or 'knowledge translation' focus. O'Brien's framework focuses on the broader purpose or orientation of the intervention as distinct from the focus on a specific target group.

In addition to the examples above, there are within the universities a range of partnerships with government departments, industry and commerce, and civil society, in the pursuance of, for example, continuing professional development, entrepreneurial innovations, public education or social services. These are related to CUE but are not usually described within a CUE discursive framework. For example, at Makerere University, there are two structures: the Makerere University Private Sector Forum (MUPSF) set up in response to the Africa-wide Smart Partnership Dialogue to bring together the public sector, the private sector and the academy to work together on issues of mutual concern; and the:

> 'Triple Helix Intervention [which] brings together actors from Government, Academia and the private sector to find innovative solutions to problems faced by business in order to improve performance and profitability and make business more competitive locally and globally. (Openjuru and Ikoja-Odongo, 2012)

NATIONAL POLICIES AND LEGISLATIVE CUE FRAMEWORKS

CUE is reflected as the 'third mission' in the policies and vision and mission statements of most African universities. Policy recommendations in CUE literature have emphasized that institutional commitment to CUE should start at the strategic planning level in order for institutions to draw on a minimal baseline for institutional support (Preece, 2011).

The national policies for higher education encourage universities to engage in community service that can address socioeconomic problems. However, there are a limited number of specific community engagement policies in Africa at the national level. The easily visible exception is South Africa, where we were able to locate a more elaborate national level policy commitment, which has in turn directly influenced the formation of academic bodies such as the South African Higher Education Community Engagement Forum (SAHECEF), founded in 2009 (Botman, 2010), and Community–Higher Education Service Partnerships, launched in 1999, supported by the Ford Foundation, in response to the call of the White Paper on the Transformation of Higher Education of 1997 (Lazarus et al., 2008). The White Paper laid the foundations for making community engagement an integral part of higher education, with one of its goals being to promote and develop social responsibility and awareness among students through community service programmes to enhance equity and democracy. The National Plan for Higher Education viewed it as a prerequisite, with the Higher Education Quality Committee requiring specific reporting on community engagement in institutional audits. Community engagement is the umbrella term, with community service-learning as just one part of this. This policy notes that it is the universities' responsibility to make a meaningful contribution to the development of the communities within their reach, and recommends that this should be achieved through the integration of teaching, learning and research in terms of internship, clinical practice, work-based education in community settings and other community-based forms of professional training (Department of Education, 1997).

In Uganda, the Universities and Other Tertiary Institutions Act of 2001, amended 2006, holds universities responsible for finding solutions to social and economic problems in the community (Government of Uganda, 2001). In other regions of sub-Saharan Africa, there are only passing policy references to community engagement, with 'service' being one of the three pillars of university education.

At the institutional level, there are a number of internal institutional impacts of CUE on research and education. For example, the mission statement of Makerere University (2007) includes the goal: 'To enhance the capacity of the university to link with and service community, private and public sectors and other universities'. The University of Malawi's strategic plan specifies 'outreach/services'. In Nigeria, both the national policy and university strategic plan identify 'community service', and in Lesotho the universities' vision and strategic plans highlight 'community service' and 'engaging in partnerships', respectively. At the University of Botswana, community service is one of the criteria for promotion of staff, and in Rwanda the Universities' mission statement refers to 'outreach' (Preece, 2011). The University of Limpopo's mission is 'A world-class African university which responds to education, research and community development needs through partnerships and knowledge generation.'

At Makerere University, it is mandatory for all programmes to include field attachment or service-learning as part of the credit. No degree programme can be designed or reviewed and approved without evidence of involving the external stakeholders in the process. There are institutional structures that have been created within universities that are specifically meant for CUE; for example, the MUPSF was created for linking with industry, complete with the appointment of non-academic honorary professors based in the community to promote CUE.

Across the board, there has, however, been persistent dissatisfaction with outcomes. Universities are at varying stages of conceptualizing community engagement practice, with some relying on volunteerism; there are few university senate committees responsible for community engagement; there is minimal government funding for it, with most innovations being driven with support from external donors, services to clients, or relationships with universities located in the north; or it is being equated to community service-learning and is then funded through normal teaching allocations. In summary, it appears that CUE is valued at a rhetorical level as it is referenced in national or university policies, but its translation into practice is often not supported institutionally through high-level senate committees or through dedicated budget allocations. There are, in some instances, offices for CUE, but many CUE initiatives are marginal to the central enterprise of the universities, or they are *ad hoc* or assumed to be integral parts of teaching and research and lack the necessary feedback loops to embed them into central activities.

Continental level networks have reinforced national- and institutional-level policy provision. For example, Africa's New Partnership for African Development (NEPAD) calls for universities and 'higher education institutions in Africa to implement curricula that produce a new generation of all-round graduates with blended entrepreneurial, vocational and intellectual competences to act as nuclei for change'. NEPAD also advocates that universities in Africa have a social obligation for knowledge generation and transfer (Makerere University, 2007, p. 7). In addition to NEPAD, the Pan-African University network, which is the AAU mission, is, 'to raise the quality of higher education in Africa and strengthen its contribution to African development'. Botman (2010) further states that the AAU acknowledges that development is linked to higher education and lists community engagement as a core function of universities, alongside teaching, learning and research.

THEMES

DEBATING KNOWLEDGE

As we have highlighted above, the question of what and whose knowledge counts runs like a fault line through discussions of CUE. Although global and long-standing debates about different forms of knowledge infuse debates about CUE in Africa as elsewhere, the cry for a recognition of indigenous knowledge and the assertion of African identity in its multiple and diverse expressions (Appiah, 1992) penetrate the debates.

A recent study by Walters et al. (2012) on promoting lifelong learning in selected African countries recognizes the importance of linking strategies for 'learning communities' with indigenous African knowledge, traditions and practices of community-based learning:

> building a learning society family by family,
> community by community, district by district through
> tapping into the long existing traditions of community
> learning and converting national policy guidelines into
> sustainable action at local levels. (Walters et al., 2012)

Enabling policies, funding, planning, expertise on the ground and relationship-building are needed to sustain such operations. Running through these are questions of identity, of 'who's knowledge' and of how the diversity of African cultural heritage can be expressed in an increasingly globalized world. The role of universities, together with government and civil society, is integral to building a 'learning society' that plays the tension between the 'modern' and the 'traditional.'

By embracing the idea of knowledge co-creation with the local communities and recognizing that knowledge also resides outside universities (Openjuru and Ikoja-Odongo, 2012), African universities are providing avenues for the acceptance of indigenous knowledge systems through this new CUE thinking.

CAPABILITIES FOR THE ADVANCEMENT OF CUE IN AFRICA

McMillan (2009) highlights the complexity of human relationships in collaboration, in particular the 'boundary work' that engagement with communities requires. This echoes Edwards's (2007) conception of 'relational agency' and the need for expertise and capacities from 'boundary spanners' (Williams, 2010); these people demonstrate strong communication skills with ongoing tolerance and a willingness to understand the cross-cultural dynamics of interactions, as well as a willingness to 'co-create hybrid cultural spaces' (Fryer, 2010) where people can collaborate to develop shared visions (Preece et al., 2012).

To counter the 'othering' of colonialism, both universities and communities need to come out of their comfort zone into 'zones of crossings', to meet on 'a bridge called home', so that new relationships can be forged that demand the fostering of creative and alternative ways of learning for a cultural (re)construction of identity and belonging (Walters, 2009).

In the range of African approaches to CUE, there are the beginnings of acknowledgement of the capabilities, skills and attitudes required to effectively negotiate and mediate the complex relationships that CUE requires, but this needs to go much deeper. There is a need for more research to assist the understanding of what these capabilities are and how they are taught and learnt.

There is also a need to create continental wide structures that can advance and support CUE in Africa. This could starts with, as Preece et al. (2012) suggest, a strengthening of the existing relationship that exists with global collaborative frameworks such as the Pascal International Observatory, which has promoted the CUE agenda globally through Pascal Universities for a Modern Renaissance. There are also national bodies such as SAHECEF, which will need to be encouraged in other African countries and from that to build regional frameworks. In universities, there is still a strong need to mainstream CUE activities in research and teaching and in the administration of universities.

SOCIAL PURPOSES

As we have signalled, there are layers of confusion and complexity in understanding what is meant by CUE – both what is meant by 'community' and what is meant by 'engagement'. At different times in Africa's history, higher education's particular social purposes have been described in multiple, contextually specific ways. In South Africa in the 1970s and 80s, for example, the UWC defined its mission and purpose in relation to the anti-apartheid struggle and attainment of social justice for the majority black population; in the late 1990s, this was redefined in terms of lifelong learning for democratic citizenship and engagement with society to enhance possibilities for redress and equity. In 2010, it strove to be an 'engaged university' within the 'global knowledge economy'. The rich case study of Makerere University in Uganda, as described by Mamdani (2008), conveys a similar movement over time, with 'community' and 'engagement' being variously interpreted in different historical periods.

Another example is CUE in the interests of building a 'knowledge economy.' In partnership with Gaborone City Council, the University of Botswana is developing a 'learning city' (Molebatsi, 2012; Ntseane, 2012), a concept that is still unknown to most universities and it is not yet the defining language for explaining their CUE (Mwaikokesya, 2012). However, 'knowledge transfer partnerships and networks' initiatives that bring together regional stakeholders, local business and community groups do exist at very rudimentary levels (Openjuru and Ikoja-Odongo, 2012). These examples illustrate that 'community' and 'social purpose' can vary greatly. As the UNESCO Declaration on Higher Education (1988) states, CUE must aim at 'Eliminating poverty, intolerance, violence, illiteracy, hunger, environmental degradation and disease'.

In the context of Africa, socioeconomic development is all important. However, which development paradigm predominates is equally important – is it within a positivist neoliberal ethic of intense, possessive individualism, or is it one that values social and environmental relationships that are marked by solidarity and a commitment to collective empowerment and the sustainability of the planet? The dominant development paradigms will invariably be reflected within approaches to CUE.

TOWARDS A CONCLUSION

African universities are increasingly seeking to have a place on the international stage (Teferra and Greijn, 2010) in a globalizing world. Preece et al. (2012) show the legacy of international influences on the curriculum and the locus of training for many African academics – along with ongoing state control where the State's development plans are themselves controlled by external funding agendas – which impinge on the 'African vision.' The Africanization of universities remains only a partially fulfilled aspiration, with very little evidence of its influence on the global stage (Teferra and Greijn, 2010).

The scholarship of CUE concerns the association between community engagement and the construction of knowledge in universities (O'Brien, 2012) but is under-theorized in Africa. The specifics of 'African learning communities in a modern sense', where smartphones and internet-based learning are the norm for increasingly urban populations, is not well known. Mobile technology is almost universal across the continent, with its use being demonstrated dramatically in the 'Arab Spring'. In addition, due to increased financial pressure, the extended family and communities operate differently from how they did a generation ago, so that the notion of 'communal' vs. 'individualist' consciousness is changing and reflects the tension between the 'modern' and the 'traditional', the 'rural' and the 'urban'. Appiah's postmodern vision of the non-existence of one single truth has been conducive to a vision of African identity as a bricolage of traditional and modern elements of culture (Muller, 2005).

There are initiatives at the local level that are grappling with these inherent tensions, where, for example, student-centred learning systems encourage ethical, decisive, innovative, adaptable and reliable graduates who aspire to blend the strong sense of African family responsibilities and values with both individual and wider social responsibilities. There are professional development initiatives for faculty staff to encourage a 'new pedagogy' that emphasizes active student involvement in an experiential, lifelong learning process where students are independent and able to challenge the status quo. Lifelong learning as a philosophy and approach for staff and students, and for the building of local, national and regional learning communities, is growing as part of the dual discourses of the 'knowledge economy' and of 'democratic and active citizenship'. CUE in Africa suggests directions for the transformation of higher education (and its diverse institutions) in their exercise of social responsibility to citizens and societies both locally and globally.

Movements towards this require enabling policies, funding, planning, expertise on the ground and relationship-building to sustain such operations. There is a need for a more coherent national higher education policy, which is translated into institutional policy and structural arrangements, for which institutions are held accountable. These structures require sufficient institutional authority in order to work across faculties and schools in coordinated and influential ways. There need to be incentives from national governments to encourage the integration of community engagement with teaching and research. It cannot be left to 'the market' alone. Relationship-building within institutions, within countries and within and across broader regions is imperative for building and strengthening CUE communities of professional practice. Top-down and bottom-up strategies are required to position CUE in Africa. This includes both high-level international acknowledgement of the importance of universities to the strengthening of societies through collaborative practices, and local 'organic intellectuals' who are activists on the ground.

ACKNOWLEDGEMENT

We wish to acknowledge the contribution of Dr Saskia van Oosterhout for her research support.

REFERENCES

Ajayi, A.J.F., Goma, L.K.H. and Johnson, A.G. (1996) *The African Experience with Higher Education*. Accra: James Currey.

Akin Aina, T. (1994) *Quality and Relevance: African Universities in the 21st Century*. Background paper for the Joint Colloquium on the University in Africa in the 1990s and beyond. Lesotho: Association of African Universities.

Alexander, L., Igumbor, E.U. and Sanders, D. (2009) 'Review: Building capacity without disrupting health services: public health education for Africa through distance learning'. *Human Resources for Health*, 7, 28.

Appiah, K.A. (1992) *In My Father's House: Africa in the Philosophy of Culture*. New York: Oxford University Press.

Auerswald, E.H. (1990) 'Towards epistemological transformation in the education and training of family therapists'. In: Mirkin, M.P. (ed.), *The Social and Political Contexts of Family Therapy*. Boston: Allyn & Bacon.

Basu, P. (2012) 'A museum for Sierra Leone? Amateur enthusiasms and colonial museum policy in British West Africa'. In: McAleer, S.L., *Curating Empire: Museums and the British Imperial Experience*. Manchester: Manchester University Press.

Botman, R. (2010) 'Hope in Africa: Human Development Through Higher Education Community Interaction-Global University Network for Innovation'. Retrieved January 30, 2013 from http://www.guninetwork.org/resources/he-articles/hope-in-africa-human-development-through-higher-education-community-interaction.

Brock-Utne, B. (2003) 'Formulating higher education policies in Africa: the pressure from external forces and the neo-liberal agenda'. *JHEA/RESA*, 1(1), 24–56.

Charmaz, K. (2006) *Constructing Grounded Theory*. Thousand Oaks, CA: Sage.

Cleaveland, T. (2008) 'Timbuktu and Walata: lineages and higher education'. In: Jeppie, S. and Diagne, S.B. (eds), *The Meanings of Timbuktu*. South Africa: HSRC Press.

Commonwealth of Learning (1994) 'Propositions related to the development of dual-mode institutions'. In: *The South African Institute for Distance Education, Opportunities for Innovation in Higher Education, Proceedings of a Workshop and Conference of Vice-Chancellors and Rectors in South African Higher Education*, Johannesburg, South Africa, November 10–12, 1994.

Department of Education (1997) *White Paper: A Programme for the Transformation of Higher Education, General Notice 1196 of 1997*, Pretoria.

Edwards, A. (2007) 'Relational agency – professional practice: a CHAT analysis'. *International Journal of Human Activity Theory*, 1, 1–17.

Favish, J. and McMillan, J. (2009) 'The university and social responsiveness in the curriculum: a new form of scholarship?' In: *London Review of Education*. London: Routledge.

Fryer, M. (2010) 'How to strengthen the third mission of the university: the case of the University of British Columbia learning exchange'. In: Inman, P. and Schuetze, H.G. (eds), *The Community Engagement and Service Mission of Universities*. Leicester: NIACE.

Goduka, M.I. (1999) *Affirming Unity in Diversity in Education: Healing with Ubuntu*. Cape Town: Juta.

Government of Uganda (2001) *Universities and Other Tertiary Institutions Act, 2001*. Ministry of Education, National Council for Higher Education. Kampala: Government Printer Entebbe.

Grant, L., Ward, K.B. and Rong, X.L. (1987) 'Is there an association between gender and methods in sociological research?' *American Sociological Review*, 52(6), 856–62.

Grossman, J. (2009) 'Domestic workers and knowledge in everyday life'. In: Cooper, L. and Walters, S. (eds), *Learning/Work: Turning Work and Lifelong Learning Inside Out*. Cape Town: HSRC Press.

Kassam, Y. and Mustafa, K. (1982) *Participatory Research: An Emerging Alternative Methodology in Social Science Research*. New Delhi: Society for Participatory Research in Asia.

Lazarus, J., Erasmus, M., Hendricks, D., Nduna, J. and Slamat, J. (2008) 'Embedding community engagement in South African higher education'. *Education Citizenship and Social Justice*, 3(1), 59–85.

Makerere University (2007) *Repositioning Makererere to Meet Emerging Development Challenges: Strategic Framework: 2007/08–2017/18*. Kampala: Makerere University Strategic Plan.

Mamdani, M. (2008) *Scholars in the Marketplace: The Dilemmas of Neo-liberal Reform at Makerere University 1989–2005*. Cape Town: HSRC Press.

Marah, J.K. (2006) 'The virtues and challenges in traditional African education'. *Journal of Pan African Education*, 1(4), 15–24.

Mbiti, J.S. (1990) *African Religions and Philosophy* (2nd edn). Oxford: Heinemann.

McMillan, J. (2009) *What Happens when the University Meets the Community? Service-learning, Activity Theory and 'Boundary Work' in Higher Education*. Seminar Paper. Cape Town: University of the Western Cape.

Modise, O. and Mosweunyane, D. (2012) 'Engagement with the city: a new paradigm for rebranding institutions of higher education'. In: Preece, J., Ntseane, P.G., Modise, O.M. and Osborne, M. (eds), *Community Engagement in African Universities: Perspectives, Prospects and Challenges*. London: NIACE.

Molebatsi, C.O. (2012) 'Needs assessment for collaboration between the University of Botswana and Gaborone City Council'. In: Preece, J., Ntseane, P.G., Modise, O.M. and Osborne, M. (eds), *Community Engagement in African Universities: Perpectives, Prospects and Challenges*. London: NIACE.

Muller, L. (2005) 'A thematic comparison between four African scholars: Idowu, Mbiti, Okot P'bitek and Appiah: what they tell us about the existence of "truth" and a "High God", and why their work is significant'. *QUEST: An African Journal of Philosophy/Revue Africaine de Philosophie*, xviii, 109–24.

Mwaikokesya, M.J. (2012) 'Scaling up the African universities' capacity for learning cities and regions: challenges and opportunities in Tanzania and East Africa'. In: Preece, J., Ntseane, P.G., Modise, O.M. and Osborne, M. (eds), *Community Engagement in African Universities: Perpectives, Prospects and Challenges*. London: NIACE.

National University of Rwanda (2013) Homepage. http://www.nur.ac.rw/.

Ng'ethe, N., Assie-Lumumba, N., Subotzky, G. and Esi-Sutheland-Addy (2003) *Higher Education Innovations in Sub-Saharan Africa, with Specific Reference to Universities*. Research Report. Tunis: Association for the Development of Education in Africa.

Nobles, W.W. (1976) 'African science: the consciousness of self'. In: King, L.M., Dixon, V.J. and Nobles, W.W. (eds), *African Philosophy: Assumption Paradigms for Research on Black Persons*. Los Angeles: Fanon Center.

Nobles, W.W. (1991) 'Extended self: rethinking the so-called negro concept'. In: Jones, R.L. (ed.), *Black Psychology* (3rd edn). Berkeley: Cobb & Henry.

Ntseane, P.G. (2012) 'Pathways to an engaged university and learning region: the case of the University of Botswana and Gaborone City'. In: Preece, J., Ntseane, P.G., Modise, O.M. and Osborne, M. (eds), *Community Engagement in African Universities: Perspectives, Prospects and Challenges*. London: NIACE.

O'Brien, F. (2010) *Grounding Service Learning in South Africa: The Development of a Theoretical Framework*. Unpublished PhD thesis, University of KwaZulu-Natal, Durban.

O'Brien, F. (2012) 'Constructing service learning in South Africa: discourses of engagement'. In: Preece, J., Ntseane, P.G., Modise, O.M. and Osborne, M. (eds), *Community Engagement in African Universities: Perspectives, Prospects and Challenges*. London: NIACE.

Openjuru, G.L. and Ikoja-Odongo, J.R. (2012) 'From extramural to knowledge transfer partnership and networking: the community engagement experience at Makerere University'. In: Preece, J., Ntseane, P.G., Modise, O.M. and Osborne, M. (eds), *Community Engagement in African Universities: Perpective, Prospects and Challenges*. London: NIACE.

Preece, J. (2011) 'Higher education and community service: developing the National University of Lesotho's third mission'. *Journal of Adult and Continuing Education*, 17 (1), 81–97.

Preece, J., Ntseane, P.G., Modise, O.M. and Osborne, M. (2012) 'The African university and community engagement in context'. In: Preece, J., Ntseane, P.G., Modise, O.M. and Osborne, M. (eds), *Community Engagement in African Universities: Perpective, Prospects and Challenges*. London: NIACE.

Saunders, C.A. (1961) *New Universities Overseas*. London: George Allen & Unwin.

Sicherman, C. (2005) *Becoming an African University: Makerere 1922–2000*. Kampala: Fountain.

Teferra, D. and Greijn, H. (2010) 'Introduction'. In: Teferra, D. and Greijn, H. (eds), *Higher Education and Globalisation: Challenges, Threats and Opportunities for Africa*. Maastricht: Maastricht University Centre for International Cooperation in Academic Development (MUNDO).

Umpleby, S., Medvedeva, T. and Oyler, A. (2004) 'The technology of participation as a means of improving universities in transitional economies'. *World Futures*, 60(1–2), 129–36.

UNESCO (1998) Declaration of the World Conference on Higher Education (WCHE), Paris, France, October 5–9, 1998.

University of the Western Cape (1992) *Colloquium: The Development of a Western Cape School of Public Health*. Unpublished document, University of the Western Cape, Cape Town.

van Oosterhout, S.A.M. and Chitsike, A.C. (2012) *Analysis of Gender Dynamics and the Potential Consequences of Transforming Goat Production and Marketing Systems for Women in Male and Female Headed Households in Mozambique and India under the IFAD/EU-funded 'imGoats' Project*. Addis Ababa: International Livestock Research Institute.

Walters, S. (2009) '"The bridge we call home": community-university engagement'. Keynote address at the University Community Engagement for Sustainability Conference, Penang, Malaysia, November 2009.

Walters, S., Yang, J. and Roslander, P. (2012) *Study on Key Issues and Policy Considerations in Promoting Lifelong Learning in Selected African Countries: Ethiopia, Kenya, Namibia, Rwanda and Tanzania*. Tunis: Association for the Development of Education in Africa.

Williams, P. (2010) 'Special Agents: The nature and role of boundary spanners'. Paper presented to the ESRC Research Seminar Series Collaborative Futures: New Insights from Intra and Inter-Sectoral Collaborations, University of Birmingham, UK.

Zeleza, P.T. (2004) 'Neo-liberalism and academic freedom'. In: Zeleza, P.T. and Olukoshi, A. (eds), *African Universities in the Twenty-first century Vol I: Liberalisation and Internationalisation*. Dakar: Council for the Development of Social Science Research in Africa (CODESRIA).

Inside View IV.2.1
Community–university engagement in South Africa

Jerome Slamat

In the introductory section of this paper, a brief historical context of South Africa and its development challenges is presented. In the second part, a systems-level view of community–university engagement in South Africa will be offered. The third section puts forward a view of community–university engagement at the individual institutional level. In the next part of the paper, a discussion follows on what is needed to go beyond existing practical arrangements and conceptual approaches,

and in the final section, pertinent conclusions and final comments are made.

INTRODUCTION
South Africa has a bitter legacy inherited from its colonial and apartheid past. All aspects of life, including higher education, are somehow shaped and directed along its current paths because of this history. The euphoria of the advent of black majority rule in 1994 was tempered by the realization of how huge

the task would be to address the widespread poverty, inequality and unemployment that is the plight of largely black majority. It was incumbent on the Mandela administration and subsequent administrations to intervene to address the huge backlogs experienced by black South Africans. Over the nearly two decades since 1994, a succession of developmental plans (the Reconstruction and Development Plan, Growth, Equity and Redistribution Policy, National Development Plan, and so on) were formulated and implemented (with mixed results) in order to fulfil the aspirations of the black majority. All these plans and implementation efforts are aimed at creating 'A better life for all', which was an election slogan of the ruling party, the African National Congress. National development and reconciliation was and still is an extremely ambitious but very necessary project in South Africa.

SYSTEMS-LEVEL VIEW: A DIFFERENTIATED HIGHER EDUCATION SYSTEM IN A DEVELOPING COUNTRY

South Africa currently has 23 public universities and a number of private higher education institutions. As part of the democratization process, new legislation governing public higher education was promulgated and restructuring of the sector occurred through processes of mergers and incorporations. The result of the restructuring process is that South Africa has a differentiated public higher education system featuring 11 traditional universities (offering theoretically oriented university degrees), 6 universities of technology (offering vocationally oriented diplomas and degrees) and 6 comprehensive universities (offering a combination of both the aforementioned types of qualification). However, there are also other bases for differentiation between universities that include the distinctions between historically disadvantaged universities and historically advantaged universities, rurally based universities and urban-based universities, as well as research-intensive universities and teaching universities (HESA, 2009). Historically, there were notions of outreach, community service or extension in most (if not all) of these types of universities in South Africa. These activities focused mostly on philanthropic, volunteer and service activities and were mostly unrelated or poorly related to the academic core functions.

The emergence of the post-apartheid developmental state in general, but specifically the *Education White Paper 3: A Programme for Higher Education Transformation of 1997*, changed all that. This document laid the basis for the Higher Education Act of 1997, which in turn made provision for the establishment of the Higher Education Quality Committee (HEQC), the body that was charged with institutional audits of universities. The White Paper included goals at a systems level, as well as institutional level goals that particularly foregrounded the social responsibility of students and universities. The HEQC, in its audit criteria, included a number of criteria that focused on community engagement. The effect of these specific audit criteria was that it steered the efforts of the universities that were audited towards social responsibility and national development.

However, care had to be taken that the role that is desired of universities in national development be a role that is aligned to the identity and self-understanding of the university and 'the identity structures of academics' in the words of Cooper (2011). It could not be enforced from outside and above, and it had to bear in mind the differentiated South African higher education system.

In terms of the development of community–university engagement in South Africa the following (updated from HEQC/CHE, 2006) can be regarded as seminal moments:

- *Education White Paper 3: A Programme for Higher Education Transformation of 1997*. This document is an example of government steering of higher education and served as an impetus for the institutionalization of community engagement. The White Paper can be downloaded from www.dhet.gov.za/Documents/Legislation/WhitePapers/tabid/191/Default.aspx.
- *The Community Engagement in Higher Education conference, Bantry Bay, Cape Town, 3–5 September 2006*. This was the first major conference on community–university partnerships in South Africa. It featured representatives from universities, different levels of government, non-profit organizations and local community partners of universities.
- *The HEQC audit of higher education institutions*. The audit process of higher education institutions can also be seen as an example of government steering of the sector. Go to www.che.ac.za/media_and_publications/frameworks-criteria/criteria-institutional-audits to view the audit criteria.
- *The launch of the South African Higher Education Community Engagement Forum (SAHECEF), Mangosuthu University of Tech-*

nology, 1–3 November 2009. The forum plays an important advocacy, networking and capacity-building building role in terms of community–university engagement on a national level. Visit the SAHECEF website at www.sahecef.ac.za.
- *Community Engagement in South African Higher Education, Kagisano No. 6, January 2010*. This booklet is the culmination of a national conversation on community–university engagement facilitated by the Council on Higher Education (CHE). The booklet can be downloaded from www.che.ac.za/media_and_publications/kagisano-series/kagisano-issue-number-6-community-engagement-south-african.
- *The National Research Foundation (NRF) Community Engagement Programme, 2010–2012*. In 2010, the Knowledge Fields Development Directorate of the NRF issued the first Community Engagement Call, which elicited a number of prime proposals from universities focusing on 'research that contributes both to knowledge production within the ambit of community engagement ...; as well as research on the processes and dynamics of engagement from the perspective of the higher education sector', in the words used in the description of the Call. See details of the NRF Community Engagement Programme at www.nrf.ac.za/projects.php?pid=49.
- *The Community Engagement: The Changing Role of South African Universities in Development conference, East London, November 2011*. This was the second major national community–university engagement conference, the first having been held in Bantry Bay in 2006. The products of this conference include a book of abstracts, as well as a special issue of the *South African Review of Sociology* (Volume 43, Issue 2) entitled 'In search of a developmental university: community engagement in theory and practice', which is available online at http://www.tandfonline.com/toc/rssr20/43/2.
- *The Trilateral Conference on Community Engagement, SA–USA–China, Durban, 11–13 December 2012*. This small conference featured representatives of the NRF (South Africa), the National Science Foun-

dation (USA) and prominent community–university engagement practitioners, from both the USA and South Africa (unforeseen circumstances unfortunately preventing the Chinese delegation from attending the conference). The findings that will come out of this kind of conversation will critically shape the future development of community–university engagement and its role in the redefinition of the university and scholarship globally.

- *Academic Interaction with Social Partners: Investigating the Contribution of Universities to Economic and Social Development.* This book, authored by Human Sciences Research Council (HSRC) researchers Kruss, Visser, Aphane and Haupt, and published towards the end of 2012, contains the results of a research study of university interaction with external social partners. It represents the first formal research study of community engagement that offers the ability to establish broad trends across the whole South African higher education system.

Because of the differentiation in the South African higher education system, different forms of community–university engagement emerged in South Africa. This is in line with the 'system of progressive self-differentiation based on varying institutional visions and missions accompanied by policies and processes that enable institutions to make meaningful progress in their distinctive developmental trajectories' that is propagated by Higher Education South Africa (HESA, 2009, p. 9).

The 2012 HSRC study employed the typology of relationships between universities and external partners that is outlined in Table IV.2.1.1. This typology corresponds to a great extent with a typology of community–university engagement that is emerging in South Africa based on the concurrent sessions of the 2006 Bantry Bay Conference, as well as the SAHECEF working groups.

Discussions in the SAHECEF Management and Governance group established that most of the institutions are involved in community engagement through teaching; in fact, the Joint Education Trust/Community–Higher Education Service Partnerships process deliberately used the tool of service-learning as an entry point

| TABLE IV.2.1.1 |
HSRC's types of university relationships with external partners
Alternative teaching
e.g. continuing education, customized training, collaborative curriculum design and alternative modes of delivery
Engaged teaching and outreach
e.g. service-learning, student voluntary outreach, community-based research, clinical services and work-integrated learning
Engaged research
e.g. collaborative R&D, consultancy, contracts, participatory research and policy research
Technology transfer
e.g. design of new technologies, technology transfer, design of new interventions and joint commercialization
Source: Adapted from Kruss et al. (2012, p. 40).

to develop community–university engagement in South Africa. Most institutions also have programmes that aim to broaden access to and widen participation in higher education, with special attention being given to interactions with disadvantaged schools. Most institutions also have active student volunteer programmes, and most are to some extent involved in regional development. A smaller number of institutions, because of their research strengths, branch out into community engagement through research. At least one South African university (North West University) has conceptualized its whole community–university endeavour as community interaction through knowledge transfer and the implementation of expertise.

INSTITUTIONAL LEVEL VIEW: INSIDE THE INDIVIDUAL SOUTH AFRICAN UNIVERSITIES

A list of good community–university engagement practices in South African universities can be accessed on the SAHECEF website www.sahecef.ac.za. The importance of these examples of good community–university engagement practice is that they confirm the fact of different institutional community engagement foci and the fact that excellence is spread all over the South African higher education system. These are exemplars that can be emulated by others who find themselves in similar contexts or have similar visions. The examples of good practice can serve to give direction and inform and inspire others in the field of community–university engagement, bearing in mind that this field of higher education is one that is relatively new, and standards need to be set in it.

Regarding good practice in individual institutions, one could ask: what are the institu-tional arrangements within individual South African universities that support engagement? Emerging practice in South Africa (as evidenced by discussions of the SAHECEF Management and Governance Work Group during 2011–2012) seems to confirm the international literature to a large extent (see, for example, Hollander et al., 2002, in this regard). The elements that are important in South African universities to support engagement appear to be the following:

- *Management support.* Community engagement in a university stands and falls by university management support. South African universities that excel in terms of community engagement all enjoy active support from top management, starting with the vice-chancellor.
- *Resources.* Adequate provision must be made in terms of financial and human resources in the main institutional budget for community engagement activities. This remains the best indicator of the importance that the institution attaches to community engagement.
- *A community engagement policy.* A community–university engagement policy that is the result of institution-wide consultation (preferably also with inputs from the major external partners) provides the formal framework to guide the implementation of community–university engagement. Such a policy is normally a mixture of conceptual commitments and practical procedures, and could be updated as institutional and external conditions change.
- *An institutional register of community–university engagement initiatives.* There has to be some form of registration mecha-

nism for community–university engagement initiatives within the institution. This can take the form of an electronic database or even printed profiles. Such a register must be regularly updated; this is a challenging task within the highly dynamic context of universities. Reports from such a register could be a valuable source of management information.

- *A senate committee.* To advance community–university engagement, it is necessary to establish a high-level committee at institutional level to oversee this function. The members of such a committee should be sufficiently senior to act as champions and to ensure that community engagement is entrenched in the institutional agenda.
- *Faculty committees and community engagement chairpersons.* To advance community–university engagement at faculty level, many South African universities have established dedicated committees for community engagement in faculties, with chairpersons, as in the case of research and teaching.
- *A central community engagement support service or unit.* The South African universities that have made significant strides in terms of community engagement have established a central support service or unit with the functions of coordination, support, monitoring and evaluation, quality assurance, training and development. At a number of universities, the head of such a unit is a senior appointment reporting to top management.
- *Recognition of community engagement.* The experience of a number of South African universities is that a formalized recognition and incentive system for faculty and students can significantly advance community engagement. Community engagement should also feature prominently in appointment, performance management and promotion procedures.

GOING BEYOND

At the heart of how universities organize themselves in terms of community engagement is their *understanding of scholarship*. In this regard, universities in South Africa seem to exhibit different kinds of approach.

For the purposes of this paper, the following three approaches can be discerned: *detached scholarship, science for society* and *engaged scholarship*:

- *Detached scholarship.* According to this view, the academic works with ideas, and the world of ideas forms a dichotomy with that of reality or practice. Objectivity, understood as neutrality, is prized above all. Knowledge is pursued for the sake of knowledge. The academic has no concern about application, that is, the business of others. This is what some have criticized as the 'ivory tower' mentality, but it could also be related to positivism, a theory of knowledge that still has a lot of currency in the academic world, in South Africa as well as elsewhere. While this kind of approach has a place in certain instances of basic science, some academics may wish to extend its applicability to all science. The human and social sciences especially suffer from continuous attempts to impose the logical form of positivism on it. Where detached scholarship reigns, there is a disdain for community engagement as being something foreign to the academy.
- *Science for society.* The common understanding in this view is that science and knowledge are owned by the university and that they are offered to and consumed by society. The university, in this view, acts as a kind of knowledge service provider. Unlike the detached scholarship view, there is an awareness of 'real-world' problems and the role that academic knowledge can play in addressing these problems. Community engagement according to the science for society view is service to society by making available university expert knowledge to solve 'real-world' problems.
- *Engaged scholarship.* This view acknowledges the existence of a knowledge ecology, of which the university and its academic knowledge is part. It takes seriously issues of cognitive justice, co-production of knowledge, transdisciplinarity, complexity and the potential of engagement for the university and its sustainability. There is a deep realization that interactions with other social partners can impact critically on the university itself and that serious

community engagement work can produce 'relational, localised and contextual knowledge' in a process of 'co-production of knowledge' (Hartley et al., 2010). In such a process, there is a multidirectional flow of knowledge as opposed to a unidirectional flow of knowledge, shared authority for knowledge creation instead of the primacy of academic knowledge, and the university seen as part of an ecosystem of knowledge production addressing public problem-solving instead of as the centre of public problem-solving (Hartley et al., 2010). Knowledge with global applicability can be generated in a local setting. (This is colloquially referred to as 'world-class science in our backyard' among colleagues at Stellenbosch University.) In such an approach, one thinks differently about scholarship and its relationship to human development. It is nothing short of a different model of scholarship from the expert model. Because it values more than academic knowledge and peer-reviewed publications, it will also need a revised incentive system. This kind of understanding of scholarship goes beyond what currently is.

A very practical example of the kind of scholarship described above is the process of writing and using the book *Sustainable Stellenbosch: Opening Dialogues*, which was launched on 30 November 2012. Co-written by Stellenbosch University academics, Stellenbosch Municipality officials and community members, this book addresses the most pressing problems of the town and offers conceptual frameworks to start thinking about possible solutions. The book marks:

> a particular moment in the evolution of a body of knowledge that is both about the material realities of the town in which the university is based and about the forging of a research practice that contributes to our global understanding of the connections between innovation, knowledge production and sustainability. (Swilling et al., 2012, p. 347)

The book will be used as the basis of several public discussions around clusters of themes that are important for the future of the town and will certainly inform public policy directions. This example shows that a move away from the traditional 'expert model' of knowledge production is not to be feared but could bring added dividends of relevance and inclusivity.

More conceptual work needs to be done, and practical measures need to be put in place to further enhance community–university engagement in South Africa. On the conceptual side, the national conversation about community–university engagement in South African higher education needs to continue, and it must continue to be driven by influential national role-players such as the CHE, NRF, HESA, Department of Higher Education and Training and SAHECEF by way of conversations, workshops, conferences, publications, and so on. In addition, the academic model and understanding of scholarship needs to be urgently deliberated and reviewed to fit the South African developmental context and to allow institutions to follow differentiated development trajectories. On the practical side, there needs to be a revision of the academic reward system that will match a revised academic model. National awards and grants (like the NRF Community Engagement Call) must be continued and expanded. The building of networks and capacity-building (professional development) in terms of community–university engagement are other important priorities to be pursued.

The one big challenge to implementing these changes is the will to do so of univer-sities and their management teams. The will and courageous leadership may be lacking because of a commitment to the current academic model and reward systems. If steering by government and other interested parties is backed up by respect for the identity and self-understanding of universities and academics, as well as by substantial monetary incentives and rewards, a different, most exciting time awaits community–university engagement in South Africa.

CONCLUSION

The South African government is, through its policies and legislation, steering universities to be more socially responsive. There is the realization that institutions within the differentiated higher education system can make a variety of possible community engagement contributions depending on their contexts, visions and missions. However, the role that the university is expected to play must keep track of its identity as an institution, as well as the identity structures of academics. Therefore, community–university engagement work must be moved into the centre of academic endeavours. There needs to be a clear realization on the part of all social partners involved in community–university engagement that the university is not a development agency; but that it has a knowledge role to play in national development and reconciliation in South Africa. What are needed are practical measures and a new academic model, with an academic incentive system that will support such a model.

REFERENCES

Cooper, D. (2011) *The University in Development: Case Studies of Use-oriented Research.* Cape Town: HSRC Press.

HESA (2009) *Pathways to a Diverse and Effective South African Higher Education System: Strategic Framework 2010–2020.* Pretoria: HESA.

Hartley, M., Saltmarsh, J. and Clayton, P. (2010) 'Is the civic engagement movement changing higher education?' *British Journal of Education Studies*, 58(4), 391–406.

HEQC CHE (2006) *Service-Learning in the Curriculum. A Resource for Higher Education Institutions.* Pretoria: Council on Higher Education.

Hollander, E., Saltmarsh, J. and Zlotkowski, E. (2002) 'Indicators of engagement'. In: Kenny, M., Simon, L., Kiley-Brabeck, K. and Lerner, R. (eds), *Learning to Serve: Promoting Civil Society Through Service Learning.* Boston: Kluwer Academic Publishers.

Kruss, G., Visser, M., Aphane, M. and Haupt, G. (2012) *Academic Interaction with Social Partners: Investigating the Contribution of Universities to Economic and Social Development.* Cape Town: HSRC Press.

Swilling, M., Sebitosi, B. and Loots, R. (eds) (2012) *Sustainable Stellenbosch – Opening Dialogues.* Stellenbosch: SUN MeDIA.

Inside View IV.2.2
Knowledge, engagement and higher education in Eastern Africa

Janice Desire Busingye

INTRODUCTION

Community engagement in Eastern Africa is informed by the historical context of education in the region. It is also informed by the need to contribute to solving social problems and to the emerging global paradigms of engagement in universities across the world. In these circumstances, institutions of higher learning have had to think globally and are still struggling to act locally. In this paper, I will descriptively landscape community engagement across nine universities drawn from the Eastern African countries of Uganda, Kenya, Tanzania, Rwanda and Burundi. I will draw on the Community Service Continuum developed by Nampota (2011, p. 110) to locate the character of community engagement in East African institutions of higher learning.

HISTORICAL CONTEXT OF COMMUNITY ENGAGEMENT IN EASTERN AFRICA

Community engagement in Eastern Africa is intertwined with the history of higher education in Africa. From the time Africa got a formalized education system in 1923 until now, the goals of community engagement and higher education have been a reflection of the needs of the wider society. For instance, during the colonial period, university and college education was purposed to serve the administrative needs of the colonial masters (Preece et al., 2012). During independence, Preece et al. (2012) have argued that university education was purposed to meet the national development needs of the countries where the universities were located. In East Africa, the De la

Warr Commission of East Africa was set up so that universities could produce good-quality leaders who would manage the affairs of their countries after colonialism (Ajayi et al.,1996). On the whole, universities were identified as ivory towers training an elite minority, detached from their own societies.

CURRENT COMMUNITY REGIME IN EASTERN AFRICA

In East African institutions of higher learning, there is no uniform understanding or practice of community engagement. Each of the nine universities closely studied has a commitment to community engagement. Community engagement in these institutions can be understood by adopting the community service continuum developed by Nampota (2010; p. 110 in Preece et al., 2012). Nampota (2010) argues that community engagement lies on a continuum with outreach at one extreme end, community engagement in the middle of the continuum and community engagement with service-learning at the other extreme end (Preece et al., 2012). In the nine universities examined, their understanding of community engagement seemed to lie along this community service continuum .

THE 'COMMUNITY OUTREACH' REGIME

Outreach was mentioned as one of the common terms that describe community engagement in several universities in East Africa. Of the nine universities examined, all three Kenyan universities were committed to outreach programmes, to which they had added extension services. For instance, Moi University, University of Nairobi and Kenyatta University have fully fledged units concerned with outreach and extension services (Kenyatta University, 2010; Moi University, 2013; University of Nairobi, 2013).

In the outreach regime, community engagement is characterized as reaching out to communities to offer services. The key issue here is to 'reach out', which can be understood as 'a one-off' activity conducted by the university to address community needs' (Preece et al., 2012, p. 152). In Kenyatta University, for example, community outreach is carried out:

> through reaching out to communities by extending knowledge, skills and other skills to help the communities to identify, mobilise

and utilise their locally available resources to improve the quality of life for individuals, families and society at large. (Kenyatta University, 2010, p. 1)

In the outreach regime, the control of knowledge and 'naming the world' (Freire, 1970, p. 60) lies in the hands of the 'ivory tower'. The universities are the creators of knowledge, and the communities are the recipients of this knowledge. Openjuru and Ikoja-Odongo (2012) have actually argued that the reason why Makerere University changed its understanding and practice of community engagement was because the communities outside the university were looked at as being the controllers of their own knowledge, technology and skills.

THE 'COMMUNITY SERVICE' REGIME

In the National University of Rwanda, the Université Lumière de Bujumbura, the Université du Burundi and the University of Dodoma, any activity with the community was referred to as 'community service' (National University of Rwanda, 2013; Université du Burundi, 2013; Université Lumière de Bujumbura, 2013; University of Dodoma, 2013). While this bears resemblance to the outreach regime, the difference lies in the intentions underlying the community engagement activities. In the outreach regime, the university community 'extends a hand' to the community, but power and control of knowledge lie in the hands of the university community. The university community involves the community as the recipients of knowledge.

In the community service regime, the university community goes into the community to work for them in order to solve a particular social problem. For instance, at the University of Rwanda, students were involved in cleaning up neighbourhoods, without the active involvement of the community members. While power was shared and the university was not represented as the only creator of knowledge, the students were not allowed to view the community as co-constructors of knowledge.

'COMMUNITY ENGAGEMENT WITH LEARNING' REGIME

The community engagement with learning regime is mainly given form and definition by the mission of the University of Dar es Salaam and Makerere University, where the commu-

nity members are looked on as co-creators of knowledge. In particular, the University of Dar es Salaam purposes in its mission to engage with communities in a process of dynamic knowledge creation (University of Dar es Salaam, 2013). Here, the power of creation of knowledge is shared between the people and the university community. In Uganda, for example, members of the private sector have been allowed to contribute to university curricula to enable them to produce graduates who are relevant to the needs of the private sector and communities around them (Makerere University, 2008).

In the community engagement regime, the university and the communities are both involved in a knowledge-generation process, with the aim of solving social problems. Power over knowledge is to a great extent shared, making it easier for communities and universities to co-create knowledge. Community engagement in this regime enables universities to be actively involved both inside and outside the walls of the university (Mwaikokesya, 2012). Such universities are taking firm steps towards engaged scholarship, in which they are producing knowledge through interdisciplinary collaboration with other actors, experiential learning and application of knowledge to action (Mwaikokesya, 2012).

CONCLUSION

Institutions of higher learning in Eastern Africa in particular are torn between serving the needs of their communities and living up to the expectations of the outside world. Community engagement is understood as community outreach, community service or community engagement with learning. In any case, what is presented in this paper shows that Eastern Africa is deliberately placing community engagement, in its different forms, within disciplines to make the content of teaching more relevant to everyday problems.

REFERENCES

Ajayi, A.J.F., Goma, L.K.H. and Johnson, A.G. (1996) *The African Experience with Higher Education*. Accra: AAU/Oxford: James Currey.
Freire, P. (1970) *Pedagogy of the Oppressed*. New York: Seabury Press.
Kenyatta University (2010) 'Community Outreach and Extension Programmes'. Retrieved June 27, 2013 from http://www.ku.ac.ke/coep.

Makerere University (2008a) *Makerere University Strategic Plan 2008/09–2018/19*. Kampala: Makerere University.

Moi University (2013) 'Extension and Outreach Centres'. Retrieved June 26, 2013 from http://www.mu.ac.ke/en/index.php/vision-missionvalues.

Mwaikokesya, J.D.M. (2012) 'Scaling up the African universities' capacity for learning cities and regions: challenges and opportunities in Tanzania and East Africa'. In: Preece, J., Ntseane, P.G., Modise, M.O. and Osborne, M. (eds), *Community Engagement in African Universities Perspectives, Prospects and Challenges*. Leicester: NIACE.

Nampota D. (2011) 'Emerging issues on the "process" and "outcomes" of community service from the experiences of eight country case studies'. In: Preece, J. (ed.), *Community Service and Community Engagement in Four African Universities*. Gaborone: Lentswe La Lesedi.

National University of Rwanda (2013) 'Community Service'. Retrieved June 26, 2013 from http://www.nur.ac.rw.

Openjuru, L.G. and Ikoja-Odongo, J.R. (2012) 'From extra-mural to knowledge transfer partnerships and networking: the community engagement experience at Makerere University'. In: Preece, J., Ntseane, P.G., Modise, M.O. and Osborne, M. (eds), *Community Engagement in African Universities Perspectives, Prospects and Challenges*. Leicester: NIACE.

Preece, J., Biao, I., Nampota, D. and Raditloaneng, W.N. (2012) 'Community engagement within African contexts: a comparative analysis'. In: Preece, J., Ntse-ane, P.G., Modise, M.O. and Osborne, M. (eds), *Community Engagement in African Universities Perspectives, Prospects and Challenges*. Leicester: NIACE.

Université du Burundi (2013) 'Community Service'. Retrieved June 27, 2013 from http://www.ub.edu.bi.

Université Lumière de Bujumbura (2013) Community Services. Retrieved June 27, 2013 from http://www.ulbu.bi.

University of Dar es Salaam (2013) 'Community Engagement'. Retrieved June 27, 2013 from http://www.udsm.ac.tz.

University of Dodoma (2013) 'Research and Public Services'. Retrieved June 26, 2013 from http://www.udom.ac.tz.

University of Nairobi (2013) 'Community Outreach'. Retrieved June 26, 2013 from http://dvcrpe.uonbi.ac.ke/node/724.

Spotlight Issues IV.2.3
Theatre for development in support of health service delivery in rural Nigeria

Oga Steve Abah

INTRODUCTION

This paper looks at the ways in which the Ahmadu Bello University, Zaria, in Nigeria has used its theatre programme to address pressing development issues in various parts of the country. It tells the story of how it has collaborated with both community and civil society to fulfil its mandate as both a research and teaching institution on the one hand, and a publicly funded academy that must give back to its benefactors on the other. Its teaching and research therefore factor into its curriculum studies that are able to meet these different demands. In a middle-income country such as Nigeria, development issues are on the front-burner of discussions.

One of the key development problems in Nigeria is health delivery. Although the problem cuts across both urban and rural areas of Nigeria, it is more pronounced in the latter. The rural communities in Nigeria are zones of endemic health problems such as malaria, dysentery and cholera, with the HIV/AIDS crisis compounding the problem. While some of these problems relate to the poor management of basic primary healthcare delivery on the part of government, there is also the problem of ignorance on the side of the rural communities. The twin problem therefore is that of service provisioning, that is, supply, and of demand. On the demand side, it has been about whether ordinary Nigerians know their health entitlements and ask for them appropriately, demanding the authorities to be responsive and accountable. In addition, when such demands are made, are the drugs available? And are they properly managed?

Therefore, in regard to health service delivery, it has been a question of how to bring the two sides on board to ensure that they both understand each other and that they have responsibilities to make the health delivery system work. Increasingly, multiple approaches involving various stakeholders such as government, development agencies, academic institutions and civil society are the preferred options, and various platforms are being explored for action.

HIGHER EDUCATION AS MULTIPLE PLATFORMS OF INTERACTION

Higher education in Nigeria is mostly funded by public money, although in the past few years several private universities have been established. Whether they are public or private institutions, they have numerous roles to play in addition to their traditional role of teaching and research. Their corporate responsibility of demonstrating their relevance to society has been on the increase, and the interaction between gown and town is of premium importance. The first stage in this has been the critical review of curricula in universities such that the relevance of courses has been scrutinized and revised accordingly. In this review, the extent to which the courses respond to community needs and to solving problems is an important consideration.

The marriage, and perhaps negotiation, that the academe has had to engage in is consequently between theory and practice. There is no doubt that the one informs the other. It is therefore the development of skills in students and researchers to move from one to the other that society is in search of. I see two essential concerns lying at the heart of this mandate for the academe: advancement and change. The word 'development' is important here, and I want to evoke Robert Chambers (2012) to ask who says that the academe in its abstract studies and aloofness has all the solutions to human/community problems? This therefore begs interaction. And this is where I pitch my tent and advocate for a practice that is creative, interactional and collective in its approach. Whereas this may not be the only approach, it is an important one that has spoken eloquently to community issues, with results to show.

THEATRE FOR DEVELOPMENT AND PARTICIPATORY DEVELOPMENT

To start with, there are two key words here: development and participation. These are very controversial words in terms of meaning and interpretation. They are controversial because they mean different things for different people, depending on which side of the equation one stands. In essence, positionality matters. But for the purpose of this discussion, I want to adopt very basic and simple working definitions. Development is seen here as the movement from one state of being or situation to a different one that signals a better standard of living. There are so many factors embedded in this very simple definition, ranging from political participation and freedom of speech to the provision of social amenities. As I have stated elsewhere:

> I would argue that in most developing countries and certainly in Nigeria, community development is seen first as how much availability there is of social amenities (schools, roads, water, electricity, hospitals and clinics and housing). (Abah, 2007a)

In the same way as when one talks about participation, there is a whole range or ladder of participation from briefing, consultation and reporting to beneficiaries on what has taken place, through to a collective process of the identification of issues, analysis and implementation. There is obviously a relationship between participation and development. The participation that would allow the above working definition to be meaningful is the ability of the beneficiaries to identify their needs and not for such needs to be imposed by an outsider. A critical element that one may use to assess whether or not participation has been part of any process or whether development has taken place is empowerment. And empowerment is seen here as the ability of the

subject to exercise choices and to take action on the choices made. Therefore, development starts from the human person and moves to material needs that he or she may identify.

The question, then, is whether all of these, outside of painting an idealistic picture, are possible. We return to the issue of negotiation and the platform on which such negotiation may be possible for the benefit of both beneficiaries and benefactors. All over Africa, a platform that has been both horizontal and empowering is Theatre for Development (TFD). TFD is the theatre practice that addresses community issues and problems using the people's language and art forms as media of expression. It also makes an analysis of such issues from the people's perspectives (at least in the first instance). It may, however, challenge the initial perspective as both animateurs and community members engage in a collective discussion and analysis of issues.

TFD is both a practice and a tool operating from the cultural matrix of the people for purposes of empowerment – knowledge, action and change in the long term. The enabling qualities of TFD include the fact that it is participatory. It is also flexible and can therefore accommodate various opinions and is indeed prepared for experimentation. The dramaturgical procedure of TFD is collective, with community members performing their problems and issues. TFD is indeed an amalgamation of traditional performance arts (songs, drumming, dance) with Western-oriented drama in the promotion of community aspirations and in aiding development (Abah, 2007b).

The flexibility of TFD has also allowed it to be used in combination with other approaches, especially the participatory learning and action methodology. It is this use in combination with other approaches that I have characterized as 'methodological conversations' (Abah, 2003, 2007b). Methodological conversation is a way of challenging the academe to go beyond its disciplinary boundaries so as to listen to others (within and outside the citadel) and to experience different stories of life. The conversations take place on different levels: between disciplines defined by the ivory tower; between the ivory tower and the community; and in ever-changing

discourse emanating from the performance in the dusty arenas of the village when practice is interrogated, when positions change, when lessons are learned and actions defined.

The Theatre for Development Centre (TFDC) at Ahmadu Bello University, Zaria, Nigeria is one such non-governmental organization that has since 2000 been working together with the university to train, undertake research and engage in community development action. In its affiliation with the Department of Theatre and Performing Arts, the TFDC trains both staff and students in TFD and participatory development approaches. It also works with development agencies to implement their intervention strategies in communities, essentially to actualize its mission of 'The promotion of participatory, gender sensitive and sustainable development through the use of TFD and other participatory strategies to build the capacity of NGOs, CBOs and women's groups so they can realize their development agendas.'

A SNIPPET OF TFD SPEAKING TO DEVELOPMENT ISSUES IN NIGERIA

The work in Jigawa State was a collaboration between Partnership for Transforming Health Systems (PATHS2) and TFDC. Its main focus was using TFD and other participatory tools to assess the performance of health service delivery in the four focal states where PATHS, a UKAid-funded programme, was in operation. The transformation sought in the health sector in Nigeria was for the health sector, especially the State Ministries of Health, to be responsive and accountable to the needs of the people. Second, the transformational marker was to be seen in the involvement of local people in the health administration (consulting with health workers and community members around local health needs; monitoring service delivery; mobilizing community resources to meet these needs; and alerting government officials if needs could not be met by the community). In order for people-oriented administration to take place, a Facility Health Committee (FHC) was set up that consisted of men and women from local communities in designated health catchment areas (Abah et al., 2011).

Whether or not such FHCs understood their roles and if they were performing well needed to be assessed. The interest for us therefore was how TFD could tell the story, not just of the performance of the FHCs, but also of the success of the initiative. Look at this:

- A nurse is busy clearing his desk to close after a long day in the hospital. A sick woman, her mother and two neighbours barge into the office. The nurse is surprised and angry. He takes his case to the audience and asks them what he is supposed to do after he has overstayed for hours attending to patients. 'Why did these people choose to come late? How can I alone cope in such a situation?' He decides he has had enough and makes to leave. One of the women blocks his path. Exasperated, he returns to the audience: 'You see!' But, in a very determined manner now, he vows that no one can make him stay any longer. He charges towards the door and the women give way to let him pass as they look helplessly, with the patient in serious pain.
- The sick woman's husband storms into the arena, waving a hoe as a weapon in the air. He has just returned from the farm to the bad news that the wife has lost the pregnancy. He threatens that hell will come down; 'Someone will have to pay for this! The health facility must close down if it cannot serve the needs of the villagers!' Friends run round to prevent him from causing harm to anyone. They head to the Sarki's house. The startled Sarki manages to calm the husband and his team down and asks what the matter is. The man narrates his ordeal and how he has lost his child and has to spend the rest of the farming season tending to crops that he mortgaged for a loan towards the referral that never prevented his child from dying; and now his wife is also dying and the health worker will not stay to help.
- One of the Sarki's advisers, who tries to rationalize and urge the man to sympa-

thize with health worker who is overworked, instantly becomes the man's target of anger for his 'insensitivity' and in fact is accused of conniving with the midwife to cheat him. (Commotion and confusion ensues!) The Sarki, in company of the husband and friends, decides to take the matter to the Director of Gunduma for intervention.

ISSUES AND IMPACT

The first issue of importance is that the scenario above was an amalgamation of stories and concerns that emerged from several processes during the field exercise that included training the members of the health facilities to understand the use of theatre and other participatory tools for analysing community issues and how they might function in their monitoring, advocacy and demand for accountability from the providers of health services. The issues that formed the content of the drama were derived from undertaking a transect walk, engaging in focused group discussion, key informant interviews, analysing issues using a problem tree, and so on. The second issue in the drama is the demonstration of an understanding of rights on the part of the community members. It also showed that they knew the channels for demanding accountability and responsiveness to their health needs.

A third point of interest is that the community members formed the story and performed it themselves. This is important in connection with development discourse and practice, which now speaks of participation, voice and agency (Holland and Blackburn, 1998). The argument that is held in respect now is that which insists that both development projects and their implementation must be demand-driven and organically situated (Cornwall and Pratt, 2003).

At the end of the day, the participants acknowledged that the training, and especially

the drama-creating process, clarified their roles and resulted in better understanding. The FHC members also acknowledged that the entire exercise allowed them to build stronger group cohesion, learning and confidence to work with each other. Reports reaching us in December 2012 indicated that progress had been made in Sankara community, where the FHC had been able to mobilize support for a laboratory to be set up in the clinic. They were now also able to ensure that the staff discharged their responsibilities appropriately, and had been known to have reported non-performing staff. In their own words: 'We are constantly climbing hills here. But we now know what we need to help us get there.'

REFERENCES

Abah, O.S. (2003) 'Methodological conversations in researching citizenship: drama and participatory learning and action in encountering citizens'. In: Abah, O.S. (ed.), *Geographies of Citizenship in Nigeria*. Zaria, Nigeria: Tamaza Publishing.

Abah, O.S. (2007a) 'Vignettes of community in action: an exploration of participatory methodologies in promoting community development in Nigeria'. *Community Development Journal*, 42(4), 435–48.

Abah, O.S. (2007b) *Performing Life: Case Studies in the Practice of Theatre for Development*. Zaria: Tamaza Publishing.

Abah, O.S. Hemmings, J. and Zakari Okwori, J. (2011) *Report of Community Sentinel Monitoring of Facility Health Committees, Jigawa State*. Abuja: PATHS2 & TFDC.

Chambers, R. (2012) *Provocations for Development*. Rugby, Warwickshire: Practical Action Publishing.

Cornwall, A. and Pratt, P. (eds) (2003) *Pathways to Participation: Reflections on PRA*. London: ITDG.

Holland, J. and Blackburn, J. (eds) (1998) *Whose Voice? Participatory Research and Policy Change*. London: ITDG.

Implementing the third mission of universities in Africa: contributing to the millennium development goals

Julia Preece

INTRODUCTION

This paper introduces a pan-African action research project entitled *Implementing the Third Mission of Universities in Africa* (ITMUA), which was funded by the Association of African Universities (AAU) during 2010 and 2011. It illustrates how four universities from Nigeria, Botswana, Malawi and Lesotho explored the mutual learning benefits of a community needs-led approach to community engagement. The engagement activities across the universities demonstrated a wide range of approaches but revealed similar issues in relation to the nature of knowledge and institutional responses to the process of engagement. A brief outline of the African context informs the partners' national and university policies for engagement, and is followed by an introduction to how the universities identified their case studies. Some illustrative learning outcomes and uses of knowledge across the case studies then preface some policy issues regarding universities and community engagement.

BACKGROUND TO THE NATIONAL AND UNIVERSITY CONTEXTS

Within South Africa, the concepts of community engagement and service learning have been enshrined in government policy since 1997 (Department of Education, 1997). There is an extensive literature in the country (see Preece's, 2013, literature review) in relation to community engagement and service learning, and a few references to learning regions or cities (Walters, 2009; Mile.org, 2010). There are fewer publications from the wider continent (see Preece et al., 2012). In spite of this, the African university has a historical commitment to nation-building (Preece et al., 2012).

The ITMUA project came about at a time of emerging interest in the revitalization of African universities and their contribution to national development (see, for example, UNESCO, 2009). The project analysed features of engagement across four different country contexts on the continent. AAU funding criteria required the study to address the Millennium Development Goals (MDGs) as a feature of its activities. The focus of the MDGs was on poverty, although other goals, such as universal primary education, global partnerships, HIV and gender concerns, were also addressed.

The participating universities were Calabar (UNICAL) in Nigeria, University of Malawi (UNIMA), National University of Lesotho and University of Botswana. Most were classified as low-income countries, ranking between 98 and 153 out of 169 countries on the human development index (Preece, 2011).

As a basis for the research, each university positioned its rationale for engagement within national policy and relevant university strategies to address development priorities. All the countries' national poverty reduction and education plans highlight concerns with poverty reduction, food security, education and health, specifically referring to the MDGs (see, for instance, Government of Botswana, 2004; Government of Lesotho, 2004, 2005).

All the university vision statements and/or strategic plans commit themselves to addressing these national priorities through lifelong learning, research and community service (for example UNICAL, 2002; UNIMA, 2004).

The study aimed to answer the following questions:

- What current engagement activities exist in each university, and in what form?
- How can university engagement be enhanced through a collaborative, community needs-led approach?
- What are the engagement learning outcomes in terms of new knowledge, skills and understanding for all participants (staff, students and the community)?
- What issues for staff, students and communities do the engagement activities raise?

An initial audit of university projects revealed a range of activities that could be classed as engagement, but no formalized coordination system for engagement was in place and participation by staff and students was seldom considered to be community-led or community-driven. In other words, communities were rarely consulted regarding the nature of engagement they wanted.

THE CASE STUDIES

The ITMUA partner universities each created two engagement case studies (Table IV.2.4.1) that met the following criteria:

- their potential for multidisciplinary involvement within the university;

TABLE IV.2.4.1

Summary of community engagement projects

Projects	Interventions
Botswana	
15–20 members of a remote rural community in D'kar	Leadership, advocacy, business skills for self-sustainability
23 women weavers in a community-owned cooperative	Marketing, entrepreneurial and management skills
Calabar	
12 female sex workers	Tailoring skills to move out of sex work, HIV awareness
15 female farmers	Production of organic fertilizers, improved planting, bookkeeping, marketing skills
Malawi	
Community-based childcare centre project with 80 children	Training in a childcare curriculum, building a borehole
Group village headmen community project with 18 villages	Irrigation farming, cropping, drug and alcohol abuse, water safety, HIV/AIDS prevention
Lesotho	
Women's self-help group with 20–40 members in 17 villages	HIV/AIDS care and prevention, income generation, business and marketing skills, building of ventilated pit latrines
Collection point for 50–200 pensioners	Health checks, income generation/savings, gardening, avocacy and support against abuse

- community identification of needs or problems to address (that is, building on existing assets or knowledge bases);
- their potential for multi-agency involvement.

The case studies were time-limited and lasted no more than six months. Most of the interventions included staff and students, although not always in the form of service-learning. On completion, all participants were interviewed in relation to the above research questions. Space prevents an elaborate discussion of the outcomes but they are summarized here.

OUTCOMES
Outcomes ranged across a variety of areas: the scientific enhancement of indigenous knowledge about organic manure for farmers; shared understandings of behaviours and their impact on each other between villagers and their leaders; increased community skills for crop production and dealing with family issues; enhanced awareness among academic staff of different cultures; local resources and skills; increased understanding by students of community concerns and coping strategies (Nampota and Preece, 2012).

Some specific issues that arose from the research findings in relation to the role of knowledge and engagement in these activities are summarized below. More detailed analysis is available in the published project report edited by Preece (2011).

ISSUES
KNOWLEDGE
Shared and mutual learning between communities and universities needs to contribute to the university knowledge base for pedagogy as well as scientific understanding – such as an improvement of indigenous fertilizers by academics and facilitating students' understanding of abuse issues experienced by pensioners.

The university curriculum needs to be flexible enough to allow opportunities for experimentation in order to open up new avenues of thinking, such as integrating a range of disciplines (for example, health, crime prevention, business management) to work together.

In order to facilitate the co-production of knowledge, agencies need to find ways of working collaboratively such as using theatre for education students to enact out community conflicts between villagers.

These forms of knowledge production are best classified as problem-based and context-specific, which develop as a result of reflexivity and an interaction with real-life situations.

ENGAGEMENT
The potential role that engagement plays for knowledge construction has to be 'sold' to staff and community members alike. It evolves over time and is based on a relationship of trust that has to be earned by all partners.

The engagement power relationship is fragile, and universities tread a fine line in promoting independence, rather than dependency, among the participating communities.

Equally, the motivation of academic staff and students to participate, in the face of competing institutional demands for international credibility, requires an institutional reward system that can measure engagement outputs and link more closely to research.

Institutional strategic goals or mission statements have to reflect organizational structures that facilitate the coordination and promotion of engagement activities, with relevant budget lines. One way of ensuring this might be to encourage government ring-fencing of some of its financial subvention to universities.

The community has to be recognized by universities as an equal partner with the assets and ability to articulate its own needs.

Engagement outcomes need to be disseminated, followed by consultations with relevant community members.

CONCLUSION
This paper has provided an example of community engagement research that took place across four countries on the African continent. The outcomes demonstrated that engagement is multifaceted but has the potential to contribute to increased knowledge and understanding across a range of levels and with mutual learning gains for both community members and university participants. However, the process of engagement tends to be uncoordinated and poorly resourced, which challenges motivation among academic staff and students. Equally, community participation requires a genuine partnership approach in order to stimulate developmental growth rather than dependency relationships.

REFERENCES
Department of Education (1997) *Education White Paper 3. A Programme for the Transformation of Higher Education*. Pretoria: Government Printers.

Government of Botswana (2004) *Poverty Reduction Strategy*. Gaborone: Government Printers.

Government of Lesotho (2004) *Poverty Reduction Strategy 2004/5–2006/7*. Maseru: Government Printers.

Government of Lesotho (2005) *Education Sector Strategic Plan 2005–2015*. Maseru: Government Printers.

Mile.org (2010) 'Welcome to MILE'. Retrieved January 2, 2012 from http://www.mile.org.za/Pages/default.aspx.

Nampota, D. and Preece, J. (2012) 'University community service and its contribution to the Millennium Development Goals: a pan-African research project'. *Journal of Education*, 55, 105–26.

Preece, J. (ed.) (2011) *Community Service and Community Engagement in Four African Universities*. Gaborone: Lentswe La Lesedi.

Preece, J. (2013) 'Towards an Africanisation of community engagement'. *Perspectives in Education*, 31(2), 114–22.

Preece, J., Ntseane, P.G., Modise, O.M. and Osborne, M. (eds) (2012) *Community Engagement in African Universities: Perspectives, Prospects and Challenges*. Leicester: NIACE.

UNESCO (2009) 'The New Dynamics of Higher Education and Research for Societal Change and Development'. Conference statement, World Conference on Higher Education, UNESCO Paris, July 5–8, 2009. Paris: UNESCO.

UNICAL (2002) *Strategic Plan 2007–2012*. Calabar: UNICAL Press.

UNIMA (2004) *University of Malawi Strategic Plan 2004/5–2009/10*. Lilongwe: UNIMA.

Walters, S. (2009) 'Learning regions in lifelong learning'. In: Jarvis, P. (ed.), *The Routledge International Handbook of Lifelong Learning*. London: Routledge.

INTRODUCTION

The concept of women's empowerment is supported on a global scale by international agencies. It is, however, interpreted differently in development agendas. So UNESCO's Education For All agenda focuses on access to schooling and adult literacy (goals 2, 4 and 5), and life skills programmes (goal 3).

The internationally agreed Millennium Development Goals include one specific reference to empowerment in goal 2 – 'Promote gender equality and empower women' – although other goals for universal primary education, reduction of poverty (goals 1 and 2) and improvement of maternal health (goal 5) have an implicit relationship with women's empowerment.

The United Nations Human Development Report (UNDP, 1995) stresses that empowerment is about participation in development decision-making, but it emphasizes developing women's capabilities to contribute to economic growth. For Oxfam, empowerment is about challenging oppression and inequality (Oxfam, 1995).

Gender empowerment indicators are often expressed in instrumental terms such as participation in schooling, levels of literacy, levels of child mortality and maternal health. So, for example, UNESCO reports that two-thirds of the world's 775 million adults who cannot read or write are women, and there are six girls for every 10 boys in secondary education in sub-Saharan Africa (UNESCO, 2013).

Women's empowerment is regarded as key to Africa's development, particularly since it is claimed that women are more likely than men to reinvest their income in the family (Wallace, 2013). It is commonly accepted that education plays a vital role in enhancing such empowerment, but it is the international adult education sector and its women's organizations who campaign most fiercely for a holistic vision in this respect:

> We need education that promotes democratic participation and solidarity, values pluralism and guarantees equal opportunities for women and girls of all ages … that understands and respects our cultural, ethnic, and sexual orientation, physical disabilities and lifestyle differences … that understands the centrality of gender relations and sexuality in the HIV/AIDS epidemic … that promotes gender justice which considers women and men as equal political and social subjects in the private and public spheres. (GEO, ICAE, REPEM, DAWN and FEMNET, 2003, p. 33)

These concerns are not limited to a once-only or linear form of education. They reflect the needs of a lifelong process of awareness-raising among men and women, whereby people learn to participate equally in community affairs, think critically and live together as equal citizens. Universities clearly have a role to play in this respect.

According to the United Nations Population Information Network (2013), women's empowerment consists of five components: a sense of self-worth; the right to have and determine choices; the right and access to opportunities and resources; the right for women to have power to control their own lives; and an ability to influence social change for economic and social justice.

The following review highlights some university engagement initiatives in African contexts that address these various components of women's empowerment. The initiatives can broadly be categorized in three ways: as service (skills and knowledge enhancement); in the form of popular education initiatives (emancipatory); and as participatory community research (enhancing ownership over decisions).

SERVICE

Since unpaid work is more traditionally a female activity, it is not difficult to find university engagement projects that work with organizations consisting almost entirely of women. As the examples cited from the Implementing the Third Mission of Universities in Africa project (see Spotlight Issues IV.2.4) demonstrate, such university interventions can range across providing enhanced knowledge and skills to female farmers, new knowledge, income-generating skills and understanding for female sex workers in Nigeria, and enhanced networking support for women's self-help groups in remote rural areas of Lesotho. These initiatives focus on the empowerment component of the right and access to opportunities and resources, with, in some cases, the right to have and determine choices. However, such interventions are small scale and time-limited. They are less likely, therefore, to influence social change or women's power to control their own lives. They often fall short of the international women's organizations' goals of promoting gender justice and democratic participation in wider society.

A more emancipatory approach to women's empowerment is often articulated in the form of popular education (Manicom and Walters, 2012).

POPULAR EDUCATION

Popular education is understood as a pedagogical approach that builds on Paulo Freire's notion of conscientization and praxis (critical awareness-raising of oppression and action to address inequalities; Manicom and Walters). It is often linked to action research – such as a University of Cape Town initiative to work in a poor community over a period of six months. This included developing a leadership course for 17 unemployed women and an HIV/AIDS and bereavement workshop for female caregivers and volunteers. The outcome was an enhanced awareness of coping strategies, understanding among the women of the forces behind their oppressed circumstances, and collective action to work for change (Ferris and Walters, 2012).

Similarly, Theatre for Development is a well-known popular education resource for challenging social awareness of important local issues. An example by Lissard (2012) shows how Lesotho's female university drama students increased their own understanding of gender power relations in relation to the country's HIV and AIDS crisis through a role-play, which they then performed for other university members, local schools and the general public – using the drama stage as 'a place to rehearse new social arrangements' (p. 99) and discuss women's empowerment issues.

These two examples demonstrate the potential for popular education engagement to address women's power to control their own lives and ability to influence social change for economic and social justice. Such outcomes require long-term involvement on the part of a variety of actors, and the extent to which awareness leads to action will depend on the quality of such sustained involvement.

A fourth aspect of community engagement that also attempts to address these latter two components of empowerment, and the centrality of gender relations in promoting democratic participation and solidarity, is often described as participatory community-based research.

PARTICIPATORY COMMUNITY-BASED RESEARCH

A core element of this kind of research is that it is both action-oriented and involves community members as partner enquirers in the research process. The extent to which this is achieved may vary, but in essence the goal is to give community members the skills to undertake their own enquiries but also be key players in providing solutions to their own problems.

An example of such an approach can be seen in a South African initiative by Mosavel et al. (2005), which attempted to address the 'intersecting roles of poverty, violence, and other cultural forces in shaping community members' health and wellbeing' (p. 2577).

The focus of the study was to develop a mutual agenda around issues of cervical cancer. The researchers emphasized that it was the community who reshaped their research focus to cervical health by taking 'ownership of the health problems and resources involved' (p. 2578), which resulted in the community members lobbying for better resources.

CONCLUSION

Women's empowerment is a multifaceted issue that cannot be addressed through a focus on access and skills alone. Education requires long-term engagement that raises awareness of the societal structures that are responsible for inequality and oppression. This in turn needs to be supported by skills, knowledge and understanding that provide women with the capacity to challenge and influence change for social and economic justice. Various forms of university engagement have been cited that contribute to the different dimensions of empowerment. A key component for change is to ensure the community's ownership of the decision-making processes that impact on their lives.

REFERENCES

Ferris, H. and Walters, S. (eds) (2012) 'Heart-felt pedagogy in the time of HIV and AIDS'. In: Manicom, L. and Walters, S. (eds), *Feminist Popular Education in Transnational Debates*. New York: Palgrave Macmillan, pp. 75–92.

GEO, ICAE, REPEM, DAWN and FEMNET (2003) 'Another education is possible'. In: Medel-Añonuevo, C. (ed.), *Women Moving CONFINTEA V: Mid-term Review*. Hamburg: UNESCO Institute of Education, p. 33.

Lissard, K. (2012) 'Women, theatre and the collapsible boundaries of silence'. In: Manicom, L. and Walters, S. (eds), *Feminist Popular Education in Transnational Debates*. New York: Palgrave Macmillan, pp. 93–109.

Manicom, L. and Walters, S. (eds) (2012) *Feminist Popular Education in Transnational Debates*. New York: Palgrave Macmillan.

Mosavel, M., Simon, C., van Stadec, D. and Buchbinder, M. (2005) 'Community based participatory research (CBPR) in South Africa: engaging multiple constituents to shape the research question'. *Social Science and Medicine*, 61, 2577–87.

Oxfam (1995) *The Oxfam Handbook of Relief and Development*. Oxford: Oxfam.

UNDP (1995) *Human Development Report*. Oxford: Oxford University Press.

UNESCO (2013) *Global Monitoring Report 2012*. Paris: UNESCO.

United Nations Population Information Network (2013) 'Guidelines on Women's Empowerment for the UN Resident Coordinator System'. Retrieved July 8, 2013 from http://www.un.org/popin/unfpa/taskforce/guide/iatfwemp.gdl.html.

Wallace, C. (2013) 'Women's empowerment key to African development'. *San Diego Union-Tribune*. Retrieved July 8, 2013 from http://www.utsandiego.com/news/2013/jul/04.

IV.2.6

Networks on community–university engagement in Africa

South African Higher Education Community Engagement Forum (SAHECEF)

SECRETARIAT: Grahamstown (South Africa).
INSTITUTION: Rhodes University.
WEBSITE: http://sahecef.ac.za/ (accessed 5 November 2012).
MEMBERS: 15 (as of 8 October 2013).

SAHECEF commits to advocating, promoting, supporting, monitoring and strengthening community engagement in higher education institutions in South Africa; furthering community engagement in higher education institutions in partnership with all stakeholders with a sustainable social and economic impact on South African society; and fostering an understanding of community engagement as being integral to the core business of higher educations.

Makerere University Private Sector Forum

Makarere University has initiated a platform through which the university can engage with the private sector to enable socioeconomic transformation. The initiative, called the Makerere University Private Sector Forum (MUPSF), was a response to the Africa-wide Smart Partnership dialogue. The main purpose of this dialogue was to work as a cross-sector forum bringing together the public and private sectors and the university to address issues of mutual concern. The university responded by setting up the Academia Network Committee to provide a structure that would work with the MUPSF. Under this initiative, prominent people in the private sector were given honorary awards by the university so as to benefit from their experiences and linkages. To understand the contribution of private–public partnership, this case highlights the experiences of Makerere University, the success points and the challenges faced in the wider context of contemporary community engagement.

Mukondeni Pottery Cooperative and the Universities of Venda and Virginia in South Africa

The Mukondeni Ceramic Water Filter Business highlights a collaboration between two international universities and the Mukondeni Pottery Cooperative in rural South Africa. Over the last two years, a multidisciplinary collection of students and staff from the University of Venda and the University of Virginia have worked with the all-female Cooperative to construct a Ceramic Water Filter Factory. The university participants represent subject areas across anthropology, architecture, biology, business, engineering and public health, all exchanging knowledge, teaching skill sets and sharing resources within the collaboration.

The filter creation process emphasizes the artistic talents and indigenous knowledge that the women have demonstrated through their pre-existing ceramic pottery business. Through empowering the women to learn new technologies, educating the community about the importance of household water quality, and building a mutually beneficial relationship, the ultimate goal of the partnership is to revive the economic stability of the Cooperative by creating a sustainable business.

The University of Cape Town, South Africa

Established in 1985, the Environmental Evaluation Unit (EEU), within the Department of Environmental and Geographical Science, is an independent, self-funded research unit based at the University of Cape Town. Its research activities are strongly rooted in the arena of sustainability and natural resource management and its interface with communities and social justice concerns.

Over the past ten years, its work has increasingly focused on enhancing understanding of the governance of complex human-ecological systems through collaborative interdisciplinary research across natural resource sectors, mostly in poor and marginalized communities. The EEU works with a range of civil society and non-government organization partners including Masifundise, Coastal Links, the Legal Resources Centre, the International Collective in Support of Fishworkers, Biowatch, the South African San Council and the Working Group of Indigenous Minorities in Southern Africa, as well as various government departments.

Social responsiveness, informed by social justice, lies at the core of all the EEU's research activities. The EEUs work focuses on four key activity areas: (1) research to inform policy; (2) research and facilitation to inform alternative natural resource management approaches; (3) academic teaching, training and capacity development interventions, and (4) advocacy to advance human and environmental rights.

The University of Ilorin, Nigeria: the COBES Program

The University of Ilorin, Nigeria, in appreciation of the multiple sites of learning and the need to produce medical doctors who are well tuned to the needs of the communities they are to serve, developed an innovative and sustainable community-based medical education programme known as Community Based Experience and Services (COBES). Under this initiative, medical students are posted to the community in the second, third, fifth and sixth years of their training, where they engage the community in identifying priority health needs and organizing a response using primary healthcare principles.

IV.3
KNOWLEDGE, ENGAGEMENT AND HIGHER EDUCATION IN THE ARAB STATES

Barbara Lethem Ibrahim

Since the end of 2010, a wave of reform and revolution has swept through the Arab region, affecting all countries to one degree or another. This major social and political upheaval is still in process, meaning that many of its outcomes and implications are still unfolding. Higher education has both played a key role in creating the generation of young Arabs who are demanding change, and is profoundly affected by the events that have been set in motion. Universities are struggling to redefine their role as educators of the new generation of active citizens, and as knowledge providers to public- and private-sector bodies.

Universities operate in three distinct settings based on the current national situation: states that are engaged in implementing gradual reforms to stave off popular challenges to authority; nations emerging from popular uprisings and now struggling through transitions to democratic governance; and states in the midst of crisis and internal struggle over the future. Patterns of policy support, academic underpinnings and the thematic areas of university civic programmes are explored across a wide diversity of those environments.

In general, Arab universities have thriving programmes of extra-curricular activities, built around cultural values stressing social solidarity and charity, to engage students and staff with their communities. Less common are engagement activities embedded in academic teaching and learning programmes. There is a serious deficit of research on universities' civic roles and very few scholars or faculty members for whom this is a primary field.

Three challenges facing progress towards engaged higher education are discussed. First is identifying the necessary intellectual tools and analysis to prepare students for an unknown future in which rapid change, contestation over the roles of religion and ethnicity, and scarce resources will be a given. Second, while evolving forms of learning and teaching are leading to a greater range of experiential learning modes

'beyond the university walls', how will these be reconciled with prevailing ideas about academic traditions? Building a body of credible evaluation research that tracks learning outcomes and longer term impacts will be essential if national policies are to become responsive to these trends. Third, the 'Arab Spring' experience has highlighted a generational divide that intersects with a rejection of traditional norms of authority: how will higher education respond to youth expectations and demands for inclusion? Throughout this paper, examples from around the region of innovation in approaches to creating more engaged higher education are highlighted.

As recent movements for governance change are transforming the Arab region, this is an opportune time to take stock of how universities are in fact playing new roles and engaging beyond their campus walls. It also presents a challenge for the authors. Whatever is captured at one point in time has a high likelihood of being outdated very shortly afterwards as the pace and arc of change accelerate. This report was also limited by the dearth of easily available information and has undoubtedly missed some of the important programmes and innovations underway across the 22 countries that make up the Arab region. By highlighting what could be found online and in existing references, the authors hope to encourage further sharing of information and successful innovation. The conditions are ripe for increased connections across the region's higher education community, who believe in the future of community-engaged universities.

INTRODUCTION AND HISTORICAL PERSPECTIVE

Since the end of 2010, a wave of reform and revolution has swept through the Arab region, affecting all countries to one degree or another. This major social and political upheaval is still in process, meaning that many of its outcomes and implications are still unfolding. Higher education has both played a key role in creating the generation of young Arabs who are demanding change and is also profoundly affected by the events that have been set in motion. Some campuses around the region are in the stages of post-uprising turmoil, while others are making strides toward innovative teaching and learning in ways that engage with the larger community. Everywhere, stakeholders in higher education are requiring more accountability from their institutions, at the same time that they are appropriating a more empowered role in the knowledge production and meaning-making of this time in history.

With a sense of urgency, new understandings of the roles and responsibilities of citizenship are emerging, albeit unevenly. Universities are acknowledged as key sites for the formation of next-generation leaders and a strong citizenry. This requires huge transformations in the existing infrastructure for higher education, coming at a time when those institutions are also struggling to become more responsive to shifting economic and labour market realities.

In some countries seeking to head off disruptive change, governments are increasing their control over university elections, publications and free expression. In countries undergoing major transitions, the tensions between religious and secular worldviews have been heightened. These polarizations are played out on campuses, where the quality of academic discourse, research and self-governance is affected. Despite stark differences among country situations, a commonality everywhere is greater stakeholder pressures for higher education that responds to contemporary economic and technological trends in society. Whereas Arab higher education was for most of the 20th century seen as the purview solely of the state, another recent development has been the growing number of alliances with private sector and civil society institutions for mutual benefit. Despite the turmoil, universities are more deeply connected to their communities than at any time in the recent past. It is a time of uncertainty and promise for Arab higher education.

A BRIEF HISTORY

Higher education has a venerable history in the Arab region. Al Qarawiyyin University in Fez, Morocco, was founded by a female benefactor in 859, followed by Al Azhar University in Cairo 75 years later, placing them among the oldest institutions of advanced learning in the world. The earliest universities (*gama'at* in Arabic, which has its root in the word for 'gathering') had strong religious foundations in Islam, grounded in reverence for learning and knowledge; the Quran

itself opens with the admonition, 'Read!' Early schools and universities were urban institutions that typically included spaces designed to serve the neighbourhood – a water fountain, hospital or soup kitchen. Academic traditions were built around pluralism and a tolerance of differing viewpoints. Al Azhar and similar Cairo *madrassa*s are laid out physically in four quadrants where students and teachers pursue the four schools of Islamic jurisprudence. Scholars were among the most highly venerated professions throughout Islamic history; for centuries until the First World War, young men were sent over thousands of kilometers to study in the capitals of the Ottoman Empire.

Universities were an integral part of the communities where they were situated. Most were sustained through religious endowments (*awqaf*) and expanded via bequests and philanthropic contributions. Instruction often took place on the ground floor in elaborately decorated halls, while a second floor housed students in small rooms ranged around a courtyard.

The 18th and 19th centuries saw new levels of engagement with Western powers and peoples. The region received waves of armies, entrepreneurs and persecuted minorities seeking safety in Cairo, Jerusalem and Beirut, while Protestant missionaries established a number of important liberal arts colleges, initially for men. Some survive today as important co-educational secular private universities, including the American University of Beirut (AUB) and the American University in Cairo (AUC).[1] Mohamed Ali, the first modernizing leader in the region, sent young Egyptians to France and England for advanced degrees in order to return and establish schools of medicine, public health and engineering back home.

As independent nation states emerged in the 20th century, universities came to be seen as a cornerstone for creating the modern citizen and replacing the primordial ties to tribes, clans and sects. New governments invested heavily in study missions to the West to train a cadre of professors in sciences, the professions and the humanities, as well as building extensive university infrastructures. These state-run universities were envisioned as a resource for policy-making and the development of modern societies. Much like the land grant colleges during the frontier era in the USA, national universities across the Arab region were funded from state budgets and commissioned to produce applied research for the improvement of health, agriculture and industry. Universities also supplied talent to nascent policy bodies and advisers to ruling elites. Law faculties, for example, provided judges, parliamentarians and foreign envoys from their ranks with regularity. Until the 1970s, the prestige of a faculty position often made up for its modest income potential.

In the desire to allow all deserving students a place in universities, quality began to suffer and classrooms became bloated. The early investments in higher education were not continued at adequate levels to assure the continuity of innovative research and teaching in countries like Iraq, Algeria, Egypt and Syria. By the 1980s, professors from low- and middle-income countries were seeking teaching positions in the rapidly developing Gulf states, where universities were newer and better funded but rarely required faculty research and publication. The value of degrees across many parts of the region began to decline, faculty morale deteriorated, and practices that undermined academic integrity – such as teachers offering private lessons or selling lecture notes to students – became widespread in some countries. Families who could afford to do so sent their children abroad or to established private universities such as AUB and AUC, further undermining the diversity and quality of public institutions.

As oil continued to drive most regional economic growth, disparities in wealth and public investment in higher education widened at the turn of the 21st century. A new phenomenon of satellite campuses affiliated to Western universities took hold in some Arab countries, most prominently in the Gulf where state subsidies were provided to bring prestigious degrees to the country. While tuition fees were high and language requirements excluded worthy Arabic-speaking students, these campuses brought new traditions to the scene, including undergraduate liberal arts curricula, service-learning and interdisciplinary professional training in applied fields such as the environment and public health. Today, there are choices among both public and private institutions of higher education in every country of the region, and many exchange programmes with European and North American campuses as well. The scene is set for real reform and development that will prepare students – and their teachers – for significant civic roles in their rapidly changing societies.

COMMON PATTERNS ACROSS THE ARAB REGION

Despite the problems noted above that challenge public higher education, especially in middle-income and poorer states, university campuses nonetheless remain places where youth congregate, discuss the issues of the day and are exposed to the social and political currents of their time. The Arab values of social solidarity and charity inspire initiatives on most campuses to serve needy students or the surrounding community. When a national or regional crisis occurs, humanitarian initiatives flower spontaneously on university campuses, usually without formal backing. A revival of religious observance in many places has contributed to informal groups of students and faculty who provide social services motivated by their faith and a sense of responsibility for those who are less fortunate.

Where national power structures still do not allow a vibrant civil society, universities play a vital preparatory role for the civic engagement of their students. This may take the form of holding student union elections, sponsoring community service clubs and allowing student initiatives such as a Model UN or Model Arab League. Campuses are in some countries one of the few venues where gathering for discussion and debate is possible, and student energy is creating more extra-curricular opportunities for civic learning to take place. Educators report that a new generation of young people is emerging that is more ready to take bold initiatives and approach civic roles in a more engaged manner than in the past.

Within universities, younger faculty members are seeking ways to make their classrooms more relevant places to learn: field observation, community service projects and practical internships are appearing as pedagogical tools alongside standard lectures and exams. Nonetheless, the overwhelming academic pattern in most public universities relies on formal lectures given in large auditoriums, a single textbook (sometimes written by the instructor) and an end-of-year examination. The opportunities for faculty to carry out community-engaged research or teaching within that tradition are very limited. Thus, the challenge to innovators is to carve out spaces for new approaches within the confines of large systems that are slow to change.

A recent encouraging sign has been the readiness of private corporate entities to invest in university programmes that may benefit future employment. An established tradition at private universities, this is now happening more regularly in public institutions where the leadership is ready to work out public–private partnerships. At Cairo University, for example, Egyptian companies are donating to help furnish laboratories and lecture halls as a way of making up for budgetary constraints. Corporate employees may lecture to students who are then offered internships in their senior year. To date, such partnerships have been largely ad hoc, only rarely supported by national policy.

Gulf universities tend to be much better resourced; they are able to support a modern physical plant and to attract international faculty who seed innovation in community-engaged practices. The generally low levels of original research output across the region, however, mean that teaching materials can be outdated and not very relevant to local contexts. By the second decade of the new century, few could argue against the urgent need for reforms to the formal academic programmes of Arab higher education.

TREMENDOUS REGIONAL DIVERSITY

We can identify three groups of countries in the Arab region for the purpose of exploring how higher education is responding during this current transformative period. *In most countries, gradual reform is still seen by leaders as a viable and preferred route to societal development.* Governments in this group of states are offering incremental openings for more citizen participation; Saudi Arabia, for example, has recently admitted 30 women for the first time to its national consultative body, the Shura Council. Morocco is encouraging some types of civil society growth. Lebanon has recently adopted a comprehensive national youth policy that encourages cross-sectoral cooperation. Universities in these countries are enjoying a period of relative openness and ability to experiment and reform, with some restrictions on free political expression.

In *countries that have come out of uprisings and are currently undergoing major governance transitions*, universities are embroiled in rapid change. This may at times involve short-lived strikes and closures, along with demands for greater institutional openness and accountability. Egyptian national university faculties, for example, are demanding the right to elect department chairs, deans and presidents. The tensions between religious and civil visions for state control have been heightened in this period of jockeying for power. With the exception of opinion polling, empirical research on these trends is rare or superficial. In the North African 'arc of transition' (Tunisia, Libya and Egypt), the middle of 2013 saw a hardening of negative stereotypes across this divide and a widening gulf between the proponents of each future imaginary. Yemen ousted a dictatorial president only to have his vice-president assume the leadership of an unstable political situation.

In transitioning countries, universities are rapidly becoming politicized spaces that reflect the conflict of ideas elsewhere in society, with all that this implies for challenges to reflection, tolerance and applying analytic rigor. At the same time, universities are struggling to achieve greater independence from central authorities in the management of their programmes. During unstable times, the likely effect is a disruption of academic scholarship, teaching and learning. As this paper was being finalized in the week of 30 June 2013, universities across major Egyptian cities were closed due to street protests, and fighting had erupted at the gates of Cairo University. Therefore, a huge challenge at the moment is to re-establish universities as places of rational discourse, synthesis, innovation and societal integration.

The third set of *countries are in the midst of political conflict or simmering civil unrest* in which universities are constrained, controlled by security forces or closed. These states are in a period of abnormal public life in which university functioning is disrupted and it is difficult to predict what the future will hold for higher education. Countries such as Iraq, Sudan and Bahrain move in and out of this category, while Palestine and Syria face prolonged struggle and violence.

COUNTRIES UNDERGOING REFORM

While the drama of the Arab Spring has attracted much media attention internationally, the fact is that most of the 22 countries forming the Arab League are in a process of instituting gradual governance and legislative reforms in order to avoid upheaval. This is true for the Gulf States, which are able to use their wealth to stem popular unrest, as well as countries with a recent violent past, like Algeria or Lebanon, where further disorder is an unattractive option for achieving participatory goals. Other countries, such as Jordan and Morocco, have young reform-minded monarchs who utilize a mix of legal reforms – Morocco recently enacted laws mandating full gender equality – and careful control of the media and the security situation to steer a gradual path forwards. Higher education in countries in this category varies widely as it includes both the wealthiest and the poorest Arab nations, those with long histories of once-renowned universities, like Sudan, and those for whom higher education was introduced only in the 1980s, as in Qatar. Nonetheless, interesting developments can be noted across this group of countries in the ways in which universities are attempting to engage their communities and to offer students learning experiences beyond the campus walls.

Commonly, engagement within universities is most highly developed in extra-curricular settings. Campuses may engage in humanitarian activities such as a blood drive in response to a crisis, or individual faculty members may provide policy advice and studies on request to government bodies. In general, a pattern can be seen where universities started out as relatively engaged institutions as part of the post-colonial state-building phase around the middle of the mid-20th century. Then, pressures of high enrolment and shrinking budgets reduced those activities to a minimum; now, the beginnings of a new trend back towards engaged learning and research may be seen, but this has not yet been widely documented. Where there are exceptions and engagement is infused in academic programmes, those can usually be traced to the specific development of an individual university rather than to current national policies in higher education.

The Gulf States have in common fairly young university systems and a generous state budget fuelled by petro-dollars. Most national education is free or highly subsidized. With the exception of Saudi Arabia, the states are small and typically support one main national university. Bahrain is a good example, with the University of Bahrain founded in 1986 as the national provider of higher education. The website (University of Bahrain, 2009) notes that:

> University of Bahrain's vision is to be an internationally recognized university for excellence in student learning, innovative research, and community engagement that contributes to the economic vitality, sustainability, and quality of life in the Kingdom, the region, and beyond.

The university also specifies its commitment to 'reaching out to the local, regional, and global communities.'

The depth of community engagement is suggested by the listing of activities: public lectures, professional development courses and the offering of consultancy services. Perhaps more is happening on campuses like this, but those efforts are not yet being publicized. Newer private universities founded in partnership with a foreign entity, such as the Royal College of Surgeons in Ireland–Medical University of Bahrain, charge higher tuition fees and offer many service clubs and opportunities for students and staff to volunteer (Royal College of Surgeons–Medical University of Bahrain, 2011). Yet it is difficult to point to one Gulf university that is actively working toward a fully engaged mission. It may be that welfare state environments do not stimulate the kinds of motivation for service that are found in places where governments have withdrawn and social problems are more pressing.

Oman's state university, Sultan Qaboos University, has established the Centre for Community Service and Continuing Education to act as a link between its various departments and the community, defined broadly as encompassing the public and private sectors, employers, children, individuals with special needs, associations and expatriates (Sultan Qaboos University, 2013). The Centre provides a wide range of external services such as short courses and workshops, but it is unclear how these programmes interface with the degree-granting programmes and the student body. Qatar University in Doha launched a Center of Volunteerism and Civic Responsibility in September 2012. Its goal is to develop 'the knowledge and skills of students to become engaged and responsible citizens in an increasingly complex, global and multicultural society' (http://www.qu.edu.qa/students/activities/volunteer-center/index.php). Through active collaboration between the institution and the community, a reciprocal benefit is expected for both partners. The Center hosts 'My Life is Volunteerism', a competition for students to submit voluntary activity ideas that compete for cash awards towards their implementation. More on Qatari universities can be found Section IV.3.2 in the spotlight on Qatar.

Saudi Arabia is the largest Gulf country, with a number of well-established national and private universities. Programmes at King Faisal University are typical, with research and extension services organized through thematic centres for agriculture, natural resource management, and so on. An innovative centre identifies gifted young Saudis and provides them with intensive science training (King Faisal University, 2010).

The United Arab Emirates (UAE) is made up of several small states with a mixture of public and private institutions of higher education. Recently, several of these universities formed the University Leadership Council, which is composed of educators from the American University of Sharjah, Masdar Institute of Science and Technology, Zayed University, UAE University, Khalifa University of Science, Technology and Research, and Abu Dhabi University. One of their first activities was to host a conference in 2013 on the vital role of philanthropy in sustainable development, with an emphasis on philanthropy-led initiatives in higher education in the UAE (Saudi Gazette, 2013).

The American University of Sharjah (AUS) has a community services office that organizes volunteer groups, social service organizations and on- and off-campus programmes. The office promotes community service as a way to 'experience the joy of helping others and giving back to society'. AUS reaches out to local non-governmental organizations (NGOs), including the Sharjah Social Empowerment Foundation, with partnership agreements to sustain its community activities (American University of Sharjah, 2013).

New York University has a branch campus in Abu Dhabi with an Office of Community Outreach that provides students with professional training and work experience to develop global leadership skills. It also organizes programmes for the campus to give back to the UAE community through public service and research. The programmes emphasize reciprocity, the idea that there are mutual benefits to philanthropy and civic engagement for both students and the community. Typical service programmes include tutoring, helping to preserve the local culture, raising environmental awareness and participating in global education conferences and workshops (New York University Abu Dhabi, undated).

Universities in Kuwait have active policy and administrative support for university civic engagement. Kuwait University has an active Deanship of Community Service and Continuing Education that sponsors student activities linked to the community. In addition, that office has created a network of community-engaged leaders from several universities around the region (Kuwait University, 2009). The American University of Kuwait is expanding its community programmes to fill important gaps. For example, it invites the community to the campus for open discussions around sensitive public issues that may not be discussed in other venues. Student groups are active in programmes to support the large and mainly impoverished community of guest workers from other countries, mainly South Asia (American University of Kuwait, 2013).

Jordan, Palestine and Lebanon comprise the countries of the Mashreq subregion, which share many historical and cultural similarities. Lebanon has the oldest universities in this group, with the AUB having been founded by missionaries in 1866 and continuing its early traditions of service into the present. The Center for Civic Engagement and Community Service (see http://www.ccecs.org/), launched in 2008, has become a model for other university programmes in the region, while the Neighborhood Initiative, begun in 2007, uses university talent and resources to support a variety of collaborative projects, including education for seniors, improved traffic flow in Ras Beirut and the creative public uses of seaside spaces (see Section IV.3.6).

The Lebanese American University established its Outreach and Civic Engagement Unit in 2010 to promote student service and community engagement with the aim of developing future leaders (Lebanese American University, undated). Since the war in July 2006, the Université Saint-Joseph has conducted Operation 7th Day (Université Saint-Joseph, 2013), which provides emergency relief, healthcare, education and civil engineering activities in war-affected areas. In 2013, a Lebanese Consortium of Universities is under development to encourage peer learning and exchange around the effective practices of community-engaged universities.

Tawasol is a European Union Tempus-supported project that links Jordanian and Lebanese Universities with European counterparts to expand community engagement programmes. The Hashemite University in Zarqa coordinates the programme in order to 'support the creation of effective cross-curricula service-learning and civic engagement centers in Jordan and Lebanon through utilizing the specialist expertise and resources of each of the partner universities'. The university works in collaboration with two Jordanian universities, Zarqa Private University and Al al-Bayt University, and two Lebanese Universities, the American University of Beirut and the University of Balamand in Tripoli. One focus is service-learning and curricular reform. The approach emphasizes 'application, reflection, practical engagement, learning by doing, civic participation, and working with local communities' (Tawasol, undated).

Al Hussein Bin Talal University sponsors a unique programme, the El-Hassan Youth Award, which offers awards to young Jordanians between the ages of 14 and 25 both in and out of university. Awards are made annually in the areas of service, expeditions, skills and physical recreation, and include a training and implementation phase as part of the programme. Work areas vary widely and give young people guided exposure to careers in public service, including health, civil defence, tourism, religious organizations, non-profit work, construction, agricultural and humanitarian volunteering activities (El Hassan Youth Award, 2012).

In North Africa, the higher education system is influenced by a French model and instruction may be in Arabic or French. Community outreach is often organized through professional faculties with an emphasis on student training. Hassan II University partners with the Moroccan Center for Civic Education to train teachers in civic education pedagogy, a relatively new subject. The goal is to 'educate younger generations to become responsible, effective and active citizens committed to democratic principles' (Moroccan Center for Civic Education, 2009). The programme extends its rigorous teacher training and implementation of civic education programmes to five out of 16 regions in Morocco, and involves the active support of the Ministries of Education, Higher Education and Scientific Research (Moroccan Center for Civic Education, 2009).

Al Akhawayn University is a private English-language university in Morocco with community engagement as part of its core mission. The Azrou Center for Community Development is an integral part of its liberal arts orientation. All students must complete 60 hours of community service before graduation, and the Azrou Center also provides education and services to community leaders in areas such as youth employment, women's literacy, education and health (Service Learning for Civic Engagement; Al Akhawayn University, 2013). In May 2013, Al Akhawayn University became a partner with CorpsAfrica, an organization that provides opportunities for students to move to an impoverished community within Morocco for one year to implement a community project. CorpsAfrica is based on the American Peace Corps movement concept with the difference that volunteers remain in their home country to provide service.

In Algeria, a number of recent programmes have linked universities around expanding their community engagement programmes. One US State Department–Middle East Partnership Initiative partnership has three components. First, the Algerian University Linkages Program develops capacity in Algerian universities to design and deliver high-quality, industry-driven programmes related to business and entrepreneurship. The Youth Centers Support Project is carried out in close collaboration with the Algerian Ministry of Youth and Sports, and focuses on interventions for at-risk youth to help them acquire marketable skills and gain access to employment and scholarship opportunities. Promoting Education, Altruism and Civic Engagement, engages Algerian university students and select young leaders with disabilities in addressing social problems within their communities. Project activities enhance the capacity of Algerian universities and civil society organizations (CSOs) to collaboratively provide students with volunteer and career opportunities and maximize future programme sustainability by building on current government and private initiatives (World Learning, 2012).

Constantine 1 University has a Sub-directorate for Scientific and Cultural Activities that aims to develop a sense of citizenship and social awareness among students by enabling them to engage in collective action, volunteering both within and beyond the university (Tempus, undated). Over 700 students participated in an on-campus clean-up campaign in early 2013.

COUNTRIES IN TRANSITION

Major political transitions provide windows of opportunity to make significant shifts at both national and institutional levels in terms of basic values and goals. This can be seen in a number of new programmes emerging in the aftermath of the Arab Spring. Both local and international partners have become motivated to reorient higher education toward the societal engagement mission that was envisioned long ago but had never been fully realized. Examples abound over the past three years, although only a few are truly multi-sectoral and involve governments, which themselves are in considerable turmoil. In Tunisia, an ambitious joint project between government, community organizations and national universities in partnership with University of Georgia, USA, is providing faculty exchanges, international service learning courses and new resources for e-learning (University of Georgia–Tunisia Partnership, 2007). At the University of Tunis, there is a topical focus on enhancing student engagement on the problems of youth unemployment and alienation, with the university maintaining a specialized youth outreach centre (University of Tunis, 2011).

As the Arab world's largest country, Egypt has 28 national universities, with multiple branches and massive student enrolments that can surpass 300,000 students on a single campus. As in many other Arab countries, university engagement has most often been defined through extra-curricular service projects such as blood drives or literacy campaigns. Since the 1980s, most national universities (including Ain Shams University, Cairo University, Beni-Suef University, Assiut University, Mansoura University and Alexandria University) have created a dedicated administrative unit, often with a vice-president position for community outreach and environmental concerns. This is the coordination office for cooperative projects with community groups, other universities and international partnerships. This office is often the focal point for university partnerships related to service, campaigns for humanitarian causes, charity efforts in the surrounding neighbourhood and awareness campaigns about community service.

Another way in which students engage beyond the campus walls is provided by student government, where elected student leaders form councils across national campuses and/or with political or social movements in the country as well. Prior to the revolutions in Tunisia, Yemen, Egypt and Libya, student unions were closely controlled by national security services and the government-appointed university administration. As a result, the post-revolutionary period has seen ongoing struggles for independence among student unions across these countries. Student union elections in 2012 and 2013 were hotly contested and reflected the broader societal splits between Islamist and civil state proponents and parties. Student strikes were also endemic in this period, usually sparked by internal grievances on matters such as tuition, free expression or food quality rather than community-wide or national concerns. However, these groups can still be seen as important training grounds for citizenship roles and future civic engagement.

Community engagement involving the academic curriculum is still rare, although one of the newest national universities in Egypt – Suez Canal University – was formed in the 1980s with that as its guiding mission. More typically, academic community engagement is an initiative at departmental or individual faculty level. Many professional programmes in health or social services, for example, maintain community clinics or service projects that double as training opportunities for students. Assiut University is another institution in Egypt with community engagement infused into its core mission under the banner of 'University without Walls'. It maintains many public programmes for the surrounding community, including a well-regarded human rights service that advises citizens on legal and rights issues without charge (Assiut University, undated).

In Tunisia, a 2006 Tempus programme worked with business schools and faculties of economics to include microfinance (with an emphasis on women borrowers) in undergraduate and postgraduate curricula. This addresses the pressing problem of unemployment across the region, as well as poverty alleviation (Tempus, 2002). Another poverty-related programme, Resala, the largest youth social service organization in Egypt, with over 100,000 volunteer members, was started by students in an engineering ethics class at Cairo University in 1999 (see Section IV.3.8). Engaged learning can extend in some cases to innovative new graduate programmes: a graduate degree in nanotechnology introduced in 2012 at Beni-Suef University (Egypt Independent, 2013) requires students to tackle a practical community problem for their MA thesis instead of completing a theoretical library research.

However, there remain many bureaucratic obstacles to making academic programmes more responsive to community and national concerns. Budgetary constraints are a common problem, even in private universities like the AUC, with an established programme of community-based learning across the

curriculum and over 40 offerings designated in the course catalogue and on student transcripts. Following the 2011 revolution, AUC faculty and students utilized these courses to reach out to communities with heightened economic needs while also helping students to achieve a deeper mastery of the course learning objectives. In some cases, faculty members provide for the incidental costs of transportation or supplies for students to regularly visit and engage with a community group. At Alexandria University, a popular debate programme is embedded in the syllabuses of courses taught in the schools of humanities and social sciences but has not spread easily to other disciplines. This disconnect between creative adaptations of the curricula locally and policy support at higher administrative levels is an ongoing concern not just in Egypt but also region-wide.

Egypt has a longer history of private universities than other transitioning countries of the region. Since legislation passed in the 1980s, a number of private universities have emerged, many with ties to an education system in Europe or North America. The oldest is the American University in Cairo, founded in 1919 by education-oriented protestant missionaries who infused the new college's mission with service and patriotism.

Following the revolutions in North Africa, interest expanded in curricular reform and civic education. In Libya, international experts were invited to advise the University of Tripoli on revamping its mandatory freshman course sequence from one focused on the writings of President Gaddhafi to broader civic education and citizenship courses. The United Nations Development Program (UNDP) has launched an ambitious programme for civic education in Tunisia titled Building Resources in Democracy, Governance and Elections (BRIDGE, 2013). The programme trains instructors to offer short courses in civics to 10,000 university students, who will then be engaged in voter education programmes in their communities.

In Yemen, universities had begun to build units and programmes for civic engagement prior to the uprising in 2011. At Taiz University, a Center for Environmental Studies and Community Services was created in 2003 to sponsor environmental research, pilot programmes and training in coordination with the government in the areas of environmental threats. It also provides technical advice to the business sector and creates awareness of civic and concerns in the community. At Queen Arwa University, Yemen's first online university, one of the institution's goals is to address the lack of qualified job entrants and to help young people improve their employment options. Programmes work closely with industry and civil society to provide scientific and social organizations with trained specialists in the areas of women's studies, environmental studies and population studies.

COUNTRIES IN CONFLICT

It is a sad reality that higher education in Palestine has been disrupted by violence and occupation for over 45 years, with half of all Palestinian youth in refugee camps or long-term diaspora. In Syria, an explosive civil war has raged since 2011. Countries such as Iraq and Sudan face more sporadic outbreaks of internal political violence, usually isolated rather than involving the entire country. In all of these cases, the effects on higher education are profound, with universities bombarded or closed, degrees delayed – sometimes for years – and insecurity robbing those institutions of the safe spaces necessary for learning, reflection and open debate that should characterize campus life.

Nonetheless, heroic efforts are made in these circumstances by university communities to persevere with teaching and learning. The disruption of normal campus life sometimes leads to real innovation and positive change, as will be seen below. It is a testament to these institutions that at one time the University of Khartoum in Sudan ranked as a leading university in the Arab world and that Birzeit, Bethlehem and Al-Quds Universities, among others in Palestine, survive and continue to produce outstanding graduates.

The toll on higher education in Syria can be seen in the drop in national budgetary allocations from $330 million in 2010 to $185 million in 2012 (as reported in *al Monitor*, 12 July 2013). Many universities have had to close due to extensive bombing damage or continuing violence. Even where classes are in still session, security checkpoints and arrests prevent students from moving in the streets to reach their campus. Despite recurrent violence in the city, the president of University of Aleppo called in 2012 for all members of the university to rebuild a system of higher education to serve the community through education, scientific research and community service. Unfortunately, while Aleppo and other universities such as Kalamoon had active extra-curricular outreach programmes prior to 2011, it has proven difficult to obtain up-to-date information on the current situation.

In Iraq, university engagement programmes focus on the aftermath of long years of conflict and on rebuilding an inclusive society. This has encouraged programmes across several universities in different regions of the country. Iraq Debate is an independent civic engagement initiative to promote open discussion and debate culture in Iraq through university venues that bring together Iraq's rich ethnic heritage: Arabs, Kurds, Chaldians, Assyrians, Turkmen, Yezidis and Armenians come together in debate workshops and tournaments. The first Iraq Debate Academy and Mesopotamia Debating Tournament was held in Duhok with students from Zakho to the Gulf coast (see http://www.iraqdebate.org/).

Another multi-university initiative is the Iraq University Linkages Program, which 'Promotes higher education reform in Iraq by working with Iraqi faculty and administrators to strengthen university curricula, enhance and update teaching methods and technology, and improve career services for students' (IREX, undated). Individual university civic programmes often address the lingering effects of civil war; at the American University of Iraq in Sulaimani, the First Stage Qalawa student club runs a weekend arts school for displaced children from Baghdad. Iraqi University makes scholarships available for disadvantaged female students to participate in the Continuing Education and Community Service Unit at the College of Education for Girls.

In Sudan, the University of Khartoum contributes to local education through maintaining model primary and secondary schools and kindergartens for the benefit of the surrounding neighbourhoods. A Peace Research Institute aims to advance a more integrated society; it organizes public seminars and workshops on politics during transitional periods and strengthening CSOs, in cooperation with the UNDP (University of Khartoum, 2013).

Afhad University for Women in Omdurman has engagement embedded in its founding mission to 'create proactive women change agents and leaders from all parts of Sudan who can participate actively in the development of their families and communities' (Stroud, 2011). Civic engagement is central to academic policy, which requires students to participate in community-based learning and research projects for graduation, and faculty to spend 6–10 hours per week in civic activities.

Palestinian higher education has shown resilience and growth in difficult political and economic circumstances punctuated by wars and uprisings. The absence of a viable state has meant that universities are dependent on outside donors, including the governments of Jordan and Egypt at some points, and more recently on international aid agencies. Palestinian culture is known for its strong commitment to education and, despite a harsh environment, universities maintain exceptional high standards and innovation. Likewise, a strong civil society has developed in part in response to the absence of a viable state, and universities are closely linked to their communities. Only a few examples among many can be provided here.

Al-Quds University in Jerusalem is a founding member of the International Talloires Network and committed to becoming a fully engaged university. Rather than locate its civic programmes in one unit, they are infused throughout the operations of the university. Student service programmes are focused on themes, human rights and pre-college education. Students are required to complete 120 hours of service for graduation, at least one-third of which should take place beyond the campus. The university notes that beyond helping to address societal problems, student service builds character traits for future citizenship, enabling volunteers to discover their talents, build self-confidence and add skills like teamwork, leadership and public speaking.

Al-Quds University's engagement activities also emphasize applied research to inform public decision-making on policy issues and conflicts such as water supply and quality. A Human Rights Clinic was established in 2006 at the Law School as the first Palestinian clinic-based legal education programme. Students practise alongside lawyers and human rights NGOs in a year-long programme of lectures, workshops, skills development and practice. In the Street Law Project, students inform residents about their rights and represent them in basic legal proceedings. Recent group research projects included a study of torture in prisons and an analysis of an urban road proposal to link Israeli settlements that would further isolate parts of East Jerusalem (Hollister, 2011).

SUMMARY OF KEY ISSUES IN SOCIETAL ENGAGEMENT FOR ARAB HIGHER EDUCATION

This overview has identified broad patterns of community and public engagement that characterize Arab higher education. Grounded in rich cultural values of social solidarity and charitable giving, most programmes are formulated around a model that provides humanitarian or developmental assistance to disadvantaged groups. Services are organized as discrete projects or activities, often through university engagement units, and student participation is typically sporadic and short term. A few universities require substantial time investments in service for graduation; even fewer have incorporated civic engagement into their mainstream academic programmes. Because

service activities are most often part of extra-curricular programmes rather than academic offerings, learning outcomes are not measured and the longer term impact on students or communities is rarely evaluated. For this paper, authors could locate only a handful of academic research papers that address aspects of service learning or broader university civic engagement, while research on programme impact is virtually non-existent.

As the effects of the Arab Spring are felt across the region, we expect a new generation of students to place even greater demands on their universities for meaningful and sustained engagements. They will expect programmes to tackle sensitive societal issues, such as labour practices, corruption or gender inequality, and to do so in ways that address the root causes and not just the symptoms of the problems. Rights, social justice and dignity, all mobilizing ideas from the recent political uprisings, will appear on campuses as themes that students expect their civic engagement activities to address. While these are daunting goals in many settings, new tools will make innovations more accessible across the region. Social media and other networking resources can enable both students and faculty to spread new ideas and learn from the experiences of other institutions despite the distances involved, and an important new publication, *Al Fanar News and Opinion*, about higher education, is widely distributed online by the Alexandria Trust (http://www.al-fanar.org/2013/09/interview-with-an-advocate-of-education-for-citizenship/). Regional networks are forming to assist in this process, and a list of those resources is found in Section IV.3.7.

For Arab higher education to respond fully to these expectations, we can point to three key challenges. The first is identifying the necessary intellectual tools and analysis to build university programmes based on respect for difference, managing the role of faith in public life, and social inclusion frameworks for development and equity. This will entail new forms of research, service and relationships to communities in times of rapid change. One promising development in this regard is that communities are beginning to approach higher education with requests for the kinds of partnerships they seek, rather than simply being the recipients of services. Shortly after the January 25 revolution in Egypt, a group of young activists approached the John D. Gerhart Center for Civic Engagement at the American University in Cairo to work with them on the design of a leadership and public service short course, one that would 'fast-track' them toward more effective public roles. They asked for exposure to differing viewpoints on Egypt's path to democracy and in 2012 welcomed diversity among the participants themselves. A real challenge now, given rising tensions around the role of religion in public life, will be to keep these programmes open to all points of view and to bridge a widening gap among Islamists and proponents of a civil state.

To date, few scholars are taking on this conceptual challenge as it relates to higher education. While it was fairly possible to find descriptive material on university civic engagement for this chapter, identifying the conceptual frameworks and desired learning outcomes that underpin them was more difficult. The region is facing critical societal rifts – over the role of gender, religion, the military and ethnic minorities – some of which can be traced to basic differences over values and goals. To find a way forward through these conflicting positions will require the application of original scholarship and creating platforms for dialogue that transcend ideological boundaries. This is an area where universities are uniquely equipped to become more engaged.

A second and more practical challenge relates to the global shifts in how learning and teaching take place, often driven by technological innovation and demand from students for more collaborative, interactive and real-world-connected classrooms. With a few exceptions, these trends have not been incorporated into the Arab region's institutions of higher education. And yet models of the engaged university provide a pathway toward these new pedagogies that do not require large investments in technology or equipment in settings where resources are limited. Having communities as integral components of the learning experience *will* require investments in teacher training and a supportive infrastructure at administrative level. The benefits for students are amply clear from those universities which support 'community-based learning'. Their students are in demand in the labour market. They rise to become civil society and government leaders by virtue of the advanced skills acquired – in problem-solving, negotiation, strategic planning and entrepreneurial outlook.

In order to 'make the case' for this shift in academic pedagogy, however, rigorous research needs to be undertaken that demonstrates both immediate outcomes and sheds light on potential longer term impacts. Involving relevant communities in that research will strengthen its outcomes and potential for policy impact. The lack of scholarship on aspects of Arab university civic engagement is a key impediment to taking the field forward and convincing policy professionals to make the investments needed at the level of national university systems.

A third major challenge in the region comes from a widening generational divide as it intersects with traditional norms of authority. Most of those in the contemporary youth generation grew up with satellite television and instantaneous means of communication beyond the confines of family and neighbourhood. They are connected regionally and globally and thus have expectations about actively influencing the course of history in the wake of the Arab Spring developments. Their impatience with slow-to-change systems of higher education will be a growing challenge to administrators and faculty alike. How will higher education respond to youth expectations for inclusion in policy-making, course design and learning outcomes?

In the traditional model, students were subordinates and passive recipients in a system of education that in many ways paralleled other patriarchal societal forms. Evidence from a number of Arab countries in the past two years suggests that challenges to this old order will continue. An argument can be made that universities could productively absorb a good deal of this youthful activism by including students fully in a major planning process around creating 'the engaged university'. Their energy and ideas would be channelled towards addressing significant community issues, and they would concurrently become aware of the realities of resource constraints, building community partnerships and aspects of the university's management usually closed to them. As engaged forms of learning, research and service emerge, students will be working side by side with faculty and community members rather than experiencing the university as a place that excludes them from authority. This model could diffuse tensions currently found on campuses where more traditional forms of higher education are still in practice.

INNOVATION

Cross-university collaboration is increasingly attractive as an effective and relatively low-cost investment in strengthening university engagement. In Yemen, four universities are collaborating with the Dutch development programme to assess models of local participation involving civil society groups, local councils and a core of trained 'mobilization facilitators', including Sana'a University, Ibb University, Mareb College and Shabwa College, In Egypt, six universities are currently cooperating to exchange and learn from each other's established civic action programmes through peer-learning workshops and case studies. The presidents held an early meeting to explore collaboration and reforms in the year following Egypt's January 25 revolution. Currently, faculty members and students come together under the umbrella of the Ma'an Arab University Alliance for Civic Engagement, established in 2008 to promote peer exchange and deepen civic engagement in higher education across the Arab region. Six case studies of unique programmes at each university are currently under preparation that will highlight the challenges to deeper engagement and creative solutions at a local level.

CONCLUSION

This necessarily brief overview has highlighted a number of issues to be considered if the rich array of university civic engagement programmes found in the Arab region are to be sustained and taken to a next level. In addition to the three major challenges described above, we can note some structural and policy issues that have arisen across several countries and higher educational systems. The first is that providing charitable services is the most prevalent mode of university civic engagement, followed by activities taking a developmental approach. The former would include visits to orphanages, blood drives, and offering free meals, clothing and medicines to those in need. The latter encompasses tutoring, community development efforts and extension services to transfer job-related skills to the community. Both of these modalities, if accompanied by guided reflection, can provide valuable learning experiences for those who participate.

However, it is those rare programmes that begin with a fact-finding or research phase and attempt to understand the root causes of a social problem before addressing it that seem to hold the most promise for transformative learning and change. These require more skill and time on the part of faculty members and probably rely on a longer intervention period than the standard semester or term. They provide opportunities for cross-disciplinary cooperation and hold the promise of significant change. The revolutionary spirit that imbues much of the Arab region at the moment may inspire more of this sort of strategic, or what some call a social justice, approach to service. Universities should certainly be one of the key institutions where deep thinking about social problems is both possible and achievable.

We have noted that many university civic engagement programmes in the region are administered in tandem with units for continuing education. There is a clear logic for this since community members are the beneficiaries of extension classes. However, it appears likely that the provision of extension services dominates programmes and resources in those settings and may prevent a fuller development of independent civic programmes reaching beyond the short course model. At least one university chose not to have a campus hub at all for their civic programmes, believing that it was better to push for the inclusion of community outreach in all units and programmes. That seems like a worthy goal for fully engaged universities. But the initial stages of mobilizing faculty, students and resources and establishing a track record may require a dedicated staff and unit. In addition, as university programmes expand, a good case may be made for one coordinating body that is alert to possible synergies and maintains quality standards.

As previously noted, extra-curricular civic programmes are far more numerous than those embedded within the academic offerings of Arab universities. Community-based learning pedagogies seem, however, to be spreading at the moment and to be in demand by a new generation of students. Where extra-curricular-only programmes are most effective, they appear to be part of graduation requirements and to have intensive faculty involvement to make sure that learning and reflection are part of the service experience. A debate is ongoing as to whether service hours should be mandated as a graduation requirement or be undertaken in a voluntary spirit. Rather than take sides on that issue, we can note from the regional overview that either seems to be working when an adequate infrastructure is in place for the activities to be meaningful, consistently carried out and of real benefit to communities as well as to the university.

Finally, it should be noted that we were not to date able to identify any faculty chair dedicated to civic engagement as a field of study, nor did we find degree programmes in civic participation or engaged citizenship. Instead, a growing number of social science and public policy courses on these topics are found in private universities and a few public universities. This is an area where some pioneering work could be undertaken to make civic engagement a proper interdisciplinary field in higher education, in much the same way that environmental studies has emerged over the last 20 years. Given the current rise in corporate social responsibility programmes ready to invest in higher education, it is conceivable that the funds needed to launch such programmes could be found locally. As universities become more effective and recognized for their community contributions, a new resource stream would very likely open up from a range of donors interested in helping to build just, prosperous and inclusive societies in the Arab region.

NOTE

1   Others, such as Robert College in Istanbul, were nationalized (this now being Boğaziçi University) but retained some of their liberal arts traditions.

REFERENCES

Al Akhawayn University (2013) 'Al Akhawayn Students Join World Top-tier Schools in the Largest Student Social Competition'. Retrieved from http://www.aui.ma/en/media-and-news/news/1299-al-akhawayn-students-join-world-top-tier-schools-in-the-largest-student-social-competition.html.

American University in Cairo (2011) 'History'. Retrieved from http://www.aucegypt.edu/about/History/Pages/history.aspx.

American University of Kuwait (2013) 'Student Affairs'. Retrieved from http://www.auk.edu.kw/student_affairs/sl_student_clubs.jsp.

American University of Sharjah (2013) 'Community Services (CS) Helps You Experience the Joy of Helping Others and Giving Back to Society'. Retrieved from http://www.aus.edu/info/200147/current_students/342/community_service/1#.UeaGfjtHLRo.

Assiut University (undated) 'University Without Walls'. Retrieved from http://www.aun.edu.eg/faculty_law/arabic/law_studies/index.htm.

BRIDGE (2013) 'Egypt, Lebanon, Jordan and Tunisia!' Retrieved from http://www.bridge-project.org/news2/arab-world/1232-egypt,-lebanon,-jordan-and-tunisia.html.

Egypt Independent (2013) 'Beni Suef University establishes Nanotechnology Faculty'. Retrieved from http://www.egyptindependent.com/news/beni-suef-university-establishes-nanotechnology-faculty.

El Hassan Youth Award (2012) 'About the Award'. Retrieved from http://hyaward.org.jo/main/en/about-the-award.html.

Hollister, R.M. (2011) 'Education and service for political change and development: Profile of Al-Quds University (OPT)'. In: Watson, D., Hollister, R.M., Stroud, S.E. and Babcock, E., *The Engaged University: International Perspectives on Civic Engagement*. New York: Routledge, pp. 83–9.

IREX (undated) 'Iraq University Linkages Program'. Retrieved from http://www.irex.org/project/iraq-university-linkages-program.

King Faisal University (2010) 'Facts and Figures'. Retrieved from http://www.kfu.edu.sa/en/Departments/knowledge Exchange/Documents/Final%20Facts%20and%20 Figures%20(executive%20Summary%20of%20KFU).pdf.

Kuwait University (2009) 'Deanship of Community Service and Continuing Education'. Retrieved from http://www.kuniv.edu/ku/Centers/CentreforCommunityServices Continuingeducation/.

Lebanese American University (undated) 'Student Engagement'. Retrieved from http://students.lau.edu.lb/student-engagement/.

Moroccan Center for Civic Education (2009) 'About Us'. Retrieved from http://civicmorocco.org/about-us/.

New York University Abu Dhabi (undated) 'Community Outreach'. Retrieved from http://nyuad.nyu.edu/campus-life/student-life/community-services-learning.html.

Royal College of Surgeons–Medical University of Bahrain (2011) 'Institutional follow-up Review Report'. Quality Assurance Authority for Education and Training, Higher Education Review Unit. Retrieved from http://en.qaa.edu.bh/UsersFiles/HERU/HERU%20english/6%20 RCSI%20EN.pdf.

Saudi Gazette (2013) 'Dubai Meeting Focuses on the Vital Role of Philanthropy in Sustainable Development'. Retrieved from http://www.saudigazette.com.sa/index.cfm?method=home.regcon&contentid=20130530167863.

Stroud, S.E. (2011) 'Empowering women as agents of change through education: Profile of Ahfad University for women (Sudan)'. In: Watson, D., Hollister, R.M.S., Stroud, E. and Babcock, E., *The Engaged University: International Perspectives on Civic Engagement*. New York: Routledge, pp. 143–50.

Sultan Qaboos University (2013) 'Centre for Community Service and Continuing Education'. Retrieved from http://www.squ.edu.om/community-service/tabid/1738/language/en-US/Default.aspx.

Tawasol (undated) 'About Tawasol.' Retrieved from http://www.tawasol.org/site/view/20/.

Tempus (2002) 'Microfinance at the University'. Retrieved from http://www.saa.unito.it/meda/objectives.htm.

Tempus (undated) 'Higher Education in Algeria'. Retrieved from http://eacea.ec.europa.eu/tempus/participating_countries/reviews/algeria_review_of_higher_education.pdf.

Université Saint-Joseph (2013) 'Operation 7th Day'. Retrieved from http://www.usj.edu.lb/7ejour/.

University of Bahrain (2009) 'Mission and Vision'. Retrieved from http://www.uob.edu.bh/english/pages.aspx?module =pages&id=1812&SID=312.

University of Georgia–Tunisia Partnership (2007) 'An International Cooperation Portfolio'. Retrieved from http://www.tunisia.uga.edu.

University of Khartoum (2013) 'Peace Research Institute'. Retrieved from: http://www.euni.de/tools/jobpopup.php?lang=en&option=showJobs&jobid=18387&jobtyp=10 &university=University+of+Khartoum&country=SD& sid=5181.

University of Tunis (2011) 'Cultural and Sport Activities'. Retrieved from http://www.utunis.rnu.tn.

World Learning (2012) 'Promoting Education, Altruism and Civic Engagement (PEACE)'. Retrieved from http://www.worldlearning.org/program-areas/international-development-and-exchange-programs/projects/promoting-education-altruism-and-civic-engagement-peace/.

INTRODUCTION

This paper traces the emergence and historical trajectory of Palestinian universities, noting the dramatic increase in student numbers over the past couple of decades. It underscores the fact that Palestinian universities have, since their creation, been concerned with regional and societal development. This feature of Palestinian higher education is then considered as part of global developments and the general move towards the third mission, assisted by the growth in information and communication technologies (ICT) and the internet. Finally, it looks at examples of regional engagement as indicated in the benchmarking exercise of the Lifelong Learning in Palestine project, which is a European Union Tempus initiative involving four Palestinian universities, two Palestinian non-governmental organizations (NGOs) and four European universities (see the Lifelong Learning in Palestine website at http://lllp.iugaza.edu.ps/en/).

GROWTH AND HISTORICAL CONTEXT

For Palestinians during the British mandate, pursuing a university education meant travelling to Beirut or Cairo. After 1948, the focus shifted to Cairo and various other universities in the Arab world. Egypt was far more in tune with Arab political aspirations. However, two-year, teacher training, technical and liberal arts colleges were established with the involvement of the United Nations Relief and Work Agency. Amidst these developments, Palestinians students were quickly developing their own sense of where they wanted to be in higher education. A Palestinian nationalist consciousness emerged. In 1967, Israel occupied the West Bank and Gaza, controlling movement in and out of the whole region. Efforts since 1967 have been almost exclusively on Palestine creating its own system of higher education.

Baramki (2010) writes that, in the early days, 'we were building a better future for our people … We needed a university to develop Palestine, train professionals, as a laboratory for ideas and create a leadership'. Since then, many universities have been established, the most recent being the University of Gaza, which was set up as a private institution. In 1948, there were around 60 higher education students, whereas today there are around 214,000 young men and women on courses in 13 universities and 50 other higher education institutions (Ministry of Higher Education, 2011). Many of the new students come from refugee camps, small villages and lower income families (Paz, 2000). Under conditions of a belligerent occupation, this increase represents quite an achievement.

FROM OSLO TO THE PRESENT

Over the period of the different Oslo agreements and under the Palestinian National Authority (PNA), the number of Palestinian students entering higher education has increased by a factor of five. This increase is without historical comparison. There has also been an incredible success in reducing illiteracy (PNA, 2008). With a single overarching legal framework being set up for all institutions, whether governmental, public, private, profit-making or non-profit-making, education came to be seen as a right (Soto, 2001). Breadth was provided in the system as well as depth, broadening the societal impact right across different socioeconomic groups. Each institution became a university, or a university college, or a polytechnic or community college (European Commission Tempus, 2012). At the same time, NGO activity increased, and in cities such as Ramallah and Jerusalem, NGOs became a strong presence. NGOs are now important partners for many universities in providing both informal and formal training and education in Palestine, which often complicates collaboration.

Higher education in Palestine operates with considerable autonomy (academic, financial and administrative) and self-management, each institution taking responsibility for admissions and staff employment policies. Autonomy no doubt contributes to the institution's self-worth (see Clark, 1971). The universities also control their own procedures for student assessments and confer their own degree awards. Boards of trustees participate exten-sively in governance, contributing a great deal to the development of strategy and missions. Universities also apply modern management principles and quality assurance standards. Outside these formal controls, universities still remain accountable to the local community by being very much an integral part of regional culture. Quality is an ongoing issue, and in 2002, the Accreditation and Quality Commission was set up, with the overarching responsibility for accrediting, assessing and evaluating programmes, subjects and institutions. This Commission is now fully functional across all institutions.

The age of students in traditional institutions is between 18 and 24 years, and over 25 in the open university system. It is a notable feature of the Palestinian system that women constitute around 55% of the student population. Yet while student numbers have increased, core funding has remained at the same level, with student fees contributing to only 60–70% of the operational budget – something in excess of 50% of students cannot pay their tuition fees. Constant financial restraints produce incredible pressures that expose almost all institutions to the risk of closure. Strikes because of the non-payment of full staff salaries are not unusual. Al-Quds University suffered particular difficulties in 2013, and financial insecurity often burdens regional involvement.

The mission statements of most institutions focus on teaching, research and community engagement. The budget targets teaching and staff salaries first, however, and these swallow up most of the budget resources. This means that only a minimum percentage of the budget is allocated to research, especially research in the community, with levels of expenditure often depending on various other sponsors. A very welcome development recently has been that the Ministry of Higher Education has specifically allocated a small budget for such research. Yet the main areas of cooperation between higher education institutions and the local community (enterprises, public institutions and NGOs) are in students' internship training, curriculum development and consultation services.

GLOBAL TRENDS AND BENCHMARKING REGIONAL ENGAGEMENT

Palestinian institutions follow international trends carefully. University centres observe the global knowledge economy, and international advisory agencies can be found working alongside many Palestinian universities. While teaching university courses in institutions such as the Islamic University of Gaza (IUG) and Birzeit observe these trends, Jongbloed (2008) comments that Palestinian institutions are now increasingly called upon to deliver education and research relevant to the global knowledge society. This is a focus for Palestine. It is also the focus of the *Arab Knowledge Report 2010/11* (Mohammed bin Rashid Al Maktoum Foundation and UNDP, 2011) which introduced its findings with the following:

> Undoubtedly, the Arab reality is thorny and problematic; this is our reality, and we know it well in detail. We have no way out but to work through this reality, with awareness and determination to overcome obstacles, and with recognition that human's worthiness is not measured by the success to adapt with reality, whatever it may be, neither by skills in managing the statuesque, but rather by the ability to develop this reality and change it for the better through serious, persistent and well thought hard work that is driven by a spirit of optimism, selflessness, and devotion. By this, change will happen and development be achieved. (page A)

It is agreed that development calls for more university involvement in the political arena through collaborations with non-profit-making organizations, social movements and a variety of different training and educational foundations (OECD, 1997). It is also agreed that the universities could play more of a role in creating social cohesion. But universities are not outside the broader political situation that isolates one area of the West Bank from the other and maintains an almost complete closure of Gaza, with nothing moving in or out of the area without prior Israeli approval. This has made the work of the Lifelong Learning in Palestine project all the more difficult. Problems have been simply with the movement of people when Europeans travel in and Palestinian colleagues travel out to different gatherings.

Knowledge exchange works through people. With strict limitations on travel, research collaborations have been patchy. Nonetheless, most Palestinian universities are embracing their 'third' mission with enthusiasm. Universities have also taken to benchmarking involvement, which was an early task of the Lifelong Learning in Palestine project. In the benchmarking exercise, considerable skills were developed and quite a lot of discussion was initiated from the results. Discussion was not limited to campus staff. Regional involvement was encouraged in the earliest of activities, and some informal learning centres took part in the discussions. Reflection on mission statements followed – prioritizing work with local companies, NGOs and civil society organizations. The benchmarking tool assessed methods of gauging community needs and informing ongoing strategies for future regional involvement.

Benchmarking asked about quality assurance procedures for community activities. Views were sought on the amount of continuing education in the region each year and also on the level of provision, culminating in university awards. Knowledge of employment and economic trends was central to the benchmarking. Details of work with enterprise, government agencies, voluntary organizations and various other organizations were solicited. Information moved around the whole question of societal development. The results did not vary a great deal, reflecting years of occupation and closure policies, which in effect meant that millions of Palestinians now connect through social media and have long conversations via mobile phones.

TECHNOLOGY

Palestinian economic, political and cultural institutional life connects to the universities, as with all other institutions, through the company Jawwal. Junka-Aikio (2012) claims that there has over the past decade been a boom in mobile phone use right across Palestine. Jawwal was licensed by the Palestinian Authority before 1999 but could not get Israel to release the needed communication frequencies. The company (a subsidiary of the Palestinian Telecommunication Group) now stands as one of the most vibrant areas of Palestinian economic life. Controversially, Junko-Aiko has argued that the impact on Palestinian subjectivities has been negative, and that Palestinians have become more and more cornered in their own individuality, so much so that old discourses about traditional identities do not endure in the way they might have done in the past.

If Junka-Aikio's thesis holds, the consequences for Palestinian higher education will not be insignificant. The telecommunications system is one of many infrastructural supports for higher education that came with the Oslo Interim Agreements, which gave the Palestinian Authority the right to build and operate a separate and independent communications system. Reliance now on this technology is shown by internet use. The demand for technological goods and services throughout Palestine is shown in Table IV.3.1.1.

TABLE IV.3.1.1 Percentage of household IT goods and services (Palestine Central Bureau of Statistics, 2011)		
Services	2004	2011
Computer	26.4%	50.9%
Internet	9.2%	30.4%
Satellite dish	74.4%	93.9%
Fixed phone line	40.8%	44.0%
Mobile phone	72.8%	95.0%

Business process outsourcing/information technology outsourcing and telecommunications technology have flourished in recent years, as the figures in Table IV.3.1.1. demonstrate. Advertising shows that Google, Cisco and various other ICT names are all active on the West Bank.

The internet is accessed for Facebook by 37%, information by 85.7%, entertainment by 79.3% and communication by 69.1% of the population. Studying and work are reasons for 49.3% and 18.2%, respectively, showing that mobile phone and internet use is on the increase, regardless of the specific purpose or use. Yet the University of Birzeit official website says that the purpose and mission of each of its centres is improving the daily realities of life in this region. Birzeit is seen by all the residents in the region to be a societal resource aiming to develop the most valuable natural resource of the area, which is the Palestinian people.

HUMAN AND SOCIAL CAPITAL DEVELOPED LOCALLY

One example of the way in which Palestinian universities are moving into regional engagement can be given with the example of the Jerusalem Community Action Center (CAC). In the Old City, the CAC functions as a Palestinian community rights-based centre, established under the umbrella of Al-Quds University (Community Action Center, 2013). The centre engages marginalized groups and empowers them to fully participate in their community. This is accomplished through individual social and legal advocacy, community organization and participation in decision-making bodies. Empowering the disadvantaged to access their social and economic rights and entitlements through democratic means is further seen as the way to develop civil society in East Jerusalem and foster equality and democracy.

Another example might be given by the Centre for Architecture Heritage, or IWAN (IWAN, 2013), which represents the community restoration of valuable architecture. In 2000, the Center was established as a small unit in the IUG's Faculty of Engineering. Its work was crucial after the 2008/2009 war on Gaza, which destroyed many of Gaza's valuable buildings. IWAN set about archiving and documenting all the damage and loss. The Center then began restoration of the Ibn Othman Mosque in Shojaeya District, the Omari Mosque in Jabalya town, the famous Hato and Ashi houses in Darag district, and numerous other houses, baths and places of different religious significance. In the process, new three-dimensional techniques of computer imaging were developed and long forgotten architectural detail was recorded for future renovation workshops and training related to the rehabilitation of old buildings, architectural conservation and restoration, redecoration and the revival of ancient ornaments, paintings, mosaics and glass drawings.

After Operation Cast Lead, IWAN organized around 12 exhibitions of its work.

The IUG has also established a unit of Business and Technology Incubators (BTI) on a community outreach basis, which aims to provide business services to young entrepreneurs who have developed their ideas beyond the early stage. The BTI provides product and marketing advice for projects with an ICT component, and works with more established regional/international investors to create funding possibilities for new companies. One of BTI's core objectives is to develop the management curriculum for new training programmes encouraging the talent to lead new Palestinian companies that can compete successfully in an international environment. The BTI has numerous collaborations with names such as Genius Soft, media eye, Tasawaq Palestine and GoCall Palestine. Through this kind of collaborative focus, the Materials and Soil Laboratories were established in 1995 for material, concrete, soil and asphalt testing. The Laboratories have established them as the best equipped material testing laboratories and offer their services to all companies across the Gaza region.

CONCLUSION

Schuetze (2010) reminds us that there are three sides to community engagement: knowledge and technology transfer, continuing education and more community-based research. An example of knowledge and technology transfer in Palestine comes in 'on the ground' networks of informal learning that need much more development. The Lifelong Learning in Palestine projects works to develop a clear national framework in which these exchanges can take place. Research collaborations, faculty consultation services, student internships, university continuing education programmes, conferences and seminars, and the exchange between the university's different professional associations are all an ongoing focus. Schuetze is keen on continuing education, described as 'recurrent professional education, public seminars and lectures, and short-term not-for-credit courses' (pp. 22–4). Palestinian universities function under conditions of a belligerent occupation but nonetheless show a remarkable degree of determination for the third mission, a fast-developing area of innovation and change. The role of the universities in moving societal change and building Palestine remains clear, but there a huge need for more international input from global networks of universities.

REFERENCES

Baramki, G. (2010) *Peaceful Resistance: Building a Palestinian University under Occupation*. London: Pluto.

Clark, B.R. (1971) 'Belief and loyalty in college organization'. *Journal of Higher Education*, 42(6), 499–515.

Community Action Center (CAC) Community Action Center. Retrieved June 14, 2013 from http://www.cac-alquds.org/index.php/en/.

European Commission Tempus (2012) 'Higher Education in the Occupied Palestinian Territory'. Retrieved June 13, 2013 from http://eacea.ec.europa.eu/tempus/participating_countries/overview/oPt.pdf.

IWAN – Centre for architectural Heritage (undated). Homepage. Retrieved June 13, 2013 from http://iwan.iugaza.edu.ps/en/Default.aspx.

Jongbloed, B. (2008) Retrieved from www.pcbs.gov.ps/Portals/_PCBS/Downloads/book1809.pdf.

Junka-Aikio, L. (2012) 'Late modern subjects of colonial occupation: mobile phones and the rise of neoliberalism in Palestine'. *New Formations*, 75, 99–121.

Ministry of Higher Education, Palestinian National Authority (2011) 'Palestinian Higher Education Statistics 2010–2011'. Retrieved June 10, 2013 from http://www.moe.gov.ps/(S(12rtcl45msgtgjjq0cv5dtqw)A(EHT_ECNIzQEkAAAAMDlIMjA2ZjUtZDgwNy00MWM5LWFlMTMtNDI4MzZlODNkYTgxhynb40Ceo96Ds2dm50cov2d-maw1))/Uploads/admin/Matweyeh2011.pdf.

Mohammed bin Rashid Al Maktoum Foundation and UNDP (2011) *Arab Knowledge Report*. Dubai: Al Ghurair Printing and Publishing.

OECD (1997) *The Response of Higher Education Institutions to Regional Needs*. Centre for Educational Research Innovation, Programme on Institutional Management in Higher Education. CERI/IMHE/DG(96)10/REV1. Paris: OECD.

Palestine Central Bureau of Statistics (2011) website. Statistical Review. Retrieved June 10, 2013 from http://www.pcbs.gov.ps/Portals/_pcbs/PressRelease/int_Pop_2012e.pdf.

Palestinian National Authority (Ghadeer Fannoun) (2008) 'The Development and State of the Art of Adult Learning and Education (ALE): National Report of Palestine'. Retrieved June 15, 2013 from http://lllp.iugaza.edu.ps/Files_Uploads/634714337651714291.pdf.

Palestinian National Authority, Ministry of Education and Higher Education (2010) 'Education Sector and Cross-Sector Strategy 2011–2013 (Preliminary Draft)'. Retrieved June 10, 2013 from http://www.mohe.gov.ps/Uploads/planning.

Paz, R. (2000) 'Higher education and the development of Palestinian economic groups'. Middle East Review of International Affairs, 4(2), 81–95.

Schuetze, H.G. (2010) 'The "third mission" of universities: community engagement and service'. In: Inman, P. and Schuetze, H.G. (eds), The Community Engagement and Service Mission of Universities. Leicester: NIACE, pp. 13–32.

Soto, J. (2001) 'The application of education rights in the occupied territories'. Florida Journal of International Law, (3), 211–29.

Inside View IV.3.2
Knowledge, engagement and higher education in Qatar

Uday Rosario

Qatar is a small country in the Arabian Gulf region that has experienced rapid growth and development over the past 20 years. Both state policy and the philanthropy of the ruling family have enhanced the spread of higher education. The national university is Qatar University (QU), founded in 1973 to produce skilled and educated Qataris for the expanding economy and social service sectors. More recently, the Qatar Foundation, lead by Her Highness Sheikha Mozah Bint Nasser, created Education City, which is composed of the satellite campuses of leading US, French and British universities. Together, these two sets of institutions are leading the way towards engaged higher education in the country.

Each institution has a unique focus that has undoubtedly been shaped by its origins. QU shows a strong commitment to partnership with key sectors in Qatari society – industry, business, government, academia and civil society. The campuses that make up Education City take the approach of developing individual students towards becoming active and engaged citizens. Education City's international make-up has encouraged a number of programmes for international service learning.

QATAR UNIVERSITY

QU, the primary institution of higher education in Qatar, joins other academic institutions in aligning its programmes, courses, research and other initiatives with objectives of the Qatar National Vision 2030, Qatar National Development Strategy, National Health Strategy and National Research Strategy. Underlying these objectives is a commitment to meet the needs of the fast-developing economy and address changes in the society's expectations, and to seek solutions to everyday challenges such as those related to education, energy, environment, health and cultural identity, to name but a few.

As the flagship national university, QU is a leading partner with government, academia, industry, business and civil society to contribute to the country's development and progress. This is apparent in the objectives listed in its Strategic Plan, its stated mission and vision, and its development of academic programmes and research initiatives.

Along with research, QU sees community service as a priority issue and adopts a holistic approach to building programmes. These can be found in the areas of national capacity-building, continuing education and professional development, volunteerism, health awareness and alumni involvement, along with other initiatives that impact positively on the community.

The Qatarization process is a critical objective by which QU serves the community through national capacity-building and matching graduates to the labour market. QU also has strong leadership programmes to maximize the capacity of Qatari faculty members as teachers, scholars and potential leaders for the university and society.

Through its Continuing Education Office, College of Pharmacy's Continuing Pharmacy Professional Development programme, National Center for Educator Development (NCED) and College of Law, QU's training and professional development activities provide members of the professional sectors in government and private-sector organizations access to up-to-date information and techniques related to their particular professions. One of QU's most recent initiatives is piloting a new human resources qualification, developed exclusively for Qatar, which is the first such training course reflecting and meeting the specific needs of the Gulf region.

Professional development and lifelong learning for teachers, educators and researchers are an important area for QU. Through its NCED programmes and annual education reform conference, the College of Education provides support to people working in the education profession – that is, teachers, school leaders, administrators, support personnel and administrative staff – to update their skills and knowledge to keep pace with the rapidly changing developments in methods, techniques and tools in the field of education.

The College of Law's continuing education initiatives are designed to engage the legal profession in Qatar in professional development activities to upgrade their skills and competencies in new and existing areas of law. An intensive three-module training programme in September–October 2012 – Advanced Intensive Skills Courses for New Lawyers and Legal Professionals in Qatar – oriented members of law firms and government and private sector legal departments on 'Advanced Contract Drafting', 'Understanding the Sources of Client Problems', and 'How to be an Excellent In-House Counsel'.

In April 2013, QU added to its portfolio the Global Changemakers' Timebank initiative (handed over from the British Council), a project developed by youth to inspire and establish a growing network of young activists, engaging them in a range of practical experiences that equip youth to become effective members in their community.

In line with the national objective to promote health, wellness and healthy lifestyles, QU engages community members in a number of health awareness activities. Blood donation campaigns in addition to obesity, diabetes, breast cancer and other health awareness campaigns, and orienting school children on medication safety, were some of the areas in which QU students played an active role.

In April 2013, the College of Education's annual Deafness Week drew a host of students, faculty, researchers, experts and policy-makers for discussion and interaction on the theme 'Early Intervention'. The event was also designed to celebrate people with hearing impairments and to continue the dialogue and share experiences on sustainable ways to engage and include them into all areas of society.

An important national health and safety issue that QU has taken on board is that of road safety. In response to the national objectives to raise awareness and implement initiatives to reduce the incidence of road and traffic accidents, the organization established the Qatar Road Safety Studies Center in 2012. Its establishment grew out of developments in Qatar – such as the increase in population and an over-concentration of vehicles on Qatar's roads – that required a specialized centre to conduct comprehensive studies on the causes of traffic accidents and an analysis of accident data and information in order to arrive at solutions to significantly reduce them.

Research and collaboration is another area of QU that impacts directly on community service. Research initiatives are aligned with the needs of the society and geared to producing solutions that will serve its

advancement and betterment. Seven specialized research centres are involved in studies and projects that address topics related to oil and gas, laboratory safety, materials processing, economic and social population surveys, mobile innovations, marine conservation and road safety.

Collaboration with other academic institutions and organizations in Qatar is an important part of QU's commitment to community engagement. This has engendered memoranda of understanding, agreements and professional Chair positions to facilitate the organization's academic and research approaches to advancing the expectations of the community and its members.

In these and the aforementioned strategies, projects and initiatives, QU continues to mount every effort to reach out to the Qatari community, to engage its needs and expectations. QU aims to increase the flow of information on trends and new developments throughout society while it brings its expertise, knowledge and experience to bear on addressing and resolving social problems.

COMMUNITY ENGAGEMENT WITHIN EDUCATION CITY

The six undergraduate universities of Education City are built on the ethos of merging academic curricula with practical experiences, with the view of shaping industry and political leaders with strong social foundations.

Most of the universities have a focus on building strong community engagement programmes either linked to their curriculum or institutionalized through student clubs. For example, students within all campuses have the opportunity to engage as volunteers, participants or programme developers for a variety of initiatives that fall within the social arms of the Qatar Foundation. Students from across the campuses participate in an adult literacy programme managed by the Reach Out To Asia Foundation. In addition, students from Georgetown University in Qatar recently created a project with a refugee camp in Gaza based on video-conferences with students studying Justice and Peace in a classroom in Doha. Other projects undertaken since 2007 include work with Palestinian and Iraqi refugees in Jordan, a disaster management trip to

China and another to New Orleans. Locally, Georgetown University has organized two 'Labor Equations' projects that are raising awareness about the important issues affecting labour migration in Qatar and the Middle East as a whole.

The six campuses also regularly engage with local humanitarian organizations such as the Qatar Red Crescent Society, Shafallah Center for Children with Special Needs or Best Buddies. Some students spend their summer break living in a foreign country and working with an international organization on service projects ranging from education and health to building and maintaining technical hardware and support systems. On the academic side, innovation in curricula and pedagogy enable students to take courses on economic development and consultancy with the option of spending between a week and two months in an international internship learning about the technical or operational aspects of civil society organizations. These experiences enable students to practise in the field the theoretical material they learn in a classroom.

'Community engagement' as an educational paradigm providing a merger between academic learning and the skills and ability to address the needs of the community. It also exposes students to the rights and responsibilities of citizenship, both locally and globally. In addition to cognitive learning, these programmes instil in students a sense of social responsibility, interconnectedness and an understanding of the intricacies of social justice. This helps students to develop an understanding of the world as an interdependent system and helps them realize the part they can play in moving towards a more fair and equitable world within their families, local communities, countries, regions and the planet.

While the administration of service learning opportunities varies across the six campuses, they share some common threads, including a focus on: (1) linking theoretical knowledge with practical skills; (2) an understanding of other cultures; (3) encouraging research practices and linking social ethics to professional study; and (4) providing an opportunity for students to critically analyse and question key societal issues and derive their own solutions.

Danielle Feinstein

The atmosphere of the Arab Spring has amplified the importance of youth enfranchisement and engagement in all parts of the Arab World, including the Hashemite Kingdom of Jordan. The events that took place in the region in 2011 contributed substantially to the public's realization that youth need to be encouraged and empowered. At the same time, social media opened the eyes of youth in Jordan to their peers' efforts throughout the region. Soon Jordan was bubbling over with new initiatives harnessing some of this energy for positive changes in Jordan. Jordanian youth feel that the sky is the limit in the demands they have for their country and futures. This dynamism is palpable in a country where 77% of youth believe that the best days are ahead of them (ASDA'A Burson-Marsteller, 2013).

One of the cradles of this energy in youth life is the university. Years spent in university serve as a formative period for every Jordanian, and the university itself acts as an essential part of community life in Jordan. Jordan is renowned in the Arab World for its educational standards and its efforts to develop its human resources for a knowledge economy. Today, Jordan ranks number one in the Arab World in education, having made great strides and significant reforms since the mid-1990s (Al-Shalabi, 2012). Jordan has 10 public universities, 17 private universities and more than 60 community colleges (EHEA, 2013). The education system has undergone rapid expansion over the past few decades, and the gross enrolment rate for the 18–25-year-old population has steadily increased since 2001. These achievements reflect a government that has supported a strong education policy and developed its human capital, which it regards as the principal source of its wealth. These are significant achievements for a country that has experienced such rapid population growth (the Jordanian population having doubled since early 1990) and absorbed waves of refugees from conflicts in the region (World Bank, 2011).

Jordan is among the top 30 countries in the world with a youth bulge (Ortiz and Cummins, 2012). Well aware of the consequences of unaddressed, jobless youth, decision-makers

in Jordan were already conscious of a need to tackle this issue prior to the Arab Spring. However, the energy of the past two years has increased the focus on youth, especially at the university level. During his speech for the 50th anniversary of the founding of the University of Jordan, His Majesty King Abdullah II (2012) declared:

It is my unshakable conviction that the youth are the engine that drives the development process; they are the vehicle and the purpose of development. Therefore, we should continue investing in the youth through education and training to equip them with skills and expertise that will nurture their creativity and enable them to excel.

This past spring, University of Jordan President Ekhleif Tarawneh also called on student bodies to launch initiatives and organize activities and events aimed at serving the university and local communities (University of Jordan, 2013). Initiatives focused on harnessing youth energy to lessen the unemployment rate, build entrepreneurial and leadership skills, and encourage greater youth participation have been prominent among government recommendations. Their importance can also be seen in various Royal Initiatives and projects initiated by The Higher Council for Youth, We Are All Jordan Youth Commission and universities, as well as in foreign donor projects funded by the United Nations, European Union and USAid (personal interview, Amman, Jordan, June 20, 2013).

Perhaps the intensified focus on youth initiatives and enfranchisement is due to the fact that the overall engagement among Jordanian students is still considered to be low. However, the rate of increasing initiatives and openness to youth engagement are promising signs for Jordan's future. One of the challenges is the scarcity of opportunities and initiatives in the various governorates in Jordan; youth opportunities tend to be centred in Amman and Irbid, and are few and far between in less densely populated governorates such as Ma'an in the south and Ajloun in the north. In focus groups conducted in these areas, youth who admitted their lack of

engagement stated that they would be more motivated to join if they were more aware of programmes running in their governorates. The test now will be to meet the needs of Jordanian youth and provide leadership skills for young people in every corner of Jordan to activate their potential.

Nonetheless, Jordan thrives with hundreds of new initiatives. Students are bridging the gap in awareness through social media, taking advantage of Facebook, Twitter and other social media tools to spread their campaigns and messages, as well as to organize public events. Listed below is a selection of initiatives by university students and administrators that reflect the diverse interests of Jordanian youth. The ingenuity and vision displayed by these initiatives are not only inspiring but also infectious, which bodes well for the future of Jordanian civic engagement and for the Kingdom.

LIMIT CHILDREN IN LABOUR INITIATIVE
DESCRIPTION
This student initiative from Hashemite University, Zarqa, was formed to tackle the issue of child labour in Jordan. It aims to apply pressure on decision-makers and officials through an online campaign to ensure children's rights in Jordan and advocate for the application of the Jordanian labour law to those businesses utilizing child labour in Jordan. The students also produced a video campaign and published it on their Facebook page. The campaign aims to reach the Jordanian parliament with this initiative and has already forged a deal with a female member of parliament to adopt the initiative and propose it as an item at an upcoming parliament session. The students also conduct numerous field activities, including a mural-painting event in a public garden in Zarqa.
Link: https://www.facebook.com/LIMIT.CHILDREN.IN.LABOR.

LAB ON WHEELS
This initiative runs country-wide at: Al-Ahliyya Amman University, Amman; Al-Balqa'a Applied University, Salt; Applied Science University, Amman; German Jordanian University, Madaba; Hashemite University, Zarqa;

University of Jordan, Amman; Jordan University of Science and Technology, Irbid; Princess Sumaya University for Technology, Amman; and Yarmouk University, Irbid.

DESCRIPTION

Lab on Wheels is a project that aims to provide young school students with the practical science experiments that are missing from many schools in Jordan, and to involve students in the demonstrative and interactive implementation of exciting projects, supplementing their theoretical learning with much-needed practical experience. This initiative is supported by a nationwide collaboration of universities and the Institute of Electrical and Electronics Engineers, a global technical professional association dedicated to advancing technological innovation and excellence for the benefit of humanity.

Link: http://www.gjuieee.com/lab-on-wheels-nationwide.

UMI 'MY MOTHER' CAMPAIGN

This is located at the American University of Madaba, Madaba; University of Jordan, Amman; and German Jordanian University, Madaba.

DESCRIPTION

The Umi Campaign grew from a partnership of four university students, three graduates and an established non-profit organization (Our Seven's World), formed to raise money for mothers in Palestinian refugee camps in Jordan. During a visit to the Al Husn refugee camp in the winter of 2012, the seven female university students and graduates became acquainted with families, especially those with mothers raising children in the camps who had no financial means. The girls decided to start a fundraising campaign to help these mothers, who were the pillars of their families. As Mother's Day approached, the Umi Campaign was founded, enabling the public to donate needed items directly to families in the camps or to buy personalized Mother's Day cards for 3 dinars apiece. In the end, the Umi Campaign fulfilled the camp's entire wish list and raised over $22,000, which was used to renovate seven homes in the camps and provide a seminar for the mothers in the camp.

Link: https://www.facebook.com/oursevens world.

IRBID CITY DEVELOPMENT

This initiative is based at the Jordan University of Science and Technology, Irbid; and Yarmouk University, Irbid.

DESCRIPTION

The Irbid City Development project seeks to transform Irbid into an advanced city by improving its infrastructure and public services, especially those dealing with waste management. Through Irbid City Development, student volunteers and associations come together to beautify their city. One of their major events was the Irbid Clean Up Marathon, where for a period of several weeks volunteers cleaned several areas of the city. The initiative will expand to reach more areas of Irbid and launch a new project named The Perfect Neighborhood.

Link: https://www.facebook.com/irbid. youth.volunteers.

STEP BY STEP

This is found at the Jordan University of Science and Technology, Irbid; and Yarmouk University, Irbid.

DESCRIPTION

The Step by Step initiative seeks to create a positive school atmosphere that inspires, motivates and excites students about education. The initiative offers extra-curricular and after-school activities such as photography, cinematography and weekly sports tournaments to strengthen the bond between students and their schools and promote a love of learning. The programme is working to create a structured curriculum that encourages students to excel alongside their studies throughout the school year.

Link: https://www.facebook.com/irbid. youth.volunteers.

SHABABSHARE

This initiative is country-wide in Jordan.

DESCRIPTION

ShababShare is a social media initiative that aims to spread a culture of 'social pioneering' and voluntary work within communities in Jordan. This initiative directs various activities that help to instil and foster these concepts within youth through social media that feature new communities, initiatives, corporations and organizations concerned with providing voluntary services and charitable work to young people. ShababShare allows representatives of youth initiatives to reach larger audiences, while enabling youth to become acquainted with their activities and achievements and facilitating the process of joining them.

Link: https://www.facebook.com/Shabab Share.

REFERENCES

Al-Shalabi, H. (2012) 'V Model of E-Learning Using Gagne Nine Steps of Education'. Last modified November 1, 2012. Retrieved from http://www.readperiod icals.com/201211/2875250991.html#b.

ASDA'A Burson-Marsteller (2013) 'Arab Youth Survey'. Retrieved from http://arabyouth survey.com/.

EHEA (2013) 'Recent Trends and Developments in Jordanian Higher Education'. Retrieved from http://www.ehea.info/ Uploads/Documents/JORDAN_recent_ trends_and_developments.pdf.

King Abdullah II (2012) 'Remarks by His Majesty King Abdullah II On the Occasion of the University of Jordan's 50th Anniversary.' Retrieved from http://kingabdullah. jo/index.php/en_US/speeches/view/ id/509/videoDisplay/0.html.

Ortiz, I. and Cummins, M. (2012) *When the Global Crisis and Youth Bulge Collide: Double the Jobs Trouble for Youth.* UNICEF Policy and Practice Division. Last modified February, 2012. Retrieved from http:// www.unicef.org/socialpolicy/files/Global_ Crisis_and_Youth_Bulge_-_FINAL.pdf.

University of Jordan (2013) 'UJ Calls Student to Launch Targeted Initiatives'. Last modified March 13, 2013. Retrieved from http://www.ju.edu.jo/Lists/SocialEvents/ Disp_Form.aspx?ID=86.

World Bank (2011) 'Project Performance Assessment Report – Hashemite Kingdom of Jordan'. Retrieved from http:// wwwwds.worldbank.org/external/default/ WDSContentServer/WDSP/IB/2011/07/08/ 000333037_20110708032128/ Rendered/PDF/627320PPAR0P060c0706 01100BOX361502B.pdf.

Civic engagement and social responsibility in Moroccan higher education is a classic case of 'good news and bad news'. To take the bad news first, it is clear from a survey of mission statements and/or president's statements from Moroccan public and private universities that civic engagement and social responsibility are not high on the list of higher education's priorities. The example of Mohamed V University, among the country's oldest public institutions, sheds some light on the priorities of higher education: (1) the intensification of Islamic and national identity; (2) the training of citizens; (3) the diffusion of knowledge; (4) scientific research; (5) the global development of the State; and (6) the development of universal values. Thus, the main thrust of higher education in Morocco can be seen as preparation for the world of work, development of the State and reinforcement of national identity. Civic engagement or social responsibility is not directly mentioned, and only in the last vague point regarding universal values can something related to this area be seen.

In addition, the conditions at the public universities particularly are fraught with challenges ranging from overcrowding with tens of thousands of students and a top-down administrative structure, to poor physical and IT infrastructure, and so on. The pedagogy itself can be considered illiberal and focused on narrow goals, with students following a prescribed set of classes assessed mainly through high-stakes examinations, leaving little chance of connecting learning to issues, social or otherwise, outside the classroom. Finally, the universities can often be places of open conflict, discord and violence between students of different political views or ethnic backgrounds, between students and teachers, and even between students and the State. An example of this is the case of Mohamed El-Fizazi, a student in Fez, who died in January 2013 from wounds sustained from the State's Quick Response Forces.

That said, there is some good news in Moroccan higher education and civic engagement. First, despite the challenges described above, the universities are dynamic areas of learning and growth for thousands of students. Moroccan citizens have a constitutional right to education and enjoy tuition-free public universities that even offer scholarships and other means of support. The private or tuition-based sector, although relatively small, is growing and bringing some innovation to higher education, including some universities that include civic concepts as a core part of their mission and practice. Indeed, each university is a locus of interaction and often activism as students and faculty vie for better study conditions within the university or seek to make societal change outside it. Thus, many universities sanction official clubs for various purposes depending on the interests of students and faculty, who may also establish or become involved in external civic organizations.

In addition, although civic engagement and social responsibility may not be seen as a direct goal of Moroccan higher education, there is a clear civic mission of schools in Morocco that starts at a young age. Moroccan public-school students have a six-year civic education curriculum in primary and middle school that is embedded in the social studies curriculum. In addition, many of the other fields, including Islamic studies, philosophy and language education, reinforce civic concepts and encourage students to actively participate in their schools and communities. Thus, when a student enters university, he or she has already formed a basis of civic concepts and actions that can be applied during the university years. Indeed, many university faculty work overtime to connect their classes to civic and social concepts, applying innovative practice such as service-learning or project-based pedagogies. Thus, the challenge for schools throughout Morocco is, therefore, not necessarily in the curriculum itself but in the application of the curriculum and its extension into higher education.

Finally, the fact that civic education and social responsibility lack focus in higher education is not lost on students, faculty or administrators, and various initiatives exist to address this issue. Just a few examples include a recent conference in Marrakesh in February 2013 that brought together university faculty, students, and researchers to discuss this issue and pose possible solutions (http://www.nrcs-center.org/scientific-events/nrcs-aeif-conference/). In addition, there are many non-governmental organizations (NGOs) that work directly in this area, such as the Institute for Leadership and Communication Studies (http://www.ilcs.ac.ma/), as well as others that that address the issue tangentially to improve civic engagement in universities or Morocco generally.

In sum, the picture of civic engagement and social responsibility in Moroccan higher education is varied and complex, with both glaring weaknesses and also many bright spots.

COMMUNITY INVOLVEMENT AND SERVICE AT AL AKHAWAYN UNIVERSITY IFRANE, MOROCCO

Al Akhawayn University's involvement stems from three areas organized by the university to promote the involvement of its students, staff and faculty. The Azrou Center for Community Development is the university's flagship institution for direct social engagement. The second instrument of engagement encompasses the university's various student clubs and organizations; these are student-led and serve purposes that are as diverse as Al Akhawayn's student body itself. The final means of promoting engagement is Al Akhawayn's Undergraduate Community Involvement Program (CIP), which has integrated community engagement into the university's curriculum through the creation of several courses.

AZROU CENTER FOR COMMUNITY DEVELOPMENT

As one of the university's most active centres of social engagement, the Azrou Center continues its ongoing outreach and community development, to benefit the local region. Based on the action plan for social development adopted by the Center for 2012–2013, programmes in education, training and health have been launched to benefit several segments of the Azrou–Ifrane population, including:

- workshops on computer networks systems, web development, programming, maintenance and commercial software, in print and web graphics;

- three seminars on technical project management and the development of entrepreneurial spirit with Agence Nationale de Promotion de l'Emploi et des Compétences, the Regional Investment Center of Meknes and Banque Populaire;
- three seminars on personal development and professional communication;
- 11 workshops on marketing, sales techniques, financial management, inventory and assets, and business planning;
- periodic training courses on socio-cultural, technical and professional themes;
- five seminars and workshops on interviewing techniques, methodology in the preparation of reports on the completion of training, and job interviews;
- participation in two hairdressing and aesthetics events (in Fez and Azrou);
- two professional sessions on various educational topics and the showing of socio-educational films (success in careers, a positive teamwork characteristic);
- two sports and cultural competitions;
- five study visits and training at various institutions and companies.

The Center has also offered regular medical consultations and organized several sexually transmitted disease awareness campaigns and screenings. To achieve its objectives, the Center has signed several agreements with the Délégation Provinciale du Ministère du Ministère de l'Education Nationale d'Ifrane, L'Association de Développement du Moyen Atlas, L'Agence du Partenariat pour le Progrès, L'Association Marocaine des Ecoles de l'Autre Chance, La Fondation Pistorio, STMicroelectronics, L'Association Marocaine d'Aide aux Enfants Diabétiques and L'Association Marocaine de Lutte Contre le SIDA.

The list below highlights the medical activities of the Center during 2012–2013, which benefitted over 3000 local residents in Azrou, Ifrane and the neighbouring villages:

- General practice medical consultations (913 people).
- A medical awareness campaign on endocrinology and hypertension in collaboration with the L'Association Marocaine d'Aide aux Enfants Diabétiques (180 people) in the town of Azrou.
- A blood donation campaign in collaboration with the Blood Center of Meknes (100 people).
- Screening for HIV/AIDS (225 people).
- Education on the means of protection against HIV/AIDS and sexually transmitted diseases (73 people).
- Thematic sessions on contraception (28 women).
- An awareness of family planning and contraceptive methods (80 women).
- A general medicine campaign for Douar Boutkho (80 people).
- A medical ophthalmology campaign in collaboration with volunteer doctors and Casa Fez (200 people) in the village of El Orjan, Outat Lhaj.
- A medical campaign in gynaecology and paediatrics in collaboration with the Association of Private Gynecologists (990 women and 595 children) in the towns of Azrou and Ain Leuh Oued Ifrane.

STUDENTS AND COMMUNITY DEVELOPMENT

Socially responsible student organizations at Al Akhawayn University

In keeping with its mission to assist the local community, Al Akhawayn University works to inculcate in its students a sense of social obligation. One of the primary vehicles of this outreach is through the many student clubs and associations that have been formed to undertake outreach and development. This year, Hand in Hand raised 630,000 MAD for the area of Dar Attalib in Dayet Aoua. The Rotaract Club raised 370,000 MAD. The Islamic Arts and Culture Club raised 10,000 MAD to buy equipment for a women's cooperative bakery in Hay Atlas neighbourhood in Ifrane. In addition to the usual donations of wood and clothing, the major events this year included two medical campaigns, one by Rotaract and the other by Leo, that served over 600 people from the Ifrane region. In addition, the Rotaract Club organized the circumcision of about 350 children in the local area.

Other prominent examples include:

- the Islamic Art and Culture club, which collected funds for Eid Al-Adha. Fifteen volunteers tutored around 50 children aged 5–16 years at Dar Al Aman orphanage in Azrou. The club also invited the children to spend a day on campus, where several cultural and sporting activities were organized for them to participate in.
- the Design for Change club, which started an EcoEcole project at Bir Anzarane Primary School focusing on water recycling, theatre, tree planting, art projects and installing a vegetable garden.

Al Akhawayn University continues to be the leading civic university in the country. Its student led associations and activities highlight its commitment to social responsibility locally, regionally and nationally.

Through community service, many student organizations, mainly Hand in Hand, Rotaract and the newly created Leo Club, have been able to make a difference by working with underprivileged children and women in an attempt to give them the chance not only to survive, but also to strive towards a healthier, happier and more productive way of life.

Al Akhawayn University's Undergraduate Community Involvement Program

The Community Involvement Program (CIP), formerly known as the Community Service Program, was launched in the fall semester of 2005 by Al Akhawayn University's former president, Dr Rachid Benmokhar. Inspired by HRM King Mohamed VI's own drive to fight poverty and empower communities through the launch of his National Initiative for Human Development in 2005, Dr Benmokhar saw the need for the Al Akhawayn University community to join this movement.

The CIP is a core curriculum component for all Al Akhawayn University undergraduate students and has three non-credited courses: CIP 1001, Human Development in Morocco; CIP 1002, The Role of Civil Society in Human Development; and CIP 2000 Community Involvement Fieldwork. CIP 2000 consists of a minimum 60-hour service placement for and under the auspices of a non-profit NGO or association accredited by the university, or one of the university departments conducting research in a social field. Alternatively, students can propose independent community service projects either in line with the mission of a student organization they are members of or as an unaffiliated group. All placements must be approved by the CIP office before commencing. CIP 2000 can be spread out as a weekly activity throughout a semester within the local Ifrane region, or as an intensive placement during a mid- or between-semester break in community partner sites spread across Morocco and, increasingly, even abroad.

Within this course, students register for a round-table session after having completed their field work; in this, in small groups, they reflect, share and question their assumptions, impressions and achievements and the unforgettable moments of their community service placement. A final report is then submitted by each student that summarizes their individual placements with an orientation towards demonstrating an understanding of human development concepts. Students do not pay for any of the three courses but the programme does appear on students' transcripts.

Students are encouraged to choose which sector of society they want to get involved in, and their interests have proved to be wide reaching. So far, students from Al Akhawayn University have joined projects that support single mothers, abused women, physically and mentally disabled children and adults, orphans, the homeless, the elderly, migrants, people with AIDS, cancer, diabetes or cardiovascular diseases, illiterate and underachieving communities, public health campaigns, human rights advocacy, environmental education and conservation, small business development and microfinance.

From 2005 up until the present day, students from Al Akhawayn University have, under the umbrella of the CIP, collectively completed over 65,000 hours of fieldwork dedicated to community action. In the 2012–2013 academic year alone, 250 undergraduate degree-seeking students completed the CIP, performing a total of 15,000 hours serving the local, national and international communities. From 2005 to 2007, Al Akhawayn University had only established 30 campus community partnerships with national NGOs, associations and institutions; this has now grown to over 330 sites and has most recently included internationally based community projects in Ghana, Senegal, Czech Republic, China, Canada and the USA, collaborating in particular with the international student-run organization, AIESEC.

Service-learning at AUI

The Al Akhawayn Language Center (LC) provides academic English preparation for Akhawayn University in Ifrane (AUI) students and has, since the spring 2012 semester, offered a service-learning programme that brings together students from the LC and the local Ifrane high school. Following a service-learning pedagogy, both groups of students are able to improve their English-language skills through engaging activities and project-based group work along with regular reflections in order to evaluate, expand and improve the programme where possible. At the core of this programme lies a team of student leaders, formed from previous programme participants, who manage all elements of the programme, from overall coordination and activity planning through to preparation of the final project, reflection and evaluation.

The LC's service-learning programme has now completed three semesters of activity and has shown considerable growth since its inception. With only one student leader and 17 AUI and 20 high-school students active in spring 2012, fall 2012 saw 15 AUI students and 7 high-school students leading a group of 50 AUI and high-school participants, and in spring 2013, the team of student leaders developed even further, creating committees to manage the programme more effectively. One of the most exciting developments in the spring 2013 semester was the commitment of several student groups to civic action projects that identified something in their community that they wanted to improve; one group repainted and stocked the high-school library; another group cleaned up a local park that had been full of trash.

For the coming fall 2013 semester, the most interesting addition to the service-learning programme will be a leadership development component in partnership with AUI's Leadership Development Institute. This comes in response to the desire of service-learning leaders to learn more about leadership itself and apply that to the service programme. It is hoped that this addition will grant added professionalism and legitimacy to the service-learning programme, for the benefit of participants and leaders alike.

In addition to the LC's growing service-learning programme, the School of Social Sciences and Humanities, in collaboration with the Office of Community Involvement, launched in summer 2013 a service-learning component to the Arabic and North African Studies programme, which is an intensive two-month Arabic language programme now in its 13th year. With the objective of enhancing students' practice of their Arabic outside of the classroom, as well as to promote cross-cultural understanding and respect, 75 international students spent every Wednesday in June and July 2013 out in the field with their professors at a community organization. Students prepared for the fieldwork in class by learning useful local vocabulary and understanding cultural customs; they also underwent reflection once they were back on campus, either by compiling a weekly journal, sharing experiences in small group discussions and/or completing relevant class projects and activities. Students were divided among 19 service sites across Ifrane and its neighbouring towns and villages.

Examples of service actions included playing sports with Moroccan youth, especially concentrating on increasing an acquisition of sports other than soccer, such as basketball, volleyball and swimming, a hands-on exchange of Moroccan and American cuisine with women and youth, school and youth centre make-overs such as painting murals, cleaning up the trash and tidying up the green spaces, teaching handicrafts and leading extra-curricular activities for young female offenders, teaching French and English to women and youth, and running Arabic language games at local summer camps.

Civic engagement partnerships

A major step towards strengthening civic engagement at AUI in 2013 included a signing of agreements between Al Akhawayn University and two not-for-profit organizations, America's Unofficial Ambassadors and CorpsAfrica. Indeed, the University's Office of

Community Involvement and Office of International Programs acted as the in-country coordinator for the America's Unofficial Ambassadors to Morocco programme that launched in July 2013. Eight female American volunteers took on individual five-week volunteer placements at different service sites within the university's neighbouring communities. Volunteers took regular Moroccan Arabic-language classes on campus throughout their internships, participated in two homestay weekends and accepted invitations to frequent tours at the homes of their service recipients during Ramadan. Two of the volunteers from America's Unofficial Ambassadors helped to run a summer soccer camp on campus in collaboration with the AUI Athletics Department. A total of 72 boys and girls from the Ifrane region had the opportunity to develop their soccer skills; 17 of these local children came from low-income families, and their attendance was sponsored by university students and campus clubs. Other actions included expanding environmental education opportunities and creating a marketing strategy for eco-tourism in the Ifrane National Park, small business development with a group of female weavers, running English- and French-language summer schools and leading summer camps for the local children of Ifrane.

AUI's work with CorpsAfrica starts in fall 2013, the two partners working together on training and assisting 10 Moroccan Fellows who will spend one year working on development projects determined by the communities themselves. CorpsAfrica intends to recruit 10 AUI graduates to be the first ever 10 Fellows of the programme, especially because the University's own CIP aspires to foster a future of civic-minded citizens.

The AUI Carbon Compensation Scheme
Under the University's commitment to corporate social responsibility and the community's local environment, the Al Akhawayn Carbon Compensation scheme will officially be launched in the fall 2013 semester. Students, faculty and staff will have the possibility to compensate their carbon emissions for their international journeys via a carbon offset button on the AUI website. Various offset options will be offered, from tree planting in the Ifrane National Park to investing in renewable energy power systems off the grid or connected to it. By reducing its carbon footprint, protecting the environment and serving the community, AUI will not only set a national example towards establishing a green and environmentally conscious Morocco, but also internationally strengthen its image of sustainability within the higher education sector.

Spotlight Issues IV.3.5
Poetry, higher education and social movements

Soheila Pashang

Growing up in a society with a history of dictatorship, revolution, war and the resultant, forced migration, I found resistance poetry to be a galvanizing expression of deep pain, hope and dreams for change. This learning came to me first from reading praxis of Iranian feminist poet Forough Farrokhzad, and later from the powerful testimonies of the exiled Mahmoud Darwish. Reciting words during a period of silence is a mode of freedom that reflects implications of injustice and oppression; and during struggle for peace, it ignites the imagination.

Walking on history

'This is my country',
he said
and pointed to the volcanic mountain

I could reach blue sky within his grasp –
a sky witness to smoke and ash,
and soaring vultures, circling for their prey
in the lush green cloud forest.

I followed him, but he was no longer here nor
   there –
the mountain had unsheathed his beginning
at a crossroad of stolen history –
I could hear the scream of burning plantations,

I could feel the war-wager's bootprints
foreclosing the town's shadow with death.

I stepped aside, and waved back at children
begging to sell coffee beans.
and hid my shame – my shame of smelling
   their sweat,
mending silence with my departure

He was searching for something –
his memories carried him towards bodies he
   buried
after each death squad –
each home mourned for someone –

for the murder of guerrilla fighters,
for victims of the drug cartels.
And women cried,
their soul narrative –
for their bodies –
for their lost virginity –
for being used as weapon of revenge.

My friend pointed in the direction of the river –
his pulse beat with the pulse of birds.
Amidst his pain,
his voice echoed
'This is my country – El Salvador!'
                                    To Francisco Rico

Others by Soheila Pashang

Resilient shadows tumble to earth –
Her beginning is like her end:
In the empty silence of sorrow
Filled with unwanted touch and fetid breath,
She echoes the sound of wind,
Sea, fire and death.
Partly destroyed, partly restored,
Her body an eternal choice –
Rising, falling,
Now with dignity,
Now a commodity –
Her voice lost in his rhythm –
Caught in a schism,
She breastfeeds her newborn
And fades from sight.
Colonized there and exploited here
Forced to migrate,
She holds hope tight.

There is no end
To the vortex of love, hate,
Power, powerlessness –
You may fail to see her
As you pass her by –
She has no definition –
Silent, yet with voice,
Unmoving, yet in motion.

Who is she?
Why is she here?
Sometimes you see her
Other times not at all.

Perhaps you know her?
By her toils,
Your coffers filled,
You sleep without guilt.
To you, she is simply, 'other' –
Beneath dark skin lurks
The pallor of fatigue,
Her body perfumed
With heavy sweat
From unrelenting shifts –
A person without intrigue,
A mother whose shoulders
Droop like thin stems on old branches.

Perhaps
You were one of them –
Then or now.
A non-status person
Present, yet ineffable as ether –
You negotiate your life,
Carving new paths
Amidst strife, enduring the pain.
You sell your body
And question your destiny,
Fighting to hope, and live again.
In your resistance
You find the strength to move on.

I worked with you
And you filled my life,
Knowing that I was once you,
Before I found my way home.
I wanted to remain faithful
To your pain,
Our historical pain –
To use my position
To battle with you for your dispossession.

Your stories opened
A window –
I saw you stealing to feed your child,
Mutilating your body to mute your guilt,
As you relived your defilement,
Your pain in watching
Your children long for things
You couldn't provide.

As I listened
I felt angry, and my eyes glistened
When I had given all the hope
I could give –
And it felt like emptiness
When you walked out the door.

In your struggle to survive,
I sought new horizons, and allies
For your journeys.
There, I met a woman,
A woman of her word,
Forthright and fearless.

A voice to lead the revival.
Her clothes are beaded,
As colourful as her heart,
And her mind discerns your pain.

Her world is bright,
Her sky is blue,
As she flies on a journey
Of praxis,
Well beyond the enemy's grasp.
She keeps her dark brown eyes
On the prize,
Constantly searching for invisibilities.
She feels the spinning
Of the world on its axis.

Her flesh is familiar
With the pain of injustice
And the freedom lost.
When she speaks of inequalities,
She mesmerizes.
Her words echo heroes,
Whose dried blood scrawled
Resistance notes
On the walls
Of distant prisons.

Her pulse
Is the heartbeat of justice
Her mind eschews the power of nations,
Rejecting cynicism,
As she flights to give power
To the stateless.
Like you,
She is a resilient fighter.
Her name is Shahrzad –
An apostle of critical feminism.

To Dr Shahrzad Mojab

INTRODUCTION

The Inclusive Neighborhood project of the American University of Beirut (AUB) offers a case study on how a university responded to a strongly felt community need (poor walkability), created an inclusive process and articulated a compelling vision, and collaborated with a variety of stakeholders to design and construct Beirut's first barrier-free street, all by engaging various academic units and mobilizing experts across the campus.

Urban universities are a special kind of anchor institution in their locales. They are not just significant contributors to the local economy by their hiring and purchasing practices. They are also able to harness the energy and brain power of academic faculty, staff and students to shed light on local problems, define solutions and contribute to change. In so doing, they can make their city a better place for all.

This paper offers a case study of how an elite private university is contributing its talents to making Beirut, Lebanon, a better place for pedestrians. The case study offers lessons on the requirements and challenges of intervening physically in the city.

THE PROBLEM

Beirut is one of the most pedestrian-unfriendly cities in the world. Sidewalks are non-existent, or broken, blocked, high or impassible due to parked cars. The situation is unsafe and unpleasant for able-bodied persons, but it severely limits the mobility of individuals with physical impairments, older people and parents with children. The fundamental right to be able to walk in one's city is simply not available to the inhabitants of Beirut. The negative situation is exacerbated by the lack of public parks and other green spaces in the city; streets and sidewalks, blocked and broken as they are, are Beirut's main public spaces.

In the past few decades, architects, product designers, urban planners and disability activist groups in many countries have advocated the adoption of government policies to encourage barrier-free environments. Originally intended to enhance accessibility for people with disabilities, recent incarnations of the barrier-free movement (Design for All, Universal Design and Age-friendly Cities) recognize that barrier-free environments provide benefits to everyone. Like many countries, Lebanon has enacted legislation (Act 220) to improve accessibility for physically impaired citizens. Non-governmental organizations (NGOs) such as the Lebanese Physical Handicapped Union and 'arcenciel' have been active advocates for the new regulations.

Some improvements have already been made in select areas of the city, notably the Beirut Central District, designed and operated by the private real estate development company Solidere, and Hamra Street, a commercial thoroughfare in the Western part of the city that was renovated a decade ago by a local businesses organization. Despite these successful examples, the vast remainder of the city offers appalling conditions to pedestrians, and advocacy and legislation have had little visible effect on the cityscape.

THE ACTORS

The AUB was founded by American Protestant missionaries in 1866, and service to the community has been an enduring theme throughout its nearly 150 years of existence (Myntti et al., 2009). To build on and consolidate this long history, university leaders decided in 2007 to create two units devoted to civic engagement. The Center for Civic Engagement and Community Service (CCECS), which is located organizationally in the Office of the Provost, promotes service-learning, extra-curricular volunteerism and development in the communities of greatest need. Projects that vary in themes include collaborations with public schools to provide educational support, between restaurants and an NGO on the development of Braille menus, and recently with refugee organizations on improvements in basic infrastructure for Syrian refugees in Lebanon in response to an emerging and pressing crisis.

The Neighborhood Initiative, located under the President's Office, is dedicated to mobilizing faculty, staff and students to solve problems of concern specifically to neighbours. The Initiative facilitates research and outreach projects with and for the district of the city just outside the university's walls. Projects tackle a wide range of problems, from noise, congestion and lack of greenery to the needs of the older population. The Neighborhood Initiative and CCECS often collaborate to address problems affecting the university's neighbourhood – a dedicated team was formed to develop the Jeanne d'Arc Street project.[1]

The Beirut Municipality, currently led by a dynamic mayor, is the lead public agency responsible for improvements to the physical realm of the city. It has an interest in collaboration with local universities to create demonstration projects for streets and public spaces in Beirut. Other stakeholders with an interest in barrier-free urban environments are individual residents and businesses, persons with mobility limitations (older people, persons with disabilities and parents with young children), and NGOs working to improve accessibility in Beirut.

THE PROJECT

The Inclusive Neighborhood project aims to create a model street for Beirut that is barrier-free and easily accessible to all pedestrians, not forgetting those with physical impairments, including of vision.

To address the problem of poor walkability, the AUB team chose to focus on one street, Jeanne d'Arc, a major thoroughfare linking the university's main gate with Hamra Street, the district's leading commercial thoroughfare. Jeanne d'Arc is similar to many congested and densely settled streets in Beirut, with a mix of land uses in addition to residential. From the beginning, the AUB team saw Jeanne d'Arc as a possible model for other streets in the city. To facilitate implementation in other parts of the city, cost and durability have been given prime consideration.

THE PROCESS

The project has unfolded through an iterative process between social research and design development, based on extensive feedback from the various stakeholders.

- January 2011: CCECS becomes interested in the problem of accessibility due to its work with an NGO addressing the needs of blind people. The Neighborhood Initiative wants to respond to neighbours' recurrent complaints about neighbourhood sidewalks. The project is conceived.
- January 2011: The research and neighbourhood outreach component is begun.
- Spring 2011: A landscape design student produces first ideas as her final year project.
- Summer 2011: The AUB designers begin developing their ideas in response to issues raised in the preliminary research.
- Summer–Fall 2011: Select neighbours in the street are consulted and feedback is solicited from street users. A documentary film is produced depicting the harshness of the streetscape for old and physically challenged people in particular.
- November 2011: The AUB team presents the design concept to the Mayor, and follows up with a written proposal after the project is adopted by the university President and senior administration, placing AUB as a 'good neighbour'.
- March 2012: The Mayor of Beirut asks the team to present the concept to the Municipal Council and clarifies the division of responsibilities: AUB will redesign the street and the Municipality will implement the design.
- March 2012: The Beirut Municipal Council takes a formal decision to develop Jeanne d'Arc Street in cooperation with AUB.
- March 2012: The AUB President responds with an official letter specifying the following deliverables: a traffic analysis report, detailed design/execution drawings, other required technical drawings and a tender file.
- Summer 2012: The AUB and other technical teams working for the Beirut Municipality meet to share information and coordinate design recommendations.
- Summer 2012: The AUB team sends letters to residents and businesses along Jeanne d'Arc Street informing them of the formal decision by the Municipal Council. Notices are also posted on building entrances.
- April 2013: The AUB team presents the project vision and design details to the Municipal Council.
- Summer 2013: Final coordination of the design with the Municipal Council and approval of the project by the Municipal Council and Governorate of Beirut.
- Fall 2013: Finalization of the design and the production of execution drawings and tender documents.
- Fall 2013: A detailed public presentation of the project's vision, process, design and works timetable to neighbours (led by Municipality with advice from AUB).
- Winter 2014 and following: Bidding for the project and selection of the contractor. Construction to begin (both to be led by Municipality, with advice from AUB as needed).

RESEARCH AND NEIGHBOURHOOD OUTREACH

The research and outreach component of the project has consisted of three strands: documentary films of wheelchair users navigating neighbourhood streets; a needs assessment using anthropological methods, including in-depth interviews with a variety of stakeholders; and design research including body-mapping of sidewalk obstructions with the assistance of a visually impaired pedestrian, a physical survey of the street, a review of existing design guidelines in Lebanon and Europe, and consultations with local experts on accessibility design.

A wide variety of stakeholders participated in the needs assessment, which articulated the main discomforts and hazards for pedestrians. Stakeholders were also asked to describe their aspirations – the essential features of a pleasant, pedestrian-friendly street. The stakeholders have included residents, local businesspeople, users of Jeanne d'Arc Street, other special groups (parents of small children, older people and persons with mobility impairments) and NGO activists on disability issues.

DESIGN PROCESS

Recommendations for Jeanne d'Arc Street were developed through an evolving process of design development with outreach to and feedback from neighbours and critiques from accessibility experts.

As the design was developed, the AUB team organized several charettes with the technical focal points from the Beirut Municipality, local urban and landscape design experts, wheelchair users and experts in accessible design. Experts suggested simple innovations not yet common in Beirut, such as elevated junctions and tactile pavers for a portion of the street. Colleagues from the Municipality challenged the AUB team to come up with a design that assumed that cars and motorcycles and shops would obstruct the walkway where and whenever possible; the design had to make it difficult for them to do so.

The Beirut Municipality provided infrastructure maps (electricity, telephone/DSL links and water and sewerage conduits) for Jeanne d'Arc Street that were necessary for the design.

DESIGN ELEMENTS

With the proposed design, Jeanne d'Arc Street will become accessible, safe and comfortable to all pedestrians. The design of the street increases foot traffic and creates an ambiance that encourages strolling, window shopping and lingering; it animates the street in a way that is good for people and good for business. The street becomes a destination, not just a passageway. Jeanne d'Arc also becomes a cost-effective model that can be replicated elsewhere in Beirut.

REFLECTIONS

Universities can generate knowledge for the public good by harnessing the talent of their faculty and students for research on problems of local concern. As more institutions, profit and non-profit alike, embrace 'corporate social responsibility' as a *modus operandi*, universities have a unique role to play by virtue of their capacity to both analyse and act for social change.

Universities must, however, be clear about their optimal role vis-à-vis other actors. They can never replace government, nor are they a typical NGO with operational flexibility. In the case of the Inclusive Neighborhood project, AUB's contribution to the city of Beirut was the design for a barrier-free city street. AUB will not construct the new street (or pay for it), which is the role of local government.

Community-based projects such as AUB's Inclusive Neighborhood project demand specific skills and attitudes among participating faculty and students. The first and foremost skill is that of listening, listening across disciplines and listening to partners in the neighbourhood, NGOs and the government itself. The process is one of mutual learning, not a one-way flow of expertise. Second, it is important to shift from a competitive attitude towards a collaborative attitude with partners. The Beirut Municipality has engaged other designers on projects such as a lighting master plan and updated urban design regulations; a collaborative attitude facilitated the sharing of knowledge and experience and the development of a coherent approach to design, which benefited everyone. The process became one of problem-solving, where everyone had something to contribute towards a shared goal.

It is important to recognize both the power and challenges of starting 'small' in a place like Beirut, where there is widespread cynicism about the possibilities of change for the public good. Additionally, and in the absence of formal design guidelines set by the Municipality on several streetscape-related components (lighting, bollards, trees, signage, and so on), the research conducted by the AUB team and others focused on adapting international standards within the local context of the city. Furthermore, the research findings and lessons learned will serve to inform the Municipality in their recent initiative to develop standard design regulations with local and international experts. From this, the Inclusive Neighborhood intervention in Jeanne d'Arc Street, although limited in geographical scope (and in time) to one street, could then have a visible and concrete impact

on the urban development of the city; it will therefore be at the forefront of advocating for a friendlier Beirut, and at the same time will conform with what is being planned and would be implemented across neighbourhoods.

Finally, communicating ideas clearly and simply to non-academic audiences is an art, and central to that is figuring out how to describe shared visions that everyone can get excited about. These skills and attitudes do not develop automatically in universities; they must be nurtured and supported by units such as AUB's Neighborhood Initiative and its CCECS.

The ultimate success of a project like the Inclusive Neighborhood is that it endures through time. Such 'durability' may require the university to play continuing but different roles over a long time period, but this period may not coincide with funders' timetables. In the case of a barrier-free street, durability has many dimensions. The Municipality has committed to constructing the new design and has indicated that it will maintain it. To keep a walkway barrier-free in Beirut, the human dimension will also be key: public education about the rights of pedestrians; enforcement of laws on parking or blockages to rights of way; awareness-raising about barrier-free design and age-friendly cities; and a street committee to promote the positive vision of the street and to deal with infractions. To make the project a success, the AUB team will

need to consider carefully what its ongoing role should be in the post-construction phase.

Finally, the outcomes of a project such as the Jeanne d'Arc Street renovation are many. The direct outcome is one Beirut street that is accessible to all pedestrians. That the street becomes a model to be replicated elsewhere in Beirut is another outcome of greater potential significance. Other outcomes are also possible. University faculty and students have gained valuable real-world experience in making change happen and reflecting on their own roles in this process. Finally, seeing change happening will also be heartening for ordinary people who live in Beirut and use the street. In a place with pervasive cynicism about the possibility of change for the public good, a new Jeanne d'Arc Street will be visible proof that it is indeed possible.

ACKNOWLEDGMENT
The authors wish to thank their colleague Tonnie Choueiri for her helpful comments on earlier drafts of this paper.

REFERENCE
Myntti, C., Zurayk, R. and Mabsout, M. (2009) *Beyond the Walls: AUB Engages its Communities.* Gerhart Center Working Paper. Cairo: American University in Cairo.

NOTE

1 The AUB Team: *CCECS*: Mounir Mabsout (Director), Rabih Shibli (Leader, Community Development Projects), Samar Kanafani (Anthropologist and Filmmaker), Ali Basma (Architect), Marwa Tannir (Final Year Project, Landscape Design and Ecosystem Management Department), Reem Fayad (Landscape Design), Siba El Samra (Landscape Design), Dalia Zein (Landscape Design); *Neighborhood Initiative*: Cynthia Myntti (Project Leader), Tonnie Choueiri (Outreach Coordinator).

IV.3.7

Networks on community engagement in the Arab states

Ma'an Arab University Alliance for Civic Engagement

SECRETARIAT: Cairo (Egypt).
INSTITUTION: The American University in Cairo, The Talloires Network.
WEBSITE: http://www1.aucegypt.edu/maan/ (accessed 4 March 2013).
MEMBERS: 11 (as of 14 March 2013).

The Ma'an Arab University Alliance shares a similar core mission and values to the Talloires Network. It is a regional association of institutions committed to strengthening the civic roles and social responsibilities of Arab higher education. They work together to implement the recommendations of the Ma'an Declaration in the Arab World, working within the Talloires Network to build a global movement of engaged universities and citizens (text taken from http://www1.aucegypt.edu/maan/Mission.html [accessed 4 March 2013]).

Kuwait University's Deanship for Community Service and Continuing Education

SECRETARIAT: Kuwait City, Kuwait.
INSTITUTION: Kuwait University.
WEBSITE: http://www.kuniv.edu/ku/Centers/
CentreforCommunityServicesContinuingeducation/ (accessed 18 June 2013).
MEMBERS: n.a.

The Center is the permanent headquarters of the Committee of Deans of the Centers for Community Service and Continuing Education in Arab Gulf countries, holding regular meetings and releasing periodic publications. For all practical purposes, the Center for Community Services and Continuing Education forms the vital conduit linking Kuwait University with the wider society, while also endeavouring to serve the society through its wide-ranging programmes, ensuring continuous development in response to emerging needs and demands (text taken from http://www.kuniv.edu/ku/Centers/CentreforCommunityServicesContinuingeducation/ [accessed 4 March 2013]).

Tawasol – Supporting Service Learning in Jordan and Lebanon

SECRETARIAT: University of Roehampton Department of Social Sciences.
INSTITUTION: University of Roehampton, Hashemite University, Jordan.
WEBSITE: http://www.tawasol.org (accessed 3 October 2013).
MEMBERS: 9 (as of 3 October 2013).

Tawasol is a network of universities working in partnership to promote civic engagement and service learning in Jordan and Lebanon. Tawasol works with academics, civil society organizations, local communities and students to support understanding of service-learning and its benefit to students, universities and the wider community in the Middle East. Participating universities provide training in service-learning to academics wishing to incorporate service-learning tools into university curricula, promotes, supports and develops student participation in university and community life, and aims to enhance the relationship between universities and the communities they serve.

IV.3.8

Good Practices

Resala, Cairo university, Egypt

Founded by a young Egyptian professor inspired by the community spirit he had seen in Canada as a graduate student, Resala began at Cairo University in 1999. It initially offered student-led volunteer activities near the campus and eventually grew into a non-profit organization that is now powered by over 100,000 young volunteers spanning 54 branches all over Egypt. It provides 20 activities for youth volunteer participation, including caring for orphans and street kids, computer training for the blind, programmes for children with special needs, blood donations, literacy campaigns and a variety of poverty alleviation activities. An innovative programme collects unused gifts and household items in well-to-do areas to redistribute to disadvantaged young couples preparing for marriage. Resala is a social service organization not formally engaged in politics. Nonetheless, its mobilized volunteers were among those who were first to organize essential support services – field hospitals, food, blankets and phone recharging stations – during the large street protests that erupted in Cairo in January 2011.

The American University in Cairo, Egypt

Without the limitations of government oversight and budgets, and with a strong donor base, the American University in Cairo (AUC) has been able to model its academic and extra-curricular programmes on liberal arts ideals. Since 2007, AUC has pioneered an academic programme of community-based learning throughout the curriculum. Student learning objectives are met through community projects tailored to the course content: rhetoric courses might record the oral histories of refugees in Cairo and publish them to raise awareness, and engineering classes help to solve energy access problems in poor communities. To date, over 40 community-based learning courses have been offered and are designated in the course catalogue and on student transcripts.

AUC also encourages and funds student-run community service clubs and civic learning projects such as the Model UN and Model Arab League. Its academic centres mix teaching, research and service objectives, including the Social Research Center, the Desert Development Center, the Center for Migration and Refugee Studies and more recently the John D. Gerhart Center for Philanthropy and Civic Engagement. The Gerhart Center helped establish the Ma'an Arab University Alliance for Civic Engagement to stimulate civic engagement across the Arab states. Newer initiatives include an entrepreneurship programme for women, a small-business incubator and a science bus that visits public schools and malls to encourage an interest in science education.

Ahfad University for Women, Sudan

In Sudan, one of the region's poorest countries, a private university for women has pioneered university commitment to quality education that is fully integrated into the wider society. Ahfad University for Women (AUW) believes that service should be a central component of academic programmes rather than an add-on activity. Every discipline major contains community-based courses, some of which are unique, such as the Family Partner Program. Medical students are paired with specific families in poor urban areas whom they meet once a month for the duration of their coursework in medical school. They focus on transferring information and skills around child, maternal and family health and assist with accessing health services (Stroud, 2011). Similarly, the School of Health Sciences is attached to health and feeding centers where students work for a month on nutrition education and child growth monitoring activities as well as community awareness. All six of AUW's schools are attached to corresponding community organizations to which students provide valuable services while mastering their course content.

Since Sudan is a largely rural society, all students must participate in the Rural Extension Program during their third year (see http://www.ahfad.edu.sd/index.php/about-us/community-outreach.html). Students actually live in rural areas and plan and participate in projects to impart knowledge and organization skills to women in rural villages. The objective is to help rural women to become change agents in their communities. While local donors are prepared to help build structures on campus, they have been less ready to support service-learning and community engagement. Donors have therefore most often been international aid organizations rather than home-grown funders.

As a private university, AUW charges a graduated tuition fee based roughly on the abilities of families to pay. In addition, AUW gives an advantage to students who are the first in their families to attend college. Special efforts are made to attract students from disadvantaged and conflict-ridden areas such as Darfur and southern and eastern areas of the Sudan. Currently, about 20% of AUW's student body are from these regions and benefit from the Tuition Waiver Program.

Al-Quds University, Palestine

Al-Quds University is a Palestinian university with a pioneering programme on ways of sustaining civic participation over time. The university has a thematic focus that cross-cuts many of its service activities on the empowerment of Palestinian women. Through the Community Action Center in the Old City, students and staff help run the Jerusalem Women's Parliament, involving women from all sectors of the community. This unique programme gives women a support network and opportunity to develop their participation in public life. In a culture where public roles were previously seen as a male arena, this programme strengthens women's self-confidence, grasp of national issues and sense of belonging to the formation of a civic culture. Students and participating women gain a better understanding of inclusion and democracy in practice within Palestinian civil society.

REFERENCE

Stroud, S.E. (2011) 'Empowering women as agents of change through education: profile of Ahfad University for women (Sudan)'. In: Watson, D., Hollister, R.M.S., Stroud, E. and Babcock, E. *The Engaged University: International Perspectives on Civic Engagement*. New York: Routledge, pp. 143–50.

IV.4

KNOWLEDGE, ENGAGEMENT AND HIGHER EDUCATION IN ASIA AND THE PACIFIC

Carol Hok Ka Ma and Rajesh Tandon

The role of higher education institutions (HEIs) has historically been recognized as a public good, with unique social responsibilities in producing knowledge for societal development and sustainability. In Asia, a region with so much disparity between rich and poor, between rural and urban, and with such diversities in religion, language and culture, inequality, poverty, insecurity, social exclusion and impropriety, the re-emphasis of principles of community engagement and participation should become the priority agenda for existing education.

However, the increased attention being paid to principles and strategies of community engagement and participation has occurred in a context in which universities are no longer the only producers of knowledge, and where they appear to be more focused on private gain rather than community benefit, on research rather than on teaching, and on raising private revenue (Boyer, 1990; Colby et al., 2003; Calhoun, 2006). In addition, competition for world-class excellence has propelled HEIs into entrepreneurial institutions commoditizing knowledge for commercialization rather than the service of humanity. Over the past decades, global development agendas and the initiatives of civil societies have increasingly challenged HEIs to develop partnerships and co-create knowledge for addressing social issues in the community.

In order to understand knowledge, engagement and higher education (HE) in the Asia-Pacific region, this paper provides an overview of the current practice of HE engagement, with reference to the need for civic education in the new economy of the Asia-Pacific region. The concept and discourse of engagement in relation to outreach/service, knowledge transfer and knowledge co-creation are then summarized, followed by a delineation of the various frameworks and approaches for HE engagement in the region. An examination, with illustrative examples, of the policies and structures or mechanisms that have emerged to support HE engagement is also presented in order to understand more about the emer-gent issues and challenges to the development of HE engagement. Future possibilities for HE engagement in the Asia-Pacific region will be discussed at the end of the paper.

INTRODUCTION

HEIs play a critical role in creating educated and responsible citizens. With diverse characteristics in the Asia-Pacific region, including inequality, poverty, insecurity and exclusion amidst abundance and prosperity, more HEIs have been pressured to develop partnerships and co-create knowledge that serves humanity. Thus, education is merely no longer transference and learning, but also emphasizes how teachers and students engage in the community through various learning methods, such as community participatory research, civic engagement activities and service-learning programmes, to build a better community.

NEEDS FOR KNOWLEDGE AND ENGAGEMENT IN THE NEW ECONOMY AND SOCIETY

Education is undoubtedly a key for developing human capital. With rapid economic development in Asia, a sustainable social and welfare system is demanded by the public. However, corporatization and competition for world-class excellence have propelled HEIs into becoming entrepreneurial institutions, commoditizing knowledge for commercialization, and training students for the demands of a globalized capitalist economy. Throughout Asia, including China, technological advancements have become a priority for universities since the turn of the millennium, and by default human developments or positions of morality tend to be neglected. A good example is the rapid adoption of human reproductive technologies (for example, sex selection) without mindfully considering the future ramifications on society. The former President of Lingnan University, Professor

Edward K.Y. Chan (Chan et al., 2009), mentioned that the modern world is facing a new economic situation, which can be characterized by digitization, globalization and a monopolization of capitalism, implying our eager preparation to face the new economy.

Rapid economic growth in the region has made some communities, regions and households substantially improve their economic status over the past two decades. Yet the region is also home to half the poor of the world (living on less than $1.25 per capita per day) as well as half of those who are illiterate (nearly five hundred million people in the region). There is also great diversity in the region in terms of basic indicators of health, education and access to drinking water, sanitation and secure livelihood. Rapid economic development has also resulted in rapid urbanization as first-generation youth come to the cities from rural areas. Serious challenges of environmental degradation afflict many parts of the region today. As a result, inequalities characterize the region. It is in this scenario that the development of HE and community engagement has to be situated.

HISTORICAL BACKGROUND OF THE ENGAGEMENT IN THE ASIA-PACIFIC REGION

Asian societies are very old settled communities; the economic, technological and educational development in these Asian societies goes back several millennia, the oldest residential universities having been located in the Indian sub-continent.

Takshila in Western region (now Pakistan) was a residential university with nearly ten thousand students and two thousand faculty between the sixth century BC and the fifth century AD. Likewise, Nalanda, in the eastern region of India, was a residential university between the fourth century BC and the sixth century AD, with several thousand students and half a dozen specializations. These universities were set up with extensive community support, and their students and faculty returned to their communities to engage with them (Tandon, 2008).

Without doubt, most Asian countries had their own traditional educational systems, for example the Confucian academies in China, the traditional *pathshalas* or *madrasahs* in India, and similar institutions in Vietnam, Cambodia and Thailand. In the 19th century, changes in the educational systems were fundamentally influenced by the colonial powers, especially during the modernization period. At that time, most of the Asian region was colonized by a few European countries, and these exported their university ideas to Asia. Those universities with colonial administration and emerging economic interests became more popular than the historical academic institutions in Asia (Altbach, 2004). For non-colonized Asian countries, too, Western culture was introduced into their education system, examples being via the Meiji Restoration in Japan and the Hundred Days' Reform in China. These marked the era of Western-style HE development in Asia.

In the 20th century, new educational philosophies evolved in the region. Nobel Laureate Rabindranath Tagore established Shantiniketan University to emphasize that HE must promote universal understanding and peace, and Mahatma Gandhi established Gujarat Vidyapith to link HE to village industry and agriculture. The societal linkages of HE were widely manifest in their educational philosophies.

With the Western cultures spreading in Asia, Christian missionaries played a significant role in education. Although these missionaries had less success in converting people to Christianity, Christian organizations set up many colleges and universities in India, China, the Philippines, Korea, and so on. Christian universities and colleges remain important in some parts of Asia. Since 1922, the United Board for Christian Higher Education in Asia has been working with HEIs in 13 countries and regions of Asia to express values such as justice, reconciliation and harmony between ethnic and religious communities, gender equity, care for the environment and civil society. The United Board has so far shown great passion in community engagement and works in partnership with over 80 HEIs in Asia.

In addition, religious influences on HEIs have been found in Indonesia since the middle of the 19th century. Unlike the private Christian universities in China (nationalized in 1949), the Islamic universities in Indonesia are public HEIs. In 1945, the year of independence for Indonesia, the Sekolah Tinggi Islam (Islamic College) was set up by the government, and the Islamic University of Indonesia was then established in 1947 (Assegaf et al., 2012).

With their government and religion background, Islamic HEIs often have the vision and mission of contributing to the community. One of the objectives of the IAIN Sunan Ampel institute is to conduct research in Islamic, social and humanities studies relevant to the needs of the community and to promote community empowerment based on religious values. Similar approaches are reported by UIN Sunan Kalijaga Yogyakarta: 'Developing research, either quantitative or qualitative, and contribute to enhancing the quality of life of the whole community through professional duties' (Assegaf et al., 2012). With approximately 150,000 students – 18% of all public university students – state-administered Islamic HE has considerable influence in Indonesian society (Kraince, 2007). The engaging university vision creates opportunities for intellectuals and students to actively participate in the community.

Another popular belief is Confucianism. Many Asians see Confucianism as one of their cultures, especially as it has been greatly emphasized in the field of education. Confucian education is all about the humanistic and the universal. As the Master said: 'A gentleman is not a tool (「君子不器」)', meaning that his capacity should not have a specific limit, nor his usefulness a narrow application. What matters is not to accumulate technical information and specialized expertise, but to develop one's *humanity*. Education is not about *having*; it is about *being* (Leys, 1997). This echoes the educational philosophy of a liberal arts education with an emphasis on whole-person development instead of specific technical knowledge. Humanist ethics are the essence of Confucianism and also give life to Chinese culture: 'With its affirmation of humanist ethics and of the universal brotherhood of man, it inspired all the nations of Eastern Asia and became the spiritual cornerstone of the most populous and oldest living civilization on earth' (Leys, 1997, p. xvi). Although the Chinese government has been promoting 'social practice' among students in HEIs since the 19th century, both teachers and students see this practice as a kind of extra-curricular activity and not necessary as fully addressing the need of the community.

Korea also holds Confucian values and strives to provide a leading edge for HEIs and regions to develop knowledge-based industries as a basis for wider engagement in HEIs. The Korean national New University for Regional Innovation (NURI) project has motivated educators to believe that HE should integrate its advanced knowledge and skills with larger social concerns.

Similarly, Indian educationists emphasize the importance of students being aware of social issues from their indigenous knowledge (Tandon, 2012a). The university was referred at *Gurukul* or 'family of the teacher' in ancient India. Students lived together with their teachers and studied grassroots knowledge related to day-to-day living (Narang, 1996). The Indian government then started the National Service Scheme in 1969 to promote the societal engagement of HE students. Although the scheme has continued, it is merely an extra-curricular activity and not integrated into the core functions of HEIs. These kinds of knowledge can be seen as belonging to 'public intellectuals', including writers, artists, traditional scholars and religious leaders, all of whom have had different kinds of role in influencing public opinion, religious and social reformation, and so on. In other words, the cultural resources, such as 'the heritage of vernacular knowledge, contemporary politics and social needs' were linked in the societies, and thus 'that tradition of intellectual and social life has not allowed Western-style universities to dominate intellectual and social life' (Nandy, 1996, p. 297).

However, the role of 'public intellectuals' began to be replaced by Western knowledge as the latter 'began to be regarded as "modern knowledge" and to be considered as superior to indigenous knowledge' (Narang, 1996, p. 259). Take India as an example. Fewer people want to acquire indigenous knowledge because of the influence of Western power. Now, most curricula only include some components of indigenous knowledge.

In this social context, the role of HE in enhancing indigenous knowledge has become important. The university can be seen as 'a key site of struggle, where local knowledge meets global knowledge in a battle to represent different worlds in different ways', since 'how we view universities around the world, and their relationships with each other, clearly depends fundamentally on how we understand culture, knowledge, education and international relations' (Pennycook, 1996, p. 64). Based on the nature of universities, the concept of 'extension work' has been introduced into the Indian social context. 'Extension work' can be seen as 'the application of classroom knowledge from the university within the community and for the community's benefit' (Narang, 1996, p. 260). Students can understand the socio-cultural reality of local communities and obtain indigenous knowledge from them.

In this Asian social and cultural context, HEIs could be a powerful tool, not only to teach the conflict between social transformation and the attainment of social justice, but also to develop teachers' and students' intellectual knowledge in order to support society's needs.

HE, COMMUNITY ENGAGEMENT AND SOCIAL RESPONSIBILITY

Traditionally, the common teaching method in HE has been academic tutorial teaching and research knowledge learning. Such traditional modes of teaching do not seem plausible in Asia, a region with an enormous economic disproportion between the rich and poor, especially in the rural and urban areas, as well as great diversities in religion, language and culture. Many often ask questions on how one can provide the ideal and necessary form of education across the region and how a giving culture can be cultivated among HEIs.

Examining historical cases in the 20th century, Hollander and Meeropol (2006) identified that there were four milestone movements that had begun in the late 1980s in the USA. We can find similar developments in Asia but in a different time frame: (1) the era of student volunteerism in the mid to late 1980s; (2) the rise of service-learning in the early 1990s; (3) the birth of the 'engaged campus' in the late 1990s; and (4) the rapid expansion of the idea of the engaged campus in the early 2000s. Universities started to focus on their civic responsibilities as well as public contributions in the areas of research and scholarship, teaching and learning, and outreach and partnership. Different terms related to the engagement of HEIs, including community participatory research, service-learning, volunteerism, science shops, civic engagement and corporate social responsibility, have become popular among HEIs in different countries as they are re-emphasizing their responsibilities to prepare students to be active and engaged citizens for contributing to our ever-changing global society (Dragne, 2007).

Alongside teaching and research, cultivating social responsibility within Asian universities is the third mission of contemporary HE. According to ISO 26000, the institution's level of social responsibility is measured by whether it has considered the impact of social and environmental outcomes. The university is one of the stakeholders in society and should bear its 'university social responsibility' (USR). Sawasdikosol proposed that the USR framework should prioritize the quality of graduate students, emphasize a sense of social awareness and resolve global warming, as well as advocate for a transparent and sufficient economy. All stakeholders, including community partners, students and teachers, and service targets, are value members for pursuing the new knowledge. Their partnership can improve the locality, society and mankind through raising, strengthening and transforming community and national potential, as well as developing local human resources, and nurturing creative and entrepreneurial leaders with quality and virtue in a society of learning and wisdom.

Obviously, the partnership between the university and the community is a very important indicator of the building and application of knowledge, which are related to how and what institutions and communities support. Tandon and Hall (2012) have stated that there are both internal and external concerns in promoting USR. Internally, USR depends on how institutions are being governed, how their values and principles of citizenship are integral to education and how institutions demonstrate respect for diversity and human rights, which are equally important in promoting USR among institutions. Externally, USR greatly depends on two-way learning, mutual respect and shared influence among different stakeholders, including academia, communities, practitioners, government and the private sector.

Many institutions in Asia are governed by the government, which also has a mission to train young people to be responsible and caring students. For example, one of the priority agendas in China is always promoting the moral and social development of university students (Wang, 2008). This shows that the government pays great attention to the development of social responsibility in HEIs. In October 2004, the government of the People's Republic of China even issued an official document titled *Guidelines on Further Intensification and Updating of Moral and Citizenship Education of University Students* to provide a national framework for the moral and social development of university students (Wang, 2008). This framework encourages HEIs to restructure their study programmes according to the country's social and economic needs. In 2013, the Chinese government has also been rethinking the mode of 'social practice', and some universities, for example South China University of Technology and South China Normal University, are even starting to integrate the concept of social practice into their curriculum. Given this opportunity, many grassroots organizations also look for partnership with HEIs in China. However, there are still some barriers as the civil society and welfare infrastructure is just starting to develop rapidly in China. Thus, many HEIs in China are still exploring effective ways to address the needs of the country.

In Hong Kong, with its relatively well-developed social welfare system and mixture of Western and Eastern cultures, another mission of HEIs alongside teaching and research is knowledge transfer. The University Grants Committee has incorporated knowledge transfer into its mission statement and institutional mission statement. Knowledge transfer means that 'the systems and processes by which knowledge, including technology, know-how, expertise and skills are transferred between higher education institutions and society, lead to innovative, profitable or economic or social improvements' (University Grants Committee, 2012). With funding support from the government, universities in Hong Kong are also willing actively to demonstrate outreach and show responsibility for the dissemination of knowledge in to society.

In Japan, the Central Council for Education has stated clearly that it is highly desirable to offer a social contribution within university-level education in order for students to become citizens who can live creatively in the 21st century. The report *A Vision for the Future of Higher Education in Japan* also expects many universities to realize the mission and integrate its content into their curriculum, including promoting human rights and peace (Todani, 2008). This movement encourages different stakeholders to rethink their partnership with the HEIs in Japan.

In South Korea, the growth and contributions of social responsibility in Korean HE started with different social movements from the 1930s to the 2000s. First was the rural enlightenment movement, which encouraged Korean universities to fulfil their social responsibility for rural community development, for instance by providing professional support towards labour services and knowledge-based activities. Second, there was a political/social movement in which professors issued a statement suggesting a constitutional amendment, which triggered the national democratization movement in June 1987 and gained a direct election for the president. Finally, Korean universities are contributing to the global movement by beginning overseas outreach through global social services in, for example, the medical, educational and cultural areas (Kim and Cho, 2008). Overall, the response from the community has been very positive as universities have addressed the community's need and are working together with the community to create a strong civic responsibility within the country.

According to UNICEF 2008, there are other examples in Asia that are supported by different stakeholders, for example different government-sponsored service programmes in Fiji, the Philippines, Malaysia, Mongolia and China; non-governmental organization (NGO)-sponsored programmes including Youth Star Cambodia, Village Focus International (Cambodia) and not-for-profit programmes in China; neighbourhood public safety campaigns supported by community and youth groups; national service projects supported by Fiji's National Youth Advisory Board, Singapore's National Youth Council and the Asian Youth Council, and so on; and youth camps with a leadership component supported by private foundations as part of the corporate social responsibility portfolio.

In preparation for the 12th Five Year Plan, the Planning Commission of the Government of India set up a committee to recommend the policies and practices necessary to further promote and deepen community engagement in HE. As a result, the current Plan (2012–2017) contains a clear emphasis on HE's social responsibility:

> In the face of growing isolation of HEIs from society, there is a need for renewed effort for HEIs for genuinely engaging with community, conduct[ing] socially relevant research and education and foster[ing] social responsibility amongst students as part of their core mission. For this purpose, a National Initiative to Foster Social Responsibility in Higher Education would be launched. An Alliance for Community engagement, an independent association of practitioners, academics and community leaders would be created to support its implementation. (Planning Commission, Government of India, 2013, p. 111)

FRAMEWORKS AND APPROACHES IN COMMUNITY ENGAGEMENT

Given the diversity of approaches and practices in the region, it is rather difficult to summarize all of them in one neat framework. However, one framework that has evolved from the perspective of actual practice on the ground is described below. This is an attempt to equate community engagement in HE with a set of principles that are holistic and synergistic (Tandon, 2012b):

- The mutually agreed interests and needs of both communities and institutions should be articulated and respected.
- Engagement must encompass all the three functions of institutions of HE – teaching, research and outreach/practice.
- Institutional engagement cutting across disciplines and faculties, including natural sciences, should be mandated and should not be restricted to the social and human sciences alone.
- Students' participation in community engagement projects should earn them credits and partially meet their graduation requirements, and should be integrated into their evaluation systems.
- Performance assessments of teachers, researchers and administrators in such institutions should include this dimension of community engagement.

The forms of engagement that Tandon (2012a) has described tend to capture that diversity:

- linking learning with community service;

- linking research with community knowledge;
- knowledge-sharing and knowledge mobilization;
- devising new curriculum with community;
- inviting practitioners as teachers;
- social innovations by students.

LINKING LEARNING WITH COMMUNITY SERVICE

In Madras Christian Collage, India, chemistry students participated in a service-learning programme aiming to preserve water resources. On the one hand, students' knowledge of water chemistry was applied within the programme; on the other, 'the residents of the local community were invite to discuss the progress of the project and their view regarding the restoration process were incorporated in the project' (Sugumar, 2009, p. 84). The involvement of local people in the programme helped as their knowledge of using a particular tree gum to remove excess iron from the water inspired the students when tackling the problem of poor water quality. The spot at which to sample the water was also suggested by the local community, which led to mutual learning between the students and the local people inhabitants.

LINKING RESEARCH WITH COMMUNITY KNOWLEDGE

The Centre for Society–University Interface and Research at Bhagat Phool Singh Mahila Vishwav-idyalaya University and the Society for Participatory Research in Asia (PRIA)/Garhwal University Mountain Research Centre in India are examples of partnerships in sharing community knowledge through various research approaches (Planning Commission, 2012).

KNOWLEDGE-SHARING AND KNOWLEDGE MOBILIZATION

These can take the form of enumerations, surveys, camps, training exercises, learning manuals and films, maps, study reports, public hearings, policy briefs, engagement with urban homeless shelters, teaching and health services in poor communities, legal aid clinics for those undergoing prosecution, and so on. The Pamulaan Center for Indigenous Peoples' Education in the Philippines is another example demonstrating how indigenous spiritual knowledge can be learned in student–community engagement process. 'Research, studies, documentation and publication of indigenous knowledge systems, stories, history, folk tales, songs, and arts' are published for both formal and non-formal education programmes (Pamulaan Center for Indigenous Peoples' Education, 2013). By conducting such research, indigenous heritage, cultures, values and customs can be learned by non-indigenous communities.

DEVISING NEW CURRICULUM AND COURSES

In consultation with local communities, local students, local community-based organizations and local government agencies, HEIs can develop new curricula for existing courses as well as design new courses. This can not only enrich the curriculum of existing courses by using locally appropriate subject matter, but also create new, locally appropriate educational programmes that will interest new generations of students (Planning Commission, 2012). The Treaty of Waitangi Research Unit, New Zealand, is an example of creating a curriculum to use traditional Maori *rongoā* (healing and medicines) to advance research aiming to change the situation of a large amount of Maori knowledge being lost in New Zealand.

INCLUDING PRACTITIONERS AS TEACHERS

Local community elders, women leaders and tribal and civil society practitioners have enormous practical knowledge on a wide variety of issues – from agriculture and forestry to child-rearing, micro-planning and project management. For example, teachers of social sciences at Lingnan University Hong Kong invited prostitutes and elderly members of the population to tell their stories to widen understanding of the social welfare of Hong Kong.

SOCIAL INNOVATIONS BY STUDENTS

In consultation with student unions, associations and clubs, students can initiate learning projects with a social impact. Shantou University in China arranged for science students to use their creativity to create a product that would help elderly people living alone in mountainous areas.

To sum up, different strategies can be employed to achieve the objectives of civic responsibilities and public contributions, including community-based research, participatory action research, knowledge creation and mobilization, educational opportunities for community members (continuous education, workshops, presentations, and so on), outreach and lifelong learning. Also used is social advocacy (which provides citizens and leaders with dependable knowledge and reliable information for reaching responsible and well-informed public judgements and decisions, and to serve as a trusted voice in public debates over controversial issues). Another approach is service-learning, which links into athletics, sports and recreational activities, health education, innovation and business/employment development, and working with special interest groups such as women, aboriginals, youth, and so on (Dragne, 2007).

HEIs can design appropriate learning curricula and facilitate lifelong educational processes through partnering with civil actors, community elders and practitioners. They can systematize the practical insights of human and social development for creating new theories and practical applications (Tandon, 2007). Meanwhile, joint research projects with civil society actors could apply for joint research funding, which is another concrete approach to producing and mobilizing knowledge .

Thus, based on the above rationales, two main community engagement approaches can be seen in Asia: community-based research and community service-learning (CSL).

The practice and promotion of *community-based participatory research* in the region dates back to the 1970s, with a regional network of participatory research active in the 1980s and 90s. PRIA grew out of this network in the early 1980s and has since been a major force for promoting the practice of participatory research in several HEIs. A recent survey indicated that participatory research as a methodology of enquiry and community engagement is being taught in nearly 40% of HEIs in the developing part of the region. This addresses real issues related to social justice, such as inclusion, poverty alleviation, environmental sustainability, gender justice, and so on. The practice facilitates the co-creation of knowledge in ways that synthesize local experiences with professional expertise (Tandon and Hall, 2012).

Community-based research can be interpreted as one kind of participatory research, challenging the hegemonic nature of knowledge and its underlying epistemology, as well as its superstructure of HEIs (Tandon, 2007). Participatory research originates from adult education. It focuses on the negative human and societal consequences of monopolistic approaches to knowledge production, which means 'knowledge-in-action and knowledge for action were important for finding solutions to the problems of societies and communities' (Tandon, 2007, p. 4). By using these methodologies, HEIs can learn from reality and mobilize academic knowledge to address social problems with or without external help.

The other approach is *service-learning*. There is much confusion over the terms 'service-learning', 'community service' and 'academic service-learning' (ASL). Two terms have been generated by experiences in some HEIs: CSL and ASL. Providence University in Taiwan has adopted these latter terms in order to create a clear understanding of what service-learning is. The definition of CSL is similar to that of service-learning and is also 'a form of experiential learning that integrates service in the community with academic courses and/or extra-curricular programmes (Angeles, 2007, pp.

78–87). Students engage in CSL work for community needs and thus have a deeper understanding of specific social issues and a higher sense of civic responsibility.

ASL is driven by the learning objectives of the course and the needs of the community (Howard, 2013). It makes sense of lives, which transforms what people learn and how information can be learnt. Both types of service-learning also include the process of mutual learning instead of the traditional approach of one-way, top-down learning. 'Reflection' is therefore emphasized in this kind of programme, in which involved participants need to go through a self-critic process.

No matter which model is employed, 'university education and research should harness specific economic and social objectives, by means of exchanging knowledge and sharing resources with mutually beneficial outcomes' (Dragne, 2007, p. 11). To demonstrate the diversity and richness of actual practices on the ground today, Table IV.4.1 illustrates various approaches and nomenclatures that have evolved in the region in community–university engagement.

Religious-based HEIs obviously remain important in some parts of Asia. There are different religious networks that also encourage and support civic engagement programmes in the region. In addition to the United Board for Christian Higher Education in Asia, mentioned earlier, the Association of Christian Universities and Colleges in Asia has organized different conferences and activities focused on service-learning, whole-person development or civic engagement. In 2012, one of its constitutional objectives was changed to foster cooperative research projects, service-learning projects, quality assurance projects and Christian character development activities among different members of the Association as well.

Other than these networks, there are also key networks and associations supporting 'engagement' exercises in Asia by emphasizing the responsibilities of HEIs to address regional challenges and generate regional knowledge and engagement programmes. For examples, the Service-Learning Asia Network (SLAN) consists of over 10 universities from the region to develop different regional service-learning programmes and research projects (International Christian University, 2009) and a Science Shop in Shanghai to motivate faculty and students to use their scientific knowledge to address the need of the community. The Universiti Kebangsaan Malaysia (or National University of Malaysia) has worked with the global Talloires Network to develop a regional partner known as the Asia–Talloires Network of Industry and Community Engaged Universities, which brings together key regional stakeholders

TABLE IV.4.1
Various types of community–university engagement

Countries/ city/region	Name of HEI	Nature of HEI	Project nature/terms	References
Private not-for-profit HEIs				
Taiwan	Fu Jen Catholic University, Taiwan	Private and Catholic university	Local and international voluntary service programmes, institutional advocacy and course-based service-learning programmes	http://slc.mission.fju.edu.tw/idea01.aspx
Taiwan	Chung Yuan Christian University, Taiwan	Private Christian university	ASL and CSL programmes	Ma (2012)*
The Philippines	Silliman University, the Philippines	Private, non-profit, Protestant university	Community engagement and international service-learning programmes	http://su.edu.ph/page/10-History
Indonesia	Petra Christian University, Indonesia	Private university	Institutional advocacy, discipline-related service-learning programmes and community-based outreach programmes	http://lppm.petra.ac.id/ppm/sl/serve_learn.html
Thailand	Payap University, Thailand	Private university	Course-related service-learning programmes and volunteer work	http://ic.payap.ac.th/graduate/mdiv/curriculum.php#
India	Madras Christian College, India	Government-aided Christian college	Course-based service-learning programmes and community engagement	Sugumar (2009); http://mcc.edu.in/
India	Lady Doak College, India	Christian university	Project-based service-learning programmes and community-based and credit-bearing outreach programmes	http://www.ladydoakcollege.edu.in/node/coslp/02
Japan	International Christian University, Japan	Private, liberal arts and Christian college	Local CSL/ASL and international service-learning programmes	http://subsite.icu.ac.jp/slc/e/about_isl.html
Korea	Seoul Women's University, Korea	Private university	Credit-bearing, community-based service-learning programmes	http://www.swu.ac.kr/english/
Public universities				
Taiwan	National Taichung University of Education, Taiwan	National public university	Community-based service-learning programmes and community-based, international and voluntary activities	http://www.ntcu.edu.tw/eng/052.htm
China	Nankai University, China	National public university	Service-learning as a public elective course, bearing 1.5 credits and lasting for one semester. The content is revised and updated each semester to maintain lasting vitality	http://www.nankai.edu.cn/english/
China	Sun Yat-sen University, China	Public university	Philanthropy courses, service-learning courses, social innovation	http://www.sysu.edu.cn/2012/cn/index.htm
China	East China Normal University	Public university	Science shop and volunteer programme	http://english.ecnu.edu.cn/
Australia	Charles Darwin University, Australia	Public university	Community-based projects	Campbell and Christie (2008); http://www.cdu.edu.au/
India	Bhagat Phool Singh Mahila Vishwavidyalaya, India	Government-funded women's university	Community-based research	Planning Commission (2012); http://www.bpswomenuniversity.ac.in/
India	Hemwati Nandan Bahuguna Garhwal University, India	Public university	Community-based research	Planning Commission (2012); http://hnbgu.ac.in/

*Carol Ma Hok Ka (2012), visiting scholar at the New England Resource Center for Higher Education (NERCHE) of the University of Massachusetts, Boston, USA, developed the table for the seminar presentation in April 2012.

from universities, industries, NGOs, communities and governments to catalyse sustainable partnerships for improving the quality of life in the region.

PRIA is an NGO that focuses on capacity-building, knowledge-building, participatory research, citizen-centric development and policy advocacy to command the strategic direction of interventions in the community. These all provide a platform to promote the engagement of HEI in Asia. For example, SLAN is formed from over 10 universities in the region to promote the common interests and networks of student exchanges, faculty research, curriculum development and programme evaluation among colleges and universities interested in service-learning in Asia. SLAN members share ideas about the development of service-learning and have united to encourage cross-national collaborations.

The Australian Universities Community Engagement Alliance (AUCEA) is a national example formed by 10 Australian universities under the leadership of the University of Western Sydney. AUCEA also aims to promote a recognition of the scholarship of engagement and facilitate collaborative research between members and their communities (Temple et al., 2005). Finally, the Service-Learning Higher Education Network in Hong Kong is a local example formed by 10 Hong Kong colleges and universities to exchange ideas on civic engagement and service-learning. These kinds of partnership also involve non-profit organizations, foundations, corporations and government as key stakeholders in civic participation.

ISSUES AND CHALLENGES

The rapid growth of enrolment in HE in the region is bringing with it a wide variety of new practices and international linkages. As a consequence, community engagement and social responsibility in HE has now begun to gain the attention of policy-makers and university administrators. However, with the rush towards economistic models of capital formation for productive purposes in the economy, it is a big challenge to adopt this as a priority agenda within the region.

One of the first sets of issues relates to the need for explicit and supportive policy and the resources to achieve this. As has been described before, several countries in the region have now put in place policies that mandate community engagement, but in reality much more needs to happen. A clear need is for more resources to be made available to position this kind of work as mainstream. Where governments have funded some innovative programmes in this direction, results have been very encouraging.

From the national experience in Thailand, the Ministry of University Affairs initiated a government-funded programme called Strengthening the Grass-roots Economy. Under this programme, 'participating institutions were funded to promote networking with local communities, conduct research on economic opportunities, and provide local training on public administration, business management, community development, etc.' (Boothroyd and Fryer, 2004, p. 15). In 2003, an avian influenza research programme was initiated as a collaboration among the different faculties from Chulalongkorn University and the University of Minnesota, with support from the Thai Government, the US National Institutes of Health and the US Centers for Disease Control and Prevention. The programme upgraded virus laboratories

to P3 bio-safety levels, and developed training activities for doctors, veterinarians, scientists and researchers, officers at the Department of Livestock Development and district officers in areas where there were repeated outbreaks. The programme also encompassed studies on surveillance in Thailand and Southeast Asia, the natural history of disease in ecosystems, animal and human genetic transformations and the development of coping measures (Suwanwela, 2007). This kind of joint government initiative in Asia is very encouraging.

In addition to the Thai case, the NURI project in Korea is another national mechanism that supports HE engagement. The Ministry of Education and Human Resource Development was responsible for a project that recruited the participation of 109 HEIs. In this project, partnerships were built between local authorities, research institutions, business and industries.

At the university level, the institutionalization of HE engagement policy is one of the key issues among different institutions in Asia. Promoting and supporting university-wide engagement from the top and among the faculties is extremely important. It is a good strategy to align the learning objectives with the university's mission (Chan et al., 2009; Xing and Ma, 2010). For example, the mission of Lingnan University in Hong Kong is 'Education for Service', the mission of Silliman University in the Philippines is 'To be of Service to Others', and the mission of Payap University in Thailand is 'Truth and Service'. Many HEIs, especially private universities with a religious background that engage widely in the community, also have mission statements driving towards civic improvements.

Meanwhile, to encourage HEI engagement, the university can set up an office to facilitate faculty and departments to have scholarship-based engagement with communities, organizations and agencies. There are several examples of central facilities that provide leadership and coordination for other departments and also are good examples for other universities to follow, especially those that want to fully engage in the community; these include the Experiential Learning Center at the University of Hong Kong, China; the Service-Learning Center at International Christian University, Japan; the Service-Learning Center at Fu Jen Catholic University in Taiwan; the Center for Professional Ethics and Service-Learning at Assumption University in Thailand; the Center for Outreach and Service-Learning Program at Lady Doak College in India; and the Community Outreach Center at Petra Christian University in Indonesia.

As has been analysed above, HEIs need to create policies and structures to promote community–university engagement efforts institution-wide. Clear incentives for teachers, researchers and students need to be evolved so that engagement becomes everybody's business all the time. Performance assessment mechanisms for students and faculty have to integrate indicators of engagement.

Another issue presently gaining great attention is the question of the public accountability of HEIs. Most of them are supported by public resources, and many have been allocated significant visibility in the country's educational programmes. Therefore, the social relevance and impact of HEIs in their neighbourhood communities is being examined. Given the growing inequality and exclusion in many parts of the region, this issue gains further significance because metropolitan locations and communities seem to benefit far more than those in the hinterland and in areas where the population is poor.

The contentious issue of indigenous knowledge and its space in the system of HEIs continues to be relevant in the region. Several HEIs have begun to showcase indigenous knowledge in courses related to health, well-being and ecology. Yet much more needs to be done to promote a coherent mutuality between these various epistemologies of knowledge that the region is known for.

One of the obstacles is that 'participation in collaborative action-research has neither the scholarly respectability of pure research nor the commercial allure of contracted research as it studies problems with the local people' (Boothroyd and Fryer, 2004, p. 17). For the same reason, the facilitation of collaborative action research is usually not recognized as teaching in academia as it does not fit well with a systematic and cumulative programme of specialized study because conventional teachers do not control the learning process. In addition, young scholars may feel uneasy acting as co-participants in social development processes when they have little power when doing such kinds of research. It seems that this kind of research is a very inefficient way to establish a scholar's publication record.

To cope with these challenges, participatory research needs to be mainstreamed in HEIs and more funding should be given to faculty members for conducting community-based research as many people would like to engage in it or are already engaging in without informing the authorities. In addition, more support and dissemination research on the impact of youth civic engagement should be encouraged.

In the region, there has been quite some debate on USR (similar to CSR). In this debate, governments have promoted university–industry engagement much more than community–university engagement. Community structures, networks and resources are rather weak. Governments need to invest in these if meaningful partnerships of engagement between communities (especially more marginalized ones) and HEIs are to be built and nurtured.

To encourage the partnership between HEIs and community agencies, greater support is also suggested. Community partners can also act proactively to engage universities to achieve good communication and make them understand the needs of the community, provide feedback or exchange information between the community and universities, and work together to conduct research for and with the community. PRIA is one of the examples of organizations that could take up this role.

On the other hand, it is not easy for a community to build relationships and partnerships with HEIs as both may have unrealistic expectations of what the partners can achieve in a certain period of time (Baum, 2006). Thus, it is suggested that universities should 'institutionalize' partnerships with the community and recognize the mutual benefits that will lead to effective and sustainable collaborations.

A major issue in the region is inadequate systematization, documentation and dissemination of practices in community engagement. As has been illustrated throughout this paper, many interesting and diverse forms of engagement are taking place, but there is not much research on this theme. A strong body of knowledge needs to be built in the future.

In addition, building on the HEI typology included in the study, we should also develop a portfolio of detailed case studies giving examples of different HEIs in the region. There are no databases or detailed case studies for reference when promoting HEI engagement. If we can also highlight the pros and cons of each approach and its appropriateness for different contexts, goals, implementing agencies and service targets, it would help stakeholders (including the government and civil society organizations, teachers and students, and so on) to decide which approaches they could considered to promote engagement exercises better.

CONCLUSION

Universities play a vital role not only in shaping the future by educating tomorrow's professionals, but also in creating a research base for sustainability efforts and in providing outreach and service to communities and nations, especially in relation to difficult sustainability issues (McKeown, 2006). According to the former President of Korea University, Sung-Joo Han, who presented at the 2005 Talloires Conference:

> universities can teach better, and students can learn better as a result of social and public engagements.

They can do better research. We have many purists who say scholars should be in an ivory tower, should not come out into the street and be involved in society. Perhaps there are different roles, depending on whether society is at a developing or developed stage, but in both cases the university (faculty and students) is an important agent of modernization and globalization, both in teaching and research. So we shouldn't worry about the conflict or competition among these three elements of teaching, research, and civic engagement. (Perold, H. & Associates, 2005, p. 21)

Greater attention to diversity of knowledge and knowledge systems and a greater focus on issues of inequality, especially gender inequality, need to be adopted in efforts to promote and deepen community engagement in the region.

In the future, HE investment in knowledge transfer, knowledge-building, knowledge application and civic/community engagement will be constantly increasing through internationalization and globalization, and the Asia-Pacific region will not be an exception to this. There are undoubtedly different cultures, different educational systems, different political systems and different stages of civic development in various countries across Asia, so it will take time for HEIs to fully accept university engagement as pedagogy or even as a curricular consideration. Since its theoretical framework and research is still in an infant stage, academia and communities need to create more joint platforms to learn and exchange each other's concerns and success stories.

REFERENCES

Altbach, P.G. (2004) 'The past and future of Asian universities'. In: Altbach P.G. and T.U. Baltimore (eds), *Asian Universities: Historical Perspectives and Contemporary Challenges.* Baltimore, MD: Johns Hopkins University Press, p. 13.

Angeles, L.C. (2007) 'The scholarship of international service learning: implications for teaching and learning participatory development in higher education'. In: *Reinventing Higher Education: Toward Participatory and Sustainable Development.* Bangkok: UNESCO, pp. 78–87.

Assegaf, A.R., Zakaria, A.R.B. and Sulaiman, A.M. (2012) 'The closer bridge towards Islamic studies in higher education in Malaysia and Indonesia'. *Creative Education*, 3(26), 986–92.

Baum, H. (2006) 'Challenges in Institutionalizing University–Community Partnerships'. *Conference on Leadership and Sustainability for Community/University Partnerships*, U.S. Department of Housing and Urban Development Office of University Partnerships, Baltimore, Maryland, March 31, 2006, p. 4.

Boothroyd, P. and Fryer, M. (2004) 'Mainstreaming Social Engagement in Higher Education: Benefits, Challenges, and Successes'. Presentation to the Colloquium on Research and Higher Education Policy: 'Knowledge, Access and Governance: Strategies for Change', December 1–3, 2004, UNESCO, Paris. Paris: UNESCO, pp. 15 and 17.

Boyer, E.L. (1990) *Scholarship Reconsidered: Priorities of the Professoriate.* San Francisco: Jossey-Bass.

Calhoun, C. (2006) 'The university and the public good'. *Thesis Eleven,* 84, 7–43.

Campbell, M. and Christie, M. (2008) 'Questionnaire summaries'. In: *Indigenous Community Engagement @ Charles Darwin University.* Australia: Charles Darwin University, pp. 6–12.

Chan, C.M., Lee, K.M. and Ma, H.K. (2009) 'Service-learning model at Lingnan University: development strategies and outcome assessment'. *Hong Kong New Horizons in Education,* 57(3), 57–73.

Colby, A., Ehrlich T., Beaumont E. and Stephens J. (2003) *Educating Citizens: Preparing America's Undergraduates for Lives of Moral and Civic Responsibility.* San Francisco: Jossey-Bass and Carnegie Foundation for the Advancement of Teaching.

Dragne, C. (2007) *Background document for the University of Victoria Task Force on Civic Engagement.* Canada: University of Victoria.

Hollander, E. and Meeropol, J. (2006) 'Engagement in teaching and learning.' In: Percy S.L., Zimpher N.L. and Brukardt M.J. (eds), *Creating a New Kind of University: Institutionalizing Community-University Engagement.* Bolton, MA: Anker Publishing, p. 6990.

Howard, J. (2013) 'Academic Service-Learning: Myths, Challenges, and Recommendations'. Retrieved March 25, 2013 from http://data.ohr.umn.edu/protected/service1.pdf.

International Christian University (2009) *Lessons from Service-learning in Asia: Results of Collaborative Research in Higher Education.* Japan: Service-Learning Center, International Christian University.

Jun Xing and Ma, H.K.C. (eds) (2010) *Service-learning in Asia: Curricular Models and Practices.* Hong Kong: Hong Kong University Press.

Kim, E.U. and Cho, Y.H. (2008) 'Social Responsibility: A Critical Role for Korean Universities in the 21st Century'. Paper presented to the Asia-Pacific Sub-regional Preparatory Conference for the 2009 World Conference on Higher Education 'Facing Global and Local Challenges: the New Dynamics for Higher Education', September 25–26, 2008, Macao, PR China. Bangkok: UNESCO.

Kraince, R.G. (2007) 'Islamic higher education and social cohesion in Indonesia'. *Prospects*, 37(3), 345–56.

Leys S. (1997) *The Analects of Confucius.* New York: W. W. Norton.

McKeown, R. (2006) Reorienting colleges and universities to address sustainability. In: Wong L. (ed.), *Globalization and Education for Sustainable Development – Sustaining the Future.* Paris: UNESCO, pp. 94–7.

Nandy, A. (1996) 'The politics of indigenous knowledge and contending ideas of the university'. In: Hayhoe, R. and Pan, J. (eds), *East–West Dialogue in Knowledge and Higher Education.* Armonk, NY: M.E. Sharpe, p. 297.

Narang, R.H. (1996) 'The integration of modern and indigenous knowledge through nonformal education'. In: Hayhoe, R. and Pan, J. (eds), *East–West Dialogue in Knowledge and Higher Education.* Armonk, NY: M.E. Sharpe, pp. 259–60.

Pacific Economic Cooperation Council Conference (2007)

'Rethinking international education engagement in the Asia-Pacific region', p. 9.

Pamulaan Center for Indigenous Peoples' Education (2013) 'The Living Heritage of Philippine Indigenous People'. Retrieved March 14, 2013 from http://pamulaan.org/programs-and-services.

Pennycook, A. (1996) 'English, universities, and struggles over culture and knowledge'. In: Hayhoe, R. and Pan, J. (eds), *East–West Dialogue in Knowledge and Higher Education*. Armonk, NY: M.E. Sharpe, p. 64.

Perold, H. & Associates (2005) *Strengthening the Civic Roles and Social Responsibilities of Higher Education. A Report on the Talloires Conference 2005*. Medford, MA: Talloires Network, Tufts University, p. 21.

Planning Commission (2012) 'Fostering social responsibility in higher education in India'. Panel Discussion at the launch of UNESCO Chair on Community-based Research and Symposium on 'Social Responsibility in Higher Education'. India: PRIA.

Planning Commission, Government of India (2013) 'Education'. In: *Twelfth Five Year Plan (2012–2017), Social sectors Volume III*. India: SAGE Publications India, p. 111.

Sawasdikosol, S. (2009) 'Driving Universities. Collaboration toward the New Era of Sustainable Social Responsibility'. Paper presented at the University-Community Engagement Conference 2009, November 23–26, 2009, Penang, Malaysia). San Francisco: University Social Responsibility Alliance.

Sugumar, R.W. (2009) 'Role of service learning in water quality studies'. *New Horizons in Education*, 57(3), 82–90.

Suwanwela, C. (2007) 'Roles of universities in sufficiency economy'. In: Haddad, C. (ed.), *Reinventing Higher Education: Toward Participatory and Sustainable Development*. Bangkok: UNESCO.

Tandon, R. (2007) 'In search of relevance: higher education for participatory research and sustainable development'. *Reinventing Higher Education: Toward Participatory and Sustainable Development*. Bangkok: UNESCO, pp. 42–50.

Tandon, R. (2008) 'Civil engagement in higher education and its role in human and social development'. In: Global University Network for Innovation (GUNI), *Higher Education in the World 3, New Challenges and Emerging Roles for Human and Social Development*. Basingstoke: Palgrave Macmillan.

Tandon, R. (2012) *Fostering Social Responsibility in Higher Education, Planning Commission*. (UNESCO) www.unescochair-cbrsr.org/.

Tandon, R. (2012) 'Fostering social responsibility in higher education in India'. India: PRIA, pp. 5–7, 11–13.

Tandon, R. and Hall, B. (2012) *UNESCO Chair on Community Based Research and Social Responsibility in Higher Education: A Framework for Action 2012–2016*. New Delhi: PRIA.

Temple, J., Story, A. and Delaforce, W. (2005) 'AUCEA: an emerging collaborative and strategic approach dedicated to community–university engagement in Australia'. In: *Proceedings of the International Conference on Engaging Communities*. Brisbane, Australia.

Todani, K. (2008) Country Report – Japan. Paper presented to the Asia-Pacific Sub-regional Preparatory Conference for the 2009 World Conference on Higher Education 'Facing Global and Local Challenges: the New Dynamics for Higher Education', September 25–26, 2008, Macao, PR China. Bangkok: UNESCO.

University Grants Committee (2012, December 27) 'Knowledge Transfer'. University Grants Committee. Retrieved March 12, 2013 from: http://www.ugc.hk/eng/ugc/activity/kt/kt.htm.

University Social Responsibility Alliance (2009, November) 'Driving Universities' Collaboration toward the New Era of Sustainable Social Responsibility'. Paper presented at University–Community Engagement Conference 2009.

Wang, L.B. (2008) 'A Country Report of the People's Republic of China'. Paper presented to the Asia-Pacific Sub-regional Preparatory Conference for the 2009 World Conference on Higher Education 'Facing Global and Local Challenges: the New Dynamics for Higher Education', September 25–26, 2008, Macao, PR China. Bangkok: UNESCO.

Xing Jun and Ma, H.K.C. (eds), (2010) *Service-learning in Asia: Curricular Models and Practices*. Hong Kong: Hong Kong University Press.

Inside View IV.4.1
The nexus between knowledge, engagement and higher education in Australia: responding to the complex challenges of our time

Michael Cuthill

The nexus between knowledge, engagement and higher education in Australia has, in one form or another, been on the national agenda for several decades now. Much of the initial discussion was informed by leading international scholars including Boyer (1990, 1996), Gibbons and associates (1994) and Holland (2005). This discussion was largely built around a deceptively simple question asked by Boyer (1996, p. 19) as to how we might best connect 'the rich resources of the university to our most pressing social, civic and ethical problems'. A strong argument for a more engaged approach to scholarship was articulated. Some of the key characteristics of this new engaged scholarship are shown in Table IV.4.1.1 (Gibbons et al., 1994; Cuthill, 2011, p. 24).

Engagement Australia (formerly the Australian Universities Community Engagement Alliance) is the lead advocate for community–university engagement in Australia. Well over half of Australia's public universities are members of Engagement Australia. Collectively, they have presented a broad argument

TABLE IV.4.1.1
Key characteristics of an engaged approach to knowledge production

Traditional concepts of scholarship	Engaged scholarship
Disciplinary	Transdisciplinary
Hierarchical	Participatory
Pure or applied	Applied
Linear	Reflexive
Quality is academically defined	Quality is academically defined and socially accountable

that an engaged university is characterized by its strong relationships and partnerships with a broad range of external communities for the mutually beneficial exchange of knowledge and expertise (Phillips KPA, 2006; Engagement Australia, 2008).

However, the Australian policy context for community–university engagement has never been well articulated (Grattan Institute, 2013). This has resulted in an uncertain practice environment within universities evidenced through quality issues, a lack of project management and collaboration skills, and the limited motivation of researchers to engage in collaborative knowledge exchange processes (Advisory Council on Intellectual Property [ACIP], 2012).

Overall, neoliberally focused Australian governments have, over the past ten years, prompted an effective reduction in public spending on higher education, coupled with a stronger focus on industry-based research that has commercialization potential. This has occurred despite the Australian Productivity Commission (2007, p. xxiii) warning that 'Even where universities undertake research that has practical applications, it is the transfer, diffusion and utilization of such knowledge and technology that matters in terms of community well-being'. Commercialization is just one way of achieving this. This underlying context has, as Peacock states (2012, p. 313), 'collectively worked to produce the "engagement" discourse now prominent in Australian University policies and strategic plans'.

As a result, the broad concept of community–university engagement remains on the periphery of mainstream Australian academia, despite the ongoing rhetoric that positions engagement as integral to teaching and research. Bradley and her colleagues (2008, p. 169), in their influential 304-page review of higher education in Australia, identify the ongoing challenge faced when trying to implement engagement innovations in Australian higher education institutions:

> Engaged teaching and research should be the norm in universities. However, institutional resources to support engagement have been placed under pressure as a result of the reductions in the real level of public funding.

However, in a somewhat contradictory statement, the Bradley report goes on to reinforce the ongoing Australian Government position stating that, 'given the integral nature of this engagement, a separate stream of funding is not desirable'.

Without this support, ongoing quality and capacity issues will remain (ACIP, 2012) thereby constraining social and economic outcomes within Australia. The apparent ambiguity between this lack of national policy and/or support, and statements relating to the importance of community–university engagement, has created a general state of confusion over how Australian universities could or should respond. While there have been good overseas examples of national government leadership in this area, Australia remains largely in a policy vacuum. Considering the influential nature of the Bradley report, it is fair to say that community–university engagement policy debate in Australia has, over the four years following this report, effectively stalled.

Perhaps the one policy initiative that has inadvertently supported a university engagement agenda over many years relates to widening participation (access to higher education for people from low socioeconomic backgrounds). The publication of *A Fair Chance for All* (Department of Employment Education and Training, 1990) promoted the development of a National Higher Education Equity Framework that continues to underpin equity and access objectives in Australian higher education. The framework identified six key equity groups as disadvantaged in terms of their under-representation in higher education: (1) people from a low socioeconomic background, (2) people with a disability, (3) people from rural or isolated areas, (4) people from a non-English speaking background, (5) indigenous people, and (6) women, particularly in non-traditional areas of study and double degrees. The Bradley report (2008) presented recommendations that provided ongoing impetus to this agenda, and the Australian Government subsequently responded with access 'targets' for individual institutions and additional institutional funding if these targets are met.

Moving from national policy to the insti-

tutional level, it is reasonable to suggest that all Australian universities have directed various levels of attention to community–university engagement (or some aspect of engagement, knowledge transfer and so on). However, few universities have made serious attempts to articulate and institutionalize their engagement in an informed and measured way. As such, community–university engagement in Australia still appears to be predominantly instigated at the individual or project level, around specific areas of interest (Cuthill, 2012). More attention to this area of activity would undoubtedly expose the excellent engagement work that is being undertaken, despite the lack of national policy and/or institutional support. Currently, little is understood or reported regarding either the quality or the impact of the engagement being implemented, and there is a scarcity of empirical evidence describing the role engagement plays in helping to achieve an institution's mission and in serving the public good. A 2013 pilot study, commissioned by the Regional Universities Network (RUN), is in the first stage of addressing this knowledge gap.

This study will explore how leveraging university assets (students, staff and facilities) through operational activities (teaching and learning, research and service) centred on an engagement paradigm producing economic, social, cultural, environmental and individual 'value' outcomes to the specific region and more broadly for Australia. These value outcomes, in a self-reinforcing, reciprocal and mutually beneficial process, provide feedback to support the university core mission (RUN Engagement Working Group, 2012).

There is strong argument that, in today's competitive market place, the viability and sustainability of much Australian higher education business heavily relies on the strong and genuine relationships developed through a diverse range of engaged scholarship initiatives (Ernst & Young, 2012). Until the Australian Government responds with clear policy direction, much of the potential offered through such initiatives will remain dormant. If we are seriously looking to address our most pressing social, economic and environmental challenges, a national policy focus on commu-

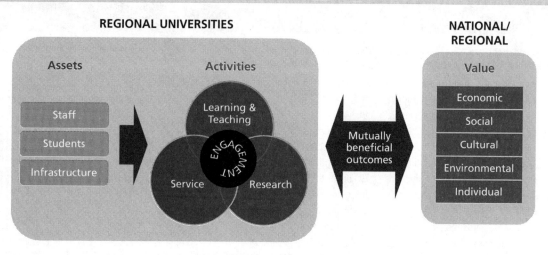

FIGURE IV.4.1.1 The value of regional universities to their region and the nation

nity–university engagement must be explicit and supportive. Such policy should provide a long-term vision and direction that recognizing that the role of the Australian university is more than that of a business enterprise, and that scholarship in Australia still has a 'public good' purpose (Cuthill, 2011).

REFERENCES

Advisory Council on Intellectual Property (2012) *Collaborations Between the Public and Private Sectors: The Role of Intellectual Property*. Final Report. Canberra: Commonwealth of Australia.

Australian Productivity Commission (2007) *Public Support for Science and Innovation: Productivity Commission Research Report Overview*. Canberra: Commonwealth of Australia. Retrieved September 2013 from http://www.pc.gov.au/__data/assets/pdf_file/0014/37121/scienceoverview.pdf.

Boyer, E. (1990) *Scholarship Reconsidered: Priorities of the Professoriate*. Princeton, NJ: Carnegie Foundation for the Advancement of Teaching.

Boyer, E. (1996) 'The scholarship of engagement'. *Journal of Public Service and Outreach*, 1, 11–20.

Bradley, D., Noonan, P., Nugent, H. and Scales, B. (2008) *Review of Australian Higher Education*. Canberra: Australian Government. Retrieved from http://www.innovation.gov.au/HigherEducation/Documents/Review/PDF/Higher%20Education%20Review_one%20document_02.pdf.

Cuthill, M. (2011) 'Embedding engagement in an Australian "sandstone" university: from community service to university engagement'. *Metropolitan Universities*, 22(2), 21–44.

Cuthill, M. (2012) 'A civic mission for the university: engaged scholarship and community based participatory research'. In: McIlrath, L., Lyons, A. and Munck, R. (eds), *Higher Education and Civic Engagement: Comparative Perspectives*. New York: Palgrave Macmillan, pp. 81–100.

Department of Employment Education and Training (1990) *A Fair Chance for All. National and Institutional Planning for Equity in Higher Education: A Discussion Paper*. Canberra: Australian Government Publishing Service.

Engagement Australia (2008) *Universities and Community Engagement: Position Paper 2008–2010*. Retrieved September 2013 from http://engagementaustralia.org.au/wp-content/uploads/2012/09/universities_CE_2008_2010.pdf.

Ernst & Young (2012) *University of the Future: A Thousand Year Old Industry on the Cusp of Profound Change*. Sydney: Ernst & Young.

Gibbons, M., Limoges, C., Nowotny, H., Schwartzman, S., Scott, P. and Trow, M. (1994) *The New Production of Knowledge: The Dynamics of Science and Research in Contemporary Societies*. London: Sage.

Grattan Institute (2013) *Mapping Australian Higher Education*. Melbourne: Grattan Institute.

Holland, B. (2005) 'Scholarship and Mission in the Twenty-first Century University: The Role of Engagement'. Paper presented to the Australian Universities Quality Forum, Sydney, Australia, July 5, 2005.

Peacock, D. (2012) 'Neoliberal social inclusion? The agenda of the Australian Universities Community Engagement Alliance'. *Critical Studies in Education*, 53(3), 311–25.

Phillips KPA Pty Ltd (2006) *Knowledge Transfer and Australian Universities and Publicly Funded Research Agencies. A Report to the Department of Education, Science and Training, March*. Canberra: Commonwealth of Australia.

RUN Engagement Working Group (2012) *Regional Universities Network Contribution to Regions and the Nation*. Pilot study January – July 2013. Unpublished tender document.

India is moving from being an information-based society to a knowledge-driven society, and higher education (HE) is seen as an important driver to ensure India's emergence as a major player in the global knowledge society. Combined with the massive growth in information technology, this has led to the democratization of knowledge, resulting in new relationships between the production, dissemination and use of knowledge. This paper argues that the response of HE in India needs to change towards greater engagement with the community, using knowledge to address the community's problems in frameworks that will facilitate a more egalitarian and non-hierarchical co-construction of knowledge by all stakeholders of the university for meaningful change.

THE HIGHER EDUCATION SCENARIO IN INDIA

The HE system in India is the third largest in the world in terms of student enrolment, second only to China and the USA. There has been a phenomenal increase in the number of HE institutions (HEIs) in India, rising from 30 universities and 695 colleges in 1950–1951 to 634 universities and 33,023 colleges with 17 million enrolled students as of 2010–2011 (University Grants Commission [UGC], 2011). There is a growing demand for HE due to the increasing youth population, improved gains in primary and secondary education, and the growing middle class and their rising aspirations (Agarwal, 2009, p. 64).

Three major developments have influenced the landscape of HE in India and India's drive towards becoming a knowledge-driven society:

- the progressive massification of HE and the diversification of its student base;
- the growth in information and communication technology, resulting in the creation of virtual worlds that weaken the relevance of physical territorial boundaries;
- accelerating globalization and a market economy that has created conditions for the commercialization of education.

By 2020, India is going to have the world's largest set of young people in the age group of 20–24 years, even as other countries such as China and others in Southeast Asia begin to age. However, as of 2007, the gross enrolment ratio, that is, the proportion of 18–23-year-olds with access to HE, was 13% – very low compared with the world average of 24% (Jeelani, 2012).

India is also one of the largest representative democracies in the world. The internet and other social and technological changes have made multiple sources of knowledge and information accessible to many more people than in the past, independent of HE, the media and the State. This has resulted in a significant change in the rules of the game pertaining to the production, dissemination and use of knowledge. On the other hand, according to the National Knowledge Commission, the major focus of HE in India is 'to make higher education institutions agents for creating knowledge that can create wealth' (Government of India, 2009). All these influences lead to the increasing commercialization and vocationalization of education. Knowledge, instead of being treated as a public good to serve the larger purpose of social well-being – is turning out to be a private good, promoted by private investment and driven by economic criteria (Altbach, 2002; Tandon, 2008).

Thus, there is a widening disconnect between society and universities as sites of learning and the production of knowledge (Yashpal Committee, 2009). Equally important is the increasing disconnect between social realities and the students entering the portals of HE institutions. For a majority of youth who come from middle-class, protective home environments, the sources of knowledge about the world outside are the internet, a sparse reading of books and conversations with peers. For some, the window for glimpsing the social realities outside – the poverty, the hunger and the disease – is their domestic servant or his or her child. In addition, there are students coming from the most deprived backgrounds who bring their own values and worldviews with differently grounded experiences.

So the question is: can an HE system based on the need to create skilled human power for the global economy incorporate scientific knowledge with people's knowledge and prepare people to be responsible citizens in a democratic society? If the answer is no, what should be the new response of HE in India to the changing realities, and how it should change?

THE CHANGING PARADIGMS OF THE CONCEPTION AND FRAMEWORK OF KNOWLEDGE

Historically in India, the production and use of knowledge remained under Brahminical domination for a long period. Even in ancient Indian universities such as Nalanda and Takshila, education was accessible only to men from some select social groups. The knowledge and experience of other social groups and genders was not taken into the formal domain of knowledge, and the value of such forms of knowledge was actively discounted. Now, the relationship between knowledge production and dissemination has undergone a radical change with the democratization of Indian society, combined with a massification of education, and information technologies. The stage of a knowledge-driven society is being replaced by a stage of knowledge democracy. Universally, knowledge democracy is characterized by the recognition that there are different types of knowledge co-constructed by stakeholders and generated from multiple sources (Veld, 2010).

As HEIs around the globe, including those in India, came under pressure to demonstrate the social relevance of the knowledge they were producing, Boyer's emphasis on the importance of university's engagement with the community gave them an opportunity to revisit their purpose and context. Boyer (1996, 1990) suggested four interrelated forms of scholarship – the scholarships of discovery, integration, application and teaching – which together have come to be known as the 'scholarship of engagement'. In this light, education, knowledge and collaboration (Tandon, 2008) are seen as the integrated purposes of HE. The multidirectional flow of knowledge and expertise between HEIs and the community was acknowledged, and community–university–civil society engagement came to be seen more as an egalitarian and collaborative construction of knowledge for meaningful change than as an interface with its overtones of superiority of academic knowledge.

THE FRAMEWORKS FOR ENGAGEMENT: SOME EXAMPLES

Several innovative examples of the community engagement of HEIs exist in India. UGC, the apex body for HE in India, has long emphasized service to the community as the 'third dimension' of HE. A few examples of community–university–civil society engagement are indicated here.

THE NATIONAL SERVICE SCHEME

The National Service Scheme (NSS) was created with inspiration from Mahatma Gandhi to foster engagement between universities/ colleges and communities, with the motto 'Education through service'. Each college has a unit of 100 volunteers, and each volunteer is expected to put in 120 weekend hours per year of voluntary engagement in community development activities. Started in 1969, the scheme grew to involve 4.9 million students by 2009, with a presence in all institutions of higher learning in India, including six union territories. Students have participated in a range of activities such as tree plantation, disaster relief and health awareness, working mostly in villages (Parasuraman et al., 2010). The NSS had now been reformulated as National Service and Skill Development Scheme, with a focus on helping learners to acquire vocational skills while rendering community service.

FIELD ACTION PROJECTS OF SOCIAL WORK EDUCATION

The social work discipline to a large extent reflects the four attributes of the scholarship of engagement. In social work, fieldwork in the form of engagement with the community forms an integral part of the curriculum. It provides the student and the teacher with an opportunity to understand the connection between theory and practice. One such innovation is the Field Action Projects in the Tata Institute of Social Sciences, which are 'unique responses to field realities and

highlight the role that HEIs can play in engaging with the community' (Dave and Raghavan, 2012, p. 454). Another example of engagement with the community for over a period of a decade has demonstrated the initiation of a micro-credit programme in the community that in turn led to the teaching of a course on the topic in Andhra University (Vijalakshmi et al., 2010).

INTERPROFESSIONAL DIALOGUES 1995–1998: PRIA'S INITIATIVE

With the changing social scenario, HEIs need to consider alternative approaches and perspectives to teaching and learning that can challenge existing educational paradigms that have become dated in terms of their transformative potential as contributors to change. With this aim, the Society for Participatory Research in Asia (PRIA), in collaboration with Association of Schools of Social Work in India, conducted a series of dialogues called the Inter Professional Dialogues on Participatory Research and Development for social work faculties in universities, creating a sizeable impact at national level (Tandon, 2008).

THE TWELFTH FIVE YEAR PLAN AND HIGHER EDUCATION

The Twelfth Five Year Plan (Government of India, 2012) has created spaces with the aim of fostering opportunities for the engagement of HEIs with the community (Box IV.4.2.1).

BOX IV.4.2.1: FOSTERING SOCIAL RESPONSIBILITY IN HIGHER EDUCATION

In the face of growing isolation of HEIs from society, there is a need for renewed effort for HEIs for genuinely engaging with community, conduct socially relevant research and education and foster social responsibility amongst students as part of their core mission. For this purpose, a National Initiative to Foster Social Responsibility in Higher Education would be launched. An Alliance for Community Engagement, an independent association of practitioners, academics and community leaders would be created to support its implementation. (Government of India, 2012, p. 11)

CONCLUSION

As HE in India is poised to move to the stage of knowledge democracy, there is an increasing disconnect between society and universities as sites of learning and nurturing of values. There is a growing recognition the world over that HE–community engagement should serve the mutually agreed interests of communities and institutions, both being seen as equal partners. Thus, if the institution of higher learning is the *jnana kshetra* (site of knowledge), the community is the *karya kshetra* (site of action), which is the field where different forms of knowledge is produced and tested. Such partnerships, if fostered, will result in the implementation of innovative solutions to real-life problems and will prepare more inclusive, connected and socially responsible learners and scholars.

REFERENCES

Agarwal, P. (2009) *Indian Higher Education: Envisioning the Future*. New Delhi: Sage.

Altbach, P.G. (2002) 'Knowledge and education as international commodities – the collapse of the common good'. *University News*, 40(22), 1–4.

Boyer, E. (1990) *Scholarship Reconsidered: Priorities of the Professoriate*. San Francisco, CA: Jossey-Bass.

Boyer, E. (1996) 'The scholarship of engagement'. *Journal of Public Service and Outreach*, 1, 11–20.

Dave, A. and Raghavan, V. (2012) 'Centrality of field action in social work education: a case study of socio-legal work'. *Social Change*, 42(4), 451–66.

Government of India (2009) *National Knowledge Commission – Report to the Nation (2006–2009)*. Retrieved from http://knowledgecommission.gov.in/downloads/report2006/eng/NKC%20Report%20to%20the%20Nation%202006.pdf.

Government of India (2012) *Twelfth Five Year Plan (2012–2017): Social Sectors*, Volume III. New Delhi: Planning Commission.

Jeelani, S. (2012) 'Strengthening higher education system in India'. *University News*, 50(43), 56–9.

Parasuraman, S., Ahmed, K., Afroz, S. and Sangita, C. (2010) 'An evaluation study of NSS in India'. *Indian Journal of Social Work*, 71(3), 417–31.

Tandon, R (2008) 'In search of relevance: higher education for participatory research and sustainable development'. In: *Reinventing*

Higher Education: Towards Participatory and Sustainable Development. Bangkok: UNESCO, pp. 42–50.

Tandon, R. (2008) 'Civil engagement in higher education and its role in human and social development'. In: GUNi (ed.) *Higher Education in the World 3*. Basingstoke: Palgrave Macmillan.

University Grants Commission (2011) *Annual Report, 2010–11*. New Delhi: Ministry of HRD.

Veld, R.J. (ed.) (2010) *Knowledge Democracy: Consequences for Science, Politics and Media*. New York: Springer.

Vijayalakshmi, B., Prasad Devi B., Bhavani, P.S.V. and Haranath, S. (2010) 'Journey with communities: engagement with SHGs from lower income neighbourhoods in Visakhapatnam'. *Indian Journal of Social Work*, 71(4), 485–516.

Yashpal Committee (2009) *Report of the Committee to Advise on Renovation and Rejuvenation of Higher Education*. Retrieved September 2013 from http://www.aicte-india.org/misyashpal.htm.

Inside View IV.4.3
Community-based learning: context as text

Betty Cernol-McCann

INTRODUCTION

Higher education institutions (HEIs) in the Philippines generally adhere to the three-pronged conventions of instruction, research and community outreach. In many HEIs, these three areas are worlds of their own with no clear mechanism for integration. At the level of the faculty, the three are entirely separate activities for which the university may assign separate merit points for teaching performance, research involvement and outreach activities.

Service-learning challenges these conventions by weaving into academic teaching and learning student-centered opportunities for practical research and community-based experience. Service-learning as an engaged pedagogy generally involves five stages: inventory and investigation, preparation and planning, action, reflection, and demonstration (Kaye, 2010). This methodology involves a careful assessment of the social situation in focus, developing a learning plan that encourages responsibility and independent study, engaging in a meaningful service that offers a safe ground for testing ideas and acquiring new skills and knowledge, providing systematic reflection on the experience and showcasing what has been learned to relevant groups in the community and the university.

EXAMPLES OF SERVICE-LEARNING IN THE PHILIPPINES

In the Philippines, a number of service-learning advocates promote experiential learning that links the classroom with the community. In Metro Manila and Luzon, several learning projects have been carried out (De la Cruz, 2013; Lappay, 2013; Libatique and Tango-

nan, 2013; Melegrito, 2013; Orsal et al., 2013). In the Visayas, community-based learning programmes have also been initiated (Del Carmen, 2013; Oracion and Ligutom, 2013; Rio, 2013). A few service-learning projects in Mindanao have also been reported (Calumpang, 2013). The paragraphs that follow describe three cases that provide an illustration.

A course entitled 'Theory and Practice of Social Development' at the Ateneo de Manila University engages students in a community service project that would benefit an urban community while honing their skills, testing ideas and acquiring new perspectives (Sescon and Tuano, 2012). Students engage in specific but interrelated service-learning activities that include development of the socioeconomic profiles of partner communities, the formulation of an alternative project intervention, and an assessment of the effectiveness of existing project interventions such as canvas bag production for senior citizens in Quiapo, Manila, and goat milk production in a farming village in Nueva Ecija. Reflection on the communities' experiences deepens students' understanding of the outcomes of poverty alleviation programmes in the country, and what made them work and what did not work, and instils in students a need to be in constant pursuit of and an active search for ways to bring about social equity, justice and fairness.

A class in Nutrition and Dietetics at Silliman University in central Philippines connects students with the mothers of malnourished preschoolers who come primarily from households where most male heads are engaged in fishing and/or construction work (Riconalla, 2013). This service-learning project involves

government and non-government agencies cooperating in activities to combat malnutrition. Specific but interconnected community activities range from nutritional assessment to the application of techniques and management of food production including product marketing. Students engage mothers and children in conversations to know more about the dietary and food preferences in local households. Students learn about local food sources rich in nutritional value, gather mothers' recipes, experiment on nutritionally enhanced food items, and develop and package food products for promotion and cooperative small-scale business production. In the process, students acquire new methods of nutritional management that are sensitive to different local conditions. Active community engagement benefits the community, while students and faculty enhance the implementation of academic programmes and learning goals, widen the scope of influence and ultimately improve the quality of education in specific disciplines.

At Trinity University of Asia in Quezon City, Developmental Communication students document the health status of households and environmental conditions in settlements along creeks in crowded city districts to demonstrate the consequences of improper waste management on the health of residents in the adopted urban communities (Orsal, 2013). In work with some faculty and students from nursing, medical technology, economics and biochemistry, the incidence of health problems such as dengue, eczema, diarrhoea and leptospirosis are reported to local health units for care and attention. Community participation in planning, implementing measures to address environmental and health issues, and setting up referral systems help to mitigate environmental degradation and health threats. Local government leaders and academics working with community residents manifest a commitment to the Philippines Agenda 21 based on the UN Conference on Environment and Development to promote a better quality of life through specific acts of care for the environment and its sustainable development.

In the examples cited here, the community projects are in support of the university's mission to engage in applied research, provide holistic education to students and extend service to needy localities. In all these examples, other faculty members and students from other disciplines as well as the non-teaching support units dedicated to community outreach programmes join forces to bring about inter-institutional, multidisciplinary and multi-agency cooperation in addressing social concerns. A collective, defined and well-organized service-learning programme within educational institutions could well lead towards new ways of thinking and articulating their role in society. Institutionalized service-learning programmes provide rich ground for the cultivation of good citizenship, relevant education and purposeful changes within the universities and their partner communities.

Oracion and Ligutom (2013) have confirmed the positive impact of service-learning on assisting students to fulfil their own learning goals, as well as the expected benefits from their participation in community engagement projects. They have reported gains in terms of relating to the community, valuing themselves and other people, applying learned skills and acquiring new knowledge. While the practice of service-learning in the Philippines is on the rise, the conduct of programme evaluation and the evaluation of learning goals by the adopters needs to keep pace in order to systematically document and review the intended outcomes.

MODELS OF SERVICE-LEARNING

Butin (2010, p. 4) suggests four 'distinct conceptualizations of how service-learning is articulated in the literature and enacted in the field: technical, cultural, political, and anti-foundational.' These various facets of service-learning are illustrated in Figure IV.4.3.1.

These models can overlap, and any practice of service-learning can contain elements of two or more of the categories. In the examples of service-learning in the Philippines that were cited earlier, the engagement with poor urban households examines poverty by relying not only on quantitative textbook definitions of poverty, but also on tangible, qualitative descriptions developed within the community (a technical perspective). The students can also empathize with those coming from urban poor communities who have less access to social services (a cultural perspective). With students reviewing the success or failure of projects intended to alleviate conditions of poverty, they could propose strategies to mitigate disparities (a political perspective). In addition, students may question their own assumptions that those who live in poverty tend to be rough and out to divest others of material things when they encounter persons in destitution who show hospitality and generosity despite their economic needs (an anti-foundational perspective).

CONCLUSION

Linking instruction to community service provides rich new opportunities to process information beyond the texts in books, journals and other published materials that are so commonly used in classroom teaching. Texts come alive and find new meaning, or perhaps even lose meaning, as they are reflected on in the context of what goes on in the real world. With rapid global changes influencing today's higher education, educators need to facilitate learners' ability to navigate between static texts and ever-changing contexts, and promote the creation of knowledge grounded on the tenet that education is for life as it is now lived.

REFERENCES

Butin, D.W. (2010) *Service-learning in Theory and Practice: The Future of Community Engagement in Higher Education.* New York: Palgrave Macmillan.

Calumpang, P.M. (2013) *Strengthening Partnerships by Theme-based Service-learning.* Progress report of Pilgrim Christian College to the United Board thru Silliman University, June 26.

De la Cruz, L.J. (2013) 'Serving Effectively Through Service-Learning: Enhancing Service-Learning Programs that Promote Innovations for Inclusive Development'. Presented to the 4th Asia Pacific Conference on Service Learning, Lingnan University, Hong Kong, June 5–7. Retrieved July 14, 2013 from http://www.ln.edu.hk/osl/conference2013/output/2E/2.%20Leland%20Joseph%20DELA%20CRUZ%20(5%20June).pdf.

Del Carmen, A.V. (2013) 'Environmental Information and Education Campaign in a Pilot Creek Community: A Civic Engagement and Learning Experience of Communication Students of the University of St.

Model	Key focus	Possibilities
Technical service-learning	Content knowledge	Cognitive progress through real-world links
Cultural service-learning	Civic and cultural competency	Expanded understanding of the self as embedded in a local and global community
Political service-learning	Social and political activism	Fostering a more equitable and socially just environment for individuals and groups
Anti-foundational service-learning	Cognitive dissonance	Expanded epistemological possibilities through questioning of a priori truth

FIGURE IV.4.3.1 Conceptual models of service-learning
Source: Service-Learning, Center for Teaching Excellence, Duquesne University.

La Salle, Bacolod City, Philippines'. Presented to the 4th Asia Pacific Conference on Service Learning, Lingnan University, Hong Kong, June 5–7. Retrieved July 14, 2013 from http://www.ln.edu.hk/osl/conference2013/output/1D/2.%20Allen%20DEL%20CARMEN.pdf.

Kaye, C.B. (2010) *The Complete Guide to Service Learning: Proven, Practical Ways to Engage Students in Civic Responsibility, Academic Curriculum, and Social Action* (2nd edn). Minneapolis, MN: Free Spirit.

Lappay, A P. (2013) 'Community Partnerships in Service-Learning: the St. Paul University Philippines' Experience'. Presented to the 4th Asia Pacific Conference on Service Learning, Lingnan University, Hong Kong, June 5–7. Retrieved July 14, 2013 from http://www.ln.edu.hk/osl/conference2013/output/3D/3.%20Allan%20Peejay%20LAPPAY.pdf.

Libatique, N. and Tangonan, G. (2013) 'Engaging Empowered Fisher-Folk and Local Communities: Engineering, Science and Humanities Students in a Lake Aquaculture Service-Learning Environment'. Presented to the 4th Asia Pacific Conference on Service Learning, Lingnan University, Hong Kong, June 5–7. Retrieved July 14, 2013 from http://www.ln.edu.hk/osl/conference2013/output/6A/3.%20Nathaniel%20LIBATIQUE%20(6%20June).pdf.

Melegrito, L.F. (2013) 'The Principle of Reciprocity in Service Learning: The Case of De La Salle University'. Presented to the 4th Asia Pacific Conference on Service Learning, Lingnan University, Hong Kong, June 5–7. Retrieved July 14, 2013 from http://www.ln.edu.hk/osl/conference2013/output/1A/2.%20Lourdes%20F.%20MELEGRITO%20(5%20June).pdf.

Oracion, E.G. and Ligutom, E.L. (2013) 'Measuring Learning Outcomes of Students in Service-Learning Considering Diversity and Degree of Experiences'. Presented to the 4th Asia Pacific Conference on Service Learning, Lingnan University, Hong Kong, June 5–7. Retrieved July 14, 2013 from http://www.ln.edu.hk/osl/conference2013/output/2A/1.%20Emervencia%20L.%20LIGUTOM%20(5%20June).pdf.

Orsal, C.D. (2013) *Enabling Community Toward a Sustainable Healthy Environment.* Progress report from the Service-Learning Team of Trinity University of Asia to the United Board for Christian Higher Education in Asia, May 20.

Orsal, C.D., Maglaque, J.I. and Cantal, D.L. Jr. (2013) 'An Impact Study on the TUA-United Board 2011 Community Project: Enabling Community Towards Sustaining a Healthy Environment'. Presented to the 4th Asia Pacific Conference on Service Learning, Lingnan University, Hong Kong,

June 5–7. Retrieved July 14, 2013 from http://www.ln.edu.hk/osl/conference2013/output/8C/2.%20Dr.%20Jean%20MAGLAQUE.pdf.

Riconalla, A.V. (2013) *Community Health and Nutrition Program.* Progress report from the Service-Learning Team of Silliman University Dietetics and Nutrition Department to the United Board for Christian Higher Education in Asia, June 28.

Rio, I.D. (2013) 'Local Governance from University to Community (The CPU Local Government Mobile Training Team Experience)'. Presented to the 4th Asia Pacific Conference on Service Learning, Lingnan University, Hong Kong, June 5–7. Retrieved July 14, 2013 from http://www.ln.edu.hk/osl/conference2013/output/2A/2.%20IRVING%20DOMINGO%20L.%20RIO.pdf.

Service-Learning, Center for Teaching Excellence, Duquesne University. 'Teaching and Learning at Duquesne University'. Retrieved July 10, 2013 from www.duq.edu/about/centers-and-institutes/center-for-teaching-excellence/teaching-and-learning.html.

Sescon, J. and Tuano, P. (2012) 'Service learning as a response to disasters and social development: a Philippine experience'. *Japan Social Innovation Journal*, 2(1), 64–71.

Spotlight Issues IV.4.4
Addressing ageing issues through elder learning in the Asia-Pacific region

Alfred Cheung-Ming Chan, Carol Hok Ka Ma, Alice Liu Cheng

AGEING IN THE ASIA-PACIFIC REGION: TRENDS, CHALLENGES AND ACTIONS

Population ageing, as an inevitable and global phenomenon, has become a major concern for the world. It is anticipated that one in five people in the world will be elderly (defined as aged 60 years and over) by 2050. The ageing problem is more severe and noticeable in the Asia-Pacific region, with 25% of the Asia-Pacific population estimated to be elderly by 2050 (Kinsella and He, 2009; United Nations, 2011). Many challenges and impacts can be raised by the ageing of the population, such as an increase in demand and costs for elderly care, concern over the physical and psychological well-being of the elderly, their financial security and social position, and so on.

Many organizations and countries have been actively preparing for and seeking solutions to the problems of ageing. For example, the Economic and Social Commission for Asia and the Pacific is continuously developing national policies on ageing and created the Macau Plan of Action on Ageing for Asia and the Pacific in 1999, which promotes productive ageing, community engagement and social support for older people (Economic and Social Commission for Asia and the Pacific, 1999). Furthermore, the World Health Organization has vigorously advocated for Active Ageing, which aims to optimize opportunities for health, participation and security in order to enhance the elderly population's quality of

life (World Health Organization, 2002). Scientific evidence also suggests that actively taking part in social and learning events could foster elders' well-being and sense of worthiness and independence (Rowe and Kahn, 1999; Matsuo et al., 2003). Thus, the concept of active ageing has become widely used as a policy framework worldwide.

Countries in Asia tend to enhance elders' social participation and engagement through different elder learning programmes as these can serve the purpose of capacity-building for the elderly in raising their self-care and participation capabilities. There are different initiators and formats of development for elder learning modes in Asia, for example elderly-

TABLE IV.4.1
Elder learning policy development in Asia-Pacific countries

Year	Country	Elder learning policy development	Initiated by
1965	Japan	Setting up of elderly colleges (*Inamino Gakuen*) at prefectural level	Government
1968	UNESCO	Advocation of the concept of lifelong learning	Government
1972	UNESCO	Publication of a report from the international Commission on the Development of Education	Government
1972	Japan	Setting up of the University of the Third Age (U3A)	Government
1972	Korea	Setting up of schools for senior citizens	Government
1981	Taiwan	Institute on Ageing founded	Government
1982	Taiwan	Setting up of the first Evergreen College	Government
1983	China	Initiation of the University for the Aged	Government
1984	Australia	Setting up of U3As – a self-help model	Community
1984	Hong Kong	Development of learning programmes for elders	NGOs
1998	Australia	Setting up of online learning	NGOs
2006	Hong Kong	Establishment of EAs	Government
2006	Nepal	Setting up of U3As	NGOs
2006	Singapore	Initiation of inter-generational learning programme	Government

colleges in Japan, schools for senior citizens in Korea, the Institute on Ageing in Taiwan, inter-generational learning programmes in Singapore, the University for the Aged on mainland China and the Elder Academy (EA) in Hong Kong (Table IV.4.1). In order to fully explain how elder learning can facilitate self-care and participation capabilities in Asia, we will highlight the characteristics of elder learning in Asia.

ACTIVE AGEING AS A POLICY FRAMEWORK TO ENCOURAGE ELDER PARTICIPATION

The Active Ageing framework has become a policy guide for encouraging active participation of the elderly in Asia. For example, governments in Hong Kong, Australia and Singapore also echo the Active Ageing initiatives and have successfully formed different modes of elder learning programmes. The Hong Kong government successfully launched the EA scheme in 2006, collaborating with over 110 local schools and non-governmental organizations (NGOs) to provide a school-based education platform for formal learning and social engagement for the elderly population through primary, secondary and tertiary education. The Singaporean and Australia governments have similar programmes integrated into their educational systems in order

to encourage more elderly people to participate in a school learning setting. After all, learning is essential for achieving a fulfilled life. Providing different elder learning courses helps to promote the message of continuous learning and encourages elders to make the best use of their time and to keep pace with modern society by acquiring new knowledge and learning new skills.

ELDER LEARNING COURSES FOR FACILITATING SELF-CARE, MUTUAL SUPPORT AND SOCIAL INCLUSION

Initially, some elder learning programmes, for example some in China, were only to develop people's interests (for example, singing or dancing) and to set up simple socializing events (such as meeting and chatting with others). After consideration of the needs of the elderly and the different cohorts of this group, many formal courses across diverse fields of study were then added to different elder learning curricula, including history, science, foreign languages, computing, painting, health, photography, and so on.

In Hong Kong, in addition to general-interest classes, there are two recommended areas of study for elderly people: health-related courses (for example, knowledge for self-health management, retirement planning courses, and so on) and computer courses (for example, how

to use a computer and how to use Facebook and email) to facilitate social inclusion and self-management knowledge for this group. The availability of different levels of course not only allows elderly people to move through a comfortable and systematic learning process, but also provides a platform for mutual support and encouragement among the elderly.

ELDER LEARNING PROGRAMMES ENCOURAGE PARTNERSHIPS BETWEEN YOUNG AND OLD

In view of the conflicts between young and old in relation to pension issues and the postponement of the retirement age in different countries, encouraging the elderly to engage in the community or in a university setting also helps to foster relationships between young and old. Traditional Asian culture values collectivism, social harmony and a hierarchical position in society (with respect for seniors and care for the young). Consistent with this cultural ideology, some elder learning programmes in Asia also feature inter-generational partnership.

In Hong Kong, elderly people are welcome to sit in on university courses and enjoy the mutual 'learning and teaching' experience with university students. Students can be tutors to teach elderly courses related to computing, communication and organizational skills, whereas older members of society can introduce and demonstrate useful daily life abilities and traditional culture to university students. The sit-in programme allows the elderly to join lectures, academic research projects and even service-learning programmes with university students. Such a dual identity of 'learning and teaching' for university and elderly students effectively trains their learning, leadership and teamwork skills. Consequently, inter-generational understanding and relationships are enhanced through mutual learning and support between young and old. This will not only expand both groups' social networks, but also promote inter-generational harmony and rapport.

ELDER LEARNING PROGRAMMES REALIZE THE OBJECTIVE OF FOSTERING A SENSE OF WORTHINESS AMONG THE ELDERLY

In addition, due to the diversity of the educational background and learning skills of the older community, it is important to provide them with different levels of learning opportunities and share their life stories with different people. Retired professors in Australia and New Zealand have, under the University of the Third Age scheme, created different platforms for educated older people to share their knowledge and demonstrate their creativity through different elder learning activities. In addition, some universities, for example Lingnan University in Hong Kong, have actively linked with local schools to implement the Through Train learning model, which offers learning and participation opportunities in primary, secondary and tertiary education for older people.

This model allows great flexibility for elders at different levels in terms of choosing courses and experiencing different study environments according to their expertise, needs and situations. For instance, elderly students can study an introductory level of computer knowledge (that is, how to utilize a keyboard and simple software such as Word and Media Player) in primary schools, whereas more advanced computer courses (that is, how to create blogs and make webpages) are available in secondary and tertiary education. Adding to this, elderly members of the community can also share their life experiences and even become the mentors for youngsters. This kind of volunteer work has enriched the life of the elderly as it creates a platform for them to further contribute to society.

ELDER LEARNING PROGRAMMES CREATE SOCIAL CAPITAL FOR THE COMMUNITY

Undoubtedly, elder learning programmes, including volunteering, teaching and learning approaches, effectively produce social capital for the community, especially when retired persons and young people become teachers and volunteers for others. The close partnerships among all the stakeholders are helpful for the effective utilization of resources (for example, shared teaching materials and facilities), knowledge exchange (for example, among the elderly, young people and the community) and better communication and understanding for stakeholders to address issues of ageing in the community. In return, society can be built up with love and care, the most important aspect being to further strengthen the ties between different stakeholders in the community.

WHAT WE CAN DO MORE IN ASIA FOR THE ELDERLY?

The launch of elder learning activities has benefited a large number of this age group in the Asia-Pacific region as it has proved to be an effective strategy not only for improving social engagement and quality of life, but also for raising capability in self-management and inclusion in the community. More of this population and even their families could benefit if there were more support from society (that is, government funding, private donations and free teaching resources), more types of learning platform (that is, online courses and long-distance programmes) and a greater involvement of social and educational institutions, which might better promote the learning and social participation of elderly Asian individuals. In addition, training elderly leaders to manage different elder learning programmes can not only increase the organizational skills and sense of achievement of the elderly, but also reduce the human resources required from other sectors of the society.

All in all, an elder learning platform is an effective way to encourage elderly individuals to be actively engaged in society. Participation in learning activities can lead to a healthy and fulfilled life. Through learning, older individuals can realize new objectives in life and enhance their sense of achievement and self-esteem in dealing with the changes occurring in their later life.

REFERENCES

Economic and Social Commission for Asia and the Pacific (1999) 'The Macau Plan of Action on Ageing for Asia and the Pacific'. Retrieved July 20, 2013 from http://www.unescap.org/ageing/macau.htm

Kinsella, K. and He, W. (2009) An Aging World: 2008. Washington, DC: National Institute on Aging and US Census Bureau.

Matsuo, M., Nagasawa, J., Yoshino A., Hiramatsu, K. and Kurashiki, K. (2003) 'Effects of activity participation of the elderly on quality of life'. Yonago Acta Medica, 46, 17–24.

Rowe, J. and Kahn, R. (1999) Successful Aging. New York: Random House.

United Nations, Department of Economic and Social Affairs, Population Division (2011) New York: World Population Prospects: The 2010 Revision, Volume 1. Retrieved July 15, 2013 from http://esa.un.org/unpd/wpp/Documentation/pdf/WPP2010_Volume-I_Comprehensive-Tables.pdf

World Health Organization (2002) Active Ageing: A Policy Framework. Retrieved July 15, 2013 from http://www.who.int/ageing/publications/active_ageing/en/index.html.

IV.4.5

Networks on community–university engagement in Asia and the Pacific

ASEAN University Network (AUN)

SECRETARIAT: Bangkok (Thailand).
INSTITUTION: Chulalongkorn University.
WEBSITE: http://www.aunsec.org/news/index.php (accessed 4 March 2013).
MEMBERS: 27 (as of 14 March 2013).

The general objective of the AUN is to strengthen the existing network of cooperation among universities in the Association of Southeast Asian Nations (ASEAN) by promoting collaborative study and research programmes on the priority areas identified by ASEAN. Its specific objectives are to promote cooperation and solidarity among scientists and scholars in the ASEAN member countries; to develop academic and professional human resources in the region; and to produce and transmit scientific and scholarly knowledge and information to achieve ASEAN's goals (text taken from http://www.aunsec.org/news/ourhistory.php [accessed 4 March 2013]).

AsiaEngage

SECRETARIAT: Selangor (Malaysia).
INSTITUTION: Universiti Kebangsaan Malaysia.
WEBSITE: http://www.asiaengage.org/ (accessed 3 December 2012).
MEMBERS: n/a.

AsiaEngage welcomes participation from private and public higher education institutions, industries, non-governmental organizations, foundations, chambers of commerce, research institutions, government agencies and other stakeholders with a commitment and passion for social responsibility and civic engagement for national and regional community development. It aims to create for its members opportunities to share innovative industry and community engagement practices, to develop regional capacity for impactful engagement, to forge collaborative industry and community-based research and to drive learning prospects as well as inspire youth volunteerism.

Asia-Pacific Community-University Engagement Network (APUCEN)

SECRETARIAT: Penang (Malaysia).
INSTITUTION: Universiti Sains Malaysia.
WEBSITE: http://apucen.usm.my/ (accessed 14 March 2013).
MEMBERS: 63 (as of 1 October 2013).

APUCEN is a regional network of higher education institutions concerned with promoting the cultural aspects of university-community engagement in a proactive, inclusive, holistic and participatory way. The network initiates collaborative efforts by leveraging each member institution's knowledge, resources and good practices to achieve mutually beneficial relationships with communities to address communities' issues and needs.

Society for Participatory Research in Asia (PRIA)

SECRETARIAT: New Delhi, India.
INSTITUTION: n/a.

WEBSITE: http://www.pria.org/ (accessed 3 June 2013).
MEMBERS: PRIA collaborates with a variety of partners and associates at the local, national and international levels.

PRIA is an international centre for learning and the promotion of participation and democratic governance. It facilitates the building of collectives and associations of citizens, enables civil society and convenes multi-stakeholder dialogues to promote citizen participation. Using the perspective that 'Knowledge is Power', PRIA builds capacities to use participatory research and training methodology and supports the enhancement of knowledge among civil society organizations, government institutions, private agencies and marginalized citizens within India and across the Asian region in Bangladesh, Nepal, Sri Lanka, Cambodia, and so on. Since 1982, it has acted as a node for the Asian Regional Network of Participatory Research and has facilitated several networks, including International Council for Adult Education and Asia South Pacific Association for Basic and Adult Education.

Service Learning Asia Network (SLAN)

SECRETARIAT: Hong Kong.
INSTITUTION: Lingnan University.
WEBSITE: http://www.ln.edu.hk/osl/slan/index.php (accessed 30 May 2013).
MEMBERS: 16 (as of 30 May 2013).

The purpose of SLAN is to promote the common interests and networks of student exchanges, faculty research, curriculum development and programme evaluation among colleges and universities interested in service-learning in Asia. SLAN members share ideas about the development of service-learning in the region and have united together to encourage cross-national collaborations (text taken from http://www.ln.edu.hk/osl/slan/about.php [accessed 30 May 2013]).

IV.4.6

Good Practices

IMU Cares Programme, International Medical University (Malaysia)

The Kampung Angkat Project, or Village Adoption Project, is part of the International Medical University (IMU) community social responsibility approach under the banner of 'IMU Cares'. The project won first place in the MacJannet Prize in 2013, organized by the Talloires Network, because of its strong university–community engagement. The University has adopted a village comprising 500, mainly indigenous, people of the Tenum ethnic group, 50% of whom are under 12 years of age, who live

with limited electricity and running water, with the nearest health clinic 20 km away.

In addressing the need of the health and social issues in the village, the University has sent medical and nursing undergraduate students to practise their knowledge and clinical skills to serve the village. The villagers have benefited from the presence of IMU students in terms of regular free health checks and health education, the treatment of minor ailments, the facilitation of referrals to appropriate health centres outside the village and the provision of free spectacles for visually impaired villagers. Students have learnt a lot through serving the villagers and have organized regular programmes with support from both the University and various governmental agencies.

See http://imunews.imu.edu.my/index.php/latest-news/imu-cares/adopted-communities/ for more information.

Service-learning Research Scheme, Lingnan University (Hong Kong)

Lingnan University is the only higher education institution to promote liberal arts education in Hong Kong. It was also the first university in Asia to launch the Service-Learning Research Scheme (SLRS) in 2004, and then established the Office of Service-Learning (OSL) in 2006, echoing the University's motto – 'Education for Service'. The OSL plays a vital role in collaborating with other academic departments to offer a real-life opportunity for students to apply the knowledge and skills that they have gained from coursework in the community, and to integrate useful knowledge with practice.

In the fast-paced modern city of Hong Kong, where people are becoming more apathetic towards public affairs, SLRS takes up its mission to cultivate social awareness and responsibility in young people. It strives to engage students from all disciplines to understand social issues not just in terms of textbook learning, but also from their experience serving the community. With SLRS fully embedded in credit-bearing courses, students work closely with community partners to design and implement service projects that address urgent needs in Hong Kong, namely poverty and housing, health and ageing, and sustainable development. Academic knowledge is then translated into quality service through students' active engagement, which creates a profound, mutually beneficial bond between the University and the community.

From 2006 to 2013, over 3,000 students have participated in over 300 service-learning projects under the SLRS scheme, contributing 85,000 service hours to over 25,500 people. Over the years, students have organized many educational or empowerment programmes for elderly individuals, low-income families, members of ethnic minorities, new immigrants, those with disabilities, teenagers and children; have drafted and implemented business plans for social enterprises; have conducted surveys and research on various topics; have taped promotion videos for non-governmental organizations; and have completed oral history writing projects for elderly people, historical heritage and the period of the SARS virus.

See http://www.ln.edu.hk/osl/ for more details.

Collaborative Campaign to End Female Foeticide and Sex-selective Abortion in Haryana (India)

The Indian constitution guarantees to every citizen the fundamental right to equality and ensures that every individual lives a life free from any discrimination based on caste, class, religion and sex. However, despite these constitutional assurances and guarantees, discrimination against women and girls continues unabated in every sphere of life, both public and private. This includes domestic violence, dowry deaths, sexual harassment and rape, kidnapping, witch-hunting and burning, trafficking and forced prostitution, and acid-burning – with the violence more pronounced in times of conflict and war.

The factors contributing to gender-based violence are varied and often deep-rooted, and this also applies to sex-selective practices of violence against girls. The factors are closely linked to social and cultural attitudes. It is often perceived that gender discrimination takes several forms among marginalized and disadvantaged communities; however, it has been observed that this particular form of violence is most dominant among the wealthy, educated and elite in society. Statistics show that the richer the state, the lower the proportion of women and girls – Punjab, Haryana and Delhi are clear proof of this reality.

The Indian government has taken measures to curb this atrocity through the Pre-Conception and Pre-Natal Diagnostic Techniques Act: 'There are clear correlations between the proliferation of sex determination tests, increase in sex selective abortions and decline in sex ratio, with urban areas showing a sharper drop in the sex ratio than rural areas'. Since the implementation of the Act, three million fewer female children than expected have been born, with one million doctors standing accused and one having been convicted of violating the Act.

The Society for Participatory Research in Asia (PRIA) has played a lead role in the programme due to its presence in the state of Haryana since 1996. It has built up a strong network and linkages with a range of groups and bodies from grassroots level up to the legal and statutory bodies of the district administration and academic institutions. The issue of sex-selective abortion has been taken up in a campaign to raise awareness and sensitize society to this critical issue that threatens the right of women to equality and even life. PRIA has worked very closely with the media as well as with local health workers and women citizen leaders in order to highlight this issue and monitor the steps being taken to reduce the incidence of female foeticide.

Over the period 2005–2007, PRIA (see www.pria.org) has partnered with twelve postgraduate colleges for women in the province and with the State Training Institute to provide capacity-building for the gender focal points of these institutes. The students, staff and faculty of the academic institutions have also been sensitized on this issue so they can understand their responsibility and the potential roles they can play in the prevention of female foeticide. As a result, they have organized activities and programmes related to the prevention of female foeticide with the students and staff of their colleges, as well as for communities within their vicinity.

IV.5

KNOWLEDGE, ENGAGEMENT AND HIGHER EDUCATION IN EUROPE

*Paul Benneworth and
Michael Osborne*

While European universities have much to offer European society in the field of community engagement, there is an urgent challenge to improve their current performance. A great deal is demanded across all walks of society for the knowledge emanating from universities, and for the exchange and co-production of knowledge with universities, and a failure to respond will undermine popular support for the sector. University work in engagement occurs against a range of competing forces, including modernization, internationalization and budget cuts. As a consequence, universities are faced with having to make strategic choices and are being overloaded with missions; seemingly less important missions risk becoming peripheral within this scenario.

Nonetheless, there is much that is outstanding in European universities in terms of community engagement, and in this chapter we provide a historical and contemporary background as well as many examples of exemplary practice. Covering a territory within which there are so many countries, and indeed regions, with distinct policies and practices is a challenge, and much has inevitably been omitted. That being said, we believe that, in most societies, the community engagement of universities in Europe is still at an early, peripheral phase, and the central challenge is in placing it at the heart of university life.

SOCIETAL ENGAGEMENT IN EUROPE

European universities have been inextricably tied up with their host societies since their foundation, and universities' institutions and ideas have evolved along with their host societies. Universities have always faced a dependency on sponsors, which has influenced their relationships with society. As Biggar (2010, p. 77) notes:

> Right from their medieval beginnings, [universities] have served private purposes and practical public purposes as well as the sheer *amor scientiae* ['knowledge for knowledge's sake'] … popes and bishops needed educated pastors and they and kings needed educated administrators and lawyers capable of developing and embedding national systems.

The scope and scale of engagement has subsequently increased from producing elites to working closely with firms and citizens,

TABLE IV.5.1
Universities between autonomy and dependency – a historical perspective

Social change	Sponsor urgent desire	'Idea' of a university	University societal engagement
Agricultural revolution	Reproducing religious administrators	Cloister (11th-century Italy)	Establishment religious elites
Emergence of nobility	Educating loyal administrators for courtly life	Free cloister (12th-century France)	Religious elites, both establishment and dissenting
Urbanization	Educated administrative elite to manage trade	Catholic University of Leuven (15th century)	Temporal elites and regulators
Sustaining national communities	Validating the state by imagining the nation	Newman's idea (from 17th century onwards)	National cultural elites 'imagining' the nation
Creating technical elite	Creating a technical elite alongside the administrative elite	Humboldtian (19th-century Germany)	Industrial elites overseeing national industrialization projects
Promoting progress	Creating economically useful knowledge	Land grant universities (19th–20th-century USA)	Mass industrial expansion through extension
Supporting democracy	Creating elites for non-traditional societal groups	Dutch Catholic Universities (20th-century Netherlands)	Political elites leading/underpinning corporatist settlements
Deliberative democracy	Equipping citizens with knowledge to function in a mass democracy	Robbins era plate glass universities (1960s UK)	Mass democratic expansion and participation

Source: Pinheiro et al. (2012).

as universities have developed relationships with and duties to religious powers, temporal authorities, cultural communities, industry and latterly civic society. This evolution is summarized in Table IV.5.1.

Universities' contributions to social progress have shaped their evolution. Some engagements have long-standing links with social movements including European popular education in the late 19th century (Steele, 2007). Continuing education brought knowledge to excluded groups (at that time, the working classes and women), providing 'enlightenment' of the masses. This emphasis on liberal adult education, based on a model of knowledge transfer from the elite to the masses, rather than on a co-production of knowledge, has contributed to the decline of continuing education in the 21st century (Osborne and Thomas, 2003).

This has partly been functional, with universities becoming part of the 'establishment' through their relations to their patrons (Daalder and Shils, 1982). But universities' engagement with marginal communities has also driven experimental practices that have changed society. Cambridge University was formed when a group Oxford scholars left dissatisfied by the religious restrictions they faced. The VU University Amsterdam was formed by orthodox Calvinists facing discrimination from the Lutheran mainstream, so that they could educate their future leaders. The Sorbonne in Paris and the Maagdenhuis in Amsterdam were flashpoints for strikes and wider social unrest driven by growing social tensions in the late 1960s regarding the closed nature of post-war society (Daalder and Shils, 1982). These struggles left us with several essential engagement repertoires such as science shops or community engagement (Gnaiger and Martin, 2001).

APPROACHES TO ENGAGEMENT WITHIN EUROPE

Contemporary university engagement in Europe began with the late 1960s 'democratic turn', in which Western European universities became highly engaged with society in many different ways and by many different mechanisms. Alongside the 1970s' general pessimism, the 'spirit of 1968' engendered much grassroots activism, this positivity driving many different kinds of innovative university engagement activity, exemplified by the Netherlands' science shops (Mulder et al., 2001), to activism and community work, through continuing and worker education, to policy advice and business consultancy. The early 1980s' report from the Centre for Educational Research and Innovation (CERI) high-

lighted the variety of institutional approaches to community engagement; CERI's typology (Table IV.5.2) remains useful for understanding those activities.

TABLE IV.5.2 University engagement with societal collectives	
Way of providing service	**Mechanism for delivering service**
University puts facilities at the disposal of the community	Use of equipment, premises and laboratories Use of teachers and students to make direct contribution Drawing on the community in delivering occupational training
Execution of orders placed by community	Offering training as occupational, continuing education or cultural University receives a payment from community for delivery of a service A near private contract between the buyer and the vendor
Analysis of needs of community	The university comes into the community as an outside expert The university provides services for the community with some reference to an 'order' by the community
Analysis of problems at request of community	University engages at community request in developing solutions University has the autonomy and freedom to suggest a range of solutions away from overarching pressure
University delivers a solution on behalf of the community	The university delivers a service for the community which is compatible with its institutional status
Source: Benneworth et al. (2013) after CERI (1982).	

CERI reported the tendencies of universities to work with nearby communities, whether based on a proximity that was geographical, ethical (for example, a common confessional position) or mission-based (for example, businesses). The report presented the best practices of university engagement, including KU Leuven R&D and the North East London Polytechnic Company. Different practical examples of institutional arrangements were presented for promoting university–business engagement, urban regeneration and community development. However, all approaches implied that public engagement was an adjunct activity to the universities' core activities, within the 'development periphery' (Clark, 1998).

From the 1980s onwards, European higher education (HE) was increasingly centralized through strategic modernization, with payment-by-results and new managerial autonomy introduced to improve the productivity and efficiency of public spending (Kickert, 1995). This profoundly affected relationships between universities and society by:

- framing universities' activities' value in cash terms;
- ranking different kinds of university activities on their strategic importance;
- encouraging universities to focus on only a few strategically important activities.

Societal engagement is increasingly managed in exclusively financial terms as a 'third mission' at a time when national HE systems face European Union (EU) pressure to prioritize the reform of teaching and research. Public engagement activities with income-generation potential (primarily business engagement) have become more important, marginalizing other engagement activities. Benneworth and Humphrey (2013, p. 182) characterize this effect in Scotland thus:

> Community engagement was based on existing activities, (continuing professional development, volunteering, widening access) rather than culturally or structurally embedded, activities that were marginal or existed to support 'core university businesses'. Research tended to be project-based and reliant on relentless income generation. 'Communities' were often restrictively defined as professional bodies, the voluntary and community sector and other organised stakeholders (companies, local authorities, NHS, Police).

In former Eastern Bloc countries, scientific academies enjoyed a degree of natural freedom from their important role in (re-)producing the cultures and narratives of national elites. However, the power of university professors was not always dependent on party structures, and therefore they were not always enthusiastic proponents of communism, representing an intelligentsia opposed to Soviet domination (Connolly, 2000). Student mobilization was an important part of power in these socialist regimes and did not always function predictably: while Polish and Czechoslovakian students opposed the socialist regime, East German students were as late as 1989 strongly supportive of it. Following a period of transition, public Eastern European universities were able to adopt very Humboldtian postures, while a huge private HE sector emerged based on immediately marketable skills. From the late 1990s, national reform efforts focused on compatibility with the Bologna Process and the European Research Area, leaving little space to develop distinctive post-socialist approaches to community–university engagement.

There is also a strong tradition of engagement in southern and Mediterranean European countries,[1] most clearly in Spain, where, in 1898, the University of Oveido adopted the proposal of *extensión universiteria*. What began as bringing community education to local industrial populations quickly moved towards addressing the atrocious living conditions of these communities. The successes of the 'Oviedo Group' led to similar efforts by the Universities of Salamanca, Seville, Valencia, Zaragoza and Santander, using HE as a progressive force in industrial communities in the next 35 years. Civil war and dictatorship halted this as universities were integrated into a single bureaucratic structure. Following the restoration of democracy, universities acquired a new societal role in decentralizing power to civil society institutions. Spanish HE reforms in a 2001 Act gave universities a substantive public and community role, including cultural enhancement, supporting regional cultural development and diffusing university values and cultures.

Looking back three decades, where the situation set out by CERI in 1982 is no longer salient for Europe is in its emphasis on citizens rather than consumers. The CERI report saw business and societal engagement as two comparable elements by which universities fulfilled their societal compacts. What has happened in that intervening period in Europe has been a massive expansion of the emphasis that all stakeholders have placed on business engagement (Zomer and Benneworth, 2011). This has been driven by the increasing dominance in Europe of the innovation imperative, a belief that as economic development depends on innovation, public expenditure should be increasingly managed to functionally drive innovation activities.

This has dominated consideration of the 'third mission' and, perhaps unsurprisingly, has seen business engagement prioritized over more diverse kinds of social engagement. Less visible has been a formalization of social engagement activities, with an increasing emphasis on working through formal, contractual relationships, often with public sector groups, this coming at the expense of less-well organized and informal community groups. The net results of these shifts has been that societal engagement either remains voluntary (in those systems that retain a high degree of academic autonomy) or has become increasingly marginalized (in those systems in which there has been a shift to managerial autonomy).

INSTITUTIONAL STRUCTURES SUPPORTING COMMUNITY ENGAGEMENT

Insofar as it is possible to talk about a European engagement tradition, it is best to talk about an informal tradition (Teichler, 1991; Schütze, 2010), that is extremely pluriform and defies simple characterization. Even in less centrally regulated systems, such as the pre-1980s UK, many activities were carried out with a sense of 'detached benevolence' (Benneworth, 2013) rather than being closely tailored to the needs and demands of external groups. In Europe, service-learning is less advanced than it is in the USA, notwithstanding programmes such as the Community-University Partnership Programme (Hart et al., 2007). The Organisation for Economic Cooperation and Development (OECD) CERI report highlighted the problems and tensions that this relative informality brought for the societal role of European universities:

> [The] question of a university's society function in the very broadest sense of the term … includes not only the development of access to qualifications, but the production of knowledge and the social significance of that knowledge. It also involves a change in the sharing of responsibility for the development of knowledge and teaching… If the university is to be effectively integrated into the community, it must no longer concern only those who attend the university, namely the teachers and the students. It should be possible to pass on one's skills without being a teacher and to receive training without being a student. (CERI, 1982, p. 13)

CERI identified many ways by which universities met societal needs but where the university and not the community often chose which activities were provided. The key challenge since then has been to integrate external stakeholders into university engagement activities, allowing these communities a right to co-determine how universities make their knowledge available to society. CERI failed to anticipate the change in relationship with the State from individuals being 'citizens' to being 'consumers'. CERI envisaged that business and societal engagement would be comparable elements but failed to foresee the belief that public expenditure should be managed to drive innovation (Kenway et al., 2012).

The emphasis placed by all European HE stakeholders on business engagement has expanded massively (Zomer and Benneworth, 2011) over more diverse social engagement. The formalization of social engagement activities has increased, favouring formal, contractual relationships with public sector groups over those with less-well-organized community groups. The net result has been that societal engagement has remained voluntary (in systems with high academic autonomy) or has become increasingly marginalized (in systems with managerial autonomy).

REGULATORY FRAMEWORKS ENCOURAGING COMMUNITY–UNIVERSITY ENGAGEMENT

Community engagement activities across European universities tend to be short-lived, with university leaders having difficulty in supporting them in the face of other more urgent pressures. This makes it important to develop resources for institutional leaders (Robinson et al., 2012), including indicators for engagement, benchmarking of community engagement, development of classifications of universities including engagement, and collective organizations such as the Global University Network for Innovation (GUNi) promoting community engagement (Conway et al., 2009; Benneworth, 2013).

Societal engagement remains implicitly important to universities today. A diversity of universities' societal missions – in contrast to their consensus around teaching and research – means that these are much less prescribed by statute than are teaching and research activities. The regulatory framework – legislation, regulation, policy, governance, finance and funding – influences institutional behaviour. Some European HE systems are naturally structurally more diverse in terms of missions and regional forms, and have different archetypes as social and economic change demands new university tasks (CEDEFOP, 2008; UNESCO, 2011).

Some of these regulatory frameworks are pan-European. Financial support for research (for example, the European Seventh Framework Programme's Science in Society strand) provides direct opportunities for a collaboration between researchers and civil society. Since 2009, this strand's 'Structuring Public Engagement in Research' has funded projects developing Mobilisation and Mutual Learning Action Plans on Societal Challenges in 2011 (European Commission, undated). Funding for three years brings researchers and a wider constellation of societal actors together to create a plan for a constructive dialogue between science and society around societal challenges, with nine consortia receiving funding in the first three rounds. In 2013, six grand challenges were targeted, namely infectious diseases, assessments of sustainable innovation, water, integrated urban development, the internet and society, and ethics assessment.

The majority of regulatory incentives are national or regional through relevant legislation, regulation and funding provision. These areas are not always equally developed – while the Netherlands, Finland and Sweden give HE institutions (HEIs) clear legal duties, they are weakly implemented financially. In contrast, in the UK, where there is no formal legal duty for engagement of universities, substantial funding has been allocated to universities for their engagement plans and, from 2014, with the Research Excellence Framework (REF), the impact of their research. France provides an example of a system with both strong duties on universities to engage as well as the relevant resources to deliver that engagement.

The Netherlands legally mandates universities' societal roles: the 1992 Higher Education Law gives universities and universities of applied sciences the mission of making their knowledge available for society (Benneworth et al., 2013; for Sweden, see Armbruster-Domeyer, 2011). But there is no funding stream for societal engagement as there has been for technology transfer activities. The net effect has been a huge amount of activity but a lack of extensive coordination, as for example in the European Higher Education and Research Areas.

Other countries also require HEIs to engage with society: Finnish universities have 'performance contracts' with the Ministry of Education and Culture, and universities have a responsibility to regional stakeholders defined as knowledge transfer aligned to regionally defined needs (Lester and Sotarauta, 2007). Within the university 'steering system', regional/local tasks fall under 'soft steering' and 'steering by information', and no indicators or results are specified in performance contracts. Universities decide their own third mission approach: some universities prioritize regional and local tasks (for example, the University of Lapland and the University of Eastern Finland), while others emphasize national or international targets.

Sweden has no financial incentives, but the Swedish Higher Education Act (1997) legally obliges universities to interact with society. This leaves room to interpret the third mission broadly from educational outreach to technology. National policy and legislation has, however, been implemented in a weak 'top-down' approach (Brundenius et al., 2011). Some institutions choose a strong approach: Mälardalen University College collaborates with several local municipalities in a formalized partnership called the *Samhällskontraktet* (Social Contract), and Karlstad University, Luleå Technical University, the University of Gothenburg and Linnæus University have similar constructions. Such work rarely involves the whole university, while collaborative action plans have little traction in university policies.

The UK by contrast has little relevant legislation as UK universities are autonomous organizations part-funded by the State to drive desired behaviours including societal engagement. One of the principal metrics used by UK funding councils to measure 'engagement' is success in recruiting from socially disadvantaged groups ('widening participation'). This has increased participation rates, although not necessarily from previously excluded communities (Osborne and Houston, 2012). Similar schemes have incentivized universities to engage with their regions or business, such as England's Higher Education Innovation Fund, a metric-based reward system stimulating a broad range of knowledge exchange activities including regional consortia. Funding has remained modest compared with teaching and research, and institutional responses were vertically differentiated: elite institutions remained aloof while more locally oriented universities engaged with non-traditional students and businesses. The 2014 REF introduced an impact element into research evaluations, partly scoring on the impacts of the research on culture, creativity and society, but the effect of the REF on public and community (as opposed to business and policy) engagement remains to be seen. One high-profile UK example is the Beacons for Public Engagement initiative, six university-based centres across the UK funded by UK Funding and Research Councils and the Wellcome Trust (see the National Co-ordinating Centre for Public Engagement homepage at http://www.publicengagement.ac.uk).

France is a clear example of both strong legislation and significant financial rewards. A range of decrees and laws mandate French universities, with associated funding at national and regional level, to engage with various communities, including working adults, the unemployed, socially excluded young people and those with disabilities. The principal emphasis has been on improving access, including university continuing education regulations permitting adult progression to higher level lifelong learning, formalized in the 2007 Law of University Responsibilities and Freedoms (the 'LRU Law'). Most well-known internationally is the Recognition of Prior Learning system, initiated by a 1985 decree and extended in 2002, which enables individuals to claim credit up to doctoral level based on their professional (paid/unpaid) experience, including in non-profit-making associations and trade unions. This has obliged many French universities to rethink their social role, with a considerable impact on academic practice.

While regulatory frameworks are vital, it is inevitable that, in the plurality of legislative models found across the countries of Europe, engagement is a choice rather than a compulsion, and that choice is often linked to the synergy that engagement has with traditional missions of teaching and research. In the next section, we will provide a typology demonstrating how that integration can come about, with some exemplars.

ARCHETYPAL PROJECTS AND ACTIVITIES FOR UNIVERSITY ENGAGEMENT

Universities respond to this highly differentiated regulatory engagement framework in a variegated manner. With few formally managed duties and responsibilities, there are few incentives for universities to institutionalize engagement. Although structures such as technology transfer offices have become pervasive (Wink, 2004), that has been much rarer for community engagement structures (Robinson et al., 2012; Powell and Dayson, 2013). Similarly units promoting widening participation (UK) or validating prior experience (France) remain peripheral to core HEI infrastructures. The typical European picture is of much activity, but greatly fragmented without overall institutional coordination.

Arguably, massification means that universities are having a greater impact on societal activity than ever before. The sector is incredibly innovative – with new kinds of engagement (Science Slam) and engagement theories (Living Laboratories and Social Innovation) emerging from universities. However, European policy-makers have had difficulty finding ways to place this university engagement with society at the heart of HE missions. Notwithstanding their lack of political traction, many good practice examples can be found across European universities, although the general peripherality of societal engagement for universities makes creating effective community engagement extremely time-consuming and place-specific.

AN OVERVIEW OF COMMUNITY–UNIVERSITY ENGAGEMENT

One way to classify university engagement is 'modes of delivery', distinguishing teaching, research, knowledge exchange and service-learning. These various kinds of potential community–university engagement are shown in Table IV.5.3 (Benneworth et al., 2009; Benneworth, 2013). Most concrete engagement initiatives have multiple aims, some covering all of these categories and involving different kinds of university activity together. Science shops include both service-learning and teaching, and may also bring elements of knowledge exchange and in some cases even research.

The precise mix of activities is in some cases driven by the universities' own supply wishes, while at the other end of this continuum are activities that are collaborative and responsive to community demands.

TABLE IV.5.3	
A typology of different kinds of university engagement activity	
Mode	**Main areas of engagement activity**
Research	Collaborative research projects
	Research projects involving co-creation
	Research commissioned by hard-to-reach groups
	Research *on* these groups then fed back
Knowledge exchange	Consultancy for hard-to-reach group as a client
	Public funded knowledge exchange projects
	Capacity building between hard-to-reach groups
	Knowledge exchange through student 'consultancy'
	Promoting public understanding and media
Service	Making university assets and services open
	Encouraging hard-to-reach groups to use assets
	Making an intellectual contribution as 'expert'
	Contributing to the civic life of the region
Teaching	Teaching appropriate engagement practices
	Practical education for citizenship
	Public lectures and seminar series
	CPD for hard-to-reach groups
	Adult and lifelong learning
Source: Benneworth et al., 2009, in Benneworth et al. (2013).	

Service-learning – taking students into communities – is less prevalent in Europe than North America, although there is a European Service-Learning Association. A recent European Commission-funded project, VALUE (Volunteering and Lifelong Learning in Universities in Europe; http://www.valuenetwork.org.uk), provides a good overview of activity across 12 countries. The case of Leuphana University (Germany) exemplifies how volunteering and service are integrally embedded into the curriculum; Reinmuth et al. (2007) provide further illustrations from Germany. Other universities such as the National University of Ireland (Galway) are also explicit about volunteering and service – its Community Knowledge Initiative allows students to obtain credit for service learning.

Science shops, first established in Europe in the 1970s in the Netherlands, are a means for a university (or non-governmental organization) to provide participatory research support to civil society groups normally excluded from specialist knowledge. Having spread internationally, they are linked through the Living Knowledge Network in Bonn, Germany. Their importance is illustrated by the considerable funding provided by the European Seventh Framework Programme for the Public Engagement with Research and Research Engagement with Society (PERARES) project. This project, coordinated by the University of Groningen Science Shop, 'aims to strengthen public engagement in research through involving researchers and Civil Society Organizations (CSOs) in the formulation of research agendas and the research process' (PERARES, 2013) and looks at 26 best-practice European science shops.

Validation of informal and non-formal learning (VNIL) provides arguably the best example of ascribing value to knowledge developed in community settings that may challenge university monopolies as the sites of knowledge production. This field has exercised the European Commission in the past decade with an emphasis on employability, with the Malta Qualifications Council (see http://www.ncfhe.org.mt/), among many such European bodies, speaking of VNIL's benefits for third-sector and voluntary organizations.

OUR CLASSIFICATION FRAMEWORK FOR COMMUNITY–UNIVERSITY ENGAGEMENT

The following sections document a range of examples of good practice in engagement that are innovative, sustainable and provide lessons for others seeking to engage. Some are drawn from recent work within the Pascal Universities Region Engagement project (Duke et al., 2013), which mapped HEI engagement systems at city and regional level in 11 European localities covering Finland, Hungary, Italy, Norway, Sweden and the UK, using a framework developed by Charles et al. (2010; following Charles and Benneworth, 2002).[2]

Societal engagement can be categorized as being directed towards economic, societal, cultural or environmental development (cf. OECD, 2007), very broad distinctions illustrating principal purposes, but in practice, engagement activities may cover multiple categories. Brennan et al. (2006) provide a framework to analyse how such work can be analysed in relation to communities that have been *disadvantaged*[3] in relation to their HE access. They refer to local and regional partnership working, cultural presence, civic roles and the provision of employment opportunities by universities. Kaunas University of Technology in Lithuania provides an all-embracing example in supporting its city to develop itself into a Learning City, covering *de facto* all potential aspects of engagement. Here the university and municipality have sought to develop

partnerships and citizens' networks to stimulate formal and non-formal learning on a city-wide basis (Eckert et al., 2012).

Another interesting example demonstrating engagement across the economic, social, cultural and environmental is the South Transdanubia region (Hungary). Community activists, including the Mayor of Karasz, work with HE in various activities seeking both to restore traditions and to generate income. Some activists have visiting faculty appointments at the University of Pécs, enabling student work experience and research project placement in the villages. They draw on university expertise, mainly from Pécs but also from the University of Kaposvár (forestry management) and two other universities with relevant specialisms, particularly in mycology. The village fruit-juicing facilities – a cooperative-style multi-supplier activity that spreads the benefit widely – even include apples from the University of Kaposvár in their mix; part of the value-added finished product is marketed in places such as Budapest.

ECONOMIC PARTNERSHIP

Universities' contributions to economic development is usually understood in terms of high-technology businesses and job creation, but these impacts often bypass excluded communities. European universities face the resultant tensions between their high-technology footprints and the ordinary economic needs of their neighbouring communities, and some have developed modes of economic engagement relevant to these ordinary communities. A key problem facing excluded communities is that of capital flight and disinvestment, so universities can make key contributions by creating new facilities in poorer areas, demand for transport and retail services of more general local benefit.

Liverpool Hope University (UK) created a new campus in England's poorest ward, Everton, with a cultural centre including arts incubator units; this campus anchors other public sector investment, including the Liverpool Philharmonic Orchestra. Another economic development problem for excluded communities is access to credit, with doorstep lending and payday loans financially burdening already indigent communities; Salford University has worked with local groups to create Moneyline, a set of community finance initiatives bringing access to credit back to ten inner city communities in England's north west (Powell and Dayson, 2013).

Universities as a whole or departmental/ faculty units may contribute directly to community partnerships or be major stakeholders in community development projects, contributing to regeneration, business development and environmental sustainability. In Helsinki (Finland), the Active Life Village is sponsored by the City of Espoo and the Laurea University of Applied Sciences with involvement from Aalto University of Technology, and service and technology companies. It supports new businesses drawing on technological innovation to provide new opportunities in the welfare sector.

Another area where universities and communities are working closely together is around creating and capitalizing on cultural assets, often supporting this with creating niche small and medium-sized enterprises in tourism and the environment, and meeting their training/development needs. Examples are:

- the University of Lecce, Puglia (Italy) – the regeneration of an abandoned factory in an urban area to make a major cultural centre;
- Buskerud University College in Buskerud County (Norway) mountain – eco-tourism;
- Mid Sweden University in Jämtland – tourism related to nature culture and indigenous peoples, local food, sport and adventure.

SOCIAL INCLUSION

Social exclusion involves individuals being systematically disadvantaged in ways that hinder their access to jobs, housing, transport, education and other services vital for participation in contemporary society (Benneworth et al., 2013). These barriers are often overlapping and self-reinforcing; university contributions to social inclusion are not just about opening education provision, but about making this sufficiently easy that people can benefit in practice. In Europe, this involves delivering education close to communities, and facilitating progression from basic to advanced educational levels. Different institutions have emphasized various dimensions, lifelong learning, learning in minority languages and flexible learning, alongside activities targeting other exclusion elements undermining participation in education, including health issues.

In Glasgow (UK), several universities have community outreach programmes encompassing the arts, culture, lifelong learning and work with poor communities. The Universities of Glasgow and Strathclyde have both made considerable provision in the liberal adult education tradition: the Senior Studies Institute at Strathclyde focuses on work with those in the 'third age', not only engaging older people through leisure courses, but also offering enhancing employment opportunities in later life (the Learning in Later Life programme). There is considerable activity across European universities in engaging with ageing

populations: a number of initiatives target in varying measure both improved labour market prospects and improved well-being. The Tertiary Higher Education for People in Mid-life Project provides cognate case studies from the Czech Republic, Germany, Hungary, Italy, the Netherlands, Spain and the UK (Krüger et al., 2014).

There is also work around health and well-being in ageing societies, with much university work inspired from a research perspective, but also integrating public engagement, as in the example of Newcastle University's Initiative on Changing Age in the UK (see http://www.ncl.ac.uk/changingage/). This programme seeks, through an engagement and education centre, to engage with voluntary sector agencies, facilitating consultation with communities around ageing and demography issues, and thereby engaging non-experts in shaping future research and policy-making.

Other targeted groups include ethnic minority groups, currently with a particular focus on the Roma people, lower socioeconomic class categories, women, those in remote regions and people with disabilities. A number of policy documents from the European Commission (EC), starting in 1991 with the *Memorandum on Higher Education in the European Community*, have emphasized the need for greater inclusiveness. This memorandum urged HEIs to widen access to higher qualifications, create opportunities for the updating and renewal of qualifications, increase preparatory courses and also do more to recognize prior learning and experience (EC, 1991). The main imperative is the need to support an increasingly knowledge-driven society, an argument that continues to resonate today.

The extent to which these various schemes for improvement are responsive to community demand and recognize communities' contribution to knowledge production is, however, debatable (Osborne, 2003). France's system of *validation d'acquis de l'expérience* (VAE) challenges what counts as valid knowledge, although ultimately HEIs still validate credits within the system. The national system provides many interesting cases, and particular institutions such as the Université des Sciences et Technologies de Lille (Lille1) are leaders in the field. Social and economic imperatives need not be contradictory: the VAE scheme encompasses both human and social capital facets, stimulating social inclusion by helping individuals improve their employability. While some commentators suggest that the scheme contains a paradox of objectives (Pouget and Figari, 2009), it is not unusual for programmes of access to focus on the improvement of individual economic prospects.

A linked notion is the recognition and exchange of indigenous knowledge that is unique to a particular culture or society (Warren, 1991) and which has been described as the social capital of the poor. Although much of the focus of debate on indigenous knowledge is not generally on Europe, we can find interesting engagements in countries such as Finland, for example at the Arctic Indigenous Peoples and Sami Research Office of the University of Lapland.

A final dimension is university involvement in community research. Spain is particularly strong in this with the Instituto Paulo Freire, a national community–university research network. This Institute supports activities in a number of Spanish universities, based on the critical pedagogy theories of Paulo Freire, and community–university participatory research is active in stimulating social engagement (Hall, 2011). In Barcelona, the Centre of Research in Theories and Practice that Overcome Inequalities is concerned with analysing social inequalities and with the consequent training needs.

Interesting cases are also found in Italy. Laura Saija (2013), for example, explains how substantial efforts by the University of Catania have contributed to driving out Mafia influence from a 1960s Sicilian new town, Librino, contributing in many ways to building a new democratic and participatory culture to replace the dominant patronage-based relationships.

CULTURE AND CREATIVITY

Universities are pipelines into other cultures in other times and places, providing lenses through which their host societies can understand these other situations and develop their own place in the world. This has not always been edifying, with universities and their scholars playing a role in some of the worst excesses of imperialism and colonialism. But universities have also been important in developing local cultures: sometimes new universities have been created explicitly to gain recognition for minority cultural groups. This activity has recently magnified in scope, partly with the explosion of 'popular culture', with universities both providing a lens to understand these cultural developments and equipping particular groups with the knowledge and tools to utilize that culture to benefit itself.

A key focus for many universities has been activities oriented towards creativity and the creative industries. These range from short courses oriented to particular interest groups, supporting the creative industries, making available cultural assets such as museums and galleries and research, development and infrastructure support linked to events on an international scale.

These activities may be facilitators of social inclusion for excluded groups, catalysts for innovation and significant elements of local, regional and even national economic development.

In Pécs, Hungary, the university has built upon the city's European Capital of Culture (ECoC) status in 2010 by offering provision linked to the wider region's multicultural heritage, including local Roma individuals being able to study in their mother tongue at the Department of Romology. The university has also created a cultural industries incubator at the Zsolnay ceramics factory, a prime objective of the ECoC: the Faculty of Arts and some departments of the Faculty of Humanities of the university are being installed in the incubator both to attract creative artists and to foster cultural tourism.

There are many other examples of universities contributing to cultural events. In the UK, the University of East London is adjacent to the 2012 Olympic Games site. The university is building on the Games' success by promoting public access to its facilities and its sports science courses, and is validating courses in sports and events management, exploiting its closeness to other large-scale cultural venues (the ExCel Exhibition Centre and the O2 Arena) and developing foundation degrees (short-cycle) in visitor management related to retail, exhibitions, tourism and hospitality. Similarly in Glasgow, the University of the West of Scotland is contributing to assessing the impact of the forthcoming 2014 Commonwealth Games on community development where students' service-learning offers a potential contributory mechanism.

SUSTAINABLE DEVELOPMENT

In contemporary Europe, the environmental costs of development are pushed onto the poorest communities that are least able to resist them (Davoudi and Brooks, 2012). Environmental justice is increasingly important for sustainable development – poor communities frequently disproportionately bear the pollution costs of urban transport systems, while at the same time, because of their limited access to transport services, they gain the lowest benefit from them. The greatest contribution that universities are making to sustainable development is therefore in terms of social and environmental justice, and fairness in the allocation of the costs and benefits of economic development. Universities are not often politically powerful actors able to change or challenge society's working; their most effective work comes in supporting grassroots mobilizations that challenge these environmental injustices.

A number of European universities have committed themselves strategically to promoting sustainable development, being active in and signatories to the Third Talloires Declaration, a set of commitments by university administrators to embed sustainable development in all their universities' activities. The Declaration evolved into the organization University Leaders for a Sustainable Future, although its spread has been less wide through Europe than other parts of the world. In the UK, a number of universities have committed themselves to a more practical sustainable development tool, the Universities that Count accreditation system, based on an index of environmental and social responsibility (ESR). This was promoted by Higher Education Funding Council for England, and a wide range of UK HEIs now follow the ESR monitoring activity to give their contribution to sustainable development a strategic focus.

The findings of Davoudi and Brooks formed part of the work of the Newcastle Fairness Commission, which was important in bringing into focus some of the injustices that exist but are often invisible or taken for granted in the distribution of environmental burdens and benefits in urban development. An important role played by universities in environmental justice is placing the demands of minority and excluded communities on wider agendas and forcing others to take notice. An obvious challenge for universities comes when this conflicts with their own corporate interests, for example around gentrification. Universities need to develop an effective ethical framework to ensure that their position as relatively strong, well-resourced actors with spatial interests does not come into conflict with their wider societal duties.

At the most basic level, much university work has focused on the universities' own management practices and on moving towards sustainable behaviour. The earlier work of GUNi notes that 'greening the campus' has been the main response in this area (Tilbury, 2012, p. 19). It is evident from earlier examples that much more than this is possible. Internal change is essential, and many practices are illustrative of what can be achieved, one example of note being the University of Plymouth (UK) with what it describes as a holistic model of change, the 4C model of Campus, Curriculum, Community and Culture.

The development of green skills has been noted in studies by CEDEFOP (2010) and the International Labour Organization (Srietska-Ilina et al., 2011) with many EU examples among the 21 country studies covering Denmark, Estonia, France, Germany, Spain and the UK. The regional government of the Ile-de-France illustrates concretely possible approaches that

can provide dialogue and action between researchers and communities in sustainable food production. The Partnerships of Institutions and Citizens for Research and Innovation was stimulated by the work of the Community-University Research Alliance to create collaborative projects between researchers and CSOs, and has sought to build an eco-region in this part of France. One subsidiary project involved developing new farming practices in managing and selecting wheat varieties for organic bread production (Gallet al., 2009).

STRATEGIES AND ACTIONS TO ADVANCE ENGAGEMENT IN EUROPE

The preceding section has told a story of engagement by European universities being an 'exceptional' activity, where a university group places additional effort into engaging with a public group to bring wider benefits from university knowledge. The challenge is bringing these activities away from universities' experimental peripheries and incorporating them into the heart of the 21st-century university, bringing various engagement projects out of their protective spaces nurtured by enthusiasts, exposing them to the reality of existence within universities. Any serious university engagement activity raises challenges and problems: contributing seriously to European society requires a commitment to address these tensions and face down interests challenged by engagement activity. In this section, we highlight some key tensions and pressures that universities experience when consolidating experimental engagement activities into holistic strategic management practices.

Universities can contribute to balancing knowledge asymmetries by mobilizing 'outsider' knowledges in peripheral communities. But this highlights the tension that the financialization of HE brings: when universities are steered through financial mechanisms, groups without financial resources have difficulty influencing strategic university decisions. The move from universal free HE to student fees and loans threatens to limit the participatory opportunities in HE to society's wealthy. With Europe undergoing financial austerity, budget cuts to universities might encourage a restriction of access to their knowledge to those able to pay. Emphasizing commercial outcomes for third mission activities can discourage community groups from working with universities – even universities' decisions on floorspace charging can drive out community groups and create additional wedges between universities and community groups.

Universities can be important in the thinking to renew society, with public intellectuals providing a useful reservoir of cultural capital contributing to civic reinvention and even resistance. But university academics also face pressure to focus on a handful of core activities that may restrict that wider public function. The relentless rise of the world-class university norm – placeless research excellence rather than community-based research relevance – represents a real threat to extending engagement. University research now focuses almost exclusively on winning research funding and on excellent publications than on making social contributions: contributing to the public intellectual realm is a second-class activity, one not valued by the universities. This risks universities abandoning their capacity to contribute to wider processes of collective reimagination and rethinking.

European universities are strong as meeting places of transcultural elite dialogue and understanding. Universities have long equipped societies with the intellectual tools to relate to other societies, and universities have been very effective in responding to challenges from fundamentalist ideologies or the rise of the so-called 'BRICs'. Universities remain marketplaces of ideas, and the European Research Area and Bologna Process have been very effective in promoting intercultural exchanges between academics and students. But the challenge in Europe is extending this from the metropolitan elite to a more demotic level. The metropolitan elite share common norms and behaviours with universities – universities are familiar to them. Bringing other kinds of community – with their own behaviours and values – into the university brings particular tensions and may conflict with university desires for universalism. But engaging in these conversations, for example around extreme right-wing nationalism, is vital for European societies, and universities have the opportunity to address the problems these communities may bring.

Universities have strong linkages with civil society, but current pressures risk universities facing a choice of ignoring civil society or treating it as a junior partner in the relationship. Engaging with a plurality of civil society interests generates conflicts and tensions with scientists' autonomy to choose their own research questions, particularly around controversial new technologies or where there are strong differences between public and private benefits. We have already seen civil society groups opposing university research into genetically modified crops because of dissatisfaction that they concentrate power unhelpfully in the hands of a few agrochemical firms. Facing such opposition, universities may restrict their engagement to those community groups who share university norms and interests. This risks confusing a general duty to support socioeconomic development with a more self-interested reading that community engagement should directly benefit the university. Although universities should engage with communities with which they share values, restricting engagement to those where there is a clear mutual benefit risks undermining universities' universality in their social mission.

CONCLUSIONS AND FINAL COMMENTS

Universities have a great deal to offer European society in terms of their engagement contributions. European universities face an urgent challenge to improve their engagement – there is great demand across society for their knowledge, and a failure to respond will undermine popular support for universities. But this is happening against a background of a range of pressures, including modernization, internationalization and budget cuts, that drive in the opposite direction. Universities are faced with having to make strategic choices and being overloaded with missions – less important missions risk becoming peripheral within universities.

Community engagement is still at an early, peripheral phase in many European universities, and the central challenge is in placing it at the heart of university life. Anyone reading the CERI report in 1982 would be surprised to see the extent to which only one element of 'community' – business communities – has been embraced and normalized by universities. Europe must likewise normalize community–university engagement, a common-sense and taken-for-granted mission rather than a special, peripheral and experimental situation. But there remains the very real problem in mainstreaming these interesting and alluring experiments, incorporating them into the mainstream of universities as institutions, organizations, companies and networks, and consolidating them to change the very nature of European HE. Indeed, if Europe's universities fail to heed this agenda and follow the seductions of ignoring the wider public, this risks undercutting the social compact by which Europe's publics provide privileged positions for its universities.

Sophisticated demands and pressures from civil society are difficult for universities as responsible actors to reject and ignore in the long term, but in Europe's increasingly individualized and consumerist society, these signals and wishes risk being lost against the noise of markets, league tables, rankings and competition. Vital to this is creating a space within Europe's 'overloaded universities' for community engagement to become important to universities. Contrary to what is sometimes claimed, it is not enough for university leaders simply to declare that 'engagement matters' (Benneworth et al., 2013). Making engagement central to a university necessitates changes in its full portfolio of activities. When students must complete a community engagement project to graduate, all staff must accept that engagement matters, rather than some staff being enthusiastic where it is voluntary. Universities must build up their capacity to:

- deliver community engagement;
- accept community engagement;
- embed community engagement within core teaching and research activities;
- make and win the ethical case for engagement within universities.

This transformation process is a journey from superficial engagement to engagement lying at the heart of universities' essence. This is a long and hard journey, and universities urgently require encouragement and support from their stakeholders along the way. Universities' existing huge contribution to societal plurality and vitality through community engagement needs be credited and celebrated. Only if European governments (and the EC) prioritize community engagement will it ever become significant for universities. As European government becomes more specialized, technocratic and deracinated, Europe's universities need to get back to their roots, roots that lie in engaging with Europe's diverse publics. Governments need to drive universities to better engage, and universities should be vocal in demanding this from them. Only when this is achieved will government and universities work better together to meet societal needs and harness the power of universities' diverse knowledge bases to drive a sustainable and inclusive Europe.

NOTES

1 This paragraph draws very heavily on the written contribution of Paul Younger to Conway et al. (2009).
2 These eight domains are regional, human capital, social capital, business, sustainable, community and cultural development and institutional development.
3 As pointed out by Brennan et al. (2006, p. 5), '"Disadvantage" is a loaded term, assuming deficit in those to whom it is ascribed and advantage to participation in higher education, both of which can be critiqued.'

REFERENCES

Armbruster-Domeyer, H., in cooperation with Hermansson, K. and Modéer, C. (2011) *International Review, Analysis and Proposals on Indicators for Measuring Public Engagement*. VA Report 2011:2. Stockholm: Vetenskap & Allmänhet (Public & Science).

Benneworth, P. (2013) 'The evaluation of universities and their contributions to social exclusion'. In: Benneworth, P. (ed.) *University Engagement with Socially Excluded Communities*. Dordrecht: Springer, pp. 309–27.

Benneworth, P. and Humphrey, L. (2013) 'Universities' perspectives on community engagement'. In: Benneworth, P. (ed.) *University Engagement with Socially Excluded Communities*. Dordrecht: Springer, pp. 165–88.

Benneworth, P.S., Charles, D.R., Conway, C., Hodgson, C. and Humphrey, L. (2009) 'How the societal impact of universities can be improved both conceptually and practically'. In: *Sharing Research Agendas on Knowledge Systems: Final Research Proceedings*. Paris, France: UNESCO.

Benneworth, P., Charles, D.R., Hodgson, C. and Humphrey, L. (2013) 'The relationship of community engagement with universities' core missions'. In: Benneworth, P. (ed.) *University Engagement with Socially Excluded Communities*. Dordrecht: Springer, pp. 85–102.

Biggar, N. (2010) 'What are universities for?' *Standpoint*, 24, 76–9.

Brennan, J., Little, B. and Locke, W. (2006) *Higher Education's Effects on Disadvantaged Groups and Communities*. London: CHERI.

Brundenius, C., Göransson, B. and Ågren, J. (2011) 'The role of academic institutions in the national system of innovation and the debate in Sweden'. In: Brundenius, C. and Göransson, B., *Universities in Transition: The Changing Role and Challenges for Academic Institutions*. Ottawa: International Development Research Centre/Springer.

CEDEFOP (2008) *Future Skill Needs in Europe: Medium-term Forecast. Synthesis Report*. Retrieved September 2012 from http://www.cedefop.europa.eu/EN/Files/4078_en.pdf.

CEDEFOP (2010) *Skills for Green Jobs – European Synthesis Report*. Luxembourg: EC.

Centre for Educational Research and Innovation (1982) *The University and the Community: The Problems of Changing Relationships*. Paris: OECD-CERI.

Charles, D. and Benneworth, P. (2002) *Evaluating the Regional Contribution of an HEI: A Benchmarking Approach*. Bristol: Higher Education Funding Council for England.

Charles, D.R., Benneworth, P., Conway, C. and Humphrey, L. (2010) 'How to benchmark university–community interactions'. In: Inman, P. and Schütze, H.G. (eds) *The Community Engagement and Service Mission of Universities*. Leicester: NIACE.

Clark, B. (1998) *Creating Entrepreneurial Universities: Organizational Pathways of Transformation*. Oxford: Pergamon/IAU Press.

Connolly, J. (2000) *Captive University: The Sovietization of East German, Czech, and Polish Higher Education*. Chapel Hill, NC: UNC Press.

Conway, C., Benneworth, P., Humphrey, L. and Charles,

D. (2009) 'Review of University Engagement'. Paper prepared for Newcastle University PVC (Engagement), Newcastle-upon-Tyne.

Daalder, H. and Shils, E. (1982) *Universities, Politicians and Bureaucrats: Europe and the United States*. Cambridge: Cambridge University Press.

Davoudi, S. and Brooks, L. (2012) *Environmental Justice and the City*. Durham: Institute of Local Governance. Retrieved November 25, 2012 from http://www.ncl.ac.uk/socialrenewal/engagement/fairnesscommission/documents/environmental-justice-and-the-city.pdf.

Duke, C., Osborne, M. and Wilson, B. (2013) *A New Imperative: Regions and Higher Education in Difficult Times*. Manchester: Manchester University.

Eckert T., Preisinger-Kleine R., Fartusnic C. et al. (2012) *Quality in Developing Learning Cities and Regions: A Guide for Practitioners and Stakeholders*. Munich: University of Munich.

European Commission (1991) *Memorandum on Higher Education in the European Community*. Brussels: CEC.

European Commission (undated) *Mobilising and Mutual Learning Action Pla*ns. Retrieved September 2013 from http://ec.europa.eu/research/science-society/index.cfm?fuseaction=public.topic&id=1226

Gall, E., Millot, G. and Neubauer, C. (2009) *Participation of Civil Society Organisations in Research*. Retrieved February 22, 2013 from http://www.livingknowledge.org/livingknowledge/wp-content/uploads/2011/12/STACS_Final_Report-Partic.research.pdf.

Gnaiger, A. and Martin, E. (2001) *SCIPAS Report No. 1. Sci Shops: Operational Options*. Improving the Human Research Potential and the Socio-Economic Knowledge Base (IHP) STRATA Action. Utrecht: Science Shop for Biology, Utrecht University. Retrieved October 11, 2012 from http://www.livingknowledge.org/livingknowledge/wp-content/uploads/2012/02/wp1-so.pdf.

Hall, B.H. (2011) 'Towards a knowledge democracy movement: contemporary trends in community-university research partnerships'. *Rhizome Freirean*, 9. Retrieved September 2013 from http://www.rizoma-freireano.org/index.php/towards-a-knowledge-democracy-movement-contemporary-trends-in-community-university-research-partnerships--budd-l-hall.

Hart, A., Maddison, E. and Wolff, D. (2007) *Community-University Partnerships in Practice*. Leicester: NIACE.

Kenway, J., Bullen, E. and Robb, S. (2012) 'The knowledge economy, the techno-preneur and the problematic future of the university'. *Policy Futures in Education*, 2(2), 330–49.

Kickert, W. (1995) 'Steering at a distance: a new paradigm of public governance in Dutch higher education'. *Governance*, 8, 135–57.

Krüger, K., Duch, N., Parellada, M., Osborne, M., Mariani, M. and Jiménez, L. (2014) 'Social efficiency of TLL'. In: UIL, *The Role of Universities in Promoting Lifelong Learning*. Hamburg: UNESCO Institute for Lifelong Learning.

Lester, R. and Sotarauta, M. (eds) (2007) *Innovation, Universities and the Competitiveness of Regions*. Technology Review 214/2007. Helsinki: Tekes.

Mulder, H.A.J., Auf der Heyde, Th., Goffer, R. and Teodosiu, C. (2001) *Success and Failure in Starting Science Shops*. Improving the Human Research Potential and the Socio-Economic Knowledge Base (IHP) STRATA Action, Utrecht. Utrecht: Science Shop for Biology, Utrecht University. Retrieved October 16, 2012 from http://www.livingknowledge.org/livingknowledge/wp-content/uploads/2012/02/wp2-so.pdf.

OECD (2007) *Higher Education and Regions: Globally Competitive, Locally Engaged*. Paris: OECD.

Osborne, M. (2003) 'A European comparative analysis of policy and practice in widening participation to life-long learning'. *European Journal of Education*, 38(1), 5–24.

Osborne, M. and Thomas, E. (2003) *Lifelong Learning in a Changing Continent: Continuing Education in the Universities of Europe*. Leicester: National Institute of Adult Continuing Education.

Osborne, M. and Houston, M. (2012) 'United Kingdom – universities and lifelong learning in the UK – adults as losers, but who are the winners?' In: Slowey, M. and Schuetze, H. (eds) *Global Perspectives on HE and Lifelong Learners*. London: Routledge.

Pinheiro, R., Benneworth, P. and Jones, G.A. (2012) 'Beyond the Obvious: Tensions and Volitions Surrounding the Contributions of Universities to Regional Development and Innovation'. Presented to the 7th International Seminar on Regional Innovation Policies, Porto, Portugal, October 7–11, 2012.

Pouget, M. and Figari, G. (2009) '*Reconnaissance des acquis: queis processus de formalisation? Complexités et tensions*'. In: Lopez, L.M. and Crahay, M. (eds) *Evaluation en tension. Entre la régulation des spprentissages et le pilotage des systémes*. Brussels: De Broeck University.

Powell, J. and Dayson, K. (2013) 'Engagement and the idea of the civic university'. In: Benneworth, P. (ed.) *University Engagement with Socially Excluded Communities*. Dordrecht: Springer.

Public Engagement with Research and Research Engagement with Society (2013) 'PERARES'. Retrieved February 21, 2013 from http://www.livingknowledge.org/livingknowledge/perares.

Reinmuth, S., Sass, C.H. and Lauble, S. (2007) '*Die Idee des service learning*'. In: Baltes, A.M., Hofer, M. and Sliwka, A. (eds) *Studierende übernehmen Verantwortung – Service Learning an deutschen Universitäten*. Weinheim: Beltz.

Robinson, F., Zass-Ogilvie, I. and Hudson, R. (2012) *How Can Universities Support Disadvantaged Communities?* York: Joseph Rowntree Foundation.

Saija, L. (2013) '"Building" engagement into the fabric of the university'. In: Benneworth, P. (ed.), *University Engagement with Socially Excluded Communities*. Dordrecht: Springer, pp. 125–41.

Schütze, H. (2010) 'The "third mission" of universities: community engagement and service'. In: Inman, P. and Schütze, H.G. (eds) *The Community Engagement and Service Mission of Universities*. Leicester: NIACE.

Steele, T. (2007) *Knowledge is Power! The Rise and Fall of European Popular Education Movements 1848–1939*. Frankfurt: Peter Lang.

Strietska-Ilina, O., Hofmann, C., Durán Haro, M. and Jeon, S. (2011) *Skills for Green Jobs – A Global View*. Geneva: International Labour Organization.

Teichler, U. (1991) 'The Federal Republic of Germany'. In: Neave, G. and van Vught F.A. (eds) *Prometheus Bound: The Changing Relationship Between Government and Higher Education in Western Europe*. Oxford: Pergamon.

Tilbury, D. (2012) 'Higher education for sustainability: a global overview of commitment and progress'. In GUNi (ed.) *Higher Education in the World 4. Higher Education's Commitment to Sustainability: from Understanding to Action.* Basingstoke: Palgrave Macmillan.

UNESCO (2011) *Trends in Diversification of Post-Secondary Education.* Paris: UNESCO.

Universities that Count. *A Report on Benchmarking Environmental and Corporate Responsibility in Higher Education.* Retrieved September 2013 from http://www.eauc.org.uk/file_uploads/he_benchmarking_project_report.pdf.

Warren, D.M. (1991) *Using Indigenous Knowledge in Agri-cultural Development.* World Bank Discussion Paper No.127. Washington, DC: World Bank.

Wink, R. (ed.) (2004) *Academia-Business Links in UK and Germany: Policy Outcomes and Lessons Learnt.* Cheltenham: Edward Elgar.

Zomer, A. and Benneworth, P. (2011) 'The rise of the university's Third Mission'. In: Enders, J., de Boer, H.F. and Westerheijden, D. (eds) *Reform of Higher Education in Europe.* Rotterdam: Sense.

Inside View IV.5.1
Knowledge production, regional engagement and higher education in Poland

Marek Kwiek

While the policy discourse in Poland is already stressing the fundamental role of universities' regional engagement in research, it is hard to assess how long it will take to develop strong links between universities and their regions. The strongest links are clearly seen in the teaching dimension of regional engagement. Regional engagement in research is a much more distant goal, and the investment of more public resources in joint programmes for universities and companies, as well as major changes in current individual and institutional research assessment formulas and academic promotion requirements, are needed.

Recent reforms of Polish higher education and research systems (2008–2011) have been based on several assumptions. The first assumption is that higher education is increasingly conceived as a vehicle for economic development of the nation and of the region in whose social and economic fabric it is embedded (see OECD, 1999, 2000). The regional mission means opening up universities to the regions in which they are located, which may result in a wide range of interactions, from cultural to social to economic (Arbo and Benneworth, 2006). The fundamental role of knowledge production in the economic growth of knowledge-driven economies puts universities and the outcomes of their teaching and research increasingly in the public spotlight (Foray, 2006; Leydesdorff, 2006; Etzkowitz, 2008; Kwiek, 2013a).

The second assumption is that the 'economic relevance' of universities, directly or indirectly, links university activities with innovations in the private sector (Geiger and

Sà, 2011). Links between higher education and the economy are tightening throughout Europe. The third assumption is that teaching is expected to be more closely linked to the needs of the labour market, avoiding the mismatch between higher education offerings and labour market needs, and research is expected to be more easily commercialized.

In Poland, following the new law on higher education of March 2011, new mechanisms to link universities and their regions include state funding for university partnerships with businesses, especially through public and private science and technology parks, new incentives for universities' regional initiatives, including for new study programmes prepared with the assistance of local and regional companies, modified requirements for the academic career ladder, and increased cooperation with local industry in university governance, with new industry representatives on universities' (still optional) boards of trustees.

The level of university responsiveness to labour market needs in Poland is still low. The level of cooperation with the business sector is also low. As a ministerial report on the barriers of cooperation between research centres and companies stresses, Polish companies need to be made more aware of the possibilities associated with cooperating with universities: approximately 20% of companies did not know that that it was possible to cooperate with the academic community, and 40% of companies had never tried to get in touch with universities. In addition, 40% of surveyed companies did not know how to reach research centres that were potentially interested in the

commercialization of research. At the same time, surprisingly, almost half of the companies surveyed that had actually been in touch with scientists (45%) reported that the initiative for cooperation came from the scientists. Companies involved in partnerships with universities were generally satisfied; the effects of cooperation with scientists were rated as 'rather positive' by 51% and 'definitely positive' by 17% of respondents. Only 3% of surveyed companies provided a 'rather negative' or 'definitely negative' assessment of a university partnership (MNISW, 2006, pp. 4–10).

The linkages between Polish universities and their economic environments are, from a comparative international perspective, weak, and international reports on Polish higher education released in the last few years stress the exceptional academic character of Polish universities, and their engagement with their own (academic) issues rather than issues of interest to, or relevant for, society and the economy. The linkages between educational offerings (especially in public institutions) and labour market needs are also weak, although both are strengthening. As an OECD report has stressed, Polish institutions are 'typically – although not always – strongly inward-looking in focus, rather than facing outward towards the wider society, including working life' (OECD, 2007, p. 77; see also World Bank/EIB 2004).

The linkages between Polish universities and their social environments are, in contrast, strong: both national metropolitan research universities and local universities engage with civil society organizations, third-sector organizations and foundations, as well as, increasingly, local governments. While higher education and research are principally funded from the national budget, European Union structural funds are disbursed regionally. Consequently, the number of initiatives between universities and local and regional governments has been on the rise in the last few years: new campuses, technology parks and research laboratories have been built in close links with local needs. In addition, new locally relevant study programmes have been developed and funded through structural funds.

The tradition of the community engagement of universities has traditionally been low as, in the communist period (1945–1989), universities were heavily politicized and, additionally, access to them was restricted. Consequently, universities, as elitist institutions (with gross enrolment rates in Poland of only about 10% in 1990 and with a steady number of students in the 1970s and 1980s), were also not involved in either service-learning or engaged scholarship. This is, however, changing in the current massified system.

Changes are slow but of consequence (Kwiek and Maassen, 2012). A governmental response to the perceived inwardness of Polish higher education includes the recent introduction of 'contracted studies' funded by the Ministry of Science and Higher Education in the strategically important areas of science and engineering. The programme of contracted studies started in 2008, and by 2013 the government will have spent 1 billion PLN (about US$330 million) on this initiative; it currently includes about 25,000 students, 10,000 of whom receive non-refundable 'motivation stipends' from 57 institutions. The programme has proved a success – in the 2010/2011 academic year, the polytechnics, for the first time in two decades, received more applicants per student place than the universities. Seven of the top twenty most popular areas of study were from the Ministry's list of 'contracted studies'.

Regional development in Poland is funded largely by regional funds, except for national, strategically important infrastructure, while public universities in Poland are funded almost exclusively by national funds. In addition, their funding does not come from student fees as studies (in major, regular track programmes) are free or tax-based. Consequently, even public funding for teaching is national. The link between fees from part-time students paid regionally and the regional relevance of teaching services is very weak in the public sector (as opposed to the Polish private sector, whose strength often derives from its regional engagement in fee-based teaching). The tensions are unavoidable: national interests represented by the national Ministry of Science and Higher Education are different from regional interests represented by regional authorities that are responsible for funding compulsory education. The difference between the public and private sectors is that national interests in funding for teaching in the public sector are different from regional interests in funding for teaching in the private sector, provided (mostly) by regional students through their fees (Kwiek, 2012, 2013b).

Private institutions are generally not involved in a prestige-seeking race for national and international research grants and for prestigious, nationally and internationally measured research output. But their teaching mission, especially in non-metropolitan areas, in institutions serving populations from rural areas and small towns and cities, is increasingly regionally oriented, especially in terms of matching local and regional labour market needs and their educational offerings. While older, more established public higher education institutions are found in the larger cities, the private sector in Poland is scattered throughout the country. Polish students are also much more attached to ideas of the labour market relevance of higher education and of closer cooperation with local and regional employers in both curricular and governance issues (for instance, tailor-made study programmes for enterprises offered by universities) than are their Western European colleagues (EC, 2009).

Polish students are very concerned with the relevance of higher education programmes for the labour market. Higher education reforms intended to link higher education more directly to the labour market have powerful social support. A large majority of Polish students surveyed (89%) agreed that it should be possible to undertake work placements in private enterprises as part of their study programmes. Almost all (97% – the highest response rate in Europe) agreed that it is important to foster innovation and an entrepreneurial mindset among students and staff. In addition, the idea of involving enterprises in higher education governance structures, curriculum design and funding is very strongly supported (at 86%, the average for Europe being 72%; EC, 2009, pp. 40–3).

This extremely positive attitude of Polish students to stronger linkages between higher education and employers does not, however, seem to be mirrored in the attitudes of the employers themselves. In contrast to student perceptions, Polish graduate recruiters (EC, 2010) are the least likely from among those of 31 countries to say that cooperation with higher education institutions is important, and most likely to say that such cooperation is not at all important. In terms of employers' satisfaction with the skills and capabilities of higher education graduates, Poland consistently ranks below the European average in terms of good literacy and numeracy skills, teamworking and communication skills, and organizational and problem-solving skills (EC, 2010).

Thus, there is a tension between the positive attitude of Polish students towards stronger higher education–employer cooperation, closely linked to the regional mission of the university, and the negative (and highly pessimistic) attitude of employers to this cooperation. Consequently, the introduction of stronger links between universities and their regional economic partners may take longer than current higher education strategies indicate. While the regional dimension of knowledge production is heavily emphasized at the national policy level in Poland, this role is still marginal in university practice (Kwiek, 2011). The strongest links between universities and their regions are seen in the teaching dimension of regional engagement, and regional engagement in research is a distant goal that requires substantial and focused funding. Recent changes in research funding modes introduced together with the opening of two new national research councils may prove highly successful in linking universities to their regions in future.

ACKNOWLEDGEMENT

The author gratefully acknowledges the support of the National Research Council (NCN) through its grant DEC-2011/02/A/HS6/00183.

REFERENCES

Arbo, P. and Benneworth, P. (2006) *Understanding the Regional Contribution of Higher Education Institutions*. Paris: OECD/IMHE.

EC (2009) *Students and Higher Education Reform*. Brussels: European Commission.

EC (2010) *Employers' Perception of Graduate Employability. Analytical Report*. Brussels: European Commission.

Etzkowitz, H. (2008) *The Triple Helix. University-Industry-Government Innovation in Action*. New York: Routledge.

Foray, D. (2006) *The Economics of Knowledge*. Cambridge, MA: MIT Press.

Geiger, R.L. and Sà, C.M. (2011) *Tapping the Riches of Science. Universities and the Promise of Economic Growth*. Cambridge, MA: Harvard University Press.

Kwiek, M. (2011) 'Universities and knowledge production in central Europe.' In: Temple, P. (ed.) *Universities in the Knowledge Economy: Higher Education Organisation and Global Change*. New York: Routledge.

Kwiek, M. (2012) 'Changing higher education policies: from the deinstitutionalization to the reinstitutionalization of the research mission in Polish universities.' *Science and Public Policy*, 39(October), 641–54.

Kwiek, M. (2013a) *Knowledge Production in European Universities: States, Markets, and Academic Entrepreneurialism*. Frankfurt: Peter Lang.

Kwiek, M. (2013b) 'From system expansion to system contraction: access to higher education in Poland'. *Comparative Education Review*, 57(3), 2–26.

Kwiek, M. and Maassen, P. (eds) (2012) *National Higher Education Reforms in a European Context: Comparative Reflections on Poland and Norway*. Frankfurt: Peter Lang.

Leydesdorff, L. (2006) *The Knowledge-based Economy: Modeled, Measured, Simulated*. Boca Raton: Universal Publishers.

MNISW (2006) *The Barriers to the Cooperation Between Entrepreneurs and Research Centers*. Warsaw: Ministry of Science and Higher Education [in Polish].

OECD (1999) *The Response of Higher Education Institutions to Regional Needs*. Paris: OECD.

OECD (2000) *The Response of Higher Education Institutions to Regional Needs*. Paris: OECD.

OECD (2007) *OECD Reviews of Tertiary Education. Poland*. Paris: OECD.

World Bank/EIB (2004) *Tertiary Education in Poland*. Warsaw: World Bank/European Investment Bank.

Inside View IV.5.2
Community–university engagement and social responsibility: community service practices by Turkish higher education institutions

Ayhan G. Hakan, Seçil Kaya and Elif Toprak

THE LEGAL BACKGROUND

According to law No. 1739 dated 1973 that regulates the Turkish education system, one of the major objectives of Turkish national education is to make individuals feel social responsibility and contribute to the well-being of their society (Kürüm, 2013). In the subject law, the emphasis on qualifications and health in every aspect and on an awareness of civic engagement can be seen.

In the 1988 Bologna Charter, approved by the Rectors of 388 European universities, it was underlined that student generations should be raised to be aware of their social environments, and that civic engagement should be one of the major functions of the higher education institutions (HEIs). In the framework of integration with the Bologna Process, the Turkish Higher Education Council (see http://www.yok.gov.tr/) identified a need to initiate 'Community Service Practices' courses at HEIs (Kaya, 2013) (Table IV.5.2.1).

The Higher Education Council's new initiative and draft for a new law on higher education has involved a special emphasis on the integration of the three functions (teaching, research and community service) of the HEIs. According to Article 44 of the Draft Law, on community services, HEIs undertake research activities, manage projects and organize activities for solving the environmental, technological, cultural and social problems of their communities. To fulfil these purposes, HEIs can set up advisory committees composed of public institutions, businesses, non-governmental organizations (NGOs) and other partners. These steps indicate the growing emphasis on the community services role of HEIs.

STUDENT CLUBS AND COLLABORATION WITH NGOS

Besides specific courses on civic engagement, universities in Turkey, in accordance with the regulations of the higher education system, have another means for realizing community services. This is the student clubs that provide another venue for students to come together and organize social services and events. These clubs provide scientific, social, cultural, artistic and sporting extra-curricular activities both on and off campus. Student clubs are defined as 'means to develop the social, artistic, cultural awareness of students and help them develop creative abilities and qualifications while spending their leisure time productively' (Kürüm, 2013) . Under the umbrella of different projects, students collaborate with different universities and even organize international events, as in the case of activities of Erasmus Student Network clubs.

Today, it is widely accepted that it is not the responsibility only of States to meet social needs. Individuals and institutions must also give support to the NGOs that are actively trying to solve problems in and meet the basic needs of society, in areas as diverse as education, health, culture, the environment and human rights.

NGOs in Turkey are divided in four categories: associations, foundations, unions and professional (occupational) associations (Erkılıç, 2013). There are in total 46 associa-

TABLE IV.5.2.1

Activities from Community Service Practices courses

Data on community services practised during 2012 for these courses have been collected by Kaya (2013). The activities listed here are examples of student practices from all over Turkey:

- Students from Eskişehir Osmangazi University found sponsors for repairing a primary school building and undertook the restoration and construction themselves, in cooperation with the Foundation for Social Services (Türkiye Toplum Hizmetleri Vakfı [TOVAK]) under the project name 'Imece' (which means 'collaboration' in Turkish).
- Students from the Faculty of Education at Pamukkale University ran a programme on the 'correct use of water and reuse of waste materials' in collaboration with the Foundation for Nature and Environment (Doğa ve Çevre Vakfı).
- Students from Karadeniz Technical University organized charity nights called 'Life Made Them Blind, Not Invisible' and 'Child Neglect and Abuse'. They also prepared a stand for informing society about cancer.
- Students from Trakya University found different ways of serving the community by preparing audio recordings of 100 books for visually impaired people, taking meals to the homes of poor and ill people who could not go to cookhouses and organizing campaigns for donations of books to be made to village schools.
- Students from Kastamonu University helped to restore a primary school and painted cartoon characters on its walls.
- At Zonguldak Karaelmas University, the Community Service Practices course in the Faculty of Education provided an opportunity to raise awareness about the needs of the hearing-impaired people in the local society. Another activity was a walk organized in cooperation with the Turkish Foundation for Combating Soil Erosion, for Reforestation and the Protection of Natural Habitats, under the motto 'No Soil, No Life'.
- Students from Adıyaman University collected 250 kg of plastic bottle caps for a nationwide campaign focused on buying wheelchairs for handicapped citizens.
- Students at Fırat University managed projects named 'Help Victims of Earthquake', 'Clean Air and Environment Around Fırat University' and 'We Stand by the Underprivileged'.
- Artvin Çoruh University's students decided to focus attention on preventing environmental pollution and cleaned their environment under the banner 'Let's Pick up the Trash'. They also started a campaign to plant trees and flowers.
- Niğde University students collaborated with the Turkish Red Crescent on a blood donation campaign, ending with contributions from 361 donors.
- Students from Maltepe University cooperated with Istanbul Marmara Education Foundation and worked as volunteers at eight primary schools in Maltepe district and at the Society for the Protection of Children.
- Students from Ceramics Department of the Faculty of Fine Arts, Anadolu University, created an atelier for socially disadvantaged children (Hakan, 2012).

Through such activities, students learn about civic engagement, face real-life and social problems and act to solve the problems together. The common characteristic of these examples is that students work under the supervision of their instructors and cooperate with the NGOs. Besides the social effects of these contributions, some activities are instructors' research projects, thus contributing to the academia as well.

tions, 48 unions and 32 occupational associations that are trying to create social awareness and organize activities that will achieve social development and progress. Most of these NGOs cooperate with HEIs in providing community services.

UNIQUE PRACTICES AT ANADOLU UNIVERSITY

Anadolu University (http://www.anadolu.edu.tr/en) is one of the world's mega-universities, with over 1.5 million students. It is a 'dual university', providing both conventional (face-to-face) and distance education. In Turkey, half of all higher education students are enrolled at Anadolu University.

As with all the other Turkish universities, the Community Service Practices course is part of the curriculum at Anadolu University. The university has signed a community service protocol with the Education Volunteers Foundation of Turkey and the Municipality of Tepebaşı that will create opportunities for students to carry out their volunteer work at different NGOs. Another practice is the inclusion of the Community Service Practices course in 'distance-learning' teacher training programmes. Through this course, different projects have, with the cooperation of the Ministry of National Education, been set up in schools in 81 provinces. These activities are evaluated in the e-portfolio systems of the subject programmes by tutors at Anadolu University.

A number of academicians from Anadolu University have collaborated with colleagues from other universities to prepare a course book on Community Service Practices. This will also be translated into an e-book format to be provided for public use within the framework

of the university's lifelong learning mission. The vision of lifelong learning vision enriches the knowledge-based and socio-cultural effects of the academicians' social responsibility projects. The university has also recently begun to disseminate its distance education e-learning materials as open educational resources through iTunes U.

Anadolu University, the Ministry of National Education and TOVAK have collaborated to select outstanding community engagement activities among the Community Service Practices courses that have been accomplished by higher education students. The Community Services Prize, named after Professor Dr Yahya Özsoy, is awarded annually.

Another important aspect of community service is university–industry collaboration. In 2013, the Anadolu University R&D and Innovation Coordination Unit has been established in order to act as an interface between the university and businesses.

SUGGESTIONS FOR INCREASING THE SOCIAL CONTRIBUTION OF HEIs

According to the report on the workshop on Faculties of Education and their Function of Community Services hosted by Ankara University in 2006, it has been suggested that units directly responsible to Rectors' offices could be founded to raise awareness and monitor activities. In the report (Ankara University Educational Sciences Faculty, 2006), it is proposed that, through such coordination, the functions and contact information of NGOs could be collected in handbooks, and project management information could be disseminated for public use.

In summary, it can be emphasized that this integration between different institutions, NGOs and individuals is vital, as is empowering their initiatives under the coordination of the universities. The basic objective of this coordination is to motivate society for cooperation and contribution.

REFERENCES

Adıgüzel, O.C., Akman Erkılıç T., Boyacı, A. et al. (2013) *Community Service Training (Topluma Hizmet Eğitimi)* (ed. Ayhan Hakan). Anadolu University Publications No. 2970. Eskişehir, Turkey: Anadolu University .

Ankara University Educational Sciences Faculty (2006) *Faculties of Education and their Function of Community Services from the Perspective of Educational Sciences Workshop.* Prepared for publication by Prof. Dr. F. Çağlayan Dinçer. Ankara University.

Erkılıç, T.A. (2013) 'Civil society and community services'. In: *Community Service Training* (Topluma Hizmet Eğitimi) (ed. Ayhan Hakan). Anadolu University Publications No. 2970. Eskişehir, Turkey: Anadolu University, pp. 57–83.

Hakan, Verdu Martinez E. (2012) 'Project of little traces'. *New Ceramics*, May/June.

Kaya, S. (2013). 'Evaluation of Community Service Practices Course'. In: *Community Service Training* (Topluma Hizmet Eğitimi) (ed. Ayhan Hakan). Anadolu University Publications No. 2970. Eskişehir, Turkey: Anadolu University, pp. 159–86.

Kürüm, D. (2013). 'Community service and the educational system'. In: *Community Service Training* (Topluma Hizmet Eğitimi) (ed. Ayhan Hakan). Anadolu University Publications No. 2970. Eskişehir, Turkey: Anadolu University, pp. 84–107.

Spotlight Issues IV.5.3
The experience of the National Co-ordinating Centre for Public Engagement in the UK

Sophie Duncan and Paul Manners

The National Co-ordinating Centre for Public Engagement (NCCPE) was established in 2008 as part of a £9.2 million project to inspire a culture change in how UK universities engaged with the public. This Beacons for Public Engagement project has provided useful insights into how to galvanize universities to embrace greater societal engagement in their work.

Hosted by the University of Bristol and the University of the West of England, the NCCPE has been working with universities across the UK to embed engagement. This article unpacks some of the learning from the project, and invites others to join in the conversation, to encourage universities to engage with society in mutually beneficial ways.

THE GENESIS OF PUBLIC ENGAGEMENT

The tradition of 'public understanding of science' within the UK was initially framed as a need for scientists to communicate their work better and to promote understanding, but the paradigm shifted in the 2000s when it was realized that such a stance implied a 'deficit' in the public. Public concerns about emerging technologies such as genetically modified foods reinforced the strategic importance of building a more robust and mutually respectful dialogue with the public in which their views should be taken account of within decision-making processes. The notion of 'public engagement' (PE) thus emerged.

Rather than being the fault of the public, a more nuanced analysis highlighted issues with the professional culture of science. An influential Royal Society report (2006) was published in which the authors interviewed researchers and identified barriers, including the research-driven culture, the fact that PE was seen to be not well regarded by peers and that it was hard to resource. This report led to the decision by the UK Research Councils, Higher Education Funding Councils and Wellcome Trust to establish Beacons for Public Engagement to 'create a culture within UK Higher Education where PE is formalized and embedded as a valued and recognized activity for staff at all levels, and for students' (HEFCE, 2006).

Six Beacons – partnerships between higher education (HE) institutions and civil society organizations – were established, along with the NCCPE, to synthesize and disseminate the learning from these projects.

The history, aims and objectives of each of the individual beacons and the NCCPE are well documented elsewhere (NCCPE, 2011). All the Beacon projects focused on critiquing, challenging and nudging their institutional systems and cultures to make them more supportive of engagement. At the heart of all the projects was an active commitment to learning and reflection. As part of this, the NCCPE invested in a national action research process, which drew on a *systemic action research* methodology to develop a systemic inquiry process (Burns, 2007). Six parallel learning streams were established, and participants with different organizational relationships to PE were drawn into small inquiry groups.

The findings from this research are summarized in a final report (Burns et al., 2011) which identified a number of barriers to change, as well as ways in which these barriers might be overcome. The report ended with seven recommendations, which accorded with much of the learning from the Beacon projects:

- While some 'third-stream' activities will need to be pursued independently of research and teaching, for most universities a focus on integrating PE into research and teaching is likely to be the most effective approach.
- PE is likely to have the greatest impact if it is focused at the level of the group (department, research and development team and/or curriculum development leaders).
- Universities should build a central support function for PE, not as the place where PE happens, but as a resource for those who are carrying it out. Key functions should include training, the development of networking opportunities, the use of space, and marketing and communications.
- Pro-vice-chancellors need to have the integration of PE into research and teaching as an explicit part of their brief.
- Expectations around PE need to be made clear to staff when they are recruited. This means building it into job descriptions and making it clear at job interviews and induction.
- Universities should pay greater attention to their accessibility, becoming more welcoming and friendly places, and thinking strategically about where the university might take its work beyond its buildings and campuses.

CHANGING CONTEXTS

While the Beacon projects were undertaking their four-year culture change programmes, the world around universities was changing dramatically.

Alongside the global economic crisis and increasing devolution between the four UK nations, UK universities also had to contend with new policy directives. These included the so-called 'impact agenda', in which research funders expect people bidding for research to articulate the engagement pathways they intend to pursue in executing their research, and the new Research Excellence Framework, which, for the first time, requires departments to submit case studies to articulate the impact of their work 'beyond academia'. A figure of 20% of the total quality assessment would be based upon that external impact. These changes brought engagement centre stage. In addition, there were profound changes to the ways students were expected to pay for their education, with fees in England tripling in most universities, creating a strong backlash against the perceived 'marketization' of HE.

The findings distilled from the Beacons projects informed the creation of a new PE Concordat (RCUK, 2010), signed by all the major research funders, which articulated their expectations of the institutions they funded:

- UK research organizations should have a strategic commitment to PE.
- Researchers should be recognized and valued for their involvement with PE activities.
- Researchers should be enabled to participate in PE activities through appropriate training, support and opportunities.
- The signatories and supporters of this Concordat will undertake regular reviews of their own progress and that of the wider research sector in fostering PE across the UK.

While the Beacons projects drew to a close, the NCCPE received funding to continue to support universities across the UK to embrace engagement as part of their work.

WHAT HAVE WE LEARNED SO FAR?

The project has elicited substantial learning to date, full details of which can be found on the NCCPE website (www.publicengagement. ac.uk).

- To embed a culture of PE, you need to consider three main areas:
  - People: involve your staff, students, and communities in helping to define what you do.

- Processes: put in place appropriate support for staff, students and partners to develop effective relationships and learn together, and reward and recognize this work in appropriate ways.
- Purpose: ensure you are clear about the strategic purpose of your engagement, communicate it effectively, and support leaders throughout the university and the community.
- Effective partnership work is at the heart of engaged practice. If you want your work to make a difference, you need to work effectively with others both inside and outside your institution, and learn to value, respect and recognize their expertise and experience.
- Funding and institutional structures mean that engagement is fragmented across institutions – from engagement with research, teaching and learning, volunteering and so-called corporate social responsibility. When considering the type of university you want to be, you need to consider these things in the round.
- Finding effective ways to evaluate and measure the impact of your engagement work is an important part of establishing effective engagement practices and protecting this work in the future.

The NCCPE's ongoing work is exploring some of the current barriers and opportunities, including the following:

- An 'Engaged Futures' consultation is exploring the interests, needs and expectations of university partners and publics. What do people really want from universities, and how could or should universities respond? (NCCPE, 2013).
- Internationally, there is much expertise and many experiences of engaged work with universities. We are keen to develop more opportunities for people passionate about this work to share their ideas and insights, and help galvanize university engagement, to the benefit of society.
- Working with a group of community partners, engaged academics and the Community University Partnership Programme at the University of Brighton, we are developing a UK Community Partner network to

share learning, build capacity and stimulate change (NCCPE, 2012).

CONCLUSION

Principles of engagement capture the imagination and commitment of many of those working in HE – at an individual level, a belief that we should 'make a difference' through our work; and at an institutional level, reconnecting to the founding principles of the institution, for instance as a 'civic' university. But this only takes you so far. Shifts in funding priorities – for instance, the expectation that impact 'beyond academia' is assessed – provide an equally important driver in the system.

Last but by no means least, what has also come sharply into focus is how engrained and embedded certain values and ways of working are that make developing open, mutually respectful collaboration both within and outside universities difficult. Idealism and coercion are potentially uneasy bedfellows. The challenge lies in building capabilities and capacities to work in more cooperative and engaged ways, where different kinds of expertise are genuinely valued. While real progress has been made to reorient HE in the UK towards a more engaged mind-set, it feels like we are still at a relatively early stage of the journey.

REFERENCES

Burns, D. (2007) *Systemic Action Research: A Strategy for Whole System Change.* Bristol: Policy Press.

Burns, D., Squires, H., with participants from the National Action Research Programme (2011) *Embedding Public Engagement in Higher Education: Final Report of the National Action Research Programme.* Retrieved from https://www.public engagement.ac.uk/sites/default/files/ Action%20research%20report_0.pdf.

HEFCE (2006) *Beacons for Public Engagement: Invitation to Apply for Funds.* Retrieved from http://www.hefce.ac.uk/ pubs/hefce/2006/06_49/06_49.pdf.

NCCPE (2011) 'Beacons for Public Engagement'. Retrieved from http://www.publi-cengagement.ac.uk/about/beacons.

NCCPE (2012) 'Community Partner Network'. Retrieved from http://www.publicengage-ment.ac.uk/about/community-partner-network.

NCCPE (2013) 'Engaged Futures'. Retrieved from http://www.publicengagement.ac.uk/engagedfutures.

RCUK (2010) 'Concordat for Engaging the Public with Research'. Retrieved from http://www.rcuk.ac.uk/per/Pages/Concordat.aspx.

Royal Society (2006) *Survey of Factors Affecting Science Communication by Scientists and Engineers*. Retrieved from http:// royalsociety.org/uploadedFiles/Royal_Society_Content/Influencing_Policy/Themes_and_Projects/Themes/Governance/Final_Report_-_on_website_-_and_amended_by_SK.pdf.

Spotlight Issues IV.5.4
OECD reviews of higher education in regional and city development

Oscar Valiente

BACKGROUND

With some notable exceptions, higher education institutions (HEIs), particularly research-intensive universities, have traditionally tended to be self-contained entities focused on the creation and development of basic knowledge for scientific purposes and prestige. This has, however, changed. The new economic paradigm, which stresses the importance of tertiary education to economic development, has stimulated the higher education sector to more directly engage in the national and/or global economy (Etzkowitz et al., 2000). Furthermore, national and regional governments and supra-national institutions such as the Organisation for Economic Cooperation and Development (OECD) or the European Union are developing regional policy frameworks, incentives and/or infrastructures to encourage HEIs to respond to local and regional needs. The recognition that higher education can play a key role in development is now a fundamental underpinning of most economic development strategies, at international, national and regional levels.

AIMS AND METHODOLOGY

Since 2005, the OECD has reviewed the role and impact of higher education in more than 30 cities and regions in over 20 countries. The *Reviews of Higher Education in Regional and City Development* have stretched over six continents, involved hundreds of universities and other HEIs, and embraced a diverse set of policy frameworks in education, science and technology, and territorial development. They have helped local, regional and national governments to mobilize higher education for skills, innovation and socio-cultural development.

The methodology of the project has consisted of the following elements: (1) a common framework for regional self-evaluation developed by the OECD task group; (2) a self-evaluation report by the regional consortium using OECD guidelines; (3) a site visit by an international peer review team; (4) a peer review report and a response from the region; and finally (5) analysis and synthesis by an OECD task group drawing upon regional case studies.

The review asked HEIs to critically evaluate with their regional partners, and in the context of national higher education and regional policies, how effective they were in contributing to the development of their regions. The OECD template guides regions to review regional development, not only along economic dimensions, but also in terms of social, cultural and environmental development. Key aspects of the evaluation were:

- human capital and skills development through interdisciplinary and entrepreneurial programmes, continuing education, professional development and lifelong learning activities;
- knowledge creation and transfer in the region through research and its exploitation via mobility programmes (work-based learning) and technology transfer (spin-out companies, intellectual property rights and consultancy);
- cultural and community development contributing to the quality of life of the local population, attracting international talent and encouraging the enterprise formation, growth, productivity and employment on which innovation in the region depends;
- capacity-building of regional governance systems through collaboration with regional stakeholders in the development of policies, strategies and practical tools.

The focus of the study was on collaborative working between HEIs and their regional partners. It sought to establish a regional learning and capacity-building process. This made it necessary to engage in participatory learning within and between regions.

The project displayed a natural evolution – beginning with centralized control and moving towards a network in which communication and knowledge-making flow in all directions. This evolution can be traced through the various dissemination meetings and the widening circles of participation that characterized the biography of the project. The wider peer learning developed as regions engaged with the work, their teams met with others, and intra- and inter-regional activities broadened the circle of those involved.

LESSONS LEARNED

Several OECD reviews have shown that city and regional engagement are not an inherent component of higher education systems (Goddard et al., 2011). It does, however, suggest that, for extensive engagement on the part of HEIs (and not just small groups of academics), strong drivers external to the higher education system are needed (OECD, 2007). Lessons learned from the OECD reviews have been articulated in policy recommendations for HEIs, regional and local authorities and national governments.

Recommendations for HEIs are as follows:

- Adopt a wide agenda of regional engagement considering the whole range of opportunities for engagement, whether these are economic, social or cultural, and then engage in a continuous improvement of these activities and a monitoring of the results.

- Focus on strengthening the regional employability and entrepreneurial skills of all graduates. Creating ties between students in fields of critical importance to the region and regional employers through internships and co-op programmes should be made a priority.
- Develop teaching methods in entrepreneurship education and support, moving away from teacher-centred learning methods. There also should be a link between entrepreneurship education and start-up support.
- Review recruitment and promotion systems for academic staff so as to include regional development agendas and entrepreneurship activity among the criteria.
- Establish special mobility programmes to link students, graduates and academic staff with local business and industry in a more systematic way.
- Reach out to socially underprivileged populations to ensure social and economic cohesion in collaboration with regional and local governments, schools and the private sector. Tertiary education institutions should also reach out and empower the migrant population to address their own challenges through community development programmes.
- Target green growth sectors and eco-innovation through collaboration with small and medium-sized enterprises in the region's green economy.
- Support cultural and creative industries in the region in collaboration with regional and local authorities and the private sector. This approach should address the needs of the diverse populations in the region and enhance the internationalization of the region.

Recommendations for regional and local authorities are also given:

- Establish a regional skills system to define region-wide goals, policies and priorities. This should include collaboration between vocational institutions and universities in developing reskilling, upskilling and continuing professional development.
- Establish a funding system for universities to engage in regional development

and collaboration with the local private and non-profit sectors. This structure will reduce the tendency of universities to measure success in innovation by the amount of public investment rather than the amount of commercial rerun generated or the number of jobs created.
- Develop a wide portfolio of robust indicators on graduate labour market outcomes and graduate destinations (possible out-migration) to support evidence-based decision-making and support targeted efforts to address human capital development needs.
- Improve internationalization of their regions and localities, their business sector and universities through attraction of talent and foreign direct investment. Policy instruments include employee tax incentives, repatriation schemes and improving the attractiveness of academic careers. These policies should be an integral part of the region's international development and cooperation strategy and should be coupled with initiatives to attract foreign investment.

Recommendations for national and federal governments include:

- Create more 'joined-up' governance (finance, education, science and technology, and industry ministries, and so on) to coordinate decisions on priorities, resources and strategic items in regional development.
- Make regional engagement and more specifically its wide agenda for economic, social and cultural development explicit in higher education legislation and encourage HEIs to address regional engagement in their mission statements and strategies.
- Further strengthen the institutional autonomy of HEIs by increasing their responsibility over curricula and the use of human, financial and physical resources, and provide incentives to exercise these responsibilities through developing long-term core funding for HEIs to support regional engagement and provide additional strategic incentive-based funding schemes.
- Strengthen the accountability of HEIs to society by developing indicators and monitoring outcomes to assess the impact of the HEIs on regional performance; in addi-

tion, require the governance of HEIs to involve regional stakeholders and encourage the participation of HEIs in regional governance structures.
- Mobilize the joint resources of the HEIs for the preparation and implementation of regional and urban strategies and encourage genuine partnerships in which HEIs are not only technical advisers for regional strategy-making, but also actors in the process and genuine stakeholders.
- Provide a more supportive environment for university–enterprise cooperation: regulatory and tax environments and accountability regimes that do not place an undue burden on HEIs and businesses.
- Continue to focus on the development of human capital through developing highly skilled graduates for the national and regional labour markets and upskilling the local labour force; improve educational opportunities through distance learning, lifelong learning and e-learning.
- Support collaboration between universities and other HEIs in the region through joint degrees, programmes, research programmes, strategies and one-stop shops for industry collaboration to improve the supply and delivery of higher education services for regional firms.

The OECD has organized different knowledge exchange activities to disseminate the lessons learned form the reviews. These activities have brought together policy-makers and practitioners, public and private bodies concerned with regional development, the leaders and managers of HEIs, and those responsible for knowledge transfer, regional development and community liaison at HEIs. All these actors have had the opportunity to share their experiences and to discuss the key themes arising from the reviews. The forthcoming OECD publication *Higher Education in Cities and Regions – For Stronger, Cleaner and Fairer Regions* will compile contributions from different international experts and the lessons learned from the second round of reviews. To find out more, go to http://www.oecd.org/edu/imhe/highereducationinregionalandcitydevelopment.htm.

REFERENCES

Etzkowitz, H., Webster, A., Gebhardt, C. and Terra, B.R.C. (2000) 'The future of the university and the university of the future: evolution of ivory tower to entrepreneurial paradigm'. *Research Policy*, 29, 313–30.

Goddard, J., Vallance, P. and Puukka, J. (2011) 'Experience of engagement between universities and cities: drivers and barriers in three European cities'. *Built Environment*, 37(3), 299–316.

OECD (2007) *Higher Education and Regions: Globally Competitive, Locally Engaged.* Paris: OECD.

IV.5.5

Networks on community–university engagement in Europe

Campus Engage: Network for the Promotion of Civic Engagement in Irish Higher Education

SECRETARIAT: Galway (Ireland).
INSTITUTION: Irish Universities Association.
WEBSITE: http://www.campusengage.ie/ (accessed 4 March 2013).
MEMBERS: Higher education institutions in the Republic of Ireland.

Campus Engage is a network of higher education institutions working together to promote civic engagement activities in Irish higher education. It aims to strengthen the relationship between higher education and the wider society by supporting the development of activities such as community-based research, service-learning/community-based learning, student volunteering and knowledge exchange, in order to increase the number of courses, activities and levels of participation in these areas across Irish higher education.

National Co-ordinating Centre for Public Engagement (NCCPE)

SECRETARIAT: Bristol (UK).
INSTITUTION: University of Bristol and University of the West of England.
WEBSITE: http://www.publicengagement.ac.uk/ (accessed 14 March 2013).
MEMBERS: n/a.

NCCPE's mission is to support universities to increase the quantity and quality of their public engagement activity. Its main objectives are: to inspire a shift in culture by supporting universities to bring change that embeds public engagement; to increase the capacity for public engagement by encouraging the sharing of effective practice; and to build effective partnerships that encourage partners to embed public engagement in their work by informing, influencing and interpreting policy and by raising the status of public engagement.

IV.5.6

Good Practices

University of Groningen Science Shops

Science shops initially emerged in the Netherlands in the 1970s, and although they are not purely a European phenomenon, this is the area where they are still most prominent. They take the form of a unit that is linked to a university department or sometimes a non-governmental organization. Their role is to offer participatory research support to civil society groups, one example being the Science Shops of the University of Groningen in the Netherlands, which have been working in this area since 1979.

The University of Groningen has five science shops: Beta (a merger of the chemistry, biology, physics and medicine Science Shops); Economy and Business; Medicine and Public Health; Education and Language; and Culture and Communication. These in turn align with three focus areas in the University of Groningen: Energy, Healthy Ageing and Sustainable Society. At the 2013 GUNi conference, Henk Mulder reported that the offer of the Science Shops at his university is made without financial barriers. Research is carried out by students as part of their normal studies and under academic supervision. Mulder has argued that this is 'an innovative way of benefitting civil society, advancing student learning and creating valuable networks for social innovation for universities'.

For more information, see http://www.rug.nl/science-and-society/science-shops/.

University of Lapland's Arctic Indigenous Peoples and Sami Research Office

Although it is less prominent than in other continents, one of the activities of some European universities is community engagement with indigenous groups. One case is provided by the Arctic Indigenous Peoples and Sami Research Office at the University of Lapland in Rovaniemi, Finland. This promotes research and educational activities in cooperation with representatives of indigenous groups, notably the Sami people.

The principal research areas of the Office are the following:

* indigenous knowledge and its utilization;
* biodiversity-related knowledge;
* natural resources and related conflicts;
* international indigenous politics;
* minority law.

Examples of the work of the office include Biological Diversity and Sami People. The aim of this project has been to investigate the form that the biodiversity-related knowledge of the Sami people in Finland takes, to determine the measures that are needed to protect this knowledge and consider how best to share its benefits. Other work has focused on the 'Prerequisites of the Sami Reindeer Herding: Meaning of Traditional Knowledge and biological diversity in the Arctic'. In this project, research was conducted with Arctic indigenous peoples in Alaska, Canada and the Russian Federation and as well as Greenland, Sweden, Norway and Finland.

More details can be found at http://www.arcticcentre.org/.

National University of Ireland, Galway's Community Knowledge Initiative

In 2001, the National University of Ireland, Galway, launched its Community Knowledge Initiative (CKI), which represents an example in Europe of a civic mission being integrated comprehensively within a university's core activities. CKI activities were viewed as 'integral to the University's strategic mission and involved a fundamental examination of the role of the University in the social fabric', and were subsequently reflected as a core priority by National University of Ireland, Galway's Academic and Strategic Plans. Civic engagement activities have been integrated into teaching, research and service at the levels of students, staff, courses, programmes and the institution as a whole.

Examples of the activities within the CKI include:

* Engaging People in Communities, which develops community–university research partnerships and public engagement between the university and the wider community;
* A Learning Initiative and the Volunteering Experience, which promotes the development of civic and leadership skills in students;
* service-learning, which 'seeks to reinvigorate the civic mission of higher education and instill in students a sense of social responsibility and civic awareness';
* the inclusive higher education project Going to College, which supports students with intellectual disabilities to participate and actively engage in all aspects of university life.

For more information, see http://www.nuigalwaycki.ie.

IV.6

KNOWLEDGE,
ENGAGEMENT
AND HIGHER
EDUCATION IN
CANADA AND THE
USA

Hiram E. Fitzgerald

This paper reviews the history and current status of engagement in higher education in Canada and the USA, and examines the diverse frameworks, approaches, policies and structures that support it. It also highlights innovative and promising practices, and identifies the actions needed to truly embed and sustain it. Community engagement scholarship (CES) is increasingly becoming central to the missions of higher education institutions (HEIs) and is essential to their very survival and relevance in a rapidly changing world. Throughout HEIs in North America, there is a call for greater collaboration, shared learning and community impact among engaged campuses, community–academic partnerships and their key stakeholders. Higher education will always have countless partnerships with communities; the real question is whether the collective impact of these partnerships advances scholarship and produces substantive community change.

NORTH AMERICA: HISTORICAL CONTEXT

Originally populated by indigenous peoples (50,000–10,000 BC), the population of North America now comprises people who have settled there from nearly every geographical region of the world. In each country, the majority population is of European heritage (Table IV.6.1), although by mid-century that will change and each country will have a non-white majority. The Aboriginal peoples of Canada (First Nations, Inuit and Métis) comprise approximately 3.8% of its population, whereas American Indians/Alaska Natives (AI/AN) comprise only 0.9% of the population of the USA. The diversity of North America is further enhanced by the number of languages spoken at home – around 200 languages in Canada and 311 in the USA. In each country, there are over 100 indigenous languages.

Strong economic ties bind the two countries: 73% of Canada's exports and 63% of its imports are to the USA, and each country is a democracy.

TABLE IV.6.1
Percentage of the population by racial category in Canada and the USA

Category	Canada	USA
White	83.8%	64.7%
Asian		4.4%
Japanese	0.3%	
Korean	0.5%	
West Asian	0.5%	
Southeast Asian	0.8%	
South Asian	4.0%	
Chinese	3.9%	
Hawaiian/Pacific Islander		0.18%
Filipino	1.3%	
Latin American	1.0%	
Hispanic		15.1%
Black	2.5%	12.9%
Arab	0.9%	
Aboriginal		
AI/AN	0.97%	
Two or more races		1.61%
Visible minority other	0.2%	
Multiple visible minority	0.4%	

Note: Canada and the USA have different approaches to categorizing races within their approaches to census.

ADVANCEMENT IN ENGAGEMENT IN THE REGION

A BRIEF HISTORY OF HIGHER EDUCATION

In Canada, the education of the settler population began in 1668 when Jesuit priests established the Quebec Seminary Latin School to educate boys into the priesthood. Université Laval (Quebec) was the first HEI in Canada (1663). In the USA, the first public educational institution was the Boston Latin School (1635). The first colleges, Harvard (1636) and William and Mary (1693), were established by religious groups primarily to educate young men for the ministry.

SCOPE OF HIGHER EDUCATION TODAY

Today, there are 14.7 million full-time students in community colleges, technical schools, colleges and universities in North America, with more women enrolled in undergraduate studies than men (Table IV.6.2). Including part-time students, the joint enrolment approaches 23 million. Canada has approximately 330 HEIs and the USA has 4,599 (universities, colleges, polytechnic, community colleges and specialized arts and cultural institutions).

TABLE IV.6.2
Enrolments in higher education (2011)

Enrolments	Total	Females	Males
Canada			
Total	1,300,000	793,000	507,000
USA			
Total	21,575,000	13,147,000	9,243,000
Full time	13,361,000	7,429,000	5,837,000
Black	3,038,000	1,949,700	1,689,100
Hispanic	2,741,400	1,586,900	1,154,660
Asian	1,282,200	681,300	600,800
AI/AN	196,400	117,600	78,800
Bi-racial	325,300	191,400	134,300
Non-resident alien	709,600	329,200	380,300

ORIGINS OF PRACTICE: HISTORICAL TO PRESENT

HISTORICAL ROOTS

Selman (2005) identified the Antigonish Movement as the best-known example of community–university engagement linked to the concept of university extension. In 1902, Father Jimmy Tompkins took up a teaching position at St. Francis Xavier University in Antigonish, Nova Scotia, and began a life time of advocacy for the development of adult education to address issues related to rural economic and community development. His advocacy was eventually linked with the building of a cooperative and credit union movement with a particular focus on fishery (Coady, 1939; Alexander, 1997). Father Tompkin's 1921 pamphlet 'Knowledge for the People: A Call to St Francis Xavier's College' might be seen as the first powerful argument for engaged scholarship in English-speaking Canada.

However, a lack of university support resulted in Father Tompkins' reassignment to a rural parish, where he continued to advocate for the use of knowledge, learning and organizing to transform the lives of people in Nova Scotia. St. Francis Xavier University eventually established an Extension Department, which Father Jimmy's cousin Moses Coady directed until his death in 1959.

The Antigonish Movement was not the only fore-runner of contemporary CES in Canada. For example, in the late 1800s, Queen's, Toronto and McGill Universities also had continuing education programmes (Archer and Wright, 1999). By the 1970s, we see the emergence of the contemporary CES in Canada with the creation of the participatory research project based at the University of Toronto and the establishment of the Service Aux Collectivités at the University of Quebec à Montreal (Hall, 2005). Community-based research (CBR) emerged within the context of indigenous scholars challenging older paradigms, the HIV/AIDS movement taking a central role in research on their own lives, and women doing research linked to their own health and their own bodies.

In 1862, the US Congress passed the Morrill Act and established the public land grant system of higher education. The Morrill Act focused on developing agricultural production and creating engineers to meet the needs of an expanding industrial society. It was an idea and a set of core values (Fitzgerald and Simon, 2012) about the ability of society to provide broad access to education. In 1887, the Hatch Act added emphasis to the importance of research in meeting the needs of American society, and in 1914 the Smith–Lever Act provided a dissemination system through the Cooperative Extension Service. A second Morrill Act (1890) provided support for HEIs in response to the needs of African-American individuals for access to higher education, and in 1994 it created a network of colleges to stimulate greater access to higher education for the AI/AN population. The Morrill, Hatch and Smith–Lever acts emphasized the teaching, research and service missions of HEIs as a public good.

As higher education continued to expand, it shifted its emphasis to graduate education, thereby propelling research to the dominant position among the teaching, research and service triad. Over time, the public came to view faculty as experts in their knowledge domains but disconnected from the community (Fitzgerald et al., 2012), and HEIs as more a private than a public good.

HIGHER EDUCATION AS A PUBLIC GOOD

Critics, notably Ernest Boyer (1990, 1996), called for renewed emphasis on the quality of the student experience, a broader definition of scholarship-based teaching, research and service, the implementation of true community–university partnerships based on reciprocity and mutual benefit (Ramaley, 2000) and an intentional focus on the resolution of a wide range of societal problems. This new engagement required institutions of higher education to rethink their structure, epistemology and pedagogy, to integrate teaching, research and service, and to review their promotion and tenure criteria (Figure IV.6.1) (Burkhart al., 2004). Boyer challenged higher education to renew its covenant with society and to embrace the problems of society with shared community partnerships. He targeted public land grant institutions in particular because they were created explicitly to serve the needs of society (Bonnen, 1998). Shortly after Boyer's calls for reform in higher education, the Kellogg Commission issued a series of reports challenging higher education to become more engaged with communities, but by working through collaborative partnerships rather than as experts with preconceived solutions to complex problems. It proposed the seven characteristics of effective societal engagement that are summarized in Table IV.6.3.

The Kellogg Commission (2000) distinguished 'engagement' from the more familiar terms of 'public service', 'outreach' and 'extension'. The Commission rejected 'outreach' as a one-way transfer of knowledge, and promoted 'engagement' as a reciprocal process of shared knowledge creation, innovation and public benefit.

TABLE IV.6.3
A seven-part test of engagement
1. *Responsiveness.* Are we listening to the communities, regions, and states we serve?
2. *Respect for partners.* Are we encouraging joint academic–community definitions of problems, solutions and definitions of success?
3. *Academic neutrality.* Engagement activities will involve contentious issues that have profound social, economic and political consequences.
4. *Accessibility.* Is our expertise equally accessible to all the constituencies of concern within our states and communities, including minority constituents?
5. *Integration.* A commitment to interdisciplinary work is probably indispensable to an integrated approach.
6. *Coordination.* The coordination issue involves making sure the left hand knows what the right hand is doing.
7. *Resource partnerships.* Are the resources committed to the task sufficient?
Source: Adapted from Kellogg Commission (2001, p. 16).

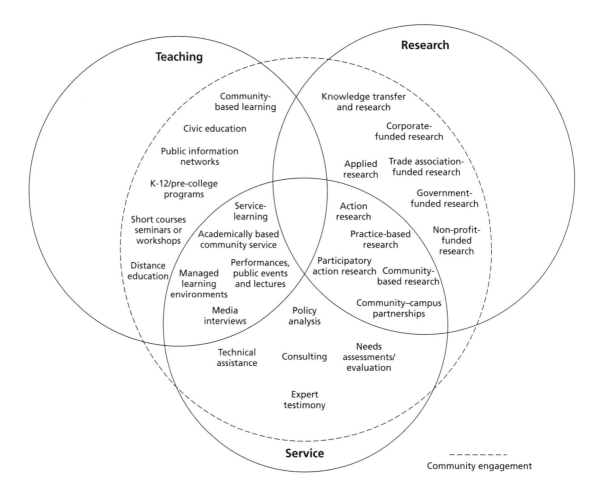

FIGURE IV.6.1 Modelling the scholarship of integration
Source: Glass and Fitzgerald (2010).

Boyer (1990) suggested that the definition of scholarship should be reframed as discovery, integration, application and teaching. The intent was to alter faculty roles so that teaching and application would be viewed as equal to research with respect to faculty responsibilities. Others argued that faculty performance should be assessed along a continuum of behaviours and social impacts, rather than by the number of publications that appear in a restricted set of discipline-defined tier journals (Glassick et al., 1997). Glassick et al. identified six standards for assessing faculty performance: clear goals, adequate preparation, appropriate methods, significant results, effective presentation and reflective critique.

CES posits a new framework for scholarship that moves standards of scholarship from emphasizing products (for example, publications) to emphasizing impact. Two approaches within CES emerged in efforts to effect sustainable positive changes in society. One approach, engaged scholarship, focuses on engagement as a partnership of university knowledge and resources with those of the public and private sectors to: enrich scholarship, research and creative activity; enhance curriculum, teaching and learning; prepare educated, engaged citizens; strengthen democratic values and civic responsibility; address critical societal issues; and contribute to the public good (Fitzgerald et al., 2005). A second approach focuses on the scholarship of engagement, on scholarly enquiry with a specific content focus on diverse forms of civic life, democratic citizenship and community engagement, including that of faculty and students in schools, colleges and universities (Stanton, 2007).

ENGAGEMENT SCHOLARSHIP IN THE 21ST CENTURY

RECONCEPTUALIZING KNOWLEDGE
The recognition that knowledge has multiple sources and is created as much outside the university as within it requires a new framework for conceptualizing the knowledge process (Sonka et al., 2000). Sonka et al. adapted Nonaka and Takeuchi's (1995) decision-making process to create a model for knowledge generation that serves community–university partnerships well. Nonaka and Takeuchi proposed that tacit and explicit knowledge were critical for decision-making. Tacit knowledge refers to the mental models that all individuals possess of how the world works. Tacit knowledge also can be thought of as stories, implicit knowledge, know-how, experience and skill.

Indigenous knowledge is a form of tacit knowledge that is deeply shaped by cultural and linguistic meaning and persists whether or not explicit knowledge leads to a sustainable solution to a societal problem.

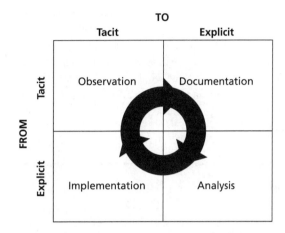

FIGURE IV.6.2 **Knowledge conversion in a knowledge-creating system**
Source: Adapted from Nonaka and Takeuchi (1995, p. 72).

Explicit knowledge is formal knowledge, systematic, with definitions and theories. There is a systemic connection between these two types of knowledge (Figure IV.6.2). Sonka and colleagues illustrate the dynamic, cyclical relationship between tacit and explicit knowledge in a system of continual knowledge creation, application and renewal. The knowledge-creation process begins with observation (tacit/indigenous knowledge), identifying problems and opportunities, generating hunches and assessing risks. Documentation is the second step and signifies the search for evidence to support observations and for designing new approaches or revising those that are not working well. Documentation is followed by analysis, accomplished by the practices of engagement scholarship or the scholarship of engagement. Finally, implementation provides the test of whether a good solution has been achieved, or whether new tacit knowledge will stimulate a new cycle of the knowledge-creation process.

PROFESSIONALIZATION OF CES
Although engagement scholarship publications can be found in journals from many disciplines, its emphasis on participatory action research (PAR), multidisciplinary collaboration, social justice, community and systems change, and blending of qualitative and quantitative methodologies prompted many scholars to create new professional organizations to guide CES,

to reshape higher education internally and to shift public policies related to the civic purpose of higher education. Table IV.6.4 provides a sample of some of the more prominent organizations, which all, although presented by within-country loci, have international memberships. As organizations formed and grew, so too did the outlets needed to communicate the results of engagement scholarship. Table IV.6.5 provides a list of peer-reviewed, open-access, online journals that publish the rich blend of scholarship that characterizes diverse engagement scholarship efforts to find solutions to the full range of local, regional and international societal problems.

TABLE IV.6.4
North American anchored organizations focused on civic and community engagement

Canada	
Association of Universities and Colleges of Canada	1914
Community-University Research Association	1999
Canadian Alliance for Community Service-Learning	2005
Global Alliance on Community-Engaged Research	2008
Community-Based Research Canada	2008
USA	
National Youth Leadership Council	1983
Campus Compact	1985
New England Resource Center for Higher Education	1988
Coalition of Urban and Metropolitan Universities	1990
Corporation for National and Community Service	1993
HBCU Faculty Development Network	1994
Community-Campus Partnerships for Health	1996
Birth2Work	1998
Community Based Collaboratives Research Consortium	1999
Engagement Scholarship Consortium	1999
Imagining America: Artists and Scholars in Public Life	1999
Talloires Network	2005
The Research University Civic Engagement Network	2005
International Association for Research on Service-learning and Community Engagement	2006
Higher Education Network for Community Engagement	2006
Coalition of Urban Serving Universities	2007
Transformative Regional Engagement Networks	2008
Academy of Community Engagement Scholarship	2013
Source: Adapted from Fitzgerald and Primavera (2013).	

TABLE IV.6.5
Journals focused on CES

American Journal of Community Psychology
Collaborative Anthropologies
Community Development Journal
Community Works Journal
eJournal of Public Affairs
Gateways: International Journal of Community Engagement and Research
Innovative Higher Education
International Journal for Service Learning in Engineering
International Journal of Research on Service-learning and Community Engagement (IARSLCE)
International Journal of Public Participation
Journal for Civic Commitment (Community College National Center for Community Engagement)
Journal of Community Engagement and Higher Education (Indiana State University)
Journal of Community Engagement and Scholarship (University of Alabama)
Journal of Community Practice
Journal of Deliberative Mechanisms in Science (DEMESCI)
Journal of Extension
Journal of Higher Education Outreach and Engagement (University of Georgia)
Journal of Public Scholarship in Higher Education (Missouri State University)
Metropolitan Universities Journal (Indiana University-Purdue University Indianapolis)
Michigan Journal of Community Service Learning (University of Michigan)
Partnerships: A Journal of Service-Learning and Civic Engagement (University of North Carolina, Greensboro)
PRISM: A Journal of Regional Engagement (Eastern Kentucky University)
Progress in Community Health Partnerships: Research, Education, and Action
Public: A Journal of Imagining America
Reflections: A Journal of Public Rhetoric, Civic Writing, and Service Learning (Syracuse University)
Science Education and Civic Engagement: An International Journal
Undergraduate Journal of Service Learning and Community-Based Research (Penn State, Berks Campus)

POLICY FRAMEWORKS SUPPORTING ENGAGEMENT

With the exception of military colleges, higher education in Canada and the USA is decentralized with respect to funding and authority over colleges and universities. Public higher education is regulated in Canada by provincial governments, and in the USA by state governments. Canada has no federal ministry or minister of higher education. Although there is no constitutional provision for higher education in the USA, in 1979 the Department of Education and its Secretary became part of the President's cabinet. With some exceptions, states have created higher education systems to oversee the operation of their state-funded public colleges and universities.

ACCREDITATION

Both Canada and the USA have institutional accreditation systems for higher education. In Canada, accreditation is conducted at the provincial level according to quality standards established by each provincial government. In the USA, the Federal Government recognizes seven private accrediting bodies, each of which independently oversees institutions within a defined region of the country. In each country, the specialized accreditation of professional programmes is conducted by a host of national associations to assure that quality standards are maintained.

ROLE OF FEDERAL GOVERNMENT

Although provincial and state governments are responsible for overseeing their public higher education systems, it would be a mistake to conclude that federal policies have no impact on higher education. In each country, federal policies that establish and regulate various funding agencies require compliance monitoring and reporting from HEIs. In most cases, but certainly not all, these involve research grants and contracts, institutional review boards for the protection of human subjects and animal welfare, conflicts of interest among researchers, funding for student scholarships or loans and other university activities. For example, in Canada, community engagement and 'partnership research' is a high priority for the Social Sciences and Humanities Research Council and knowledge translation is central to the Canadian Institutes for Health Research.

In the USA, community engagement in one form or another is a priority for the National Institutes of Health, the Centres for Disease Control, the National Science Foundation, the Administration for Children and Families and nearly all federal agencies that provide grants and contracts for community-based initiatives. For example, the seven leading multi-university research clusters in the USA received $115.5 billion to support research and development in 2011, the majority of which was directed to the life sciences (57%), engineering (15%), physical sciences (7%), environmental sciences (5%) and maths/computer science (4%). The National Institutes of Health publishes a guidebook for CBR, including community-based participatory research (CBPR), with a heavy emphasis on its application in public health initiatives.

State, provincial and federal agencies could play a more positive role by expanding funding for early career investigators for CES, providing funding to support their community partners, strengthening support for CBPR approaches to scholarship, targeting funds to community–university partnerships for economic development, including engagement criteria in performance agreements, and creating incentives to stimulate university investments in their communities (Dubb, 2007). Much could also be said of the corporate sector and the non-profit and foundation sectors.

APPROACHES TO ENGAGEMENT

SERVICE-LEARNING

In both counties, every form of community engagement is practised to one degree or another (Holland et al., 2010; Schuetze, 2010). Community-engaged teaching and learning involves curricular, co-curricular, continuing education, online courses and degree programmes, alternative spring breaks, study abroad and employee and alumni volunteer programmes. For North America, the question is not one of student interest, but of university investment in increasing service-learning and civic engagement opportunities (Bringle and Hatcher, 2011). The importance of service-learning is well captured by President and Vice Chancellor Axworth of the University of Winnipeg (2009): 'Community learning … recognizes the responsibility of the university to function in an accessible manner and to open itself up to the wide diversity of knowledge and experience represented within society.'

The J.W. McConnell Family Foundation's National Community Service-Learning Program provided resources to ten universities to strengthen or expand service-learning. The programmatic efforts varied among the institutions. For example, the University of Alberta expanded its service-learning unit to create a university-wide network of service-learning, Wilfred Laurier University established a service-learning centre, and Nipissing University expanded its programmes affecting literacy and numeracy skills for children in the Northern region. The Canadian Alliance for Community Service-Learning published a framework to guide the development of community service-learning in Canada (Gemmel and Clayton, 2009).

In the USA, Campus Compact (CC) has 1,100 member institutions serving six million students. A study of 400 CC institutions indicated that there were an average number of 125 partnerships. Extrapolating this to the 1,100 member institutions would produce a conservative estimate of 137,500 partnerships. The estimate is conservative because CC member institutions represent only 25% of HEIs in the USA. Although only 34 of 50 states have CC Affiliates, service and service-learning activities or programmes can be found in all 50 states and all USA Territories. Ninety-one per cent of CC HEIs have a mission statement that includes service, service-learning or civic engagement, and the percentages are higher for faith-based (93%) and minority-serving (95%) institutions (Table IV.6.6). Eighty-one per cent of HEIs solicit community feedback when evaluating partnerships. Eighty-nine per cent of HEIs classified by the Carnegie Foundation for the Advancement of Teaching's engaged institutions were also CC institutions (277 of 311). Ninety-four per cent of CC HEIs offer service-learning courses. The estimated annual value of student service and service-learning to communities is estimated to be $9.1 billion (CC, 2011).

TABLE IV.6.6
Percentage of minority-serving (MHEIs) and other institutions (OHEIs) requiring and supporting service-learning in the USA (2005)

Service-learning	MHEIs	OHEIs
Require service for graduation	18%	8%
Require service-learning for graduation	17%	9%
Have a service-learning office	96%	83%
Have a service-learning director	92%	80%
Have partnerships with K-12 schools	100%	93%
Have partnerships with faith-based institutions	90%	69%

BOX IV.6.1

IMPACT: Individuals Moving People and Community Together – 6,717 Auburn University students participated in 13,434 hours of community service involving elementary schools, retirement homes and humane society.

Beyond Auburn. Auburn University's Outreach Scholarship Magazine (Fall/Winter, 2012)

IMPACT: Simon Fraser University – Intellectual Property Issues in Cultural Heritage. Archaeologist George Nichols leads a team from nine Canadian and 19 international universities and 20 Canadian and international organizations across eight countries in an effort to clarify intellectual property rights associated with cultural tourism, the use of rock art and other images, open versus restricted access to information, applications in new products, bio-archaeology and the uses of ancient genetic data, customary versus legal protections, and research premissions and protocols.

Simon Fraser University News Online: Who owns the past? (2008).

ACADEMIC SERVICE-LEARNING

The CC survey also indicated that 55% of HEIs require academic service-learning as part of the core curriculum, with slightly higher percentages in faith-based (61%) and business, professional and tribal colleges (60%). Approximately 7% of faculty in traditional colleges and universities participate in academic service-learning. The participation rates increase for tribal (15%), historically black colleges and universities (HBCUs) (15%) and faith-based (13%) institutions, but are lower in two-year community colleges (3%). Students report that much of what they learn in service-learning has more to do with non-academic outcomes than course-based materials. Specifically, students report outcomes related to civic knowledge (83%), critical thinking (88%) and service to the community, education for global leadership, student leadership development and student civic learning (all more than 67%). Students' critical reflections are consistent with student-preferred service-learning interest areas: K-12 education (92%), hunger (89%), poverty (88%), housing/homelessness (88%), mentoring (85%), and tutoring (85%). Canadian students apparently 'also achieve significant outcomes in terms of skill development and competencies, workplace experience, understanding of non-profit management and governance, career development, and fulfilment of their "change the world aspirations"' (Gemmel and Clayton, 2009, p. 5).

ALTERNATIVE SPRING BREAK

Seventy-three per cent of CC institutions support alternative spring breaks for students to travel to national or international sites for work on community projects. Student-driven, most alternative spring break projects focus on social justice issues related to poverty and exclusion from full participation in society.

AMERICORPS VISTA

Since 1965, the US government has supported a programme that places students in non-governmental organizations (NGOs) and public agencies for one-year assignments to focus on literacy, health services, employment, housing access, recidivism and access to technology in rural and urban areas of poverty and low income.

STUDY ABROAD

During 2011, 273,996 US students participated in study abroad programmes ranging from several weeks to full semesters. With origins over 100 years ago at Indiana University and the University of Delaware, study abroad has grown significantly during the past

IMPACT: The Montana State University (MSU) Student Chapter of Engineers Without Borders (EWB) is a student-initiated partnership between Montana State University and the people of the Khwisero District of Western Province, Kenya. The organization's primary mission is to bring potable water and clean sanitation facilities to 58 primary schools and the surrounding communities of Khwisero. MSU's project necessitates building sustainable relationships across race, class and cultural difference. Today, EWB is the largest and most successful student-led organization at MSU, with more than 60 active students representing every college within the university. With local fundraising and grant-writing, the group has raised over $375,000 for project implementation, drilled wells at seven primary schools, constructed composting latrines at five schools and a biogas latrine at another, designed a distribution pipeline to link one of the wells to additional schools, a health clinic and a market, and sent over 75 MSU students to collaborate with the people of Khwisero in their development efforts.

Leah Schmalzbauer, Associate Professor, Sociology, Montana State University

IMPACT: York University's Experiential Education program links high-school students with undergraduate students and faculty to provide opportunities to expand high school students' knowledge of real-world situations in information technology, marketing, human resource management and public policy and administration. The Thornlea Secondary School's Specialist High Skills Majors Program is an initiative developed by Ontario's Ministry of Education.

York University's yFile News Service

decade as increasing numbers of students seek cultural, linguistic, and pre-professional experiences prior to graduation (Box IV.6.3). In contrast to an alternative spring break, study abroad tends to focus more on the students' learning experiences than on efforts to improve local conditions through service.

Study abroad – The College of Saint Benedict and Saint John's University offer 19 semester-long study abroad programmes in 15 countries on six continents. Most programmes are faculty-led, a model that is unusual among baccalaureate institutions. In addition, they sponsor dozens of short-term and service learning overseas trips, as well as internship and volunteer opportunities.

COMMUNITY-BASED RESEARCH

The various forms of PAR are especially important for effective community–university partnerships (Flicker et al., 2008). Action research is a process for blending stakeholders and university partners to identify problems of mutual interest, to design action plans to stimulate change, and to determine the methods that will be used to analyse progress and outcomes (Foster-

Fishman and Watson, 2010). PAR is a co-creative effort recognizing that partnerships must be inclusive, democratic and anchored in multiple forms of knowledge. A form of PAR – CBR – is a widespread practice in HEIs across North America. Less common are the participatory versions of CBR, such as PAR and CBPR.

CBPR emphasizes processes that embed co-creation. Combined with CBPR practices, the knowledge-creation process ideally enriches engagement and integrates discovery and learning to allow for a more effective creation, application and then re-creation of knowledge that serves society's needs (Minkler et al., 2012). CBPR involves individuals from higher education and the community working side by side to define the questions and methods (blending tacit/indigenous knowledge), implement the research (explicit knowledge), disseminate the findings and apply them, and determine what new tacit knowledge has been discovered through the scholarship of application (Galliher et al., 2012). CBPR approaches are especially of interest to HEIs that are not funded as major research universities because they provide unique opportunities for faculty to engage students in evidence-based practices through service-learning and academic service-learning (Fletcher, 2003; Gemmel and Clayton, 2009).

When partnerships focus on systemic action research (SAR), they must first determine the current structure of the system in order to leverage changes in components that may influence systems change. Because community–university partnerships increasingly involve community-based initiatives, it is important that they implement SAR practices – identify systems norms, identify system resources, identify system regulations, identify system power operations and identify system interdependencies (Foster-Fishman and Watson, 2010) – before constructing theories of change. These issues are critically important for partnerships with indigenous communities (Sahota, 2010; Fletcher, 2011; NCAI Policy Research Centre, 2012).

INSTITUTIONAL STRUCTURES SUPPORTING ENGAGEMENT

Most engagement activities in Canada and the USA are supported institutionally within the office of the president/chancellor or within the office of the provost. In most cases, each of the administrators responsible for facilitating the implementation of the institution's engagement mission is supported by a small staff, but in some instances universities invest heavily in senior-level support or through a workforce of outreach/engagement staff distributed throughout the institution. For land grant institutions in the USA or for Canadian institutions with an extension mission, a considerable infrastructure exists to support engagement efforts. In the USA, land grant universities have extension programmes funded in the millions of dollars, for example consisting of a combination of federal, state, university and community investments, and these programmes literally reach every corner of the State.

ORGANIZATIONAL STRUCTURES

Although there are countless ways in which universities partner with diverse communities, Hall et al.'s (2009) analysis generated four major types of partnerships. Type one involves individual faculty working with community partners to achieve common goals that are important to them, but no institutional role is associated with the partnership. This is probably the most common form of community–university partnership because it spans the broadest domain of engaged research, teaching and service.

Type two refers to centres and institutes that emerge with institutional support, most commonly bound to a particular discipline or set of disciplines focused on a specific content domain. This type of partnership is also referred to as co-optive (Martinez, 2005). Co-optive approaches are characterized by investments in centres and institutes, each of which has a targeted

mission such as environmental toxicology, maths and science education, public health, community and economic development, or service-learning. In fact, in many research universities there may be more centres and institutes than disciplinary departments. Many centres and institutes conduct basic research, but many others have an explicit scholarship of application mission. Many engaged organizations are increasingly moving towards the CBPR side of the CBR continuum of methods. Many were developed to play a key role in government- or business-funded areas of concern (environmental toxicology, food safety, air-borne or virally transmitted disease).

The third type of partnership identified by Hall et al. (2009) refers to an inclusive investment at the institutional level to define engagement scholarship as central to the mission of the university.

Inclusive institutions are more likely to embrace the concept that engagement cuts across the teaching, research and service components of mission, incorporating both types one and two and aligning the institution fully, and supporting faculty engagement scholarship through the promotion and tenure process. These institutions often have an infrastructure support staff who serve as boundary-spanners, or connectors, linking faculty and academic staff with community partners. Finally, type four partnerships involve multi-university collaborations with community partners from significantly diverse places but united in a common concern, such as preservation of the Great Lakes, food production in Africa or biotechnologies and renewable energies.

How particular institutions organize their commitments to CES varies more within Canada and the USA than it does between the two countries. Indeed, this comment applies to nearly every comparison of higher education between the two countries. Mirza's (2011) scan of the engagement structures of 32 universities in Canada suggests that most universities locate engagement in specific offices or institutes (co-optive), whereas Guelph, Alberta, Memorial, Toronto, Victoria and Windsor universities reflect more of the inclusive or mixed approaches. Moreover, the analysis clearly indicates that all would qualify for inclusion in the Carnegie Foundation's engaged university classification. Many of Canada's several hundred colleges are most likely also to have active programmes in continuing education and/or service-learning. In the USA, over 300 institutions now hold the Carnegie classification of engaged university, which represents an underestimate of the number of 4,500 institutions of higher education that most likely practise at least one of the four modes of engagement.

INSTITUTIONAL REVIEW BOARDS

The diversity of CES has led many Institutions to develop separate institutional review boards for community research. Many larger community NGOs and schools maintain their own community review boards, as do many First Nations and AI/AN communities (Albert Einstein College of Medicine, 2012).

MUSEUMS, PERFORMING ARTS CENTRES AND FESTIVALS

Many universities support museums, performing arts centres, departments of theatre and/or music and athletics, all of which provide public access. There are at least 22 HEI museums in Canada. The USA has 444 HEI museums and galleries, the vast majority specializing in art and cultural heritage. Many museums sponsor folk, science or music festivals in partnership with local communities in addition to presenting on-campus and travelling exhibits in the art, folk, cultural, history and natural science domains. There are slightly more than 100 museums that are affiliates of the Smithsonian Museum in Washington, DC.

MEASUREMENTS AND METRICS

Assessing the impact of community–university partnerships for effecting sustainable change is difficult (Lall, 2010). At the project level, outcomes generally can be tied rather closely to the methods used to determine whether interventions have achieved their desired outcomes. Prevention studies ordinarily take a considerable time to determine whether the desired outcomes have been achieved. At the level of systems change, the determination of transformative change may take years to observe 'causal' relationships between partnership efforts and the desired outcomes. It is essential that partners determine expected outcomes from the beginning of any project and continue to monitor change processes throughout. Another aspect of assessment is related to transformative change in the students, faculty and academic staff involved in the partnerships. Wenger and MacInnis (2011) conducted an intensive review of assessment tools related to CES and provide a significant resource to guide contextually appropriate assessments. Similarly, Granner and Sharpe (2004) provide a detailed review of measurement tools used to evaluate community coalitions and partnerships.

MAIN TOPICS/THEMES TACKLED IN THE REGION

ECONOMIC DEVELOPMENT

In both countries, research-intensive universities have developed corporate research parks to stimulate private–public partnerships to facilitate the transfer of science and technology discoveries at the universities to private companies. During the past five years, many universities have developed community-based innovation and entrepreneurial centres in partnership with local, regional and state government agencies and chambers of commerce in order to stimulate economic development.

In both countries, HEIs are engines of economic growth and community development. In many cases, HEIs are the longest standing institutions in the community, hire the most employees and, through their students and employees, generate enormous economic impact for local merchants in the apparel, housing and food industries. Many institutions rent or purchase buildings in urban or rural areas remote from the main campus in order to support faculty and students when working in communities remote from campus. Many institutions also form inter-university partnerships to address critical problems that are multi-region in scope, such as water quality, air quality and wind and solar energy, capitalizing on multidisciplinary teams and the inclusion of community voices in order to model contextual variations across states or geographies, or cultures. The major areas of economic activity are: (1) direct economic support (employment, purchasing and resources-sharing); (2) human capital (educating students, staff and community members; (3) knowledge transfer (patents, application of knowledge and business partnerships); and (4) investments in innovation (university research parks for private–public partnerships, innovation centres and economic zones).

An analysis of one state's trio of public research-intensive universities indicated that their combined economic impact in 2011 was $15.5 billion, producing a 17:1 return for investments in funding relative to income generated for the State. The Anderson Report noted that the three universities employed 52,200 people (11,400 faculty and 40,800 support staff) and paid $4.6 billion in salaries. Alumni from the three universities living in the state number 590,000 and had a combined income of $29.2 billion in 2011. When these impacts are projected to the top 100 research universities in the USA, the economic impact of HEIs is extraordinary. Nearly all universities have policies and practices that assure inclusive access from businesses for bids related to contractual work with universities.

INTERNAL IMPACT OF CES

Aligning the institution to incorporate CES into its mission requires leadership from the president/chancel-

lor and the provost (or other chief academic officer) of
the university if the deans, chairs and directors are to
seriously consider its value relative to the institutional
mission (Albert, 1985; Burkhart et al., 2004: Furco,
2010). Many of the professional associations noted in
Table IV.6.4 are HEI-member rather than individual
member organizations, and nearly all require the president or chancellor to endorse their membership. Senior-
level administrators must also publically articulate the
institution's engagement mission. The Association of
American Colleges and Universities, the Canadian
Alliance for Community Service-Learning and the
University of Victoria have published frameworks
for infusing civic engagement throughout academic
life. Moreover, one cannot underestimate the impact
of statements such as that offered by the Governor
General of Canada (26 May 2012):

> As a scholar – a Canadian scholar – I believe we
> must reconsider the role of scholarship in how we
> apply our learning, in how we make knowledge more
> widely available to Canadians, and in how we further
> democratize knowledge for all people.

OUTREACH CONNECTORS AND BOUNDARY-SPANNERS

Top-level administrators can articulate the vision, but
for faculty to be successful in engagement efforts,
the university needs to have a cadre of staff who can
play key roles in building connections between the
university and the diverse communities with whom the
university partners (Boyte, 2004). These individuals
span boundaries that separate community members or
organizations and universities from one another. Often
boundary-spanners have rich personal experience in
communities before being hired into university positions, for example hiring a retired or available former
vice-president of a drug company to head up a university entity established to facilitate technology transfer
or to connect businesses to university faculty, or hiring
a former deputy director of a state department of education to be an outreach coordinator for K-12 education.
Boundary-spanners are an integral component of the
engagement process because they can readily translate
their knowledge of community and university to each
side of the partnership.

CURRICULAR DEVELOPMENT AND TEACHING PRACTICES

There are three significant trends in instructional development related to CES. First, the number of academic
service-learning courses is increasing dramatically.
Second, there is a significant increase in the role of
community partners in shaping course contents to

support the skills needed for 21st-century information technology jobs. Third, there is an explosive interest in open educational resources, which refers to 'free online resources for learning, including courses and course-based materials, textbooks, video and audio, multimedia applications, educational websites, reference works, games, simulations, self-assessments, and more' (Weiland, 2012, p. 5). While these avenues to knowledge may promote readiness and self-learning, it is not yet clear how they integrate easily into CES, service-learning and civic engagement.

PROFESSORIATE

Aligning HE to an engagement mission requires a change in the criteria for promotion and the review of tenure. A key first step is to redefine what kinds of scholarship flow from CES, particularly when CES is viewed as cutting across the teaching, research and service triad that defines faculty work (Table IV.6.7). Imagining America's taskforce on promotion and tenure guidelines for art and design is one example of a national effort to transform faculty performance evaluations. Michigan State University, Portland State University, Pennsylvania State University and Syracuse University were among institutions that broadened the criteria for assessing faculty scholarship during the 1990s. Table IV.6.8 provides a summary of the four aspects of engaged scholarship that are assessed at Michigan State University. Faculty are provided with a rich set of qualitative and quantitative indicators of each of the four core components of the 'Points of Distinction'. Community-Campus Partnerships for

---

TABLE IV.6.7
Types of CES

Engaged research and creative activity	Engaged teaching and learning	Engaged service
CBR	Online and off-campus education	Technical assistance
Applied research	Continuing education	Consulting
Contractual research	Occupational short courses, certificates and licensure	Policy analysis
Demonstration projects		Expert testimony
Needs and assets assessments	Contract instructional programmes	Knowledge transfer
Programme evaluations	Participatory curriculum development	Commercialization of discoveries
Translation of scholarship through presentations, websites and publications	Non-credit classes and programmes	Creation of new ventures
	Conferences, seminars and workshops	Clinical services
Exhibitions and performances	Educational enrichment programmes for the public and alumni	Human and animal care
		Service-learning, study abroad, pre-college programmes

Michigan State University, University Outreach and Engagement 2009.

TABLE IV.6.8
Points of Distinction: selected exemplars from the matrix for evaluating quality outreach for promotion and tenure

Dimension	Components	Qualitative indicators	Quantitative indicators
Significance	Goals/objectives of consequence	Narrative discussing scope and potential impact All stakeholders understand the goals and objectives as stated Increased visibility in the community or profession; new structures created, new skills developed and knowledge generated	Projections of scope and potential impact Degree of opportunity to change the situation Objectives achieved
Context	Appropriateness of methods	Evidence of scholarship on the application of the method to related issues Narrative showing degree of fit between project needs and expertise deployed	Number of instances of innovations in delivery, for example student involvement or use of technology Number of stakeholders in leadership roles
Scholarship	Knowledge generation	Assessment of scholarly merit by an internal peer review process External review of performance by stakeholders	Number of times the project is cited; publications, speaking engagements, requests for consulting, exhibits
Impact	Sustainability and capacity-building	Inventory of new or developed skills Technology adopted and maintained Networks activated, activities and processes institutionalized	Quantitative changes in skills, technologies, behaviours, activities, etc. Amount of resources generated to sustain the project Amount of resources leveraged

Source: Zimmerman © 1996, 2000, Michigan State University Board of Trustees. Adapted with permission.

Health has prepared an in-depth set of tools for advising HEIs on integrating engagement scholarship into the promotion and tenure review process across broad disciplines (Jordon, 2007). The National Review Board (University of Georgia) provides non-tenured faculty with evaluative feedback on their promotion portfolios prior to standing for the review process.

FACULTY RECRUITING

Hiring practices are increasingly embracing efforts to shift towards multidisciplinary research areas (neurosciences, food production, transport, safety and security, water quality and use, land use, toxicology, non-carbon energy sources, regional economic development and transformational changes in urban core centres). Not only has there been an increase in the hiring of public sociologists, public anthropologists, community psychologists and community physicians, but many HEIs are also hiring new faculty who have joint appointments from the outset of their careers (Boyte, 2004).

AWARDS

Higher education is increasingly including awards and recognitions for community–campus partnerships at the same level as other institutional awards, and is adding endowed professorships in areas where CBR is explicitly critical to the resolution of societal problems and to the university's mission. Nearly all universities now recognize various aspects of engagement scholarship with awards to students for exemplary participation or practice. Faculty members are recognized for leadership in advancing student civic learning, CBPR, reciprocal practices in community–university partnerships and building institutional commitment to service-learning (Martinez-Brawley, 2003). Such awards also exist at the national level, for example the McConnell Foundation Community Service Award in Canada, and in the USA the President's Higher Education Community Service Honor Roll, the W.K. Kellogg regional and Peter Magrath national awards for engagement scholarship, and the CC Thomas Ehrlich Civic Engagement awards are among the most prestigious recognitions given at the national level.

ALUMNI

The most significant movement in the USA is Citizen Alum. This is a programme from the American Commonwealth Partnership promoted by the White House (ACPonline at DemocracyU) that stresses building connections with alumni based not on their donor potential, but on their ability to give public visibility by facilitating their involvement in participatory research and community engagement involving local people as well as current university students. Giving purpose to the millions of alumni across the expanse of North America could mobilize an enormous force for community engagement. Citizen Alum is currently housed at the University of Michigan.

MAIN SOCIAL ACTORS

In North America, the CES movement touches every component of the four helixes of systems change: civil society, business, government and higher education. Partnerships with segments of civil society tend to focus on issues of social justice, with a heavy emphasis on families living in circumstances ranging from poverty to the working poor, and on minority populations that have experienced historical injustices. Partnerships with businesses focus on regional economic development, technology transfer, information technology, food production and distribution, healthcare and alternative energy. Partnerships with government focus on early childhood and K-12 public education, with special emphasis on STEM disciplines, workforce development and economic development. Partnerships with higher education revolve around multi-university collaborations that bring clusters of universities and community partners together to solve complex interactive problems.

STRATEGIES AND ACTIONS TO ADVANCE THE REGION

Higher education in Canada and the USA collectively has embraced engagement scholarship as an avenue to building successful community–university partnerships across all forms of engagement and involving every disciplinary field in the academy.

CIVIC EDUCATION

The US National Task Force on Civic Learning and Democratic Engagement's *A Crucible Moment* report advanced specific recommendations related to HEI's responsibilities for integrating civic learning fully within all disciplines and activities involving student life (National Task Force on Civic Learning and Democratic Engagement, 2012). The report provided guidelines for addressing the question, 'What would a civic-minded campus look like?' (Box IV.6.6). The report is clear in advocating the centrality of engagement for every student as fundamental for instilling and preserving the core values of democracy and democratic processes in civic society.

BOX IV.6.6: WHAT WOULD A CIVIC-MINDED CAMPUS LOOK LIKE?

CIVIC ETHOS GOVERNING CAMPUS LIFE

The infusion of democratic values into the customs and habits of everyday practices, structures, and interactions; the defining character of the institution and those in it that emphasizes open-mindedness, civility, the worth of each person, ethical behaviors, and concern for the well-being of others; a spirit of public-mindedness that influences the goals of the institution and its engagement with local and global communities.

CIVIC LITERACY AS A GOAL FOR EVERY STUDENT

The cultivation of foundational knowledge about fundamental principles of debates about democracy expressed over time both with in the United States and in other countries; familiarity with several key historical struggles, campaigns, and social movements undertaken to achieve the full promise of democracy; the ability to think critically about complex issues and to seek and evaluate information about issues that have public consequences.

CIVIC INQUIRY INTEGRATED WITHIN THE MAJORS AND GENERAL EDUCATION

The practice of inquiring about the civic dimensions and public consequences of a subject of study; the exploration of the impact of choices on different constituencies and entities, including the planet; the deliberate consideration for differing points of view; the ability to describe and analyze civic intellectual debates within one's major or areas of study.

CIVIC ACTION AS LIFELONG PRACTICE

The capacity and commitment both to participate constructively with diverse others and to work collectively to address common problems; the practice of working in a pluralistic society and world to improve the quality of people's lives and the sustainability of the planet; the ability to analyze systems in order to plan and engage in public action; the moral and political courage to take risks to achieve a greater public good.

Source: National Task Force on Civic Learning and Democratic Engagement (2012, p.15).

CENTRALITY OF ENGAGEMENT IN HEIs

Faculty and academic staff individually and in teams will continue to be at the fore with respect to community–university engagement partnerships. But universities need to provide mechanisms to create backbone support in order to monitor the collective impact; otherwise, it is unlikely that collaborative partnerships will achieve transformative systems change.

Higher education needs to be innovation-focused, doing things differently from in the past. If past attempts to correct a societal problem have failed, new innovations are needed to move to second-order transformations. And innovation must come from multidisciplinary teaming as well as from community–university partnerships that embrace co-creation as core to problem-solving, and collective impact as a big idea desired outcome.

Higher education must also be knowledge-driven, making greater use of the interplay between tacit and explicit knowledge and continuing to seek evidence to guide data-driven decision-making in partnership with the community. Higher education must make wise

decisions along the risk-to-resilience continuum, while cautiously making risk–benefit analyses before taking on wicked problems, that is, those problems for which there are no good ideas about causal factors, nor any good ideas about possible solutions. Higher education must focus on evidence-based practice, making sure that research and scholarly engagement with communities interlocks community needs with disciplinary interests.

Higher education needs to recognize that sustainability for community–university partnerships is a two-way street. Programmatic efforts to effect change in some part of a complex system must involve knowledge transfer to and from community as well as to and from faculty if true innovation is to be achieved. Higher education must establish innovative and entrepreneurial opportunities wherever possible, and focus on outcomes as much as it focuses on individual programme outcomes so that programmes are aligned to the system in which they are embedded.

Finally, higher education must embrace a range of epistemologies in order to guide its efforts, but the common thread is to bind students and communities into experiences that give meaning to democracy, deliberative dialogue, and commitment to civil discourse and to transformative change (Dibos, 2002; Boyte, 2004).

DIVERSITY AND ENGAGEMENT

The critical question for each country concerns the role that HEIs play in transforming societies into a population mix that will be majority–minority within the next generation. What do HEIs hope to gain by having faculty and students working on projects in diverse community contexts (Dibos, 2002)? Is work in these communities designed to serve faculty needs, or is the intent to work with communities to make sustainable and transformative change?

Having a project partnership with a First Nations or American Indian early childhood programme may produce gains for the children in the project, but unless the successful programme is taken to scale, little will occur to transform the systemic conditions that keep First Nation or Tribal children and their families so vulnerable to the injustices of racial and social inequity (Fitzgerald and Farrell, 2012). If there is a great partnership between a faculty member and a small business which enables that business to successfully expand, how does this success go to scale and fuel community-wide economic growth? Higher education needs to focus on collective impacts so that individual programme initiatives contribute to systems change guided by the same tacit/indigenous-explicit approaches that work for individual community–university partnerships.

SYSTEMS CHANGE: COLLECTIVE IMPACT

Most of the problems in contemporary programmes consist of what Ackoff (1999) refers to as messes, or complex interacting problems. Co-creative problem-solving can be especially helpful for efforts to achieve sustainable solutions to complex situations. So, the critical question for higher education and engagement scholarship is: how do we go about building community–university partnerships to solve messes? Transforming community, economic, family life, health and education issues requires systems-framed efforts to guide more narrow programme-focused preventive interventions that have not proven to be successful in producing systems change. So, to play an effective role in solving messes, partnerships need to be driven by big ideas and creative systems thinking (Patton, 2012) (Figure IV.6.3). Longitudinal efforts to build sustainable and evidence-driven

change models will require a deeper discussion of the promotion and tenure process as well as criteria that are indicative of success. At all times, partners need to remember that 'A partial solution to a whole system of problems is better than whole solutions of each of its parts taken separately' (Alpaslan and Mitroff, 2011, pp. xiii–xiv).

METRICS: HOW WILL WE RECOGNIZE SUCCESS?

What common metric will inform all of the partnerships about the collective transformational changes occurring as a result of their efforts? What feedback does each partnership receive that may inform it about conflicts caused by the partnerships themselves? Kania and Kramer (2013) offer a recipe for building assessment into systems efforts to track collective impact:

● Develop a common agenda so that there is a shared vision for change.
● Develop a shared measurement procedure so that data collection and measurement are consistent.
● Use mutually reinforcing activities so that varied activities are coordinated through a plan of action (for example, through an overall logic model or theory of change).
● Maintain continuous communication to build and reinforce trust to support mutual objectives and common motivation.
● Have backbone support consisting of an organization and skilled staff to coordinate the effort. Community–university partnership teams can serve as the backbone support to continuously monitor the project's progress and the collective impact of the overall system.

CONCLUSION

In North America, society requires that its community of scholars develops innovations to resolve a variety of problems across multiple contexts. These problems relate to: competitiveness in a global economy; the quality of early childhood, pre-K and K-12 education; healthcare access and delivery; the stability and security of families and the community; the security of food and water supplies; effective land use and sustainable, built environments; community and interpersonal violence and antisocial behaviour; and tolerance for diversity in all of its forms. Community change requires a much broader conceptualization of the community of scholars, one that recognizes non-academic, experiential knowledge as being equally as important as campus knowledge for the resolution of

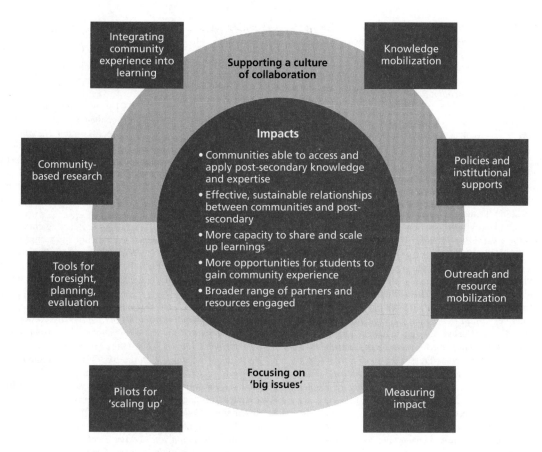

FIGURE IV.6.3 Community–campus collaboration initiatives
Source: United Way—Centraide Canada. One World, Inc. 2012.

community problems. The resolution of societal problems will not come from the community of scholars or from politicians, school superintendents, fire marshalls, social critics or corporate CEOs alone. Evidence clearly indicates that HEIs in North America have committed to the transformative changes necessary to democratize knowledge, to instil a deeper sense of civic purpose in all community–university partnership participants, to give voice and effort to rectify historical practices that have created deeply ingrained social injustices, and to stand strong in support of democratic principles in both Canada and the USA.

REFERENCES

Ackoff, R.L. (1999) *Re-Creating the Corporation.* New York: Oxford University Press.

Albert, D. (1985) 'Performance and paralysis: the organizational context of the American research university'. *Journal of Higher Education,* 56, 241–81.

Albert Einstein College of Medicine, Bronx Health Link and Community-Campus Partnerships for Health (2012) *Community IRBs and Research Review Boards: Shaping the Future of Community-engaged Research.* Bronx, NY: Albert Einstein College of Medicine, Bronx Health Link and Community-Campus Partnerships for Health.

Alexander, A. (1997) *The Antigonish Movement: Moses Coady and Adult Education Today.* Toronto: Thompson Educational Publishing.

Alpaslan, C.M. and Mitroff, I.I. (2011) *Swans, Swine and Swindlers: Coping with the Growing Threat of Mega-crises and Mega-messes.* Stanford, CA: Stanford University Press.

Archer, W. and Wright, K. (1999) 'Back to the future: adjusting university continuing education research to an emerging trend'. *Canadian Journal of University Continuing Education,* 25, 61–84.

Axworth, L. (2009). 'The University and Community Learning: An Evolving Mission'. Presented at the Canadian Club Luncheon, November 27.

Bonnen, J.T. (1998) 'The land-grant idea and the evolving outreach university'. In: Lerner, R.M. and Simon, L.A.K. (eds) *University-Community Collaborations for the 21st Century.* New York: Garland, pp. 25–70.

Boyer, E.L. (1990) *Scholarship Reconsidered: Priorities of the Professoriate.* San Francisco: Jossey-Bass.

Boyer, E.L. (1996) 'The scholarship of engagement'. *Journal of Public Service and Outreach,* 1(1), 11–20.

Boyte, H.B. (2004) *Going Public: Academics and Public Life.* Dayton, OH: Kettering Foundation.

Bringle, R.G. and Hatcher, J.A. (2011) 'Student engagement trends over time'. In: Fitzgerald, H.E., Burack, C. and

Seifer, S.D. (eds) *Handbook of Engaged Scholarship: Contemporary Landscapes, Future Directions*, Volume 2: *Community–Campus Partnerships*. East Lansing, MI: Michigan State University Press, pp. 411–30.

Burkhart, M.J., Holland, B., Percy, S.L. and Zimpher, N. (2004) *Is Higher Education Ready to Commit to Community Engagement?* Racine, WI: Wingspread.

Campus Compact (2011) *Deepening the Roots of Civic Engagement*. Annual Membership Survey. Boston: Campus Compact.

Coady, M. (1939) *Masters of their Own Destiny: The Story of the Antigonish Movement of Adult Education Through Economic Cooperation*. New York: Harper & Brothers.

Dibos, A. (2002) 'Democracy as responsibility, meaning, and hope: introductory reflections on a democratic project in education'. *Journal of Thought*, 37(1), 11–24.

Dubb, S. (2007) *Linking Colleges to Communities*. College Park, MD: Democracy Collaborative, University of Maryland.

Fitzgerald, H.E. and Farrell, P. (2012) 'Fulfilling the promise: creating a child development research agenda with native communities'. *Child Development Perspectives*, 6, 75–8.

Fitzgerald, H E. and Primavera, J. (eds) (2013) *Going Public: Civic and Community Engagement*. East Lansing, MI: Michigan State University Press.

Fitzgerald, H.E. and Simon, L.A.K. (2012) 'The world grant ideal and engagement scholarship'. *Journal of Higher Education Outreach and Engagement*, 16(3), 31–53.

Fitzgerald, H.E., Smith, P., Book, P., Rodin, K. and CIC Committee on Engagement (2005) *Draft CIC Report: Resource Guide and Recommendations for Defining and Benchmarking Engagement*. Champaign, IL: Committee on Institutional Cooperation.

Fitzgerald, H.E., Bruns, K., Sonka, S.T., Furco, A. and Swanson, L. (2012) 'Centrality of engagement in higher education'. *Journal of Higher Education Outreach and Engagement*, 16(3), 1–30.

Fletcher, C. (2003) 'Community-based participatory research relationships with Aboriginal communities in Canada: an overview of content and process'. *Pimatisiwin: A Journal of Aboriginal and Indigenous Community Health*, 1, 27–62.

Fletcher, M.L.M. (2011) 'The Indian Child Welfare Act: implications for American Indian and Alaska Native children and their families'. In: Sarche, M.C., Spicer, P., Farrell, P. and Fitzgerald, H.E. (eds) *American Indian and Alaska Native Children and Mental Health: Development, Context, Prevention and Treatment*. Santa Barbara, CA: ABC/CLIO Praeger, pp. 269–84.

Flicker, S., Savan, B. and Mildenberger, M. (2008) 'A snapshot of community-based research in Canada: Who? What? Why? How?' *Health Education Research*, 23, 106–14.

Foster-Fishman, P. and Watson, E.R. (2010) 'Action research as systems change'. In Fitzgerald, H.E., Burack, C. and Seifer, S. (eds) *Handbook of Engaged Scholarship: Contemporary Landscape, Future Directions*, Volume 2. East Lansing, MI: Michigan State University Press, pp. 235–25.

Furco, A. (2010) 'The engaged campus: toward a comprehensive approach to public-engagement'. *British Journal of Educational Studies*, 58(4), 375–90.

Galliher, R.V., Tsethlikai, M.M. and Stolle, D. (2012) 'Perspectives of native and non-native scholars: oppor-

tunities for collaboration'. *Child Development Perspectives*, 6, 66–74.

Gemmel, L.J. and Clayton, P.H. (2009) *A Comprehensive Framework for Community Service-learning in Canada*. Ottawa: Canadian Alliance for Community Service-Learning.

Glass, C.R. and Fitzgerald, H.E. (2010) 'Engaged scholarship: historical roots, contemporary challenges'. In: Fitzgerald, H.E., Burack, C. and Seifer, S. (eds) *Handbook of Engaged Scholarship: Contemporary Landscapes, Future Directions*, Volume 1: *Institutional Change*. East Lansing, MI: Michigan State University Press.

Glassick, C., Huber, M. and Maeroff, G. (1997) *Scholarship Assessed: Evaluation of the Professoriate*. San Francisco: Jossey-Bass.

Granner, M.L. and Sharpe, P.A. (2004) 'Evaluating community coalitions characteristics and functioning: a summary of measurement tools'. *Health Education Research: Theory and Practice*, 19, 514–32.

Hall, B. (2005) 'In from the cold? Reflections on participatory research 1970–2005'. *Convergence*, 38(1), 5–24.

Hall, B., Tremblay, C. and Downing, R. (2009) *The Funding and Development of Community University Research Partnerships in Canada: Evidence-based Investment in Knowledge, Engaged Scholarship, Innovation and Action for Canada's Future*. Victoria, BC: Office of Community Based Research, University of Victoria.

Holland, D., Powell, D.E., Eng, E. and Drew, G. (2010) 'Models of engaged scholarship: an interdisciplinary discussion'. *Collaborative Anthropologies*, 3, 1–36.

Jordon, C. (ed.) (2007) *Community-engaged Scholarship Review, Promotion and Tenure Package. Peer Review Workgroup, Community-engaged Scholarship for Health, Collaborative Community-Campus Partnerships for Health*. Washington: Community-Campus Partnerships for Health.

Kania, J. and Kramer, M. (2013) 'Embracing emergence: how collective impact addresses complexity'. *Stanford Social Innovation Review*, January.

Kellogg Commission (2000) *Renewing the Covenant: Learning, Discovery, and Engagement in a New Age and Different World*. Washington: National Association of State Universities and Land Grant Colleges.

Kellogg Commission (2001) *Returning to our Roots: Executive Summaries of the Reports of the Kellogg Commission on the Future of State and Land Grant Universities*. Washington, DC: National Association of State Universities and Land Grant Colleges, p. 16.

Lall, N. (2010) 'Measuring the impact of university-community research partnerships: a literature review of theories, concepts, tools and practices'. In: Inman, P. and Schuetze, H.G. (eds) *The Community Engagement and Service Mission of Universities*. Leicester: NIACE, pp. 87–102.

Martinez, R.O. (2005) 'Latino demographic and institutional issues in higher education: implications for leadership development'. In: D. Leon (ed.), *Lessons in Leadership: Executive Leadership Programs for Advancing Diversity in Higher Education*. Oxford: Elsevier Science, pp. 17–55.

Martinez-Brawley, E.E. (2003) 'The scholarship of engagement in a research university: faculty incentives and disincentives'. *Metropolitan Universities Journal: An International Forum*, 14(4), 116–30.

Minkler, M., Garcia, A.P., Rubin, V. and Wallerstine, N. (2012) *Community-based Participatory Research: A Strategy for Building Healthy Communities and Promoting*

Health Through Policy Change. Berkeley, CA: School of Public Health, University of California Berkeley.

Mirza, R. (2011) *Scan of Engagement Structures in Canadian Universities*. St John's, NL: Memorial University Office of Engagement.

National Task Force on Civic Learning and Democratic Engagement (2012) *A Crucible Moment: College Learning and Democracy's Future*. Washington, DC: Association of American Colleges and Universities, p. 15.

NCAI Policy Research Center and MSU Center for Native Health Partnerships (2012) *Walk Softly and Listen Carefully: Building Research Relationships with Tribal Communities*. Washington, DC/Bozeman, MT: NCAI Policy Research Center/MSU Center for Native Health Partnerships.

Nonaka, I. and Takeuchi, H. (1995) *The Knowledge Creating Company*. New York: Oxford University Press.

Patton, M. (2012) 'How to Evaluate Interventions in Complex Dynamic Environments'. Webinar, February 28, 2012.

Ramaley, J. (2000) 'Embracing civic responsibility'. *AAHE Bulletin*, 52(7), 9–13.

Selman, M. (2005) 'An identity for Canadian university education'. *Canadian Journal of Continuing Education*, 31(1), 19–27.

Sahota, P.C. (2010) *Community-based Participatory Research in American Indian and Alaska Native*

Communities. Washington, DC: NCAI Policy Research Center.

Schuetze, H.G. (2010) 'The 'third mission' of universities: community engagement and service'. In: Inman, P. and Schuetze, H.G. (eds) *The Community Engagement and Service Mission of Universities*. Leicester: NIACE, pp. 13–31.

Sonka, S.T., Lins, D.A., Schroeder, R.C. and Hofing, S.L. (2000) 'Production agriculture as a knowledge creating system'. *International Food and Agribusiness Management Review*, 2(2), 165–78.

Stanton, T.K. (2007) *New Times Demand New Scholarship: Research Universities and Civic Engagement: Opportunities and Challenges*. Los Angeles: University of California.

Weiland, S. (2012) *Open Educational Resources: Online Learning, Open Courseware, and Work Force Development*. East Lansing, MI: Michigan State University, EDA University Center for Regional Economic Innovation.

Wenger, L. and MacInnis, A. (2011) *Inventory of Tools for Assessing University Capacity, Support for, and Outcomes of Community/Civic Engagement and Community-engagement Scholarship*. Washington, DC: Association of Public and Land Grant Universities.

Zimmerman, D. L. (ed.) (1996, 2000) *Points of Distinction: A Guidebook for Planning and Evaluating Quality Outreach*. East Lansing, MI: Michigan State University Press.

Inside View IV.6.1
Research and training beyond the university walls

Sylvie B. de Grosbois and Yves Mauffette

Université du Québec à Montréal (UQAM) is an urban, comprehensive, public French-language university. Since its foundation, UQAM has been engaged in research and training activities with non-profit organizations. An institutional policy on community services was adopted in 1979, which led the way to several approaches indented to support faculty members participating in partnership projects. These institutional approaches are presented here. Community–university engagement (CUE) initiatives are also being developed in other higher education institutions in Quebec; a few examples will be presented here, along with their specific features. Challenges for future development are also discussed.

INTRODUCTION

Involved since its foundation in 1969 in rethinking engagement and the social responsibility of higher education institutions, UQAM has developed institutional approaches intended to support faculty members implicated in partnership projects with non-governmental organizations (NGOs). Designed to facilitate involvement, these approaches aim to recognize

engagement as part of the first two missions of universities (research and teaching), which are often perceived as the most important aspects for academics' tenure tracks. These approaches were developed on the premises that such an engagement would contribute to a better knowledge-based society and to improvements in teaching and research functions for the institution. UQAM remains the only higher institution in Quebec offering such institutional support. Other universities in Quebec have developed CUE initiatives, mainly through training programmes (adapted to specific populations or co-op-based) or research projects carried out by institutes, centres or research chairs.

This paper aims to present: (1) UQAM's institutional approaches for facilitating community–university partnerships engaged in co-creating and exchanging knowledge; (2) examples of other CUE initiatives in Quebec; and finally (3) challenges for future development.

UQAM'S INSTITUTIONAL APPROACHES

UQAM, an urban, comprehensive, public

French-language university, was founded with the mandate of making higher education more accessible and more democratic. Accessibility was defined in a broad sense to encompass sectors of the community not usually served by universities, mainly NGOs, women's groups and unions involved in collective advancement. An institutional policy on community services (see http://www.instances.uqam.ca/ReglementsPolitiquesDocuments/Pages/Politiqueno41.aspx), which promotes the democratization of access for these groups, was adopted in 1979, and concrete approaches were implemented to facilitate and encourage community–university partnerships. This institutional policy was developed based on several founding principles:

- the recognition of NGOs and other groups as full and effective partners of the university in terms of training and research activities;
- a recognition that this strategic partnering, based on intellectual inputs and knowledge-sharing, would enable all the partners to pool their resources to achieve results they could not attain alone;

- a project-by-project approach in which the identification of partners, objectives and methods had to be agreed upon prior to the development of each project;
- the necessity of setting up institutional procedures and criteria to ensure both the social relevancy and the scientific quality of projects;
- the recognition that training as well as research or creative activities carried out with NGOs would be integrated into the regular duties of a faculty member, namely teaching and research, and not relegated solely to a third mission promoting the diffusion of knowledge;
- the importance of knowledge mobilization to achieve engagement and social responsibility at UQAM.

Recognizing and integrating these activities as part of regular task of faculty members was structured as follows.

BOARD OF COMMUNITY SERVICES
The creation of the Board of Community Services (BCS), co-governed by eight in-house and eight NGO representatives, followed shortly after the adoption of UQAM's institutional policy. Its mandate is to provide recommendations on UQAM's institutional priorities on community engagement and to evaluate the different projects that are presented for institutional support (training or research and creative activities).

TRAINING OR RESEARCH ACTIVITIES
Nine hundred hours of training or research activities are made available yearly. Therefore, a faculty member involved with NGOs in providing training or research activities can be exempted from one of their regular teaching assignments (at UQAM, each teaching assignment comprises a total of 45 hours) to participate in such activities. This 'exemption' allows resources to be redirected towards needs expressed by the NGOs. These activities must be recognized and sanctioned by the BCS; evaluation will be based on the scientific and social relevancy of activities.

SEED MONEY ALLOCATED TO RESEARCH AND CREATIVE PROJECTS
Annually, an institutional budget of about

$100,000 is allocated to support projects conducted in partnership with NGOs. This money is mainly devoted to supporting students engaged in these projects. Projects must demonstrate their social pertinence as well as their scientific quality. This seed money often provides leverage for more substantial financial support from federal or provincial granting agencies.

COMMUNITY SERVICES UNIT
The operationalization of CUE at UQAM is made possible by the Community Services Unit (CSU; or Service aux Collectivités). Its mandate is to promote and coordinate training and research activities to be carried out by faculty members in collaboration with NGOs, women's group and unions. The role of the coordinator, acting as the intersection between the community and the university, is critical for implementing collaborative, sustainable relationships between the parties. Coordinators provide the main entry point for NGOs in the university, will help with finding faculty members interested in the project and will assist with writing the memorandum of understanding. They will act as conciliators and facilitators throughout the different stages of the co-developed project, helping to define research objectives and methodologies based on a common understanding of the expressed needs, and are actively involved in knowledge mobilization. Coordinators also assure the establishment of a partner's follow-up committee, which meets regularly.

Since its foundation, the CSU has initiated more than a thousand research and training activities. Based on a cross-cultural perspective – scientific and practitioner views – academics, NGOs, trade unions and women's movements have established through these projects a 'knowledge dialogue' based on mutuality. Two fundamental premises have been necessary to achieve this goal:

- trust and mutual respect from both parties;
- a recognition of each party's input into the project.

The CSU was the first structure created in Canada for CUE, years before the current generation of structures. It was the CSU, together with the science shops and participatory research network of the 1970s, that led

directly to the creation in 1998 of the Community-University Research Alliances (CURA) funding envelope of the Social Science and Humanities Research Council (SSHRC).

EXAMPLES OF OTHER CUE INITIATIVES IN QUEBEC
CUE initiatives were developed in past years with support from the CURA programme, private foundations and other provincial funding sources. Engagement can embrace multi-faceted strategies and CUE initiatives through training programmes or research projects, mostly carried out by institutes, centres or research chairs. This paper is not intended to present a compendium of such initiatives but will give a broad overview and succinctly present their distinctive features.

Regional universities (see, for example, http://www.uquebec.ca/reseau/ and http://www.usherbrooke.ca/irecus/accueil/) can foster a structuring networking role to support local and regional development. Therefore, regional CUE initiatives are often related to specific economic, social, local and regional needs. Examples from the eastern coastal part of Quebec can be provided by CURA's programme Challenges of Coastal Communities of the Estuary and Gulf of St. Lawrence at a Time of Climate Change, which promotes the co-production of knowledge, skills and methods that will stimulate the emergence of innovative approaches reinforcing communities' capacities to develop strategies to adapt to climate change and to participate in the decision-making process (see http://www.defisdescommunautescotieres.org/definitionaruc/en). A second example from Eastern Quebec can be provided by the work conducted by the Canada Research Chair on Regional and Land Development, which studies the social dynamics and processes surrounding resource and regional development, particularly in outlying and non-metropolitan regions (see http://www.chairs-chaires.gc.ca/chairholders-titulaires/profile-eng.aspx?profileId=2239).

In Abitibi-Témiscamingue, a northwestern region near several First Nations communities, sustainable forestry is an important local issue. The Canada Research Chair in Aboriginal Forestry (see http://www.chairs-chaires.

gc.ca/chairholders-titulaires/profile-eng. aspx?profileId=2493) was developed to take into consideration the past, present and future in setting up sustainable forestry management strategies that respect the Aboriginal viewpoint and culture. Also in the Abitibi-Témiscamingue region, an interesting adapted training programme, respectful of Aboriginal perspectives, that is contributing to the improvement of living conditions for Aboriginal people has been developed by the First Peoples' University (see http://www.uqat.ca/en/services/firstpeoples/).

Urban universities also contribute to the development of their surrounding or more remote communities. Embedded in the community-based participatory research paradigm, and promoting the collaboration of those affected by the issue being studied for purposes of education and taking action for effective social change, these projects cover topics as diverse as health (http://pram.mcgill.ca/), First Nations issues (http://www.reseaudialog.ca/; http://www.mcgill.ca/cine/) and the social development of communities (http://www4.uqo.ca/crcoc/), among others.

CUE is favoured by training programmes adapted to specific needs or populations, for example: Quebec's First Nations and Inuit Faculties of Medicine (http://old.cssspnql.com/eng/sante/faculte.htm); experiential learning, adult learning and transformational learning (http://chrcs.concordia.ca/about/); community economic development (http://scpa-eapc.concordia.ca/en/graduate-diploma-in-ced/); and diverse co-op programmes (https://oraprdnt.uqtr.uquebec.ca/pls/public/gscw030?owa_no_site=1280; http://www.usherbrooke.ca/ssp/en/).

Other forms of CUE include public conversations in community spaces across Montreal (see http://www.concordia.ca/extended-learning/community-development/univcafe/).

CHALLENGES FOR FUTURE DEVELOPMENT

One of the challenges that UQAM and other institutions are facing is to increase the number of faculty members willing to engage their research activities in these non-traditional approaches, and in addition to gain recognition institutionally and among their peers for their work. For example, at UQAM in 2011, 60 out of 1,000 faculty members were involved in 82 projects; the majority of these academics originated from the social sciences and humanities. The number of 60 professors involved is certainly impressive, but there is still room for improvement.

A major stumbling block remains the lack of recognition by the granting agencies of such partnerships, mainly in the natural sciences and engineering, and the evaluation of academia's scientific production based almost solely on mainstream peer-reviewed publications. Only a few programmes from the SSHRC, such as CURA, have encouraged and recognized community–university partnerships and evaluated scientific production in a different way. However, this programme has recently been replaced by others (see http://www.sshrc-crsh.gc.ca/funding-financement/umbrella_programs-programme_cadre/connection-connexion-eng.aspx#.

UQAM provides an example of successful CURA alliances in social economy. Research related to social economy that is useful to the community was developed by coordinating networks of researchers and community partners. Sharing knowledge and practices between universities and communities stimulated engagement by bridging spheres of research and action:

over 100 research projects were completed, which led to the publication of research findings and the organization of seminars,

workshops, and conferences. These activities were carried out by more than 160 researchers and partners who are active in the social economy, from universities, research centres, and various collective businesses and non-profit organizations, mostly based in Québec, but also in the rest of Canada and many other countries. (http://www.aruc-es.uqam.ca/Portals/0/docs/Information%20%28english%29.pdf)

Another challenge is related to the complexity of issues brought up by community partners that often require accompanying follow-up measures. An example is provided by the project A Pension Plan Made to Measure, which was set up to remedy the lack of a pension plan for 80,000 employees, mostly women, in Quebec's NGOs and social economy sector. With the support of CSU resources, a pension plan adapted to the community movement's needs and constraints was elaborated; it manages CAD$15 million and has a growing membership of 3,210 employees from 416 different community and women's groups (see www.regimeretraite.ca). Given the complexity of the issue, university resources are still involved in the project to ensure knowledge transfer on a continuous basis to the other pension plan trustees.

The CUE experiences described in this paper were all beneficial for the community partners, the researchers and the institutions themselves. As the enrichment has benefited all three parties, the commitment to pursue collaboration has been rendered easier. However, difficulties related to different organizational cultures – different approaches to learning, action and time, for example – remain. Therefore, academia's engagement and social responsibility must be supported, and a clear institutional commitment must be put forward to ensure the success of these ventures.

Spotlight Issues IV.6.2
Bringing community and university scholars together on a national stage:
the Canadian Community–University Exposition experience

Joanna Ochocka

The purpose of this article is to share the Canadian experience of a successful community–campus engagement event in Canada. A national innovation, the Community-University Exposition (CU Expo) brings together community and university scholars, activists and leaders every two or three years to address the critical issues faced by local and global communities. Established in 2003 as a breathing space for researchers conducting community-based research, it has become a critical community–campus engagement movement in Canada and internationally. This paper provides a short overview of five CU Expos and discusses the outcomes of the movement.

BACKGROUND

Canada has entered a new phase in the development of the architecture of knowledge creation. A recent review of some partnership research projects funded by the Social Science and Humanities Research Council (SSHRC) has demonstrated a new trend in our nation. We are moving from a historical phase of engaged scholarship based largely on the work of a number of committed individual scholars and their personal connections to community, towards an institutional approach with the creation of new structures and networks to facilitate the creation of community–university research partnerships (Hall and Tremblay, 2012).

Community–university research partnerships provide the opportunity for community members to work directly with experienced researchers to define a problem, conduct research, interpret the findings and apply the results to bring about positive change. This approach involves using creative methods of research to meet community needs and to produce results that are important and useful to community, academics and policy-makers.

Canada has a strong tradition of community–university partnership research. The creation in 1998 of the Community-University Research Alliances (CURA) grant by the SSHRC, the current SSHRC Partnership Development Grants, the Canadian Institutes of Health Research's Community Alliances for Health Research grants and current Community-based

Research and Knowledge Transfer programmes are examples of this. The future of social science is quickly moving towards community–campus engagement, as evidenced by the SSHRC's most recent thrust to promote community–campus collaborations (Gaffield, 2011).

The CU Expo is a leading illustration of community–campus engagement in Canada. It is a Canadian-led international conference designed to showcase the best practices in community–university partnerships worldwide, in response to critical issues facing our local and global communities. The conference has been held every two or three years over the past decade in different provinces – Saskatchewan, Manitoba, British Columbia, Ontario and Newfoundland. This event draws people who are passionate about the power of community–campus partnerships as a vehicle for social change and who use building knowledge to transform our systems and lives. It is more than the conference … it is a movement.

HISTORY

The CU Expo movement began in Western Canada as a response to individual university scholars who needed a forum to share their experiences, struggles and ideas when conducting community-based research. Community-based research is research that strives to be:

- *community-situated* – it begins with a research topic of practical relevance to the community and is carried out in community settings;
- *collaborative* – community members and researchers equitably share control of the research agenda through active and reciprocal involvement in the research design, implementation and dissemination;
- *action-oriented* – the process and results are useful to community members in making positive social changes and promoting social equity (Ochocka et al., 2010). The funding for the first two CU Expos was directly linked to the CURA funding programme offered by the SSHRC.

CU Expo is organized jointly by universities and colleges, communities, government and

non-profit organizations and attracts a considerable number of people. In 2003, the first CU Expo, *Community-University Research: Partnerships, Policy and Progress*, was hosted by University of Saskatchewan and the community of Saskatoon. It assembled approximately 350 individuals from across Canada and elsewhere, and offered over 70 presentations in addition to site visits with local organizations. The main goal was to examine the unique research partnerships needed to tackle a wide variety of issues, such as child poverty, social housing, cultural, Aboriginal, gender and environmental concerns.

CU Expo 2005, *Community-University Research Partnerships: Leaders in Urban Change*, was hosted by the Winnipeg Inner-City Research Alliance. Approximately 300 people attended from across Canada and abroad. They presented over 45 sessions that helped to strengthen the effectiveness of community-based research. The conference sought to strengthen the understanding of, and support for, action-oriented research initiatives involving collaboration between university and community partners. The themes of the conference brought together an examination of research partnership strategies with urban issues such as poverty alleviation, community capacity-building, affordable housing, homelessness, education, social marginalization and community economic development.

CU Expo 2008, *University-Community Partnerships: Connecting for Change*, hosted by the Office for Community-Based Research at the University of Victoria and the United Way of Greater Victoria, attracted almost 600 people. The conference themes included community-engaged scholarship, knowledge exchange for making a difference in areas of sustainability, poverty, housing and homelessness, healthy living, climate change, community economic development, social economy, food security, arts-based activism, and Aboriginal leadership in research. The conference stressed that many researchers work in collaboration with community partners and that this kind of collaboration is fundamental to respectful and productive civic engagement. The university was challenged as an institution to make civic engagement a core university objective and thus enhance the quality and purpose of research.

CU Expo 2011, *Community-University Partnerships Expo 2011: Bringing Global Perspectives to Local Action*, was hosted by the communities of Waterloo Region. The Centre for Community Based Research, a not-for-profit research institute, took on the organizing challenge, attracted 550 participants from Canada and 16 other countries and featured 250 sessions. The planning goal of CU Expo 2011 was to strengthen the 'C' in community–university research partnerships. The conference was organized across eight themes inspired by the UN Millennium Development Goals and by three streams: Community Voice and Relevance, Partnership and Collaboration, and Action and Change.

CU Expo 2013, *Engaging Shared Worlds*, was hosted by Grenfell Campus, Memorial University of Newfoundland, the city of Corner Brook and the provincial government Office of Public Engagement. The Expo drew 450 people from Canada and around the world. The key themes for the conference were engaging knowledge, engaging voices and engaging transformation.

CU EXPO MOVEMENT

From the beginning, CU Expo was not a typical academic conference but an exposition of community–campus partnerships. Pre- and post-conference round-table discussions, innovative presentation formats that fostered community involvement (for example, engagement sessions that are interactive and include two-way dialogue and learning from each other), engagements with local communities (site/field visits, community dinners, events, and so on) and original ways to disseminate knowledge (for example, theatre productions, music and poetry) are some of the distinctive features of each conference. Since 2011, CU Expo has developed its own brand.

CU Expo has become an important forum for networking. The third CU Expo 2008 launched two large networks: the Pan-Canadian Coalition on Community-Based Research, called Community-Based Research Canada, and the Global Alliance on Community-Engaged Research. Both have been intended to enable

and empower citizens across Canada and globally 'to access, produce, and put into action knowledge that will make their communities more sustainable, fairer, safer, healthier, and prosperous' (http://web.uvic.ca/~cuexpo08/index. php). Over time, CU Expos have started to be a convening space for other networks, such as the Canadian Alliance for Community Service Learning (www.communityservicelearning.ca), Research Impact (www.researchimpact.ca), Community-Campus Partnerships for Health (http://depts.washington.edu/ccph/), the Living Knowledge Network (www.livingknowledge. org), the National Coordinating Centre for Public Engagement in the UK (www.publicengagement.ac.uk) and University–Community Partnerships for Social Action Research network (http://ucpsarnet.iglooprojects.org/).

Strengthening the 'C' in community–university research partnerships, the conference planning processes have themselves been showcases of community–university engagement since 2008. Local steering committees have been developed to guide conference planning and delivery, including establishing goals and objectives, resources and promotion, site visits with local initiatives and other community-based events (www. CUExpo2011.ca). Local media and organizations have been involved as co-sponsors and partners. Advisory groups of previous CU Expo organizers have been involved in planning to lead up to the conference event. The close working relationship with the provincial government of Newfoundland and Labrador was an innovative feature of CU Expo 2013 (www.CUEXpo2013.ca).

Funds to deliver the last three CU Expos have been raised through sponsorships and grants, making the events an entrepreneurial undertaking. The hosting organization(s) assume responsibility for organizing the conference, including the planning, fundraising and delivery. Since 2011, there has been a formal application process to host future CU Expos.

OUTCOMES

CU Expo has proven to be an effective conference. It is the largest and only national forum to gather students, community leaders, researchers, educators, funders, policy-makers and others invested in community-building

to showcase the exemplars in community–university partnerships worldwide, and to explore creative ways of strengthening our local and global communities. This forum creates opportunities for sharing, dialoging, reflecting and working together through innovative new collaborations.

CU Expo promotes transdisciplinary, partnership research that is both academically excellent and community relevant, as well as other types of community–campus engagement (such as science shops, community service-learning and knowledge mobilization impact). It is the primary vehicle for disseminating new knowledge produced with and for society, and for recognizing the role of art, creativity and imagination in initiating action and change. CU Expo strengthen networks and produces collective declarations to inspire, advance thinking and advocate for systemic changes.

CONCLUSION

Complex social issues require global perspectives to inform local action. Community–university partnerships are an effective way to stimulate innovative solutions for the pressing concerns within our communities both locally and globally. The potential for such solutions is maximized when diverse partners come together to re-imagine the relationship between the higher education institutions and the community, and in the process create new possibilities.

The momentum of community–university partnerships and the spirit of sharing and dialogue should continue. CU Expo is a critical forum for the community–campus engagement movement in Canada and internationally. It is an excellent model that could be repeated in every country of the world.

REFERENCES

Gaffield, C. (2011) 'Research key to vibrant communities'. *SSHRC/CRSH Newsletter Dialogue*, (Spring), 1.

Hall, B. and Tremblay, C. (2012) *Learning from SSHRC Funded Partnerships: Community Outcomes and Conditions for Success.* Victoria, BC: University of Victoria.

Ochocka, J., Moorlag, E. and Janzen, R. (2010) 'A framework for entry: PAR values and engagement strategies in community research'. *Gateways: International Journal of Community Research & Engagement*, 3, 1–19.

Spotlight Issues IV.6.3
Strategic initiatives to impact the institutionalization of community engagement
at a public research university
Andrew Furco

Community partnerships have always been a part of higher education. Most, if not all, higher education administrators can point to numerous community-engaged projects and initiatives on their campuses. However, despite their long-standing presence in higher education, community engagement activities have held only marginal status within the academy. In many cases, higher education institutions do not have an intentional community engagement agenda; rather, the presence of community engagement is the result of specific projects championed by individual personnel or initiatives promoted by particular campus units.

Additionally, community-engaged work may be viewed to have limited relevance for the broader institution because it is highly associated with the work of specific disciplines (for example, professional degree programmes), personnel with certain titles or responsibilities (for example, 'professors of the practice' or clinical faculty) or in-the-moment situations (for example, mobilizing institutional resources to assist restoration efforts following a local natural disaster) (O'Meara et al., 2005; Marrero et al., 2013). And while individual community engagement projects and activities can endure for years on a campus and in essence become sustained practices that receive ongoing institutional support, such efforts do not always reach the stricter threshold of institutionalization. The institutionalization of community engagement requires an intentional agenda for more deeply embedding the work into the institution's academic culture and everyday practice.

Unlike more marginalized practices that are episodic, isolated, at risk and lack status, institutionalized practices are widespread, legitimized, expected, supported and resilient to changes at the institution (Kramer, 2000). The concept of institutionalization goes beyond the notion of programme sustainability to suggest a deeper acceptance and valuing of a practice across the institution. Tenure, publishing, awarding of academic credit for courses, and lecturing are just some of the practices in higher education that can

be considered institutionalized. Albeit not without controversy, they enjoy widespread adoption, are legitimized by the institutional power structures, are expected practices that are widely supported by key stakeholders and remain relatively unchanged despite shifts in institutional leadership, funding and focus. Institutionalized practices are the default practices to which institutions revert when innovations and other new initiatives fail (Trowler, 2008). For community engagement to move from the margins to become a fully institutionalized practice, it needs to find deep grounding within the institutional culture and operational values structure (Lazarus et al., 2008; Sandmann, 2008).

Studies of higher education have identified a set of components that, when fully in place, further the institutionalization of community engagement on campuses. These institutionalization components are organized within five dimensions: philosophy and mission, faculty involvement and support, student involvement and support, community partnerships and institutional support (Table IV.6.3.1).

Through the operationalization of these components, the institutionalization of community engagement moves through three stages of development (*critical mass-building, quality-building* and *sustained institutionalization*), each of which is estimated to occur over a five-to seven-year period (Bell et al., 2000). While these components are universal in their application to community-engaged work, the ways in which each is operationalized at an institution will be influenced a campus's unique and idiosyncratic culture (Kezar and Eckel, 2002). Study findings suggest that it takes 15–20 years to progress through these three stages and to achieve the full institutionalization of community engagement (Letven et al., 2001; Sandmann et al., 2009; Furco, 2010).

For the University of Minnesota, Twin Cities, in the USA, it has been a 13-year strategic and concerted effort to advance and institutionalize community engagement that has moved the institution into the *sustained institutionalization* phase of its community engagement agenda. With over 50,000

graduate and undergraduate students enroled across 17 schools and colleges and over 300 academic programmes, this comprehensive, public research university is a good example of how a strategic focus on implementing the institutionalization components presented in Table IV.6.3.1 has helped to advanced community engagement across the three stages of development, moving it away from the margins and closer into the mainstream.

While this over 150-year-old university has had a long tradition of supporting and conducting community-partnered work, the community engagement efforts had become somewhat marginalized over the years as the university's research profile grew substantially. In 2001, the university launched a campaign to transform it in ways that would reinvigorate the institution's public engagement mission (*institutionalization components 2 and 3*). This campaign focused on instituting a contemporary approach to public and community engagement that would: (1) focus on making community engagement as integral to research and teaching as it was to the university's public service/outreach mission; (2) be integrated more intentionally and fully with academic programming; (3) become part of everyone's work, not just the work of those who work in traditional outreach units and programmes; (4) emphasize mutually beneficial partnerships acknowledging the assets and knowledge in the community; (5) focus on working 'with' the community and not just doing 'to', 'for' or 'in' the community; and (6) move from supporting discrete, independent, time-limited projects to supporting multifaceted, interdisciplinary 'partnerships' addressing grand challenges and broad societal issues (for example, poverty, health, education, and so on) (*institutionalization components 6, 10, 14 and 15*).

Over the next few years, this 21st-century approach to 'public engagement' would be discussed and vetted across the campus, with the goal of securing input and buy-in from as broad-based a constituency as possible (*components 7, 11, 15, 20 and 21*). In 2002, a campus-wide Council on Public Engage-

TABLE IV.6.3.1

Dimensions and components that promote the institutionalization of community engagement in higher education

Dimension	Components
Philosophy and mission	1. Clear definitions and purposes for community-engaged work 2. A long-term vision and strategic plan for community engagement 3. Direct ties to the institutional mission 4. Seen as a strategy (rather than a 'programme') to accomplish institutional goals
Faculty involvement and support	5. Clarity and awareness among faculty regarding the principles of engaged scholarship 6. Faculty involvement in engaged teaching and research 7. Influential, well-respected faculty members who champion community-engaged teaching and research 8. Faculty incentives and rewards that support and recognize high-quality community-engaged work (for example, promotion, tenure and so on)
Student involvement and support	9. Institution-wide mechanisms that promote student awareness of community engagement opportunities 10. Availability of community engagement opportunities for students from across the institution 11. Encouragement of students to serve as advocates and ambassadors for institutionalizing community engagement at the institution 12. Formal mechanisms (for example, catalogued lists of service-learning courses, transcript notations, and so on) that encourage and reward students to participate in community engagement
Community partnerships	13. Community awareness of the institution's goals for community engagement and the full range of engagement opportunities at the institution 14. Mutual understanding between community circles and the institution regarding the goals, purposes, promise and limitations of the institution's engagement work 15. Community agency representatives are welcomed and encouraged to serve as leaders, advocates and ambassadors for institutionalizing community engagement at the institution
Institutional support	16. The presence of a coordinating unit that assists various constituencies in engagement programming and institutionalization efforts 17. A unit that makes institutional policies supporting the advancement of community engagement 18. The institution houses and funds an appropriate number of permanent staff and/or faculty members with appropriate titles who understand community engagement 19. Community-engaged work supported primarily by hard dollars from the institution 20. Explicit and implicit support for institutionalizing community engagement provided by administrators and other campus leaders 21. Academic departments (faculties) value and fund community engagement opportunities as part of the core academic programme 22. Ongoing, systematic effort in place to account for the number, quality and impact of community-engaged activities

ment was established (*component 17*), and in 2004, a formal university-wide definition for public engagement was adopted (*component 1*).[1] In 2006, a university-wide Office for Public Engagement was established to provide senior leadership (through an Associate Vice-president for Public Engagement) on policy issues concerning the aforementioned goals and the work to secure the university's status as fully engaged.

At the time, the university had in operation over one thousand community partnership activities that were organized and implemented through more than 200 units, offices and centres within and across collegiate units

(*components 16, 18 and 19*). What the university lacked was a strategic plan and key initiatives to harness and systematize the university's broad-based engagement programming.

In 2007, the university revised its promotion and tenure guidelines to support faculty engaged scholarship (*components 8 and 20*). And in 2008, the Office for Public Engagement developed a Ten-Point Plan for Advancing and Institutionalizing Public Engagement (*components 2 and 4*). This plan sought to enhance the university's capacity to conduct high-quality community engagement in ways that would ensure the success of the university's public engagement campaign (goals mentioned

above). Intentionally designed to advance many of the institutionalization components identified in Table IV.6.3.1, the Ten-Point Plan focuses on: (1) enhancing the scholarly value of community engagement; (2) strengthening the university's capacity to measure the scale, scope and impact of its engagement work; (3) building systems that provide more articulated and advanced opportunities for students' community engagement; (4) securing mutually beneficial, reciprocal partnerships with participating community members; (5) cultivating the leadership and capacity of the professionals on campus who lead engaged programmes and units; (6) raising the visibility and value of community-engaged activities; (7) securing better internal alignment of the many engagement initiatives; (8) integrating public and community engagement practices into key university-wide priorities (for example, internationalizing the curriculum, enhancing interdisciplinary research, and so on); (9) connecting with and learning from national and international community engagement-focused associations and networks; and (10) leveraging available extramural support, resources and funding for community engagement initiatives. Since its inception, the plan has served as a road map for making strategic investments in the institutional structures, activities and support mechanisms that can best ensure the fulfillment of the university's public engagement goals.

This strategic approach to advancing community-engaged work has begun to pay off. The institutionalization work that has grown out of the early engagement work and the Ten-Point Plan has helped to:

- increase the number of faculty at the university who conduct community-engaged scholarship (*component 6*);
- further embed community engagement practices into the academic programmes of 21 academic units that have been designated as 'engaged departments' (*component 21*);
- strengthen the institution's capacity to measure the scope and impacts of the university's community engagement practices (*component 22*);
- move the institution from a focus on community-based 'projects' to community 'partnerships' (*component 13*);

- cultivate engagement efforts that both honour the knowledge within the community and focus on working 'with' community rather than doing 'to' or working 'in' the community (*components 14 and 15*);
- raise the visibility and strengthen the scholarly legitimacy of public and community engagement across the institution (*components 5 and 19*).

Today, more faculty members than ever are reporting their community-engaged research and community-engaged teaching work in their scholarly portfolios. The university now awards the President's Award for Community-Engaged Scholarship, which goes to one faculty member whose body of work exemplifies the principles of community-engaged scholarship. The number of undergraduate and graduate students involved in community-engaged experiences continues to grow. Student demand for community-engaged experiences continues to rise. The University of Minnesota, Twin Cities, was one of only a handful of research universities in the USA to receive the Carnegie Community Engagement Designation in 2006 (an elective classification given by the Carnegie Foundation for the Advancement of Teaching). And in 2011, the university received its largest single-institution research grant in the history of the university ($51 million); this was a grant from the US National Institutes of Health to increase community involvement in the research process and the efficiency and speed with which the results of clinical trials translate into new treatments, cures and improved health outcomes. Among the reasons the research grant was awarded was the university's strategic and deep commitment to reciprocal community partners that advance the university's capacity to conduct rigorous scientific research of significance that provides tangible benefits to society.

This grant and all of the aforementioned accomplishments have helped to further spread community-engaged work across the institution. They have deepened the legitimization of high-quality community-engaged scholarship as a scholarly pursuit. They have helped community engagement to become an expectation in various collegiate units (for example, the College of Food, Agriculture and National Resources Sciences, in which the entire undergraduate curriculum is being redesigned to embed experiential, community-based and interdisciplinary learning opportunities across all departments). In assessing the current status of community engagement at the University of Minnesota, Twin Cities, many of the elements (for example, widespread, legitimized, expected, supported and resilient) that characterize true institutionalization are now present.

While much progress has been made at the university in advancing community engagement along the institutionalization continuum, there are still issues that need to be addressed. Within some academic units, junior faculty members remain unsure of whether their community-engaged scholarship will be accepted by their influential peers. The quality of community-engaged courses (for example, service-learning, internships, and so on) offered across the institution is uneven, and the standards of quality need to be more fully and broadly understood and practised. The large, decentralized and entrepreneurial nature of the campus sparks many new community engagement efforts and initiatives, but this sometimes occurs at the expense of community members' capacities. The institution continues to work to find the right balance between expanding engagement opportunities while simultaneously strengthening the internal alignment and efficiencies of the existing engagement work. Finally, measurement of the impacts of community engagement on students, faculty, the institution and the community continues to be elusive given the many potential outcomes that might be measured. The university has made a concerted effort to develop a campus-wide public engagement metric framework that prioritizes engagement metrics according to broader university goals and priorities. But the operationalization of this engagement metrics framework remains slow to develop as broad institutional buy-in and support for the priorities still need to be garnered.

As the university approaches its 14th year of concentrated work to advance the public engagement agenda, it is taking stock of how best to sustain the energy and enthusiasm for a further advancement of community-engaged work. Reform fatigue is legendary in higher education; indeed, too few educational reform efforts have had staying power (Levine, 1980; Curry, 1992). In looking to the future, the key issue for the campus will be to stay the course in its commitment to further the institutionalization of public engagement. Success will lie in the university's focus on promoting public engagement as an important 'strategy' to accomplish broad institutional goals (for example, doing more interdisciplinary work, improving student learning and on-time graduation, internationalizing the curriculum, deepening the societal impact of faculty research, improving town–gown relationships, and so on).

Ultimately, the goal is *not* to do community engagement, but rather to use community engagement as one valued vehicle to advance institutional priorities. As the institution continues to evolve and the institutional priorities shift over time, the goals of and purposes for community engagement will need to be adjusted accordingly. Given the strong foundation for public engagement that the university has built over recent years, there is much hope and continued enthusiasm across the institution that community-engaged research, teaching and outreach will continue grow and thrive as the University of Minnesota enters its next phase of work.

REFERENCES

Bell, R., Furco, A., Sorgen, V., Ammon, M.S. and Muller, P. (2000) *Institutionalizing Service-learning in Higher Education: Findings from a Three-year Study of the Western Region Campus Compact Consortium*. Berkeley, CA: University of California.

Curry, B.K. (1992) *Instituting Enduring Innovations. Achieving Continuity of Change in Higher Education*. ASHE-ERIC Higher Education Report No. 7. Washington, DC: Association for the Study of Higher Education.

Furco, A. (2010) 'The engaged campus: toward a comprehensive approach to public engagement'. *British Journal of Educational Sciences*, 58(4), 375–90.

Kezar, A.J. and Eckel, P.D. (2002) 'The effect of institutional culture on change strategies in higher education: universal principles or culturally responsive concepts?' *Journal of Higher Education*, 73(4), 435–60.

Kramer, M. (2000) *Make it Last Forever: The Institutionalization of Service Learning in America*. Washington, DC: Corporation for National and Community Service.

Lazarus, J., Erasmus, M., Hendricks, D., Nduna, J. and Slamat, J. (2008) 'Embedding community engagement in South African higher education'. *Education, Citizenship and Social Justice*, 3(1), 57–83.

Letven, E., Ostheimer, J. and Statham, A. (2001) 'Institutionalizing university–community engagement'. *Metropolitan Universities: An International Forum*, 12(3), 63–75.

Levine, A. (1980) *Why Innovation Fails*. New York: SUNY Press.

Marrero, D.G., Hardwick, E.J., Staten, L.K. et al. (2013) 'Promotion and tenure for community-engaged research: an examination of promotion and tenure support for community-engaged research at three universities collaborating through a Clinical and Translational Science Award'. *Clinical and Translational Science*, 6(3), 204–8.

O'Meara, K., Rice, R.E. and Edgerton, R. (2005) *Faculty Priorities Reconsidered: Rewarding Multiple Forms of Scholarship*. San Francisco, CA: Jossey-Bass.

Sandmann, L.R. (2008) 'Conceptualization of the scholarship of engagement in higher education: a strategic review, 1996–2006'. *Journal of Higher Education Outreach and Engagement*, 12(1), 91–104.

Sandmann, L.R., Thornton, C.H. and Jaeger, A.J. (2009) *Institutionalizing Community Engagement in Higher Education: The First Wave of Carnegie Classified Institutions*. San Francisco: Jossey-Bass.

Trowler, P. (2008) *Cultures and Change in Higher Education: Theories and Practices*. Basingstoke: Palgrave Macmillan.

NOTE

1   At the University of Minnesota, public engagement is 'the partnership of university knowledge and resources with those of the public and private sectors to enrich scholarship, research, and creative activity; enhance curriculum, teaching and learning; prepare educated, engaged citizens; strengthen democratic values and civic responsibility; address critical societal issues; and contribute to the public good.'

IV.6.4

Networks on community–university engagement in North America

Canadian Alliance for Community Service-Learning (CACSL)

SECRETARIAT: Ottawa (Canada).
INSTITUTION: n/a.
WEBSITE: http://www.communityservicelearning.ca/en/ (accessed 6 March 2013).
MEMBERS: 35 (2010/2011 financially supporting members).

CACSL is a national alliance established to support the active participation of students, educators and communities in community service-learning (CSL) by providing resources and support to CSL practitioners in the post-secondary and non-profit sectors supporting local, regional, national and international networks of individuals and organizations involved in CSL practice and research; investigating, celebrating, promoting and strengthening promising community-centered CSL practices that contribute to positive social change; advocating for CSL in Canadian post-secondary institutions as a complement to existing teaching, learning and research; and advocating for the integration of CSL into planning and practices within organizations in Canada's non-profit sector, as a complement to their own existing strategies to educate on social issues, implement programmes and manage resources (text taken from http://www.communityservicelearning.ca/en/about_vision.htm [accessed 6 March 2013]).

Jonathan M. Tisch College of Citizenship and Public Service

SECRETARIAT: Medford, MA (USA).
INSTITUTION: Tufts University.
WEBSITE: http://activecitizen.tufts.edu/ (accessed 2 October 2013).
MEMBERS: n/a.

The Jonathan M. Tisch College of Citizenship and Public Service is a national leader in civic education, whose model and research are setting the standard for higher education's role in civic engagement. Serving every student at Tufts University, Tisch College prepares young people to be lifelong active citizens and creates an enduring culture of active citizenship.

The Tisch College Model is that Tisch College is a catalyst for active citizenship at Tufts and is the only university-wide programme of its kind. By continuously developing and introducing new active citizenship programming in collaboration with Tufts schools, departments and student groups, Tisch College builds a culture of active citizenship throughout the university. This entrepreneurial approach grows the university's capacity for engagement, and allows the college to reach every student at all of Tufts' schools.

Community-Based Research Canada (CBRC)

SECRETARIAT: Victoria and Kitchener-Waterloo (Canada).
INSTITUTION: University of Victoria, Centre for Community-Based Research, Carleton University, Université du Québec à Montréal.
WEBSITE: http://communityresearchcanada.ca/ (accessed 2 July 2013).
MEMBERS: n/a.

CBRC is a national network of people and organizations engaged in community-based research to meet the needs of people and communities and to build research capacities. The intent of CBRC is to grow an inclusive and open network by engaging already existing networks and by building support for community–university partnerships in community-based research and community engagement. CBRC also provides secretariat support to Community University Exposition, a biannual, Canadian-led international conference designed to showcase best practices in community–university partnerships worldwide, in response to critical issues facing our local and global communities. At the international level, this effort is mirrored by the Declaration of the Global Alliance on Community-Engaged Research (GACER), which influences international discussions on the future role of higher education in meeting global needs for sustainable development.

Community-Campus Partnerships for Health (CCPH)

SECRETARIAT: Seattle, WA (USA).
INSTITUTION: n/a.
WEBSITE: http://www.ccph.info/ (accessed 6 March 2013).
MEMBERS: Over 2,000 individuals and organizations in countries on six continents, primarily in the USA and Canada.

CCPH's mission is to promote health equity and social justice through partnerships between communities and academic institutions. Its goals are to leverage the knowledge, wisdom and experience in communities and in academic institutions to solve pressing health, social, environmental and economic challenges; to ensure that community-driven social change is central to the work of community–academic partnerships; and to build the capacity of communities and academic institutions to engage each other in partnerships that balance power, share resources and work towards systems change. CCPH advances its mission and goals by mobilizing knowledge, providing training and technical assistance, conducting research, building coalitions and advocating for supportive policies (text taken from http://depts.washington.edu/ccph/principles.html [accessed 6 March 2013]).

Engagement Scholarship Consortium (ESC)

SECRETARIAT: Michigan (USA).
INSTITUTION: Michigan State University.
WEBSITE: http://engagementscholarship.org/ (accessed 17 May 2013).
MEMBERS: 27 universities.

ESC is a non-profit educational organization composed of a mix of state/public and private higher education member institutions. Its goal is to work collaboratively across all disciplines to build strong community–university partnerships anchored in the rigor of scholarship and designed to help build community capacity and advance the engagement scholarship mission of higher education throughout the world (text taken from http://engagementscholarship.org/about [accessed 17 May 2013]).

Imagining America

SECRETARIAT: Syracuse, NY (USA).
INSTITUTION: Syracuse University.
WEBSITE: http://imaginingamerica.org (accessed 6 March 2013).
MEMBERS: 91 (as of 14 March 2013).

Imagining America advances knowledge and creativity through publicly engaged scholarship that draws on humanities, arts and design. It catalyses change in campus practices, structures and policies that enables publicly engaged artists and scholars to thrive and contribute to community action and revitalization (text taken from http://imaginingamerica.org/about/our-mission/ [accessed 6 March 2013]).

National Collaborative for the Study of University Engagement (NCSUE)

SECRETARIAT: East Lansing, MI (USA).
INSTITUTION: Michigan State University.
WEBSITE: http://ncsue.msu.edu/ (accessed 6 March 2013).
MEMBERS: n/a.

NCSUE strives to be a pre-eminent innovator within the scholarly movement of engagement in higher education. NCSUE deepens the study of and discussion about two key principles – engaged scholarship and the scholarship of engagement – to inform and advance the national agenda. It seeks a greater understanding of how university engagement enhances faculty scholarship and community progress. The Collaborative convenes scholars and community fellows to explore ways of creating institutional support for building truly collaborative arrangements. NCSUE supports research studies and dissemination through publications, data collection instruments, educational programmes, conferences, presentations and workshops (text taken from http://ncsue.msu.edu/about/ [accessed 6 March 2013]).

Project Pericles

SECRETARIAT: New York, NY (USA).
INSTITUTION: n/a.
WEBSITE: http://www.projectpericles.org (accessed 6 March 2013).
MEMBERS: 29 (as of 15 March 2013).

Project Pericles encourages and facilitates commitments by colleges and universities to include social responsibility and participatory citizenship as essential elements of their educational programmes. To be identified as a Periclean, an institution must abide by certain distinctive Policies (Institutional Commitment, Program, Constituency Involvement, Central Administration, Cooperation and Collaboration). These policies are designed to cultivate a learning environment that integrates issues of civic and social responsibility into the academic and co-curricular experiences of students, while respecting the character, resources and traditions of each institution (text taken from http://www.projectpericles.org/projectpericles/about/ [accessed 6 March 2013]).

ResearchImpact

SECRETARIAT: n/a.
INSTITUTION: York University and University of Victoria (Canada).
WEBSITE: http://www.researchimpact.ca/home/ (accessed 5 July 2013).
MEMBERS: 10 (as of 5 July 2013).

ResearchImpact is Canada's knowledge mobilization network, which provides knowledge mobilization services that connect university researchers with community and government organizations to support the use of research in decision-making about social programming, public policy and professional practice (text taken from http://www.researchimpact.ca/about/vision/index.html [accessed 5 July 2013]).

The Research University Civic Engagement Network (TRUCEN)

SECRETARIAT: Boston, MA (USA).
INSTITUTION: Campus Compact.
WEBSITE: http://www.compact.org/initiatives/trucen/ (accessed 6 March 2013).
MEMBERS: 36 (as of 15 March 2013).

TRUCEN works to advance civic engagement and engaged scholarship among research universities and to create resources and models for use across higher education. It calls upon research university colleagues to embrace a bold vision for civic and community engagement and work to bring it about. Through scholarship that combines rigorous academic standards with community collaboration, broadly defined, research universities can deepen our understanding of issues and develop practical solutions that will make a difference. TRUCEN is committed to helping research universities understand and meet their responsibility, which is to help us understand our world; that understanding is enhanced through engagement with communities in solving the world's greatest problems, in ways that will make them better institutions of higher learning making a greater difference in the world (text taken from http://www.compact.org/initiatives/trucen/ [accessed 6 March 2013]).

IV.6.5

Good Practices

Institute for Studies and Innovation in Community-University Engagement, University of Victoria, British Columbia, Canada

The Institute for Studies and Innovation in Community-University Engagement (ICUE) emerged in 2013 from the former Office of Community Based Research and the strategic commitment of the University of Victoria to civic engagement. It is a centre for action and research into the theoretical and practical aspects of community–university engagement. Using an innovative structure of joint community and university governance and collaboration, the Institute provides a space for the study and practice of engaged scholarship and inter-disciplinary innovation. Focused on engagement, the Institute harvests new knowledge that will contribute to solutions for community issues focused on sustainability, public policy development and improved theory and practice.

Some of its current work is in the fields of community mapping, food security and indigenous-led research on child protection and sustainability. ICUE responds to the University of Victoria's desire to strengthen the links between teaching and research, to the interest in increased service-learning opportunities for students, and to building research capacity within communities. There is a strong focus on the engage-

ment of Aboriginal community partners. ICUE provides support to Community-Based Research Canada and to British Columbia networks of community-based research. ICUE also works closely with the UNESCO Chair in Community-Based Research and Social Responsibility in Higher Education, which is based at both at the University of Victoria and at PRIA in New Delhi, India.

For more information, go to www.uvic.ca/cue, or contact lbrown@uvic.ca.

The Riverworks at Sturgeon City, North Carolina State University, USA

Transforming the environmental and economically devastated Wilson Bay section of Jacksonville, NC into the Riverworks at Sturgeon City community centre required a partnership between the city, the community and the university. A large-scale effort was launched to improve water quality, including decommissioning the wastewater plant, reducing local run-off and the removal of an old dock leaching hazardous creosote byproducts. Wetlands were re-established, and oysters were deployed to serve as a living water filter. The NC State faculty organized community charrettes and student 'design studios', with students presenting alternative visions for reuse to the city council. A broadened partnership – including three universities, two community colleges, Camp Lejeune Marine Corps Base, the New River Foundation, numerous local businesses and local residents – now supports the site, which has become a major recreational, learning and local economic development asset for the city and county.

For more information, contact Jay_Levine@unsu.edu.

Healthy Transitions, University of Tennessee, Knoxville, USA

In 2007, Burundians resettling in Knoxville faced systems unprepared for their arrival and transition. The faculty and students of University of Tennessee, Knoxville, launched a community-based service-learning and research initiative to develop an infrastructure for community-based programming and research. The Burundian community named the new organization SODELA (Solidarity, Development, and Light Association) and defined its mission as 'to support the healthy transition of refugees through the promotion of education, employment, cultural preservation, and the long-term sustainability of families resulting in better personal adjustment to resettlement and positive mental and physical health.' All Burundian children in Knoxville now go to school, while the adults take English classes, pre-GED test classes and computer classes. Many Burundian families already have a car, and some have been accepted by the Habitat for Humanity programme. Despite the serious language barrier, most Burundians now know where to go for healthcare, insurance and groceries. They have contact with churches and are socializing with people outside the Burundian community.

For more information, contact dbates2@utk.edu.

A Long History of Social Responsibility, Extension and the Coady International Institute at St. Francis Xavier University, Nova Scotia, Canada

The idea of the social responsibility of the university to engage with the community has strong historical precedents. In 1918 – almost a century ago – in the rural province of Nova Scotia, Canada, Dr Jimmy Tompkins, then a professor at St. Francis Xavier University, wrote a series of articles entitled 'For the People'. He argued that our 'colleges must catch the spirit of service – service of the whole people in matters national, civic, educational and social' (Laidlaw, 1961, p. 63). In 1920, St. Francis Xavier University held its first 'People's School' for rural leaders, using adult education methods to help address local economic and community development issues. From this beginning was born a movement for self-reliance based on principles of cooperation known as the Antigonish Movement, which spread rapidly across Canada.

By 1928, St. Francis Xavier University had established an extension department, led by Dr Moses Coady, reflecting its ongoing commitment to adult education and collective action. As it grew, the Antigonish movement also attracted international attention. In 1959, the University established the Coady International Institute, which has continued over more than five decades to bring community leaders from around the world to the university's campus to gain leadership skills for community self-reliance. The Institute now has over 6,000 graduates in 130 countries, and serves, along with the university's Extension Department, as a global exemplar of what a university can do 'for the people'.

For further information, see http://coady.stfx.ca/.

REFERENCE
Laidlaw, A.F. (1961) *The Campus and the Community: The Global Impact of the Antigonish Movement.* Canada: Harvest House.

Latin America has a strong century-old tradition of civic and social engagement in higher education, but the depth and diversity of the regional experience and its original theoretical reflections are generally overlooked in the global north.

Language and cultural issues are central to the discussion, so this paper will open with a brief discussion of some key elements of related language in the region. Some of the landmark events in the history of engagement in Latin American universities are presented, including the 1918 'Reform' movement that promoted 'extensionism' throughout the region. The Mexican Social Service policy of 1945 and other mandatory mechanisms and long-standing national policies promoting engagement are also presented.

This paper presents current regional thoughts on engagement and studies, debates and initiatives relating to the regional understanding of concepts such as 'social responsibility', 'social engagement' and 'solidarity service-learning'.

The distinctive features of university engagement and its impact in the region will be analysed with special reference to policy frameworks, recent trends towards the integration of teaching and research missions with significant social programmes and the institutionalization of service-learning practices.

Finally, a brief state of the question on the vitality of regional networks and practices and current challenges in the advancement of higher education engagement will be presented.

ENGAGEMENT OF THE LATIN AMERICAN UNIVERSITY: ROOTS AND CONTEMPORARY DEVELOPMENTS

'SOLIDARITY' OR 'SERVICE': THE LANGUAGES OF ENGAGEMENT

I would like to start this paper with a brief reflection on the linguistic implications of the word 'engagement', inspired perhaps by the fact that although I am writing in Castilian Spanish, this paper will be read in English.

In the Castilian Spanish of Latin America, very similar social engagement practices are named in various manners: 'social service' in Mexico, 'communal work' in Costa Rica, 'solidarity practices' in Argentina. Terms usually used in Chile and Peru, such as 'university social responsibility' (USR), may appear 'politically incorrect' in Argentina and Uruguay (see p. 274).

And if understanding is difficult within the same language, it is obviously even more difficult to express the culture of engagement in other languages. *Solidaridad* (solidarity) is a common term in Castilian Spanish and Portuguese, one that implies working together for the common good, and is not, in our context, a 'radical' term – as it sometimes sounds for native English speakers; nor can it be literally translated as 'service' or 'care' (Tapia, 2000). *Militancia* (militancy) is not exactly the same as 'activism', nor is *protagonismo juvenil* quite the same as 'youth leadership'.

Only in recent years has reflection upon the linguistic and cultural differences involved in the discussion of 'engagement' come to the fore (McBride et al., 2003; Perold et al., 2003; McIlrath et al., 2012). A recognition and evaluation of these enormously complex differences can contribute to a better reciprocal understanding and can help to establish a more solid basis for comparative studies of engagement in higher education.

Elements of the vast and valuable bibliography on engagement available in Spanish and Portuguese have only rarely been translated, and the English-speaking world tends to overlook texts not written in English. As a result, I especially value the opportunity offered by this collective work to attempt to give a voice – at least synthetically – to the complex and very diverse region of Latin America and the Caribbean, and to its '*solidario y militante*' (solidarity-giving and militant) university engagement.

(see p. 274)

IV.7
KNOWLEDGE, ENGAGEMENT AND HIGHER EDUCATION IN LATIN AMERICA AND THE CARIBBEAN

María Nieves Tapia

THE SOCIAL ENGAGEMENT OF HIGHER EDUCATION IN LATIN AMERICA: A RICH AND COMPLEX HISTORY

It is possible to state that engagement in the region has cultural roots as old as the communitarian tradition of the original peoples and the early incoming 'criollo' culture (Bertín Ramírez, 2000; Ighina, 2012). From the late 18th century, universities such as Chuquisaca (Bolivia) spread Suárez's theory on popular sovereignty and trained many of the young leaders of the pro-independence revolutions.

In the postcolonial phase of the 19th century, the establishment of 'national' universities formed part of the organizational process in many of the new States: a new lay educational system was established, aimed at training the ruling classes, generally under a State monopoly. Almost inevitably, these tended to imitate the structures and programmes of the European universities, without too many adaptations to local issues and situations (García Garrido, 1999; Vessuri, 2008).

The words of the rector of the Universidad Nacional Autónoma de México (UNAM), José Vasconcelos, in 1920 – 'I come not to work for the university, but to ask the university to work for the people' (RHEL, 2005, p.181) – somehow express the tension between the expectation that universities should contribute to the progress of the recently established republics and the agendas of the institutions that conceived of themselves as 'temples' of a supposedly 'neutral' but often alien knowledge: studying the medicine of countries with no tropical diseases, or teaching construction with marble and brick while overlooking the sustainable qualities of native adobe (UCP, 2001; Tapia, 2009).

In the early years of the 20th century, university extension began to spread. The term 'extension' had arisen in Cambridge, in 1867, as a synonym for scientific and cultural dissemination activities (Labrandero and Magdalena-Santander, 1983). The first manifestation of this in Latin America was the founding of the Universidad Nacional de La Plata in 1905, with an inbuilt 'extension department'. Its first rector pointed out that while extension in English universities has been voluntary, here the experience 'is resolutely established as a permanent function' of the university (González, 1907; Sanllorenti, 2009).

The affirmation of extension as the 'third column' of university life was precisely one of the main banners of the 'University Reform' movement. Initiated in 1918 with a student uprising in the University of Cordoba, Argentina, the Reform movement expanded rapidly throughout the region (Cúneo, 1978; Ciria and Sanguinetti, 1987), favouring extension as a form of engagement with national situations on the ground and the

development of social initiatives. This vision inspired the creation of extension departments in hundreds of universities, and progammes such as the mandatory Social Service in Mexico (De Gortari Pedroza, 2005).

The Reform established autonomous public universities managed through shared governance between teachers, students and graduates and funded by the State, guaranteeing free access to public higher education in most of our countries. In such a vast and diverse region, the Reform soon generated an inter-institutional network that extended across national frontiers and disseminated an ideology of a democratic and politically and socially committed university that was not easy to sustain within the framework of the hard vagaries of the century.

In fact, and with some national variations, it can be said that throughout the 20th century there was an oscillation between three opposed situations, which Hernández Gurruchaga defined as the foundational 'ivory tower', the agitated 'militant university' and the repressed 'university under surveillance' (UCP, 2001, p. 8).

Even though the inertia of the 'ivory tower' never completely disappeared, the situation of universities surveilled and repressed by dictatorships or authoritarian establishments was practically the 'norm' in the region before and during the Cold War. Meanwhile, some of the forms of 'militant university', with their broad ideological exclusions, were not exactly well-disposed towards constructive academic debate either. Much can be said for the solidarity of the Latin American culture, in that students did not cease their work on social engagement, even as limited or clandestine initiatives in the bloodiest times.

Within this framework, from the 1960s, new tendencies occurred, such as popular education and action research (see p. 273) and 'the second university reform' – that of 'commodification and dual public, private education' (Rama Vitale, 2006, p. 14). Almost all countries permitted the establishment of private universities and reduced State funding, allowing many higher education institutions (HEIs) to start to focusing on the production of knowledge and services for corporate 'clients' rather than the public interest.

From the 1980s, with the processes of the transition to democracy and increased social and civic participation, social and civic engagement activities were revitalized and became more complex within the HEIs, bringing the traditional concept of 'extension' into debate (see p. 273).

In the present day, within the framework of the 'third reform' – that of mass education, regulation and internationalization (Rama Vitale, 2006) – social engagement is increasingly strongly postulated as a cross-cutting criterion for the indication of quality for HEIs as a group (see p. 279).

POLITICAL FRAMEWORKS FOR ENGAGEMENT IN HIGHER EDUCATION

NATIONAL POLICIES FOR THE PROMOTION OF VOLUNTARY ENGAGEMENT

While it is impossible to present the full variety and complexity of the legislation on engagement in universities for all 38 states of Latin America and the Caribbean here, it can be confirmed that every country in the region has laws to regulate higher education, and almost all of these provide in one form or another some details of their social mission, extension, engagement or necessary contribution to national development and the dissemination of culture (REDIVU, 2009).

State responsibility for the partial or total funding of public higher education is established in long-standing mandates within constitutional law or legislation. Thanks to these contributions, the public HEIs in the region – with the exception of isolated cases such as Chile – provide free education or charge almost symbolic fees. The free nature of public higher education, guaranteed by law in Argentina, Brazil, Mexico, Uruguay, Venezuela and other countries, has been and continues to be a central element as a vehicle for upward social mobility and for the creation of the middle-classes in the region (Pérez, 2000; Rama Vitale, 2006).

In this context, the idea of using the knowledge acquired thanks to public funding to 'give back' to society' is at the forefront of discourse and debate within the HEIs and beyond (De Gortari, 2009, p. 2; García de Berríos et al., 2011, p. 2). State funding of public HEIs generally includes funds for the implementation of university extension and volunteering programmes.

MANDATORY STUDENT SOCIAL SERVICE ON A NATIONAL LEVEL

An original trait in the region can undoubtedly be seen in the number of countries that have established obligatory student service of some sort as a requirement for graduation from higher education. These requirements are generally founded on both the idea of 'giving back' the support received to society, and also on the pedagogical goal of training professionals capable of contributing to the resolution of specific problems within these countries in a way that will contribute to national development.

The oldest of these schemes was the Mexican 'Social Service', established in Article 5 of the 1917 Constitution as obligatory 'professional social services'. The constitutional mandate was brought into regulation in 1945, establishing the completion of 300 hours of 'social service' by students as a requirement for graduation. Costa Rica (1974), El Salvador (2004), Venezuela (2005), Colombia (2007) and Panama (2009) have also established national legislation that demands the fulfilment of a varying numbers of hours of mandatory social service (Ochoa, 2010).

TENDENCIES, DEBATES AND VARIOUS APPROACHES TO UNIVERSITY ENGAGEMENT

THE UNDERLYING DEBATE: THE 'COMMITTED' AND THE 'SERIOUS'

In Latin America and the Caribbean, it would be difficult to overlook the value of the contribution of engagement programmes of HEIs to communities, but there is still an ongoing debate over their significance for research, teaching and institutional management. Those involved in social activities frequently complain of a lack of interest and participation from other academics, while some faculty and researchers criticize more 'engaged' members for their lack of 'scientific rigour' (Martínez Martín, 2009).

This traditional tension is added to – within the framework of the increasing globalization of higher studies – by the fact that the HEIs of the region are under pressure to conform with patterns defined by the rankings developed in the global north on the basis of northern priorities (Vessuri, 2008), which do not tend to include engagement among the evaluation factors. In this context, many institutions feel the pressure to review their policies and to pay closer attention to northern requirements than to their own Latin American tradition.

In the tension between the 'committed' and the 'serious', the 'three pillars' paradigm would tend to relegate the third pillar to a position peripheral to the daily life of academia. From the mid-20th century, this model has come into question through the dissemination of hybrid or coordinated activities, such as participatory action research (investigación-acción participativa; Fals Borda, 1987; Ander Egg, 2003; Flores-Kastanis et al., 2009) or research and solidarity service-learning programmes (Herrero, 2002; Edusol, 2008; Tzhoecoen, 2010; CLAYSS, 2012).

The current debate is taking place on the epistemological plane, targeting the concept of academic 'excellence' itself. From the 1960s, the critical pedagogy of Freire and his disciples questioned the 'banking' concept of the production and reproduction of knowledge in the formal education system, and the separation between the types of knowledge: academic, popular and that of the indigenous peoples (Freire, 1973, 1974; de Souza Santos, 2005). In Freire's 'praxis' (reflection + action), there is no separation between theory and practice, rigorous knowledge and social militancy; rather, 'the practice of revealing reality constitutes a dynamic and dialectical unity with the practice of transforming reality' (Freire, 2002, pp. 98–9).

Today, an increasing number of engaged academics are making more systematic links between their social interventions, teaching and research activities (Tzhoecoen, 2010; CLAYSS, 2012) and are questioning criteria of 'excellence' that do not include evaluation of the social relevance of the knowledge produced. Increasing numbers of universities consider publication alone to be insufficient for a good academic, stating that there must be some evaluation of whether the knowledge produced is significant and relevant for local and regional development, and for the societies that definitively sustain higher education. In fact, these criteria are currently being considered for the evaluation and promotion of teachers in institutions such as the Universidad Señor de Sipán in Peru and in some national scientific policies: the National Scientific and Technical Research Council of Argentina includes 'social relevance' among the criteria for the assignation of funds to research proposals.

INTERNAL DEBATE: 'EXTENSION', 'RESPONSIBILITY' OR 'ENGAGEMENT'

As has already been indicated above, 'extension' is the oldest and most widely disseminated concept in the region for expressing the social mission of the university (in some countries, synonyms such as 'projection' are used). In most HEIs, extension sectors cover voluntary engagement programmes, cultural dissemination activities, university publishing houses and the sale of services and consultancy.

In recent years, even faculty involved in extension have come to the conclusion that there is a problem with the 'conceptual weakness' of extension and the lack of consensus in its definition (García, 2010). There is still an open debate between those supporting 'traditional extension' – limited to voluntary work and dissemination in parallel to academic areas – and those who promote a form of extension that actively seeks to coordinate the social mission with the teaching and research missions (Camilloni, 2010; García, 2010). In recent years, this weakness in the concept of extension has led to a quest for more specific definitions of the

element in terms such as the social 'responsibility' or 'engagement' of the university.

The concept of USR, with its various regional aspects and hues (Kliksberg, 2000, 2011; Vallaeys and Carrizo, 2006; Vallaeys et al., 2009; Jiménez, 2008; see also http://www.ausjal.org/responsabilidad-social-universitaria.html) began to spread in the 1990s, establishing the importance of evaluating the impact of university management on the environmental, social and political context. At the same time, the concept of 'engagement' (de Souza Santos, 2005; Rojas Mix, 2008; Cecchi et al., 2009) has been growing in strength, especially since the early 21st century, in the wake of the crisis in the neoliberal model in many of our countries, and following denunciation of the serious associated social gap that persists despite sustained economic growth, placing a greater emphasis on the political participation of the university.

Both concepts aim to generate a university that is more ethically involved with its context and that has improved integration between the three great missions. In some countries, these are used as synonyms, while in others they have become the object of inflamed debate, due to both the ideological implications attributed to the discussion and the practical consequences in terms of institutional management. This debate is installed deep within the bosom of some universities, where a variety of stances to these models are being held at the same time.

Beyond all the debate, not all of the institutions that have embraced one or another of the conceptualizations are actually implementing the same institutional policies, nor do they obtain similar results in terms of the social and environmental impact of their efforts. More research and rigorous evaluation still remain to be completed on the institutional practices associated with models for extension, USR and university engagement in the region.

MODALITIES OF ENGAGEMENT IN HIGHER EDUCATION IN LATIN AMERICA

It is difficult to fit the vast and complex range of activities undertaken in the HEIs of the region into the framework provided by the conceptualizations and debates imported from the global north. However, beyond the linguistic and ideological barriers, the following could be stated:

- The concept of 'community-based research' is strongly paired with the Latin American and 'participatory action research' movement. Since the 1970s, generations of researchers in the region have been undertaking research of this type, and concepts such as 'participatory diagnosis', 'integration of popular and indigenous knowledge' and others are commonly used in most of our universities, even if they are not always implemented with equal rigour.

- The concept of 'engaged research' is not so well disseminated in Spanish as in the English-speaking world, although its practice is widespread. In the region, the language more frequently used discusses the 'production of relevant knowledge' or the 'social pertinence of research' contributions (Garrocho Rangel and Segura Lazcano, 2011, pp. 1–2; Naidorf et al., 2007, pp. 4–5), as a fundamental dimension in evaluating the quality of scientific production and also as a 'priority ethical mandate' (Orozco Silva, 2010, p. 32).
- The concepts of 'knowledge mobilization', 'implementation science' and 'research utilization' could be translated into Latin American Spanish using the concepts of '*transferencia*' (transferral) and '*extensión*' (extension). As has already been explained, these are the most widely disseminated practices in the region, even in those HEIs with lower levels of institutional engagement.
- The concept of 'science shop' networks is practically unknown in Latin America. However, research in the service of social organizations is a common and long-standing practice.
- One of the most widespread concepts used in the region to express the necessary coordination between academic knowledge and social practices is that of 'solidarity service-learning' (*aprendizaje-servicio solidario*), a pedagogy with common points with, but also with significant differences from, the global north's model of 'service-learning' (McIlrath et al., 2012, p. 8).

In fact, the adjective 'solidarity' (see 1.a) indicates some distance from the concept of 'service' in the 'vertical', paternalistic, aid-based and individualistic sense that some critics identify with the English term 'service-learning', compared with a more 'horizontal' concept of solidarity. This can be understood as working 'with' the community and not only 'for' it, aiming not only at the autonomous development of individuals and communities (Tapia, 2003; Baggio, 2006; Roche Olivar, 2010), but also at the leading role of children and youth from more vulnerable sectors in solidarity service-learning projects (Massat, 2012).

As a result of the more generalized consensus is in the region, we understand practices of 'solidarity service-learning' to include any that simultaneously cover at least the three characteristics of:

- solidarity-based service aiming to deal with real and felt needs in a limited but effective manner *with* a community, and not only *for* it;
- active protagonism by students from planning through to evaluation;
- intentional coordination with learning, involving curriculum content, reflection on practice, the development of skills for citizenship and work, and research links to solidarity-based practice (Tapia, 2006; Tzhoecoen, 2010; CLAYSS, 2012).

THE POLITICS OF ENGAGEMENT
THE GOVERNMENT OF ENGAGEMENT

For the reasons outlined on p. 272, the public universities of Latin America were historically constituted with vice-rector's offices or secretariats for extension, and they include social engagement or responsibility as one of the main axes of their institutional mission. Private HEIs tend to replicate the institutional models of the public institutions and have the same type of centralized governance of engagement activities, even though there are enormous differences between those universities with the longest and most solid tradition of social engagement and other more recently founded institutions, some of which do not have defined areas or policies, either due to a lack of resources, or because they prefer to replicate institutional models from the global north that do not include the Latin American tradition of extension.

HEIs containing specific bodies to coordinate social engagement policies can today be grouped into three typologies:

- *HEIs in which engagement policies are implemented in a coordinated manner*, from the rector's office and the higher councils, with agreements between the academic areas and those coordinating extensions, USR or engagement. An increasing number of the more prestigious public and private universities are found in this group.
- *HEIs in which the three 'missions' are not coordinated* and where guidance on engagement policies comes from entities peripheral to the central decision-making structure, or is fragmented between entities dependent on various authorities. In some cases, the extension entity does have sufficient decision-making capacity over policy and economic resources to implement valuable activities in social engagement, but these are isolated from the academic areas. In recent years, conceptual debates have led to the coexistence in some institutions of 'extension' areas alongside independent USR centres and with service-learning programmes dependent on academic areas. This dispersal generally conspires

against any possibility of developing more effective and coordinated engagement policies. It could be said that a high percentage of the HEIs in the region are today located in the second group.

- *HEIs with no institutional policies on social engagement*, where the activities depend totally or almost exclusively on teacher or student initiatives. This is a minority group in relation to the other two on a regional level.

POLICIES RELATING TO THE COMMUNITY AND THE IMPACT OF THE COMMUNITY ON THE HEIs

In the traditional perspective, the university 'extended' to where the 'outside' was considered to exist and 'bridges were built', assuming institutions as 'islands' essentially isolated from their contexts. Social projects were planned from the university perspective, and the beneficiaries tended to be considered passive receivers. Even where these views continue to exist to some extent, an increasing number of HEIs currently recognize themselves as part of a territory where they aim to build networks and establish alliances and forms of collaborative work with non-governmental organizations (NGOs) and community leaders.

Even though there are still many programmes based on the dissemination of knowledge produced within the faculties, there has in recent decades been a growing openness to dialogue with popular knowledge, the tradition or knowledge of indigenous people and knowledge produced from civil society. Especially in Mexico, Ecuador and Bolivia, significant advances have been made in the recognition of traditional healing and other areas of knowledge of the indigenous peoples.

The strengthening of NGOs specializing in specific issues in the region – such as the environment or inclusive education – with their own resources and research teams, has allowed more horizontal dialogue to be established between traditional academia and these new spaces for knowledge production.

The established 50-year-old regional tradition of popular education movements has gradually permeated academic settings, and, in an increasing number of cases, working with real problems in local settings through engagement or solidarity service-learning has led to a modification of the academic curricula, either through the adaptation of content, the incorporation of new knowledge or even the reorientation of professional profiles. For example, support practices in vulnerable contexts have led to an increasing number of teacher training institutions reconsidering pedagogical models built on suppositions carried over from the urban middle-class context, leading them to suggest

specific undergraduate and postgraduate courses for education in diverse contexts.

The implementation of policies linking the university with local, regional and national surroundings tends to cause tension between two aspects:

- *Aid for social and natural emergencies and the establishment of programmes targeting local development*. An increasing number of HEIs in the region continue to sustain voluntary projects dedicated to the collection of food and to disaster response, but they have also established medium and long-term programmes to target more structural questions alongside relief activities (see p. 278).
- *Free initiative or focused approach*. Openness to the free initiative of professors and students can generate a broad and creative variety of projects, but can also disperse efforts and resources, while a focused approach and coordination on the basis of institutional policies ruling all available human and economic resources in one or several locations can generate a great impact on local development, but also limit innovation. In general, the more committed HEIs simultaneously run a selection of highly significant programmes focused on one location or one type of work – such as the Universidad de Buenos Aries (UBA) programme focused on Vulnerable Neighbourhoods, or the UNAM programme to support municipalities – with other more spontaneous initiatives.

THE VOLUNTARY OR MANDATORY NATURE OF STUDENT SERVICE

Apart from the countries where mandatory service requirements have been established (see p. 273), HEIs have predominantly voluntary policies. Even universities with obligatory service also have institutional volunteer programmes, as is the case with the Universidad de Costa Rica. The volunteer programmes are promoted and funded by some national governments, as is the case with the National University Volunteer Programme in Argentina. These are often promoted by NGOs, such as Servicio País in Chile, Universidade Solidária (UniSol) in Brazil, Opción Venezuela and others.

At the same time, and especially in the last decade, some HEIs have introduced different forms of mandatory social service, even when national legislation does not demand this. Some require the fulfilment of a given number of hours of service within the framework of social programmes organized by the institution or in social organizations recognized by it, as is the case in several Argentinean universities (Seltzer and Puglisi, 2009; García, 2010).

On top of the various institutional policies in the region that have already been mentioned, there are a further two that have been proven to be the most effective:

- *Institutional programmes for the training of teachers and local partners in engagement.* These range from congresses and courses organized in various areas to institutional systems for continuing training, such as the noteworthy programme for service-learning faculty training of the Universidad Católica de Chile or diplomas in USR organized by some Jesuit Universities.

- *Recognition and visibility systems.* In the Universidad Central de Venezuela, the mandatory Community Service section holds an annual good practices fair organized by the rector's office. Some universities include participation in engagement programmes as elements to be evaluated in faculty promotion, and others have annual prizes for the most committed professors, as is the case in the Monterrey Institute of Technology and Higher Education. In a small but growing number of HEIs in the region, this engagement is given some value in faculty evaluation and promotion processes.

THE IMPACT OF UNIVERSITY ENGAGEMENT IN LOCAL AND NATIONAL CONTEXTS

Lacking all-inclusive quantitative or qualitative regional studies, the following section will present some practices that we hope will provide a better idea of the impact of the vast and complex solidarity action of HEIs in their communities and countries.

CONTRIBUTIONS TO THE RESOLUTION OF SPECIFIC ISSUES

The social engagement projects of HEIs in the region cover an extremely broad range of questions. We shall concentrate on only four of the most frequently approached issues.

Education

One of the main contributions made to our societies by HEIs in the region probably relates to inclusive education through literacy campaigns, school support actions in community organizations and the tutoring of youth and children to avoid school abandonment. Examples are the UNAM 'Peraj-Adopta un amigo' (Adopt a Friend) programme, or the 'Adopta un herman@' (Adopt a Brother/Sister) programme developed by the Fundación para la Superación de la Pobreza de Chile (Foundation for Overcoming Poverty in Chile), in which 50 HEI students help to deliver the service in 80 schools and 21 municipalities throughout the country.

In recent years, the number of literacy and information technology inclusion programmes has also increased (Viola and Rosano, 2004; EDUSOL, 2009). All of these practices are especially significant in institutions training future teachers as part of their preparation in the development of effective educational inclusion strategies (EDUSOL, 2007).

Some HEIs are also developing institutional programmes to encourage inclusion in higher education itself, as is the case in the Universidad de Chile, where the Educational Equity Priority Entry System reserves spaces for excellent student graduates of municipal establishments who have not achieved the necessary score in the traditional and extremely selective Chilean entrance examination. The highlight of the UBA is the UBA XXII Programme, which offers the possibility of graduating in several careers in academic units within various federal prisons, and the 'secondary distance learning' initiative, implemented to allow non-teaching staff with incomplete studies to complete these while working, making use of the equipment and tutors provided by the university.

Indigenous people continue to be to a large extent excluded from higher education, not only due to economic issues, but also because of the lack of bilingual teaching and the poor or lack of attention to their cosmovision and ancestral knowledge. In recent years, some efforts have been initiated to approach this situation on the national and institutional levels. Mexico has played a pioneering role in creating nine 'inter-cultural public universities' between 2001 and 2006. The academic offer of these universities includes the study of indigenous languages and offers courses such as sustainable development, alternative tourism, community forest engineering and inter-cultural health.

In a context of rapid expansion of university enrolment, graduation rates are still relatively low even in the countries with the best results: 34% in Panama, 23% in Barbados, 21% in Cuba and 19% in Mexico (UNESCO, 2009). On this front, an increasing number of HEIs are proposing new internal strategies and new support programmes for secondary or preparatory schools as a contribution to the democratization of higher education.

Health

Many health-related university careers deliver programmes that benefit public health. As well as the free clinics and prevention and assistance campaigns sustained by many universities, community practices have frequently been incorporated into the curriculum, as is the case with the health sciences course at the Universidad Javeriana de Cali (Colombia). In the Universidad Central del Este (Dominican Republic), the cycle for internship rotations includes a month in community medicine. The Universidad Nacional de Tucumán (Argentina) demands a final semester of placements in rural health centres and outlying urban areas.

Dentistry courses in the region tend to include a 'social dentistry' assignment or practice, and it is very common for students and teachers to undertake prevention and care campaigns in rural areas where no dentistry services are available.

Housing

Many universities in the region have been implementing programmes on this issue for decades, for example designing popular housing (II Encuentro Internacional de Rectores de Universia, 2010, pp. 39–44), reconditioning or building affordable housing – as is the case with the obligatory 'Social-housing Service' module within the architecture school of the Universidad Católica de Córdoba (EDUSOL, 2009; PWC-CLAYSS, 2009). They also contribute to town planning in populations with no professional resources, for example UNAM (De Gortari, 2009) and the Universidad Central de Venezuela (FAU-UCV, 2008), or design and build anti-earthquake housing for those affected by earthquakes, as with the Universidad Católica de Occidente in El Salvador.

Many of these experiences are linked to the Regional Network of Housing Faculties (ULACAV), which specifically aims at the exchange of knowledge and good practices, and at promoting the incorporation of curriculum content and programmes linked to the social habitat into higher education.

In recent years, many students and university leaders have participated in the 'Un techo para mi pais' (a roof for my country) construction campaigns – an NGO founded in 1997 by university students in Chile, and which is currently seeing mass dissemination throughout the region. More than 86,000 emergency homes have been built.

Social economy: micro-businesses, sustainable agricultural development and food sovereignty

The idea of 'teaching a man to fish' rather than distributing fish is not new, but it has been deployed in recent decades in many projects aimed to train the most vulnerable populations to sustain themselves with dignity.

Programmes aiming to achieve 'food sovereignty' and sustainable agricultural development include the

research and promotion of initiatives for urban agriculture and the network of organic gardens with unemployed neighbours of the Universidad Nacional de Mar del Plata, Argentina (EDUSOL, 2007). Others are the dissemination of hydroponic gardening in vulnerable communities by the Universidad Católica del Ecuador in Manabí, and programmes to promote family and community agriculture in Brazilian universities linked to the Unisol network.

The many experiences of advice and training for micro-business leaders in urban and rural contexts include students from the University of Monterrey (Mexico) participating in the 'Mujer emprende' (Woman entrepreneur) institutional programme to train and advise female entrepreneurs. Students in the economic and administrative sciences faculty of the Universidad Javeriana de Cali (Colombia) undertake valuable voluntary practice running a 'school for shopkeepers', accredited by the university, which provides training for small business owners in the most marginalized neighbourhoods of the city, offering technical assistance to improve their small businesses.

Programmes managing micro-credits and providing advice and training in accountancy administration to community organizations are also common, as in the case of the programme to support small and medium-sized enterprises and social entities that is run by the University of Costa Rica.

IMPACTS ON LOCAL DEVELOPMENT

In recent years, there has been a proliferation of projects aimed at the sustainable development of an entire territory, dealing simultaneously with issues linked to care of the environment, the preservation and promotion of cultural heritage and sustainable development. This type of programme works in the medium and long term rather than on an emergency basis, and tends to require greater institutional involvement and alliances with governmental entities, civil society organizations, companies and other social actors.

Within the local development programme of the Universidad Señor de Sipán de Chiclayo, Peru, for instance, all schools organize programmes serving local municipalities, especially aimed at the recovery of the indigenous Mochica culture and the economic and educational development of the region, with support from national and international cooperation funding. Fieldwork, service-learning projects and research on local issues is supported by offices that operate on the periphery of the campus, the community development centres, which facilitate interdisciplinary work and direct links with local actors.

The Universidad Nacional de General Sarmiento (Argentina), established in 1992 in a suburban area of extreme poverty, was designed to promote the inclusion of young people from the region and to deal with the many problematic issues of the urban areas around Buenos Aires. All of the schools' curricula include participation in interdisciplinary 'laboratories' that undertake research in the service of local municipal entities and community organizations (Fournier et al., 2012). For example, the Environmental Diagnosis Laboratory offers municipalities with few professional resources diagnostic reports on their environmental issues, an extremely valuable resource for local management (PWC-CLAYSS, 2010).

NATIONAL IMPACTS

In some of our countries, the HEIs' engagement contribution has also had a significant impact at national level.

We need only think of the advances made in literacy in Cuba by the 'literacy brigades' that enrolled more than 100,000 secondary and university students as literacy teachers, especially for rural communities (Gómez García, 2005), or the more than 70,000 students in Ecuador who participated in the Monseñor Leonidas Proaño National Literacy Campaign (1988–1990), both of which made a significant impact at national level (Torres, 2004).

Much of the research undertaken in the HEIs has had an impact on public policy design, from housing policies inspired by 'self-build' programmes with advice from the HEIs, to health and environmental conservation policies. But more difficult to quantify, although equally significant, is the impact of the thousands of hours of social work undertaken by the hundreds of thousands of students who have performed their obligatory social or solidarity service-learning over the last century on a most diverse range of issues in the most underdeveloped regions of Mexico, Costa Rica, Venezuela and other countries with mandatory student service.

SOCIAL ENGAGEMENT IN TEACHING AND RESEARCH
SOLIDARITY SERVICE-LEARNING, CURRICULUM INNOVATION AND SOCIALLY COMMITTED RESEARCH
Within teaching structures still heavily marked by the encyclopaedic approach, extremely discursive teaching styles and a wide gap between theory and practice, the solidarity service-learning practices (see p. 274) disseminated in recent years have led to innovations in both teaching practices and curriculum development. Social engagement is now present in teaching and research in five basic formats:

- *Courses in regular disciplines.* Teachers incorporate voluntary or obligatory community practice to enrich the normal course. The 'audiovisual production' course in the Monterrey Institute of Technology and Higher Education (Mexico) requires the final production of a video serving a local community organization in order to pass the course. Similarly, in the Engineering School of the Universidad de Salta (Argentina), students design, build and install solar energy devices in isolated communities in the province's mountains as part of the renewable energy course. These examples could be multiplied across a wide variety of disciplines.

- *Multidisciplinary programmes.* As courses in different disciplines get in touch with a specific community, a need often arises to approach complex problems from a multidisciplinary perspective and to organize projects between various departments or schools. The Interdisciplinary Seminar for Social Emergency was a course designed to draw together advanced students from all the careers in the UBA School of Architecture, Design and Urban Planning. Taking various community organizations on as 'clients' each semester, the architecture students have designed plans for the construction of a community centre, the graphic design students have produced promotional material for an NGO, and the industrial design students have created wooden toy designs that can be reproduced by local entrepreneurs. In the more than 10 years that this project has been running, the initiative has gradually involved philosophy and literature students as support workers with school children in the community centres, and combined projects have been organized with the service-learning sections of the veterinary and social sciences faculties to work in the same neighbourhoods (Frid and Marconi, 2006).

- *Courses on USR or ethical training for citizenship.* In recent years, some HEIs have introduced courses on USR, ethical training for citizenship or social training, in which curriculum content is linked to social engagement, and solidarity-based practices are undertaken. The USR studies course in Concepción (Chile) is just such a case, where students identify local needs and design interdisciplinary projects for prisoners, students with special educational needs and other target groups (Navarro Saldaña, 2009).

- *Pre-professional placements and practices in the community.* Many HEIs are authorizing placements in community organizations. No predefined work positions are identified within these entities, but students will be expected to deal with problematic issues in challenging contexts. This requires the interns to respond creatively and plan their own activities, thus developing valuable competencies that cannot always be deployed in internships on the lower levels of the corporate ladder.

Similarly, many courses are introducing socially oriented pre-professional practices in community environments. For example, the Instituto Superior de Formación de Docente de Educación Física de Rosario (Higher Institute of Teacher Training in Physical Education of Rosario; Argentina) has a final teaching practice that is only partially performed in schools. In order to graduate, students must work on a project alongside a community organization, planning and evaluating activities such as keep fit for the elderly, neighbourhood sporting activities and many other elements. Community practice has contributed to an improved quality of life for hundreds of local residents in the peripheral areas of the city, and has also broadened the profile of the graduates to new horizons of activity (EDUSOL, 2006).

● *Thesis and research programmes coordinated with solidarity service-learning practices.* The number of undergraduate and postgraduate theses based on solidarity service-learning experiences has begun to multiply in recent years. Many of the research projects that have arisen on the basis of service-learning programmes have been published in specialized academic journals across a wide range of disciplines, making it difficult to systematize the number and impact of this research. Networks of researchers linked to service-learning or social engagement programmes have recently begun to emerge. In 2012, the II Jornada de Investigadores sobre Aprendizaje-Servicio (Second Service-learning Researchers Conference) was held in Buenos Aires, with the participation of around a hundred researchers and specialists from nine countries (CLAYSS, 2012).

In many cases, it is clear that rigorously performed research linked to social problems allows for the demands of social groups and academic careers to be approached simultaneously. Many socially committed teachers view this as a significant change, meaning that they will be able to focus all their energies on a specific community problem, exercising their role as teacher and researcher around the same cause, whereas the traditional approach to 'extension' tended to leave them overwhelmed by having to run their research and teaching tasks in parallel to their social engagement.

Many testimonials have been collected on the impact of these practices on the teachers themselves. The most common of these include the generation of new sense and motivation for their teaching role, the creation of less stereotypical relationships with students and satisfaction from the results obtained both from the academic point of view and within the communities (EDUSOL, 2008).

On both the world (Eyler and Giles, 1999; Billig and Eyler, 2003; Furco, 2005) and regional levels, there is evidence of the impact of social engagement in the development of professional competencies and those linked to citizen participation (Tapia, 2006; Folgueiras Bertomeu and Martínez Vivot, 2009; Martínez Vivot and Folgueras Bertomeu, 2012). Especially significant are those impacts where students have effectively been the protagonists from the project design phase through to evaluation rather than simply a 'free workforce' obeying orders.

Their engagement also helps to broaden their perspectives on the areas in which they aim to practise a profession. Many graduates state that their professional and personal career paths have been marked by their social engagement experiences. In the words of the students themselves:

These practices in which we participated allow us to have another view of reality. We acquired experience to complement the theory received in our classrooms. We left our books and went into practice. We discovered that dialogue is always possible with others, that we can all do something and produce transformation together with others.[1]

SOCIAL ENGAGEMENT NETWORKS

Regional integration processes have accelerated in recent years, and Latin American and Ibero-American networks in the higher education sector have strengthened. The creation of various networks relating to the engagement issue reflects the different points of view expressed in the current debate, already discussed on p. 274. It is no surprise, then, that the most long-standing of the regional networks are those relating to extension, while the more recent creations tend to relate to other conceptualizations.

Practically all countries of the region have national networks for extension, service-learning and/or USR. There are also thematically grouped regional networks, such as the housing group ULACAV, previously mentioned, the social odontology network, veterinary medicine service-learning networks and others. The section on regional networks includes links to some of the most important of them.

SOME CHALLENGES AHEAD

In spite of a 100-year tradition of social engagement in our HEIs and the great advances made in recent decades, a number of challenges undoubtedly remain. A good synthesis of the situation was expressed by the rectors of Latin America and the Caribbean in the Belo Horizonte Declaration of 2007, which issued a call to:

Promote a qualitative leap in social engagement of Universities, stimulating the production of strategic changes, such as:

– From voluntary work and philanthropy, to ethical engagement with social justice and the exercising of rights.

– From short term, disperse and episodic action, to far-reaching lines of programming.

– From the implementation of social engagement activities at low hierarchical levels within the institutions, to their incorporation within the institutional mission statements themselves.

– From isolated and sector-based action, to synergies, based on country projects.

– From extension as a transfer service, to social meetings, knowledge dialogue, the construction of appropriate knowledge, participation in non-exclusive social projects.

Here, we will discuss some of the most significant challenges and their implications.

EFFECTIVE ARTICULATION OF ENGAGEMENT IN THE THREE MISSIONS

In the quest to overcome the tension between the 'engaged' and the 'serious' (see p. 273), and to effectively articulate all the institutional missions, some of the strategies that have proven most successful have been to the following:

- Strengthening the coordination between theory and practice, between scientific training and training for active citizenship, through solidarity service-learning projects and programmes strongly anchored in the curriculum and linked to research projects, both throughout the training course and in final professional practices.
- Offering specific training instances for faculty, researchers and authorities on relevant issues related to engagement.
- Promoting the visibility of good practices on engagement at the institutional level – prizes and acknowledgements allow the valuable work of faculty and students to be recognized, and they also contribute to the documentation and systemization of practices, the building of databases of experiences that facilitate policy articulation and the establishment and dissemination of quality parameters for engagement.
- Reviewing systems for the evaluation and promotion of all faculty and researchers, incorporating criteria relevant to the pertinence and social relevance of the research and teaching practices and their contributions to the social and civic engagement of the university.
- Facilitating interdisciplinary dialogue relating to local sustainable development issues, aiming to generate cross-cutting, socially committed research and service-learning programmes that run throughout the entire institution.
- Developing more research and studies on the state of the social engagement and service-learning practices within the university. All too often, fieldwork does not allow time for recording of the work undertaken, or for reflection or systematic evaluation. More systematic connections will be needed between already existing national and international database, and implied methodological challenges must be assumed. A greater amount of rigorous research would be required into the social problems in which we are becoming involved, and also into the impacts of solidarity practices on communities, student education and the university organization itself.
- As well as producing rigorous knowledge around engagement, volunteering and service-learning, more openings must be found for these studies to be made known and discussed. Even though, in recent years, some regional peer-reviewed publications on engagement have been produced, it would be critical to have specialized academic publications in Spanish and Portuguese, as well as for a greater number of articles on engagement to be published in academic journals relating to the various disciplines.

ADOPT ENGAGEMENT AS 'INTEGRATED REFORM'

When an institution defines itself as 'committed' or 'responsible' (see p. 274), institutional practices must support these declarations, and we understand that, in order to do this, it is important to demonstrate and evaluate practices that effectively transform modes of management and that have a positive impact on the training of students and the real lives of peoples within both frameworks. The following issues, among others, would have to be approached or further discussed:

- the effective inclusion of young people from vulnerable social sectors, indigenous populations and their cultures within higher education;
- the environmental and social impact of the campus or buildings on their surroundings;
- the review of internal policies that may contradict the principles of justice and respect for the rights of students, teaching and non-teaching staff, and the community in general.

STRENGTHEN WORK WITH LOCAL NETWORKS AND STRENGTHEN REGIONAL NETWORKS

There is also a need to deepen reflection on dialogue between academic, local and ancestral knowledge, and to rethink social contexts as settings for learning and the transformation of reality, not only considering them from the utilitarian outlook of collecting research data. The establishment of sustainable networks for local development that provide a voice and a leading role for local actors themselves continues to present a challenge.

There is a need to strengthen and, above all, link the already existing engagement networks at a regional level, especially to contribute to the visibility and impact of good practices, and to provide solidity to the field on the basis of theoretical and methodological frameworks fitted to the regional reality.

DEEPEN SOUTH–SOUTH DIALOGUE

In recent years, the experiences of HEIs in Africa and Southeast Asia have been closer and more significant to the Latin American experience than those of their peers in the developed north. Despite the geographical and cultural distances, our countries share a similar colonial history, in that they have fought – and are still fighting – for effective independence, the stability of democratic systems fitted to our own traditions and sustainable development on the basis of our resources. Our peoples have faced civil wars and their consequences, economic crises and natural disasters with resilience, and they continue to fight poverty with enormous energy and admirable creativity.

Without failing to recognize what we have already learned and still could learn from the north, we have in recent years become increasingly aware of how much we could learn from each other. The south is finding its own voice and, perhaps for the first time, is starting to feel that someone is listening. We understand that the strengthening of south–south dialogue between institutions and the engagement networks is fundamental in allowing the exchange of good practices, research and

theoretical reflection, and for the empowering of an inter-regional movement that will allow the global south to increasingly air its own voice in world dialogue.

CONCLUSION AND FINAL COMMENTS

Since the early 20th century, and even earlier still, Latin America and the Caribbean have developed their own forms of social and civic engagement with original outlooks and institutional models and good practices that tend not to be known enough outside the region, despite their significance. We understand that collective works like the present report represent a significant step forward in international dialogue on the engagement of HEIs.

Perhaps the current context of crisis in the global north is making our region's experience more relevant, accustomed as we are to starting projects with no economic resources, to approaching issues where no State involvement has been seen and where we daily recognize the failure of pure theory to meet the clamouring of those with no homes, no bread and no work.

Within the limitations placed upon this text by the process of synthesis and translation, I sincerely hope that the resilience, creativity and spirit of solidarity in the regional experience may serve as an inspiration for both south and north.

NOTES

1   Final declaration of participants and experiences winning the presidential prize for solidarity-based educational practices in higher education, 2010. XIII International seminar of solidarity service and learning, Buenos Aires, August 2010. Unpublished document of the National Programme for Solidarity Education, Ministry of Education, Republic of Argentina, 2010.

REFERENCES

II Encuentro Internacional de Rectores de Universia (2010) *Documento de conclusiones. Agenda de Guadalajara.* Retrieved October 2012 from http://www.universia.net/nosotros/files/Agenda_Guadalajara.pdf.

Ander-Egg, E. (2003) *Repensando la Investigación-Acción Participativa.* Buenos Aires: Grupo editorial Lumen Humanitas.

Baggio, A.M. (ed.) (2006) *El principio olvidado: la fraternidad. En la Política y e Derecho.* Buenos Aires: Ciudad Nueva.

Bertín Ramírez, G.I. (2000) *El servicio social en México.* In: Maldonado Pérez, M. de la Cruz, Hoyo García de Alba, L.E. and Martínez de la Torre, E. (eds) *El Servicio Social:*

Institución para el Desarrollo Municipal. Mexico: Colección Documentos, ANUIES.

Billig, S. and Eyler, J. (eds) (2003) *Deconstructing Service-learning: Research Exploring Context, Participation, and Impacts.* Advances in Service-Learning Research. Greenwich, CT: Information Age Publishing.

Camilloni, A. (2010) '*Calidad académica e integración social. Ponencia en el IV Congreso Nacional de Extensión Universitaria. Mendoza, Universidad Nacional de Cuyo, November 10, 2010*'. Retrieved October 2012 from http://www.uncu.edu.ar/extension/upload/Alicia_Camilloni.pdf.

Cecchi, N., Lakonich, J.J., Pérez, D.A. and Rotstein, A. (2009) *El compromiso social de la Universidad latinoamericana del siglo XXI. Entre el debate y la acción.* Buenos Aires: IEC-CONADU.

Ciria, A. and Sanguinetti, H. (1987) *La Reforma Universitaria.* Volumes I and II. Buenos Aires: Centro Editor de América Latina.

CLAYSS (2012) CLAYSS and Red Iberoamericana de aprendizaje-servicio. '*Actas de la II Jornada de investigadores sobre aprendizaje-servicio. Buenos Aires, August 22, 2012*'. Retrieved October 2012 from http://www.clayss.org.ar/06_investigacion/jornadas/Libro_IIJIAS_COMPLETO.pdf.

Cúneo, D. (1978) *La reforma universitaria (1918–1930).* Caracas: Biblioteca Ayacucho No. 39. Retrieved October 2012 *from* http://www.bibliotecayacucho.gob.ve/fba/index.php?id=97&backPID=87&begin_at=32&tt_products=39.

De Gortari, A. (2009) '*De la gestión al establecimiento de redes sociales a través de la participación de jóvenes universitarios*'. Paper presented to the Seminario Internacional Políticas e Instrumentos de Gestión para Potenciar el Voluntariado Universitario. Escuela Universitaria Iberoamericana de Compromiso Social y Voluntariado de la REDIVU, Universidad Autónoma de Madrid, November 16–18, 2009. Retrieved October 2012 from http://www.redivu.org/eventos_congresos.html.

De Gortari Pedroza, A. (2005) *El Servicio Social Mexicano: diseño y construcción de modelos.* In: Ministerio de Educación, Ciencia y Tecnología. UPE, Programa Nacional Educación Solidaria, *Aprendizaje y servicio solidario en la Educación Superior y en los sistemas educativos latinoamericanos. Actas del 7mo. Seminario Internacional Aprendizaje y Servicio Solidario.* Argentina: Ministerio de Educación, Ciencia y Tecnología, pp. 111–13.

De Souza Santos, B. (2005) *La Universidad en el Siglo XXI. Para una reforma democrática y emancipadora de la Universidad.* Mexico City: UNAM.

EDUSOL (2006) Programa Nacional Educación Solidaria. *Experiencias ganadoras del Premio Presidencial 'Prácticas Solidarias en Educación Superior'.* UPE. Buenos Aires: Ministerio de Educación, Ciencia y Tecnología.

EDUSOL (2007) Programa Nacional Educación Solidaria. *Experiencias ganadoras del Premio Presidencial 'Prácticas Solidarias en Educación Superior' 2006.* UPE. Buenos Aires: Ministerio de Educación, Ciencia y Tecnología.

EDUSOL (2008) Programa Nacional Educación Solidaria. *Aprendizaje-servicio en la Educación Superior. Una mirada analítica desde los protagonistas.* UPE. Buenos Aires: Ministerio de Educación.

EDUSOL (2009) Programa Nacional Educación Solidaria. *Experiencias ganadoras del Premio Presidencial 'Prác-ticas Educativas Solidarias en Educación Superior'.* Buenos Aires: Ministerio de Educación.

Eyler, J. and Giles, D. (1999) *Where's the learning in service-learning?* San Francisco: Jossey-Bass.

Fals Borda, O. (1987) *Investigación Participativa.* Montevideo: Ediciones de la Banda Oriental.

FAU-UCV (2008) *Presentación en las V Jornadas de Extensión UCV,* March 6, 2008. Caracas: Universidad Central de Venezuela.

Flores-Kastanis, E., Montoya-Vargas, J. and Suárez, D.H. (2009) '*Investigación-acción participativa en la educación latinoamericana: un mapa de otra parte del mundo*'. *Revista mexicana de investigación educativa,* 14(40), 289–308. Retrieved October 2012 from http://www.scielo.org.mx/scielo.php?script=sci_arttext&pid=S1405-66662009000100013&lng=es&tlng=es.

Folgueiras Bertomeu, P. and Martínez Vivot, M. (2009) *El desarrollo de competencias en la universidad a través del Aprendizaje y Servicio Solidario.* In: Revista Interamericana de Educación para la Democracia (RIED). Retrieved October 2012 from http://www.ried-ijed.org/spanish/articulo.php?idRevista=9&idArticulo=28.

Fournier, M., Abramovich, A.L. and Da Representaçao, N. (eds) (2012) *Aprender haciendo con otros.* Buenos Aires: Universidad de General Sarmiento.

Freire, P. (1974) *La educación como práctica de la libertad.* Buenos Aires: Siglo XXI.

Freire, P. (1973) *Pedagogía del oprimido.* Buenos Aires: Siglo XXI.

Freire, P. (2002) *Pedagogía de la esperanza. Un reencuentro con la Pedagogía del oprimido.* Buenos Aires: Siglo XXI.

Frid, J. and Marconi, E. (2006) *Universidad y urgencia social.* Buenos Aires: UBA-CBC-FADU.

Furco, A. (2005) *Impacto de los proyectos de aprendizaje-servicio.* In: Programa Nacional Educación Solidaria. UPE. *Aprendizaje y servicio solidario en la Educación Superior y en los sistemas educativos latinoamericanos. Actas del 7mo. Seminario Internacional 'Aprendizaje y Servicio Solidario'.* Buenos Aires: Ministerio de Educación, Ciencia y Tecnologia, pp. 19–26.

García, O. (2010) '*La Extensión Universitaria y su impacto curricular*'. Paper presented to the IV Congreso Nacional de Extensión Universitaria. Mendoza, Universidad Nacional de Cuyo, November 10, 2010. Retrieved October 2012 from http://www.uncu.edu.ar/extension/upload/Oscar_Garc%C3%ADa.pdf.

García de Berríos, O., Berríos García, F.J. and Montilla, J.M. (2011) Artículos Arbitrados. Venezuela. *La socialización en educación universitaria: una forma de servicio comunitario. Educere,* May–August, 389–97.

García Garrido, J.L. (1999) *La universidad en el siglo XXI.* Madrid: UNED.

Garrocho Rangel, C. and Segura Lazcano, G.A. (2011) *Análisis de pertinencia social para la universidad pública en materia de investigación científica.* Universidad Autónoma del Estado de México-Universidad Wëin, Hermenéutica de la Cotidianidad. Cuerpo Interdisciplinario e Interinstitucional. Retrieved October 2012 from http://www.uaemex.mx/SIEA/hermeneutica/docs/60/PYE_AP.pdf.

Gómez García, C. (2005) '*La alfabetización en Cuba, inicio de un proceso de culturización de las masas populares*'. *Achegas, Revista de Ciência Politica,* 23. Retrieved October 2012 from http://www.achegas.net/numero/vinteetres/carmen_garcia_23.htm.

González, J.V. (1907) *'Inauguración de las Conferencias de Extensión Universitaria, La Plata, 1907'*. In: Universidad Nacional de La Plata. *Extensión universitaria: conferencias de 1907 y 1908*. La Plata: Talleres Gráficos Christmann y Crespo, 1909.

Herrero, M.A. (2002) *El 'problema del agua'. Un desafío para incorporar nuevas herramientas pedagógicas al aula Universitaria*. Tesis para la especialidad en docencia universitaria. Universidad de Buenos Aires: Facultad de Ciencias Veterinarias.

Ighina, D. (2012) *La brasa bajo la ceniza: la fraternidad en la historia del pensamiento latinoamericano*. Buenos Aires: Ciudad Nueva.

Jiménez, M. (2008) *'¿Cómo medir la percepción de la responsabilidad social en los diversos estamentos de la universidad?: una experiencia concreta'*. In: ESS *Educación Superior y Sociedad*. Nueva Época, 13(2), *El movimiento de responsabilidad social de la universidad: una comprensión novedosa de la misión universitaria*. Caracas: IESALC-UNESCO, pp. 139–62.

Kliksberg, B. (ed.) (2000) *Capital Social y Cultura. Claves estratégicas del desarrollo*. Mexico: Fondo de Cultura Económica.

Kliksberg, B. (2011) *Emprendedores Sociales. Los que hacen la diferencia*. Buenos Aires: Temas.

Labrandero, I. and Magdalena-Santander, L.C. (1983) *'Extensión académica: una función del sistema universitario'*. In: Revista de la Educación Superior. ANUIES (Asociación Nacional de Universidades e Instituciones de Educación Superior), Mexico, July–September. Retrieved October 2012 from http://www.anuies.mx/servicios/p_anuies/publicaciones/revsup/res047/txt4.htm.

McIlrath, L., Lyons, A. and Munck, R. (eds), (2012) *Higher Education and Civic Engagement. Comparative Perspectives*. New York: Palgrave Macmillan.

Martínez Martín, M. (ed.) (2009) *Aprendizaje Servicio y Responsabilidad Social de las Universidades*. Barcelona: Octaedro.

Martínez Vivot, M. and Folgueiras Bertomeu, P. (2012) *'Competencias genéricas y específicas adquiridas por estudiantes de Veterinaria en un proyecto de aprendizaje-servicio'*. In: Herrero, M.A. and Tapia, M.N., *Actas de la II Jornada de Investigadores sobre Aprendizaje-Servicio*, August 22, 2012. Buenos Aires: CLAYSS-Red Iberoamericana de aprendizaje-servicio.

Massat, E. (ed.) (2012) *Siete experiencias innovadoras en educación*. Buenos Aires: CLAYSS-Natura Creer para Ver.

McBride, A.M., Benitez, C., Sherraden, M. et al. (2003) *The Forms and Nature of Civic Service: A Global Assessment*. Washington University in St Louis: Global Service Institute, Center for Social Development.

Naidorf, J., Horn, M.A. and Giordana, P. (2007) *'Las tensiones y complejidades de la noción de pertinencia'*. Paper presented to the V Encuentro Nacional y II Latinoamericano 'La universidad como objeto de investigación', August 30 – September 1, 2007. Tandil: UNICEN, Facultad de Ciencias Humanas.

Navarro Saldaña, G. (2009) *'Aprendizaje y servicio; una estrategia metodológica para la formación de profesionales socialmente responsables'*. Presented to the XII Seminario Internacional de aprendizaje y servicio solidario, Buenos Aires, August 20–21, 2009.

Ochoa, E. (2010) *'Aprendizaje-servicio en América Latina. Apuntes sobre pasado y presente'*. In: Tzoecoen, *Revista científica, No. 5. Número especial dedicado al aprendizaje-servicio*, editado por Universidad Señor de Sipán USS Chiclayo-Perú, Centro Latinoamericano de Aprendizaje y Servicio Solidario CLAYSS Buenos Aires-Argentina, Organización de Estados Iberoamericanos OEI Oficina Regional Buenos Aires-Argentina. Chiclayo, Peru: Universidad Señor de Sipán, pp. 108–25.

Orozco Silva, L.E. (2010) *'Calidad académica y relevancia social de la educación superior en América Latina'*. *Revista Iberoamericana de Educación Superior*, 1(1). Retrieved October 2012 from http://ries.universia.net/index.php/ries/article/view/22.

Pérez, C. (2000) *'La reforma educativa ante el cambio de paradigma'*. EUREKA. Caracas: Universidad Católica Andrés Bello.

Perold, H., Sherraden, M. and Stroud, S. (eds) (2003) *Service Enquiry: Service in the 21st Century*. Johannesburg: Global Service Institute, USA and Volunteer and Service Enquiry Southern Africa.

PWC-CLAYSS (2009) *Premio PriceWaterhouseCoopers a la Educación. Quinta Edición-Año 2008. Emprendimientos universitarios de aprendizaje y servicio solidario en alianza con organizaciones comunitarias. 'La Universidad al servicio del desarrollo local'*. Buenos Aires: PWC-CLAYSS.

PWC-CLAYSS (2010) *Premio PriceWaterhouseCoopers a la Educación. Sexta Edición-Año 2009. Experiencias de aprendizaje-servicio solidario para la preservación y promoción del cuidado del medio ambiente. 'Cuidemos el mundo entre todos'*. Buenos Aires: PWC-CLAYSS.

Rama Vitale, C. (2006) *'La tercera reforma de la educación superior en América Latina y el Caribe: masificación, regulaciones e internacionalización'*. *Revista Educación y Pedagogía*, XVIII(46), 11–24.

REDIVU (2009) *'Observatorio Iberoamericano de Compromiso Social y Voluntariado Universitario'*. Retrieved October 4, 2012 from www.redivu.org/observatorio.php.

RHEL (2005) , *Revista Historia de la Educación Latinoamericana*, 7. Turja, Colombia: Universidad Pedagógica y Tecnológica de Colombia.

Roche Olivar, R. (2010) *Prosocialidad: nuevos desafíos. Métodos y pautas para la optimización creativa del entorno*. Buenos Aires: Ciudad Nueva.

Rojas Mix, M.A. (2008) In: ESS *Educación Superior y Sociedad*. Nueva Época. 13(2), *El movimiento de responsabilidad social de la universidad: una comprensión novedosa de la misión universitaria*. Caracas: IESALC-UNESCO, pp. 175–90.

Sanllorenti, P. (ed.) (2009) *'El Compromiso Social de la Universidad Latinoamericana del Siglo XXI. Entre el debate y la acción'*. IEC–CONADU. Retrieved October 2012 from http://www.iec-conadu.org.ar/e/?p=268.

Seltzer, S. and Puglisi, S. *'Prácticas comunitarias como requisito curricular. Facultad de Ciencias Económicas y Sociales, Universidad Nacional de Mar del Plata'*. Paper presented to the 12mo. Seminario Internacional 'Aprendizaje y Servicio Solidario', Buenos Aires, August 20–21, 2009. Retrieved October 2012 from http://www.slideshare.net/extensionmdp/prcticas-comunitarias.

Tapia, M.N. (2000) *La Solidaridad como Pedagogía*. Buenos Aires: Ciudad Nueva.

Tapia, M.N. (2003) *'"Servicio" and "solidaridad" in South American Spanish'*. In: Perold, H., Sherraden, M. and Stroud, S. (eds) *Service Enquiry: Service in the 21st Century*. Johannesburg: Global Service Institute, USA and Volunteer and Service Enquiry Southern Africa, pp. 139–48.

Tapia, M.N. (2006) *Aprendizaje y servicio solidario en el sistema educativo y las organizaciones juveniles*. Buenos Aires: Ciudad Nueva.

Tapia, M.N. (2009) *Aprendizaje-servicio y calidad educativa*. In: Ministerio de Educacion. Programa Nacional Educación Solidaria. *Excelencia académica y solidaridad. Actas del 11o. Seminario Internacional 'Aprendizaje y Servicio Solidario'*, Argentina, September 2009, pp. 37–67. Retrieved October 2012 from www.me.gov.ar/edusol.

Torres, R.M. (ed.) (2004) *'Educación, movilización social y formación de opinión pública. La experiencia de la Campaña Nacional de Alfabetización 'Monseñor Leonidas Proaño' del Ecuador (1988–1990)'*. Entrevista con Rosa María Torre. Reedición anotada de una entrevista de Elie Ghanem y Vera Masagão Ribeiro, CEDI, Sao Paulo, Brazil, May 21,1993; Buenos Aires, November 6, 2004. Retrieved October 2012 from http://es.scribd.com/doc/19336400/Ecuador-La-experiencia-de-la-Campana-Nacional-de-Alfabetizacion-Monsenor-Leonidas-Proano-del-Ecuador-19881990-veinte-anos-despues.

Tzhoecoen (2010) *Revista científica, No. 5. Número especial dedicado al aprendizaje-servicio*, editado por Universidad Señor de Sipán USS Chiclayo-Perú, Centro Latinoamericano de Aprendizaje y Servicio Solidario CLAYSS Buenos Aires-Argentina, Organización de Estados Iberoamericanos OEI Oficina Regional Buenos Aires-Argentina. Chiclayo, Peru: Universidad Señor de Sipán.

UCP (2001) *Asumiendo el país: Responsabilidad Social Universitaria. 13–14 de junio de 2001*. Proyecto Universidad: Construye País. Santiago de Chile: Corporación Participa-AVINA, 2001.

UNESCO (2009) Instituto de Estadística. *Compendio mundial de la educación 2009. Comparación de las estadísticas de educación en el mundo*. Montreal. Retrieved October 2012 from www.uis.unesco.org/publications/GED2009.

Vallaeys, F. and Carrizo, L.(2006) *Responsabilidad Social Universitaria-Marco conceptual, Antecedentes y Herramentas*. Red Ética y Desarrollo, BID.

Vallaeys, F., De La Cruz, C. and Sasia, P.M. (2009) *Responsabilidad social universitaria: manual de primeros pasos*. Mexico: BID-McGraw Hill Interamericana.

Vessuri, H. (2008) *De la pertinencia social a la sociedad del conocimiento*. In: Tünnermann Bernheim, C. (ed.) *La educación superior en América Latina y el Caribe: diez años después de la Conferencia Mundial de 1998*. Colombia: Pontificia Universidad Javeriana Colombia-IESALC-UNESCO, Capítulo X, pp. 459–78.

Viola, M.C. and Rosano, N. (2004) *'Formación de animadores comunitarios de lectura'*. In: *Revista Lectura y vida*, 25(1). Buenos Aires: Universidad Nacional de La Plata, Facultad de Humanidades y Ciencias de la Educación.

Inside View IV.7.1
Knowledge, engagement and higher education in the Caribbean

Patricia Ellis

INTRODUCTION

The English-speaking Caribbean consists of a number of islands and two mainland countries: Belize in Central America and Guyana in South America. The islands, most of which are independent nations, include Anguilla, Antigua and Barbuda, the Bahamas, Barbados, the Cayman Islands, Dominica, Grenada, Carriacou and Petit Martinique, Jamaica, Montserrat, St Kitts and Nevis, St Lucia, St Vincent and the Grenadines, the Turks and Caicos Islands, the Virgin islands and Trinidad and Tobago.

The emergence of globalization and of knowledge-based economies and societies, of the information age, and of the information, communication and technological revolution has highlighted the need for new kinds of knowledge and triggered an increase in demand. Reflection on these phenomena has heightened awareness of the critical role that education has to play in the creation and increase of knowledge, and in empowering people so that they can improve their lives. As the generators and transmitters of knowledge higher education, institutions have a fundamental role to play in the expansion of knowledge and the development of intellectual capacity, and in creating individuals who can adjust to the changing demands of economies and who can build and maintain democratic societies.

THE CHANGING ROLE OF HIGHER EDUCATION

In a world that has changed and continues to change at a rapid pace, societies must now be better equipped to function in a globalized environment and to compete and succeed in changed economic and social realities. Citizens must therefore be well equipped with large amounts of different kinds of knowledge and possess a wide variety of skills. It is therefore important to build knowledge societies in which citizens have access to education that provides them with the knowledge and skills to be innovators, entrepreneurs and active contributors and participants in the development of their country.

While primary and secondary education provides individuals with basic knowledge and skills, it is exposure to higher education that will provide the knowledge and skills needed to contribute to the creation and building of knowledge economies and societies. This new role for higher education therefore goes beyond preparing individuals for degrees, diplomas and certificates. Higher education institutions must now concentrate on fostering a desire and a hunger for knowledge, must increase intellectual capacity and must engage individuals in creating new and different types of knowledge. They must also encourage a commitment to lifelong learning and to sharing and using knowledge for the development of society.

To perform this role, higher education institutions must reach out to larger segments of the population, including 'non-traditional' students. Consequently, they have had to rethink the types and numbers of programmes that they offer, they have had to be more flexible in the way they operate, and they have had to use new and innovative teaching methods and approaches, including new information and communication technologies, to make their programmes more accessible and to deliver them to people wherever they are. They are now placing a greater emphasis on learning and on learning to learn rather than on teaching, on using more interactive methods such as peer tutoring, self-directed and problem-based learning, and on reflective proactive critical self-awareness. Their extensive use of technology, including computers, the internet, online distance education and social media, has revolutionized and is rapidly replacing former traditional delivery systems.

HIGHER EDUCATION IN THE CARIBBEAN

As a result of globalization and other changes, the small island developing states of the Caribbean are now expected to function in the global arena and to compete with larger and more developed countries. This means that their populations have to be well equipped with relevant and new knowledge, and, given the new role of higher education, larger numbers of people will have to become engaged with and participate in higher education programmes.

Higher education in the Caribbean is provided by public, private and foreign institutions operating at the local and regional levels. It is provided by 150 institutions, 60% of which are public, 30% private and the rest private but with some support from government. The private institutions include some 'offshore' institutions from North America and the UK.

The largest institution and provider of higher education is the University of the West Indies (UWI), with its main campuses in Jamaica, Trinidad and Barbados, and with an Open Campus and Open Campus Centres in 14 countries. Other universities include the University of Technology in Jamaica, and the Universities of Belize, Guyana, Trinidad and Tobago, and the Virgin Islands. Community colleges, technical and vocational institutes, teachers' training colleges and theological colleges also offer higher education programmes.

There are also over 70 foreign institutions that provide higher education and offer mostly medical programmes for non-Caribbean students. While most private institutions provide non-university programmes, a few have established links with UWI and with universities in the UK, and offer programmes leading to degrees from these universities. Together, the institutions of higher education provide a wide range of programmes that include certificate, diploma and degree programmes as well as professional and para-professional training,

technical and vocational education and training, and continuing education.

Most of the institutions of higher learning are members of the Association of Caribbean Tertiary Institutions, which facilitates cooperation, collaboration and articulation between its members, and provides a forum for discussion and problem-solving.

ENGAGEMENT IN HIGHER EDUCATION IN THE CARIBBEAN

In 1997, fewer than 10% of adults in the region were enrolled in higher education programmes and a target of 15% was set to be achieved by 2015. Since then, several initiatives have been taken to achieve this goal.

In the last decade, there has been a rapid increase in the demand for higher education, and the characteristics of individuals making the demands have changed. More individuals in their late twenties and early thirties and more mature persons are now participating in higher education programmes. Expansion in provision and greater and easier access have also increased opportunities for individuals from diverse groups, including people with disabilities, and those from different socioeconomic backgrounds, to participate in programmes of higher education. UWI's outreach programme 'The University in the Community', with lectures on and discussions of topical issues, is also attracting and increasing public participation.

Students are now also more likely to question the relevance of programmes, to demand that they respond to the needs of their career paths and of the workplace, and to expect that digital communication technologies will be used to facilitate learning. Through institutional links and partnerships, students now have access to programmes via multiple pathways, and they can use prior learning in one institution to gain access to another at a higher level without loss of time or credits.

Higher education institutions are now also more aware of the importance of linking their programmes to the demands of the labour market, of making them more relevant to the needs of the workers in key sectors of the economy and of offering programmes that provide the population with the knowledge and skills they need to function in these

sectors. Emphasis is therefore now being placed on tourism and hospitality studies, offshore financial services, management and professional development, human resource management, immigration studies, public sector management and the acquisition of multiple literacies, including economic and technological literacy.

Although face-to-face methods still have a place and are still used to deliver programmes, new modes of delivery are now common. The introduction of distance education, including tele- and video-conferencing, the availability of online courses and virtual education have all contributed to major changes in the way programmes are now being delivered. The result is an increase in the number of people of all ages who are engaged in formal and non-formal higher education programmes and in informal education and learning.

While larger numbers of people in the region are participating in higher education programmes, there is a concern that more females than males are enrolled in the available programmes. Throughout the region, evidence of this can be seen in the large numbers of females in classes of higher education programmes and in an increase in the number of females who are accessing and participating in technical and vocational programmes that were previously believed to be for males. At the same time, in many higher education programmes there are also more female instructors, lecturers and tutors than there are male.

CONCLUSION

In the Caribbean, universities are still regarded as the pinnacle of higher education, and some people still believe in an elitist education and that not everyone is 'suited' to university or higher education. However, the increase in other institutions, such as community colleges and technical vocational education and training institutes, working alone or collaborating with the universities, has broadened the concept of higher education, increased outreach to all sectors of the population and increased the type and number of programmes being offered.

This has not only improved the status of non-university institutions, but also gradually led to a change in attitudes towards larger segments of the public who are now engaged in the pursuit of higher education. Consequently, there has been a significant increase in the number of individuals at all levels of society who are now increasing their knowledge through engagement in higher education programmes.

Inside View IV.7.2
Extramural studies and experiences of learning and service-learning against the logic of university marketization in Brazil

Katia Gonçalves Mori

This paper argues in favour of a humanizing education, jointly responsible for the construction of a democratic state. The point of departure is the current scenario, which is heavily influenced by Brazil's rapid economic growth and the expansion of higher education as a lucrative business for market investors. In response to the 'marketization' of the university, the extramural studies programme and experiences of learning and service-learning are presented as possible alternatives to rescue the social purpose of quality in higher education in order to achieve the desired critical-emancipatory training.

The history of higher education in Brazil is quite recent. The first universities were established in the early 20th century, for example University of Rio de Janeiro (1920) and University of São Paulo (1934). Movements such as the 1932 Manifesto of the Pioneers of National Education, which called for compulsory, free basic public education for all, resulted in a rise in enrolments. Pressure for university posts for recent graduates in basic education moved the government to create facilities to expand the network of private higher education courses, resulting in uncontrolled growth.

In the early 1960s, 40% of enrolments in higher education were in the private sector, driven by economic growth. During the military dictatorship (1964–1965), the privatization rate rose to 65%. After a period of decline (around 5%) in the 1980s, the country sustained renewed growth with the introduction of neoliberalism, reaching practically 70% by around 2000 and 75% in 2009 (Otaviano, 2011).

Entrepreneurs are currently interested in higher education as a 'growth market' that moves around US $53 billion per year, or the equivalent of 7% of the country's gross domestic product, and receives investments in the order of US $16.2 billion per year, according to Hoper Educacional, the institution that provides consultancy services in this area (Osman, 2008). Higher education became a lucrative business, despite being considered non-profit, a sector not lacking in 'consumers' with the acceleration of the Brazilian economy and the rising income of social classes C and D seeking qualifications in an expanding labour market.

For Marilena Chauí (2003, p. 6), the higher education crisis in Brazil may be a reflection of national politics, which, based on reform justified as overthrowing a 'paternalistic and state-subsidized regime', redefined state sectors, placing education in the designated non-exclusive services sector; education was no longer considered a guaranteed right but a service that can be private or privatized.

The transition of the concept of university as a social institution into a service-providing organization, in the midst of a capitalist system, shatters the vision of social responsibility. Whether private or public, a university education should provide an opportunity not only for academic and scientific learning and for the labour market, but also for the construction of a democratic state:

> If we want to take the public university in a new direction, we need to begin by demanding, above all, that the state does not view education from the perspective of public spending but as a social and political investment, which is only possible if education is considered a right and not a privilege or a service. ... It is through the allocation of public funds to social rights that the democratisation of a state is measured and with it the democratisation of the university. (Chauí, 2003, p. 8)

Our objective is to rescue the role of the university and the quality of university training, which is in crisis. For Boaventura de Sousa Santos, the 'marketization' of universities affects the quality of education provided on two levels, transforming it into a field of evaluation of 'educational capitalism'. On the first level, marketization consists of ensuring that the university establishes partnerships with capital, particularly industrial capital, in order to generate its own revenue. On the second level, private and public universities together evolve into a company, which not only produces for the market, but also 'produces itself as a market, a market of university management, curricula, certification, and assessment of teachers and students' (de Sousa Santos, 2005, p. 12).

This capitalist and productivist pressure has distanced the university from its humanistic and cultural function. Scientific and technological production cannot cause the breakdown of critical-emancipatory education, surrendering to the demands of the economy. If we want a less unequal world, it will not be achieved through consumption but through citizenship. The quality of education must be based primarily on ethical and political training, in favour of a dignified life for each and every person.

Along these lines, in 1987 the National Forum of Pro-Rectors of Public Universities in Brazil decided on the creation of extra-mural studies, defined as 'a cultural, educational and scientific process that indivisibly links teaching and research and paves the way for a transformative relationship between university and society.[1] Subsequently, in 1999, the concept of university extra-mural studies was included in the National Plan for Extramural Studies: 'university extramural studies are a cultural, educational and scientific process that indivisibly links teaching and research and paves the way for a transformative relationship between university and society'.[2]

The principle of indissolubility (teaching–research–extra-mural studies) reaffirmed extra-mural studies as an academic process, justifying the adjective 'university', which in all extra-mural activities must be linked to the training process of individuals and to knowledge generation, and placing students at the centre of their technical training; in this way, they can obtain the expertise required for professional performance and citizenship education, a guarantee of rights and duties, assuming a transformative vision:

University extramural studies are a cultural, educational and scientific process that indivisibly links teaching and research and paves the way for a transformative relationship between university and society. Extramural studies are a two-way street that guarantees traffic flow for the academic community, which will encounter, in society, the opportunity to develop the practice of academic knowledge. In the return to university, teachers and students will convey learning that, once subjected to theoretical reflection, will enhance that knowledge.

This flow, which establishes the exchange of academic or popular systematised instruction, will lead to the production of knowledge resulting from confrontation with Brazilian and regional reality, the democratisation of academic knowledge and the effective participation of the community in university performance. In addition to the instrumental nature of this dialectic process of theory/practice, extramural studies are an interdisciplinary operation that enhances the integrated vision of the social dimension. (FORPOREX, 2012, p. 8)

University extra-mural work promotes the acquisition of scientific and technical expertise through community service activities and, to a certain extent, overlaps with the concept and practice of service-learning (Tapia, 2006), whereby students are stimulated during their period of academic training to apply academic knowledge to solve real social problems that they have previously identified. Such experiments are beginning to gain social recognition and importance. Through them, young people are encouraged to think and act in favour of a better quality of life for the community, which denotes a better quality academic training (Tapia, 2001, 2006). Thus, there is no dichotomization between professional training, and political and civic awareness training, from the perspective of ethical instruction and for the construction of knowledge-emancipation (de Sousa Santos, 2009).

The fundamental challenge to university extra-mural studies (although mainly between public universities) is currently 'the defence of public policies, by participating in the formulation, follow-up and appraisal of these policies in every sphere of the federation and sectors of activity, particularly those related to the guarantee of rights' (Soares, 2007, p. 2).

Civil society initiatives, such as the Universidade Solidária (UniSol), established in 1995, have contributed by promoting joint community–university projects (private and public companies, tertiary sector organizations and communities), conceived as learning and service-learning, with a direct impact on local development, reinforcing university research and extra-mural studies, and citizenship education. UniSol aims to stimulate leadership in university students, principally to provide a more matter-of-fact view of Brazilian social reality, as well as to strengthen community organization by seeking solutions to local problems, promoting improved quality of life and sustainable development.

In the 16 years since its creation, the UniSol programme has mobilized 23,865 students and teachers from 214 universities, who have undertaken projects in 1,336 communities throughout the country. This has benefited over two million people with projects in several areas of knowledge wholly based on the premises of networking and partnerships between various sectors to find solutions to social problems (see www.unisol.org.br).

FINAL CONSIDERATIONS

A continental country like Brazil, the world's seventh largest economy but ranked 85th in the Human Development Index, shows that economic growth does not automatically result in quality of life for its people. And to achieve that aim, there is still much to be done. It is not enough to merely acknowledge social inequality, injustice, corruption and so many other social ills. We cannot allow higher education to become one big growth market for investors or to be accessory to the regulation of the unjust established order.

The public significance of education, its function in shaping a society that accepts the responsible undertaking of constructing a democratic state must be included on the agenda of university education. It is the responsibility of society as a whole to demand that the university show transparency and commitment to the quality of life of the community. To that end, one alternative might involve including extra-mural studies and service-learning experiences in the curriculum, therefore making them an inherent part of the initial training process, mainly in teacher training courses.

In short, according to de Sousa Santos (2011), experiences that overcome the separation of academic and popular knowledge, of learning produced at university and the real social problems of the community, of knowledge regulation and knowledge emancipation, must be the result of education by intention. In a society that desires greater fairness, the university cannot reproduce science and technology without ethical and socially responsible objectives. On the contrary, such responsibility must lead to mutual understanding and transnational solidarity.

REFERENCES

Chauí, M. (2003) *A universidade pública sob nova perspectiva*. Conferência na sessão de abertura da 26ª Reunião Anual da ANPEd, Minas Gerais.

de Sousa Santos, B. (2005). *A universidade no Século XX: Para uma reforma democrática e emancipatória da Universidade*. Brasilia: Ministério da Educação.

de Sousa Santos, B. (2009). *A crítica da razão indolente: contra o desperdício da experiência*. São Paulo: Cortez.

de Sousa Santos, B. (2010). *Pela mão de Alice. O social e o político na pós modernidade*. São Paulo: Cortez Editora.

de Sousa Santos, B. (2011). *A encruzilhada da universidade europeia. Revista Ensino Superior*, 41 (July–August–September).

FORPOREX (2012) '*Política nacional de extensão universitária*'. Retrieved September 2013 from http://www.proec.ufpr.br/downloads/extensao/2012/legislacao/

Politica%20Nacional%20de%20Extensao%20Universitaria%20maio2012.pdf.

Osman, R. (2008) 'Lições da educação'. Retrieved September 2013 from http://www.istoedinheiro.com.br/noticias/3855_LICOES+DA+EDUCACAO.

Otaviano, H (2011) 'A privatização do ensino superior'. Retrieved September 2013 from http://www.brasildefato.com.br/node/7136.

Soares, L.T. (2007) Prefácio: Direitos humanos políticas públicas e extensão universitária. In: Direitos humanos, violência e pobreza na América Latina contemporânea. Rio de Janeiro: Letra e Imagem.

Tapia, M.N. (2001) La solidaridad como peda-gogía: el 'aprendizaje-servicio' en la escuela (2nd edn). Buenos Aires: Ciudad Nueva.

Tapia, M.N. (2006) Aprendizaje y servicio solidario en el sistema educativo y las organizaciones juveniles. Buenos Aires: Ciudad Nueva.

NOTES

1   This definition was published by FORPO-REX (the National Forum of Pro-Rectors of Public Universities in Brazil), an organization dedicated to articulating and defining academic policies on extra-mural studies, committed to social transforma-tion for the full exercise of citizenship and the reinforcement of democracy, an organization that is dedicated to articulat-ing and defining academic policies for extra-mural studies.

2   See http://www.renex.org.br/documentos/Colecao-Extensao-Universitaria/01-Plano-Nacional-Extensao/Plano-nacional-de-extensao-universitaria-editado.pdf.

Inside View IV.7.3
The social responsibility of higher education in Chile: AEQUALIS, the higher education forum

Mónica Jiménez de la Jara

The day at the dawning of the 21st century on which we created a consortium of 13 universities as part of the 'Universidad Construye País' (University Builds Country) project now seems far off. At the time, we defined the social responsibility of universities as:

the university's ability to disseminate and put into practice a set of general and specific principles and values, through four key processes: management, teaching, research and university extension, in response to the university community and the country in which it is based. (Universidad Construye País, 2006)

For many years, higher education institutions in Chile operated reactively. In other words, they tried to survive in the face of increasing student demand and to adapt to the resulting requirements. However, this role was challenged by a reduction in state involvement in education and the emergence of a highly deregulated market, the appearance of private educational offerings, the diversification of funding, internationalization, rankings and accreditation for quality assurance.

Despite the slow pace of the transformations, a new, more proactive attitude and greater commitment can today be observed. Universities are trying to anticipate society's demands. To achieve this, universities need to be close to society and interact with it. They must listen to, join with and even be an agent of the diverse voices of which society is composed. Despite the various forces that aim to diminish this effort, we can see a strengthening of the universities' social role, which has begun to transform all of their main functions, including 'university extension'. In the past, the public were considered to be 'consumers' of culture in extension activities, rather than active, participating agents who can create and generate it.

Talk of the 'social and civic commitment' of universities involves fostering and promoting a more equal relationship of mutual need and interdependence. Universities are no longer seen as institutions that have and 'generously share' knowledge. They are institutions that are learning, that are open, that listen and discover more relevant ways of serving society. In other words, there is a paradigm shift at whose heart is the joint creation of knowledge. We are moving on from the 'ivory tower' to modes of relations characterized by a continuous interaction with actors situated in the surrounding area. Thus, universities will become important agents of the synergistic development of knowledge.

The challenge of interacting with relevant actors in the surrounding area is not limited to universities; it also applies to vocational schools that provide professional training at all levels. Such schools form relations in a different way from universities as a result of their function and mission. Their objectives focus on helping students to join the labour market and on promoting technological innovation. Consequently, the challenges require commitment to the local and regional area in which the schools operate. Local actors will reduce the need to increase the diversity of the higher education system and thus extend the content of development beyond the universities. In fact, each function that the various institutions carry out contributes in its own way to the process of modernization of societies and the development that supports this process. To bring about this change, a new approach needs to be taken by the authorities, academic bodies, administrative organs and, of course, the students.

In Chile, the students have clearly taken the lead: they are claiming their citizenship, as well as their civil, political, economic, social and cultural rights. They are not only asking for better living conditions for themselves, but also organizing protests to demand profound changes in society. They are calling for the State to play a greater role, for recognition of the right to education and health, for an end to profit in education, and for deep changes in the economy, social relations and citizen participation. In addition, they are pushing for a different conception of democracy – supported by an integral vision of human life – that would involve a series of civic responsibilities and not just politics.

In this approach, the State is associated with the democratic regime for at least three reasons. First, it is the entity that demarcates citizens' electoral participation. Second, it is responsible for the legal system that sanctions the civil liberties without which the democratic regime would not exist. Third, it is reflected in a bureaucratic structure that gives continuity and certainty to political processes.

Before the start of the student protests in 2011, a group of one hundred academics from various regions, who had a range of ideological and religious opinions and worked in different vocational and academic higher education institutions, got together and formed AEQUALIS, the Higher Education Forum.

This wide-ranging, diverse, innovative forum has systematically dealt with the various problems of Chilean higher education, and considers that social commitment is expressed in concern for the education system in general and the higher education system in particular. At this time, there is no better way to demonstrate social responsibility than by acting on the education system and by carrying out the reforms that society is crying out for.

This energy has driven the work of AEQUALIS (2013) in the last four years, in the process of which the characteristics of the new kind of students have been discussed, as well as the changes that institutions must undergo to ensure the admission, progression and appropriate qualification of these people. The subject of equity has been conceptualized, and opinions have been formed on entry mechanisms for higher education, with a focus on the need to adapt these mechanisms to make them more inclusive and integrative as this is an essential factor in all social systems. The forum has also discussed the main supports of the higher education system's structure in order to redefine them so that the public sphere is taken into account at all levels.

One concept that should be reconsidered is that of the 'autonomy' of higher education institutions. The idea is to foster a kind of institutional autonomy that considers in internal decision-making processes the mid- and long-term effects of decisions on the entire system. In other words, we must assume that an institution is not simply a private entity that offers products and processes them for a group of 'consumers'. Instead, it belongs to a system whose survival depends on the responsible participation of all components. This responsibility is not only to the student or the internal community, but also to the rest of the actors in the surrounding area, including other institutions of the same type.

Likewise, it is essential to increase the spaces in institutions' internal communities that are available for deliberation, discussion and, of course, decision-making. A higher education system that is constituted from the public sphere must recognize joint decisions taken about strategic areas. In fact, internal communities, which are constituent parts of the institutional project, should decide on an institution's future: empowerment of the institution's actors is a vital device for internally legitimating the project that is being promoted. In this context, the Talloires Network, which operates worldwide, states clearly that:

something revolutionary is occurring at global level: students and teachers are working together and are becoming active agents in the life of their communities. They are feeling the solitude of the ivory tower and have opened the gates. Enthusiasm for flourishing civic commitment is common today in US colleges and universities and is redefining the relationships between academia, public interest, and all those who are concerned about social justice, the environment, human and general development, and the social and economic challenges of development. (Talloires Network, 2010)

These winds of change create a suitable setting for pursuing the structural reforms that education systems must at times undergo. Higher education institutions in Latin America have felt the pressure to change, and, each in its own context, are working to attain greater legitimation of their decisions and actions.

REFERENCES

AEQUALIS (2013) *Hacia una nueva arquitectura del sistema de educación superior: el régimen de lo público.* Chile: AQUALIS, Foro de Educación Superior

Universidad Construye País (2006) *Responsabilidad Social Universitaria: Una Manera de Ser Universidad. Teoría y Práctica en la Experiencia Chilena.* Chile: Universidad Construye País.

Talloires Network (2010) www.tufts.edu/talloiresnetwork.

Spotlight Issues IV.7.4
The role of the university in the transformation of a territory of poverty[*]

Paulo Speller, Sofia Lerche Vieira and Stela Meneghel

This paper reflects on the role and contribution of the university in areas of poverty and discusses the case of the University of International Integration of the Afro-Brazilian Lusophony (UNILAB). Recently created in the city of Redenção[1] (Ceará state), located in northeast Brazil,[2] UNILAB is a federal university designed to build a historical and cultural bridge between Brazil and the Portuguese-

* This paper has been developed under a project receiving financial support from the National Council for Scientific and Technological Development (CNPq).

speaking countries (the Community of Portuguese Language Countries) and strengthen cooperation with the African continent. Within its two years of existence, it has played a unique role in the higher education scenario, expressing the significant potential of institutions with cooperation for solidarity as a main goal. The paper presents a few aspects of UNILAB's project and figures, as well a brief portrait of higher education in Brazil.

BRIEF TRENDS OF HIGHER EDUCATION IN BRAZIL

Since the first institutions whose origins date back to the Middle Ages, the link between universities and urban centres has been significant and important. In most countries, there have been strong trends and traditions to create them in areas of cultural, social and/ or economic interest, although it is possible to observe, in various contexts, some exceptions to this rule. In Brazil, the movement for the creation of higher education institutions (HEIs) had a similar trajectory, so that the first of these were created in the early 19th century by the State in the capitals of the most developed states, to act as vocational schools. It was only in the 1940s that they started to become universities, effectively carrying out research[3] (Cunha, 2007).

In the 1970s, there was a large expansion in the further education system, with vocational training being offered through the private sector, which has since become hegemonic in the provision of further education. However, during this same period, the federal government created some mechanisms and institutions (development agencies, in particular) in order to make some public HEIs 'centres of excellence' in research. As a result, the country now has a majority of private institutions, concerned with certification for professional careers (colleges and schools and with fewer than 3,000 students), while at the same time there are a few research-driven public institutions – universities – that are located in major urban centres and engaged in postgraduate training and the generation of knowledge (Meneghel, 2001).

From the mid-1990s, there was a strong new wave of expansion of higher education exclusively in the private sector. However,

new policy frameworks have been designed in recent years,[4] leading to a renewed growth of federal higher education institutions and a reversal in the trend of establishing them in the state capitals, seeking a differentiated profile. The expansion process was from then on directed primarily at sparsely populated locations as well as border areas (a movement called 'interiorization'), with a strong focus on social inclusion. In addition, there was another peculiarity: two universities were created focusing on international integration. This is the case of UNILAB, the last of 14 federal universities created during this period, which aims to:

> offer further education, develop research in various fields of knowledge and promote university extension, with the specific institutional mission of qualifying human resources to contribute to the integration between Brazil and other members of the Community of Portuguese Speaking Countries (CPLP), especially those in Africa, and to promote regional development and cultural, scientific and educational exchange. (Law No. 12.289/2010, Art. 2; Brazil Presidência da República, 2010)

Therefore, UNILAB's creation as an educational, research and extension institution was geared to building close ties with the specific reality of the region where it was founded, while at the same time promoting international cooperation with Portuguese-speaking countries.

UNILAB'S PROJECT

UNILAB's project aims for integration in a broad sense. Its mission is based upon the principle of cooperation for solidarity, within the context of the internationalization of higher education. Three principles guide its actions both nationally and internationally:

- higher education aligned with the demands and needs of the Brazilian Northeastern region and partnering countries, with a special focus on the Baturité Massif, the Portuguese-speaking African countries and East Timor;
- student education, established in partnership with education institutions in the partnering countries, in order to allow an exchange of

experiences, professors' and students' mobility and the qualification of the staff;
- an effective absorption of graduate professionals into the world of work in their home countries – based upon an extensive network of cooperation, UNILAB intends to support students as they pursue a professional career and may contribute to the development of their regions and countries.

As a result of a process of dialogue with UNILAB's partners, a few appropriate topics were identified to foment the exchange of knowledge, in harmony with the national demands and the relevance of policies for economic and social development. The following areas were initially prioritized: collective health, teacher training, rural development, sustainable development and technologies, humanities and languages, and public management. The undergraduate courses now offered are: Public Management, Agronomy, Humanities, Natural Sciences and Math, Nursing, Energy Engineering and Letters/Portuguese Language. All of these have a significant percentage of foreign students from partner countries.

One of UNILAB's goals is to attract half of its student body from partner countries and half from its surrounding area. Out of the 1,387 students regularly enrolled at UNILAB, 1,087 are Brazilian. The others are from Angola (27), Cape Verde (39), Guinea-Bissau (134), Mozambique (5), São Tomé and Príncipe (23) and East Timor (72). The number of foreign students tends to increase as new students come with each academic term. Enrolment in distance education consists of 350 students in undergraduate courses and 681 in graduate courses. UNILAB's current staff consists of 85 professors (74 Brazilians and 11 from other countries) and 89 other professionals working in administrative activities. (For further information, see: www.unilab.edu.br.)

UNILAB's present image is that of a melting pot of cultures and races expressed in the composition of those who belong to its staff or are enrolled there. Its students, who come from a variety of contexts, some of which involve significant economic constraints, have the opportunity to change their future in ways that were never dreamed of by those who, at the end of the 19th century, pursued the abolition of slavery in Redenção. The challenge is, at the same time, to promote an academic environment of excellence through its teaching, research and extension activities, and a culture of citizenship values in a world of change and uncertainty.

Although it is too early to tell what the future will bring out of this original institutional project, it is certain that it will play an important role in the context of cooperation for solidarity and the reduction of poverty in poor areas. If the goals set for UNILAB's mission are achieved, there will be new lessons to be learned from its experience.

REFERENCES

Brazil Presidência da República (2010) 'Casa Civil. Subchefia para Assuntos Jurídicos. Lei No. 12.289, de 20 de julho de 2010. Dispõe sobre a criação da Universidade da Integração Internacional da Lusofonia Afro-Brasileira e dá outras providencias'. Retrieved June 20, 2013 from http://www.planalto.gov.br/ccivil_03/_Ato 2007-2010/2010/Lei/L12289.htm.

Cunha, L.A. (2007) A universidade reformanda: o golpe de 1964 e a modernização do ensino superior (2nd edn). São Paulo: UNESP.

Meneghel, S.M. (2001) A crise da Universidade moderna no Brasil. Doctoral thesis, UNICAMP, Campinas.

NOTES

1   The city of Redenção was chosen as the main campus of UNILAB due to its special role in the movements against slavery in the 19th century, being the first Brazilian city to abolish slavery.
2   UNILAB was created in August 2010 and started work in May 2011. Its objective is to promote south–south interaction through cooperative solidarity between the Community of Portuguese Language Countries: Angola, Cape Verde, Guinea-Bissau, Mozambique, São Tomé and Principe, and East Timor, as well as Portugal.
3   A few further education institutes started as universities, as did the University of Brasília, whose founding coincided with the building of the city that became the capital of the Republic in 1961.
4   UNILAB was created under President Luiz Inácio Lula da Silva's government (2003–2010).

Spotlight Issues IV.7.5
The Social Entrepreneurship Lab

Luz Arabany Ramírez

The Social Entrepreneurship Lab (SEL) of the National University of Colombia Campus Manizales began its activity in August 2012 with the purpose of eliminating poverty in Caldas, Colombia. The SEL provides academic activities to the local community through teaching, investigation and outreach projects for students, entrepreneurs, private organizations and the local government.

The introduction of concepts of social entrepreneurship has provided the region's population with an alternative to working in or creating traditional businesses. The SEL supports students, entrepreneurs and local governments. It offers students the opportunity to participate in courses in social entrepreneurship. To local entrepreneurs, the SEL offers support and guidance to steer their organizations towards social entrepreneurship. Similarly, the SEL provides local government research with results that measure the level of and reduction in poverty in order to formulate new projects and design public policies.

For the future, the SEL proposes holding a permanent forum to design social entrepreneurship solutions that will address financial, educational, managerial and public policies.

POVERTY IN COLOMBIA AND CALDAS

Poverty is unavoidable when modes of production are insufficient to give the population a comfortable standard of living. Over the last few years, reducing poverty has become a major goal for many international organizations, so much so that there are global millennium development goals to completely eliminate poverty over the next few decades.

Since the late 1990s, important economic sectors in Colombia have experienced economic recession, worsening the situation of poverty in the country. The most affected sectors are the agricultural, manufacturing, transportation and construction industries, which are the main sources of employment in the country. Caldas, with its municipal capital Manizales, is a department of Colombia and part of the famous Colombian coffee-growing region. The population of Caldas is 1,030,062 over an area of 7,291 km^2, with 47% of its population located in rural areas.

The National Administrative Department of Statistics reports that poverty in Colombia has decreased gradually and slowly in the past few years. A press release delivered on 2 January 2013 presents the following numbers for 2011 (Departamento Administrativo Nacional de Estadística, 2013, p. 8):

- The national poverty index decreased 3.0%.
- The extreme poverty index decreased 1.7% in Colombia and 1.3% in Caldas.
- The national Gini coefficient decreased 0.012 and 0.007 in Caldas.

When Manizales is excluded from statistics for Caldas, the regional poverty index increases to 49.9% (that is, one in three people in Caldas is poor) and the regional extreme poverty index increases to 15.4% (Gobernación de Caldas, 2012). In other words, Manizales has many possibilities to reduce poverty. In spite of these numbers, Colombia is one of the most economically unequal countries in Latin America.

The Development Plan of Caldas 2012–2015 proposes that the poverty seen in Caldas is caused by the lack of sources of income and employment opportunities. It is therefore necessary to implement strategies and projects to remedy that situation (Gobernación de Caldas, 2013). One of the objectives of the Development Plan of the City of Manizales 2012–2015 is to create projects that will favour social inclusion and employment opportunities to improve quality of life and well-being in order to reduce poverty (Municipio de Manizales, 2012). The creation of the SEL has been proposed as one of the goals of the Social Entrepreneurship for Eliminating Poverty in Caldas project, in addition to local governmental initiatives to reduce regional poverty and in line with the mission of the National University of Colombia.

OBJECTIVES OF THE SEL

The SEL focuses on academic activities to promote and develop a culture of social entrepreneurship. It offers training, consultation, research and the development of projects with public and private organizations interested in generating new ideas, and with businesses that provide social value and reduce the vulnerability of poor communities.

DESCRIPTION OF THE INITIATIVE

Social Entrepreneurship for Eliminating Poverty in Caldas won the First Pro Bono Outreach UN Contest and received financial support. The project activities included:

- support for formal education programmes in social entrepreneurship;
- the diffusion of social entrepreneurship;
- non-degree education in social entrepreneurship;
- the creation of the SEL.

The SEL is proposed as one action line of the Management Consulting Office (MCO) of the Management School. The MCO has provided support to entrepreneurship activities for 20 years in traditional, technology-based and cultural entrepreneurship.

At the SEL, we believe that the traditional business methods and traditional mindset of non-governmental organizations need to change. Charity has proven to be insufficient when it comes to reducing poverty in the long term, and the willingness to help our communities has been increasing. We should develop new and interesting methods to include and work with the community. The SEL defines social entrepreneurship as an innovative activity with social value that reduces negative aspects and strengthens a community's development possibilities. It is an activity that emerges from a person or an organization, public or private, and produces a business. Once that innovative idea demonstrates its social validity, the business can be replicated and adapted in other contexts.

The members of the SEL are scholars, students and freelancers who develop academic activities:

- *Education.* The goal of this activity is to share and transfer experience and project results and research conducted by the SEL to undergraduate and graduate students.
- *Research.* This area focuses on the development of research projects with the purpose of building theoretical and practical elements to expand the development of social entrepreneurship in Caldas and Colombia:
  - Define social entrepreneurship as well as the structure and operation of businesses with a social emphasis to show the differences between traditional businesses and businesses with a social purpose.
  - Identify and develop social entrepreneurship trends and models (entrepreneurship ecosystems and clusters, among others).
  - Measure the effectiveness of activities related to social entrepreneurship (for example, studies to determine potential markets and consumers of products and services provided by businesses with a social emphasis).
  - Identify best practices of social entrepreneurship and determine the characteristics and results needed to replicate them in different contexts and conditions.
- *Community outreach projects.* The function of this activity is the projection of topics of academic interest and the relation to the surroundings:

- Elaborate and develop non-degree programmes in social entrepreneurship.
- Develop joint projects with public and private organizations.
- Provide counselling to social entrepreneurs throughout the entire social entrepreneurship value chain (awareness, training, recognition, guidance and formulation, among others).
- Offer relevant counselling in the formulation of public policies in social entrepreneurship at local, regional and national levels, based on previous experiences, success stories and the development of cross-functional activities of social entrepreneurship.
- Offer educational events (such as forums, meetings and congresses) that promote and provide networking opportunities to interested organizations and people interested in social entrepreneurship in the region.

Other activities that are part of the SEL are:

- identifying and presenting social entrepreneurship projects in order to obtain financial awards;
- writing articles and presenting talks in order to share the results of the SEL's activity.

Based on the combined efforts of the initiatives and activities mentioned above, for the next year the SEL proposes to hold a permanent monthly forum that includes a cross-functional participation of different members to design social entrepreneurship solutions addressing financial, educational, managerial and public policies.

OUTCOME OF THE SEL INITIATIVE

Social entrepreneurship is a growing movement in the world and relatively new in Colombia. The National University of Colombia has the opportunity to be one of the Colombian pioneers guiding where this movement will go. In addition, the University Campus Manizales is the first institution in the region to create an SEL that supports students, entrepreneurs and public and private organizations throughout the entire social entrepreneurship value chain. The SEL has shown a strong positioning since it began its activities. It has held the first two social entrepreneurship meetings (with the support of Grameen Caldas and the Catholic University of Manizales) in the region, with over 540 participants.

REFERENCES

Departamento Administrativo Nacional de Estadística (2013) *Comunicado de Prensa* *sobre la Pobreza en Colombia Años 2010–2011*. Bogota: DANE.

Gobernación de Caldas (2013) *Plan de Desarrollo del Departamento de Caldas 2012–2015 Compromiso de Todos*. Retrieved September 2013 from http://gobernacion decaldas.gov.co/images/plandedesarrollo/plan2012completo.pdf.

Municipio de Manizales (2012) *Plan de Desarrollo Municipio de Manizales 2012–2015 Gobierno en la Calle*. Retrieved September 2013 from http://www.manizales.gov.co/dmd/pd/ACUERDO0784/PLANDEDESAR ROLLOGOBIERNOENLACALLE.pdf.

Spotlight Issues IV.7.6
The Indigenous Intercultural University network – a place for dialogue on knowledge

Claudia Stengel

The Indigenous Intercultural University (IIU) is a collectively constructed regional academic initiative that promotes and accompanies the social transformation that is being led by the Fund for the Development of the Indigenous Peoples of Latin America and the Caribbean (Indigenous Fund) by offering specific postgraduate formation and promoting epistemic pluralism in academic spheres.

The IIU Network consists of more than 20 academic centres that offer eight different postgraduate courses to indigenous leaders and professionals from the whole Latin American continent. Since its start in 2005, more than 500 men and women from more than 85 indigenous peoples have graduated. One aspect of the innovative IIU approach is the Cátedra Indígena Itinerante (CII, the Itinerant Indigenous Faculty), which is an integral part of postgraduate courses aimed at the dissemination, exchange and collective and systematic building of indigenous knowledge and wisdom, in which debate, shared learning and active participation are promoted among students.

BACKGROUND

As part of their processes of modernization and democratic consolidation, many Latin American countries have passed laws recognizing indigenous peoples as an integral part of their multicultural societies. Indigenous organizations realize that, in order to improve their participation in the government, economy and society, they need more people with professional training. At present, they do not have enough qualified specialists with leadership skills who are capable of working successfully in the political arena and, above all, ensuring effective coordination between the State and society.

However, existing education systems have not yet met the demand for training for indigenous people in either quantitative or qualitative terms. Indigenous people do not have the same opportunities to pursue higher education, and there are few universities offering degrees and programmes focused on subjects that are important to them. The problem, in terms of quality, is that current university education systems focus on subjects and methodologies that do not respond to the interests of indigenous peoples or value the contributions they make.

Extensive discussions have taken place within this context. Indigenous people consider that higher education in and for their communities must be structured around the transmission of integrated systems of holistic knowledge and draw on the wellsprings of indigenous spirituality. They believe that higher education should not only be realistic and pragmatic, but also reflect the spiritual richness of indigenous cosmogonies and philosophies, which are inexhaustible sources of wisdom and harmonious balance between the people and the land in their communities. These concerns stem from criticism levelled by indigenous people at formal education at all levels. They feel that it has contributed to the loss of their peoples' identity, offers knowledge and skills that they cannot apply and results in a loss of respect for their way of life, including their leaders, culture and ancestral wisdom. There are also demands for full indigenous participation in the formal state education system, which has not yet been achieved. Consequently, the dialogue between indigenous and academic knowledge is not yet satisfactory.

In this respect, one of the challenges facing higher education programmes for indigenous people is the recording, application, protection and transfer of knowledge that exists and is commonly used in their communities. The knowledge of each indigenous people is unique, traditional and local. It covers all aspects of community life, including their relation with the natural environment.

THE IIU NETWORK

In 2005, to respond this challenge and to address the 30 years of demands of the continental indigenous organizations, the Indigenous Fund called for the formation of the regional IIU Network. Its aim is to contribute to the formation of qualified indigenous professionals with leadership capacity, so they can take on coordination, participation and decision-making tasks from an inter-cultural perspective, and exercise positive influence over the political, economic and social organization of their respective societies.

To respond the demand for academic formation with identity and from an indigenous perspective, the CII was created as an integral part of postgraduate courses aimed at the dissemination, exchange and collective and systematic building of indigenous knowledge and wisdom, in which debate, shared learning and active participation are promoted among students. Developed by indigenous specialists and wise men and women, the purpose of the CII is to offer a conceptual and political framework to help each postgraduate programme develop its themes by integrating the perspective of indigenous experience and knowledge.

In 2007, the IIU launched several blended postgraduate programmes, incorporating the CII as part of the study programme and getting several virtual platforms up and running at the universities responsible for each programme. These platforms make it possible to carry out the virtual activities that form part of the blended mode of learning that characterizes this education project, since part of the course is carried out face to face (with the CII) and part is completed by distance learning. The virtual learning component is based on a methodology called 'collaborative learning'. From this perspective, knowledge is built with the participation and contribution of all involved; the teacher is not seen as the owner of the information, but rather as the facilitator of the learning process.

Since its outset, the IIU has been able to provide relevant, quality programmes that respond to the expectations and demands of indigenous peoples. The current offer includes the following courses:

- Inter-cultural Bilingual Education
- Inter-cultural Health
- Indigenous Rights
- Governance, Indigenous Peoples, Human Rights and International Cooperation
- Development with Identity for Communitarian Well Being–Good Living

- Linguistic and Cultural Revitalization
- Good Governance and Public Administration with Indigenous Perspective
- Indigenous Women's Leadership.

To finance the studies, the Indigenous Fund established a special scholarship programme that had, up to 2012, enabled the successful participation of more than 500 men and women.

Another important cornerstone is the recovery and production of knowledge in order to promote an integrated development and an affirmation of the identity of the region's indigenous peoples and ethnic groups, generating knowledge and information arising from research studies and the systematization of the traditional wisdom of indigenous cultures, and from inter-cultural relations. The research focuses on actions to bring about social transformation, under the Well Being–Good Living paradigm. The IIU also promotes the publication of educational materials and specialized texts.

IIU'S OUTCOMES

The students, who are mostly indigenous people (just under 15% of the participants being non-indigenous), come from 20 different countries, mainly in Latin America and the Caribbean. Many (52%) of the 500 students who graduated between February 2007, when the first postgraduate course on inter-cultural bilingual education started, and 2012 now hold positions of responsibility in the government of their country or in other institutions where they are able to influence the definition, formulation and implementation of public policies concerning the rights of indigenous peoples.

IMPACTS ON IIU'S PARTNERS

It can be said that the main impact of the integral IIU approach is that it helps to broaden traditional academic models of university education by offering a different option based on the experiences, practices, struggles and history of indigenous peoples. Another specific impact of this process lies in encouraging students to engage in reflective analysis, with a view to decolonizing university and academic knowledge by incorporating approaches based on spirituality, citizenship, gender equality and inter-culturality.

The CII leads through personal changes in terms of *individual* identity and the reassertion of *collective* identity. Students confirm that their self-esteem improves through a recognition and appreciation of the cultural, economic, environmental and spiritual elements of their cultures.

The contacts and exchanges among leaders and local actors from different countries are contributing to building knowledge with different ideological, political, social, cultural and spiritual contexts.

LESSONS LEARNT

Higher education for indigenous peoples should be made by indigenous peoples responding to their own spirituality and epistemology. An alternative higher education needs alternative institutional structures. One of the challenges facing higher education programmes for indigenous people is the recording, application, protection and transfer of knowledge that exists and is commonly used in their communities.

For more information, contact formacion@fondoindigena.org, or go to www.fondoindigena.org.

IV.7.7

Networks on community–university engagement in Latin America and the Caribbean

América Solidaria

SECRETARIAT: Chile.
WEBSITE: http://www.americasolidaria.org (accessed 17 May 2013).
MEMBERS: n/a.

América Solidaria's mission is to build networks that cooperate among the American nations to strengthen local projects with volunteer professionals, with the goal of enhancing the quality of life of the poorest and most excluded people in the continent (text taken from http://www.americasolidaria.org/home/quienes-somos-2/#gen [accessed 17 May 2013]).

Asociación de Universidades Confiadas a la Compañía de Jesús dn América Latina (AUSJAL)

SECRETARIAT: Caracas (Venezuela).
WEBSITE: http://www.ausjal.org (accessed May 17, 2013).
MEMBERS: 30 universities and higher education institutions. (HEIs) from 14 countries in Latin America.

Its mission is to strengthen the networking of partners in order to promote the integral development of the students, the training of scholars and collaborators in the Christian and Ignatian identity inspiration, the research that influences public policy on issues related to Jesuit universities, and the collaboration with other networks or areas of the Society of Jesus. The network has an area dedicated to university social responsibility (text taken from http://www.ausjal.org/Misi%C3%B3n_y_Visi%C3%B3n.html [accessed 17 May 2013]).

Centro Latinoamericano de Aprendizaje y Servicio Solidario (CLAYSS)

SECRETARIAT: Buenos Aires (Argentina).
WEBSITE: http://www.clayss.org/ (accessed 4 March 2013).
MEMBERS: A non-governmental organization and an independent research centre, CLAYSS serves as the Secretariat for the Iberican-American Service-learning Network and the Latin American Hub of the Talloires Network (see below).

Founded in 2002, CLAYSS' mission is to contribute to the growth of a fraternal and participative culture in Latin America through the development of educational social engagement projects. Its institutional goals are to promote the development of the pedagogical proposal of service-learning in Latin America; to offer training to faculty and community leaders to develop service-learning projects and to aid in the formation of pro-social attitudes; and to develop solidarity service-learning projects in schools, higher education institutions, universities and youth organizations (text taken from http://www.clayss.org/01_quienes/mision.htm [accessed 4 March 2013]).

Latin American and Caribbean hub of the Talloires Network

SECRETARIAT: CLAYSS, Buenos Aires (Argentina).
WEBSITE: http://www.clayss.org.ar/talloires.htm (accessed 25 May 2013).
MEMBERS: 42 universities.

This is the hub of the Talloires Network for Latin America and the Caribbean (see http://talloiresnetwork.tufts.edu/; accessed 30 May 2013).

Red Iberoamericana de Aprendizaje-Servicio/ Iberian-American Service-Learning Network

SECRETARIAT: Buenos Aires (Argentina).
WEBSITE: http://www.clayss.org/redibero.htm (accessed March 4, 2013).
MEMBERS: Around 90 civil society organizations, HEIs, governmental organizations and cooperation agencies in Latin America and the Caribbean, Spain and USA, as well as national networks that promote service-learning.

Founded in 2005, the Network facilitates the dialogue among service-learning leaders in the region. Among other common endeavours, the Network has contributed to two collective publications: a special number of academic journal *Tzhoecoen* (2010; http://www.clayss.org/04_publicaciones/TZHOECOEN-5.pdf; accessed 30 May 2013), and the procedures of the Second Service-learning Researchers Meeting (2012; http://www.clayss.org/06_investigacion/jornadas/Libro_IIJIA-S_COMPLETO.pdf; accessed 30 May 2013).

Observatory on Social Responsibility in Latin America and the Caribbean (ORSALC-IESALC)

SECRETARIAT: Venezuela.
WEBSITE: http://www.iesalc.unesco.org.ve (accessed 17 May 2013).
MEMBERS: n/a.

The UNESCO International Institute for Higher Education in Latin America and the Caribbean (IESALC) has launched an Observatory on Social Responsibility for Latin America and the Caribbean (ORSALC), which is working with the broad network of Columbus Universities and ODUCAL. The main goal of the Observatory is to actively follow up on the development of situations that compromise an aspect of culture, education or university institutional life in any of the Latin America and the Caribbean countries (text taken from http://www.iesalc.unesco.org.ve/index.php?option=com_content&view=article&id=2860:sobre-el-observatorio697&catid=207&Itemid=965&showall=&limitstart=2&lang=es [accessed 17 May 2013]).

Unión Latinoamericana de Extensión Universitaria (ULEU)

SECRETARIAT: Ecuador.
WEBSITE: http://www.uleu.org (accessed 17 May 2013).
MEMBERS: n/a.

Founded in 1994, ULEU has since 1996 organized annual regional conferences on extension. The presidency and location of these conferences rotate among the members of Latin America and the Caribbean.

Costa Rica: 40 years of uninterrupted community service as an obligatory part of professional training

The Trabajo Comunal Universitario (TCU, or University Community Work) programme in the Universidad de Costa Rica (UCR) demands 300 hours of community work in order for students to graduate. Established in 1974 in the organic statute of the UCR, the requirement was extended to private universities throughout the country by law in 1981.

From the outset, the TCU aimed towards the application of the specific knowledge and competences learned in each course within the framework of interdisciplinary projects. The university offers a variety of interdisciplinary programmes each year allowing students to fulfil their hours of service. In UCR, the TCU is associated with two sections of the curriculum that are common to all courses in the 'National Situation Seminars', which provide lectures and training sessions to accompany community practice.

The TCU runs hundreds of projects throughout all regions of the country, with contributions of knowledge from around 200 teachers and 3,000 students each year. Perhaps the most significant of these are the interdisciplinary primary oral healthcare programmes in the zones of Grecia, Palmares and San Ramón, which have led to an almost total reduction in the number of caries in school children in some of the locations, as well as many environmental and cultural heritage conservation projects in Costa Rica.

For more detail, see http://accionsocial.ucr.ac.cr/web/tcu/.

Research linked to local needs

In 1993, Jaime Ferreira, a biologist, genetics professor and researcher at the Universidade Federal de Santa Catarina (Florianopolis, southern Brazil), established a Laboratory of Marine Molluscs. His research allowed him to suggest mussel-farming initiatives in the region using the seed produced in the laboratory. With the support of the university and the local authorities, he overcame the initial scepticism of the fishermen on the island, and these fishermen began to farm the molluscs, earning a greater income from less effort in farming than they had from the traditional fishing techniques they had been using. At present, the marine molluscs laboratory has a multidisciplinary team of 40 people, including teachers, technicians and students, who have helped 6,000 families to live from mollusc-farming in the state of Santa Catarina, helping to improve the quality of life of the traditional fishermen, whose low levels of productivity had been forcing them to either change profession or emigrate. The experience has also been exported to all the other coastal states of Brazil.

For more information, see http://www.lmm.ufsc.br/index.php?area=54.

Medical students in the public health service

At the medical faculty of the Universidad Nacional de Tucumán (Argentina), future doctors are expected to complete a classic internship in a teaching hospital, but must also spend a semester on a 'placement' involving practice and research in provincial health centres in rural areas and the urban periphery in northeastern Argentina.

During the years of a national crisis, 2001–2003, child deaths from malnutrition reached epidemic proportions in the province. A programme known as 'Búsqueda – Identificación – Nutrición' ('Search – Identification – Nutrition') was run for at-risk children within the framework of the placements. Once it had been shown that the deaths from malnutrition had generally occurred because the babies had already reached an irreversible condition before their first consultation, the students formed teams working from the health centres and going out into the neighbourhoods and rural areas most affected by the socioeconomic crisis. They offered to examine all the children in every house, and when the symptoms of malnutrition were identified in a child, the team adopted them as a patient. The programme helped to channel the food and medicine provided by the government to families and children, accompanying them through recovery to full health. During the years of the crisis, the programme helped to diagnose almost 500 children and remove them from danger (EDUSOL, 2006).

Research undertaken within the framework of the programme helped to identify a poor dissemination of breast-feeding in the peripheral urban areas, so the faculty established breast-feeding promotion programmes in public hospitals in the city of Tucumán over the following years (EDUSOL, 2009). The incidence of prostate cancer in rural areas was also reduced as a result of the placement initiative.

For further information, see http://www.pperiurbana.ecaths.com/.

Socially committed research and service-learning

A good example of coordination between service-learning practices and research programmes can be seen in the experience implemented in the veterinary science faculty of the Universidad Austral, Temuco, Chile. This department studied horse pathologies and initiated community practices with students dealing with the horses of the *carretoneros*, the families who live by collecting recyclable materials from the household waste of others, who often use horse-drawn carts to extend their collection area. These horses live in the same precarious and overcrowded conditions as their owners, and the diseases they presented were uncommon to professionals and students accustomed to studying and treating racehorses, polo horses or farm horses. While improving the quality of life of the *carretoneros*, the project has also over the last ten years served as the subject of many theses, research papers, publications and presentations at congresses on issues not previously studied.

More information can be found at http://www.uctemuco.cl/medicina-veterinaria/consultorio_caballos_carretoneros.php.

REFERENCES

EDUSOL (2006) *Experiencias ganadoras del Premio Presidencial 'Prácticas Solidarias en Educación Superior'*. UPE. Buenos Aires: Ministerio de Educación, Ciencia y Tecnología.

EDUSOL (2009) *Experiencias ganadoras del Premio Presidencial 'Prácticas Educativas Solidarias en Educación Superior'*. Buenos Aires: Ministerio de Educación.

PART V
FUTURE VISIONS AND AGENDA FOR ACTION

AN INVITATION

As we know, knowledge is power and knowledge has power. Knowledge has the power to transform lives, institutions and societies. We can address the power of knowledge to build the world we want. A world where social, economic and ecological justice includes all citizens irrespective of class, ethnicity, race, gender and age. A world in which life is respected no matter what form it takes. A world that shares an understanding of the interdependence of the social, human and environmental dimensions and that the key of our collective success is cooperation.

This report and the associated 6th International Barcelona Conference on Higher Education has been, is and will be an invitation to each of us to imagine three things:

- the kind of world that we want for future generations;
- the role of knowledge in the creation and representation of that world;
- the role of institutions of higher education in the re-enchantment of our world.

This report and the associated conference has been a collective project of hundreds of women and men from more than 50 nations. We are students, administrators, foundation leaders, government officials, researchers, social movement activists, professors, networkers and more. We share a common concern that the civilizational paradigm that brought us through the 19th and 20th centuries is in crisis. It is no longer a tide that floats all boats. To be blunt … the world is not OK.

When we reflect on the state of the world at the present time, we can be critical of the uses to which knowledge has been put and the role that knowledge in the academy has played. Who is knowledge serving? For what purposes is knowledge created today? We are now calling on scholars and policy-makers to put knowledge at the service of positive social transformation.

But we are also aware of hundreds and thousands of people who are, as we read these words, reinventing or recreating the world in smaller and larger ways. We are aware of transformative visions about who creates knowledge and how to use knowledge for change. We see people in the community working in new ways with higher education institutions (HEIs). And we see convincing evidence of positive changes in HEIs and a new openness to address social responsibility. The winds of change are upon us and we invite ourselves, our readers, those in our communities, institutions and networks, to set sail together towards the world we imagine.

HEIs can and must play a significant role as agents of social change. Institutions can help societies in facing local and global challenges, and help to generate new solutions to the most pressing economic, social and ecological problems of our times. The visions and actions of HEIs could reinforce their roles towards the creation and distribution of socially relevant knowledge in education and research and in relationships with communities. They can and must support, and even anticipate, ways of acting to play a proactive and committed roles to transform societies.

Several years ago, a new conversation on the role of engagement emerged worldwide in hundreds of universities, community organizations and social movements. Originating mostly from personal positions, ethics and values, individual scholars started a new way of thinking and acting, according to a new sense of social responsibility. These people met with leaders in civil society and started to turn the conversation into a movement. Now is the moment to build on these conversations and take them into the heart of our HEIs, to institutionalize and normalize these new ways of working. These practices have several common characteristics:

- a new conception of the relationship with communities as equal partners;
- new conceptions of what knowledge is, giving equal value to the different kinds and sources of knowledge;
- new ethics and values for knowledge democracy;
- new perceptions of what societies could be, and new values regarding life;

V.1
TRANSFORMATIVE KNOWLEDGE TO DRIVE SOCIAL CHANGE: VISIONS FOR THE FUTURE

Budd L. Hall, Cristina Escrigas, Rajesh Tandon and Jesús Granados Sánchez

- new perceptions on what education, in particular higher education, should mean.

SOCIAL RESPONSIBILITY OF HIGHER EDUCATION

If higher education has a role to play with its mandate of generating and disseminating knowledge for all of society, it should be to serve the common public good, at a time when what we understand by 'good' and by 'common' is difficult to define (Taylor, 2008a).

As previous GUNI reports stressed, largely and with exceptions, HEIs are not at the centre of either the development agenda or the debates about changes and crisis that are transforming the world. This is partly due to the fact that, in recent decades, HEIs have been forced to focus their efforts on survival. The expected role for HEIs today within the dominant economic model is to contribute to making national economic systems globally competitive. The model of global economic growth has imposed particular priorities and has introduced competitive dynamics into higher education systems.

According to the analysis of the several recent GUNi reports (GUNi, 2006, 2007, 2008, 2009), the last three decades have brought a number of factors that are influencing higher education across the world. Although there are significant differences between systems, especially between those in developing countries and those in developed countries, the following trends have affected all higher education systems in some way:

- a massive expansion in demand;
- a reduction in the role of the state and the emergence of the market;
- the emergence of private education and the diversification of providers;
- a diversification of funding sources;
- internationalization and cross-border education;
- accreditation for quality assurance and rankings.

The interrelation between the global context and the context of higher education leads to tensions about the social function of higher education. These tensions reproduce the general dynamics present in contemporary society:

- the capacity to be proactive and anticipatory institutions versus reactive ones;
- the pressure for profitability versus the social value of knowledge; the knowledge economy versus the knowledge society and the knowledge democracy;
- the debate regarding public goods versus private goods (including the meaning of 'public good');
- social and ecological relevance versus competition and competitiveness.

As Nayaar (2008) states:

markets and globalization are influencing universities and shaping education, in terms of not only what is taught, but also what is researched. Student employability is not simply a force that is pushing to create more places for vocational courses in higher education. It is also inducing universities to introduce new courses for which there is a demand in the market, because these translate into lucrative fees as a major source of income. Similarly, markets are beginning to exercise an influence on the research agenda of universities.

The social responsibility of universities implies their relevance and contributions to the future development of individuals and societies; it implies that teaching and research as the core functions of a university are linked closely with the elaboration and promotion of shared societal visions and common public goods. Its fundamental objective is to promote the social usefulness of knowledge, and its relevance goes beyond responding to the needs of economic development. It requires a two-way perspective between universities and society, which involves directly multiplying the critical uses of knowledge in society (Herrera, 2008).

Relevance, in its local and global dimensions, is the concept to be analysed and debated. If relevant means appropriate to the context, then what is appropriate to the current context? How can higher education serve the needs of different levels of the context in which all the institutions and higher education systems are immersed simultaneously: local, national, regional and global levels? How can we work so that cooperation between institutions leads to higher education systems that are relevant in their places?

The answers to these questions, the resolution of the inherent tensions of the education system and the development of a consensus on emerging proposals should provide a range of useful alternatives for redesigning institutional missions and actions. The vision and mission for higher education roles in society could be reoriented beyond the paradigm of the 'ivory tower' or the 'market-oriented university', to reinvent an innovative and socially committed response that anticipates and adds value to the process of social transformations, strengthening their social responsibility (Escrigas and Lobera, 2009).

We have to put these issues in the centre of the academic agenda and to generate debate regarding new approaches of social responsibility, setting these issues in the international forums on higher education.

Several global and regional frameworks for reflection and action can be found listed in this report.

Furthermore, community–university engagement (CUE) implies a reformulation of the pertinence of HEIs and their activities in the face of these new conceptions of social responsibility. The main contribution of civic engagement in terms of social responsibility is the idea of serving society at large, dealing with real problems of common people and communities, under a vision of ethics and values. It is a higher education contribution to build a just and inclusive world through knowledge democracy. We encourage the academic community to take up these issues and this report as a collective contribution for a better world.

ELEMENTS OF A VISION

Over the past several years, thousands of us have been immersed in conversations scattered around the world about the concepts of CUE, broader notions of knowledge, the nature of transformation and resilience within our communities and our institutions, the kinds of policies needed at the State level and at the level of our institutions, and what role the various networks in this field can play going forwards. Our report strives to represent the energy of these engagements and social responsibility narratives of recent years. We have strived to give at least a glimpse of the small and large ideas that are driving what many of us call a movement. We have strived to be inclusive and to listen to the voices at the margins, as those are the places where the new ideas often come from. We will of course have failed to reach every new source of energy or wisdom. We will fail to be as inclusive as we wish. But recognizing the incompleteness of our knowledge is one of the powerful lessons we are learning.

TRANSFORMATIVE KNOWLEDGE TO DRIVE SOCIAL CHANGE

There is a tacit agreement on what is relevant to do and to know to live, develop and prosper in contemporary societies. Reading reality, it is relevant to ask: what knowledge do we emphasize in our education systems as the most useful and useful for what purpose? Are we preparing people to understand and to live in contemporary society? Are we preparing people who are able to use their professional practice to actively participate in the positive transformation of our societies? What ethics and values do we transmit in the current educational processes? What are we valuing as knowledge, and which kinds of knowledge do we appreciate as

most relevant? Which are the most common criteria that guide the investment in knowledge creation? Who do we recognize as legitimate knowledge producers in our societies?

In our emerging knowledge societies, there is a need for a deeper understanding of knowledge itself. To imagine a different world, we need to consider what knowledge is needed and generated for what kind of society. Knowledge, as we understand it, needs to be understood as a contribution to human heritage.

Transformative and democratic approaches to knowledge democracy refer to acknowledging the existence of multiple epistemologies or ways of knowing, affirming that knowledge is both created and represented in multiple forms including text, image, numbers, story, music, drama, poetry, ceremony, meditation and more, and understanding that knowledge is a strategic element for taking action to deepen democracy and to struggle for a fairer and healthier world. Transformative knowledge links the values of democracy, respect and action to the process of using knowledge.

There is a global dividing line that separates the visible constituents of knowledge and power from those that are invisible. Popular, lay, plebeian, peasant, indigenous, the knowledge of the disabled and more cannot be fitted in any of the ways of knowing on the side of the line where power is present. These other knowledge systems exist on the other side of the line. And because of this invisibility, they are beyond truth or falsehood. As de Sousa Santos (2007) notes, 'Global social injustice is therefore intimately linked to global cognitive injustice. The struggle for global social justice will, therefore, be a struggle for cognitive justice as well.' We see a way forward in the concept of 'ecologies' of knowledge. An ecology of knowledge allows the vast diversity to be acknowledged.

We need to challenge ideas about 'dominant knowledge' residing in the hands of experts and engage with the majority in ways that make connections between knowledge, action and consciousness (Taylor, 2008a). We also have to question the dominance of the rational-scientific paradigm as the only valid knowledge system. We need to understand the relationships between scientific knowledge and other forms of knowledge, and reconsider the value we attribute to different types and sources of knowledge. We need to go deeper in the ways in which ethics and values should be addressed, recognizing their inherent existence and questioning the idea of an absolute truth, dealing openly with complexity and uncertainty.

Other pathways for a future related to knowledge and society have to lie in the analysis of the implications of the advance of knowledge. On a global scale, only a small percentage of all of the resources invested in science and technology is allocated to the analysis of its ethical, environmental and social implications. A first step is recognizing that science, technology and society are topics of research and education that require urgent attention, in order to close the gap between the scientific production of knowledge and reflections on the impacts of this production.

As Jassanof (2008) points out, technologies clearly incorporate design choices that reflect prior cultural assumptions about what is desirable or possible to achieve in society. To meet the challenges head on, universities will need to develop a fuller, more historically informed sense of their own institutional missions, not only as incubators of the production of new scientific knowledge and technological know-how, but also as sites of capacity-building for social analysis, critical reflection and democratic citizenship.

In synthesis, we have to build transformative knowledge to drive social change. According to Granados and Escrigas in this publication, transformative knowledge implies six deep changes in the way we perceive value and create knowledge. These changes imply to move from a mono-culture of scientific knowledge to an ecology of knowledge; from rational knowledge to integral human knowledge; from descriptive knowledge to knowledge for intervention; from partial knowledge to a holistic and complex knowledge; from an isolated creation of knowledge to a social co-creation of knowledge; from a static use of knowledge to a dynamic and creative knowledge.

This report has introduced quite a number of papers that bring fresh and innovative ideas about knowledge creation and recognition. A task for the immediate future is dealing openly with these issues.

WHEN CUE INFORMS THE EDUCATION PROCESS

Higher education should prepare students to gain a critical consciousness of the world they inhabit and help them to better anticipate, articulate and animate alternative processes to build better societies.

According to Bawden (2008), higher education should prepare humanity to deal with contemporary issues that, in their complexity, represent clear threats to sustainable ways of being. Such issues require us to embrace moral, aesthetic and even spiritual dimensions in equal part to their intellectual aspects. HEIs should appreciate the vital importance of a focus on contextual human and social development, and accept it as their primary educative purpose.

Universities educate citizens, who will build the social, economic, human systems that future generations will inherit. The current education model is based on training competitive human resources. It is appropriate to encourage an evolution towards a system that educates global citizens, builders of inclusive, just and fair social systems, with ethical criteria, which can understand reality from a holistic perspective and prepare us to act with patterns of trust and collaboration. This more global, holistic perspective of the educative purpose is the central contextual challenge of today.

It could be discussed that the central educative purpose of HEIs ought to be the explicit facilitation of reflexive, critical, transformative learning that leads to responsible paradigms for living, and for 'being' and for 'becoming', both as individuals alone and collectively as communities (Taylor, 2008a).

In short, higher education systems worldwide have to go beyond educating professionals to educating citizens with an ethical awareness and civic commitment. This deep change in the purpose of education implies a change in curriculum contents, in the educative offer and in the conception of what a degree is and what it is preparing students for, that should no longer be disciplinary. It implies new ways of educating that demand deeper changes in pedagogies. New approaches for learning based on dialogical, co-learning, participatory and problem-oriented methods are also required. Disciplinary studies should make connections with real world and real-time issues in the future. New, critical and reflexive learning systems need also to be incorporated (Taylor, 2008b).

Institutions could not do this without reducing the supremacy of technological knowledge, putting it at the same level as social, ecological and humanitarian knowledge and facilitating a productive dialogue in the way that these areas of knowledge have to work together in the solution of real human and social problems. All these changes require inner movements of comprehension that will create new forms of external action.

Higher education can be focused on training professionals as value-neutral technicians, or on educating citizens capable of using their professional skills for the benefit of all of society and not just the few. That transformation requires a deep sense of citizenship as an active way to contribute to a wide range of collective goals. Being prepared as a citizen who will interact with society through the exercise of a profession means educate for *glocality*, democracy, intercultural relations, peace-building and a deep understanding of life's dynamics. These changes are reflected in the Communiqué of the 2009 UNESCO World Conference of Higher Education:

Higher education institutions should increase their interdisciplinary focus and promote critical thinking and active citizenship. This would contribute to sustainable development, peace, wellbeing and the realization of human right … [Higher education] must not only give solid skills for the present and future world but must also contribute to the education of ethical citizens committed to the construction of peace, the defence of human rights and the values of democracy. (UNESCO, 2009)

Proposing individual and collective responsibility in professional decision-making within new global ethical paradigms will be a subject for the near future.

The ethical dimension must be introduced in all the disciplines as something inherent to the use of knowledge. This requires a non-separation between the use of knowledge and the impacts of that knowledge. Our higher education systems are mostly focused on the academic contents of a disciplinary approach: little relevance has been given to the impact of the fragmented comprehension of reality that is inherent in our education system. Today, we know that reality is complex, that any phenomenon, problem or situation we live or create is multidimensional. We are educating people outside this understanding, teaching a partial understanding with a partial toolbox for professional activities, far from real problems and predominantly looking at the profit capacity of our studies. This is an inappropriate way to prepare people to live in our world, which we have to describe as being in a state of crisis.

Globalization threatens to impose a damaging cultural uniformity. The cultivation and dissemination of our own identities and values must be closely linked to the local, regional and national community, in order to prepare citizens who can commit themselves to the world's problems and appreciate and value cultural diversity as a source of enrichment and world heritage.

As Delanty (2008) notes, globalization is a term used to describe an interconnected world, not a single world. According to Delors (1996), people gradually need to become world citizens without losing their roots, and still need to continue to play an active part in the life of their nation and their local community. A key dynamic is the integration of citizenship at several levels simultaneously – from local to global. Globalization challenges the current world structures and brings a post-cosmopolitan citizenship (Dobson and Bell, 2006) equipped with a social consciousness (Goldberg, 2009), which will act and participate with their agency, and together with other people, social stakeholders and organizations, in the construction of a new world order by developing partnerships for solving problems and creating things for the appropriate scales and communities.

Universities are located in a space that is local, national and global. This multi-level feature places universities in an appropriate position to help in bridging the gap of connecting different administrations and issues that are of different scales. Therefore, they can be seen as having a particularly significant role to play as the facilitators of post-cosmopolitan identities.

More emphasis should be placed in the education process on emotional intelligence, the knowledge and opportunity to adapt to and function in unfamiliar contexts, and collaborative skills for work in groups, often with members from highly diverse backgrounds and perhaps even from across former conflict lines. All this facilitates an inter-cultural dialogue and understanding among different backgrounds and cosmovisions.

CUE, through its rich and continually evolving practices, is the way to connect the three institutional missions: teaching, research and service. Some ways and practices of CUE such as service-learning, community-based research, engaged scholarship or academic enterprise, to mention just a few, are currently linking engagement within the teaching and research dimensions. The challenge of CUE is the development of initiatives that enable the integration of the three dimensions enhancing teaching, research and outreach or service. CUE and its different expressions are one of the clear ways in which HEIs have to unsettle the inertia of the education system. Service learning and community-based research most often deal directly with the day-to-day challenges facing our communities.

PARTNERSHIPS: ESTABLISHING COMMUNITY– UNIVERSITY DIALOGUE

Constructive criticism and the creation of new ideas and practices are needed to better contribute to a transition to a better future for the human community. Much has been done to recognize what does not work any more, but the huge task is to propose ways to transcend what has been shown to be obsolete. There is a need to create a true democratic knowledge society through engagement with a broad set of social actors to deal with the problematic issues of the day.

Citizen groups, associations, non-governmental organizations (NGOs), not-for-profit research institutes and independent think-tanks, as civil society actors, have taken a leading role in identifying, analysing and articulating national and transnational debates on positive social transformation in the last few decades.

HEIs should establish stronger relationships with civic associations and with social movements in order to democratize access to knowledge and to co-create knowledge. Participatory action research and science shop experiences worldwide are but two of many promising ways to move forwards.

Civil society should take a lead in calling on universities to become partners with which to imagine and develop cooperation and new knowledge and action alliances. New approaches to knowledge mobilization and transfer are needed between institutions and their communities, related to real problems. Greater coordination is needed between governments, civil society, educative institutions and the private sector in order to achieve this social transformation.

In the context of the knowledge society, HEIs also have an important role to play in linking technology to citizenship and in bringing about a democratization of science and technology. This significance lies in their ability to produce democratic discourse and enhance citizen participation in the field of knowledge production.

One of the challenges of the university today is to become a cosmopolitan actor in the global knowledge society by forging new links between knowledge and citizenship (Delanty, 2008). In the context of a democratic knowledge society, the question of technological citizenship is particularly important if the university is to define a new identity for itself. Technology, especially technoscience, is shaping the world according to the dictates of global market forces and is one of the major societal discourses today in which rights and democracy are framed. Universities have an important role to play in linking technology to citizenship and in bringing about a democratization of science and technology.

There are a range of actions that would contribute to a more democratic and engaged knowledge system:

- quickly making new knowledge available on an open-access basis for society while improving its application;
- understanding transformative knowledge as being a co-construction as well as being a two-way flow between the university and the community;
- emphasizing interdisciplinary and integrated approaches to knowledge creation within a problem or issue-based approach;
- making explicit the links between technological knowledge and the ability to act on that knowledge;
- sustaining discussions among diverse knowledge systems in relation to the grand challenges of our communities;

- generating knowledge strategies for informing political decision-making that affect local or global populations;
- creating cosmopolitan centres of global public culture, building bridges and connecting different cultures and sources of knowledge, and participating in the debate on its social relevance.

The existence and quality of relationships between partners outside higher education and those within it lie at the very heart of our collective capacity to transform our institutions of higher education into truly 'engaged' universities. Without transforming the ways in which community–university partnerships have historically evolved, we will not achieve the changes that we aspire to. In looking to the future, we are calling for a world where a new set of partnership principles are the rule rather than the exception. Community organizations are calling for new forms of partnership. They are calling for a move away from partnerships based on notions of 'noblesse oblige' on the part of the HEIs to ones based on principles of reciprocity, mutuality, respect, an acknowledgement of the differences of knowledge cultures in communities and universities and long-term, not project-funded partnerships. A good partnership is one where the diverse knowledge forms and systems of the community and the academic partners are recognized and where we listen to each other, laugh together and support each other in difficult times.

In our future vision, we see that many things will have changed. The strategic plans and mission statements of universities will be aligned with the engagement agenda. Community stakeholders will be involved in strategic planning. We will have effective tools to evaluate the collective impact of our work together. The infrastructure and support to strengthen engaged learning and teaching will be in place, and core and donor funding will be there to support the partnerships.

But the challenges for knowledge partnerships between academics and those working in community sectors are substantial. To begin with, the 'knowledge culture' within higher education and community organizations is dramatically different. Knowledge is a product to be generated within the academy almost without regard for its eventual impact or role in the community. But knowledge is also a commodity that, among other things, plays a critical role in the career structure of most academics. Promotion and advancement along a career path as an academic is closely tied to the provision of evidence of a certain kind of knowledge production. In the commodification of knowledge within the academy, less attention is paid to the application or impact of new knowledge that is created than to its representation in the form of articles for peer-reviewed elite journals or books or success in getting research grants from research-granting agencies.

Knowledge in a community agency is a practical tool. It is seen as a way of making decisions about which kinds of action are more likely to be successful. It is seen as a way of assessing progress over time in the sectors in which the organization is engaged. It may also be seen as a way of validating the work of the agency so that its application for further funding might find favour. The knowledge that is needed has to be quickly available and clear on the directions that should be taken in developing programming. A community–university research partnership from the community point of view may be seen as a way of accessing resources such as space, networks, student researchers, access to databases, and so forth.

But more problematic is the unequal nature of the knowledge-generating capacities of civil society organizations and academic institutions. Academic institutions have knowledge generation as one of their central goals. A part of the time of most academics is devoted to research. They are paid to do research whether they do it in cooperation with community groups or whether they sit in their homes or offices or libraries and write entirely by themselves. Knowledge-workers are few and far between in civil society organizations. Only the largest NGOs will have specialized staff available to work permanently on research projects, and these people will most likely be working on either evaluation tasks or funding proposals. So when an HEI invites a community group to become a partner in a project, it becomes a very difficult decision to join unless there is additional funding provided to the community group. Even the time to meet with academics can be problematic in an era where community groups are more and more taking up the slack that the state has abandoned in terms of social welfare.

BROADENING THE CONCEPT OF COMMUNITY: HIGHER EDUCATION'S ROLE IN ADDRESSING MAJOR GLOBAL ISSUES

When we think of community, we most often think of the physical space near our institutions of higher education, but community can also apply more broadly to a sense of communal responsibility on a national or even international scale.

Over the past 30 years, we have seen many initiatives to bring attention to mobilizing resources in the face of the global challenges that have been facing us as people around the world. Whether within the framework of the UN system of agencies or otherwise, the leadership in these campaigns and global initiatives has come from the civil society side, from the NGOs and social movements. They have been openly leading as engines of social criticism and transformation. HEIs, however, have much to offer to these internationally agreed global challenges, which include the Millennium Development Goals and Education for All. A global agenda for CUE should reflect these realities (UNESCO, 2009).

Higher education has the opportunity, in collaboration with civil society and other knowledge-workers, to lead society in generating global knowledge to address global challenges such as food security, climate change, water management, intercultural dialogue, renewable energy and public health (UNESCO, 2009). Linking research agendas to collective challenges and the global development agenda, making evident connections between academic activity and societal needs, is also a challenge for the near future.

This approach implies redefining multiple and simultaneous spaces that could all be called 'community' at diverse levels. We must assume that these diverse levels of communities are interdependent and that no real solutions will be sustainably reached if we do not work on all them simultaneously. The main tools to deal with the global community are the same as the local ones, some of them being described in this report. Structures of interconnection have emerged that allow for the simultaneous overlay of local and global communities to take place, what Castells (2012) calls of 'Networks of outrage and hope'. South–south and north–south networks are examples of these new structures of communication and action. These broader structures of partnership, with the intention of solving global community challenges, have a need for a knowledge strategy, both a way of generating new forms of transformative knowledge and a strategic vision of how to use knowledge to organize for real change. Here again, a range of diverse social actors should be involved as real partners, in equal conditions, to create and spread relevant knowledge.

NEW POLICIES: HIGHER EDUCATION AND THE STATE
PROFESSIONAL CAREERS IN HEIs

There is considerable turmoil in relation to knowledge, engagement and career advancement within our institutions of higher education. Within the world of what are referred to as 'research-intensive' universities, debates about the role of the various global ranking systems are ever present. Global ranking systems currently recognize specific forms of knowledge representation – traditional peer-reviewed articles published in scholarly journals – as evidence of achievement. At the same time, there is a powerful current of interest in the 'open-access' publishing of research findings. Open access refers to digital publishing in ways that allow the findings to be viewed free of charge anywhere internet access is available. The Wellcome Trust in the UK made headlines when they announced that all research funded by them must be published in open-access formats. The International Development Research Centre in Canada stipulates the same. In the Mpumalanga Traditional Knowledge Commons in South Africa, knowledge is described as 'An outcome of virtuous relationships with the land, the plants and the animals. It is not property to bought and sold. It is simultaneously cultural and spiritual and its movement and application promotes a kind of virtuous cohesiveness' (Abrell, 2009).

Engaged scholarship and community-based research further complicate the knowledge–engagement–career picture. In some institutions, young scholars are discouraged from following an engaged scholarship career pathway; they are told that only publishing in traditional academic reviews will allow them to advance. We are, however, optimistic about the future. The evidence from the participants of the Barcelona conference and from the other elements found in this report is that the policy climate within the academic world about how to recognize excellence in community-based research and engaged scholarship is advancing.

The Community-Campus Partnerships for Health network operating in both the USA and Canada has produced a kit that provides support to academics wishing to provide evidence of the quality of their community-based research when going forward for merit reviews or promotion. The Research Assessment Exercise in the UK now requires scholars to document the 'impact' of their research so much innovation on how to do that is emerging. New journals, many of them open access, are emerging within the field of CUE scholarship, and we see this expanding dramatically as the years go by. The National Coordinating Committee for Public Engagement in the UK is a good example of a national structure that raises these matters effectively at a national level. We are confident that these new ways of working will in time drive a change in how we measure the impact of scholarship. The policies to support these changes are already emerging and will continue to do so.

GOVERNMENTAL POLICIES

In 1998, the Government of Canada's Social Sciences and Humanities Research Council (SSHRC) initiated a category of research funding called the Community–University Research Alliance (CURA). In order to be eligible to apply for these research funds, academics had to be in a research alliance with one or more community organizations. Over a period of 10 years, the SSHRC invested over $120 million in CURA projects covering a wide range of community challenges, launching an era of unprecedented attention to and interest in community-based and engaged scholarship. There was so much interest in these collaborative co-construction research projects that within a few years CURA grants became the most competitive of all the SSHRC categories of funding. In the end, the principles of partnership were applied to the majority of all research funding on offer. This policy decision can be said to mark the beginning of the modern era of engaged scholarship in Canada.

Each five years, the Government of India engages itself in a massive and complex central planning exercise to produce its next Five Year Plan. In 2011, preparatory work was underway to introduce some new ideas to the higher education plan of 2012–2017. The India Planning Commission created a sub-committee to give some consideration to how the Five Year Plan might support CUE. In spite of the fact that universities in the days of Gandhi were intimately engaged in the independence movement and that student service schemes were created post-independence, higher education in the 1980s, 1990s and 2000s had lost the map to the communities where they were physically located. No pathways to the urban slums or to the villages could be found. With involvement from the civil society organization the Society for Participatory Research in Asia and several other university vice-chancellors, the working group on higher education and engagement came up with a strong set of recommendations to the entire public university sector. And, much to the surprise of some seasoned observers, the Government of India endorsed the suggestions, which these are now part of the official plan. These are high-level recommendations that will, over the span of the plan, create the kind of policy environment that will allow CUE structures and practices to grow and develop in one of the most populous nations on Earth.

BUILDING THE MOVEMENT: ROLE OF NETWORKS

The transformation of a competitive model into a cooperative model is one of the strategic opportunities that universities have in the recreating of their social role in a globalized world.

In order to face global issues as well as local knowledge needs, HEIs are developing flexible nodes and spaces of cooperation, exchange and co-creation of knowledge. These links may be permanent clusters, ad hoc clusters or complementary networks in which interdisciplinary partnerships can be formed for specific projects. The aim is to reclaim a role in defining and collectively solving social, environmental and economic problems. Whether such problems are local or national, they can no longer be tackled without a critical consideration in the wider global context.

Numerous national, regional, sectoral and global networks have emerged over past years with an overall objective of building the movement of CUE for purposes of being better able to contribute to meeting the critical issues of our times. These networks have several goals: building the institutional capacity for CUE, building capacity among community groups, development knowledge systems, policy development and advocacy and providing opportunities for collaboration. The constellation of CUE networks provides a kind of circulation system for ideas, good practices, policy language and simply inspiration. The coverage of networks is, however, uneven in terms of both global distribution and sectoral focus. North America has the largest number of national networks and is the home of several of the global networks. Africa as a region is the least well served from a network perspective.

Challenges for our networks include how to continue to build the CUE movement across the different terminologies and narratives. Is there an overarching narrative for the way in which knowledge, higher education and society might be seen to interact, or is that even desirable? Will Africa see a more developed communications capacity? Will we be able to unlock the rich wellspring of information circulating in Spanish and Portuguese in Latin America? We expect in the future to see further collaboration and common action among the various networks. There are over 5,000 universities represented, for example, through the existing networks in over 100 nations. How can these networks create a common project where the combined resources and imagination of all the parties might be brought to bear?

If the spirit and the content of this world report are to have influence beyond the narrow professional interests of the higher education world, the various global networks that have contributed to the report itself are best placed to take these lessons forwards. We call on all our HEIs to organize debates and discussions around the spirit and content of this report. We call for regional and national conversations to take place. There could be space in each of the thousands of specialist gatherings of higher educators to take up the issues outlined in this report. How can our many networks collaborate, taking up some common action within the framework of the movement? National research councils, ministries of higher education or post-secondary education, municipal and state or provincial governments all have an opportunity to advance the agenda.

A CALL TO ACTION

We are excited about the prospects of deepening the contributions of transformative knowledge to drive social change in the world today. We are fully aware of the growing potential of higher education to make sustained and meaningful contributions towards identifying, elaborating, designing and catalysing various elements of a desirable social change agenda for the future of all humanity. We are confident that HEIs have the capacity, resources and mandates to demonstrate their social responsibility through meaningful community engagement. This report, its messages and exemplars provide the visions to those pathways towards such a meaningful set of contributions to social change.

We invite each of you to explore what you can do in your own part of the world, your own community, your own organization, your own network, your own government position, your own civil society organization, your own social movement, your own classroom, your own research centre or even your own foundation or business to do what you can to advance the movement of transformative knowledge to drive social change.

REFERENCES

Abrell, E. (2009) *Imagining a Traditional Knowledge Commons. A Community Approach to Sharing Traditional Knowledge for Non-commercial Research*. Rome: International Development Law Organization.

Bawden, R. (2008) 'The educative purpose of higher education for human and social development in the context of globalization'. In: GUNi, *Higher Education in the World 3*. Basingstoke: Palgrave Macmillan, pp. 65–73.

Castells, M. (2012) *Networks of Outrage and Hope: Social Movements in the Internet Age*. London: Polity Press.

Delanty, G. (2008) 'The university and cosmopolitan citizenship'. In: GUNi, *Higher Education in the World 3*. Basingstoke: Palgrave Macmillan, pp. 28–31.

Delors, J. (1996) *Learning: The Treasure Within. Report to UNESCO of the International Commission on Education for the Twenty-first Century*. Paris: UNESCO.

de Sousa Santos, B. (2007) 'Beyond abyssal thinking: from global lines to ecologies of knowledge'. *Review*, XXX(1), 45–89.

Dobson, A. and Bell, D. (eds) (2006) *Environmental Citizenship*. London: MIT Press/University of Edinburgh.

Escrigas, C. and Lobera, J. (2009) 'New dynamics for social responsibility'. In: GUNi, *Higher Education at a Time of Transformation*. Basingstoke: Palgrave Macmillan, pp. 3–13.

Goldberg, M. (2009) 'Social conscience. The ability to reflect on deeply-held opinions about social justice and sustainability'. In: Stibbe, A. (ed.) *The Handbook of Sustainability Literacy. Skills for a Changing World*. Devon: Green Books, pp. 105–10.

GUNi (2006) *Higher Education in the World 2006: The Financing of Universities*. Basingstoke: Palgrave Macmillan.

GUNi (2007) *Higher Education in the World 2007: Accreditation for Quality Assurance: What is at Stake?* Basingstoke: Palgrave Macmillan.

GUNi (2008) *Higher Education in the World 3. Higher Education: New Challenges and Emerging Roles for Human and Social Development*. Basingstoke: Palgrave Macmillan.

GUNi (2009) *Higher Education at a Time of Transformation. New Dynamics for Social Responsibility*. Basingstoke: Palgrave Macmillan.

Herrera, A. (2008) 'Social responsibility of universities'. In: GUNi, *Higher Education in the World 3*. Basingstoke: Palgrave Macmillan, pp. 176–7.

Jasanoff, S. (2008) 'Ethical, environmental and social implications of science and technology: challenges for the future'. In: GUNi, *Higher Education in the World 3*. Basingstoke: Palgrave Macmillan, pp. 137–41.

Nayaar, D. (2008) 'Globalization and markets: Challenges for higher education'. In: GUNi, *Higher Education in the World 3*. Basingstoke: Palgrave Macmillan, pp. 40–50.

Taylor, P. (2008a) 'Introduction'. In: GUNi, *Higher Education in the World 3*. Basingstoke: Palgrave Macmillan, pp. xxiv–xxvii.

Taylor, P. (2008b) 'Higher education curricula for human and social development'. In: GUNi, *Higher Education in the World 3*. Basingstoke: Palgrave Macmillan, pp. 89–101.

UNESCO (2009) *2009 World Conference on Higher Education: The New Dynamics of Higher Education and Research for Societal Change and Development*. Paris: UNESCO. Retrieved September 2013 from http://www.unesco.org/fileadmin/MULTIMEDIA/HQ/ED/ED/pdf/WCHE_2009/FINAL%20COMMUNIQUE%20WCHE%202009.pdf.

PART VI
FURTHER READING

INTRODUCTION

This recommended selection of bibliography illustrates one of the most significant trends in higher education over the past 10–15 years: the growth of the theory and practice of community–university engagement (CUE) as a key feature in the evolution of higher education.

CUE is a multifaceted, multidimensional umbrella term that may be applied to a vast range of activities, as well as to a certain view of the role that the university has to play in society that underlies them. Some scholars speak of a CUE movement (Talloires), of engaged scholarship (Boyer, 1996; Fitzgerald et al., 2012), of the 'engaged university' (Watson et al., 2011), of 'public engagement in higher education' (NCCPE, 2010), of service-learning (Campus Compact, McIlraath and Mac Labhrainn, 2007) of community-based research (Strand et al., 2003), of community–university research partnerships (Hall et al., 2013), and more.

The practices, mechanisms and structures of CUE are rich and continually evolving. The bibliography illustrates this with general literature that provides global ideas, followed by a section with concrete and specific literature from the different world regions, which illustrates peculiarities, differences and similarities.

The bibliography also shows the concept of CUE from a vision that goes beyond what is often called the 'third mission' of universities, to a contribution that improves higher education institutions. The challenge for CUE is to integrate all the missions of higher education institutions, exploring ways in which engagement enhances teaching and research and ways that accept the multiple sites and epistemologies of knowledge, as well as the reciprocity and mutuality in learning and education.

GENERAL

Academic Ranking of World Universities (2013) '2012 World University Rankings'. Shanghai: Shanghai Jiao Tong University, Graduate School of Education. Retrieved October 2013 from http://www.shanghairanking.com/index.html

Adıgüzel, O.C., Akman Erkılıç T., Boyacı, A. et al. (2013) *Community Service Training (Topluma Hizmet Eğitimi)* (ed. Ayhan Hakan). Anadolu University Publications No. 2970. Eskişehir, Turkey: Anadolu University.

Ander-Egg, E. (2003) *Repensando la Investigación-Acción Participativa*. Buenos Aires: Grupo editorial Lumen Humanitas.

Angeles, L.C. (2007) 'The scholarship of international service learning: implications for teaching and learning participatory development in higher education'. In: *Reinventing Higher Education: Toward Participatory and Sustainable Development*. Bangkok: UNESCO, pp. 78–87.

Ansley, F. and Gaventa, J. (1997) 'Researching for democracy and democratizing research'. *Change: The Magazine of Higher Learning*, 29(1), 46–53.

Arbo, P. and Benneworth, P. (2006) *Understanding the Regional Contribution of Higher Education Institutions*. Paris: OECD/IMHE.

Armbruster-Domeyer, H. in co-operation with Hermansson, K. and Modéer, C. (2011) *International Review, Analysis and Proposals on Indicators for Measuring Public Engagement*. VA Report 2011:2. Stockholm: Sweden Vetenskap & Allmänhet (Public & Science).

Banks, S. et al. (2011) *Community-based Participatory Research: Ethical Challenges*. AHRC Connected Communities Scoping Study. Durham: Durham University, Centre for Social Justice and Community Action.

Barker, D. (2004) 'The scholarship of engagement: a taxonomy of five emerging practices'. *Journal of Higher Education Outreach and Engagement*, 9(2), 123–37.

Bartha, M. (2010) 'Serious work: public engagement and the humanities'. *Western Humanities Review*, 64(3), 85–104.

Bauer, M.W. and Jensen, P. (2011) 'The mobilization of scientists for public engagement'. *Public Understanding of Science*, 20(1), 3–11.

Baum, H. (2006) 'Challenges in Institutionalizing University-Community Partnerships'. Conference on Leadership and Sustainability for Community/University Partnerships, US Department of Housing and Urban Development Office of University Partnerships, Baltimore, Maryland, March 31, 2006, p. 4.

Beere, C.A., Votruba, J.C., Wells, G.W. and Shulman, L.S. (2011) *Becoming an Engaged*

Campus: A Practical Guide for Institutionalizing Public Engagement. San Francisco: Jossey-Bass.

Benneworth, P. (2009) The Challenges for 21st Century Science: A Review of the Evidence Base Surrounding the Value of Public Engagement by Scientists. Enschede, the Netherlands: Universiteit Twente, Center for Higher Education Policy Studies.

Benneworth, P. (2013) 'The evaluation of universities and their contributions to social exclusion'. In: Benneworth, P. (ed.) University Engagement with Socially Excluded Communities. Dordrecht: Springer, pp. 309–27.

Benneworth, P. and Humphrey, L. (2013) 'Universities' perspectives on community engagement'. In: Benneworth, P. (ed.) University Engagement with Socially Excluded Communities. Dordrecht: Springer, pp. 165–88.

Benneworth, P.S., Charles, D.R., Conway, C., Hodgson, C. and Humphrey, L. (2009) 'How the societal impact of universities can be improved both conceptually and practically'. Sharing Research Agendas on Knowledge Systems: Final Research Proceedings, UNESCO: Paris, France.

Benneworth, P., Charles, D.R., Hodgson, C. and Humphrey, L. (2013) 'The relationship of community engagement with universities' core missions'. In: Benneworth, P. (ed.) University Engagement with Socially Excluded Communities. Dordrecht: Springer, pp. 85–102.

Benneworth, P.S., Conway, C., Charles, D., Humphrey, L. and Younger, P. (2009) Characterising Modes of University Engagement with Wider Society: A Literature Review and Survey of Best Practice. Newcastle: Newcastle University Office of the Pro-Vice Chancellor.

Benyon, J. (2009) 'Developing greater dialogue: knowledge transfer, public engagement and learned societies in the social sciences'. Twenty-First Century Society, 4(1), 97–113.

Bickerstaff, K., Lorenzoni, I., Jones, M. and Pidgeon, N. (2010) 'Locating scientific citizenship: the institutional contexts and cultures of public engagement'. Science, Technology & Human Values, 35(4), 474–500.

Biegelbauer, P. and Hansen, J. (2011) 'Democratic theory and citizen participation: democracy models in the evaluation of public participation in science and technology'. Science and Public Policy, 38(8), 9.

Billig, S. and Eyler, J. (eds) (2003) Deconstructing Service-Learning: Research Exploring Context, Participation, and Impacts. Advances in Service-Learning Research. Greenwich, CT: Information Age Publishing.

Bivens, F.M. (2011) Higher Education as Social Change: Seeking a Systemic Institutional Pedagogy of Social Change. PhD thesis, Institute of Development Studies, University of Sussex, Brighton. Available online from http://sro.sussex.ac.uk/6942/.

Bjarnason, S. and Coldstream, P. (eds) (2003) The Idea of Engagement: Universities in Societies. London: Association of Commonwealth Universities.

Bonnen, J.T. (1998) 'The land-grant idea and the evolving outreach university'. In: Lerner, R.M. and Simon, L.A.K. (eds) University-Community Collaborations for the 21st Century. New York: Garland, pp. 25–70.

Boothroyd, P. and Fryer, M. (2004) 'Mainstreaming social engagement in higher education: benefits, challenges, and successes'. In: Colloquium on Research and Higher Education Policy: 'Knowledge, Access and Governance: Strategies for Change', 15, 17.

Boyer, E.L. (1990) Scholarship Reconsidered: Priorities of the Professoriate. Princeton, NJ: Carnegie Foundation for the Advancement of Teaching.

Boyer, E.L. (1996) 'The scholarship of engagement'. Bulletin of the American Arts and Sciences, 49(7), 18–33.

Boyte, H.B. (2004) Going Public: Academics and Public Life. Dayton, OH: Kettering Foundation.

Brennan, J. and Teichler, U. (2008) 'The future of higher education and of higher education research'. Higher Education, 56(3), 259–64.

Brennan, J., Arthur, L., Little, B. et al. (2010) Higher Education and Society: A Research Report. London: CHERI.

Bringle, R.G. and Hatcher, J.A. (2002) 'Campus-community partnerships: the terms of engagement'. Journal of Social Issues, 58(3), 503–16.

Bringle, R.G. and Hatcher, J.A. (2011) 'Student engagement trends over time'. In: Fitzgerald, H.E., Burack, C. and Seifer, S.D. (eds) Handbook of Engaged Scholarship: Contemporary Landscapes, Future Directions, Volume 2: Community-Campus Partnerships. East Lansing, MI: Michigan State University Press, pp. 411–30.

Brown, L.D. and Gaventa, J. (2008) 'Constructing transnational action research networks: observations and reflections from the case of the Citizenship DRC'. IDS Working Paper. Brighton: University of Sussex, Institute of Development Studies. See also (2009), Journal of Action Research, 8(1), 5–28.

Brukardt, M.J., Holland, B., Percy, S.L. and Zimpher, N., on behalf of the Wingspread Conference participants (2004) Calling the Question: Is Higher Education Ready to Commit to Community Engagement? Milwaukee: University of Wisconsin-Milwaukee, Milwaukee Idea Office. Retrieved October 2013 from http://www.uwm.edu/MilwaukeeIdea/elements/wingspread.pdf.

Burns, D. and Squires, H. with Programme Participants (2011) Embedding Public Engagement in Higher Education: Final Report of the National Research Programme. Bristol: NCCPE. Retrieved October 2013 from http://www.publicengagement.ac.uk/how-we-help/our-publications/embedding-pe.

Butin, D. (2007) 'Focusing our aim: strengthening faculty commitment to community engagement'. Change, 39, 34–9.

Butin, D.W. (2010) Service-Learning in Theory and Practice: The Future of Community Engagement in Higher Education. New York: Palgrave Macmillan.

Calhoun, C. (2006) 'The university and the public good'. Thesis Eleven, 84(1), 7–43.

Calumpang, P.M. (2013) Strengthening Partnerships by Theme-based Service-learning. Progress report of Pilgrim Christian College to the United Board thru Silliman University, June 26.

Campus Compact (2011) Deepening the Roots of Civic Engagement. Annual Membership Survey. Boston, MA: Campus Compact.

Carnegie Foundation for the Advancement of Teaching (2012) 2015 Documentation Reporting Form: First Time Classification Documentation Framework. Stanford, CT: Carnegie Foundation for the Advancement of Teaching.

Carnegie Foundation for the Advancement of Teaching (2013) Community Engagement Classification. Retrieved October 2013 from http://classifications.carnegiefoundation.org/descriptions/community_engagement.php?key=1213.

Centre for Urban and Regional Development Studies (2012).

Culture, Creativity and Education in Schools and Civic Universities and the Contribution to Social Innovation: An Exploratory Study (Proposal). Newcastle-upon-Tyne: Newcastle University, Centre for Urban and Regional Development Studies.

Charles, D. and Benneworth, P. (2002) *Evaluating the Regional Contribution of an HEI: A Benchmarking Approach*. Bristol: Higher Education Funding Council for England.

Charles, D.R., Benneworth, P., Conway, C. and Humphrey, L. (2010) 'How to benchmark university-community interactions'. In: Inman, P. and Schütze, H.G. (eds) *The Community Engagement and Service Mission of Universities*. Leicester: National Institute of Adult Continuing Education.

Chilvers, J. (2013) 'Reflexive engagement? Actors, learning and reflexivity in public dialogue on science and technology'. *Science Communication*, 35(3), 283–310.

Clark, J. and Laing, K. (2011) *The Involvement of Children and Young People in Research within the Criminal Justice Area*. AHRC Connected Communities Review. Newcastle-upon-Tyne: Newcastle University, Research Centre for Learning and Teaching.

Clinical and Translational Science Awards (CTSA) (2011) *Principles of Community Engagement* (2nd ed.). Durham, NC: NIH Publications, Duke University. Retrieved from http://www.atsdr.cdc.gov/communityengagement/pdf/PCE_Report_508_FINAL.pdf.

Commission on Community-Engaged Scholarship in the Health Professions (2005) *Linking Scholarship and Communities: Report of the Commission on Community-Engaged Scholarship in the Health Professions*. Seattle, WA: Community-Campus Partnerships for Health.

Conway, C., Benneworth, P., Humphrey, L. and Charles, D. (2009) *Review of University Engagement*. Paper prepared for Newcastle University PVC (Engagement). Newcastle-upon-Tyne: Newcastle University.

Cortegodo, A., Sarachu, G. and Pereyra, K. (2012) *Prácticas Académicas Integrales en el Cono Sur. Colección temática PROCOAS: Universidad y Trabajo asociado*. Montevideo: Comisión Sectorial de Extensión y Actividades en el Medio.

Cunningham, K. and Leighninger, M. (2010) 'Research for democracy and democracy for research'. *New Directions for Higher Education*, (152), 59–66.

Cuthill, M. (2010) 'Working together: A methodological case study of 'engaged scholarship''. *Gateways: International Journal of Community Research and Engagement*, 3, 20–37.

Cuthill, M. (2012) 'A civic mission for the university: engaged scholarship and community based participatory research'. In: McIlrath, L., Lyons, A. and Munck, R. (eds) *Higher Education and Civic Engagement: Comparative Perspectives*. New York: Palgrave Macmillan, pp. 81–100.

Dahlgren, P. (2012) '*Mejorar la participación: la democracia y el entorno de la web*'. In: Champeau, S. and Innerarity, D., *Internet y el futuro de la democracia*. Barcelona: Paidós.

Davies, S.R. (2013) 'The rules of engagement: power and interaction in dialogue events'. *Public Understanding of Science*, 22, 65–79.

Delanty, G. (2001) *Challenging Knowledge: The University in the Knowledge Society*. Buckingham: Society for Research into Higher Education/Open University Press.

Dempsey, S.E. (2010) 'Critiquing community engagement'. *Management Communication Quarterly*, 24(3), 359–90.

de Sousa Santos, B. (2005) *La universidad en el siglo XXI. Para una reforma democrática y emancipadora de la universidad*. Argentina: Miño y Dávila editores.

de Sousa Santos, B. (2006) The University in the 21st Century: Towards a Democratic and Emancipatory University Reform. In Rhoads, R. and Torres, C.A. (eds) *The University, State, and Market. The Political Economy of Globalization in the Americas*. Stanford, CA: Stanford University Press, pp. 60–100. Retrieved October 2013 from http://www.ces.uc.pt/bss/documentos/university11Feb(2005).pdf.

de Sousa Santos, B. (2007) 'Beyond abyssal thinking: from global lines to ecologies of knowledges'. *Review*, XXX(1), 45–89.

de Sousa Santos, B. (2009) 'A non-occidentalist West? Learned ignorance and ecology of knowledge'. *Theory, Culture and Society*, 26(7–8), 103–25.

de Sousa Santos, B., Nunes, J.A. and Meneses, M.P. (2007) 'Opening up the canon of knowledge and recognition of difference'. In: de Sousa Santos, B. S. (ed.) *Another Knowledge is Possible*. London: Verso, pp. xix–lxii.

Didriksson, A. (2007) *Universidad y Sociedades del Conocimiento*. Mexico: UNESCO-México.

Dragne, C. (2007) *Background document for the University of Victoria Task Force on Civic Engagement*. Victoria, BC: University of Victoria.

Driscoll, A. (2008) *Carnegie's Community-Engagement Classification: Inventions and Insights*. Stanford, CT: Carnegie Foundation for the Advancement of Teaching.

Dubb, S. (2007) *Linking Colleges to Communities*. College Park, MD: University of Maryland, Democracy Collaborative.

Duke, C. (2008) 'University engagement: avoidable confusion and inescapable contradiction'. *Higher Education Management and Policy*, 20(2), 87–97.

Duke, C. (2011) 'Winning the university engagement narrative'. *International Journal of Lifelong Education*, 30(5), 701–9.

Duke, C., Osborne, M. and Wilson, B. (eds) (2005) *Rebalancing the Social and Economic: Learning, Partnership and Place*. Leicester: National Institute of Adult Continuing Education.

Duke, C., Osborne, M. and Wilson, B. (2013) *A New Imperative – Regions and Higher Education in Difficult Times*. Manchester: Manchester University Press.

Durie, R., Lundy, C. and Wyatt, K. (2011) *Researching with Communities. Towards a Leading Edge Theory and Practice for Community Engagement*. Connected Communities Review. Swindon: AHRC. Retrieved from: http://www.ahrc.ac.uk/Funding-Opportunities/Research-funding/Connected-Communities/Scoping-studies-and-reviews/Documents/Researching%20with%20Communities.pdf.

Durose, C., Beebeejaun, Y., Rees, J., Richardson, J. and Richardson, L. (2011) *Towards Co-Production in Research with Communities*. AHRC Connected Communities Review. Swindon: AHRC.

Eckerle-Curwood, S., Munger, F., Mitchell, T., MacKeigan, M. and Farrar, A. (2011) 'Building effective community-university partnerships: are universities truly ready?' *Michigan Journal of Community Service Learning*, 17(2), 15–26.

Etzkowitz, H. and Leydesdorff, L. (eds) (1997) *Universities in* the *Global Economy: A Triple Helix of University-Industry-Government Relations*. London: Cassell Academic.

Etzkowitz, H., Webster, A., Gebhardt, C. and Terra, B.R.C. (2000) 'The future of the university and the university of the future: evolution of ivory tower to entrepreneurial paradigm'. *Research Policy*, 29, 313–30.

Facer, K., Manners, P. and Agusita, E. (2012) *Towards a Knowledge Base for University-Public Engagement: Sharing Knowledge, Building Insight, Taking Action.* Bristol: NCCPE.

Favish, J. and McMillan, J. (2009) 'The university and social responsiveness in the curriculum: a new form of scholarship?' *London Review of Education*, 7(2), 169–79.

Fitzgerald, H.E. and Simon, L.A.K. (2012) 'The world grant ideal and engagement scholarship'. *Journal of Higher Education Outreach and Engagement,* 16(3), 31–53.

Fitzgerald, H.E., Smith, P., Book, P., Rodin, K. and CIC Committee on Engagement (2005) *Draft CIC Report: Resource Guide and Recommendations for Defining and Benchmarking Engagement.* Champaign, IL: Committee on Institutional Cooperation.

Fitzgerald, H.E., Bruns, K., Sonka, S.T., Furco, A. and Swanson, L. (2012) 'The centrality of engagement in higher education'. *Journal of Higher Education Outreach and Engagement,* 16(3), 7–27.

Folgueiras Bertomeu, P. and Martínez Vivot, M. (2009) 'Development of competencies at the university through service-learning'. In: *Revista Interamericana de Educación para la Democracia*, 2(1), 56–76. Retrieved from http://scholarworks.iu.edu/journals/index.php/ried/article/view/142/1060.

Fournier, M., Abramovich, A.L. and Da Representaçao, N. (eds) (2012) *Aprender haciendo con otros.* Buenos Aires: Universidad de General Sarmiento.

Freire, P. (1973) *Pedagogía del oprimido.* Buenos Aires: Siglo XXI.

Freire, P. (1974) *La educación como práctica de la libertad.* Buenos Aires: Siglo XXI.

Frid, J. and Marconi, E. (2006) *Universidad y urgencia social.* Buenos Aires: UBA-CBC-FADU.

Fryer, M. (2010) 'How to strengthen the third mission of the university: the case of the University of British Columbia learning exchange'. In: Inman, P. and Schuetze, H.G. (eds) *The Community Engagement and Service Mission of Universities.* Leicester: National Institute of Adult Continuing Education.

Furco, A. (2002) *Self-assessment Rubric for the Institutionalization of Service-Learning in Higher Education.* Campus Compact Engaged Scholar. Berkeley, CA: University of California, Berkeley, Service-Learning Research & Development Center.

Furco, A. (2005) *Impacto de los proyectos de aprendizaje-servicio.* In: Programa Nacional Educación Solidaria/UPE/Ministerio de Educación, Ciencia y Tecnologia. *Aprendizaje y servicio solidario en la Educación Superior y en los sistemas educativos latinoamericanos. Actas del 7mo. Seminario Internacional 'Aprendizaje y Servicio Solidario'.* Argentina, pp. 19–26.

Furco, A. (2010) 'The engaged campus: toward a comprehensive approach to public-engagement'. *British Journal of Educational Studies,* 58(4), 375–90.

Gaventa, J. and Barret, G. (2010) *So What Difference Does it Make? Mapping the Outcomes of Citizen Engagement.* Research Summary of Working Paper No. 347. Brighton: University of Sussex, Institute of Development Studies.

Gaventa, J. and Bivens, F. (2011) '*Co-Constructing Knowledge for Social Justice: Lessons from an International Research Collaboration. Social Justice and the University'.* Knoxville, University of Tennessee. On-line speech available at http://160.36.161.128/UTK/Viewer/?peid=37ef5f56055149a785b21401feaead3d.

Gibbons, M. (1994) *The New Production of Knowledge: The Dynamics of Science and Research in Contemporary Societies.* London: Sage.

Gibbons, M., Nowotny, H. and Scott, P. (2001) *Rethinking Science, Knowledge and the Public in an Age of Uncertainty.* Cambridge, UK: Polity Press.

Gibson, M. and Campus Compact (eds) (2006)' New times demand new scholarship'. In: *Research Universities and Civic Engagement. A Leadership Agenda. Report of the 2005 Conference on Research Universities and Civic Engagement, Tufts U., Medford, MA.* Retrieved from http://www.compact.org/wpcontent/uploads/initiatives/research_universities/Civic_Engagement.pdf.

Goddard, J., Kempton, L. and Vallance, P. (2011) *The Civic University: Connecting the Global and the Local.* Newcastle-upon-Tyne: Newcastle University.

Granados, J. (2011) *La evaluación de iniciativas de aprendizaje participativo para una acción responsable y de servicio.* In: Miralles, P., Molina S. and Santisteban, A. (eds) *La Evaluación en el Proceso de Enseñanza y Aprendizaje de las Ciencias Sociales.* Murcia: APUDCS, pp. 343–52.

Granner, M.L. and Sharpe, P.A. (2004) 'Evaluating community coalitions characteristics and functioning: a summary of measurement tools'. *Health Education Research: Theory and Practice*, 19, 514–32.

GUNi (2008) *Higher Education in the World 3. Higher Education: New Challenges and Emerging Roles for Human and Social Development.* Basingstoke: Palgrave Macmillan.

GUNi (2009) *Higher Education at a Time of Transformation: New Dynamics for Social Responsibility.* Basingstoke: Palgrave Macmillan.

Hagedoorn, J., Link, A.N. and Vonortas, N.S. (2000) 'Research partnerships'. *Research Policy*, 29, 567–86.

Hakan, V. Martinez Ezgi (2012) 'Project of Little Traces'. *New Ceramics*, May/June, 38–9.

Hall, B.L. (2005) 'In from the cold? Reflections on participatory research 1970–2005'. *Convergence*, 38(1), 5–24.

Hall, B.L. (2009) 'Higher education, community engagement, and the public good: building the future of continuing education in Canada'. *Canadian Journal of University Continuing Education*, 35(1), 11–23.

Hall, B. (2011) 'Towards a knowledge democracy movement: contemporary trends in community university research partnerships'. In: *Rizoma Freireano*, 9 (Special Issue).

Hall, B.L. (2011) 'Towards a knowledge democracy movement: 'Antyodaya' and higher education'. In: *Becoming Visible 2011 – A Knowledge Democracy Movement.* Retrieved from http://www.aletmanski.com/al-etmanski/2011/02/bud-hall-becoming-visible-2011-a-knowledge-democracy-movement.html.

Hall, B.L., Jackson, E.T., Tandon, R., Lall, N. and Fontan, J.-M. (eds) (2013) *Knowledge, Democracy and Action: Community University Research Partnerships in International Perspectives.* Manchester: Manchester University Press.

Hall, M. (2010) 'Community engagement in South African higher education'. *Kagiso*, 6, 1–52.

Hart, A., Maddison, E. and Wolff, D. (eds) (2007) *Community-University Partnerships in Practice*. Leicester: National Institute of Adult Continuing Education.

Hart, A., Northmore, S. and Gerhardt, C. (2009) *Auditing, Benchmarking and Evaluating Public Engagement*. Bristol: NCCPE.

Hart, A., Ntung, A., Millican, J. et al. (2011) *Community-University Partnerships Through Communities of Practice*. AHRC Connected Communities Review. Swindon: AHRC.

Hartley, M. and Huddleston, T. (2010) *School-Community-University Partnerships for a Sustainable Democracy: Education for Democratic Citizenship in Europe and the United States*. EDC/HRE Pack, Tool 5. Strasbourg: Council of Europe.

Hartley, M., Saltmarsh, J. and Clayton, P. (2010) 'Is the civic engagement movement changing higher education?' *British Journal of Education Studies*, 58(4), 391–406.

Hazelkorn, E. (2009) 'Community engagement as social innovation'. In: Weber, L. and Duderstadt, J. (eds) *The Role of the Research University in an Innovation-Driven Global Society*. Economica. Retrieved from: http://arrow.dit.ie/cgi/viewcontent.cgi?article=1013&context=cserbk.

Hikins, J.W. and Cherwitz, R.A. (2010) 'The engaged university: where rhetorical theory matters'. *Journal of Applied Communication Research*, 38(2), 115–26.

Helene Perold & Associates (2005) *Strengthening the Civic Roles and Social Responsibilities of Higher Education: Building a Global Network*. Medford, MA: Talloires Network.

Higher Education Quality Committee/Council for Higher Education (2006) *Service-Learning in the Curriculum. A Resource for Higher Education Institutions*. Pretoria: Council on Higher Education.

Holland, B. (2005) 'Scholarship and Mission in the Twenty-first Century University: The Role of Engagement'. Paper presented to the Australian Universities Quality Forum, Sydney, Australia.

Holland, B. and Gelmon, S. (1998) 'The state of the engaged campus: what have we learned about building and sustaining university and community partnerships?' *AAHE Bulletin American Association for Higher Education*, 51(1), 3–6.

Holland, D., Powell, D.E., Eng, E. and Drew, G. (2010) 'Models of engaged scholarship: an interdisciplinary discussion'. *Collaborative Anthropologies*, 3, 1–36.

Hollander, E. and Saltmarsh, J. (2000) 'The engaged university'. *Academe*, 86(4), 29–32.

Hollander, E., Saltmarsh, J. and Zlotkowski, E. (2002) 'Indicators of engagement'. In: Kenny, M., Simon, L., Kiley-Brabeck, K. and Lerner, R. (eds) *Learning to Serve: Promoting Civil Society Through Service Learning*. Boston, MA: Kluwer Academic.

Holliman, R., Collins, T., Jensen, E. and Taylor, P. (2009) *ISOTOPE: Informing Science Outreach and Public Engagement. Final Report of the NESTA-funded ISOTOPE Project*. Milton Keynes, UK: Open University Press.

Howard, J., *Academic Service-Learning: Myths, Challenges, and Recommendations*. Retrieved March 25, 2013 from http://data.ohr.umn.edu/protected/service1.pdf.

Inman, P. and Shutze, H. (2011) *The Community Engagement and Service Mission of Universities*. Leicester, UK: National Institute for Adult and Continuing Education

Innerarity, D. (2011) *La Democracia del Conocimiento. Por una Sociedad Inteligente*. Barcelona: Editorial Planeta.

Jackson, E.T. (2010) 'University capital, community engagement and continuing education: blending professional development and social change'. *Canadian Journal of University Continuing Education*, 36(2), 1–13.

Jay, G. (2010) 'The engaged humanities: principles and practices for public scholarship and teaching'. *Journal of Community Engagement and Scholarship*, 3(1), 55–63.

Jensen, E. (2011) 'Sounding off: we need to evaluate engagement'. *People and Science*, June, 29.

Jensen, E. and Buckley, N. (2012) 'Why people attend science festivals: Interests, motivations and self-reported benefits of public engagement with research'. *Public Understanding of Science*, epub ahead of print.

Jordan, C. (ed.) (2007) *Community Engaged Scholarship Review, Promotion and Tenure Package*. Peer Reviewed Work Group, Community Engaged Scholarship for Health Collaborative. Seattle, WA: Community-Campus Partnerships for Health.

Jordan, C., Gelmon, S., Ryan, K. and Seifer, S.D. (2012) 'CES4Health.info: a web-based mechanism for disseminating peer-reviewed products of community-engaged scholarship. Reflections on year one'. *Journal of Higher Education Outreach and Engagement*, 16(1), 47.

Kania, J. and Kramer, M. (2013) *Embracing Emergence: How Collective Impact Addresses Complexity*. Stanford Social Innovation Review. Standford, CT: Stanford University.

Kassam, Y. and Mustafa, K. (1982) *Participatory Research: An Emerging Alternative Methodology in Social Science Research*. New Delhi: Society for Participatory Research in Asia.

Kaye, C.B. (2010) *The Complete Guide to Service Learning: Proven, Practical Ways to Engage Students in Civic Responsibility, Academic Curriculum, and Social Action* (2nd edn). Minneapolis, MN: Free Spirit.

Kellogg Commission (1999) *Returning to Our Roots: The Engaged Institution, Third Report of the Kellogg Commission on the Future of State and Land-Grant Universities*. Retrieved October 2013 from http://www.aplu.org/NetCommunity/Document.Doc?id=183.

Kellogg Commission (2000) *Renewing the Covenant: Learning, Discovery, and Engagement in a New Age and Different World*. Washington, DC: National Association of State Universities and Land Grant Colleges.

Kenway, J., Bullen, E. and Robb, S. (2012) 'The knowledge economy, the techno-preneur and the problematic future of the university'. *Policy Futures in Education*, 2(2), 330–49.

Kezar, A.J. and Eckel, P.D. (2002) 'The effect of institutional culture on change strategies in higher education: universal principles or culturally responsive concepts?' *Journal of Higher Education*, 73(4), 435–60.

Kindon, S., Pain, R. and Kesby, M. (2007) *Participatory Action Research Approaches and Methods: Connecting People, Participation and Place*. London: Routledge.

King, R. (2009) *Governing Universities Globally. Organizations, Regulation and Rankings*. Cheltenham: Edward Elgar.

King, R., Marginson, S. and Naidoo, R. (eds) (2011) *Handbook of Higher Education and Globalization*. Cheltenham: Edward Elgar.

Kruss, G., Visser, M., Aphane, M. and Haupt, G. (2012) *Academic Interaction with Social Partners: Investigating the Contribution of Universities to Economic and Social Development*. Cape Town: HSRC Press.

Lall, N. (2010) 'Measuring the impact of university-community research partnerships: a literature review of theories, concepts, tools and practices'. In: Inman, P. and Schuetze, H.G. (eds) *The Community Engagement and Service Mission of Universities*. Leicester: National Institute of Adult Continuing Education.

Leach, M. and Scoones, I. (2007) *Mobilising Citizens: Social Movements and the Politics of Knowledge*. IDS Working Paper No. 276. Brighton: University of Sussex, Institute for Development Studies.

Letven, E., Ostheimer, J. and Statham, A. (2001) 'Institutionalizing university-community engagement'. *Metropolitan Universities: An International Forum*, 12(3), 63–75.

Lindblom, C. (1965) *The Intelligence of Democracy: Decision Making Through Mutual Adjustment*. New York: Free Press.

Lutz, J.S. and Neis, B. (eds) (2008) *Making and Moving Knowledge – Interdisciplinary and Community-based Research in a World on the Edge*. Montreal: McGill Queen's University Press.

Manson O'Connor, K., Lynch, K. and Owen, D. (2011) 'Student-community engagement and the development of graduate attributes', *Education + Training*, 53(2/3), 100–15.

Marrero, D.G., Hardwick, E.J., Staten, L.K. et al. (2013) 'Promotion and tenure for community-engaged research: an examination of promotion and tenure support for community-engaged research at three universities collaborating through a clinical and translational science award'. *Clinical and Translational Science*, 6(3), 204–8.

Marres, N. (2009) 'Testing powers of engagement: green living experiments, the ontological turn and the undoability of involvement'. *European Journal of Social Theory*, 12(1), 117–33.

Martinez-Brawley, E.E. (2003) 'The scholarship of engagement in a research university: faculty incentives and disincentives'. *Metropolitan Universities Journal: An International Forum*, 14(4), 116–30.

Martínez Martín, M. (ed.) (2009) *Aprendizaje Servicio y Responsabilidad Social de las Universidades*. Barcelona: Octaedro.

Marullo, S. and Edwards, B. (2000) 'From charity to justice: the potential of university-community collaboration for social change'. *American Behavioral Scientist*, 43, 895–912.

McBride, A.M., Benitez, C., Sherraden, M., with Danso, K., Castaño, B., Johnson, L. et al. (2003) *The Forms and Nature of Civic Service: A Global Assessment*. St Louis, MO: Washington University in St. Louis, Global Service Institute, Center for Social Development.

McCormick, A.C. and Zhao, C.M. (2005) *Rethinking and Reframing the Carnegie Classification*. Stanford, CT: Carnegie Foundation for the Advancement of Teaching.

McIlrath, L. and Mac Labhrainn, I. (eds) (2007) *Higher Education and Civic Engagement: International Perspectives*. Aldershot: Ashgate.

McIlrath, L. (2012) 'Community perspective on university partnership—prodding the sacred cow'. In: McIlrath, L., Lyons, A. and Munck, R. (eds) *Higher Education and Civic Engagement – Comparative Perspectives*. New York: Palgrave Macmillan.

McIlrath, L., Lyons, A. and Munck, R. (2012) *Higher Education and Civic Engagement: Comparative Perspectives*. New York: Palgrave Macmillan.

McMillan, J. (2009) *What Happens When the University Meets the Community? Service-learning, Activity Theory and 'Boundary Work' in Higher Education*. Seminar Paper, University of the Western Cape.

Michael, M. (2012) 'What are we busy doing?: engaging the idiot'. *Science, Technology & Human Values*, 37, 528–54.

Millican, J. and Bourner, T. (2011) 'Student-community engagement and the changing role and context of higher education'. *Education + Training*, 53(2/3), 89–99.

Modise, O. and Mosweunyane, D. (2012) 'Engagement with the city: a new paradigm for rebranding institutions of higher education'. In: Preece, J., Ntseane, P.G., Modise, O.M. and Osborne, M. (eds) *Community Engagement in African Universities: Perspectives, Prospects and Challenges*. London: NIACE.

Murphy, D., Scammell, M. and Sclove, R. (eds) (1997) *Doing Community Based Research: A Reader*. Amherst, MA: Loka Institute.

Nandy, A. (1996) 'The politics of indigenous knowledge and contending ideas of the university'. In: Hayhoe, R. and Pan, J. (eds) *East-West Dialogue in Knowledge and Higher Education*. Armonk, NY: M.E. Sharpe, p. 297.

NCCPE (National Coordinating Committee for Public Engagement in Higher Education) (2010) *The Engaged University: Manifesto for Public Engagement*. Bristol, UK: NCCPE.

NCCPE (2013) *Engaged Futures*. Retrieved October 2013 from http://www.publicengagement.ac.uk/engagedfutures.

Neresini, F. and Bucchi, M. (2010) 'Which indicators for the new public engagement activities? an exploratory study of European research institutions'. *Public Understanding of Science*, 20(1), 64–79.

Nyden, P. and Percy, S. (2010) 'Documenting impacts: engaged research centers and community change'. In: Fitzgerald, S.D., Burack, H.E., Siefer, C. (eds) *Handbook of Engaged Scholarship: Contemporary Landscapes, Future Directions*, Volume 2, pp. 311–32. East Lansing, MI: Michigan State University Press.

Ochocka, J., Moorlag, E. and Janzen, R. (2010) 'A framework for entry: PAR values and engagement strategies in community research'. *Gateways: International Journal of Community Research & Engagement*, 3, 1–19.

OECD (2007) *Higher Education and Regions: Globally Competitive, Locally Engaged*. Paris: OECD.

OECD, Centre for Educational Research and Innovation (2009) *Higher Education to 2030*, Volume 2: *Globalisation*. Paris: OECD.

O'Meara, K., Rice, R.E. and Edgerton, R. (2005) *Faculty Priorities Reconsidered: Rewarding Multiple Forms of Scholarship*. San Francisco, CA: Jossey-Bass.

Ostrom, E. (1990) *Governing the Commons. The Evolution of Institutions for Collective Action*. Cambridge, UK: Cambridge University Press.

Pahl, K. and Pool, S. (2011) 'Living your life because it's the only life you've got'. *Qualitative Research Journal*, 11(2), 17–37.

Pennycook, A. (1996) 'English, universities, and struggles over culture and knowledge'. In: Hayhoe, R. and Pan, J. (eds) *East-West Dialogue in Knowledge and Higher Education*. Armonk, NY: M.E. Sharpe, p. 64.

Percy, S.L., Zimpher, N.L. and Brukardt, M.J. (eds) (2006) *Creating a New Kind of University. Institutionalizing Community-University Engagement*. Bolton, MS: Anker.

Perold, H., Sherraden, M. and Stroud, S. (eds) (2003) *Service Enquiry: Service in the 21st Century*. Johannesburg:

Global Service Institute, USA and Volunteer and Service Enquiry Southern Africa.

Powell, J. and Dayson, K. (2013) 'Engagement and the idea of the civic university'. In: Benneworth, P. (ed.) *University Engagement with Socially Excluded Communities*, Dordrecht: Springer, pp. 143–63.

PytlikZillig, L.M. and Tomkins, A.J. (2011) 'Public engagement for informing science and technology policy: what do we know, what do we need to know, and how will we get there?' *Review of Policy Research*, 28(2), 21.

Rice, R.E. (2002) 'Beyond scholarship reconsidered: toward an enlarged vision of the scholarly work of faculty members'. *New Directions for Teaching and Learning*, Summer (90), 7–8.

Robinson, F., Zass-Ogilvie, I. and Hudson, R. (2012) *How Can Universities Support Disadvantaged Communities?* York: Joseph Rowntree Foundation.

Roche Olivar, R. (2010) *Prosocialidad: nuevos desafíos. Métodos y pautas para la optimización creativa del entorno*. Buenos Aires: Ciudad Nueva.

Rowe, G. and Frewer, L. (2005) 'A typology of public engagement mechanisms'. *Science, Technology & Human Values*, 30(2), 251–90.

Rowe, G., Horlick-Jones, T., Walls, J., Poortinga, W. and Pidgeon, N.E. (2008) 'Analysis of a normative framework for evaluating public engagement exercises: reliability, validity and limitations'. *Public Understanding of Science*, 17(4), 419–41.

Rowe, G., Rawsthorne, D., Scarpello, T. and Dainty, J.R. (2009) 'Public engagement in research funding: a study of public capabilities and engagement methodology'. *Public Understanding of Science*, 19(2), 225–39.

Ryan, K.E. and Hood, L.K. (2004) 'Guarding the castle and opening the gates'. *Qualitative Inquiry*, 10(1), 79–95.

Saija, L. (2013) '"Building" engagement into the fabric of the university'. In: Benneworth, P. (ed) *University engagement with socially excluded communities*. Dordrecht: Springer, pp. 125–41.

Salmi, J. (2009) *The Challenge of Establishing World-class Universities*. Washington, DC: World Bank.

Sandmann, L.R. (2008) 'Conceptualization of the scholarship of engagement in higher education: a strategic review, 1996–2006'. *Journal of Higher Education Outreach and Engagement*, 12(1), 91–104.

Sandmann, L.R., Thornton, C.H. and Jaeger, A.J. (2009) *Institutionalizing Community Engagement in Higher Education: The First Wave of Carnegie Classified Institutions*. San Francisco: Jossey-Bass.

Schneller, C. and Thöni, E. (eds) (2011) Knowledge Societies: Universities and their Social Responsibilities, 2nd Asia-Europe Education Workshop, Innsbruck, Austria, June 5–7, 2011.

Schuetze, H.G. and Inman, P. (eds) (2010) *The Community Engagement and Service Mission of Universities*. Leicester: National Institute of Adult Continuing Education.

Schütze, H. (2010) 'The "third mission" of universities: community engagement and service'. In: Inman, P. and Schütze, H.G. (eds) *The Community Engagement and Service Mission of Universities*, Leicester: National Institute of Adult Continuing Education, pp. 13–32.

Sörlin, S. and Vessuri, H. (eds) (2007) *Knowledge Society vs Knowledge Economy*. Paris: UNESCO.

Staniszewska, S., Adebajo, A., Barber, R. et al. (2011) 'Developing the evidence base of patient and public involvement in health and social care research: the case for measuring impact'. *International Journal of Consumer Studies*, 35(6), 628–32.

Stanton, T.K. (2007) *New Times Demand New Scholarship: Research Universities and Civic Engagement: Opportunities and Challenges*. Los Angeles, CA: University of California.

Staudt, K. and Thurlow Brenner, C. (2000) 'Higher Education Engagement with Community: New Policies and Inevitable Political Complexities'. Paper presented to *COMM-ORG: The On-line Conference on Community Organizing and Development*. Retrieved October 2013 from http://comm-org.wisc.edu/papers2002/staudt.htm.

Steinberg, K.S., Bringle, R.G. and Williams, M.J. (2010) *Service-learning Research Primer*. Scotts Valley, CA: National Service-Learning Clearinghouse. http://servicelearning.gov/filemanager/download/Service-Learning_Research_Primer.pdf.

Strand, K., Marullo, S., Cutforth, N., Stoecker, R. and Donohue, P. (2003) 'Principles of best practice for community-based research'. *Journal of Community Service Learning*, 9(3), 5–15.

Sunstein, C.R. (2006) *Infotopia: How Many Minds Produce Knowledge*. Oxford: Oxford University Press.

Talloires Network (2005) Talloires Declaration. Retrieved October 2013 from http://talloiresnetwork.tufts.edu/wp-content/uploads/TalloiresDeclaration2005.pdf.

Tandon, R. (2007) 'In search of relevance: higher education for participatory research and sustainable development'. *Public Responsibility for Higher Education*, 4(10), 1–13.

Tandon, R. (ed.) (2008) *Participatory Research: Revisiting the Roots*. Delhi: Mosaic Books.

Tandon, R. (2008) *Civil engagement in Higher Education and its role in human and social development*. In GUNi, *Higher Education in the World 3: New Challenges and Emerging Roles for Human and Social Development*. Basingstoke: Palgrave Macmillan.

Tandon, R. and Farrell, M. (2008) 'Collaborative participatory research in gender mainstreaming in social change organisations'. In: Shani, A.B., Mohrman, S.A., Pasmore, W.A., Stymne, B. and Adler, N. (eds) *Handbook of Collaborative Management Research*. Thousand Oaks, CA: Sage Publications, p. 289.

Tandon, R. and Hall, B. (2012) *UNESCO Chair on Community Based Research and Social Responsibility in Higher Education: A Framework for Action 2012–2016*. New Delhi: PRIA.

Tapia, M. Nieves (2000) *La Solidaridad como Pedagogía*. Buenos Aires: Ciudad Nueva.

Tapia, M. Nieves (2006) *Aprendizaje y servicio solidario en el sistema educativo y las organizaciones juveniles*. Buenos Aires: Ciudad Nueva.

Tapia, M. Nieves (2009) *Aprendizaje-servicio y calidad educativa*. In: Ministerio de Educacion, Programa Nacional Educación Solidaria, *Excelencia académica y solidaridad. Actas del 11o. Seminario Internacional 'Aprendizaje y Servicio Solidario'*. Argentina, pp. 37–67. Ministerio de Educación, Gobierno de Argentina. Retrieved from: http://www.me.gov.ar/edusol/archivos/2010_actas_12.pdf.

Timotijevic, L., Barnett, J. and Raats, M.M. (2011) 'Engagement, representativeness and legitimacy in the development of food and nutrition policy'. *Food Policy*, 36(4), 490–8.

Turner, N.J., Marshall, A., Thomson, J.C. (EDŌSDI), Hood, R.J., Hill, C. and Hill E.A. (2008) 'Ebb and flow: transmitting environmental knowledge in a contemporary Aboriginal community'. In: Lutz, J.S. and Neis, B. (eds) *Making and Moving Knowledge – Interdisciplinary and Community-based Research in a World on the Edge*. Montreal: McGill Queen's University Press, p. 51.

Tzhoecoen (2010), *Revista científica*, No. 5. *Número especial dedicado al aprendizaje-servicio.* Editado por Universidad Señor de Sipán USS Chiclayo-Perú, Centro Latinoamericano de Aprendizaje y Servicio Solidario CLAYSS Buenos Aires-Argentina, Organización de Estados Iberoamericanos OEI Oficina Regional Buenos Aires-Argentina. Universidad Señor de Sipán, Chiclayo, Perú.

University of Glasgow (2009) *Shaping Metrics for HEI Cultural Engagement – Knowledge Transfer*. AHRC Project Report. Swindon: AHRC.

University Social Responsibility Alliance (2009) 'Driving Universities' Collaboration toward the New Era of Sustainable Social Responsibility'. Paper presented to the University-Community Engagement Conference, November.

Vallaeys, F. (2011) *Les Fondements Éthiques de la Responsabilité Sociale.* PhD thesis, Université Paris Est. Retrieved October 2013 from http://tel.archives-ouvertes.fr/tel-00704533.

Vallaeys, F., de la Cruz, C. and Sasia, P. (2009), *Responsabilidad Social Universitaria, Manual de Primeros Pasos.* Mexico: McGraw-Hill Interamericana Editores, Banco Interamericano de Desarrollo. Retrieved October 2013 from http://idbdocs.iadb.org/wsdocs/getdocument.aspx?docnum=35125786.

Veld, R.J. (ed.) (2010) *Knowledge Democracy: Consequences for Science, Politics and Media*. New York: Springer.

Vessuri, H. (2008) *De la pertinencia social a la sociedad del conocimiento*. In: Tünnermann Bernheim, C. (ed.) *La educación superior en América Latina y el Caribe: diez años después de la Conferencia Mundial de (1998).* Colombia: Pontificia Universidad Javeriana Colombia-IESALC-UNESCO, Capítulo X, pp. 459–78.

Vijayalakshmi, B., Devi, P., Bhavani, P.S.V. and Haranath, S. (2010) 'Journey with communities: engagement with SHGs from lower income neighbourhoods in Visakhapatnam'. *Indian Journal of Social Work*, 71(4), 485–516.

Walters, S. (2009) '"The Bridge We Call Home": Community-University Engagement'. Keynote Address at the University Community Engagement for Sustainability Conference, Penang, Malaysia, November 2009.

Watson, D. (2007) *Managing Civic and Community Engagement*. Maidenhead, UK: McGraw-Hill/Open University Press.

Watson, D. (2010) 'Universities' engagement with society'. In: Peterson, P., Baker, E., McGaw, B. and Peterson, P. (eds) *International Encyclopedia of Education,* Volume 4. Oxford: Elsevier, pp. 398–403.

Watson, D., Hollister, R., Stroud, S.E., and Babcock, E. (eds) (2011) *The Engaged University: International Perspectives on Civic Engagement.* Abingdon, UK: Routledge, Routledge/Taylor & Francis.

Wenger, L. and MacInnis, A. (2011) *Inventory of Tools for Assessing University Capacity, Support for, and Outcomes of Community/Civic Engagement and Community Engaged Scholarship.* Campus Community Partnerships for Health and the Institute for Community Engaged Scholarship, Univesity of Guelph. Retrieved October 2013 from http://cescholarship.ca/resources.

Willke, H. (2007) *Smart Governance: Governing the Global Knowledge Society*. Frankfurt: Suhrkamp.

Wink, R. (2004) (ed.) *Academia-Business Links in UK and Germany: Policy Outcomes and Lessons Learnt*. Cheltenham: Edward Elgar.

World Learning (2012) 'Promoting Education, Altruism and Civic Engagement (PEACE)'. Retrieved October 2013 from http://www.worldlearning.org/program-areas/international-development-and-exchange-programs/projects/promoting-education-altruism-and-civic-engagement-peace/.

Younger, P. (2009) *Characterising Modes of University Engagement with Wider Society: A Literature Review and Survey of Best Practice.* Retrieved October 2013 from http://talloiresnetwork.tufts.edu/wp-content/uploads/Characterisingmodesofuniversityengagementwithwidersociety.pdf.

Zomer, A. and Benneworth, P. (2011) 'The rise of the university's Third Mission'. In: Enders, J., de Boer, H.F. and Westerheijden, D. (eds) *Reform of Higher Education in Europe*. Rotterdam: Sense Publishers.

REGIONAL PERSPECTIVES

AFRICA

Abah, S.O. (2007) 'Vignettes of community in action: an exploration of participatory methodologies in promoting community development in Nigeria'. *Community Development Journal*, 42(4), 435–48.

Abah, S.O. (2007) *Performing Life: Case Studies in the Practice of Theatre for Development*. Zaria: Tamaza Publishing.

Abah, S.O., Hemmings, J. and Zakari Okwori, J. (2011) *Report of Community Sentinel Monitoring of Facility Health Committees, Jigawa State.* Abuja: PATHS2/TFDC.

Ajayi, A.J.F., Goma, L.K.H. and Johnson, A.G. (1996) *The African Experience with Higher Education*. Accra/Oxford: James Currey.

Akin Aina, T. (1994) *Quality and Relevance: African Universities in the 21st Century*. Background paper for the Joint Colloquium on the University in Africa in the 1990s and beyond, Association of African Universities, Lesotho.

Cooper, D. (2011) *The University in Development: Case Studies of Use-oriented Research*. Cape Town: HSRC Press.

Department of Education (1997) *A Programme for the Transformation of Higher Education*. White Paper. General Notice 1196 of 1997, Pretoria.

Harley, A. (2012) '"We are poor, not stupid": learning form autonomous grassroots social movements in South Africa'. In: Hall, B.L., Clover, D.E, Crowther, J. and Scandrett, E. (eds) *Learning and Education for a Better World: The Role of Social Movements*. Rotterdam: Sense Publishers.

Lazarus, J., Erasmus, M., Hendricks, D., Nduna, J. and Slamat, J. (2008) 'Embedding community engagement in South African higher education'. *Education Citizenship and Social Justice*, 3(1), 59–85.

Marah, J.K. (2006) 'The virtues and challenges in traditional African education'. *Journal of Pan African Education*, 1(4), 15–24.

Mosavel, M., Simon, C., van Stadec, D. and Buchbinder, M. (2005) 'Community based participatory research (CBPR) in South Africa: engaging multiple constituents to shape the research question'. *Social Science and Medicine*, 61, 2577–87.

Mwaikokesya, M.J. (2012) 'Scaling up the African universities' capacity for learning cities and regions: challenges and opportunities in Tanzania and East Africa'. In: Preece, J., Ntseane, P.G., Modise, O.M. and Osborne, M. (eds) *Community Engagement in African Universities: Perpectives, Prospects and Challenges*. London: NIACE.

Nampota, D. and Preece, J. (2012) 'University community service and its contribution to the Millennium Development Goals: a pan-African research project'. *Journal of Education*, 55, 105–26.

Ng'ethe, N., Assie-Lumumba, N., Subotzky, G. and Sutheland-Addy, E. (2003) *Higher Education Innovations in Sub-Saharan Africa, with Specific Reference to Universities*. Research Report. Tunis: Association for the Development of Education in Africa.

Ntseane, P.G. (2012) 'Pathways to an engaged university and learning region: the case of the University of Botswana and Gaborone City'. In: Preece, J., Ntseane, P.G., Modise, O.M. and Osborne, M. (eds) *Community Engagement in African Universities: Perspectives, Prospects and Challenges*. London: NIACE.

O'Brien, F. (2010) *Grounding Service Learning in South Africa: The Development of a Theoretical Framework*. Unpublished PhD thesis, University of KwaZulu-Natal, Durban.

O'Brien, F. (2012) 'Constructing service learning in South Africa: discourses of engagement'. In: Preece, J., Ntseane, P.G., Modise, O.M. and Osborne, M. (eds) *Community Engagement in African Universities: Perspectives, Prospects and Challenges*. London: NIACE.

Openjuru, G.L. and Ikoja-Odongo, J.R. (2012) 'From extramural to knowledge transfer partnership and networking: the community engagement experience at Makerere University'. In: Preece, J., Ntseane, P.G., Modise, O.M. and Osborne, M. (eds) *Community Engagement in African Universities: Perpective, Prospects and Challenges*. London: NIACE.

Preece, J. (2011) 'Higher education and community service: developing the National University of Lesotho's third mission'. *Journal of Adult and Continuing Education*, 17(1), 81–97.

Preece, J. (ed.) (2012) *Community Service and Community Engagement in Four African Universities*. Gaborone: Lentswe La Lesedi.

Preece, J. (2013) 'Towards an africanisation of community engagement and service learning'. *Perspectives in Education* (forthcoming).

Preece, J., Idowu, B., Nampota D. and Raditloaneng W.N. (2012) 'Community engagement within African contexts: a comparative analysis'. In: Preece, J., Ntseane, P.G., Modise, O.M. and Osborne, M. (eds) *Community Engagement in African Universities: Perpective, Prospects and Challenges*. London: NIACE.

Preece, J., Ntseane, P.G., Modise, O.M. and Osborne, M. (2012) 'The African university and community engagement in context'. In: Preece, J., Ntseane, P.G., Modise, O.M. and Osborne, M. (eds) *Community Engagement in African Universities: Perpective, Prospects and Challenges*. London: NIACE.

Preece, J., Ntseane, P.G., Modise, O.M. and Osborne, M. (eds) (2012) *Community Engagement in African Universities: Perspectives, Prospects and Challenges*. Leicester: National Institute of Adult Continuing Education.

Robins, S. (2010) 'Mobilising and mediating global medicine and health citizenship: the politics of AIDS knowledge production in rural South Africa'. In: Gaventa, J. and Tandon, R. (eds) *Globalising Citizens*. London: Zed Books, p. 56.

Salmat, S. (2010) 'Community engagement as scholarship: a response to Hall'. In: Hall, M. *Community Engagement in South African Higher Education*. South Africa: Council on Higher Education.

ARAB STATES

Afifi, R. (2011) *Youth Challenges in Social Transformations in the Arab Region*. In: UNESCO (2011) *Arab Youth: Civic Engagement and Economic Participation*. Beirut: UNESCO Regional Bureau, pp. 8–15. Retrieved from http://www.unesco.org/new/fileadmin/MULTIMEDIA/FIELD/Beirut/pdf/YCE%20_EN.pdf.

European Commission – Tempus (2012) *Higher Education in the Occupied Palestinian Territory*. Retrieved October 2013 from http://eacea.ec.europa.eu/tempus/participating_countries/overview/oPt.pdf.

European Higher Education Area (2013) Recent Trends & Developments in Jordanian Higher Education. Retrieved October 2013 from http://www.ehea.info/Uploads/Documents/JORDAN_recent_trends_and_developments.pdf.

Hollister, R M. (2011) 'Education and service for political change and development: profile of Al-Quds University (OPT)'. In: Watson, D., Hollister, R.M., Stroud, S.E. and Babcock, E. (eds) *The Engaged University: International Perspectives on Civic Engagement*. New York: Routledge, pp. 83–9.

King, N. (2005) *Education under Occupation ...: Learning to Improvise*. UK: Discovery Analytical Resourcing.

Kuwait University (2009) 'Deanship of Community Service and Continuing Education'. Retrieved October 2013 from http://www.kuniv.edu/ku/Centers/CentreforCommunityServicesContinuingeducation/.

Ma'an (2009) 'Towards Civic Engagement in Arab Higher Education'. Retrieved October 2013 from http://www1.aucegypt.edu/maan/expanding.html.

McNitti, C. (2009) 'Through thick and thin: the American University of Beirut engages its communities'. In: McIlrath, L., *Higher Education and Civic Engagement: Comparative Perspectives*. New York: Palgrave Macmillan, pp.205–19.

Mercy Corps (2012) 'Civic Engagement of Youth in the Middle East and North Africa: An Analysis of Key Drivers and Outcomes'. Retrieved October 2013 from http://www.mercycorps.org/research-resources/civic-engagement-youth-middle-east-and-north-africa.

Myntti, C., Mabsout, M. and Zurayk, R. (2009) *Beyond the Walls: AUB Engages its Communities*. Gerhart Center Working Paper. Cairo: American University in Cairo.

Paz, R. (2000) Higher Education and the Development of Palestinian Economic Groups. *Middle East Review of International Affairs*, 4(2).

Shibli, R. and Comer, B. (2013) 'Role of Academia in the

Aftermath of the Arab Spring: A Case Study Collaborative Course Between AUB and AUC'. Paper Presented at Takaful: Third annual conference on Arab Philanthropy and Civic Engagement, Tunis, Tunisia.

Underwood, C. and Jabre, B. (2010) 'Reflections on Civic Participation and Emerging Leadership in the Arab World'. Paper prepared for the Appreciating and Advancing Leadership for Public Wellbeing workshop, sponsored by NYU Abu Dhabi Institute.

UNESCO, (2011) *Arab Youth: Civic Engagement & Economic Participation*. Beirut: UNESCO Regional Bureau.

ASIA AND THE PACIFIC

Altbach, P.G. (2004) The past and future of Asian universities. In: Altbach, P.G. and Umakoshi, T. (eds) *Asian universities: Historical perspectives and contemporary challenges*. Baltimore: Johns Hopkins University Press, pp. 13–32.

Australian Universities Community Engagement Alliance. (2008) Universities and Community Engagement: Position Paper 2008–2010. Retrieved October 2013 from http://engagementaustralia.org.au/wp-content/uploads/2012/09/universities_CE_2008_(2010).pdf.

Cuthill, M. (2011) "Embedding engagement in an Australian 'sandstone' university: from community service to university engagement". *Metropolitan Universities*, 22(2), 21–44.

Eui, Y.K. and Young, H.C. (2009) *Social Responsibility: The Critical Role for Korean Universities for the 21st Century*. Retrieved October 2013 from http://www.unescobkk.org/fileadmin/user_upload/apeid/workshops/macao08/papers/3-c-1.pdf.

International Christian University (2009) *Lessons from Service-Learning in Asia: Results of Collaborative Research in Higher Education*. Japan: International Christian University, Service-Learning Center.

Jeelani, S. (2012) 'Strengthening higher education system in India'. *University News*, 50(43), 56–9.

Jun Xing and Ma, Hok Ka C. (eds) (2010) *Service-Learning in Asia: Curricular Models and Practices*. Hong Kong: Hong Kong University Press.

Patel, P.J. (2012) 'Academic underperformance of Indian universities, incompatible academic culture, and the societal context'. *Social Change*, 42(1), 9–29.

Peacock, D. (2012) 'Neoliberal social inclusion? The agenda of the Australian Universities Community Engagement Alliance'. *Critical Studies in Education*, 53(3), 311–25.

Phillips KPA Pty Ltd (2006) *Knowledge Transfer and Australian Universities and Publicly Funded Research Agencies*. A report to the Department of Education, Science and Training, March, Commonwealth of Australia, Canberra.

Planning Commission (2012) Fostering Social Responsibility in Higher Education in India. The Society for Participatory Research in Asia, 14–15. Retrieved from: http://www.google.es/url?sa=t&rct=j&q=&esrc=s-&source=web&cd=2&ved=0CDUQFjAB&url=http%3A%2F%2Funescochair-cbrsr.org%2Fpdf%2Fresource%2FFostering%2520Social%2520Responsibility%2520in%2520Higher%2520Education%2520in%2520India.docx&ei=ZyF9UtWvIcv07Ab004HABw&usg=AFQjCNFDAQds2ejMP_pwTmhDOIJS7eGQfg&sig2=n

vSPSF8CUNaAloVoUZ7WsA&bvm=bv.56146854,d.ZGU.

Sescon, J. and Tuano, P. (2012) 'Service learning as a response to disasters and social development: a Philippine experience'. *Japan Social Innovation Journal*, 2(1), 64–71.

Temple, J., Story, A. and Delaforce, W. (2005) AUCEA: An emerging collaborative and strategic approach dedicated to university-community engagement in Australia. Retrieved October 2013 from http://eprints.qut.edu.au/2350/1/2350.pdf.

EUROPE

Boland, J. (2006) 'Pedagogies for civic engagement in Irish higher education: principles and practices in context'. In: *Democracy, Citizenship and Higher Education: Dialogue between Universities and Community. Vytautas Magnus University Kaunas, Lithuania, November 23–24*.

Department of Education (1997) *A Programme for the Transformation of Higher Education Education*. White Paper 3. Government Gazette No. 18207 15 August 1997. Pretoria: Government Printers.

European Commission (2003) The Role of the Universities in the Europe of Knowledge. Brussels: European Commission.

Gaete, R. (2011) *La responsabilidad social universitaria como desafío para la gestión estratégica de la Educación Superior: el caso de España. Revista de Educación*, 355 (May–August), p.141

Goddard, J., Vallance, P. and Puukka, J. (2011) 'Experience of engagement between universities and cities: drivers and barriers in three European cities'. *Built Environment*, 37(3), 299–316.

Kwiek, M. (2011) 'Universities and knowledge production in Central Europe'. In: Temple, P. (ed.) *Universities in the Knowledge Economy: Higher Education Organisation and Global Change*. New York: Routledge.

Kwiek, M. (2012) 'Changing higher education policies: from the deinstitutionalization to the reinstitutionalization of the research mission in Polish universities.' *Science and Public Policy*, 39 (October), 641–54.

Kwiek, M. (2013) *Knowledge Production in European Universities: States, Markets, and Academic Entrepreneurialism*. Frankfurt: Peter Lang.

Lyons, A. and McIlrath, L. (2011) *Survey of Civic Engagement Activities in Higher Education in Ireland*. Galway, Ireland: Campus Engage.

Manners, P. and Duncan, S. (2012) 'Embedding public engagement within higher education: lessons from the beacons for public engagement in the United Kingdom'. In: McIlrath, L., Lyons, A. and Munck, R. (eds) *Higher Education and Civic Engagement – Comparative Perspectives*. New York: Palgrave Macmillan.

Mulder, H.A.J., Auf der Heyde, Th., Goffer, R. and Teodosiu, C. (2001) *Success and Failure in Starting Science Shops*. SCIPAS Report No. 2. Improving the Human Research Potential and the Socio-Economic Knowledge Base (IHP) STRATA Action. Utrecht: Science Shop for Biology, Utrecht University. Retrieved from http://www.livingknowledge.org/livingknowledge/wp-content/uploads/2012/02/wp2-so.pdf.

National Coordinating Centre for Public Engagement (2013) *The EDGE Self-Assessment Tool for Public Engage-*

ment. Bristol: University of Bristol/University of West England.

NCCPE (2011) 'The Beacons Project'. Retrieved October 2013 from http://www.publicengagement.ac.uk/about/beacons.

NCCPE (2012) 'Community Partner Network'. Retrieved October 2013 from http://www.publicengagement.ac.uk/about/community-partner-network.

Osborne, M. (2003) 'A European comparative analysis of policy and practice in widening participation to lifelong learning'. *European Journal of Education,* 38(1), 5–24.

Osborne, M. and Houston, M. (2012) 'United Kingdom – Universities and lifelong learning in the UK – adults as losers, but who are the winners?' In: Slowey, M. and Schuetze, H. (eds) *Global Perspectives on HE and Lifelong Learners.* London: Routledge.

Osborne, M. and Thomas, E. (2003) *Lifelong Learning in a Changing Continent: Continuing Education in the Universities of Europe.* Leicester: National Institute of Adult Continuing Education.

PERARES (2013) 'PERARES'. Retrieved October 2013 from http://www.livingknowledge.org/livingknowledge/perares.

RCUK (2010) 'Concordat for Engaging the Public with Research'. Retrieved October 2013 from http://www.rcuk.ac.uk/per/Pages/Concordat.aspx.

Rowe, G., Horlick-Jones, T., Walls, J. and Pidgeon, N. (2005) 'Difficulties in evaluating public engagement initiatives: reflections on an evaluation of the UK GM Nation? Public debate about transgenic crops'. *Public Understanding of Science,* 14(4), 331–52.

UNESCO (2005) *Towards Knowledge Societies.* Paris: UNESCO.

Watermeyer, R. (2011) 'Challenges for university engagement in the UK: towards a public academe?' *Higher Education Quarterly,* 65(4), 386–410.

Wynne, R. (2009) *The Civic Role of Universities: General Concepts and Irish Practices* Unpublished EdD thesis, University of Sheffield.

LATIN AMERICA AND THE CARIBBEAN

Cecchi, N., Lakonich, J.J., Pérez, D.A. and Rotstein, A. (2009) *El compromiso social de la Universidad latinoamericana del siglo XXI. Entre el debate y la acción.* Buenos Aires: IEC-CONADU.

CLAYSS-Natura Creer para Ver. (2012) *Siete experiencias inspiradoras en educación.* Buenos Aires: Natura Cosméticos S.A./CLAYSS.

CLAYSS and Red Iberoamericana de aprendizaje-servicio (2012) *Actas de la II Jornada de investigadores sobre aprendizaje-servicio.* Buenos Aires: Argentina. Retrieved October 2013 from http://www.clayss.org.ar/06_investigacion/jornadas/Libro_IIJIA-S_COMPLETO.pdf.

Didriksson, A. (2008) 'Contexto Global y Regional de la Educación Superior en América Latina y el Caribe'. In: Gazzola. A.L.and Didriksson, A., *Tendencias de la Educación Superior en América Latina y el Caribe.* Caracas: IESALC-UNESCO.

Flores-Kastanis, E., Montoya-Vargas, J. and Suárez, D.H. (2009) 'Investigación-acción participativa en la educación latinoamericana: un mapa de otra parte del mundo'. *Revista Mexicana de Investigación Educativa,* 14(40), 289-308. Retrieved October 2013 from http://www.scielo.org.mx/scielo.php?script=sci_arttext&pid=S1405-66662009000100013&lng=es&tlng=es.

Jiménez, M. (2008) *¿Cómo medir la percepción de la responsabilidad social en los diversos estamentos de la universidad?: una experiencia concreta.* ESS *Educación Superior y Sociedad,* 13(2), 139–62.

Martínez Vivot, M. and Folgueiras Bertomeu, P. (2012) *Competencias genéricas y específicas adquiridas por estudiantes de Veterinaria en un proyecto de aprendizaje-servicio.* In: Herrero, M.A. and Tapia, M.N. *Actas de la II Jornada de Investigadores sobre Aprendizaje-Servicio.* Buenos Aires: CLAYSS-Red Iberoamericana de aprendizaje-servicio.

Meneghel, S. (2001) *A crise da Universidade moderna no Brasil.* Campinas: UNICAMP.

Ochoa, E. *Aprendizaje-servicio en América Latina. Apuntes sobre pasado y presente.* Tzohecoen, 3(5), 108–25.

Orozco Silva, L.E. (2010) *Calidad académica y relevancia social de la educación superior en América Latina. Revista Iberoamericana de Educación Superior,* 1(1). Retrieved October 2013 from http://ries.universia.net/index.php/ries/article/view/22.

Sanllorenti, P. (ed.) (2009) *El Compromiso Social de la Universidad Latinoamericana del Siglo XXI. Entre el debate y la acción.* IEC – CONADU. Retrieved from http://biblioteca.clacso.edu.ar/Argentina/iec-conadu/20100317010331/2.pdf.

Tapia, M. Nieves (2003) 'Servicio' and 'solidaridad' in South American Spanish. In: Perold, H., Sherraden, M. and Stroud, S. (eds) *Service Enquiry: Service in the 21st Century, First Edition.* Johannesburg: Global Service Institute, USA and Volunteer and Service Enquiry Southern Africa, pp. 139–48.

Tapia, M. Nieves (2012) 'Academic excellence and community engagement: reflections on the Latin American experience'. In: McIlrath, L., Lyons, A. and Munck, R. (eds) *Higher Education and Civic Engagement – Comparative Perspectives.* New York: Palgrave Macmillan.

Universidad Construye País (2001). *Asumiendo el país: Responsabilidad Social Universitaria.* June 13–14. Santiago de Chile: Ediciones Proyecto Universidad Construye País.

Universidad Construye País (2006) *Responsabilidad Social Universitaria, Una Manera de Ser Universidad. Teoría y Práctica Chilena.* Retrieved from http://rsuniversitaria.org/web/images/stories/memoria/UCP%202006.pdf.

CANADA AND USA

Bell, R., Furco, A., Sorgen, V., Ammon, M.S. and Muller, P. (2000) *Institutionalizing Service-learning in Higher Education: Findings from a Three-year Study of the Western Region Campus Compact Consortium.* Berkeley, CA: University of California.

Castleden, H., Morgan, V.S. and Lamb, C. (2012) '"I spent the first year drinking tea": exploring Canadian university researchers' perspectives on community-based participatory research involving indigenous peoples'. *Canadian Geographer / Le Géographe canadien,* 56(2), 160–79.

EDUSOL (2006) *Experiencias ganadoras del Premio Presidencial 'Prácticas Solidarias en Educación Superior'.* Buenos Aires: Ministerio de Educación, Ciencia y Tecnología.

EDUSOL (2007) *Experiencias ganadoras del Premio Presi-*

dencial 'Prácticas Solidarias en Educación Superior' (2006) Buenos Aires: Ministerio de Educación, Ciencia y Tecnología.

EDUSOL (2008) Aprendizaje-servicio en la Educación Superior. Una mirada analítica desde los protagonistas. UPE. Buenos Aires: Ministerio de Educación.

EDUSOL (2009) Experiencias ganadoras del Premio Presidencial 'Prácticas Educativas Solidarias en Educación Superior'. Buenos Aires: Ministerio de Educación.

Fitzgerald, H.E., and Farrell, P. (2012) 'Fulfilling the promise: creating a child development research agenda with Native communities'. Child Development Perspectives, 6, 75–8.

Fletcher, C. (2003) 'Community-based participatory research relationships with Aboriginal communities in Canada: an overview of content and process'. Primatziwin: A Journal of Aboriginal and Indigeneous Community Health, 1, 27–62.

Flicker, S., Savan, B. and Mildenberger, M. (2008) 'A snapshot of community-based research in Canada: Who? What? Why? How?' Health Education Research, 23, 106–14.

Galliher, R.V., Tsethlikai, M.M. and Stolle, D. (2012) 'Perspectives of native and non-native scholars: opportunities for collaboration'. Child Development Perspectives, 6, 66–74.

Gemmel, L.J. and Clayton, P.H. (2009) A comprehensive framework for community service-learning in Canada. Ottowa: Canadian Alliance for Community Service-Learning.

Hall, B. and Dragne, C. (2008) 'The role of higher education for human and social development in the USA and Canada'. In: GUNi (2008) Higher Education in the World 3. Basingstoke: Palgrave Macmillan.

Hall, B. and Tremblay, C. (2012) Learning from SSHRC Funded Partnerships: Community Outcomes and Conditions for Success. Victoria, BC: University of Victoria.

Hall, B., Tremblay, C. and Downing, R. (2009) The Funding and Development of Community University Research Partnerships in Canada: Evidence-based Investment in Knowledge, Engaged Scholarship, Innovation and Action for Canada's Future. Victoria, BC: University of Victoria, Office of Community Based Research.

Kramer, M. (2000) Make it Last Forever: The Institutionalization of Service Learning in America. Washington, DC: Corporation for National and Community Service.

Minkler, M., Garcia, A.P., Rubin, V. and Wallerstine, N. (2012) Community-based Participatory Research: A Strategy for Building Healthy Communities and Promoting Health Through Policy Change. Berkeley, CA: University of California Berkeley, School of Public Health.

Mirza, R. (2011) Scan of Engagement Structures in Canadian Universities. St John, NL: Memorial University Office of Engagement.

NCAI Policy Research Center and MSU Center for Native Health Partnerships (2012) Walk Softly and Listen Carefully: Building Research Relationships with Tribal Communities. Washington DC/Bozeman, MT: Authors.

Sahota, P.C. (2010) Community-based Participatory Research in American Indian and Alaska Native Communities. Washington DC: NCAI Policy Research Center.